HANDBOOK OF ANNOTATED FINANCIAL FORMS

HANDBOOK OF ANNOTATED FINANCIAL FORMS

Robert P. Vichas

Prentice-Hall, Inc., Englewood Cliffs, New Jersey

Prentice-Hall International, Inc., *London*
Prentice-Hall of Australia, Pty. Ltd., *Sydney*
Prentice-Hall of Canada, Ltd., *Toronto*
Prentice-Hall of India Private Ltd., *New Delhi*
Prentice-Hall of Japan, Inc., *Tokyo*
Prentice-Hall of Southeast Asia Pte. Ltd., *Singapore*
Whitehall Books, Ltd., Wellington, *New Zealand*

©1981, *by*
Order of the Cross Society

Library of Congress Cataloging in Publication Data

Vichas, Robert P
    Handbook of annotated financial forms.

    Includes index.
    1. Finance--Forms, I. Title.
HG174.V5   658.1'5   80-20895
ISBN 0-13-374009-9

/

Printed in the United States of America

The Author

Dr. Robert P. Vichas has accumulated widespread experience, in the United States and abroad, in financial planning and analysis, credit, collections, and administration. Besides having managed his own businesses, he has been a consultant, financial and credit analyst, and commodity research director. He has also taught business strategy and policy, free enterprise economics, and financial management at several universities, including the University of Connecticut, Catholic University, East Carolina University, and Northwood Institute.

His articles have appeared in the *Journal of Management Studies, Human Events, Tradelook, The Envoy, Managerial and Decision Economics, Long Range Planning,* among others.

Published books include:

Handbook of Financial Mathematics, Formulas, and Tables. Englewood Cliffs, N.J.: Prentice-Hall, Inc.
Getting Rich in Commodities, Currencies, or Coins. New Rochelle, N.Y.: Arlington House Publishers.
Coeval Economics. Berkeley, CA: McCutchan Publishing Co.

TO
    MY
        WIFE
            DOLORES

A Word from the Author

The threads that link the more than 550 field-tested financial forms in this handbook to the successful operations of your organization are:

- COST CONTROL
- PROFIT PROTECTION
- FINANCIAL PLANNING.

Because of business and financial uncertainties, a debilitating inflation, and politically induced instabilities in the markets for resources, goods, and funds, today's successful manager necessarily aims at control of operational and administrative costs. *Cost control* is essential for any firm operating in a highly competitive industry. *Cost analysis* is necessary to protect potentially profitable projects. *Cost planning* precedes financial planning for future survival and growth. Effective cost control intensifies gains of a profitable endeavor; it can turn an ineffectively managed organization into a profit giant.

Writing of profits, are you happy with your firm's profit performance? If you are, then you will want to *protect* them *from profit leaks.* If you're not, this is the moment to initiate your own profit enhancement program by borrowing all ideas in this manual that can be turned into money in your pocket. Without profits, growth is stymied, jobs are not created, businesses fail. With profits, management is obliged to carefully protect and nurture them and employ them in more efficient, high-return undertakings.

Planning for cost control and profit protection is central in financing the means to achieve corporate objectives. On the cost side, planning denotes finding the most economical means for implementing decisions. On the profit side, planning stands for financing growth efficiently. *Financial planning* is continuous. It relies on a two-way flow of information at all levels. Many forms in this handbook can become valuable tools both in formulating and in communicating corporate plans. Without fairly accurate data, clearly and simply presented, financial planning will be less effective.

With today's corporate concern about cost control, profit analysis, and financial planning of resource use and asset acquisition, the financial management and planning staff and corporate controller hold the spotlight. From somewhere on this team will arise the wizard of profit maximization. With focus on technology in the 1950s, the R & D people rode the crest. In the quest for new and expanding markets in the 1960s, high performance was expected from marketing. Today, the influence of the financial officer pervades corporate operations, and his or her team has moved away from traditional accounting, credit, cash control functions into long-range planning and measurements of effectiveness of invested funds.

This handbook of financial forms was designed precisely for these critical areas that influence *costs, profits,* and *planning* decisions but without disdain for more traditional areas, still of major importance to successful and competent operation. Consequently, many benefits can be gained from an effective application of this guide:

◆ Time saver—ergo, money saver.
◆ Source book of ideas.
◆ Adds professionalism to any operations.
◆ Raises office efficiency.
◆ Eliminates confusion on forgotten points.
◆ An idea-sparker, when an idea is desperately needed.
◆ Increases profits.
◆ Standard reference when checking on others.
◆ Raises the user's prestige.

The purpose of the handbook is to provide a quick, efficient, accurate reference to material familiar and not so familiar. Therefore, anyone, from president to clerk, will want to place this volume between a dictionary of the English language and the companion volume, *Handbook of Financial Mathematics, Formulas, and Tables* by Robert P. Vichas (published by Prentice-Hall, Inc.)—i.e., in a key spot in your private library—because its proper use can:

✓ • enrich profits by avoiding costly errors;
✓ • reduce costs by saving on search time;
✓ • serve as a supplementary training reference for new employees;
  • save face (who wants to admit not knowing?);
✓ • eliminate guesswork on crucial matters;
  • increase the opportunity for promotion.

Collected together in a single source are more than 550 forms, checklists, and organizers selected to improve the quality and effectiveness of transmitting financial information most critical to an operational financial officer in his role as controller, planner, and decision-maker. Many of these forms have proven their worth in money saved several times over. Some have been standardized to conform with common business, legal, and administrative law requirements. Forms in this handbook represent the culmination of many years of experimentation and experience of business enterprises protecting profits and investments, nonprofit organizations controlling costs, governmental entities concerned with information flow, consultants and others with experience in the field, including the writer, involved in planning.

No business information is costless, although some persons mistakenly believe otherwise. Sloppy communication of the information may prove disastrously costly. Or presentation of summary data incomprehensible to the ultimate decision-maker, or user of it, is a nonproductive expenditure.

The purpose behind any form, memo, checklist, and the like, is to communicate precisely, to produce a sufficient quantity of information at a reasonable cost. Unfortunately, too many corporations experience communication problems of all types at most levels because they may not have clearly defined informational needs and data base requirements.

A form should communicate a reasonable amount of data in an intelligible and practical design so that such information may be profitably incorporated into business decisions. Too much information is expensive to collect and analyze, and difficult to digest, communicate, and absorb. Therefore, a financial form should meet basic requirements similar to those of a well-written letter, essay, or memo, because forms are "written" communications, even though they may be a computer readback and printout.

Forms, too, should be interesting to look at, attractive enough in organization to invite study and response. Of course, the configuration of a form may be dictated in part by the type of data to be communicated, the need to be concise, the vehicle for communicating or analyzing it, and its underlying purposes.

Consequently, the forms and information in this manual will profit just about anyone in a business organization linked to profit analysis, accounting, financial planning and control, money management, legal matters, systems analysis, *et al.* Even financial officers of nonprofit organizations, including churches, foundations, hospitals, universities, and governmental officials as well, will discover a standard reference for effective communications of financial data and cost efficiencies. Outside of the organizational structure, this book adds professionalism to any consultant's, lawyer's, or accountant's operations.

In review, this handbook segments the more than 550 forms into 11 sections:

- ◆ COST CONTROL to improve efficiency and asset use.
- ◆ PROFIT ANALYSIS to keep the enterprise on target.
- ◆ FINANCIAL PLANNING to reduce risks, raise yields.

◆ ASSET ACQUISITION, LEASING, and MERGERS to sustain growth.

◆ REAL ESTATE forms to protect profits.

◆ INVESTMENT INSTRUMENTS to raise funds.

◆ INTERNATIONAL CASH MANAGEMENT to shield foreign currency investments.

◆ CASH and CREDIT MANAGEMENT to reduce working capital needs.

◆ PAYROLL forms to control labor costs.

◆ ACCOUNTING forms to analyze profitability.

◆ NONPROFIT organization forms to aid in control and planning.

Because all of the above areas rather directly influence the balance sheet and income statements, using or adapting the forms in this handbook for internal application will provide valuable information on controlling *costs*, analyzing *profits*, and *planning* efficient use of financial resources for future growth.

Robert P. Vichas

Table of Contents

How to Locate a Form Quickly

There are several ways to locate a valuable form in this handbook besides random selection.

(1) The handbook is subdivided into 11 sections. From the Table of Contents, determine the section most appropriate to your needs.

(2) Preceding each section is a list of forms enumerated in order of appearance. Scanning this list you may locate a form that will produce the desired profitable results.

(3) Each section opens with textual matter. Reading the narrative you may discover the form or group of forms that will yield cost-saving results.

(4) Forms are clustered in logical sequence. By turning several pages forward or backward around your general problem area, you can develop the system or routine that is most efficient for your organization.

(5) A comprehensive index lists all forms by subject matter.

(6) The Locat-o-Matic on the following pages catalogs 70 categories for fast referral to pertinent forms.

Each form in this handbook has been labeled with a letter and a number. The letter indicates the major section, the number the form's position within the section.

A — Cost
B — Profit
C — Planning
D — Assets
E — Real Estate
F — Investments
G — International
H — Cash and Credit
I — Payroll
J — Accounting
K — Nonprofit

The Locat-o-Matic lists those forms which seem most applicable to each category. Simply look up the heading, and note the forms enumerated under it. For rapid identification and greater versatility, use the Locat-o-Matic Form Finder.

LOCAT-O-MATIC FORM FINDER

ACCOUNTS RECEIVABLE
H-45, H-46, H-55, H-56, H-60, J-1, J-2, J-3, J-4, J-28, J-29.

ASSET REPLACEMENT, ACQUISITION AND CONTROL
D-1, D-2, D-3, D-4, D-5, D-6, D-10, D-12, D-13, D-14, D-15, D-16, D-17, D-21, D-22, D-23, D-42, K-18, K-30, K-41.

ASSIGNMENTS
E-12, F-21, F-22, F-24, H-50, H-53, H-67.

BANK TRANSACTIONS
F-4, F-5, G-12, G-13, H-8, H-11, H-12, H-13, H-14, H-15, H-16, H-17, H-18, H-19, H-24, H-25, H-27, H-49, I-27, J-27, J-30, J-41, J-51, J-52.

BIDS
B-13, B-14, C-40, D-46, E-24, E-27.

BILLS OF LADING
A-13, A-14, G-42, J-15, J-16, J-17, J-18, J-19.

BONDS (FIDELITY OR INSURANCE)
E-17, E-18, H-65, H-66.

CASH FLOW CONTROL AND MANAGEMENT
C-1, C-2, C-3, C-4, C-5, C-7, C-8, C-9, D-44, G-1, G-5, G-7, G-8, G-9, G-10, H-1, H-3, H-7, H-10, H-11, H-20, H-21, H-24, H-28, J-25, J-26, J-32, J-46, K-17, K-29.

CASH TRANSFERS
B-17, G-2, G-6, H-4, H-5, H-6, H-11, H-22, H-23, H-24, H-27, H-32, I-27, J-31, J-33, J-34.

CONTRACTS
A-57, B-14, C-40, D-40, E-7, E-22, E-25, E-26, E-28, E-29, E-32, E-34, E-36, H-50, H-51, H-52, H-54, J-6.

CREDIT AND COLLECTIONS
H-37, H-38, H-39, H-40, H-43, H-44, H-46, H-49, H-57, H-58, H-59, H-60, H-63, H-64, H-65, H-66, J-44, J-45, J-46, J-47, J-48.

DEBT
C-34, C-35, D-24, D-28, D-31, D-32, D-39, E-3, E-6, E-8, E-10, E-13, F-11, F-12, F-13, F-14, F-15, F-25, F-26, F-27, F-31, F-32, F-33, G-55, H-14, H-15, H-53, H-61, H-62, H-63, H-64, J-51, J-52.

DEEDS

E-15, E-16, E-17, E-18, E-19, E-20.

DIVIDENDS

F-5, F-20, H-1.

EFFICIENCY ANALYSIS

A-48, A-49, A-64, A-65, G-52, K-41.

EMPLOYEE DISABILITY AND RETIREMENT

I-30, I-31, I-32, I-33, K-38.

ESTIMATED COSTS

A-53, A-60, A-63, A-64, A-66, B-7, B-13, E-12, G-53, G-57, G-60, I-1, K-10, K-11, K-12, K-13, K-15, K-32.

EXEMPTIONS

I-24, J-9, K-19, K-20, K-21, K-22, K-24.

EXPENSE REPORTS

A-38, A-39, A-40, B-7, J-35, J-36, J-37, J-49, K-14.

EXPORT FORMS

G-38, G-39, G-44, G-45, G-46, G-47, G-48, G-49.

FINANCIAL ASSET MANAGEMENT

D-25, D-26, D-27, F-1, F-2, F-3, F-4, F-6, F-9, F-10, F-15, F-16, F-18, F-19, F-20, F-21, F-22, F-23, F-24, F-28, F-29, F-34, G-3, G-16, G-17, G-19, G-20, G-21, G-24, G-25, G-26, G-56, H-9, H-27, H-29, I-28, J-56, J-57.

FINANCIAL INSTRUMENTS

F-5, F-8, F-11, F-12, F-13, F-14, F-17, F-30, F-31, F-33, G-4, G-14, G-15, G-16, G-18, G-23, H-6, H-9, H-24, H-25, H-26, H-30, H-31, H-35, H-36, H-50, H-51, H-52, H-54, H-61, H-62, K-28.

FINANCIAL REPORTS AND ANALYSIS

B-18, B-26, B-40, C-7, D-37, G-53, G-54, H-41, H-42, J-44, J-45, J-46, J-47, J-48, J-50, J-55, J-56.

FINANCIAL SOURCES

See Sources of Funds.

FRANCHISING

F-41, F-56, G-50.

FREIGHT

A-13, A-14, A-15, G-38, G-42, G-43, G-44, J-13, J-14, J-15, J-16, J-17, J-18, J-19, J-20, J-21.

GROWTH

B-45, C-21, C-23, D-4, D-6, D-7.

MORTGAGE DEBT

PERFORMANCE REPORTS

PERSONNEL

PLEDGES

PRESENT VALUE ANALYSIS

PRICING

PRODUCTION SCHEDULING

PRODUCTIVITY ANALYSIS

PROFIT ANALYSIS

PURCHASE AND PRODUCTION ORDERS

QUOTATIONS

RECEIVING

REGISTRATION

REQUISITIONING MATERIALS/SUPPLIES

RETURNS OF MERCHANDISE

RETURN ON INVESTMENT

B-19, B-20, B-21, B-23, B-24, B-25, B-45, B-46, C-20, C-31, C-32, C-33, D-6, D-7, D-42, F-32, F-35, G-22, G-53, J-56.

REVENUE

See Sales.

RISK ANALYSIS

C-31, C-33, G-53, G-54, H-41, H-42.

SALES

A-66, B-4, B-5, B-6, B-8, B-9, B-29, B-30, B-35, B-37, B-40, C-6, C-12, C-13, C-14, C-21, C-23, C-24, D-9, E-23, E-28, E-29, E-30, E-31, E-32, H-39, H-40, H-45, H-46, J-29, K-16.

SALARIES

See Wages.

SHIPPING, RECEIVING, INSPECTIONS, RETURNS

A-11, A-12, A-13, A-14, A-15, A-17, A-18, A-20, A-21, A-22, A-23, A-51, A-52, A-58, G-40, G-42, G-43, J-10, J-13, J-14, J-15, J-16, J-17, J-18, J-19, J-21, J-22, J-23, J-24.

SOURCES (EXTERNAL) OF FUNDS

C-36, D-24, D-26, D-27, D-41, F-5, F-7, F-8, F-11, F-12, F-13, F-14, G-55, J-46, J-50.

SYSTEMS ANALYSIS

A-65, C-47, D-45, F-1, G-37, H-1, H-2, I-41, J-25, J-43, J-53.

TAXATION

E-21, I-14, I-24, J-9, J-41, J-54, K-26, K-27.

VARIANCE ANALYSIS

A-64, B-22, B-30, C-10, G-62.

WAGES AND SALARIES

I-5, I-6, I-8, I-9, I-10, I-11, I-12, I-13, I-14, I-22, I-23, I-35, J-40, J-41, J-42, K-36, K-37.

WORKING CAPITAL

C-4, C-8, C-11, C-18.

YIELDS

B-20, B-23, B-24, B-25, B-46.

Acknowledgments

This handbook contains financial forms that represent many years of development, experience, and efforts to solve basic communication problems relating to cost control, profit analysis, and financial planning. Many forms have been created and recreated by businessmen with requirements unique to their line of activities, by systems analysts who have worked toward the development of a frictionless flow of financial information, by form-printing companies that have catered to general business needs and have standardized and streamlined forms to conform with common business, legal, and government agencies' requirements.

The author especially acknowledges the support of many fine organizations which contributed to the success of this undertaking.

Abba Co. (New Jerusalem)
Aer Lingus Irish Airlines (New York City)
Airborne Freight Corporation (Seattle, Washington)
Alerion Standards Co. (Miami, Florida)
All State Legal Supply Co. (Mountainside, New Jersey)
American Express Company (New York City)
The Asbury Graphite Mills, Inc. (Asbury, New Jersey)
Bankers Leasing Corporation (San Mateo, California)
Barclays Bank International Limited (New York City)
Bellaire Aluminum Products, Inc. (Bradenton, Florida)
Beta Gamma Sigma (St. Louis, Missouri)
Burroughs Corporation Office Products Group/Business Forms Division
Cleaveland Legal Blank Service, Inc. (East Hartford, Connecticut)
Eagle Lake Rod and Gun Club (Maine)
Electro-Methods, Inc. (South Windsor, Connecticut)
Fibre-Matte Mfg. Co. (Dallas, Texas)
The First National Bank of Boston (Massachusetts)
First National Bank of Kansas City (Missouri)
G. Fox & Co. (Hartford, Connecticut)
Garden Way, Incorporated (Connecticut)
Har-Conn Chrome Co. (West Hartford, Connecticut)
Indian Hill Country Club, Inc. (New Jersey)
Jackson & Son Quality Roofing Co. (Harrisburg, Pennsylvania)
Japan Air Lines (New York City)
Joske Bros. Co. (San Antonio, Texas)
Lexington Gardens, Incorporated (Connecticut)

Linwood Golf and Country Club (Linwood, New Jersey)
Litton Office Product Centers (Hartford, Connecticut)
Marathon Oil Company (Findlay, Ohio)
Marine Sales Company (South San Francisco, California)
Marlborough Farms (Marlborough, Connecticut)
Moore Business Forms, Inc. (Toronto, Ontario)
Murray Electric Plumbing & Heating (Chillicothe, Missouri)
New England Business Service, Inc. (Groton, Massachusetts)
Northeast Chemical & Supply Co., Inc. (Lansford, Pennsylvania)
Northeast Utilities (New England)
Northwestern National Bank of Minneapolis (Minnesota)
Oak Crest de Nicaragua (Managua, Nicaragua)
Pepperidge Farm, Inc. (Clinton, Connecticut)
Petroleum Equipment Sales and Service (Salisbury, Maryland)
Rediform Office Products (Paramus, New Jersey)
Regent Standard Forms, Inc. (Bellmawr, New Jersey)
Reliable Finance Corporation (New York)
Saint George Greek Orthodox Church of Passaic and Bergen County, Inc.
Ted's Market (Hebron, Connecticut)
Trans World Airlines, Inc. (New York City)
The Travelers Insurance Co. (Hartford, Connecticut)
United Technologies (Hartford, Connecticut)
The University of Connecticut (Storrs)
Wightman Farms, Inc. (Morristown, New Jersey)
Wilson Jones Company (Chicago, Illinois)

Since individuals, not organizations, make things happen, the author wishes to gold-star several part-time researchers: Steve Aronson, Dennis D'Angelo, Mietek Duzny, Ernest Ferrari, Peter Griggs, George Riggs, Dolores Vichas. The author is also most grateful to those persons who took time from their busy schedules to answer inquiries and questions.

Frank Aldrich, Senior Vice President
L.L. Allison
Robert C. Aronson, Assistant Treasurer
Steve Aronson
John S. Beckman, Sales Development Manager
Howard K. Clery, Jr., President
Dennis D'Angelo
Gerald O. Desplaines
Mietek Duszny
Jack Ellis, Vice President & General Manager
James N. Farrell, Sales Development Manager
Ernest Ferrari
Robert N. French, Treasurer, Metropolitan District, Hartford
Bernard Goldman, President
Bruce Goodpasture, Principal Technical Writer
P.C. Grassick, General Sales Manager

Charles E. Greenway, Vice President
John C. Griggs, Vice President
Peter Griggs
Paul Keller, Comptroller
Paul Levy, Sales Promotion
Martha Lewis, Manager, Business Development
James R. Livsey, Financial Analyst
Charles M. Mabon, Senior Vice President
Simon N. Mennell, Corporate Business
C.K. Morgan, Treasurer
Valerie E. Morgan, Senior Supervisor, International Banking
J.W. O'Leary, Group Vice President
Lori Proctor, Forms Management
George Quaggi, Assistant Administrator
Gordon Ramsay, Vice President, Cleaveland Legal Blank Service, Inc.
George Riggs, CPA, Rosen, Lasoff, & Plaster, P.C.
William Rogal, Retail Store Manager, Plimpton's
Elliot Jay Rosen, Controller
G. Gilbert Rosen, Executive Vice President
Robert W. Spaulding, Manager, Advertising & Sales Promotion
A.T. Stanger, Vice President
Marion Stanger, Office Manager
Gregory R. Stelmak, CPA
Lars H. Thunell, Director of Planning, American Express Company
Dolores Vichas
Jane Westrich, Corporate Research

Several governmental agencies also contributed forms, and the author wishes to acknowledge their assistance.

Alaska Department of Commerce & Economic Development
California Department of Corporations
Office of the Secretary of State of Connecticut
Delaware Division of Corporations
Florida Division of Corporations
Metropolitan District, Hartford, Connecticut
Secretary of State of Illinois
Secretary of State of Indiana
Secretary of State of Minnesota
Secretary of State of Massachusetts
New Jersey Department of State
Secretary of State of Ohio
Small Business Administration, Washington, D.C.
Texas Secretary of State's Office
U.S. Department of Commerce
Wisconsin Office of the Commissioner of Securities
Office of the Secretary of State of Wisconsin

Also, the author wishes to thank Prentice-Hall, Inc., Englewood Cliffs, New Jersey, for permission to reprint copyrighted material:

> *Budget Principles and Procedures* by John R. Bartizal.
> *Handbook of Financial Mathematics, Formulas, and Tables* by Robert P. Vichas

Although a particular form may no longer be used by a contributing organization, it is exhibited because it may be just the form, or checklist, or organizer, or idea-sparker, needed for *internal use* in *your* business, and it may provide the best solution to your communication problem. Of course, for quantities of preprinted forms, a commercial supply house can create and print forms for your internal needs (gleaned from ideas you drew on in this reference book), or from their supply stock, assuming availability.

Finally, the success of this volume depends not only on the suppliers of forms, materials, and ideas, but also on the reader and user. The author wishes to thank personally the purchaser of this handbook, and hopes that he or she profits by it. He also wishes to thank, in advance, those persons who are interested in sending ideas and forms for use in future revisions.

HANDBOOK OF ANNOTATED FINANCIAL FORMS

"That every man should eat and drink, and enjoy the good
of *all* his labour, it is the gift of God."

(*Ecclesiastes* 3:13)

"That no man should blame us in this abundance which
is administered by us."

(II *Corinthians* 8:20)

COST CONTROL, ANALYSIS, AND PLANNING

Cost Control, Analysis, and Planning

Control and planning of operations: these are the central purposes for accumulating, using, and analyzing cost data.

With cost data in hand management can better plan expansion of existing lines, new product introduction, evaluation of operational efficiency, pricing of products and services, investment decisions, product, department or divisional discontinuances; or better choose among techniques of production; or accurately charge customers for services or time; etc.

Cost control is essential for any firm operating in a highly competitive industry. For example, in broiler production, cost control down to fractional pennies per chicken marks the difference between profits and bankruptcy; marketing commands less prestige here because the firm exerts limited sway over prices of undifferentiated products. The same holds true for firms selling into controlled markets. Periods of recessions, more inflation (a tax), and political uncertainty encourage greater cost control in planning for future growth.

Cost analysis and control march with management every step from production to the office. Minor cost reductions magnify profits of an already profitable firm. But effective cost control can turn even a poorly managed concern into a profit giant.

The forms in this section represent some steps toward better control of costs and expenditures. Mostly they apply to materials, inventory and labor. Other forms, more analytical in nature, focus on management effectiveness or cost variance or material scheduling, production, pricing, or when to harvest a forestal product.

The finished goods inventory is a function of sales and the finished goods inventory requirements, anticipated price changes and shortages (or surpluses), supplier relationships, *inter alia.* After calculation of inventory and material requirements, actual commitments for material purchases and supplies may flow through any one of several possible systems. For example, material procured on receipt of a Materials Requisition

A-1
A-2
form (A-1), or a Stock Requisition form (A-2), places responsibility for raw materials INVENTORY CONTROL on production management. Purchasing and receiving, passive in the ordering function, are still responsible for checking. This system demands close coordination between changes in sales, work-in-process, and production requirements. Notice additional detail in the first form (A-1) required for BUDGET CONTROL purposes, viz., an allowance figure for the period, residual balance before ordering, value of current order, and sum available after ordering. The second form (A-2) treats this type of information differently, with accounting done elsewhere. A third

A-3
illustration (A-3), a shortened version, serves the same purpose. All forms provide for a signature from the person or department head ordering and the individual who approves

A-4
the requisition. Supplies (A-4), office or maintenance, are ordered on request, for the most part.

A-5
Part of an effective COST CONTROL system on purchases is a Request for Quotation (A-5) on products or services sold in competitive markets. A request for quotation, not a commitment to buy, assigns responsibility to the seller to meet competition. The form illustrated consists of four copies. The first and last pages are of equal length; the middle pages are of shorter and different lengths. This format permits individual typing of each recipient's name (and address). Each carbon copy accommodates the common information, description and quantity of material desired. In response to this request, the

A-6
firm will receive a Quotation form (A-6) indicating quantity, description, and unit price of the material, terms of sale, and approximate shipping date after receipt of order.

A-7
An effective purchasing system uses a Purchase Order (A-7) to request materials. Terms and conditions indicated on the form stipulate that the vendor transmits invoices in triplicate, the buyer be notified of any delay in shipment, unordered merchandise be returned at the seller's expense, the seller warrants the quality of merchandise, the order and amounts due may not be assigned, the price must not exceed that shown on the quotation, and the buyer retains the right to make periodic changes. There are distinct advantages to a centralized purchasing function. Because purchasing specialists are developed, COSTS ARE CUT through:

- reduction of clerical output;
- better inventory control;
- improved price negotiations (and discounts).

A-8
A shortened version of a purchase order also appears (A-8). The displayed copies are for *production control* and *quality control.* For *financial control* other copies should be routed to receiving, accounting, and purchasing, in addition to copies retained by the originator of the order and the original to the supplier. When changes become necessary

due to an increase or decrease in sales or specification modifications, a Purchase Order Change Notice (A-9) is sent to the seller, which notice amends the initial purchase order. Sometimes such changes compel an equitable adjustment between buyer and seller.

A-9

Sometimes material which does not conform to required specifications may be permitted, in which event the buyer will authorize the supplying manufacturer to ship nonconforming material (A-10). Two points are noted:

A-10

(a) Final acceptance of material is subject to buyer's inspection and testing.
(b) The buyer does not obligate himself to accept future shipments that may deviate from the standard.

Smaller manufacturers may find this type of authorization a keyhole opportunity to supply a large enterprise on a regular basis while ironing out internal production matters.

The supplier may complete an Order Form (A-11) like the one shown, which is actually a two-section form with four copies attached to the left-hand stub and two copies to the right-hand one. The purpose of this system is to SAVE TIME and CUT order processing COSTS. The four-copy set consists of an original, one for inventory, another to sales, and the last to billing. The second set is inserted between pages two and three and comprises one copy for accounting and a second for back order. Both sets together create a system of cost control without duplication of effort and without leaving one department or another aphotic. In other words, a good COST CONTROL SYSTEM begins with the receipt of an order and ends when the money is collected.

A-11

Shipment preparation will require several more documents. A Packing Slip (A-12) may be enclosed for control at the supplier's end and comparison of invoices and materials received at the buyer's end. Also, a Bill of Lading (A-13) will be prepared. Two examples appear (A-13, A-14), practically identical in content. This document, issued by the carrier, may be completed by the shipper. The bill of lading serves at least three purposes:

A-12

A-13
A-14

(a) It is receipt signed by the carrier for receipt of specific merchandise.
(b) It defines the terms of contract between shipper and carrier.
(c) It is the certificate of ownership covering merchandise represented by the document.

A straight bill of lading is non-negotiable in any country. Usually the buyer can obtain possession of the merchandise without presenting the bill of lading. With shipments by air, the shipper will issue a Letter of Instruction (A-15) along with an Air Waybill (illustrated in Section G) and other documents. If the merchandise is to be exported, even to Puerto Rico or the Virgin Islands, other documents (discussed in Section G) must accompany the letter of instruction.

A-15

After supplies are requested (A-16) and shipped, at the receiving end, a clerk will complete a Receiving Form (A-17). Adequate COST CONTROL PROCEDURES call for comparing number of packages, weight, and type of goods against the Purchase Order

A-16
A-17

A-18   (A-7) with notation as to whether freight was prepaid or collect. On a daily basis the shipping department will complete a Daily Report (A-18) that details from whom goods were received, carrier, number of packages, weight and quantity, description of merchandise, freight charges, and to what department delivered. Tight control lessens the chance of misrouting or pilfering and INCREASES PROFITS.

A-19   For routine follow-ups on goods ordered, a Rapid Follow-Up form (A-19) will suffice. It's a real time-saver. This form applies for purchase orders and changes, incorrect or incomplete invoices, partial shipments, delays, back orders, and other routine matters.

A-20
A-21
A-22
A-23   At some point it become necessary to inspect merchandise to ascertain whether it measures up to specifications (A-20). If goods and equipment have been sold to a government agency, inspection may well occur on the manufacturer's premises. It is sound policy to check goods before payment of invoice. It is sound policy to check merchandise for resale before reshipping it to customers. For equipment not measuring up to required standards, a Nonconformance Report (A-21) is completed. If parts and equipment are returned, a Returned Goods Report (A-22) may accompany them. Similarly, if work in process does not measure up to standards, a Material Rejection Ticket (A-23) is completed and filed. Information required includes description of the deviation from acceptable standards, reason for rejection, disposition of the material, and, most importantly, COST COMPUTATION, an important step to REDUCE PROFIT LEAKS and provide input for analysis of budgeted versus actual expenses.

An adequate control procedure for supply inventories as well as finished goods supports supply costs analysis. Close control tends to restrain usage and inventory buildup. A concern may establish minimum-maximum levels for certain articles or categories of items. Further, control helps to determine the rate of use for key items. It means better timing of purchases, taking advantage of quantity discounts. Controlling production activity is especially significant for total cost determination.

A-24   One simple control form is an Inventory Tag (A-24) for either specific items or categories of articles. It records considerable information in rather limited space. Since all tags are numbered, all must be accounted for. This simplifies the inventory-taking process, or it may be supplemental to computerized inventory records. Space is provided for the following information, front and back sides:

    (a)   Article or class of material.
    (b)   Quantity, size, and building or warehouse location.
    (c)   Unit price and total value.
    (d)   Who counted the stock, who priced it, and who checked it.
    (e)   Date and amount in, out, and balance.

A-25   Material removed requires a Stores Requisition (A-25). The form registers the quantity, size, description, and part or pattern number of the article, who received it, and who approved the order. The department subsequently is charged by accounting. The stock clerk uses data from the form to update inventories.

Manufactured material moving into inventory begins with a Production Order (A-26). **A-26**
Notice that for control purposes the material requisition numbers are also recorded for
later comparison. The production manager authorizes initiation of work when inventory
buildup is required or when a job is ready for production. This system establishes
priorities; it facilitates planning for all departments and operators; the production
manager can readjust job sequence by periodically reviewing job orders in order to
SCHEDULE OPERATIONS EFFICIENTLY, *lower costs, enrich profits.* Also
illustrated is a Dual Purpose Document Card (A-27) from engineering. **A-27**

Closely monitor inventory for sale as well. Some products lend themselves to daily or
weekly inventories (A-28). The modeled form provides for the previous inventory **A-28**
balance, minus transfers to other locations plus deliveries, and total inventory on hand
matched against total weekly sales. In this particular case, the unit manager responds for
the inventory count. If merchandise is transferred to another unit or if new merchandise is
received, this information must equate with data on the transfer and new stock forms (A-29). **A-29**

Another variation of the inventory control form (A-30) provides for an indication of the **A-30**
age of stock and markdowns. After a physical count is completed of the number of items
on hand, and unit cost computed, extensions are then made of the total cost of each item
on hand. These total cost figures are compared with balances shown in stock ledger
records. The data provide analytical input on the average age of inventory and degree of
obsolescence, identification of slow-moving or hot items, and basis for working with sales
to move overstocked items.

With the theater example, management can shift stock around among units to prevent
staleness and discards, while nonperishables may be marked down in value. Stock
rotation, usually preferred, may be assisted with a Rotated Unit Control Board (A-31), or **A-31**
a Stock Control Record by Department, Classification, and Description (A-32), or a **A-32**
Stock Ledger Card (A-33). The accounting clerk posts information from approved **A-33**
invoices onto the stock ledger card. A separate card is maintained for each article or kinds
of articles, parts, or raw materials. The clerk enters the voucher number, number of units
received, unit price, and total cost in the received section. The balance on hand is the
adjusted amount. For control purposes, the sums of the received sections on all stock
ledger cards should agree with the total of all charges posted from the voucher register to
the inventory control accounts in the ledger.

The purposes of these forms have been:

◆ to plug profit leaks at the source, the user level;
◆ to make COST CONTROL an ongoing system of PROFIT PLANNING.

The most effective point at which to stop excess expenditures is *before* the purchase order
is written. Productivity is essential. Productivity measurement depends on an accurate
and complete Job Material and Labor Record (A-34) to catalog the amount of material, **A-34**
price per unit, and total material cost *plus* labor by individual or category and additional

job expenses. Profits depend upon proper pricing. Pricing depends upon adequate cost data. Sales depend upon competitive pricing and cost minimization. And *cost minimization translates into profit maximization.* Nonperformance, poor utilization of time, too much time spent on low payoff situations apply to nonmanufacturing endeavors as well.

A-35

A-36
A Daily Time Record (A-35) aids in productivity analysis and correct billing of customers. Where a client buys a service expressed principally in time, a Time Charge Record (A-36) presents a complete picture, minimizes disputes over billings, and IMPROVES PROFITS. Also, the firm's management can determine, from an analysis of billing records, whether it handles its resources in the most productive manner.

A-37

A-38
An effective cost control system must be specific, addressed to potential and actual problem areas, not to a general policy statement that "costs must be cut." The translating of general policy into specific action usually originates with a determination of where spending seems excessive or out of line, and this begins with adequate record keeping. For example, a detailed Expense Report (A-37) is a must for travelers. The front page of the form breaks down expenses into categories; but entertainment, automobile and miscellaneous expenses require more specific input and should be supported, whenever feasible, by receipts. The reverse side of the form is for recording expenses not reimbursed and credit card expenses by day of the week and then totaled for the week. A variation of the Expense Report (A-38) provides space for home office approval of certain expenses and further details on telephone, entertainment, and miscellaneous expenditures. Charge items are itemized by category rather than by firm.

Unfortunately, cost control is not cost free. Requiring forms and records does help to establish which costs wander out of line or are abnormal in any accounting period, and it also discourages free use or misuse of company facilities.

A-39
For example, a long-distance telephone log (A-39) discourages employees from using telephones for long-distance personal calls, encourages the caller to keep the call short and to the point, provides space to register to whom the call is made (and possibly even why) and the telephone number, and to whom the expense should be charged. Some organizations compel employees to make only person-to-person calls, limit all calls to, say, ten minutes, and record time and charges. This control system of operator-assisted calls may cost more than it was designed to save. Unless a specific client is being charged for calls, time and charges can be estimated and then matched against telephone company statements.

A-40
Another profit leaker is overuse of photocopy or other duplicating equipment. Aside from the problem of personal use, free and easy access to this equipment may encourage extravagant and even unnecessary output. The Xerographic Request and Charge Slip (A-40) serves the dual purpose of work order and instruction to charge the appropriate department or client to be billed.

For a jobbing plant, the focal point of the cost system is the job cost record, whether for a departmentalized plant (A-41) or a nondepartmentalized plant (A-42). For a given job, the job cost record catalogs all costs associated with a particular job up to that date— direct labor and materials, and overhead. From the firm's viewpoint, this represents work in progress. The work-in-progress account is the CONTROL ACCOUNT because its balance should equal the total of all costs of uncompleted jobs in the cost ledger; or work in progress may more conveniently be subdivided into labor in process, materials in process, and overhead in process for finer analysis and better cost control of the components. Fundamental to any job cost record are:

A-41
A-42

    (a)   identification of the job;
    (b)   periodic entries for direct labor costs;
    (c)   data on direct material costs;
    (d)   computation of applicable overhead costs;
    (e)   a summary of total costs.

IMPROVED COST CONTROL means controlling material usage (A-43). This may translate into less waste or changing the combination or mix of materials. There are really two mixes involved at this level. A product can frequently be produced by more than one combination of materials. It can also be produced by varying combinations of labor (of differing skills and quality) together with various combinations of material and machinery. Obviously, COST CUTTING means finding a LEAST COST COMBINATION, or something approaching it, given production and quality constraints. The financial form enumerates data on amount of material consumed and cost analysis for each class of materials. Variance between actual and standard is then accounted for. Improved cost control also means labor use records (A-44). The Direct Labor summary (two variations reproduced) provides for the same type of information as the material usage report. Again an analysis of differences appears.

A-43

A-44

Another cost control form, the Job Cost Estimate (A-45), similar to the job cost record, calls for information on costs to date, including shop labor and material costs and subcontract expenses, plus estimated costs to finish the job. The inventory value of work in progress is figured as of a specific date, whether or not there has been a partial shipment, with space to indicate if there are job delays.

A-45

After job completion, entries appear on a production control record, summarized on a monthly Production Cost Summary (A-46), data being taken from a job cost record. This information is then available for appropriate accounting entries on finished goods and work-in-process inventories and for COST ANALYSIS. In addition, a Shop Job Log (A-47) keeps track of job orders by customer and also provides space for billing information, the invoice number and amount billed. This simple system helps control work flow and trace customer inquiries.

A-46

A-47

The monthly Departmental Budget Performance Report (A-48) summarizes actual and budgeted expenses for each expense category. An analysis of budgeted performance by department provides some measure on EFFICIENCY OF ASSET USE. Tying bonuses

A-48

to budget performance may provide additional incentive to manage effectively those costs under departmental control or influence.

A-49

A-50

Another cost analysis form, the Manpower Loading Report (A-49), caters to a month-by-month analysis of a long-term project. Estimated number of labor hours and activity slack (converted into weeks) show up in the analysis. Yet another type of labor analysis, a Daily Summary Control (A-50), highlights *sales productivity,* as important to cost control and efficiencies as shop labor analysis. This particular form summarizes the daily activities of individual salespeople. From it is derived an analysis of the number of sales calls, number of new orders and new accounts opened (i.e., productivity), service calls, and dollar value of sales efforts (i.e., efficiency). The daily record is summarized at the bottom in a monthly tally.

A-51

A-52

Besides labor productivity, cost analysis entails material analysis (A-51). Materials that do not measure up to standards elevate costs to the user; and if nonconforming materials are accepted, appropriate adjustments may be forthcoming. Similarly, finished goods inventory shortages reduce profits and raise costs. The worksheet for shortage rate calculations (A-52) pinpoints monthly shortages, permits analysis of deviation from historical norms, and prepares the way for management to take appropriate action to REDUCE these LOSSES.

A-53

A-54

PLANNING FOR PROFITS begins with PLANNING COST CONTROL and ANALYSIS. The difference between estimated and actual costs (A-53) determines the extent of profits or losses per job, project, or program. The indicated form enumerates estimated amounts and costs of materials, labor, and subcontracting on the left and actual data on the right. The profit (or loss) summary—the good (or bad) news—appears on the far right. Planning for profits is not unique to any industry, activity, or organization, and imposes proper invoicing of labor and material costs (A-54). The form depicted requests complete details on parts, price per unit, total amount, and summary of labor services performed. This information allows for:

- ◆ further analysis;
- ◆ subsequent adjustments in pricing policies;
- ◆ checking for proper billing;
- ◆ inventory control and planning.

A-55
A-56

Other examples of this type of form are the Auto Repair Order (A-55) and the Electronic Repair Order (A-56). Of course, if this information sits idly by and is not conscripted for analysis and planning, then a valuable information source is being underutilized, or even overlooked. Planning includes cost control, inventory management, sales analysis, and expansion or contraction of services and parts.

Cost control also means planning for future contingencies. An honest supplier-customer relationship dictates adequate understanding of contractual relationships. A Contingent

Fee Agreement (A-57) establishes the parameters for final price settlement when there are unknowns. Unknowns may include price change or interest rate swings, special material purchases, or court settlements, for example.

A-57

Additionally, cost control means monitoring freight charges. The examples in A-58 reproduce file memos on spot and relet shipping rates and destinations. A Billing Log (A-59) keeps track of invoice numbers and dates by customer, job number, date shipped and by whom, and information on freight billing. The check off on the right-hand side is a time-saving checklist and update reminder.

A-58

A-59

Another aspect of planning for cost control springs from the PERT/Cost Estimating Form (A-60). PERT is an acronym for Program Evaluation and Review Technique, a network planning of objective-oriented work. PERT establishes a basis for effective cost control and replanning and bringing together raw material components in an orderly and cost efficient manner. Notice in the form that PERT time estimates call for best possible and worst possible times together with an estimate of the most likely outcome.

A-60

But control and planning of costs need not be so sophisticated. The Service Station Day Sheet (A-61), a basic format, contributes information for analysis and planning for PROFITABLE OPERATIONS. With adequate data, computations on a Pricing Cost Sheet (A-62) will yield a selling price that COVERS COSTS and captures a desired return on investment. The calculations derive from sufficient data on material and labor costs, overhead and shipping expenses, plus sufficient markup to cover other costs.

A-61

A-62

Where time and costs work against a producer, there is (a) a best time to sell, and (b) a point beyond that time where costs continue to rise. For example, growers of flowers or plants or Christmas trees try to calculate the optimum time to sell. At some point costs rise faster than the increase in value so that time alone works against the grower. A Christmas tree grower, in planning for cost control, will want to compute the present value of current and future outlays per acre (A-63) and compare the total results to projected incomes in various periods. Similar techniques are employed by whiskey, wine, and cheese agers as well.

A-63

Another planning form is used for pharmacy costs, production, and variance analysis (A-64). The first section deals with production, the number of prescriptions filled per month, which is compared with planned output. Then the percent of plan achieved is computed both monthly and cumulative to date. The second section covers cost. Costs are analyzed to discover whether they are over- or underplanned. The third section analyzes costs per prescription filled, and once again actual is compared with planned-per-unit cost.

A-64

The next form (A-65) supplies analysis of cost data, along the same lines, by subsidiary, of a large retail enterprise. This semiannual appraisal compares data against the previous

A-65

year's results. Of course, the end purpose of each of these forms differs, but the techniques are similar. They can be adapted to any parallel purpose.

A-66   The last form in this section is a Cost/Income Format (A-66). This is the format prescribed by corporate management for budgets submitted to them by operating divisions. The first page contains instructions for completing the statement form and requests that supporting schedules be attached. After corporate management has reviewed the inputs, data will be analyzed and spun out for planning costs and profits.

Figure A-1: REQUISITION ON PURCHASING DEPARTMENT
(From the book <u>Business Finance Handbook</u> by Lillian Doris, Editor. © 1953 by Prentice-Hall, Inc. Published by Prentice-Hall, Inc., Englewood Cliffs, New Jersey 07632.)

Figure A-2: STOCK REQUISITION FORM
(Courtesy of Regent Standard Forms, Inc., Bellmawr, New Jersey 08031.)

purchase requisition

Supplier_____   Purchase
_____   Order No._____

PURCHASING DEPT: please order for dept._____   Requisition No._____

Deliver to_____Notify_____   Date _____19_____

For use on_____On hand_____One month usage_____Charge No._____Date Wanted_____

Quantity	Description	Price

Remarks

Approval (Final)	Signed
Approval (Supt.)	

WilsonJones Division of Swingline Inc.   GrayLine Form 601-03 c 1975 Printed U.S.A.

Approval (Final)	Signed
Approval (Supt.)	

WilsonJones Division of Swingline Inc.   GrayLine Form 601-03 c 1975 Printed U.S.A.

Figure A-3: PURCHASE REQUISITION FORM
(Copyright 1975 by Wilson Jones Company. All rights reserved. Forms may be obtained, subject to supply, from Wilson Jones Company, 6150 Touhy Avenue, Chicago, Illinois 60648.)

REQUISITION FOR SUPPLIES

TO PURCHASING AGENT: Date .... No. ....

Please furnish the following: To Be Used For ....

QUANTITY	PART OR CAT. NO.	SIZE	FULL DESCRIPTION	✓
			When Wanted	

Deliver To .... Dept.   Charge To .... Acct. No..............

Source of Supply ....   P. O. No. ....

Make this form in duplicate — Retain one for reference.   Signed .... Approved ....
Use a separate sheet for each kind of goods.   For Dept.

STANDARD FORM 645
REGENT STANDARD FORMS, INC., PENNSAUKEN, N. J. 08109

Figure A-4: REQUISITION FOR SUPPLIES
(Courtesy of Regent Standard Forms, Inc., Bellmawr, New Jersey 08031.)

Request For Quotation
Inquiry Only
This Is Not An Order

To:
1 :

To:
2 :

To:
3 :

	Summary Of Quotations			
Item	Quantity	No. 1	No. 2	No. 3
Other Information				
Delivery				
F.O.B.				
Terms				

Inquiry No.

Date

To Receive Consideration, Your Quotation Must
Be Received By

Please Quote Unit Price, Shipping Point, Terms, F.O.B. and delivery on the following:

Item	Quantity	Description and Delivery Required

Special Notice to Vendor

1. IF UNABLE TO QUOTE, PLEASE ADVISE AT ONCE AND RETURN BLUE PRINTS, SPECIFICATIONS, ETC.
2. SHOW ABOVE INQUIRY NUMBER ON ALL QUOTATIONS.
3. ITEMIZE ALL UNIT PRICES, DISCOUNTS, TERMS AND CHARGES. SHOW TAXES SEPARATELY, IF APPLICABLE.
4. ATTACH COMPLETE SPECIFICATIONS FOR ANY SUBSTITUTIONS OFFERED.
5. WE RESERVE THE RIGHT TO ACCEPT OR REJECT YOUR QUOTATION.
6. ALL QUOTATIONS SUBJECT TO ACCEPTANCE ON OUR USUAL PURCHASE ORDER FORM.

By _____

WilsonJones GRAYLINE FORM 44-152 4-PART
© 1976 · PRINTED IN U.S.A

Figure A-5: REQUEST FOR QUOTATION

Quotation

ELECTRO-METHODS, INCORPORATED
P. O. BOX 54   330 GOVERNORS HIGHWAY
SO. WINDSOR, CONNECTICUT 06074

DATE:

QUOTATION NO. ✳ 874

YOUR INQUIRY NO.

In response to your inquiry, we submit the following quotation:

QUANTITY	DESCRIPTION	PRICE

TERMS:	F.O.B.	ESTIMATED SHIPPING DATE:

We are a small business as defined by the Small Business Administration.
We are an Equal Opportunity Employer.

By _____

Figure A-6: QUOTATION
(Courtesy of Electro-Methods, Inc., South Windsor, Connecticut.)

ELECTRO-METHODS, INC.

P.O. BOX 54, 330 GOVERNORS HIGHWAY, SOUTH WINDSOR, CONN. 06074

TEL. (203) 289-8661 · TWX (710) 425-6016 · DWNS-00-144-7762

VENDOR •

PLEASE ENTER OUR ORDER FOR THE FOLLOWING, SUBJECT TO INSTRUCTIONS HEREIN AND ALL TERMS AND CONDITIONS PRINTED ON THE REVERSE SIDE:

DATE OF ORDER	REQUISITION NO.	TERMS	F.O.B. SOUTH WINDSOR, CONN. OR	SHIP VIA	PREPAY ALL SHIPMENTS

ITEM	QUANTITY	PATTERN NO. (PART NO.)	DESCRIPTION OF MATERIALS AND OR SERVICES TO BE SUPPLIED	PRICE

IMPORTANT INSTRUCTIONS:

1— PLEASE COMPLETE AND RETURN ACKNOWLEDGMENT PLY IMMEDIATELY CONFIRMING PRICE AND INDI-CATING EARLIEST SHIPPING DATE OF EACH ITEM.
2— RENDER INVOICES PROMPTLY AND IN TRIPLICATE.
3— THIS ORDER IS SUBJECT TO THE TERMS AND CON-DITIONS PRINTED ON THE REVERSE SIDE HEREOF, AND NO EXCEPTIONS WILL BE ALLOWED WITHOUT WRITTEN PERMISSION OF THE PURCHASING DEPART-MENT.

ELECTRO-METHODS, INC.

_____
PURCHASING

ACKNOWLEDGEMENT

ELECTRO - METHODS, INC.

P.O. BOX 54, 330 GOVERNORS HIGHWAY, SOUTH WINDSOR, CONN. 06074

TEL. (203) 289-8661
TWX (710) 425-6016

ITEM	SHIPPING DATE	PRICE	ITEM	SHIPPING DATE	PRICE
1			5		
2			6		
3			7		
4			8		

PLEASE RETURN IMMEDIATELY CONFIRMING PRICE AND INDICATING EARLIEST SHIPPING DATE OF EACH ITEM.

WE ACCEPT YOUR ORDER SUBJECT TO THE TERMS AND CONDITIONS PRINTED ON THE VENDOR COPY OF YOUR PURCHASE ORDER, AT THE PRICE AND SHIPPING DATE INDICATED ON THIS ACKNOWLEDGEMENT.

VENDOR _____

PER _____ DATE _____

Figure A-7: PURCHASE ORDER
(Courtesy of Electro-Methods, Inc., South Windsor, Connecticut.)

47

ELECTRO-METHODS, INC.

P.O. BOX 54, 330 GOVERNORS HIGHWAY, SOUTH WINDSOR, CONN. 06074

TEL. (203) 289-8661
TWX (710) 425-6016

VENDOR •

PURCHASE ORDER

THIS NUMBER MUST APPEAR ON ALL INVOICES, PACKING SLIPS, PACKAGES AND CORRESPONDENCE RELATIVE TO THIS ORDER

CONN. STATE TAX EXEMPTION CERTIFICATE # 0658-559

THIS ORDER TAX EXEMPT: ☐ YES ☐ NO

DATE SHIPMENT REQUIRED AT ELECTRO-METHODS, INC.

•

PLEASE ENTER OUR ORDER FOR THE FOLLOWING, SUBJECT TO INSTRUCTIONS HEREIN AND ALL TERMS AND CONDITIONS PRINTED ON THE REVERSE SIDE:

DATE OF ORDER	REQUISITION NO.	TERMS	F.O.B. SOUTH WINDSOR, CONN. OR	SHIP VIA	PREPAY ALL SHIPMENTS

ITEM	QUANTITY	PATTERN NO. / PART NO.	DESCRIPTION OF MATERIALS AND OR SERVICES TO BE SUPPLIED	PRICE

IMPORTANT INSTRUCTIONS:

1— PLEASE COMPLETE AND RETURN ACKNOWLEDGMENT PLY IMMEDIATELY CONFIRMING PRICE AND INDICATING EARLIEST SHIPPING DATE OF EACH ITEM.

2— RENDER INVOICES PROMPTLY AND IN TRIPLICATE

3— THIS ORDER IS SUBJECT TO THE TERMS AND CONDITIONS PRINTED ON THE REVERSE SIDE HEREOF, AND NO EXCEPTIONS WILL BE ALLOWED WITHOUT WRITTEN PERMISSION OF THE PURCHASING DEPARTMENT.

ELECTRO-METHODS, INC.

_____ PURCHASING

PRODUCTION CONTROL

QUALITY CONTROL

Figure A-8: PURCHASE ORDER (SHORT FORM)
(Courtesy of Electro-Methods, Inc., South Windsor, Connecticut.)

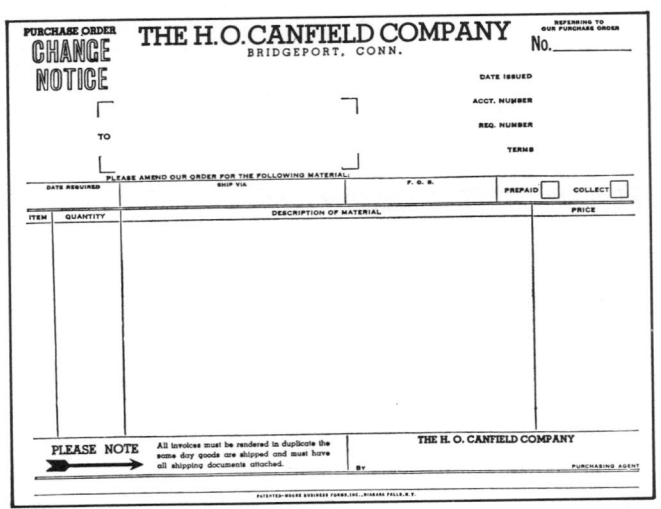

Figure A-9: PURCHASE ORDER CHANGE NOTICE
(From the book Business Finance Handbook by Lillian Doris, Editor, © 1953 by Prentice-Hall, Inc. Published by Prentice-Hall, Inc., Englewood Cliffs, New Jersey 07632.)

Pratt & Whitney Aircraft DIVISION OF UNITED AIRCRAFT CORPORATION

No. 35181

EXPERIMENTAL PURCHASING SECTION
AUTHORIZATION TO SHIP NONCONFORMING MATERIAL

VENDOR QUALITY CONTROL SURVEILLANCE	YES ☐	NO ☐	*If "NO", then Q.C.R. blocks not applicable.*

VENDOR NAME & ADDRESS	PART NAME		PWA RECEIVING DESTINATION	PAGE ___ OF ___
	PART NO.	PURCHASE ORDER	SERIAL NO.	PACK. SLIP NO.
	(PART OR MATERIAL) COMPLETE TO B/P SPECIFICATION YES ☐ NO ☐		FURTHER OPERATIONS REQUIRED AT PWA YES ☐ NO ☐	

DESCRIPTION AND DRAWING LOCATION OF EACH NONCONFORMANCE:

HAVE SAME NONCONFORMANCES OCCURRED BEFORE: NUMBER OF TIMES

ENGINEERING AUTHORIZATION	PURCHASING AUTHORIZATION TO SHIP	VENDOR REPRESENTATIVE	DATE
TYPED OR PRINTED NAME OF PWA Q.C.R.	PWA Q.C.R. SIGNATURE	TIME	DATE

VENDOR IS AUTHORIZED TO SHIP CONDITIONALLY FOR REVIEW AND SUBJECT TO FINAL ACCEPTANCE BY PWA PARTS WHICH HAVE BEEN FULLY INSPECTED AND PRESENTED TO V.Q.C. IF DEVIATE IT SHOULD BE NOTED THAT ACCEPTANCE OF THIS MATERIAL ESTABLISHES NO PRECEDENCE FOR CONTINUED ACCEPTANCE OF THESE PARTS IN A SIMILAR CONDITION.

PWA FORM 4085   REV. 2-68 (FORMERLY 1652B)

2. PURCHASING—BUYER MAIL TO P M C ENG.

3. PURCHASING-BUYER

4. P W A INSPECTION—SHIP WITH MATERIAL & PACKAGING SLIP

5. V.Q.C.

**Figure A-10: EXPERIMENTAL PURCHASING—AUTHORIZATION TO SHIP
NONCONFORMING MATERIAL**
(Courtesy of Electro-Methods, Inc., South Windsor, Connecticut.)

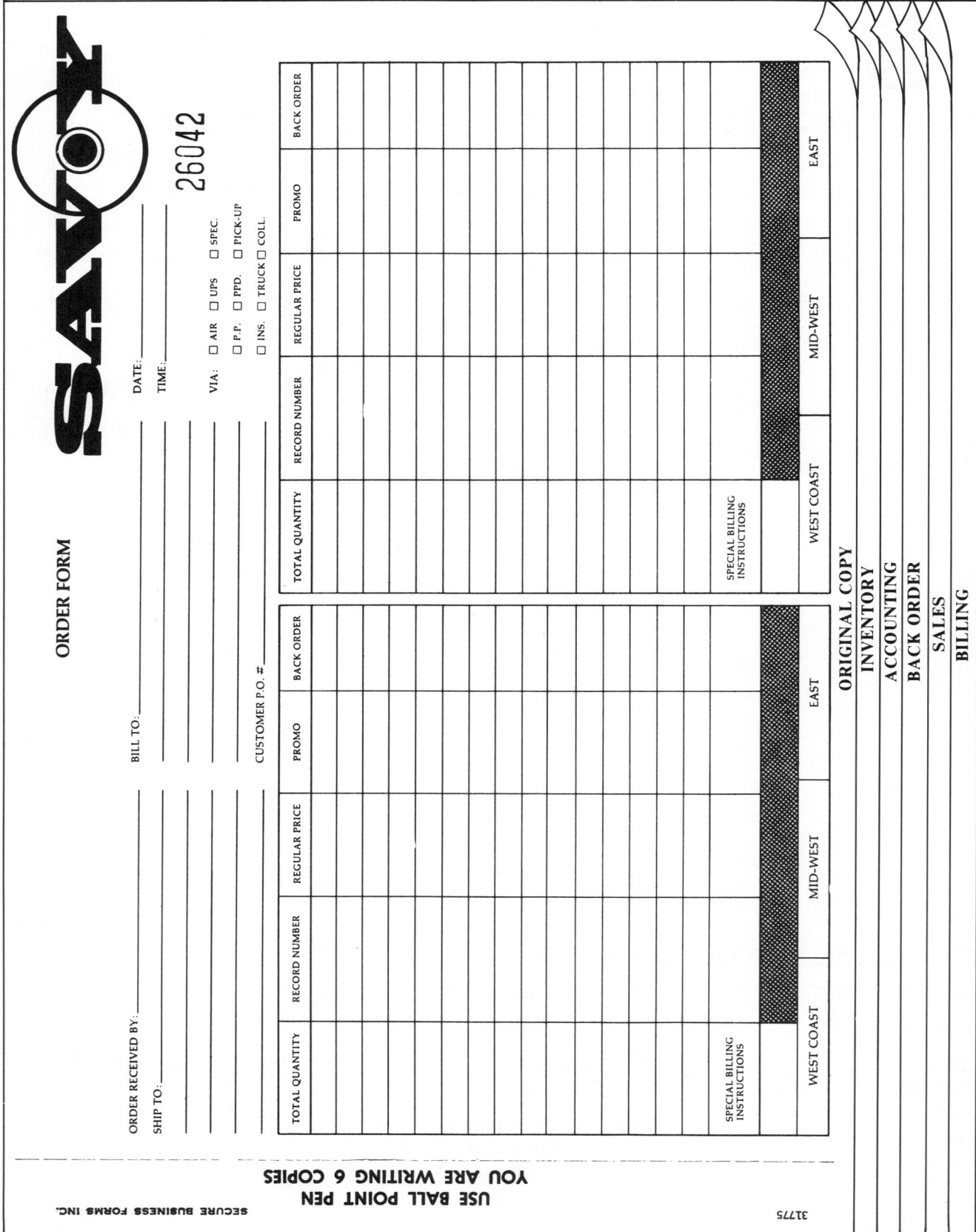

Figure A-11: SHIPPING, INVENTORY, ACCOUNTING, SALES, BILLING FORM

PACKING SLIP

FROM
ELECTRO-METHODS, INC.
P.O. BOX 54, 330 GOVERNORS HIGHWAY, SOUTH WINDSOR, CONN. 06074

PURCHASE ORDER NO.	CUSTOMER'S NO.	JOB NUMBER	DATE	o
				19

Sold To

Address

Ship To

Address

QUANTITY	DESCRIPTION

PACKED BY	CHECKED BY	CARTONS-PKGS.	TOTAL WEIGHT	SHIPPED VIA

PLEASE NOTIFY US IMMEDIATELY IF ERROR IS FOUND IN SHIPMENT

No. 05232

UARCO Business Forms

PLEASE NOTIFY US IMMEDIATELY IF ERROR IS FOUND IN SHIPMENT

No. 05232

UARCO Business Forms

Figure A-12: PACKING SLIP
(Courtesy of Electro-Methods, Inc., South Windsor, Connecticut.)

STRAIGHT BILL OF LADING—ORIGINAL—Not Negotiable

Shipper's no. N⁰ 12141

RECEIVED, subject to the classifications and tariffs in effect on the date of the Issue of this Bill of Lading.

Company _____ Agent's No. _____

At _____ 19 ___ From **ARI   RECORDS**   Norwalk, Conn.

the property described hereon, in apparent good order, except as noted (contents and condition of contents of packages unknown), marked, consigned, and destined as indicated below, which said company (the word company being understood throughout this contract as meaning any person or corporation in possession of the property under the contract) agrees to carry to its usual place of delivery at said destination, if on its own road, or its own water line, otherwise to deliver to another carrier on the route to said destination. It is mutually agreed, as to each carrier of all or any of said property over all or any portion of said route to destination, and as to each party at any time interested in all or any of said property, that every service to be performed hereunder shall be subject to all the conditions not prohibited by law, whether printed or written, herein contained, including the conditions on back hereof, which are hereby agreed to by the shipper and accepted for himself and his assigns.

Consigned to _____

(Mail or Street Address of Consignee—for purposes of notification only.)

Destination _____ State _____ County _____

Route _____ Delivery Address★ _____

(★To be filled in only when shipper desires and governing tariffs provide for delivery thereat.)

Delivering Carrier _____ Car or Vehicle Initials _____ No. _____

No. Packages	Description of Articles, Special Marks, and Exceptions	*Weight (Sub. to Cor.)	Class or Rate	Check Column	Subject to Section 7 of Conditions of applicable bill of lading, if this shipment is to be delivered to the consignee without recourse on the consignor, the consignor shall sign the following statement: The carrier shall not make delivery of this shipment without payment of freight and all other lawful charges.
	FBD/BXS. — Talking Machine or Phonograph				
	Records, Plastic, Non-Breakable, Disc-Type				(Signature of Consignor.)
					If charges are to be prepaid, write or stamp here, "To be Prepaid."
					Received $ _____ to apply in prepayment of the charges on the property described hereon.
					Agent or Cashier
					Per _____ (The signature here acknowledges only the amount prepaid.)
					Charges Advanced: $

*If the shipment moves between two ports by a carrier by water, the law requires that the bill of lading shall state whether it is carrier's or shipper's weight.
NOTE—Where the rate is dependent on value, shippers are required to state specifically in writing the agreed or declared value of the property.
The agreed or declared value of the property is hereby specifically stated by the shipper to be not exceeding
_____ per _____

† "The fibre containers used for this shipment conform to the specifications set forth in the box maker's certificate thereon, and all other requirements of Rule 41 of the Uniform Freight Classification and Rule 5 of the National Motor Freight Classification." ‡ Shipper's imprint in lieu of stamp; not a part of bill of lading approved by the Interstate Commerce Commission.

ARI   RECORDS _____ Shipper _____ Agent _____   **1**

Norwalk, Conn. _____ Per _____ Per _____

Permanent post-office address of shipper.

ARI.   RECORDS _____ Shipper _____   **2**

Norwalk, Conn. _____ Per _____ ☞ Agent must detach and retain this Shipping Order and must sign the Original Bill of Lading.

Permanent post-office address of shipper.

ARI   RECORDS _____ Shipper _____ Agent _____   **3**

Norwalk, Conn. _____ Per _____ Per _____

Permanent post-office address of shipper.

Figure A-13: STRAIGHT BILL OF LADING

RAPIDFORMS® NO. 12003
BILL OF LADING

REORDER FROM REGENT STANDARD FORMS, INC., INTERSTATE INDUSTRIAL PARK, BELLMAWR, N.J. 08031

STRAIGHT BILL OF LADING—SHORT FORM—ORIGINAL—NOT NEGOTIABLE

DESIGNATE WITH AN (X)

RECEIVED, subject to the classifications and tariffs in effect on the date of issue of this Original Bill of Lading.

BY TRUCK ☐   **FREIGHT** ☐

the property described below, in apparent good order, except as noted (contents and condition of contents of packages unknown), marked, consigned and destined as indicated below, which said carrier (the word carrier being understood throughout this contract as meaning any person or corporation in possession of the property under the contract) agrees to carry to its usual place of delivery at said destination, if on its route, otherwise to deliver to another carrier on the route to said destination. It is mutually agreed, as to each carrier of all or any of said property over all or any portion of said route to destination, and as to each party at any time interested in all or any of said property, that every service to be performed hereunder shall be subject to all the terms and conditions of the Uniform Domestic Straight Bill of Lading set forth (1) in Uniform Freight Classification in effect on the date hereof, if this is a rail or a rail-water shipment, or (2) in the applicable motor carrier classification or tariff if this is a motor carrier shipment.

Shipper hereby certifies that he is familiar with all the terms and conditions of the said bill of lading, including those on the back thereof, set forth in the classification or tariff which governs the transportation of this shipment, and the said terms and conditions are hereby agreed to by the shipper and accepted for himself and his assigns.

From   HAR-CONN CHROME CO.

At   603 New Park Ave. • West Hartford, CT 06110
(Mail or street address of consignee—For purposes of notification only.)

DATE	19	SHIPPER'S NO. 1125

CARRIER ↓   CARRIER'S NO.

BY

CONSIGNEE AND DESTINATION

ROUTE   DELIVERING CARRIER

CAR OR VEHICLE INITIALS & NO.

NO. PACKAGES	HAZARDOUS MATERIALS	DESCRIPTION OF ARTICLES, SPECIAL MARKS AND EXCEPTIONS	*WEIGHT (SUBJECT TO CORR.)	CLASS OR RATE	✓	
						Subject to Section 7 of conditions of applicable bill of lading, if this shipment is to be delivered to the consignee without recourse on the consignor, the consignor shall sign the following statement.
						The carrier shall not make delivery of this shipment without payment of freight and all other lawful charges.
						Per_____ (Signature of Consignor)
						If charges are to be prepaid, write or stamp here, "To be Prepaid."
						Received $_____ to apply in prepayment of the charges on the property described hereon.
						Agent or Cashier.
						Per_____ (The signature here acknowledges only the amounts prepaid.)

Charges Advanced:

SHIPPERS CERTIFICATION: This is to certify that the above-named materials are properly classified, described, packaged, marked and labeled, and are in proper condition for transportation according to the applicable regulations of the Department of Transportation.   SIGNATURE_____   TITLE_____

$_____

* If the shipment moves between two ports by a carrier by water, the law requires that the bill of lading shall state whether it is "carrier's or shipper's weight."
† Shipper's imprints in lieu of stamp; not a part of Bill of Lading approved by the Interstate Commerce Commission.
Note — Where the rate is dependent on value, shippers are required to state specifically in writing the agreed or declared value of the property.
The agreed or declared value of the property is hereby specifically stated by the shipper to be not exceeding

C.O.D. SHIPMENT

C.O.D. Amt_____

| THIS SHIPMENT IS CORRECTLY DESCRIBED. | † The fibre boxes used for this shipment conform to the specifications set forth in the box makers certificate thereon, and all other requirements of the Consolidated Freight Classification. | | Collection Fee_____ |
| CORRECT WEIGHT IS _____ LBS. | | Per_____   Shipper | Total Charges_____ |

HAR-CONN CHROME CO.
603 New Park Ave. • West Hartford, CT 06110

Shipper, Per_____   _____ Agent, Per_____

Permanent post office address of shipper

[]

FORM 12003, REGENT FORMS. BELLMAWR, N.J. 08031

Figure A-14: STRAIGHT BILL OF LADING—SHORT FORM
(Courtesy of Regent Standard Forms, Inc., Bellmawr, New Jersey 08031.)

AIRBORNE FREIGHT CORPORATION
190 QUEEN ANNE AVENUE NORTH
P.O. BOX 662
SEATTLE, WASHINGTON 98111

☐ Designates AIRBORNE SERVICE
☐ Other_____

FREIGHT CHARGES	SHIPPER REQUESTS INSURANCE	SHIPPER'S REFERENCE NUMBER

FREIGHT CHARGES
PREPAID ☐   COLLECT ☐

SHIPPER REQUESTS INSURANCE
(If neither is checked, shipment is NOT insured.)   YES ☐   NO ☐   AMT. $_____

DECLARED VALUE FOR CARRIER
$

SHIPPER'S C.O.D. (If any)
$

SHIPPER'S LETTER OF INSTRUCTION
It is not necessary for Shipper to complete shaded areas.

FROM (U.S. port of export)_____

METHOD OF TRANSPORTATION (Check one):
☐ VESSEL (incl. ferry)   ☐ AIR   ☐ OTHER (Specify) _____

EXPORTING CARRIER (If vessel, give name of ship, flag and pier number. If air, give name of airline.)_____

EXPORTER (Principal or seller — licensee)_____   ADDRESS (Number, street, place, State)_____

AGENT OF EXPORTER (Forwarding agent)_____   ADDRESS (Number, street, place, State)_____

AIRBORNE FREIGHT CORPORATION

ULTIMATE CONSIGNEE_____   ADDRESS (Place, country)_____

INTERMEDIATE CONSIGNEE_____   ADDRESS (Place, country)_____

FOREIGN PORT OF UNLOADING (For vessel and air shipments only)_____   PLACE AND COUNTRY OF ULTIMATE DESTINATION (Not place of transshipment)_____

INLAND ROUTING INFORMATION:
SHIPPED TO AIRBORNE: PREPAID ☐   COLLECT ☐   DATE_____   VIA (CARRIER)_____   B/L No._____   FROM (SUPPLIER)_____
INLAND CHG. ONLY:

SHIPPER'S INSTRUCTIONS IN CASE OF INABILITY TO DELIVER AS CONSIGNED: ABANDON ☐   RETURN TO SHIPPER ☐   DELIVER TO_____

MARKS AND NOS.	NUMBER AND KIND OF PACKAGES, DESCRIPTION OF COMMODITIES, EXPORT LICENSE NUMBER	SHIPPING (GROSS) WEIGHT IN POUNDS	Specify D or F	SCHEDULE B COMMODITY NO.	NET QUANTITY IN SCHEDULE B UNITS	VALUE AT U.S. PORT OF EXPORT

VALIDATED LICENSE NO._____   OR GENERAL LICENSE SYMBOL_____

AIR WAYBILL NUMBER_____

The undersigned hereby authorizes AIRBORNE to act as forwarding agent for export control and customs purposes

AIRBORNE FREIGHT CORPORATION

(ADDRESS - NUMBER, STREET, PLACE, STATE)

EXPORTER_____

IMPORTANT

Shipper must sign (1) below where indicated and (2) on lines 18 and 19 where indicated on next copy which becomes Original Export Declaration.

FOR_____
(Name of corporation or firm, and capacity of signer; e.g., secretary, export manager, etc.)

ADDRESS_____

SPECIAL INSTRUCTIONS AND REMARKS:_____

SHIPPER'S SIGNATURE
X_____   DATE:_____

AFC AGENT SIGNATURE
X_____   DATE:_____

	ATTACHED	PREPARE
EXPORT DECLARATION	☐	☐
COMMERCIAL INVOICE	☐	☐
CERTIFICATE OF ORIGIN	☐	☐
CONSULAR INVOICE	☐	☐
EXPORT LICENSE	☐	
IMPORT LICENSE	☐	

FORM 407 REV. 10/78

SHIPPER'S COPY

Figure A-15: SHIPPER'S LETTER OF INSTRUCTION
(Courtesy of Airborne Freight Corporation, Seattle, Washington.)

STANDARD FORM 197
REGENT STANDARD FORMS, INC., PENNSAUKEN, N. J. 08109

RECEIVING FORM

RECEIVED FROM _____

Address _____

Receipt No. _____

Date _____

Shipper's No. _____

Shipping Date _____

CASES	CARTONS	PACKAGES	ROLLS	BUNDLES	PREPAID	COLLECT
					$_____	$_____

QUANTITY	PART NO.	WEIGHT	DESCRIPTION	POSTED STORES RECORD

Our P. O. No. _____   Freight ☐   Express ☐   Truck ☐   Parcel Post ☐

Our Job No. _____   Received by _____

Partial Shipment ☐   O.K'D by _____

Complete Shipment ☐   Rejected by _____ Reason _____

Figure A-16: STOCK REQUISITION FORM
(Courtesy of Regent Standard Forms, Inc., Bellmawr, New Jersey 08031.)

RECEIVING DEPARTMENT MASTER

PURCHASE ORDER

CONN. STATE TAX EXEMPTION
CERTIFICATE # 0658-559

THIS ORDER TAX EXEMPT: ☐ YES ☐ NO

DATE SHIPMENT REQUIRED AT
ELECTRO-METHODS, INC.

VENDOR

PLEASE ENTER OUR ORDER FOR THE FOLLOWING, SUBJECT TO INSTRUCTIONS HEREIN AND ALL TERMS AND CONDITIONS PRINTED ON THE REVERSE SIDE:

DATE OF ORDER	REQUISITION NO.	TERMS	F.O.B. SOUTH WINDSOR, CONN. OR	SHIP VIA	PREPAY ALL SHIPMENTS

ITEM	QUANTITY	PATTERN NO. (PART NO.)	DESCRIPTION OF MATERIALS AND/OR SERVICES TO BE SUPPLIED	

DATE RECEIVED	1. DATE			2. DATE			3. DATE			4. DATE			5. DATE			6. DATE		
ITEM	QTY. REC'D.	WEIGHT	BAL. DUE	QTY. REC'D.	WEIGHT	BAL. DUE	QTY. REC'D.	WEIGHT	BAL. DUE	QTY. REC'D.	WEIGHT	BAL. DUE	QTY. REC'D.	WEIGHT	BAL. DUE	QTY. REC'D.	WEIGHT	BAL. DUE
1																		
2																		
3																		
4																		
5																		
CARRIER	PPD.	COL.		PPD.	COL.		PPD.	COL.		PPD.	COL.		PPD.	COL.		PPD.	COL.	
REC'D. BY																		

DATE RECEIVED	7. DATE			8. DATE			9. DATE			10. DATE			11. DATE			12. DATE		
ITEM	QTY. REC'D.	WEIGHT	BAL. DUE	QTY. REC'D.	WEIGHT	BAL. DUE	QTY. REC'D.	WEIGHT	BAL. DUE	QTY. REC'D.	WEIGHT	BAL. DUE	QTY. REC'D.	WEIGHT	BAL. DUE	QTY. REC'D.	WEIGHT	BAL. DUE
1																		
2																		
3																		
4																		
5																		
CARRIER	PPD.	COL.		PPD.	COL.		PPD.	COL.		PPD.	COL.		PPD.	COL.		PPD.	COL.	
REC'D. BY																		

Figure A-17: RECEIVING DEPARTMENT MASTER
(Courtesy of Electro-Methods, Inc., South Windsor, Connecticut.)

Figure A-18: DAILY REPORT OF GOODS RECEIVED
(Courtesy of Regent Standard Forms, Inc., Bellmawr, New Jersey 08031.)

MAKE REPORT IN DUPLICATE
RETAIN ONE FOR REFERENCE

DAILY REPORT OF GOODS RECEIVED

RECEIVING CLERK

DATE

SHEET No

RECEIVED FROM	VIA	NO. PKGS.	WEIGHT	QUANTITY	DESCRIPTION OF GOODS	P O OR REQ NO.	CHARGES PAID	DELIVERED TO

REMARKS

STANDARD FORM 910
REGENT STANDARD FORMS, INC. BELLMAWR, N.J. 08031

57

PLEASE REPLY IMMEDIATELY TO

MARINE SALES COMPANY
324 LITTLEFIELD AVE.
SOUTH SAN FRANCISCO, CA 94080
(415) 871-2290

RAPID FOLLOW-UP
N⁰ 3073

THIS IS OUR   REQUEST FOR INFORMATION

PLEASE REPLY TODAY VIA –

☐ THIS FORM   ☐ WIRE

☐ TELEPHONE   ☐ RETURN ENVELOPE ENCLOSED

DATE	QUOTATION REQUEST NO.
PURCHASE ORDER NO.	INVOICE NO.
INVOICE DATE	INVOICE AMOUNT

FOLD

PLEASE REFER TO
⟵
IN REPLY TO YOUR REFERENCE
☐

☐ 1. When are you shipping? These goods are urgently needed!

☐ 2. Goods have not been received. Please trace shipment.

☐ 3. If shipment has been made, please mail invoice today.

☐ 4. Please send a receipted freight bill.

☐ 5. Please send a certified weight slip.

☐ 6. Please CHANGE ORDER as noted below and acknowledge.

☐ 7. Can you meet our shipping date?

☐ 8. Release shipments as shown under "Our Remarks" below.

☐ 9. Please send ACCEPTANCE COPY of our Purchase Order.

☐ 10. Please acknowledge our order, giving shipping date.

☐ 11. Can you give a more specific shipping date?

☐ 12. When will the balance of our order be shipped? (FOLD)

☐ 13. Please rush prices requested.

☐ 14. Please send us a shipping notice.

☐ 15. Please put our P.O. No. on papers enclosed or referred to.

☐ 16. We have no record of the transaction covered by your invoice. Please give us order date, date shipped, P.O. No., name of person placing the order and/or signed delivery receipt.

☐ 17. SHIP THIS ORDER TO address shown in "Our Remarks" below.

☐ 18. YOUR INVOICE IS RETURNED for the reason checked.

☐ 19. We require _____ copies of each invoice.

☐ 20. Price or discount does not match your quotation.

☐ 21. Terms on invoice do not match our Purchase Order.

☐ 22. Enclosed invoice was sent to us in error.

☐ 23. Quantity differs from our Purchase Order.

☐ 24. Unit Price is incorrect.

☐ 25. Extension is incorrect.

☐ 26. Our Purchase Order No. is lacking or incorrect.

☐ 27. Sales Tax (does) (does not) apply.

☐ 28. Order should be billed F.O.B. destination.

☐ 29. Have you considered this order complete?

☐ 30. Please be sure to SHIP VIA _____

☐ 31.

☐ 32.

☐ 33.

☐ 34.

OUR REMARKS

YOUR REPLY

FORM 15253 REGENT FORMS, BELLMAWR, N.J. 08030

WHITE COPY is for your records.   RETURN PINK COPY with your reply.

SENDER: Snap Out YELLOW COPY only. Send WHITE & PINK COPIES with carbon intact.

Figure A-19: RAPID FOLLOW-UP ON GOODS ORDERED
(Courtesy of Regent Standard Forms, Inc., Bellmawr, New Jersey 08031.)

MATERIAL INSPECTION AND RECEIVING REPORT	1. PROC. INSTRUMENT IDEN(CONTRACT)		(ORDER) NO.	6. INVOICE NO.	7. PAGE	OF
				DATE	8. ACCEPTANCE POINT	

2. SHIPMENT NO.	3. DATE SHIPPED	4. B/L TCN		5. DISCOUNT TERMS

9. PRIME CONTRACTOR	CODE		10. ADMINISTERED BY	CODE

11. SHIPPED FROM (If other than 9)	CODE	FOB:	12. PAYMENT WILL BE MADE BY	CODE

13. SHIPPED TO	CODE		14. MARKED FOR	CODE

15. ITEM NO.	16. STOCK/PART NO. DESCRIPTION (Indicate number of shipping containers - type of container - container number.)	17. QUANTITY SHIP/REC'D *	18. UNIT	19. UNIT PRICE	20. AMOUNT

21. PROCUREMENT QUALITY ASSURANCE	22. RECEIVER'S USE
A. ORIGIN ☐ PQA ☐ ACCEPTANCE of listed items has been made by me or under my supervision and they conform to contract, except as noted herein or on supporting documents. / B. DESTINATION ☐ PQA ☐ ACCEPTANCE of listed items has been made by me or under my supervision and they conform to contract, except as noted herein or on supporting documents.	Quantities shown in column 17 were received in apparent good condition except as noted.

21. PROCUREMENT QUALITY ASSURANCE

A. ORIGIN
☐ PQA ☐ ACCEPTANCE of listed items has been made by me or under my supervision and they conform to contract, except as noted herein or on supporting documents.

B. DESTINATION
☐ PQA ☐ ACCEPTANCE of listed items has been made by me or under my supervision and they conform to contract, except as noted herein or on supporting documents.

DATE	SIGNATURE OF AUTH GOVT REP	DATE	SIGNATURE OF AUTH GOVT REP
TYPED NAME AND OFFICE		TYPED NAME AND TITLE	

22. RECEIVER'S USE

Quantities shown in column 17 were received in apparent good condition except as noted.

DATE RECEIVED   SIGNATURE OF AUTH GOVT REP

TYPED NAME AND OFFICE

* If quantity received by the Government is the same as quantity shipped, indicate by (✔) mark, if different, enter actual quantity received below quantity shipped and encircle.

23. CONTRACTOR USE ONLY

DD FORM 250   1 NOV 68   REPLACES EDITION OF 1 AUG 67 WHICH MAY BE USED

Figure A-20: MATERIAL INSPECTION AND RECEIVING REPORT
(Courtesy of Electro-Methods, Inc., South Windsor, Connecticut.)

ELECTRO-METHODS REPORT
OF NONCONFORMANCE

O. NUMBER

1. SUPPLIER'S RPT. NO. 2. SUPPLIER'S CODE 3. PART NUMBER CLASS CHG. LTR. P.I.A. NUMBER CHG. LTR.

4. SUPPLIER'S NAME AND ADDRESS

PAGE OF PAGES

5. RECEIVING 6. ENGINE MODEL 7. PART NAME 9. ATTEN. TO

10. NONCONFORMANCE

11. PCS. INSP. 11A. PCS. NONCONF 11B. PCS. AFFECTED 12. CHARACT. NO.

13. CAUSE — CORRECTIVE ACTION AND DATE OF IMPLEMENTATION

NONCONFORMANCE

PCS. INSP. PCS. NONCONF. PCS. AFFECTED CHARACT. NO.

CAUSE — CORRECTIVE ACTION AND DATE OF IMPLEMENTATION

NONCONFORMANCE

PCS. INSP. PCS. NONCONF. PCS. AFFECTED CHARACT. NO.

CAUSE — CORRECTIVE ACTION AND DATE OF IMPLEMENTATION

15. SUPPLIER'S REP DATE 16. E.M. CONT. REP. 17. GOV'T REP. 18. E.M. ENG. DATE EXT.

ITEM	CHG. CODE	DISP. CODE	NONCONFORMANCE CODE	DWG. LOC.	CHARACTER-ISTIC NO.	PIECES N/C	21. REPAIR DWG OR MRB INDEX NO.	EXTENT ALLOWED	PIECES/DATE ALLOWED	SCHEDULE
A										
C										

QRC REP. DATE 25. MR ENGINEER DATE 26 GOV'T REP. DATE 23.

SUPPLIER WARRANTS THAT MATERIAL MEETS PURCHASE ORDER SPECIFICATIONS EXCEPT NONCONFORMANCES (1) AS LISTED HEREON, OR (2) PREVIOUSLY ACCEPTED. ELECTRO-METHODS INC. QUALITY REVIEW AUTHORIZATION ON THIS FORM PERMITS SUPPLIER TO SHIP MATERIAL HEREON LISTED TO ELECTRO-METHODS INC. SUBJECT TO DISPOSITION CONDITIONS. ANY SUPPLIER AGREEMENT ESTABLISHING A TIME LIMIT FOR THE RETURN OF PARTS OR MATERIALS BY EM FOR CREDIT SHALL NOT APPLY TO SHIPMENTS MADE AGAINST THIS FORM. THIS DOCUMENT NULL AND VOID AFTER ONE YEAR.

Figure A-21: REPORT OF NONCONFORMANCE
(Courtesy of Electro-Methods, Inc., South Windsor, Connecticut.)

RAPIDFORMS NO 19002
RETURNED GOODS REPORT

REORDER FROM REGENT STANDARD FORMS, INC.
INTERSTATE INDUSTRIAL PARK, BELLMAWR, N.J. 08031

RETURNED GOODS REPORT   No.

RECEIVED FROM

ADDRESS

CUST. ORDER NO.	OUR ORDER NO.	DATE RECEIVED	

		PREPAID	COLLECT
☐ U.P.S. ☐ PARCEL POST		$	$
☐ TRUCK ☐ FREIGHT			

REASON RETURNED

NO.	QUANTITY	DESCRIPTION	CONDITION

CREDIT TO

REMARKS

RECEIVED BY

FORM 19002 REGENT FORMS BELLMAWR N J 08031

Figure A-22: RETURNED GOODS REPORT
(Courtesy of Regent Standard Forms, Inc., Bellmawr, New Jersey.)

MATERIAL REJECTION TICKET	Nº 96967		
PART NO.	NAME	QUANTITY	
		ORIG. LOT	REJECTED
DATE	LOCATION	W. O. NUMBER	LAST OPER. COMPLETED

DESCRIPTION OF DEVIATION:

DEFECT DUE TO		QUANTITY	
OPERATION RESPON.	EMP. NO. RESPON.		
		REWORK	SCRAP

REASON FOR REJECTION							
	V	DEPT. NO.	Acc't. No.		V	DEPT. NO.	Acc't. No.
OPERATOR				ENG. CHANGE			
METHODS				INSPECTION			
TOOLING				OTHER			

MRB DISPOSITION		COST COMPUTATION		
			UNIT COST	EXT'N
ACCEPT	QTY.	RAW MAT.		
		PCH. PARTS		
REWORK	QTY.	LABOR		
		BURDEN		
SCRAP	QTY.	DEV. TOOLS		
SALVAGE INSP.		DEV. ENG.		
		SUNDRY		
CHIEF INSP.		TOTAL		
FOREMAN		SUPERV. RESP.		

E-1032

DISPOSITION:
1ST STAGE — FINISHED PARTS STORES
2ND STAGE — TABULATING
3RD STAGE — PRODUCTION CONTROL

1

Figure A-23: MATERIALS REJECTION TICKET
(From the book Business Executive's Handbook, 4th Edition, by Stanley M. Brown and Lillian Doris, Editors. © 1953 by Parker Publishing Company, Inc. Published by Parker Publishing Company, Inc., West Nyack, New York 10994.)

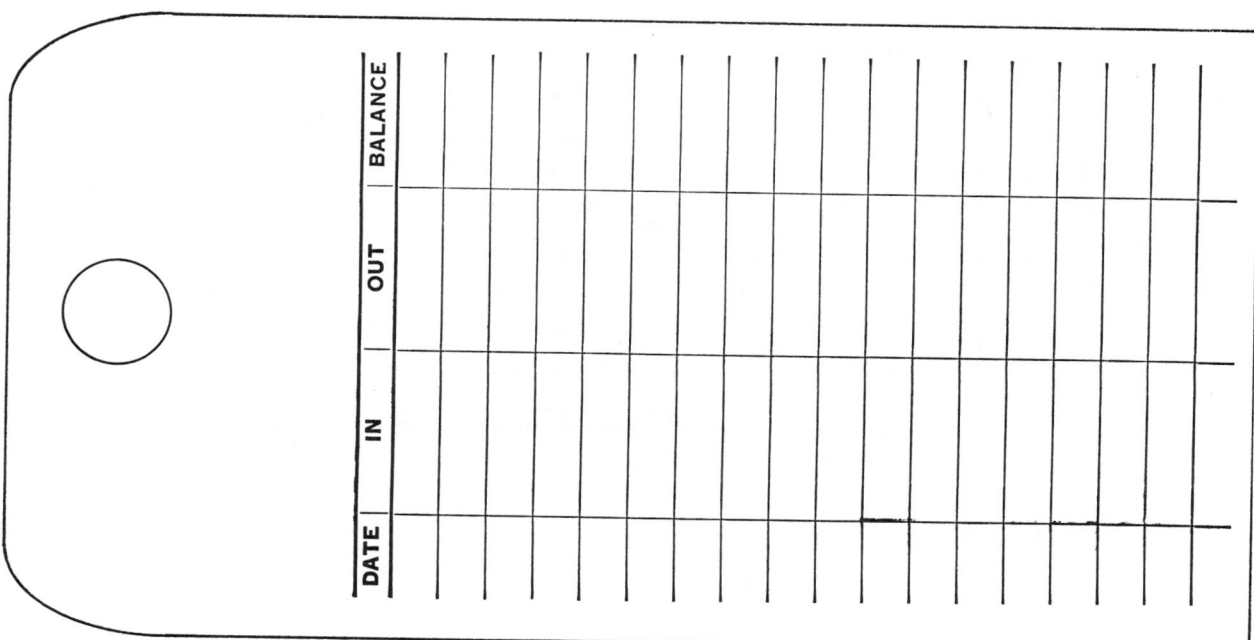

Figure A-24: INVENTORY CONTROL TAB
(Courtesy of Regent Standard Forms, Inc., Bellmawr, New Jersey 08031.)

STORES REQUISITION

Date .... No. ....

Deliver To ....

To Be Used For .... Order No. ....

QUANTITY	PART OR CAT NO.	SIZE	FULL DESCRIPTION	FOR OFFICE USE		

Remarks ....

Filed By .... Signed .... Approved ....

For Dept.

STANDARD FORM 840
REGENT STANDARD FORMS, INC., PENNSAUKEN, N. J. 08109

Figure A-25: STORES REQUISITION FORM
Courtesy of Regent Standard Forms, Inc., Bellmawr, New Jersey 07031.)

PRODUCTION ORDER

ORDER NO. _____ DATE ISSUED _____

FOR _____ OR STOCK_____
          PURCHASER

SCHEDULED COMPLETION DATE _____

PRODUCT DESCRIPTION _____

NO. OF ITEMS_____ DRAWING NO._____ PATTERN NO._____

MATERIAL REQUISITION NOS._____

INSTRUCTIONS:

DATE COMPLETED_____
NO. OF GOOD UNITS _____
NO. OF DEFECTIVE UNITS _____ FOREMAN OR SUPERVISOR

Figure A-26: PRODUCTION ORDER
(From the book Cost Accounting for Small Manufacturers, 2nd Edition, by R. Lee Brummet and Jack C. Robertson. © 1972. Published by Small Business Administration.)

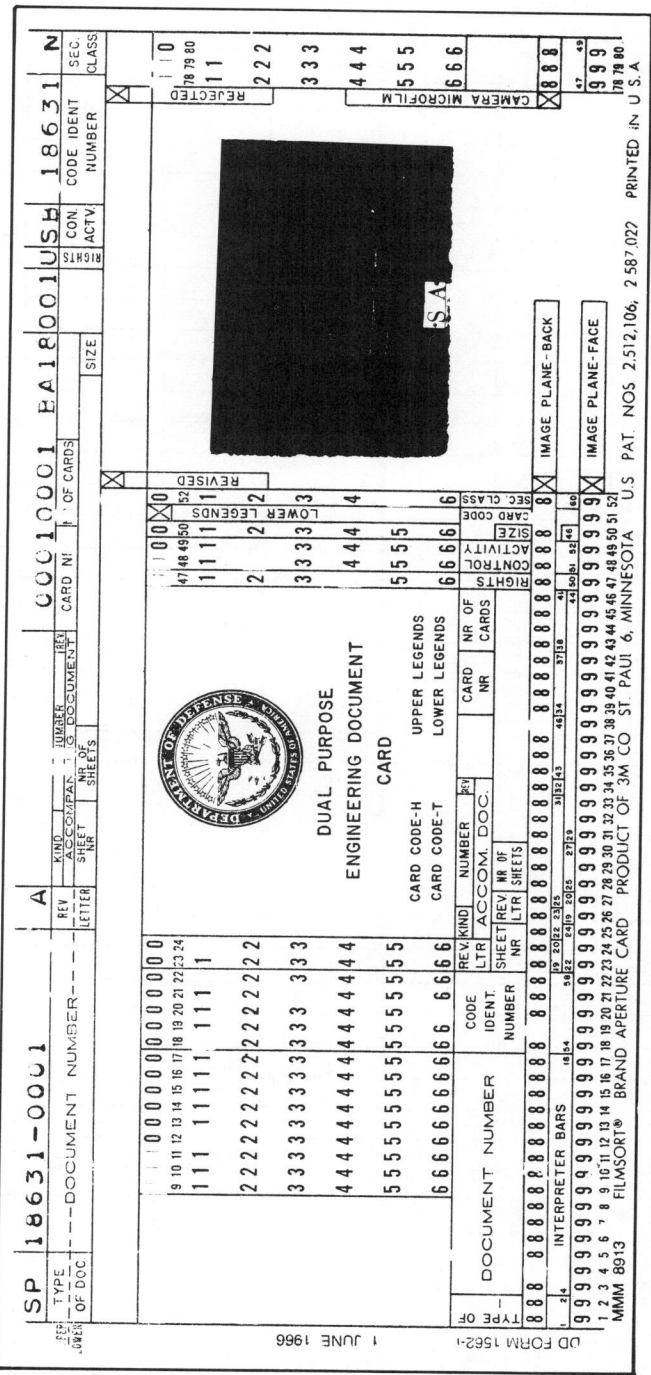

Figure A-27: DUAL PURPOSE DOCUMENT CARD

65

THEATRE CIRCUIT

WEEKLY ITEMIZED INVENTORY   WEEK ENDING: _____

THEATRE ....   TOWN ....

Item	@	Previous Inventory	Deliveries or Transfers		Total	Weekly Inventory ct.	Sold	Cash
Root Beer Drops	.30							
Lemon Drops	.30							
Cherry Drops	.30							
Sweetarts	.30							
Starburst	.35							
Char. Chews	.35							
Butt. Fingers	.40							
Baby Ruth	.40							
Baz Peanuts	.40							
Hershey Plain	.40							
Kit Kat	.40							
Milky Way	.40							
Heide Drops	.60							
Ju-Ju Fruit	.60							
Red Hot $	.60							
Milk Duds	.70							
Malt Balls	.70							
Peanut Chews	.70							
Jordon Almond	.70							
Raisinettes	.75							
Goobers	.75							
Sno Caps	.75							
Twizzlers	.75							
Good & Plenty	.75							
Orange Slices	.75							
Spearmint	.75							
M & M Plain	.75							
M & M Peanut	.75							
Choc. Almonds	.80							
Jr. Mints	.80							
Pom-Poms	.80							
Bridge Mix	.80							
Peanut Butter	.85							
Fruit Slices	.85							
Chunky	.85							
Popcorn 24 oz.	.60							
" 46 oz.								
" 83 oz.	1.25							
Ice Cream	.40							

SIGNATURES (Name Not Initials)

....

Inventory Taken By Manager ....

Figure A-28: WEEKLY INVENTORY CONTROL FOR THEATERS

Figure A-29: INTRACOMPANY STOCK TRANSFER

Inventory 44-292

Inventory

Page No. _____

Sheet No. _____

_____ 19 _____

Department _____ Priced By _____ Checked By _____

Location _____ Extended By _____ Checked By _____

Called By _____ Entered By _____ Totalled By _____ Examined By _____

Quantity	Unit	Description/Stock Number	Price	Unit	Extension	Time In Stock	Marked Down Value		√
							Price	Extension	
		Brought Forward							
		Carried Forward							

Figure A-30: INVENTORY CONTROL AND MARKDOWNS

ROTATED UNIT CONTROL RECORD

ROTATED UNIT CONTROL					1	2	3	4	5	6	7	8	9	10	11	12	13	TOTAL Quarterly sales
STYLE	size / min qty	min pack / del time	cost / retail	date	2/2	2/16	2/30	3/19	3/27	4/11	4/25	5/8	5/22	6/5	6/18	7/3		
WHITE BUTTON DOWN	15-36 / 12	4 / 1 WK.	28.50 DOZ. / 3.95	on hand	24	23	22	22	20	19	20	17	17	15	16	16		
				on order														
				rec'd														this year 8
				sales	1	1	0	2	1	-1	3	0	2	-1	0	0		last year 9
DOWN COLLAR	15½-30 / 24	4 / 1 WK.	28.50 DOZ. / 3.95	on hand	39	32	28	28	25	24	26	30	27	28	29	25		
				on order						8	8							
				rec'd														this year 26
				sales	7	4	0	3	1	-2	4	3	1	-1	4	2		last year 31

Figure A-31: ROTATED UNIT CONTROL RECORD

DEPARTMENT   CLASSIFICATION   DESCRIPTION

	WEEK ENDING					WEEK ENDING					WEEK ENDING				
price	number units sold	units in stock	open to buy	on order	price	number units sold	units in stock	open to buy	on order	price	number units sold	units in stock	open to buy	on order	

Figure A-32: STOCK CONTROL RECORD BY DEPARTMENT, CLASSIFICATION, AND DESCRIPTION

STOCK LEDGER CARD

ARTICLE DESCRIPTION _____ SPECS. _____

MAXIMUM NUMBER OF UNITS _____ MINUMUM NUMBER OF UNITS _____

DATE	RECEIVED				ISSUED				BALANCE		
19 —	VO. NO.	UNITS	PRICE	AMOUNT	REQ. NO.	UNITS	PRICE	AMOUNT	UNITS	PRICE	AMOUNT

Figure A-33: STOCK LEDGER CARD
(From the book Cost Accounting for Small Manufacturers, 2nd Edition, by R. Lee Brummet and Jack C. Robertson. © 1972. Published by Small Business Administration.)

JOB MATERIAL and LABOR RECORD

JOB NAME	JOB NUMBER	DESCRIPTION OF WORK	DATE	19
ADDRESS	PHONE			☐ DAY WORK ☐ CONTRACT ☐ EXTRA

QTY.	MATERIAL	PRICE	AMOUNT	QTY.	MATERIAL	PRICE	AMOUNT

TIME AND LABOR RECORD

WORKMAN	DATE	IN	OUT	IN	OUT	HOURS	RATE	AMOUNT
							TOTAL	

MISCELLANEOUS JOB EXPENSES

DESCRIPTION	AMOUNT
TOTAL	

TOTAL MATERIAL	
TOTAL LABOR	
MISC EXPENSES	
TOTAL	

SIGNATURE

FORM 340 REGENT STANDARD FORMS, INC. BELLMAWR, N.J. 08030

Figure A-34: JOB MATERIAL AND LABOR RECORD
(Courtesy of Regent Standard Forms, Inc., Bellmawr, New Jersey 08031.)

72

ALL-STATE LEGAL SUPPLY CO.
269 Sheffield St., Mountainside, N. J. 07092

Daily Time Record of _____

Day _____ Date _____

TIME	Kind of Work	IN RE	Basic Time Charge	TIME	Kind of Work	IN RE	Basic Time Charge
A. M. 8.00				P. M. 1.00			
8.10				1.10			
8.20				1.20			
8.30				1.30			
8.40				1.40			
8.50				1.50			
9.00				2.00			
9.10				2.10			
9.20				2.20			
9.30				2.30			
9.40				2.40			
9.50				2.50			
10.00				3.00			
10.10				3.10			
10.20				3.20			
10.30				3.30			
10.40				3.40			
10.50				3.50			
11.00				4.00			
11.10				4.10			
11.20				4.20			
11.30				4.30			
11.40				4.40			
11.50				4.50			
12.00				5.00			
12.10				5.10			
12.20				5.20			
12.30				5.30			
12.40				5.40			
12.50				5.50			
1.00				6.00			
Long Distance Phone Calls				Over Time			
REMARKS:							

C. C.—Common Pleas Court   B. C.—Bankruptcy Court   C.—Consultation
O. C.—Orphans' Court   P. P.—Preparing Papers   T.—Telephone Conversation
F. C.—Federal Court   L. L.—Looking up Law   L.—Letters

Figure A-35: DAILY TIME RECORD
(Courtesy of All State Legal Supply Co., Mountainside, New Jersey 07092.)

454 T C—TIME-CHARGE RECORD   ALL-STATE LEGAL SUPPLY CO.   269 SHEFFIELD STREET, MOUNTAINSIDE, N.J. 07092

CLIENT _____   MATTER: _____   19 ____

TIME FROM ____ TO ____ TOTAL ____   PHONE NO. _____   FILE NO. _____

REMARKS

HOURS   CHARGE

☐ ____ TELEPHONE $ ____
☐ ____ INTERVIEW $ ____
☐ ____ DICTATION $ ____
☐ ____ CONSULTATION $ ____
☐ ____ CONFERENCE $ ____
☐ ____ RESEARCH $ ____
☐ ____ APPEARANCE $ ____
☐ ____ CLERICAL $ ____
☐ ____ TRAVEL $ ____

DISBURSEMENTS $ ____   TOTAL $ ____

BY: _____   BILL ☐ $ ____

Figure A-36: TIME CHARGE RECORD
(Courtesy of All State Legal Supply Co., Mountainside, New Jersey 07092.)

74

Figure A-37: REIMBURSABLE AND NONREIMBURSABLE EXPENSE REPORT

(Copyright 1978 by Wilson Jones Company. All rights reserved. Forms may be obtained, subject to supply, from Wilson Jones Company, 6150 Touhy Avenue, Chicago, Illinois 60648.)

CAUTION. DO NOT WRITE ON THIS SHEET WITHOUT PROTECTING FRONT OF SHEET FROM CARBON.

MEMO OF CREDIT CARD EXPENSES

EXPENSES NOT REIMBURSED

SUNDAY			
MONDAY			
TUESDAY			
WEDNESDAY			
THURSDAY			
FRIDAY			
SATURDAY			
		TOTAL	

Figure A-37—Reverse Side

expense report

DUP

EXPENSE REPORT FOR RECORDING I.R.S. DATA

001261

| PRINT NAME | DEPT. OR SALES OFFICE | DATE OF TRIP } FROM / / | TO / / |

BUSINESS PURPOSE:

SALES CODE

CASH ADVANCED BY THE COMPANY ➡ $

ITEMS DATES	1. AUTO EXPENSE ONLY (RATE ___ ¢MI.)	2. OTHER TRANSPOR-TATION (ATTACH RECEIPTS)	3. TAXI LIMOUSINE BUS SUBWAY	4. HOTEL (ATTACH RECEIPTS)	5. MEALS (INCLUDE TIPS)	6. ✶✶ TELEPHONE TELEGRAM	7. PARKING AND TOLLS	8. TIPS (OTHER THAN MEALS)	9. ✶✶ ENTERTAIN-MENT	10. ✶✶ MISC.	DO NOT INCLUDE ITEMS CHARGED TO THE COMPANY. (THESE ARE TO BE RECORDED IN SPACES PROVIDED BELOW.)
SUN. /											
MON. /											
TUES. /											
WED. /											
THUR. /											
FRI. /											TOTAL ▼
SAT. /											
ITEM TOTALS ▶											

HOME OFFICE APPROVAL

REMARKS:	INV. NO.	ACCOUNT DISTRIBUTION	BALANCE DUE EMPLOYEE
	PAY BY		$
	VENDOR		BALANCE DUE COMPANY
APPROVED BY:	APPROVED		
DATED	DATED		$

✶EXPLAIN ITEMS 1, 2 AND 3 IN DETAIL BELOW

ITEM		SUN.	MON.	TUES.	WED.	THURS.	FRI.	SAT.
1 AND 2	FROM							
	TO							
	TO							
	TO							
	AUTO MILEAGE							
3	FROM							
	TO							
	FROM							
	TO							

CHARGES TO THE COMPANY (EXCLUDE CASH ADVANCES) | AMOUNT | **TRIP COST SUMMARY**

A. AIR TRAVEL (TICKET NO.'S_____)$_____ | TOTAL EXPENSES REPORTED ABOVE $

B. CAR RENTAL (AGENCY AND INVOICE NO._____)$_____ | TOTAL CHARGES TO COMPANY $

C. HOTEL (NAME AND TOTAL AMOUNT_____)$_____ | TOTAL COST OF TRIP $

D. OTHER (EXPLAIN_____)$_____

✶✶ EXPLAIN ITEMS 6, 9 AND 10 IN DETAIL BELOW (ATTACH RECEIPTS FOR ALL EXPENDITURES OF $25.00 OR MORE)

ITEM	DATE	EXPLANATION	AMOUNT	ITEM	DATE	EXPLANATION	AMOUNT

SIGNED _____ DATE _____ | APPROVED BY _____ DATE _____

PART 1 WITH RECEIPTS ATTACHED TO APPROPRIATE OFFICE

REDIFORM. 9S978

POLY PAK (50 SETS) 9P978

PART 2 RETAINED AS YOUR RECORD OF EXPENSE.

Figure A-38: EXPENSE REPORT FOR RECORDING IRS DATA
(Courtesy of Rediform Office Products, Paramus, New Jersey 07652.)

LONG DISTANCE PHONE CHARGES

CALLS MADE BY ....   DATE .... 19 ....

TIME	PARTY CALLED	TELEPHONE AREA CODE & NUMBER	CHARGE TO	AMOUNT
FROM: A. M. P. M. TO: A. M. P. M.				

LD 5—LONG DISTANCE PHONE CHARGES

© 1976 ALL-STATE LEGAL SUPPLY CO.
269 SHEFFIELD STREET, MOUNTAINSIDE, N. J. 07092

Figure A-39: DAILY CHARGE FOR LONG-DISTANCE TELEPHONE CHARGES
(Courtesy of All State Legal Supply Co., Mountainside, New Jersey 07092. Copyright 1976.)

XEROGRAPHIC REQUEST & CHARGE SLIP .... 19 ....

Please make .... copies of .... originals ☐ Xerox ☐ Other ....

☐ RUSH, To be completed by ....

Collate ☐ and   Clip ☐   Staple ☐   Spiral Bind ☐

Size: 11" ☐   13" ☐   14" ☐   Other ☐ ....

2 Hole ☐   3 Hole ☐   Use Backer ☐ ....

COLOR, SIZE, ETC.

Charge
Client ....   Client No. ....

Matter ....   File No. ....

Instructions ....

Operator ....   Total No. of Pages ....   @ .... ¢ = Total Charge $ ....

REQUESTED BY ....   DELIVER TO ....

XC-14 - XEROX CHARGE SLIP   © 1976 ALL-STATE LEGAL SUPPLY CO., 269 SHEFFIELD ST., MOUNTAINSIDE, N. J. 07092

Figure A-40: XEROGRAPHIC REQUEST AND DEBIT SLIP
(Courtesy of All State Legal Supply Co., Mountainside, New Jersey 07092. Copyright 1976.)

JOB COST RECORD

FOR _____ ORDER NO. _____

PRODUCT _____ QUANTITY _____

DATE WANTED _____ DATE STARTED _____ DATE COMPLETED _____

DIRECT MATERIALS

DATE	DEPT.	REQ. NO.	STORES NO.	QUANTITY	COST PER UNIT	TOTAL COST

DIRECT LABOR

DATE	DEPT.	TIME CARD NO.	DESCRIPTION	HRS. OR PCS.	RATE	TOTAL COST

APPLIED OVERHEAD

DATE	DEPT.	BASIS	RATE	TOTAL COST

SUMMARY FOR ORDER NO. _____

DIRECT MATERIALS _____

DIRECT LABOR _____

APPLIED OVERHEAD _____

TOTAL FACTORY COST _____

FACTORY COST PER UNIT _____

Figure A-41: JOB COST RECORD FOR DEPARTMENTALIZED PLANT
(From the book Cost Accounting for Small Manufacturers, 2nd Edition, by R. Lee Brummet and Jack C. Robertson. © 1972. Published by Small Business Administration.)

JOB COST RECORD

FOR _____ ORDER NO. _____

PRODUCT _____ QUANTITY _____

DATE WANTED _____ DATE STARTED _____ DATE COMPLETED _____

DIRECT MATERIALS			DIRECT LABOR			APPLIED OVERHEAD		
DATE	REQ. NO.	AMOUNT	DATE	TIME CARD NO.	AMOUNT	BASIS	RATE	AMOUNT

SUMMARY FOR ORDER NO. _____

DIRECT MATERIALS _____

DIRECT LABOR _____

APPLIED OVERHEAD _____

TOTAL FACTORY COST

FACTORY COST PER UNIT

Figure A-42: JOB COST RECORD FOR NONDEPARTMENTALIZED PLANT
(From the book Cost Accounting for Small Manufacturers, 2nd Edition by R. Lee Brummet and Jack C. Robertson. © 1972. Published by Small Business Administration.

MATERIAL USAGE REPORT

DEPT. NO. _____ DEPT. NAME _____ DATE _____

	PRODUCTION			MATERIAL USAGE											
				A		B		C		D		TOTAL			
	GOOD	SCRAP	TOTAL	POUNDS	PER CWT.	POUNDS	PER CWT.	POUNDS	PER CWT	POUNDS	PER CWT.	POUNDS	PER CWT.		
ACTUAL															
STANDARD															
VARIANCE															

	COST			VARIANCE DUE TO			
MATERIAL	ACTUAL	STANDARD	VARIANCE	SCRAP	SHRINKAGE	MIX	OTHER
A							
B							
C							
D							
TOTAL							
REMARKS:							

Figure A-43: MATERIAL USAGE REPORT
(From the book Corporate Treasurer's and Controller's Handbook by L. Doris, Editor. © 1950 renewed 1978 by L. Doris, Editor. Published by Prentice-Hall, Inc., Englewood Cliffs, New Jersey 07632.)

		DIRECT LABOR SUMMARY								
		PERIOD _____								
DEPT. NO	DEPARTMENT	HOURS			DOLLARS			COST	
		ACTUAL	STANDARD	% OF EFF'CY	ACTUAL	STANDARD	VARIANCE	PER ACT. HOUR	PER ST'D HOUR

		DIRECT LABOR SUMMARY								
		PERIOD _____								
DEPT NO	DEPARTMENT	HOURS						PER CENT		
		(1) TOTAL	(2) STAN-DARD	(3) ACTUAL	(4) OFF ST'D	(5) INDIRECT	(6) MAKE-UP	EFF'CY 2/3	OFF ST'D 3/1	DIR TO INDIR.-5/3

Figure A-44: DIRECT LABOR SUMMARY

(From the book Corporate Treasurer's and Controller's Handbook by L. Doris, Editor. © 1950 renewed 1978 by L. Doris, Editor. Published by Prentice-Hall, Inc., Englewood Cliffs, New Jersey 07632.)

JOB COST ESTIMATE

Job # _____

Shop labor to date (_____)   _____

Subcontract and raw material to date   _____

Estimated labor to complete (_____)   _____

Estimated raw material and subcontract to complete   _____

Estimated total cost when complete   _____

S/P of remaining units   _____

   Less:
      Cost to complete (see above)   _____

      G & A @ _____ of S/P   _____

Inventory value as of _____   _____

Balance of order worth _____ (S/P)

÷ total order worth _____ = _____ % value still on hand

WIP value of parts shipped = _____ % × _____ = _____

Job in hold—no additional work or material since _____

Figure A-45: JOB COST ESTIMATE

| | | | | PRODUCTION COST SUMMARY FOR MONTH OF _____ | | | | |
| | | | | FOR DEPARTMENT _____ | | | | |
DATE COMPL.	ORDER NO.	PRODUCT	QUANTITY	DIRECT MATERIALS	DIRECT LABOR	APPLIED OVERH'D	TOTAL COST	COST PER UNIT

Figure A-46: PRODUCTION COST SUMMARY

(From the book <u>Cost Accounting for Small Manufacturers</u>, 2nd Edition, by R. Lee Brummet and Jack C. Robertson. © 1972. Published by Small Business Administration.)

SHOP JOB LOG

						Billing	
Job Ticket	Date of Order	Customer	Purchase Order Number	Date Started	Date Shipped	Invoice Number	Amount

Figure A-47: SHOP JOB LOG

DEPARTMENTAL BURDEN BUDGET PERFORMANCE REPORT

DEPARTMENT_____

MONTH_____

STANDARD CAPACITY_____ (DIRECT LABOR HOURS) HOURS OPERATED_____ % of CAP. _____

	CURRENT MONTH			PERIOD (MOS.)		
	ACTUAL	BUDGET	OVER -(UNDER)	ACTUAL	BUDGET	OVER -(UNDER)
Indirect Labor						
Supplies						
Repairs & Maintenance						
Product Control						
Other						
TOTAL VARIABLE EXPENSE						
Salaries						
Depreciation						
Taxes						
Insurance						
Other						
TOTAL FIXED EXPENSE						
Total Indirect Expense						
GRAND TOTAL EXPENSE						

Analysis of Indirect Labor and Supplies

Indirect Labor						
Supervision						
Scrap Handling						
Equipment Cleaning						
Quality Control						
Truck and Service						
TOTAL INDIRECT LABOR						
Supplies						
Fabrics						
Tape						
Adhesives						
Alcohol						
Abrasives						
Cleaning Supplies						
Small Tools						
TOTAL SUPPLIES						

Figure A-48: DEPARTMENTAL BURDEN BUDGET PERFORMANCE REPORT
(From the book Business Finance Handbook by Lillian Doris, Editor. © 1953 by Prentice-Hall, Inc. Published by Prentice-Hall, Inc., Englewood Cliffs, New Jersey 07632.)

MANPOWER LOADING REPORT		SKILL: 16
PROGRAM: MWS	REPORT DATE: 3/31/	
PROJECT: A10 VEHICLE	CONTRACT	
LEVEL: (3) PROPULSION	NUMBER:	98-7865

Month	Performing Unit	Charge No.	Estimated Man-hours	Activity Slack (weeks)
6/2	6821	39786340	1000	-4.0
	6821	39782191	2000	8.0
	5211	39784213	4000	12.0
			7000*	
7/2	6821	39782315	800	1.0
	5821	39782191	1000	8.0
	5211	39784213	200	12.0
			2000*	

Figure A-49: MANPOWER LOADING REPORT

DAILY SUMMARY CONTROL

REVISED 11-1-78
FORM 6 1-011-A

POST DAILY TOTALS FROM DAILY CALL REPORT | DAILY RECORD | USE SUNDAY LINE FOR WEEKLY TOTALS

| A | 1 | 2 | 3 | 4 | 5 | 6 | 7 | 8 | 9 | 10 | 11 | 12 | 13 | 14 | 15 | 16 | 17 | 18 | 19 | 20 | 21 | 22 | 23 | 24 | 25 | 26 | 27 | 28 | 29 |

DAILY CALL REPORT | INSPECTION SLIPS | 5 x 3 PROSPECT SLIPS

PROSPECTS

DAY	NO. CALLS	NO. ORDERS	NO. NEW ACCTS SOLD	NO. DIFF RECORD FORMS SOLD		SALES THIS MONTH		NO. INSPECTIONS MADE				NUMBER DEVELOPED CURRENT MONTH									DISPOSITION-CUR. MO.					TOTAL EST. VALUE ON HAND			
				STOCK	SPEC	DAY	TO DATE	SAL.	STO.	LED.	FIL.	FIL.	LED	SAL	STO PUR	FUR	SER		MISC	TOTAL	SOLD	LOST	DROP	TOTAL	TOTAL ON HAND	EST. VALUE DEV.	EST. VALUE DIS.	TOTAL EST. VALUE	% SOLD TO NO. ON HAND

NUMBER
1
2
3
4
5
6
7
8
9
10
11
12
13
14
15
16
17
18
19
20
21
22
23
24
25
26
27
28
29
30
31
T

MONTHLY RECORD

REMARKS

| B | 30 | 31 | 32 | 33 | 34 | 35 | 36 | 37 | 38 | 39 | 40 | 41 | 42 | 43 |

THIS INFORMATION FROM SALES RECORD

MONTH	TOTAL NAMES IN FILE	NO. CALLED ON THIS MONTH	NO. NOT CALLED ON IN 6 MONTHS	% TO TOTAL NAMES IN FILE	NO. SOLD THIS MONTH	NO. SOLD THIS YEAR	NO. OF ACCOUNTS SYSTEMS PRODUCTS SOLD TO THIS YEAR				NO. OF INSTALLATIONS SOLD TO THIS YEAR			
							VRS.	VER.	L. L.	S. C.	SALES	STOCK	LEDGE	FILING
T														

SALESMAN | OFFICE | MONTH

Figure A-50: DAILY SUMMARY CONTROL
(From the book Business Executive's Handbook, 4th Edition, by Stanley M. Brown and Lillian Doris, Editors. © 1953 by Parker Publishing Company, Inc. Published by Parker Publishing Company, Inc., West Nyack, New York 10994.)

REPORTS, MATERIALS CONTROL LABORATORY
PRATT & WHITNEY AIRCRAFT
(Plant to which material is shipped)

This is to certify that Paragraph Number (s) .... apply to the shipment described below: (insert at least one of the first 4, plus 5 if applicable.)

1. (Applicable to all raw material, to parts made from raw material furnished or purchased by vendor, or to assemblies of which some or all components are made from raw material furnished or purchased by vendor.) Material, parts, or components of assemblies have been inspected and accepted to the specifications involved, and results of tests required by Pratt & Whiteny Aircraft are as shown herein.

2. (Applicable to parts or assembly components made from raw material furnished by Pratt & Whitney Aircraft and not chemically or metallurgically treated by vendor so as to change surface or internal condition significantly.) Parts or assemblies have been machined or formed from material furnished by Pratt & Whiteny Aircraft, to make these parts or components of asemblies.

3. (Applicable to parts or assembly components made from raw material furnished by Pratt & Whitney Aircraft and chemically or metallurgically treated by vendor so as to change surface or internal condition significantly.) Parts or components of assemblies have been made from raw material furnished by Pratt & Whitney Aircraft to make these parts or ocmponents of assemblies. Parts, components of assemblies, or assemblies have been inspected and accepted to the specifications involved, and results of tests required by Pratt & Whitney Aircraft are as shown herein.

4. (Applicable to repaired or reworked raw material, parts, or assemblies.) The raw material, parts or assemblies have been reworked or repaired in accordance with Pratt & Whiteny Aircraft instructions, and are the same material, parts or assemblies returned for such reworking or repair, except for replacement of assembly components, in which case paragraphs 1 and 5 are also applicable.

5. (Applicable to all assemblies, and to parts when specifically authorized by purchaser.) Results of all chemical and physical tests not shown below, as well as all other evidence which shows acceptability of raw materials and assembly components, are on file and available for inspection at any reasonable time.

PART OR ASS'Y NO. *(Size, if no Part No.)*		CHG. LTR.	SUF. NO.	SPECIFICATIONS, AS ORDERED*		
QUANTITY	DATE SHIPPED		LOCATION OF PWA PLANT SHIPPED TO		PACK. SLIP NO.	P.O. NO.
HEAT, LOT, CODE OR BATCH NO.		RAW MATERIAL VENDOR		TYPE—COMPOUND OR CASTING	PWA HEAT CODES *(If required)*	

*If material, parts or assemblies do not entirely conform to specification requirements, the deviation, and authority for furnishing such material, are indicated below:

RESULTS OF TESTS *(Use reverse side if necessary)*

VENDOR NAME	BY *(Authorized Agent)*
VENDOR ADDRESS	

PWA FORM 3279 REV. 11-72

Figure A-51: REPORT ON RAW MATERIAL ANALYSIS
(Courtesy of Electro-Methods, Inc., South Windsor, Connecticut.)

WORKSHEET—SHORTAGE RATE CALCULATION
(000's)

☐ Spring
☐ Fall   19_____

LINE NO.		(1)	(2)		LINE NO.

I. FORMULA FOR DETERMINATION OF FIRST 5 MONTHS SHORTAGE RATE:

	YEAR	ANNUAL SHORTAGE RATE
1	19 ———	%
2	19 ———	
3	19 ———	_____
4	TOTAL	%
	(÷ 3)	
5	AVERAGE RATE	%

II. CALCULATION OF PLAN SHORTAGE:

	MONTH	SALES	RATE BASED ON FORMULA	ALTERNATIVE RATE	SHORTAGE DOLLARS	PLAN RATE	
1	FEB/AUG						1
2	MAR/SEP						2
3	APR/OCT						3
4	MAY/NOV						4
5	JUN/DEC						5
6	JUL/JAN						6
7	SEASON TOTAL						7

III. MAJOR EXCEPTIONS:

	CORPORATE COMPARISON	FORMULA RATE	ALTERNATIVE RATE	
1				1
2				2
3				3
4				4
5				5
6				6
7				7
8				8

Figure A-52: SHORTAGE RATE CALCULATION

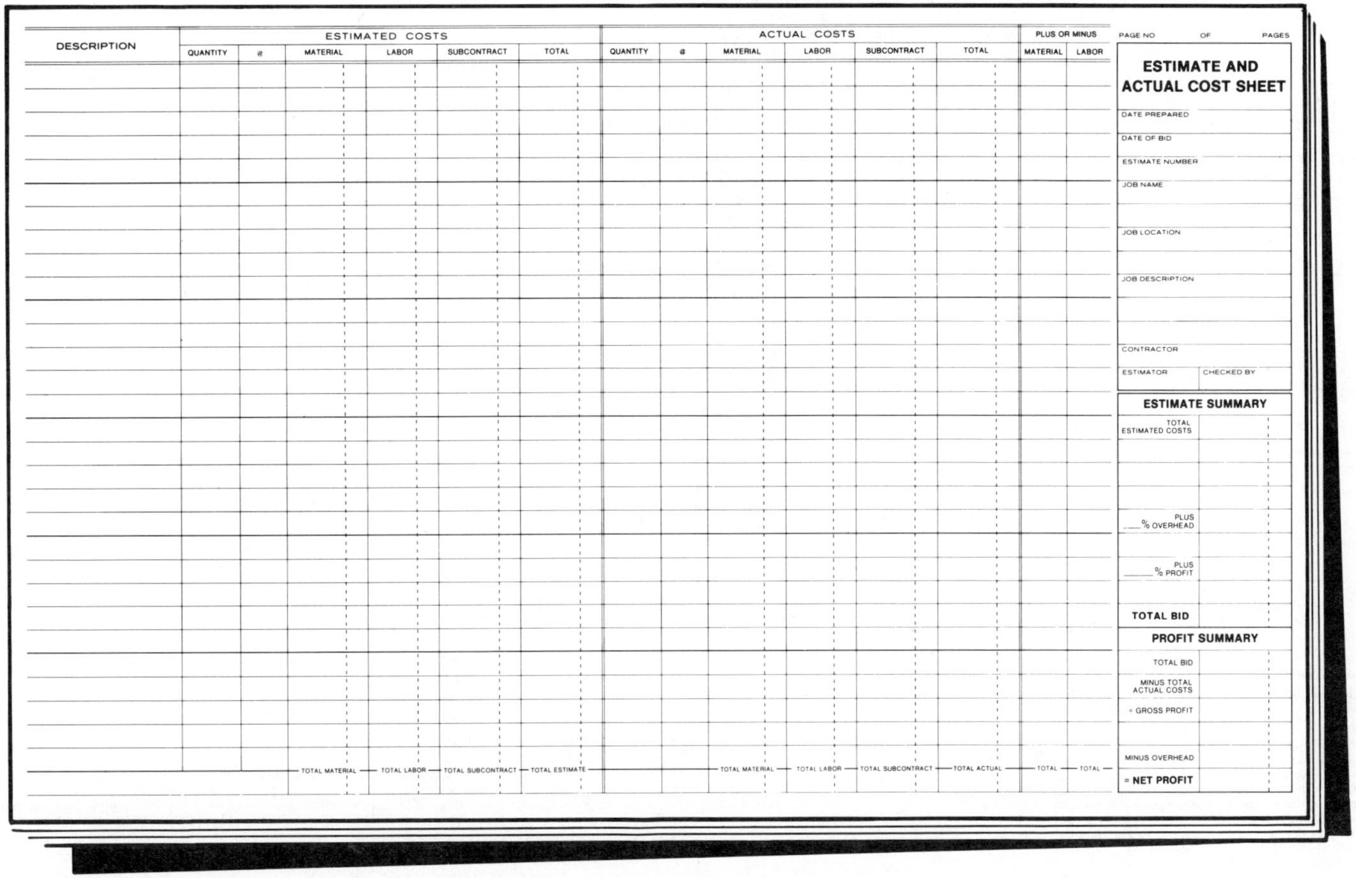

ESTIMATE AND ACTUAL COST SHEET

PAGE NO ___ OF ___ PAGES

DESCRIPTION	ESTIMATED COSTS					ACTUAL COSTS					PLUS OR MINUS	
	QUANTITY	@	MATERIAL	LABOR	SUBCONTRACT	TOTAL	QUANTITY	@	MATERIAL	LABOR	SUBCONTRACT	TOTAL	MATERIAL	LABOR

Column footers: TOTAL MATERIAL — TOTAL LABOR — TOTAL SUBCONTRACT = TOTAL ESTIMATE

TOTAL MATERIAL — TOTAL LABOR — TOTAL SUBCONTRACT = TOTAL ACTUAL

DATE PREPARED
DATE OF BID
ESTIMATE NUMBER
JOB NAME
JOB LOCATION
JOB DESCRIPTION
CONTRACTOR
ESTIMATOR   CHECKED BY

ESTIMATE SUMMARY

TOTAL ESTIMATED COSTS
PLUS ____% OVERHEAD
PLUS ____% PROFIT

TOTAL BID

PROFIT SUMMARY

TOTAL BID
MINUS TOTAL ACTUAL COSTS
= GROSS PROFIT
MINUS OVERHEAD
= NET PROFIT

Figure A-53: ESTIMATE AND ACTUAL COST SHEET
(Available from New England Business Service, Inc., North Main Street, Groton, Massachusetts 01450; 1-800-225-6380.)

89

OFFICE COPY

SEE STATEMENT ON REVERSE SIDE

FORM 2585A, REGENT FORMS, BELLMAWR, N.J. 08031

PETROLEUM EQUIPMENT SALES & SERVICE
321 LAKE ST. P. O. BOX 1936
SALISBURY, MD 21801
(301) 749-7156

ESTIMATE **669**
$

ESTIMATE INCLUDES:
☐ SERVICE CALL   ☐ REMOVAL
☐ SHOP LABOR   ☐ REINSTALLATION.
☐ PARTS ☐ OTHER:

CUSTOMER O.K.   DEPOSIT $

REVISED ESTIMATE   TIME AND DATE CALLED
$

CUSTOMER O.K.   CALLER

ACKNOWLEDGEMENT: I have read and understand the above estimate and terms and authorize the removal of the above described equipment for purposes stated. I also understand when authorized repairs along with necessary materials are completed, an express repairman's lien is hereby acknowledged on equipment to secure the amount of repair thereto.

CUSTOMER'S SIGNATURE   DATE

BROUGHT IN BY   DATE

CALL TAKEN BY   DATE

MAKE   MODEL   SERIAL NO.

DATE PROMISED   ☐ PICK UP   ☐ DELIVER

☐ SERVICE   ☐ CASH ☐ CHARGE   WARRANTY INFO.
☐ INSTALLATION ☐ CHECK ☐ C.O.D.   ☐ PARTS   DATE PURCHASED
SERVICE REQUESTED BY CUSTOMER   ☐ LABOR NAME

ADDRESS

CITY   PHONE NUMBER

SERVICE RECOMMENDED BY TECHNICIAN

NOTE:
WE DO ☐ DO NOT ☐
CARRY FIRE, THEFT AND
VANDALISM INSURANCE

NOTE: If equipment is returned at customer request before authorized service is performed, a diagnosis and handling charge of $_____ will be made.

RECEIVED BY
TECHNICIAN X

QUAN.	PART NUMBER	PART DESCRIPTION	PRICE	AMOUNT

PARTS TOTAL →

LABOR PERFORMED   AMOUNT

SAMPLE FORM ONLY
REGENT STANDARD FORMS, INC.

SUBJECT TO TERMS AND CONDITIONS
ON REVERSE SIDE

SERVICE PERFORMED

DATE COMPLETED   TECHNICIANS
                        SIGNATURE: X

REPAIRS SATISFACTORILY COMPLETED AND OLD PARTS RETURNED
CUSTOMERS SIGNATURE: X
RETURN OF PARTS WAIVED
CUSTOMERS SIGNATURE: X

CONSUMER STATEMENT:
An estimate where requested or required for repair and parts necessary for a specific job shall be given to the customer by the service dealer in writing, and the service dealer may not charge for work done or parts supplied in excess of the estimate without prior consent of the customer. The service dealer may charge a reasonable fee for making the estimate. For information, contact your state's Bureau of Repair Services, Department of Consumer Affairs.

TOTAL LABOR	
SERVICE CHARGE	
REMOVAL & REINSTALLATION	
TOTAL PARTS	
TAX	
TOTAL AMOUNT	

GUARANTEE: WE ARE PLEASED TO GUARANTEE ALL MATERIALS LISTED ABOVE FOR 90 DAYS UNLESS OTHERWISE SPECIFIED. CUSTOMER WILL BE CHARGED ONLY FOR LABOR REQUIRED.

Figure A-54: LABOR AND MATERIAL COST AND INVOICE
(Courtesy of Regent Standard Forms, Inc., Bellmawr, New Jersey 08031.)

REPAIR ORDER

auto repair order

REDIFORM
4S 479
Poly Pak (50 sets) 4P479
OFFICE COPY

003263

QUAN.	PART NO.	NAME OF PART	SALES AMOUNT	COST

Name

Address

Phone No._____ Date_____

Speedometer Reading_____ Serial No._____

MAKE AND MODEL	LICENSE NO. AND STATE	MOTOR NO.

OPERATION NUMBER	INSTRUCTIONS	AMOUNT

LUBRI-CATE ☐   CHANGE OIL ☐   FLUSH TRANS. ☐   FLUSH DIFF. ☐   WASH ☐   POLISH ☐

RETAIN PARTS FOR INSPECTION ☐   DISCARD PARTS ☐

	Total Labor	
TOTAL PARTS	ESTIMATE AMOUNT PARTS AND LABOR	Total Parts
Gals. Gas @	Revised Estimate TIME BY	Gas, Oil, Grease
Qts. Oil @	Revised Estimate	Accessories
Lbs. Grease @		Tires, Tubes
Total Gas-Oil-Grease	ESTIMATE TOTAL ▶	Outside Work
		TOTAL
		TAX
		TOTAL AMOUNT

I hereby authorize the above repair work to be done along with the necessary material, and hereby grant you and/or your employees permission to operate the car, truck or vehicle herein described on streets, highways or elsewhere for the purpose of testing and/or inspection. An express mechanic's lien is hereby acknowledged on above car, truck or vehicle to secure the amount of repairs thereto.

Work Authorized by X_____ Date Promised_____

Delivered to_____ Date Delivered_____

Figure A-55: AUTO REPAIR ORDER
(Courtesy of Rediform Office Products, Paramus, New Jersey 07652.)

ELECTRONIC REPAIR ORDER

INVOICE NUMBER

3616

STATE REGISTRATION NO.

| ☐ SERVICE ☐ INSTALL | ☐ WILL CALL ☐ DELIVER | BROUGHT IN BY | ☐ CASH ☐ CHECK | ☐ CHARGE ☐ C.O.D. | DATE __/__/__ |

N
A
M
E
A
D
D
R
E
S
S

APT.

PHONE

MAKE

MODEL

SERIAL

REPAIRS DONE (IF OTHER IS MARKED GIVE ADDRESS BELOW)

○ AT SHOP IN HEADING   ○ IN HOME   ○ OTHER

The deposited property is ☐ is not ☐ insured or protected to the amount of the actual cash value against loss occasioned by theft, fire, or vandalism.

QUAN.	DESCRIPTION OF PARTS-TUBES-MATERIALS	AMOUNT

SERVICE PERFORMED:

	TOTAL PARTS	
	TAX	
	TECHNICAL CHARGES	
	SERVICE CHARGE	
	TOTAL	

NATURE OF SERVICE REQUEST

ESTIMATE $	CUSTOMER'S O. K.	CHGS. IF NOT REPAIRED $	DEPOSIT $
REVISED ESTIMATE $	TIME & DATE CALLED		BY WHOM
INVOICE WRITTEN BY:	TECHNICIAN SIGNATURE	REPAIRS SATISFACTORILY COMPLETED & OLD PARTS RETURNED	
		CUSTOMER SIGNATURE	

Rediform®

4S 459

Poly Pak (50 sets)

4P459

GUARANTEE: We are pleased to guarantee all materials listed above for 90 days unless otherwise specified. Customer will be charged only for labor required.

SEE BACK OF SHEET 1 OR 2 FOR ADDITIONAL INFORMATION

ELECTRONIC REPAIR ORDER ORIGINAL

Rediform®

4S 459

Poly Pak (50 sets)

4P459

GUARANTEE: We are pleased to guarantee all materials listed above for 90 days unless otherwise specified. Customer will be charged only for labor required.

SEE BACK OF SHEET 1 OR 2 FOR ADDITIONAL INFORMATION

CUSTOMER'S INVOICE

3616

Rediform • 4S 459   Poly Pak (50 sets) 4P459

GUARANTEE: We are pleased to guarantee all materials listed above for 90 days unless otherwise specified. Customer will be charged only for labor required.

CUSTOMER CLAIM CHECK

Figure A-56: ELECTRONIC REPAIR ORDER
(Courtesy of Rediform Office Products, Paramus, New Jersey 07652.)

CONTINGENT FEE AGREEMENT

(ATTORNEY - CLIENT)

KNOW ALL MEN BY THESE PRESENTS, That the undersigned, residing or located at

herein referred to as the client, hereby retains

as the attorney(s) for the client in the handling or prosecution, trial or settlement of any claim the client may have against

for injuries and damages sustained by reason of

with full power and authority to appear on behalf of the client in any Court of record, administrative proceedings or any other proceeding whatsoever, and to do and perform all and every act and thing whatsoever that may be requisite and necessary to be done therein as fully as the client might or could do if personally present; hereby ratifying and confirming all that such attorney(s) shall lawfully do or cause to be done therein by virtue of these presents.

The client agrees that the attorney(s) shall receive in full payment for such professional services, per cent of the amount recovered by settlement before suit, or per cent of the amount recovered after institution of suit, plus costs and disbursements.

IN WITNESS WHEREOF, this instrument has been signed and sealed this

day of , 19

Witnesses:

....

....

....

Figure A-57: CONTINGENT FEE AGREEMENT
(Copyright 1976 by All State Legal Supply Co., Mountainside, New Jersey 07092.)

FILE MEMO

SPOT IN

Vessel: _____

Load: _____

Load At: _____

Going To: _____

Arrive: _____

Payment: _____

FILE MEMO

RELET OUT

Vessel: _____

Load: _____

Load At: _____

Going To: _____

Arrive: _____

Receipt: _____

Figure A-58: MEMOS (2) FOR SPOT AND RELET CARGO SHIP SPACE

BILLING LOG

Invoice Number	Invoice Date	Customer	Job Number	Date Shipped	Freight Company	Freight Re-billed	White Sent	CHECK-OFF Job Log Posted	Job Folder Updated

Figure A-59: BILLING LOG

PERT/COST ESTIMATING FORM

RESPONSIBLE UNIT: DATE: CHARGE NO.

DESCRIPTION   SUMMARY NO.

EVENT NO.

PERT TIME ESTIMATES

Beginning: (first)
Ending: (last)

Optimistic:
Most Likely:
Pessimistic:

SCHEDULED ELAPSED TIME   SCHEDULE

Start Date:
End Date:

IDENTIFICATION

cc Hours or $ Code	cc-cc Performing Unit	cc-cc Resource Code

ESTIMATED MANPOWER (HRS.) AND DIRECT COSTS ($)

MONTHS beginning with start date

cc-cc 1	cc-cc 2	cc-cc 3	cc-cc 4	cc-cc 5	cc-cc 6	cc-cc 7	cc-cc 8	cc-cc 9	cc-cc 10	cc-cc 11	cc-cc 12

— START DATE occurs during this month.

"H" = Man-hours
"D" = Direct Dollars
"T" = Total Dollars

ESTIMATOR _____

APPROVED _____

DATE _____

Figure A-60: PERT/COST ESTIMATING FORM

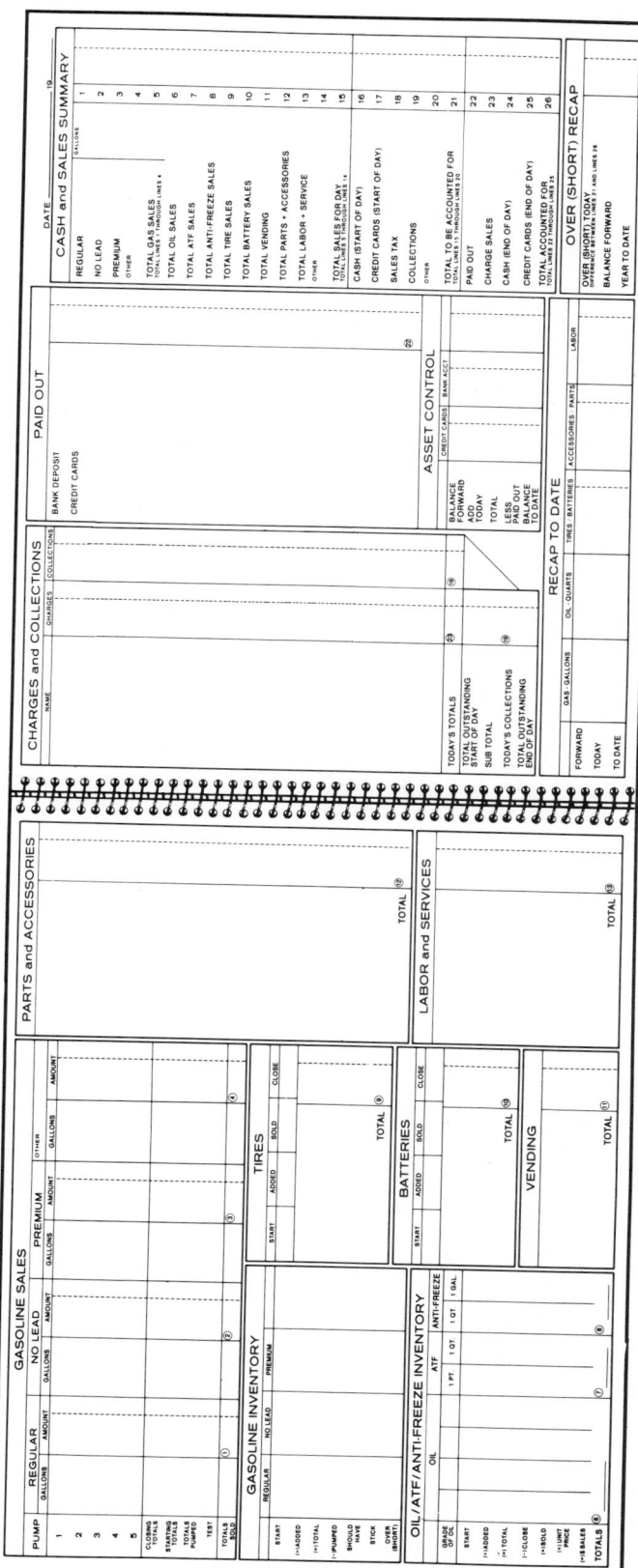

Figure A-61: SERVICE STATION DAY SHEET
(Available from New England Business Service, Inc., North Main Street, Groton, Massachusetts 01450; 1-800-225-6380.)

PRICING COST SHEET

PRODUCT: _____

      Size of Order   100 Units 500 Units _____

A. MATERIAL

      Pens @ _____ per gross

      Ink @ _____ per lb.

      + setup waste

      + running & cleanup wastes

          Total Material Cost

B. DIRECT LABOR

      Setup time

      Adjustments time

      Running time

      Cost @ _____ per hour

C. PACKAGING AND SHIPPING

      @ _____ per unit

D. TOTAL COST TO MANUFACTURE

E. PLUS MARK UP (covers SAG costs)

F. SELLING PRICE

      Per unit

      Total

Figure A-62: PRICING COST SHEET

ESTIMATED CHRISTMAS TREE PRODUCTION COSTS PER ACRE

					costs incurred in year				
	1	2	3	4	5	6	7	8	9
SITE PREPARATION									
SEEDLINGS									
PLANTING COSTS									
WEED CONTROL									
INSECT CONTROL									
FENCING									
PRUNING									
FIRE PROTECTION									
TAXES									
SALES COSTS									
CUTTING COSTS									
TRANSPORTATION									
OTHER LABOR COSTS									
MISCELLANEOUS									
TOTAL									

MARLBOROUGH FARMS

Figure A-63: ESTIMATED CHRISTMAS TREE PRODUCTION COSTS PER ACRE

PHARMACY SERVICE: BASE W

Prescriptions Filled

		ITEM		JULY	AUG	SEPT	OCT	NOV	DEC
OUTPUT-PRESCRIPTIONS FILLED (NUMBER)	**MONTHLY**	PLAN	01	4866	4520	4051	4780	4920	4315
		ACTUAL	02	4866	4372	4873			
		VARIANCE (02–01)	03	--	−148	822			
		% OF PLAN (02 ÷ 01)	04	100	97	120			
	CUMULATIVE	PLAN (CUM 01)	05	4866	9386	13437	18217	23137	27452
		ACTUAL (CUM 02)	06	4866	9386	14111			
		VARIANCE (06–05)	07	--	−148	674			
		% OF PLAN (06 ÷ 05)	08	100	98	105			
COST (THOUSANDS OF DOLLARS)	**MONTHLY**	PLAN	09	5.8	5.8	5.9	6.4	6.4	6.4
		ACTUAL	10	5.5	7.1	9.9			
		VARIANCE (10–09)	11	−0.3	1.3	4.0			
		% OF PLAN (10 ÷ 09)	12	95	122	168			
	CUMULATIVE	PLAN (CUM 09)	13	5.8	11.6	17.5	23.9	30.3	36.7
		ACTUAL (CUM 10)	14	5.5	12.6	22.5			
		VARIANCE (14–13)	15	−.3	1.0	5.0			
		% OF PLAN (14 ÷ 13)	16	95	109	129			
COST PER PRESCRIPTION FILLED (CENTS)	**MONTHLY**	PLAN (09 ÷ 01)	17	119	128	146	134	130	148
		ACTUAL (10 ÷ 02)	18	113	162	203			
		VARIANCE (18–17)	19	−6	34	57			
		% OF PLAN (18 ÷ 17)	20	95	127	139			
	CUMULATIVE	PLAN (13 ÷ 05)	21	119	124	130	131	131	134
		ACTUAL (14 ÷ 06)	22	113	136	159			
		VARIANCE (22–21)	23	6	12	29			
		% OF PLAN (22 ÷ 21)	24	95	110	122			

Figure A-64: PHARMACY COSTS, PRODUCTION, AND VARIANCE

ANALYSIS OF CENSUS BY HUNDRED GROUP

Company _____

☐ Preliminary

☐ Final

☐ Spring

☐ Fall   19 _____

| | | PLAN | | | LY | | B/(W) THAN LAST YEAR | |
| | | (1) | (2) | (3) | (4) | | (5) | (6) |
	EXPENSE CENTER	TY TOTAL	NEW STORES	EXISTING STORES	TOTAL		EXISTING STORES	TOTAL
1100	General Management							
1150	Security & Shortage							
	GEN. MGMT. — TOTAL 1000							
2110	Control & Gen. Acctg.							
2150	Mail and Messenger							
2250	Payroll							
2300	Accounts Payable							
2500	Sales Audit							
2600	EDP Processing							
	CONTROL — TOTAL 2000							
3210	Pre-Billing							
3200	Accts. Rec. & File							
3230	Bill Adjustments							
3310	Credit Development							
3320	Collections							
3330	Cashiers Office							
	CREDIT — TOTAL 3000							
4200	General Publicity							
4240	Radio Advertising							
4250	Direct Mail							
4260	TV Advertising							
4300	Shows and Exhibits							
4410	Display Production							
4450	Sign Shop							
4600	Eagle Stamp							
	PUBLICITY — TOTAL 4000							

Rev:

DATE RECEIVED BY CORPORATE _____

Figure A-65: ANALYSIS OF MANAGEMENT EFFECTIVENESS

ANALYSIS OF CENSUS BY HUNDRED GROUP

Company _____

☐ Preliminary

☐ Final

☐ Spring

☐ Fall   19 _____

	EXPENSE CENTER	PLAN			LY	B/(W) THAN LAST YEAR	
		(1) TY TOTAL	(2) NEW STORES	(3) EXISTING STORES	(4) TOTAL	(5) EXISTING STORES	(6) TOTAL
5100	Serv. & Operations						
5200	Supply Purchasing						
5250	Print Shop						
5500	Gen. Telephone Service						
5700	Cleaning						
5810	Maintenance of Property						
	OPERATIONS — TOTAL 5000						
6100	Pers., Empl. & Training						
6300	Supplemental Benefits						
	PERSONNEL — TOTAL 6000						
7300	Rec., Chkg., & Marking						
7500	Transfer Hauling						
	MER. HANDLING — TOTAL 7000						
8050	Selling Supervision						
8100	Dir. Selling — Owned						
8200	Maintenance of Stock						
8250	Customer Service						
8340	Mail & Telephone Order						
8450	Free Customer Parking						
8500	Pay Customer Parking						
8670	Wrap and Pack						
8700	Delivery						
8850	Truck and Garage						
4410	SELLING — TOTAL 8000						
9100	Merchandise Management						
9210	Buying						
9300	Buying Office						
9400	Merchandise Control						
	MERCHANDISING — TOTAL 9000						

Rev:

Figure A-65 (continued)

Cost/Income Statement Format

PMA Marketing Division

Attached is a blank copy of the current financial statement. This should be the format that you use in submitting your budgets to us. Certain items may not yet readily be available as they are related to the activities in other divisions. Where this information is not available, please note and we will fill them in when all the information is gathered.

Certain other items on this statement are combinations and will require additional analysis.

For instance, publication advertising income is a combination of GWM reimbursable advertising expense plus the gross publication revenues from NPC. The mailing categories include all the different types of mailings including, but not limited to, inquiry, owner, direct mail and 1st and 2nd follow-ups. Other reimbursables are combinations of many relatively small items. Please refer to attached schedules for details.

One question that needs to be resolved will be the treatment of the APC computer costs. Let's discuss statement format before the budget is prepared.

For your fringe benefits budget please use 55% of payroll.

Please let us know what relevant statistics you would like to see on the new financial statement.

I will be pleased to work with you as closely as possible on this budget.

Denholtz   *Prophet*

Figure A-66: COST/INCOME STATEMENT FORMAT
(Courtesy of Garden Way, Incorporated.)

PRECISION MARKETING ASSOCIATES
PMA Marketing Division

INCOME
Marketing fee   —GWMC
      "   "   —GWR & GWP
      "   "   —GWLC
Publication advertising
Cooperative advertising programs
Mailings
Computer services & salaries
Other reimbursable income
Miscellaneous income

    Total Income

DIRECT EXPENSES
Publication advertising
Cooperative advertising programs
Mailings
Computer services
Other Reimbursable Expenses

    Total Direct Expenses

    Gross Profit

OPERATING EXPENSES
Salaries - Regular
Fringe benefits
Office expenses
Professional services
Occupancy expenses
Legal and Accounting Fees
Selling & Marketing Expenses

    Total Operating Expenses

    Net Income or (Loss)

Figure A-66 (continued)

PRECISION MARKETING ASSOCIATES

OCCUPANCY EXPENSES

OCCUPANCY EXPENSES
Rent
Business insurance
Utilities
Repairs & Maintenance
Depreciation–Leasehold improvements
        –Furniture & fixtures
Equipment rental
Property tax
Storage charges

Total Occupancy Expenses

ALLOCATION OF OCCUPANCY EXPENSES
PMA Marketing
PMA Lettershop

Total

Figure A-66 (continued)

PRECISION MARKETING ASSOCIATES

OFFICE EXPENSES

OFFICE EXPENSES
Temporary manpower
Office supplies & expenses
Dues and subscriptions
Bank service charges
Telephone
Recruiting expenses
Employment agency fees
Sales tax expense
Travel & Entertainment
Depreciation - Automobiles
Miscellaneous
Postage

Total Office Expenses

Figure A-66 (continued)

PRECISION MARKETING ASSOCIATES
Corporate Expenses

CORPORATE EXPENSES

Stockholders life insurance
Directors fees
Contributions
Trustees fees
Investment management fees
Meeting house operating expenses
Miscellaneous corporate taxes

Total Corporate expenses

Figure A-66: (continued)

SAMMZY MY MANUFACTURING CO.   1976 PROFIT PLAN   09/11/75

CONTROL ACCOUNT 752   PMA. ADMIN.
___

ACCT NUM. ACCOUNT	AUG. 75 YTD ACT	DEC /	JAN /	FEB /	MAR /	APR /	MAY /	JUNE /	JULY /	AUG /	SEPT /	OCT /	NOV /
					-------1976 DEPARTMENTAL BUDGET-------								
509	0.	*	*	*	*	*	*	*	*	*	*	*	*
586 INQUIRY TE	30,498.	*	*	*	*	*	*	*	*	*	*	*	*
587 LETTER SHO	42,000.	*	*	*	*	*	*	*	*	*	*	*	*
588 PMA. PROF S	33,366.	*	*	*	*	*	*	*	*	*	*	*	*
589 PMA EXP AC	100,000.	*	*	*	*	*	*	*	*	*	*	*	*
590 MMT FEE FM	1,285,234.	*	*	*	*	*	*	*	*	*	*	*	*
591 COMPUTER S	202,218.	*	*	*	*	*	*	*	*	*	*	*	*
592 MINI TILL	17,987.	*	*	*	*	*	*	*	*	*	*	*	*
593 W/HOUSE RE	12,000.	*	*	*	*	*	*	*	*	*	*	*	*
594	0.	*	*	*	*	*	*	*	*	*	*	*	*
595 GWA EXP. P	255,601.	*	*	*	*	*	*	*	*	*	*	*	*
596	0.	*	*	*	*	*	*	*	*	*	*	*	*
598 MAL HSE NA	209.	*	*	*	*	*	*	*	*	*	*	*	*
601 TRAVEL & E	52,362.	*	*	*	*	*	*	*	*	*	*	*	*
606 ART, TYPE	30,185.	*	*	*	*	*	*	*	*	*	*	*	*
608 PRINTING M	49,587.	*	*	*	*	*	*	*	*	*	*	*	*
790 TELEPHONE	983.	*	*	*	*	*	*	*	*	*	*	*	*
T O T A L	2,159,100.	*	*	*	*	*	*	*	*	*	*	*	*

THIS ORIGINAL BUDGET PAGE TO BE RETU SED 66   + +   ON OR BEFORE 10/24/75

Figure A-66 (continued)

XXXXXX   MANUFACTURING CO.   1976 PROFIT PLAN   09/11/75   Page   PAGE 121

CONTROL ACCOUNT 763   PMA INC. ACC. & MATL

ACCT NUM. ACCOUNT	AUG. 75 YTD ACT	1976 DEPARTMENTAL BUDGET											
		DEC	JAN	FEB	MAR	APR	MAY	JUNE	JULY	AUG	SEPT	OCT	NOV
736 INQUIRY TE	11,812.	*	*	*	*	*	*	*	*	*	*	*	*
586 MGL NGE NA	66,727.	*	*	*	*	*	*	*	*	*	*	*	*
595 MAL KSE NA	42,611.	*	*	*	*	*	*	*	*	*	*	*	*
600 SGST MAIL.	726,655.	*	*	*	*	*	*	*	*	*	*	*	*
652 PUBLIC. AC	341,355.	*	*	*	*	*	*	*	*	*	*	*	*
663 MGGR. ADV.	365,728.	*	*	*	*	*	*	*	*	*	*	*	*
68 M A CIS. A	67,565.	*	*	*	*	*	*	*	*	*	*	*	*
655 INC. FELL.	383,475.	*	*	*	*	*	*	*	*	*	*	*	*
T O T A L	1,940,935.	*	*	*	*	*	*	*	*	*	*	*	*

THIS ORIGINAL BUDGET PAGE TO BE RETU SED 6 6 + +   ON OR BEFORE 10/24/75

Figure A-66 (continued)

109

PROFIT PROTECTION, ANALYSIS, AND PLANNING

SECTION **B** FORMS

Profit Protection, Analysis, and Planning

113

Profit Protection, Analysis, and Planning

Other people's profits have been the cause of much supposed unhappiness in this world, so much so that endless schemes have been devised to appropriate the profits of others. Most of what passes for profits in business operations are really returns to owners in payment for invested capital, which should include an adequate return for the use of capital (i.e., savings), compensation for the amount of risk the investor assumes, and adjustment for price-level changes induced by inflation (i.e., loss of purchasing power). If anything is left over after paying all suppliers of materials, labor and management services, and after compensating the real risk-takers (the investors), then we can talk about profits—if indeed there are any at all.

Tax collectors deliberately define profits as what remains after most, if not all, suppliers are paid—except suppliers of capital. This is an incorrect concept. Heavy taxation of profits, however they are defined, discourages investment and job creation.

Replacement, of course, can materialize out of depreciation return of existing capital in a profitable endeavor, but growth relies on savings. Profits are one form of savings. Consequently, profits must be protected, analyzed, and planned for. When planning time also embraces protection from tax collectors, valuable business resources are diverted from productive to nonproductive activities, and red tape machinations result in an additional burden, or tax, upon the enterprise. The forms in this section have helped some organizations to preserve income; however, the tax question is not treated in this handbook, although it is recognized as an integral part of investment and profit planning.

PROFIT PROTECTION is really PROFIT CONTROL. Profit control springs from efficient cost control (portrayed in Section A) and financial planning (illustrated in Section C). Thus, this section begins with some forms on merchandise control systems.

115

B-1 The first, a Rotated Merchandise Control Record (B-1), hinges on physical inventory enumeration on a rotated or staggered basis. Subtracting each inventory count from the previous balance, and including additions to inventory, produces a theoretical sales figure. The system offers several advantages:

(a) The record allows for comparative sales figures, significant in forecasting.
(b) It simplifies routine ordering that can be done by a lower cost employee.
(c) Salespersons maintaining the count become more familiar with the merchandise and inventory movements (even if this supplements a computer-based system).
(d) It pins down the rate of pilfering when compared with central records.

B-2 In addition to this method, a Seasonal Item Control Report (B-2) lists sales and inventories by classification and price line, month by month, for an entire season. This

B-3 procedure is vital for review purposes. The other aid is a Style Activity Record (B-3), a complete history of the item from order to sales. These forms are especially useful in the apparel trade where fashion changes during a brief marketing season. Positive feedback urges quick response to PROTECT ACCUMULATED PROFITS or GENERATE MORE PROFITS when a firm is on the right side of a trend.

Profit protection means control; control means analysis; analysis results in better planning. For example, movie theater management demands an Hourly Box Office

B-4 Report (B-4). This information, when charted, begins to form distinct cyclical patterns by hour of day and by day of week. It provides close control over numbered tickets. It furnishes the basis for investment decisions and innovative alternatives to INCREASE PROFITS. It also helps to nail down pilferers. Theaters typically separate the ticket sales function from the ticket-taker to control free entries. But if these two persons cooperate, the ticket-taker can recycle used tickets to the sales booth, and they split the proceeds, while the theater manager accurately matches ticket numbers with ostensible revenue. However, with an historical box office record, the manager can quickly FERRET OUT PROFIT LEAKS. This information is summarized, together with other income sources,

B-5 in the Box Office Statement (B-5), which is forwarded to the corporate office for PROFIT REVIEW.

Further examples of profit protection are forms recording Daily Sales and Stock Report

B-6 (B-6) and a Weekly Report (B-7). The Daily Sales and Stock Report lists all items sold on
B-7 the previous sales day. To be valuable, any unusual activity that can INCREASE PROFITS should be observed and acted upon. Similarly, a weekly report will reveal any imbalance in merchandise assortment. The Weekly Carbon Report doubles as a cost control device and registers any interruptions that may adversely affect long-run profits.

B-8 The monthly Sales and Stock Plan Report (B-8) focuses on comparative sales and profit potentials over a longer time period than weekly reports. It compares last year's sales with this year's and differences between planned and actual sales as well as deviations in inventory purchases and investment, a *key item to profit control.*

A different kind of sales activity report is an Insurance Production Report (B-9). Being intangible, policy sales activity and profit measurement are adjusted to company requirements. But for firm measuring sales and profit movement by jobs, projects, or programs, a Project Status Report (B-10) identifies progress relative to cost accumulation and helps to identify profit leaks.

B-9

B-10

Profits may be substandard compared with the rest of an industry if worker productivity is too low in relation to wage costs. A Productivity and Employment Costs Analysis (B-11) registers total production divided by number of hours worked. When this is done over a long enough period, periodic percentage changes are also figured. Such an analysis is fruitful when results are compared with industry-wide averages. Cost increases must be adjusted for price-level changes caused by inflation in order to determine whether cost accretion per unit of production actually reflects a fall in productivity. Productivity may be rising along with rising nominal costs but falling real costs (i.e., adjusted).

B-11

A different type of form relating to production generates figures for client billing for specific types of labor and professional services. The Analysis of Final Billing (B-12) summarizes (1) total number of hours worked by employee or professional, (2) the hourly rate to customers, and (3) a comparison of deal fees to billed fees. If the ideal too often exceeds billed fees, there may be a problem of (a) completion, (b) inadequate analysis of service, (c) over-optimism, or (d) poor marketing.

B-12

Profits are protected when costs for labor, materials, and subcontract labor are adequately accounted for. An Estimate Sheet (B-13) enrolls these costs, covers overhead, and includes an adequate profit. If bids are missed, profits are missed. If bids are too low, profits are missed. But wrong accounting of overhead also leaks profits. The fate of profits is sealed when the bid is submitted (B-14), and the firm's reputation and future profits result from honest relationships.

B-13

B-14

A Job Cost Record (B-15) adds up cost inputs on a particular job; the lower right-hand section calls for a summary of gross and net profits before taxes. Another variation of this form is a Job Envelope (B-16), which preserves cost data and profit analysis on the outside, and holds receipts, correspondence, and contracts relating to the specific job inside the card-stock envelope. These data can be extracted later and rearranged for profit analysis. Also in line with profit control, payments are usually covered by a purchase order for parts and supplies. However, especially with several subsidiaries and centralized accounting, one technique to handle situations not covered by a purchase order, an Intercompany Check Request Form (B-17), covers these situations while PROTECTING PROFITS.

B-15

B-16

B-17

Another form for profit analysis, a Financial Report (B-18), dissects an operation by departments and begins with an analysis of targeted income vis-a-vis actual income, then does the same with expenses. Expenses are itemized and compared with budget

B-18

allocations of largely fixed expenses in seven categories: fuel, utilities, insurance, taxes, leases, interest, depreciation. The form also accommodates capital expenditures and payments on principal.

B-19 Where interest expenses are paramount, seasonal analysis of Interest Expense and Return on Equity (B-19) crops up. The form modeled, not a worksheet, represents the culmination of considerable investment in time:

    (a)   Section I itemizes uses of funds.
    (b)   Section II examines investment by layer, i.e., in terms of time.
    (c)   Section III classifies interest expenses by layer, corresponding to investments in II.
    (d)   Section IV analyzes return on equity.

The entire season (if business is seasonal as in the example) is then analyzed according to planned and actual results for each unit or subsidiary, and final results are submitted for corporate-wide review.

B-20 Profit analysis may mean measurement of Return on Inventory (B-20), computed as gross profit times inventory turnover. The gross profit rate is annual gross profit divided by sales; inventory turnover is annual sales divided by average inventory investment; and return on inventory is the annual gross profit rate divided by average inventory. If return on inventory is too low, then the focus is on improvement of gross profit. Improvement may result from better cost control (Section A), or centralized purchasing, or more efficient inventory management, or revenue analysis.

B-21 The Passenger Revenue Analysis and Rate of Return on Total Operations (B-21), while less concerned with gross profits and inventory costs, does focus on load factors. Pricing and scheduling nucleate around an attempt to exceed the break-even load factor; and marginal pricing, not presented here, may be the method to raise rate of return on total operations. (For a succinct treatment of marginal pricing with specific reference to airline operations, see Robert Vichas, *Handbook of Financial Mathematics, Formulas, and* **B-22** *Tables,* published by Prentice-Hall, Inc., Chapter 6.) Variance Analysis (B-22) of summary data by using averages of income and cost data contributes toward developing adequate PROFIT PLANNING.

There are at least two important relationships in profit planning:

    ◆   the relation of profits to investment;
    ◆   the relation of profits to alternative revenue and cost structures.

In other words, a close link arises among profit planning, capital investments, and cost control and analysis discussed in Section A. Achieving the best, if not optimum, cost mix and best product or services mix influences cost, volume and revenues, and ultimately affects return on investment.

Calculating Return on Investment (B-23), although requiring time to generate the data, need not be presented in a complicated format. The form exhibited provides for quick communication, getting to the heart of the matter, viz., return on investment. This analysis of an investment in a subsidiary, based on original investment in the acquired firm, compares two fiscal periods. Total investment figures as the original investment plus earnings and intercompany loans, minus dividends. Return on investment analysis subdivides the subsidiary's operation into three components, plus a total for all operations, and records percent profit on net sales after taxes, net sales divided by net assets, and return on investment.

B-23

Return on equity under differing assumptions about the future and under differing assumptions of capital structure (B-24) fills more than idle time, for it may provide some real insight into viable options during periods of instability. A high degree of leverage may be more practical under cyclical upturns than under downturns. The analysis focuses on return on equity by changing six variables, but long-term profit planning means correct financial policy for survival during uncertain times to balance the various risks inherent in any business operation.

B-24

Profitable cash management, an important aspect of financial policy under any economic conditions, is singularly significant when another currency is involved. The Canadian Cash Management form (B-25) registers average daily bank balances and investment portfolio of accounts expressed in Canadian dollars on a monthly basis along with the effective yield on investment accounts. The manager is required to state why there are changes in average daily investments and in the portfolio yield.

B-25

Of course, PROFIT PLANNING relies on financial statements and analysis. The 14 pages of the form shown (B-26) represent how one diversified firm tackled this problem. The format calls for an exposition of sales and revenues by corporate division along product/service lines and a few key liquidity ratios. The remaining 13 pages are consigned to budgeted-versus-actual comparisons for the current period under probe, year to date, and actual results of a prior year. The first two pages divulge data on marketing expenses and an ordering of costs per inquiry. The next page links sources and uses of funds and an examination of changes in working capital, followed by a corporate balance sheet, an inquest on prepaid expenses, and combined statement of net operating profit. The remainder of the form particularizes details on income and expenses by activity.

B-26

Another way to fractionalize production activity is via the Detailed Project Status Report (B-27), which pairs the time and cost status of each project underway. Of course, a firm engaged in silvaculture desires information in a format that rearranges time and costs. The form exhibited (B-28) applies present value analysis to costs that occur in different years, or over several years, to unearth the best or optimum time to sell and to determine when, in time, the discounted value of costs exceeds potential income.

B-27

B-28

B-29   Sales Analysis (B-29) is fundamental to many successful profit plans. This form compares both dollar amounts and percentages for each period of credit plan sales and mail and telephone plan sales. Each of these categories is related to total sales. Variance analysis of sales data can generate information on quantity variance, price variance, quantity-price variance, and total variance; that is, any of these factors or combinations may produce variations in the total cost of goods sold. Separation of these effects is attempted in a

B-30   Three-Way Sales Variance Analysis (B-30). Variance resulting from quantity changes applies to absorption costing where quantity relates to the effect of changes from the planned sales volume to the fixed cost component in costs per unit. These are all part of ANALYSIS OF PROFITABILITY.

B-31   Revenue may be strengthened by expanding volume at the same price; but at some point the firm will meet resistance, and further volume growth can be achieved only by intensified marketing efforts (product differentiation, additional services, etc.) at higher costs, or by lowering price. The Pricing Formula (B-31) represents one approach to tagging on a price sufficiently high to achieve desired profits. And profits are the objective, not a buildup in physical volume, per se. Nor is profit per unit sold the final objective. The purpose of profit scrutiny is to INCREASE TOTAL PROFITS.

B-32   Which does not exempt from analysis Profits Per Unit (B-32). This form segregates products or services (or classes of products) by total sales, costs, and contribution per product and then on a per-unit basis. This analysis is repeated for as many categories as necessary (not necessarily limited to three as illustrated) and then summed to yield total sales and administrative expenses and net profits, which can be computed by subtracting fixed manufacturing and S & A costs from variable profits.

B-33   Sales can also be reviewed in terms of inventories and markdowns, and profits analyzed
B-34   as a percent of plan and markdowns as a percent of sales (B-33). Then the merchandise plan summarized by group (B-34) yields information on group markdowns, gross margins, shortages, and inventory turnover. The monthly profit plan for the season (B-
B-35   35) is segmented by sales, gross margin, operating and interest expenses, earnings compared to last year (LY) and flow-through. Finally, profit contribution is figured
B-36   according to space required for merchandise (B-36), which provides data on new product expansion, or product elimination, to INCREASE PRODUCTS WITHOUT INCREASING REQUIRED SPACE.

B-37   Sales and profits may be bettered through improved customer-employee relationships (B-37)—particularly through emphasis on courtesy and accuracy. If errors occur, they are itemized by department, the item and correct price are shown, and reason for error is noted.

B-38   Neither are the bosses exempt from evaluation. They may choose auto-evaluation or prefer to evaluate each other (B-38). Obviously this must be done with tact. Substandard contributions to the management team or poor relationships with employees and customers—all damage profits. The biggest profit leak of all may well be an owner of the business. Profits may multiply with a change in attitude. And profits may also be enhanced by controlling costs and losses on each job (B-39) completed by a manufacturing concern.

B-39

The Contribution Approach to Budget Income Statements (B-40) calls for an analysis of variable and fixed costs. The first problem arises with finding a working definition of variable and fixed costs. Some get around this problem by dividing costs into *variable, semi-variable,* and *fixed;* but for a starter, variable costs are those which vary directly with production. Raw material, manufacturing, and some labor costs are obviously variable; other labor costs are less obvious. In a theoretical sense, or with *zero-based budgeting,* variable costs may enjoy a broader range definition of labor services. However, no decision begins at zero once an operation is initiated, so that all decisions are made at the margin; for instance: What will an *additional* investment yield? What will it contribute to profits? The objective of this type of profit analysis is to isolate variable costs and undertake those projects which at least will cover variable costs and contribute something toward the reduction of fixed costs (*fixed* being fixed whether the firm operates at a high or low volume). That is, the additional contribution INCREASES PROFITS. Naturally, sooner or later all fixed costs must be covered if operations are to be profitable; but the analysis here is for the purpose of determining whether losses are being minimized with each additional undertaking, until total fixed costs are covered, and then how much each additional job will add to profits.

B-40

Time spent on budgeting is a painful experience for many managers. If mere collection of data were the end, work on a budget would dismay most production-oriented persons. The Performance-to-Budget Report (B-41) reflects the efficiency of the operating manager. Has he lived within his means? Has he saved anything from allocation allowances? Some similar reports will require considerably more feedback than appears here.

B-41

Minimal information on a performance-to-budget report will include:

(a) cost accounts on the department's budget;
(b) actual outflows for the period;
(c) budgeted allowance for the period;
(d) extraordinary expenditures;
(e) difference between actual and budgeted amounts;
(f) cumulative data on year to date:
    (i) the variance for year to date;
    (ii) the actual expenditures for year to date.
(g) The foregoing is on an individual item basis; totals are shown for all accounts.

The Profit Plan illustrated is for a Departmental Budget Package (B-42). The guidelines demonstrate how to help department managers furnish the quality of information essential to profit analysis and planning. The first six guidelines cover treatment of labor costs; the seventh one embraces manufacturing costs and expense account numbers used

B-42

for standardization. The next page casts dates for meeting various phases of profit-plan development. Appendices supply the profit plan parameters and a calendar of events. The last form in this set is a Manpower Needs Forecast by month and pay grade.

B-43   In a subsequent Profit Plan (B-43), the same firm modified its earlier format. The revised parameter requirements begin with a statement of goals and objectives. The unit profit plans must then conform to corporate objectives. Sales are stated in probabilistic terms, disclosing high and low extremes of the range of sales and then the most likely, or targeted, outcome. Departmental managers must furnish profit-plan parameters by a deadline date to the Financial Planning, Analysis, and Review Group, for inclusion in the budget package.

Can a corporation realistically meet its long-run growth objectives? The forecasted growth rate, if constant, can be projected at a compounded rate into the future. The **B-44**   difference between actual and forecasted (B-44) performance is the gap. If the difference is significant, the company will want to revise either its goals or its strategy. If goals have been carefully formulated, then shift in strategy is called for. Strategy in this sense means the method(s) or path which management chooses to meet stated objectives

Finally, in profit planning, management will want to examine carefully the performance of subsidiaries, its investment portfolio, and possible acquisitions. (Sections D and E include forms on asset and firm acquisitions and real estate acquisitions.) The Normal **B-45**   Value of a Growth Stock (B-45) is calculated by estimating earnings and the forecasted growth rate plus a quality factor and the nongrowth price-earnings ratio. Normal growth is then defined as the product of the growth factor times the quality factor times the **B-46**   nongrowth price-earnings factor. Corporate Investment Analysis (B-46) is divided into two categories: (1) an analysis of earning power, and (2) an analysis of financial factors. These data are projected as far into the future as is plausible. Despite an unknowable future, financial planning for profitability and cost control ranks high in priority.

ROTATED UNIT CONTROL RECORD

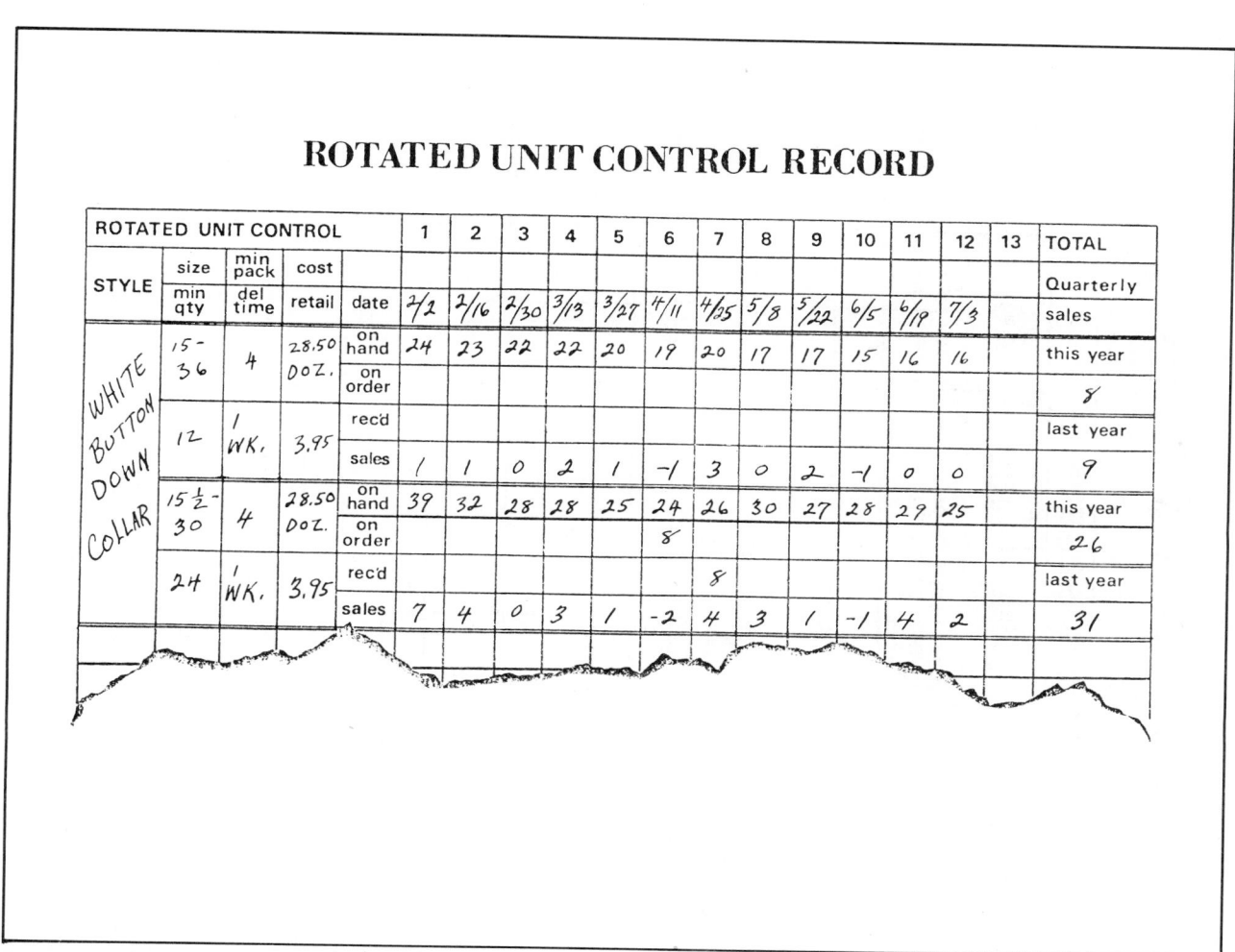

ROTATED UNIT CONTROL					1	2	3	4	5	6	7	8	9	10	11	12	13	TOTAL
STYLE	size	min pack	cost															Quarterly
	min qty	del time	retail	date	2/2	2/16	2/30	3/13	3/27	4/11	4/25	5/8	5/22	6/5	6/19	7/3		sales
WHITE BUTTON DOWN COLLAR	15-36	4	28.50 DOZ.	on hand	24	23	22	22	20	19	20	17	17	15	16	16		this year
				on order														8
	12	1 WK.	3.95	rec'd														last year
				sales	1	1	0	2	1	-1	3	0	2	-1	0	0		9
	15½-30	4	28.50 DOZ.	on hand	39	32	28	28	25	24	26	30	27	28	29	25		this year
				on order						8								26
	24	1 WK.	3.95	rec'd							8							last year
				sales	7	4	0	3	1	-2	4	3	1	-1	4	2		31

Figure B-1: ROTATED UNIT CONTROL BOARD

SEASONAL ITEM REPORT CONTROL BOARD

SEASONAL ITEM REPORT

SELLING SEASON

Classification	FEB		MARCH		APRIL		MAY		JUNE		JULY		AUG		seasonal summary	
PRICE	stock units	sold units	stock units	sold units	stock units	sold units	stock units	sold units	stock units	sold units	stock units	sold units	stock units	sold units	sold units	end stock

Figure B-2: SEASONAL ITEM REPORT CONTROL BOARD

| UNIT CONTROL RECORD | | | | | | | | | | | | | | SOURCE: | | | | | | | |

RECEIVED			CLASSIFICATION NO.								STYLE		RETAIL						COST	ON ORDER	
date	no. units	to date	sales week begin	M	T	W	T	F	S	sales to date	units on hand	sales week begin	M	T	W	T	F	S	sales to date	units on hand	date	no. units

| RECEIVED | CLASSIFICATION NO. | STYLE | RETAIL | COST | ON ORDER |

Figure B-3: MODEL ACTIVITY RECORD

HOURLY BOX OFFICE REPORT

_____ THEATRE

DAY _____ DATE _____

	PRICE	OPENING NUMBER	CLOSING NUMBER	SOLD	TOTAL SOLD PER HOUR		PRICE	OPENING NUMBER	CLOSING NUMBER	SOLD	TOTAL SOLD PER HOUR	
12 TO 1												5 TO 6
1 TO 2												6 TO 7
2 TO 3												7 TO 8
3 TO 4												8 TO 9
4 TO 5												9 TO 10

TOTAL MATINEE		TOTAL EVENING
PROGRAM		TOTAL FOR DAY
		BOX OFFICE OPENING TIME
		BOX OFFICE CLOSING TIME

Figure B-4: HOURLY BOX OFFICE REPORT

THEATRE CIRCUIT • BOX OFFICE STATEMENT

Theatre

Day

Date

CO

Feature

Co-Feat Subjects

Subjects

Matinee

Sold	Price	Net	Tax @	Tax	Total
C	Child				
O	PASS				
C	XX				
O	A C				
C					
O					
C					
O	Adult				
C					
O					
Mat Totals	XX XX		—		

Change of Mat. to Eve. is 5:00 p.m.

	Starting Bank	$	Finish Bank	$
Matinee Cashier				
Evening Cashier	Starting Bank	$	Finish Bank	$

Evening

Sold	Price	Net	Tax @	Tax	Total
C	Child				
O	Pass XX				
C	AC				
O					
C	Student				
O	Adult				
C					
O					
C					
O					
Eve. Totals	XX XX				
Mat. Totals	XX XX				
Refunds *			—		
Day Totals	XX XX				

Other Income (Specify)

Adjustments (Explain)

+ or

Engagement to Date   W T F S S M T $

Deposit ▲

Run to date total must NOT include tax

Soda Machine
Present Mo.
Last Mo.   X   c — $

Explain *
Refunds

Opposition

Remarks

Weather

MANAGER
OR
ASSISTANT MANAGER _____

CONCESSIONS

CANDY STAND			
CANDY MACHINE			

Adjustments (Explain)   + or —

Stand
Per Capita   Deposit ▲

Figure B-5: DAILY BOX OFFICE REPORT

DEPARTMENT		CLASSIFICATION		DESCRIPTION
WEEK ENDING		WEEK ENDING		
PRICE		PRICE		
MON		MON		
TUE		TUE		
WED		WED		
THU		THU		
FRI		FRI		
SAT		SAT		
TOTAL		TOTAL		

Figure B-6: DAILY SALES AND STOCK REPORT

THEATRE CIRCUIT

WEEKLY CARBON REPORT

THEATRE   LOCATION   WEEK ENDING

	POS.	NEG.	Show Time Hrs.	Min.	INTERRUPTIONS	REASONS.
WEDNESDAY						
THURSDAY						
FRIDAY						
SATURDAY						
SUNDAY						
MONDAY						
TUESDAY						
TOTAL............						

	POS.	NEG.
OPENING STOCK		
ADDED		
TOTAL		
CLOSING STOCK		
USED		

POS. RATE, per hour	
NEG. RATE, per hour	
TOTAL...........	

..................................Projectionist

..................................Manager.

Remarks.

GIVE TWO COPIES OF THIS REPORT TO
YOUR MANAGER EACH WEEK AND KEEP ONE
FOR YOUR OWN FILE.

Figure B-7: MONEY-SAVING CHECKLIST—WEEKLY CARBON REPORT

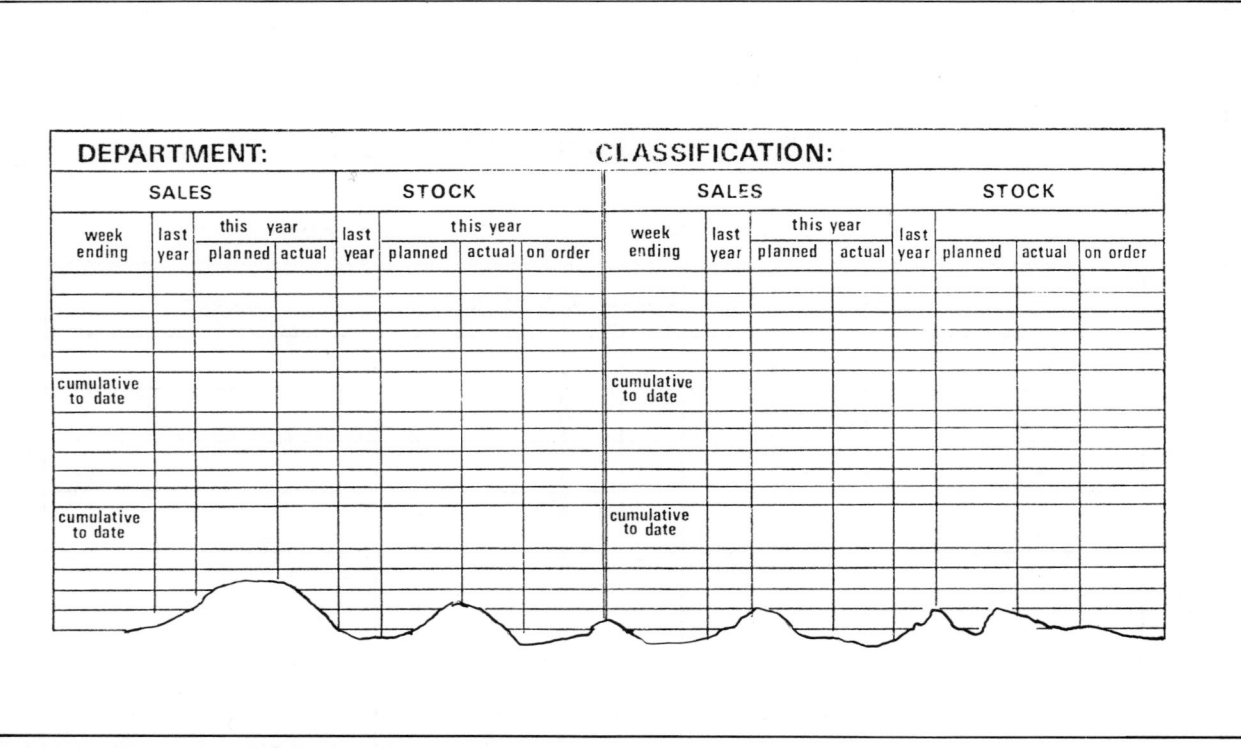

Figure B-8: MONTHLY SALES AND STOCK PLAN REPORT

	LIFE DEPARTMENT—002			
	LIFE LINES			
	Life Other—PTD			
	Life Other—Death			
01-02	Total Life Other			
05-06	Group Life			
	Total Life Lines			
	ACCIDENT LINES			
07	Group Acc. & Health			
70-79	Other Accident Only			
71	Non Cancellable Acc. & Health			
72-75	All Other			
73-77	Guaranteed Renewable			
74	Collectively Renewable			
76	Non Renewable for SRO			
	Total Individual A & H			
	Total Accident Lines			
	Total Life Department			
	TICORI—INDV. HEALTH—027			
70-79	Other Accident Only			
71	Non Cancellable Acc. & Health			
72-75	All Other			
73-77	Guaranteed Renewable			
74	Collectively Renewable			
	Total TICORI Indiv. Health			
	TICORI—HEALTH—028			
07	Group Acc. & Health			
	Total TICORI—Health			
	TLICC GRP & CORP DEPT.—LIFE—035			
05-06	Group Life			
	Total TLICC Grp & Corp. Dept. Life			
	TLICC GRP & CORP. DEPT—NON-LIFE—036			
07	Group Acc. & Health			
	Total TLICC Grp & Corp. Non-Life			
	TLICC INDIVIDUAL—LIFE—037			
	TLICC INDIVIDUAL—NON-LIFE—038			
	TRAV. IND OF ILL.—HEALTH—039			
07	Group Acc. & Health			
	Total Ind. of Ill.—Health			
	TRAV. INS. CO. OF ILL.—GROUP DEPT—042			
05-06	Group Life			
07	Group Acc. & Health			
	Total Trav. Ins. Co. of Ill.—Group			
	TRAV. LIFE & ANNUITY CO.—054			
	Individual Annuity			
	Group Annuity			
	Total Trav. Life & Annuity Co.			

M-3727 REV. 8-74 PRINTED IN U.S.A.

Figure B-9: INSURANCE PRODUCTION REPORT
(Courtesy of the Travelers Insurance Company.)

PROJECT: MARK 93 GROUND SUPPORT			CONTRACT NO. 98-7865					REPORT DATE: 11/30/			
IDENTIFICATION				TIME STATUS					COST STATUS			
Charge or Summary No.	Level*	Begin Event No.	End Event No.	Sched. Elapsed Time (weeks)	Date Completed	Earliest Completion Date (S_E)	Latest Completion Date (S_L)	Activity Slack (weeks) ($S_L - S_E$)	Actual To Date $	Contract Estimate $	Latest Revised Estimate $	Overrun/(Underrun) $
71831070	6	598	599	9.0	11/30/	12/21/	12/30/	1.3	5.600	5.600	5.600	
71831072	6	601	602	1.0		05/03/	03/30/	-4.8		1.450	1.650	200
670057	5	590	602			05/03		-4.8	5.600	28.300	24.20C	(4.100)
71831083		565	568	6.0		04/02/	04/27	3.6				
		577	578	1.0		05/09/	04/27/	-1.7				
	6	565	578			05/09		-1.7	2.740	14.700	14.000	
670037	5	590	610			05/27			29.000	60.000	657.960	(12.100)
670016	4	001	999			01/31/		-4.8	69.000	540.000	665.200	25.600

*SUMMARY LEVEL
{ 6. Charge Level
{ 5. Time and Cost Summary at Major Hardware Level
{ 4. Time and Cost Summary at Subsystem Level

Figure B-10: PROJECT STATUS REPORT

PRODUCTIVITY, EMPLOYMENT COSTS, AND STEEL PRICES FOR PERIOD ENDING

DATE	INGOT PRODUCTION	TOTAL WAGE-HOURS WORKED	INGOT TONS ÷ HOURS WORKED	ANNUAL PERCENTAGE CHANGE	AVERAGE TOTAL EMPLOYMENT COST PER HOUR	ANNUAL PERCENTAGE CHANGE	STEEL PRODUCTS PRICE INDEX	ANNUAL PERCENTAGE CHANGE

COMPARISON WITH INDUSTRY AVERAGE (U.S.)

COMPARISON WITH INDUSTRY AVERAGES (WORLDWIDE)

COMPARISON WITH MOST SIGNIFICANT COMPETITOR

Figure B-11: FORM FOR COMPARISON OF PRODUCTIVITY, LABOR COSTS, AND INDUSTRY PRICES

DATE	EMPLOYEE NAME & HOURLY RATE		TOTAL HOURS	IDEAL FEE	BILLED FEE

CLIENT: _____

JOB TITLE: _____

PERIOD COVERED: _____

Figure B-12: ANALYSIS FOR FINAL BILLING

ESTIMATE SHEET

PAGE NO. _____ OF _____ PAGES

JOB NAME	CONTRACTOR	ESTIMATE NO.
LOCATION	ARCHITECT	DATE
ESTIMATOR	CHECKED BY	BID DATE
JOB DESCRIPTION		

FORWARD ▶

DESCRIPTION	QUANTITY	@	MATERIAL	LABOR	SUBCONTRACT	TOTAL

TOTAL COSTS

MISC. JOB EXPENSES	AMOUNT		
		OVERHEAD	%
		PROFIT	%
TOTAL		BID SUBMITTED OR TOTAL FORWARD ▶	

FORM 378 REGENT STANDARD FORMS INC. BELLMAWR N.J. 08030

Figure B-13: BID SHEET WITH ESTIMATE OF OVERHEAD AND PROFIT
(Courtesy of Regent Standard Forms, Inc., Bellmawr, New Jersey 08031.)

JACKSON & SON QUALITY ROOFING CO.
628 MACLAY STREET
HARRISBURG, PA 17110
(717) 236-6297

ESTIMATE & AGREEMENT

№ 022

DATE:

To

BID: We hereby propose to furnish material and labor to complete the work outlined herein for the sum of:

_____ dollars

($ _____) Payment to be made as follows:

_____ _____

We hereby submit specifications and bid for:

SAMPLE FORM ONLY
REGENT STANDARD FORMS, INC

CONTRACTOR'S GUARANTEE

We guarantee all material used in this contract to be as specified above and the entire job to be done in a neat, workmanlike manner. Any variations from plan or alterations requiring extra labor or material will be performed only upon written order and billed in addition to the sum covered by this contract. Agreements made with our workmen are not recognized.

DATE | SIGNED

ACCEPTANCE OF BID

The above specifications, terms and contract are satisfactory, and (I) (we) hereby authorize the performance of this work.

DATE

SIGNED

THIS CONTRACT IS VOID 30 DAYS FROM DATE UNLESS PINK COPY IS SIGNED AND RETURNED TO BIDDER
WE COMPLY WITH ALL WORKMAN'S COMPENSATION & PROPERTY DAMAGE LIABILITY INSURANCE LAWS.

Figure B-14: ESTIMATE AND AGREEMENT
(Courtesy of Regent Standard Forms, Inc., Bellmawr, New Jersey 08031.)

JOB COST RECORD

DESCRIPTION	QUANTITY OR HOURS	@	MATERIALS	LABOR	OTHER EXPENSES	TOTAL COST
TOTAL →						

REMARKS

TOTAL SELLING PRICE	
LESS TOTAL COST	
GROSS PROFIT	
LESS OVERHEAD COSTS ____ % OF SELLING PRICE	
NET PROFIT	

Figure B-15: PROFIT ANALYSIS AND JOB COST RECORD
(Courtesy of Regent Standard Forms, Inc., Bellmawr, New Jersey 08031.)

JOB NAME		JOB NUMBER
JOB LOCATION		
BILL TO		
DATE STARTED	DATE COMPLETED	DATE BILLED

JOB COST SUMMARY

TOTAL SELLING PRICE		
TOTAL MATERIAL		
TOTAL LABOR		
INSURANCE		
SALES TAX		
MISC. COSTS		
TOTAL JOB COST		
GROSS PROFIT		
LESS OVERHEAD COSTS ____ % OF SELLING PRICE		
NET PROFIT		

REORDER FROM REGENT STANDARD FORMS, INC., BELLMAWR, N.J. 08030

JOB ENVELOPE

FORM 715 PRINTED IN USA

Figure B-16: JOB COST SUMMARY AND PROFIT (ENVELOPE)
(Courtesy of Regent Standard Forms, Inc., Bellmawr, New Jersey 08031.)

CHECK REQUEST FORM

COMPANY

ELECTRO _____

BAUER _____

JETAIR _____

E.M. INT'L _____

TO: _____   PAYMENT DATE _____

_____   INVOICE DATE _____

_____   NO. OF DAYS _____

_____

AMOUNT $ _____

DISTRIBUTION ACCOUNT # _____

REASON

VOUCHER # _____   APPROVAL _____

THIS CHECK REQUEST FORM IS TO BE USED FOR DISBURSEMENTS NOT COVERED BY A PURCHASE ORDER.

Figure B-17: INTERCOMPANY CHECK REQUEST FORM
(Courtesy of Electro-Methods, Inc., South Windsor, Connecticut.)

INDIAN HILL COUNTRY CLUB, INC.
FINANCIAL REPORT

DATE _____ 19 ___

	PROSHOP	GREENS	LOCKER	BAR	REST	ADM	TOTAL
BUDGETED INCOME	,000		,000	,000	,000	,000	$
ACTUAL INCOME							
BUDGETED EXPENSES							
ACTUAL EXPENSES							
ITEMIZED EXPENSES							
SALARIES & WAGES							
OUTSIDE HELP							
CHEMICALS & FERT.							
MAINT. OF GROUNDS							
MAINT. OF EQUIP.							
MAINT OF BLDG.							
TOWELS & LINEN							
SUPPLIES							
MISCELLANEOUS							
COST OF FOOD & LIQ. Tournament Comm. Postage & publ.							
LEGAL & AUD.							
BUDGET ITEM. EXP.							
BUDGET. ALLOC. EXP.							
ACTUAL ITEM. EXP.							
ACTUAL ALLOC. EXP.							

ALLOCATED EXPENSES

	FUEL	UTIL.	INS.	TAXES	LEASE	INT.	DEPR.	TOTAL
BUDGETED EXPENSES								
ACTUAL EXPENSES								

CAPITAL EXP. _____

PRINCIPAL PAYM. _____

Figure B-18: FINANCIAL REPORT

Figure B-19: INTEREST EXPENSE AND RETURN ON EQUITY

(\$000's omitted)

INTEREST EXPENSE & RETURN ON EQUITY

Company _____

☐ Spring
☐ Fall

PR-12
WORKSHEET

19 _____

LINE NO.		MAR/SEP (1) PLAN	(2) LY	(3) PY	APR/OCT (4) PLAN	(5) LY	(6) PY	MAY/NOV (7) PLAN	(8) LY	(9) PY	JUN/DEC (10) PLAN	(11) LY	(12) PY	JUL/JAN (13) PLAN	(14) LY	(15) PY	(16) PLAN	(17) LY	(18) PY	SEASON AVERAGE (19) PLAN	(20) LY	(21) PY
	I. INVESTMENT																					
1	Cash																					
2	Net Accts. Receivable																					
3	Inventories																					
4	Fixed Assets																					
5	Accounts Payable																					
6	Deferred Taxes																					
7	Other Assets																					
8	Other Liabilities																					
9	TOTAL																					
	II. INVESTMENT BY LAYER																					
10	1971 and prior																					
11	1972 + 1973																					
12	1974																					
13	1975 + 1976																					
14	1977 + 1978																					
15	1979																					
16	TOTAL																					

III. INTEREST RATES BY LAYER

LINE NO.	LAYER	4 WK	5 WK				TOTAL EXPENSE															
17	1971 and prior	.14%	.18%																			
18	1972 + 1973	.36%	.44%																			
19	1974	.45%	.56%																			
20	1975 + 1976	.50%	.63%																			
21	1977 + 1978	.35%	.42%																			
22	1979	.35%	.42%																			
23	Interest Expense																					
24	Reclassified from Rent																					
25	Tot. Interest Expense																					

IV. RETURN ON EQUITY

LINE NO.		(1)	(2)	(3)	(4)	(5)	(6)	(7)	(8)	(9)	(10)	(11)	(12)	(13)	(14)	(15)	(16)	(17)	(18)	SEASON AVERAGE (19)	(20)	(21)
26	Investment (line 9)																					
27	Capitalized Leases																					
28	Total Investment																					
29	Cum YTD Investment																					
30	Ave YTD Investment																					
31	Equity %	53%	53%	53%	53%	53%	53%	53%	53%	53%	53%	53%	53%	53%	53%	53%	53%	53%	53%			
32	Equity																					
33	Earnings (PR-2)																					
34	Earnings YTD																					
35	Income Tax Comple.																					
36	Net Income (34 × 35)	.52	.52	.52	.52	.52	.52	.52	.52	.52	.52	.52	.52	.52	.52	.52	.52	.52	.52			
37	YTD ROE (36 ÷ 32)																					
38	Month ROE																					

DATE RECEIVED BY CORPORATE _____

Rev: 8/8

141

FIGURE B-20.   RETURN ON INVENTORY ANALYSIS

ITEM: _____   AMOUNTS STATED IN: $ _____

DATE: _____ QUARTER: _____   BY: _____

COMMENTS: _____

	FIRST MONTH	SECOND MONTH	THIRD MONTH	QUARTER GOAL
INITIAL GROSS PROFIT (%):				
Goods on Order (%)				
Goods on Hand (%)				
Demand to Date				
DISCOUNT SALES (%) (Loss to G.P.)				
FINAL GROSS PROFIT (%)				
INITIAL INVENTORY TURNOVER				
TURNOVER LOST (By Cancellations)				
FINAL INVENTORY TURNOVER				
RETURN ON INVENTORY (%)				
GROSS PROFIT TO DATE ($)				

Figure B-20: RETURN ON INVENTORY ANALYSIS

142

PASSENGER REVENUE ANALYSIS AND RATE OF RETURN ON TOTAL OPERATIONS

DATE	EXPENSE PER AVAILABLE TON-MILE	AVERAGE TOTAL SCHEDULED PASSENGER REVENUE PER PASSENGER-MILE	BREAK-EVEN LOAD FACTOR	EXPENSES PER REVENUE TON-MILE	PASSENGER REVENUE/REVENUE TON-MILE				RATE OF RETURN ON TOTAL OPERATIONS
					First Class	Coach Class	Economy Class	Total Operating Revenues	
AVERAGES FOR PER.									

PREPARED FOR _____

PREPARED BY _____ TITLE _____ DATE _____

DERIVED FROM DATA AUDITED _____ ON _____

EXPLANATORY NOTES:

Figure B-21: REVENUE AND RATE OF RETURN ANALYSIS ON TOTAL OPERATIONS

VARIANCE ANALYSIS

	ACTUAL	FORECAST	VARIANCE CAUSED BY PRICE	VARIANCE CAUSED BY VOLUME	NET VARIANCE (negative)
SALES					
VARIABLE COSTS:					
Material					
Transformation					
TOTAL VARIABLE COSTS					
MARGINAL INCOME					
FIXED COSTS:					
Operating					
Administrative					
Marketing					
Other					
TOTAL FIXED COSTS					
PROFIT (Before Taxes)					
Income Taxes					
Foreign Taxes					
PROFIT (After Taxes)					

Figure B-22: VARIANCE ANALYSIS

PEPPERIDGE FARM, INCORPORATED

Based on Original Campbell Soup Company Investment

RETURN ON INVESTMENT
(Million Dollars)

	Through July 19	Through July 19
Original Investment (Total Purchase Value– 357,413 shares @ $65.00)	$23.2	$23.2
Earnings		
Acquisition Through July 19	19.9	19.9
19 - Fiscal Year	—	6.8
Less: Dividends		
Acquisition Through July 19	10.7	10.7 (1)
19 - Fiscal Year	—	1.0 (2)
Plus Inter-Company Loans:		
Through July 19	0	0
Through July 19	0	0
Total Investment	$32.4	$38.2
Net Income for Year		
19 -	$ 5.5	—
	—	$ 6.8
Return on Investment	17.0%	17.8%

Note (1): Dividends based on Campbell Soup Co. dividend rates per share
Note (2): Actual dividends paid by Pepperidge Farm, Inc., to Parent Company

PEPPERIDGE FARM, INCORPORATED
RETURN ON INVESTMENT

Based on Net Assets on Pepperidge Farm Books

19 - Fiscal Year

	Bakery	Biscuit	Frozen Food	Total
% Profit on Net Sales After Taxes	5.5%	6.4%	9.8%	7.1%
Net Sales divided by Net Assets	2.43	3.24	3.50	2.84
Return on Investment	13.4%	20.7%	34.3%	20.1%

Figure B-23: RETURN ON INVESTMENT ANALYSIS

RETURN ON EQUITY UNDER DIFFERENT ASSUMPTIONS
(state in thousands or millions)

FOR _____ 198____ ASSUMED TAX RATE _____ %

	LOW LEVERAGE FACTOR ____%	HIGHER LEVERAGE FACTOR ____%	HIGH LEVERAGE FACTOR ____%

I. ASSUMPTION OF RECESSION

Rate of Return on Total Assets (%) (w/o interest)
Amount of Return on Total Assets (w/o interest)

Total Earnings
Less: Interest Expense

GROSS INCOME

Income Taxes
Amount Available to Equity

PERCENT RETURN ON EQUITY

II. ASSUMPTION OF LOW REAL ECONOMIC GROWTH (0% - 2%)

Rate of Return on Total Assets (%) (w/o interest)
Amount of Return on Total Assets (w/o interest)

Total Earnings
Less: Interest Expense

GROSS INCOME

Income Taxes
Amount Available to Equity

PERCENT RETURN ON EQUITY

III. ASSUMPTION OF HIGH REAL ECONOMIC GROWTH (3%+)

Rate of Return on Total Assets (%) (w/o interest)
Amount of Return on Total Assets (w/o interest)

Total Earnings
Less: Interest Expense

GROSS INCOME

Income Taxes
Amount Available to Equity

PERCENT RETURN ON EQUITY

Figure B-24: RETURNS TO EQUITY UNDER DIFFERENT ASSUMPTIONS OF LEVERAGE AND ECONOMIC CONDITIONS

CANADIAN CASH MANAGEMENT

Average daily bank balance and investment portfolio for the Canadian accounts for the month of

_____ were as follows:

	Average Daily Bank Balance	Average Daily Investments	Total Interest	Effective Yield %
	_____	_____	_____	_____
	_____	_____	_____	_____
	_____	_____	_____	_____

TOTAL

The average bank balance for   and   decreased/increased _____% and _____%

respectively from the month of _____ .

_____ bank balance decreased/increased _____ over the previous month.

Average daily investments of C$_____ million represents a _____%

decrease/increase over the month of _____ level of C$_____ million.

The decrease/increase in average daily investments is due primarily to _____

_____

_____ .

The effective portfolio yield decreased/increased to _____% from _____% for the month of

_____ .

Remarks:

**Figure B-25: YIELD ANALYSIS OF CANADIAN DAILY BANK BALANCE
AND INVESTMENT PORTFOLIO**

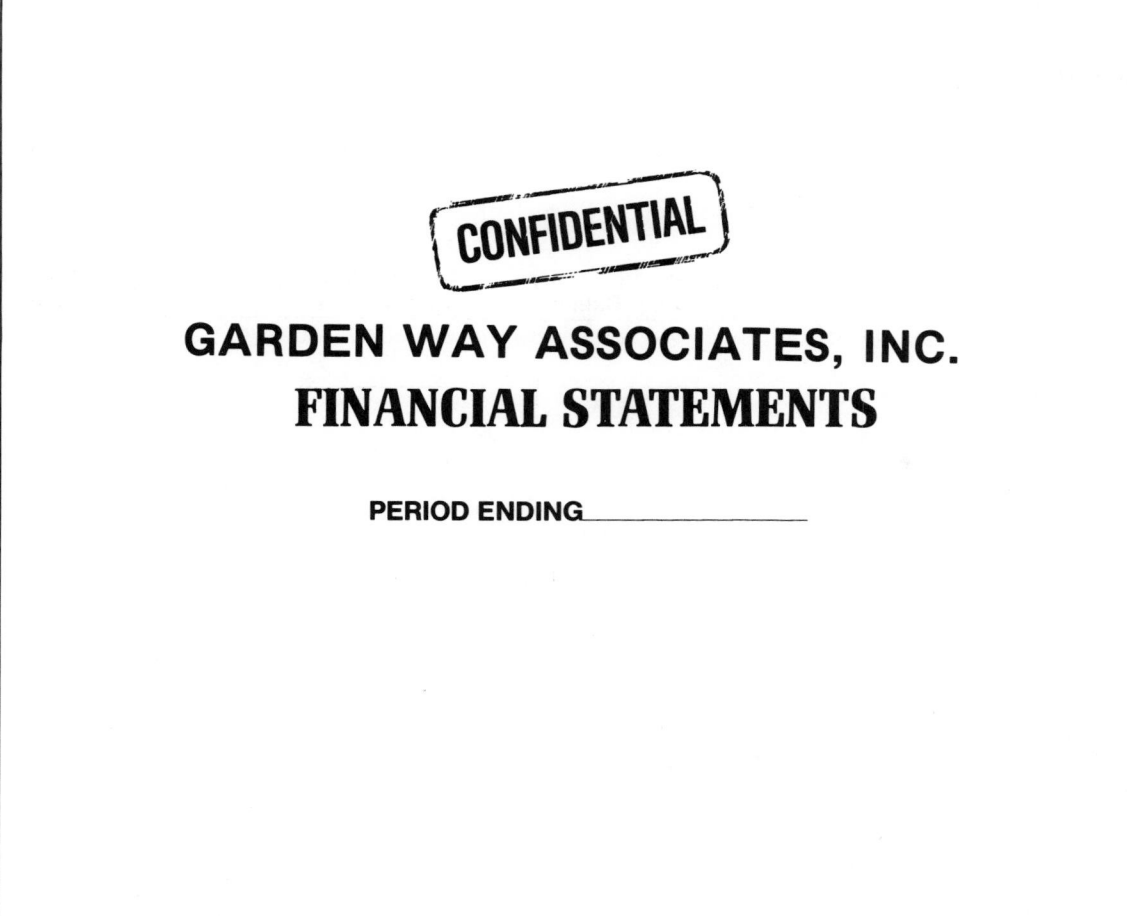

Figure B-26: FINANCIAL STATEMENT AND ANALYSIS
(Courtesy of Garden Way, Incorporated.)

GARDEN WAY ASSOCIATES, INC.
FINANCIAL PERSPECTIVES
(000's Omitted)

	Year to Date		Year Ago
	Budget	Actual	Actual

GWA Billings & Sales by Division
GWA - Marketing
    - Lettershop
    - Computer Services
Gardeners' Marketplace
Garden Way Research
Garden Way Publishing
        Catalog
        Associates
        CO-OP Services
        Stickler

New Programs

Total GWA Billing & Sales

Net Earnings (Loss) after tax

Total Assets Employed

Working Capital
  (Current Assets-Current Liab.)

Liquid Assets
  (Cash, investments & Receiv.)

Liquid Ratio
  (Liquid Assets)
  (Current Liabilities)

Number of Employees by Division	Total	F/T	P/T	Total	F/T	P/T
GWA Mktg.						
Lettershop						
Comp. Svc.						
GMP						
GWR						
GWP						
GWC						
GWA						
Total						

Figure B-26 (continued)

GARDEN WAY ASSOCIATES, INC.
ANALYSIS OF BUDGETED & ACTUAL BILLING TO GWMC

CURRENT PERIOD			YEAR TO DATE		Prior Year
Budget	Actual		Budget	Actual	Actual

Direct Marketing Expenses
Marketing Fee
GWLC 2% Mgmt. Fee
Publication Advertising
Cooperative Advertising - Catalog Inserts
                             Package   "
Direct Mail
TV Advertising
Newspaper Inserts
New Inquiry Follow-up
Mailings to Inqs - Re-Inquiry
              GFO Mailings
GFO Mailing to Owners
T-BON
After Market Promo - Direct Mail
                          T-BON
Other Direct incl. DSC's, Fairs, Buddy
                   Cards, Custom Till,
                   Dealer Support, Etc.
International - Canada
Two Way Tiller Exp.

   Total Direct Expenses

Other Marketing Expenses
Lettershop Fee & Whse Rent
Professional Services
Computer Services & Salaries
Market Research
GWA Expense & Salaries
Less: List Rental Income
Travel & Entertainment
Misc. Expenses - ATP, PTG. & Misc.
Printing of Owners' Manuals

   Total Other Mktg. Expenses

   Total GWA Marketing Expense

Figure B-26 (continued)

GARDEN WAY ASSOCIATES, INC.
ANALYSIS OF TILLER STATISTICS

CURRENT PERIOD				YEAR TO DATE		Prior Year
Budget	Actual			Budget	Actual	Actual

Total GWA Billings to GWMC

Orders Received - Net of cancellations

GWA Billing per Orders Rec'd

Tillers Shipped - Including no charge

GWMC Net Sales

Total GWA Billing to GWM net sales

Inquiries received by Category
Publication Advertising
CO-OP - Catalog Inserts
        - Package "
Direct Mail
TV/Radio Advertising
Newspaper Inserts
JOG Book Buddies
Fairs, Shows, & DSC's

    Total

Costs Per Inquiry
Publication Advertising
Cooperative   " - Catalog
               - Package
Direct Mail
TV/Radio Advts.
Newspaper Inserts
JOG Book Buddies
Fairs, Shows & DSC's

    Total Cost Per Inquiry

NOTE: Gross orders received thru _____ were _____
               GWA billings per gross order is $ _____

Figure B-26 (continued)

GARDEN WAY ASSOCIATES, INC.
STATEMENT OF CHANGES IN FINANCIAL POSITION

	CURRENT PERIOD				YEAR TO DATE		
	Budget	Actual			Budget	Actual	Prior Year

FUNDS PROVIDED:
  From Operations
    Net Income (Loss)
    Add changes not requiring Funds
      Depreciation & Amortization
    (Gain) Loss on Disposition-Ppty & Inv.

  Funds Provided

FUNDS APPLIED:
  Additions to property & equip.
  Increase in other Assets
  Decr. in Long Term Liab. & RE Adj.
  Incr. in Cash Surrender Value-Life Ins.
  Decrease in Deferred Comp.

  Funds Applied

Increase (Decrease) in Working Capital

CHANGES IN WORKING CAPITAL

  Increase (Decrease) in Current Assets
    Cash
    A/R-Net-Related
    A/R-Net-Trade
    Prepaid Exp.
    Inventory
    Total Incr. (Decr.) in Current Asts.
  Increase (Decrease) in Current Liab.
    Accounts Payable (Trade)
    Advances from customers
    Postal Advances
    Accrued Taxes & Expenses
    Accrued Profit Shar., Bonus & ESP
    Total Incr. (Decr.) in Current Liab.
  Increase (Decrease) in Working capital

Figure B-26 (continued)

GARDEN WAY ASSOCIATES, INC.
BALANCE SHEET

Exhibit A

CURRENT ACTUAL						COMBINED		
GWA	GWR	GWP	GWC			BUDGET	ACTUAL	PRIOR YEAR

ASSETS
Current Assets
Cash
Investments
A/C Rec. - GWI
       - GWM
       - Trade-Net of Res.
Inventory
Prepaid Expenses
  Total Current Assets
Property & Equip, Land & Bldg.
  Less Accum. Dept. Rec.
Net
Intra-Company Rec.
OTHER ASSETS
Loans & Exch. & CSV
Deferred Taxes

  Total Assets

LIABILITIES & EQUITY
Current Liabilities
Accounts Payable
Notes & Mtge Payable
Customer advances
Postal Advances
Accrued taxes & exp.
Accrued Prof. Share, Bonus & ESP

  Total Current Liabilities

Intracompany Payables
Deferred Compensation
Mortgage Payable

STOCKHOLDERS EQUITY
Common Stock-pd in capital
Retained Earnings
Net Earnings-YTD (Ls)
Stockholders Equity

  Total Liab. & Equity

Figure B-26 (continued)

153

GARDEN WAY ASSOCIATES, INC.
Analysis of Prepaid Expense
GWA Division Only

	Current	Prior Year
Prepaid Expenses - Garden Way Associates		
Federal Tax Refund Due		
Current Years provision for Corporate Income Tax Estimated Refund due as of		
Postal Deposits		
Postal advances from GWMC - Normal Credit Balance		
Other prepaid expenses		

Figure B-26 (continued)

GARDEN WAY ASSOCIATES, INC.

Combined Statement of Operating Profit

Exhibit B

CURRENT PERIOD			YEAR TO DATE		
Budget	Actual		Budget	Actual	Prior Period

NET OPERATING PROFIT (LOSS) BY DIVISION

GWA Marketing Division	C	
GWA Lettershop "	D	
GWA Computer Services	E	
Gardener's Marketplace	F	
Newspaper Inserts	G	
Garden Way Research	H	
Garden Way Publishing	I	
Garden Way Associates	J	
Garden Way Catalog	K	
GWA Kitchen Carousel		
GWA Gardening Catalog		
Other Programs–Readers Digest		

Total Operating Profit

OTHER EXPENSES

Empl. Stock Plan & Stock Bonus
GWA Corporate Exp. - Interest Exp.
Legal & Accounting
GWI Fee
    Total Expenses
    Net Profit (Loss)

OTHER INCOME

Gain or (Loss) on Sale of Assets
Interest Income
    "   " - Intracompany
Net Rental Income (Expense)

    Total Other Income

Net Profit before future Compen. Pmts.

Provision for Future Compensation Pmts.

Net Profit (Loss) before Taxes

Provision for Income Taxes

Net Earning (Loss) after Tax

Figure B-26 (continued)

GARDEN WAY ASSOCIATES, INC.
GWA MARKETING DIVISION

Exhibit C

CURRENT PERIOD							PRIOR	
BUDGET	ACTUAL	%	BILLINGS		BUDGET	ACTUAL	%	YEAR	%

BILLINGS
Marketing Fee - GWMC
           - GWR
           - GWP
           - GWLC
           - GWC
           - GMP
    Total Fees
GWMC Billed - Direct Expense
           - Operating "
Miscellaneous Income

    Total Billings

DIRECT EXPENSES
Publication Advertising -   GWMC
Radio, TV & Newspaper Ins.   "
Cooperative Advtg   "
Mailing - Inq. & Owner   "
DSC's & Dealers   "
After Market   "
Two-Way   "
Other reimbursable expenses   "

    Total Direct Expenses

    Gross Profit

OPERATING EXPENSES
Salaries - Regular
Fringe benefits
Office expenses
Occupancy expense
Free Lance services

    Total Operating Expense

    Net Profit or (Loss)

Figure B-26 (continued)

GARDEN WAY ASSOCIATES, INC.
GWA LETTERSHOP OPERATION

Exhibit D

CURRENT PERIOD					YEAR TO DATE			PRIOR	
BUDGET	ACTUAL	%			BUDGET	ACTUAL	%	YEAR	%

BILLINGS
Lettershop Income GWMC
"   GWR
"   GWP
"   GWC
"   NPC
"   Others
Lettershop Fee
Storage Fees

   Total Billing

DIRECT EXPENSES
Salary Administrative
Fringe Benefits
Lettershop payroll
Fringe benefits
Management fee - NPC
Occupancy expenses
Office   "
Depreciation

   Total Direct Expenses

   Net Profit or (Loss)

Figure B-26 (continued)

GARDEN WAY ASSOCIATES, INC.
GWA COMPUTER OPERATION

CURRENT PERIOD				YEAR TO DATE				
BUDGET	TOTAL	%	BILLINGS	BUDGET	ACTUAL	%	YEAR	%
			Computer Service - GMP					
			- GWMC					
			- GWR					
			- GWP					
			- GWC					
			Total Computer Services					
			Salaries & Fringes GWM					
			Total Billings					
			EXPENSES					
			Salaries					
			Fringes					
			Computer Rental					
			Computer Supplies					
			Office Expense					
			Depreciation					
			Total Expenses					
			Net Cost absorbed by GWA					

Figure B-26 (continued)

GARDEN WAY ASSOCIATES, INC.
GARDENER'S MARKETPLACE DIVISION

Exhibit F

CURRENT PERIOD				YEAR TO DATE			PRIOR	
BUDGET	ACTUAL	%		BUDGET	ACTUAL	%	YEAR	%

BILLINGS
Gross Billings - Trade
  Less: Negotiated Discounts
        15% Agency Commissions
        2% Prompt Payment Disct.

Net Billings - Trade
            - Intra-Company
Other - Newsstand sales & list ren.
Newspaper Pre-Print
Total Net Billings

DIRECT EXPENSES
Printed materials purchased
Letttership expense
Postage
List Rental Exp.
Other - Misc.-Can. Tax-Contest
  Total Direct Expenses

  Gross Profit or (Loss)

SELLING & MARKETING EXPENSES

  Net Income or (Loss) bef. Op.

OPERATING EXPENSES
Salaries
Fringe benefits
Office expenses
Occupancy expenses

  Total Operating Expenses

  Net Profit or (Loss)

  5% Mktg. Fee Trade only

  Net Profit or (Loss)

Figure B-26 (continued)

159

GARDEN WAY ASSOCIATES, INC.
NEWSPAPER INSERTS

Exhibit G

CURRENT PERIOD					YEAR TO DATE			PRIOR	
BUDGET	ACTUAL	%			BUDGET	ACTUAL	%	YEAR	%

BILLINGS
Gross Billings - Trade
Less:

Net Billings - Trade
          - Intra-Company

Total Net Billings

DIRECT EXPENSES
Printed materials purchased
Distribution Expense
Newspaper Insert Expense
Radio & TV Expense
Other - Postage & Lettershop

  Total Direct Expenses

  Gross Profit or (Loss)

SELLING & MARKETING EXPENSES

  Net Income or (Loss) bef. Op.

OPERATING EXPENSES
Salaries
Fringe benefits
Office expenses
Occupancy expenses

  Total Operating Expenses

  Net Profit or (Loss)

Figure B-26 (continued)

GARDEN WAY ASSOCIATES, INC.
GARDEN WAY ASSOCIATES

Exhibit I

CURRENT PERIOD				YEAR TO DATE		PRIOR
BUDGET	ACTUAL			BUDGET	ACTUAL	YEAR

BILLINGS

Reimbursable Expenses - GWM
      "   Expenses - GWI

Total Sales

OPERATING EXPENSES
Salaries - Administrative
Fringe benefits
Freelance Services
Research & development expenses
Office expenses
Occupancy expenses
Legal
Miscellaneous

    Total Operating Expenses
    Net Profit or (Loss)

Figure B-26 (continued)

DETAILED PROJECT STATUS REPORT

PROJECT—

CONTRACT NUMBER—

REPORT DATE—

UNIT—

Identification			Time Status				Cost Status		
ACCOUNT NUMBER	LEVEL	EVENT No.	SCHEDULE ELAPSED TIME (DAYS)	DATE COMPLETED	EARLIEST COMPLETION DATE	LATEST COMPLETION DATE	ACTUAL TO DATE	CONTRACT ESTIMATE	LATEST REVISED ESTIMATE	OVERRUN (UNDERRUN)

ABBA Co.

162

Figure B-27: DETAILED PROJECT STATUS REPORT

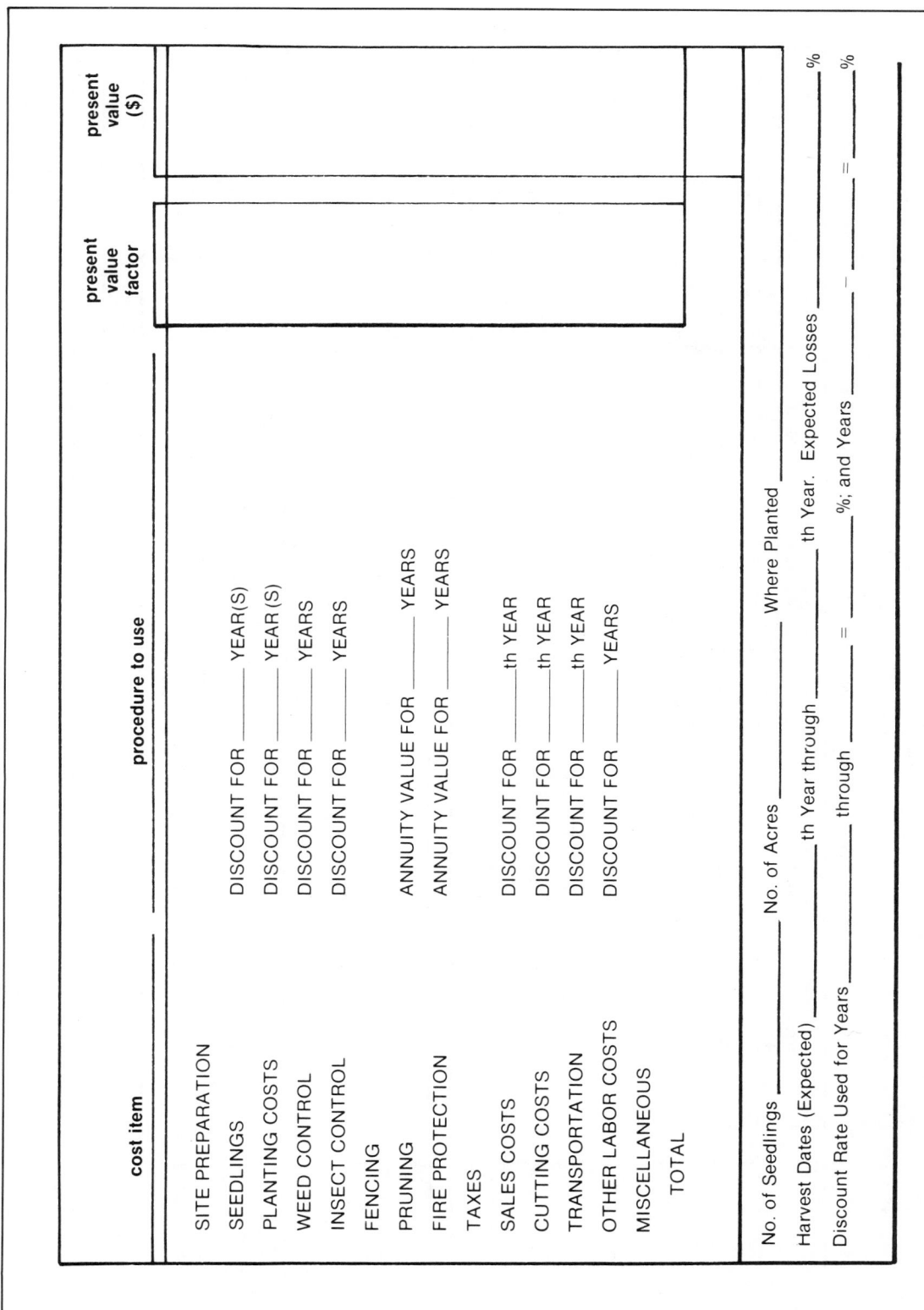

cost item	procedure to use	present value factor	present value ($)
SITE PREPARATION			
SEEDLINGS	DISCOUNT FOR _____ YEAR(S)		
PLANTING COSTS	DISCOUNT FOR _____ YEAR (S)		
WEED CONTROL	DISCOUNT FOR _____ YEARS		
INSECT CONTROL	DISCOUNT FOR _____ YEARS		
FENCING			
PRUNING	ANNUITY VALUE FOR _____ YEARS		
FIRE PROTECTION	ANNUITY VALUE FOR _____ YEARS		
TAXES			
SALES COSTS	DISCOUNT FOR _____ th YEAR		
CUTTING COSTS	DISCOUNT FOR _____ th YEAR		
TRANSPORTATION	DISCOUNT FOR _____ th YEAR		
OTHER LABOR COSTS	DISCOUNT FOR _____ YEARS		
MISCELLANEOUS			
TOTAL			

No. of Seedlings _____ No. of Acres _____ Where Planted _____

Harvest Dates (Expected) _____ th Year through _____ th Year. Expected Losses _____ %

Discount Rate Used for Years _____ through _____ = _____ %; and Years _____ - _____ = _____ %

MARLBOROUGH FARMS

Figure B-28: DETERMINATION OF PRESENT VALUE OF CHRISTMAS TREE PRODUCTION COSTS

163

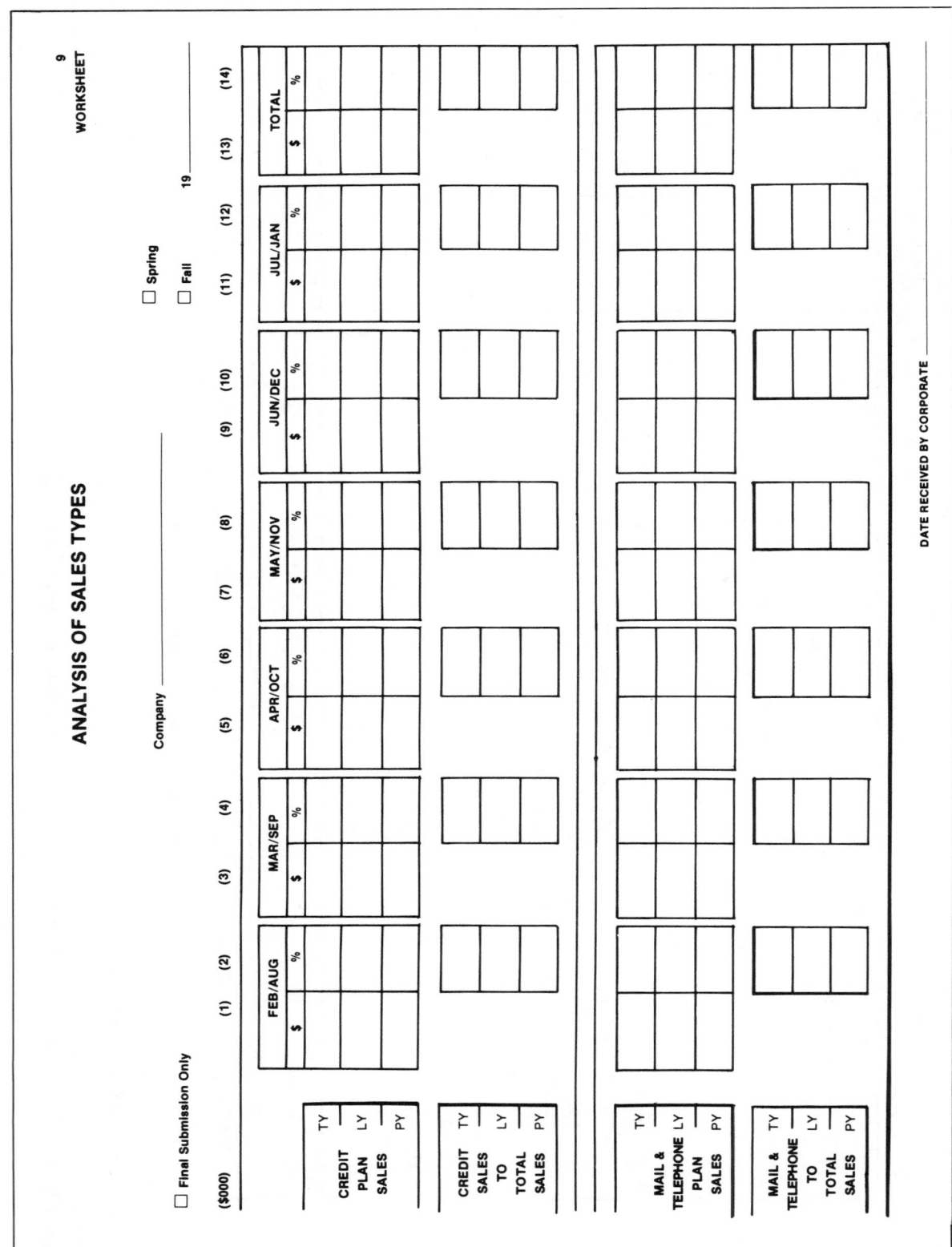

Figure B-29: ANALYSIS OF SALES TYPES

MARLBOROUGH FARMS

Post Office Box 238

Marlborough

Tel. 203+228-0286

Connecticut 06447

SALES VARIANCE ANALYSIS

SALES REVENUE FOR CURRENT YEAR ....

SALES REVENUE FOR LAST YEAR ....

SALES REVENUE VARIANCE ....

Quantity Factor:

NUMBER OF UNITS SOLD IN CURRENT YEAR ....

NUMBER OF UNITS SOLD LAST YEAR ....

INCREASE IN NUMBER OF UNITS SOLD ....

INCREASE IN SALES REVENUE DUE TO QUANTITY FACTOR ($P \times Q$) ....

Price Factor:

UNIT SELLING PRICE THIS YEAR ....

UNIT SELLING PRICE LAST YEAR ....

INCREASE IN UNIT SELLING PRICE ....

INCREASE IN SALES REVENUE DUE TO PRICE FACTOR ($Q \times P$) ....

Quantity-Price Factor:

INCREASE IN QUANTITY SOLD ....

INCREASE IN UNIT SELLING PRICE ....

INCREASE IN SALES REVENUE DUE TO QUANTITY-PRICE FACTOR ....

Three-Way Sales Variance Analysis:

QUANTITY VARIANCE ....

PRICE VARIANCE ....

QUANTITY-PRICE VARIANCE ....

TOTAL VARIANCE ....

Figure B-30: THREE-WAY ANALYSIS OF SALES VARIANCE

OAK CREST DE NICARAGUA, CIA. LTDA.

APARTADO:
1003

MANAGUA, D. N., NICARAGUA
CENTRO AMERICA

TELEFONOS:
91228 - 96547

PRICING FORMULA

DIRECT LABOUR:

_____ Hours @ $ _____ per hour   =   _____

OVERHEAD @ _____ %   =   _____

          SUBTOTAL --   _____

MATERIALS   =   _____

          SUBTOTAL--   _____

GENERAL & ADMINISTRATIVE EXPENSES @ _____ %   =   _____

          SUBTOTAL --   _____

PROFIT @ _____ %   =   _____

          TOTAL PRICE PER UNIT--------------------------   _____

AVICULTURA   -   AGRICULTURA   -   COMERCIO

Figure B-31: PRICING FORMULA
(Courtesy of Oak Crest de Nicaragua.)

PROFITS PER UNIT—BUDGETED VOLUME AND MIX

PRODUCTS: _____ _____ _____

							ALL PRODUCTS	
	TOTAL	PER UNIT	TOTAL	PER UNIT	TOTAL	PER UNIT	TOTAL	PER UNIT
1) Unit Sales								
2) Dollar Sales								
VARIABLE COSTS:								
3) Labor								
4) Materials								
5) Manufacturing Exp.								
6) Sales & Admin.								
7) TOTAL								
8) Variable Margin								
MANUFACTURING COSTS:								
9) Variable								
10) Fixed								
11) TOTAL								
12) Contribution								
13) Sales & Adm. Fixed								
14) NET INCOME								
15)								

Figure B-32: PROFITS PER UNIT—BUDGETED VOLUME AND MIX

OWNED RETAIL DEPARTMENTS STOCK & GROSS MARGIN PLAN
TOTAL COMPANY COMPARABLE BASIS

Form PR-3A
MANAGEMENT

☐ PRELIMINARY _____ DATE

☐ FINAL _____ DATE

($000)

☐ Spring

☐ Fall   19 _____

Company _____

MONTHLY PLAN		FEB/AUG		APR/SEPT		APR/OCT		MAY/NOV		JUN/DEC		JUL/JAN		SEASON TOTAL	
		$	%	$	%	$	%	$	%	$	%	$	%	$	%
RETAIL SALES $ % OF CHANGE	MDSE PLAN														
	L.Y.														
	P.Y.														

STOCK PLAN BEGINNING OF SEASON		PLAN		L.Y.		P.Y.								SEASON AVG. STOCK	
PLAN EOM STOCK $ AND WEEKS OF SUPPLY	OPEN STORES														
	LY OPEN STORES														
	PY OPEN STORES														

STOCK TURN OPEN STORES	MDSE PLAN														
	L.Y.														
	PRIOR YEAR														

MARK-DOWNS $ % TO SALES	MDSE PLAN														
	L.Y.														
	PRIOR YEAR														

Figure B-33: STOCK AND GROSS MARGIN PLAN

SUMMARY OF MERCHANDISE PLAN BY GROUP

☐ FINAL _____
DATE
TIES WITH
PR-3 DATED _____

☐ Spring
☐ Fall   19_____

FORM PR-5
MANAGEMENT

Company _____

DATE RECEIVED BY CORPORATE _____

	GROUP	ORD SALES PLAN			GROSS MARGIN	IMO & CD	MARKDOWNS		SHORT-AGE	AVERAGE STOCK	RECEIPTS (OPEN STORES)	STOCK TURN
		($000)	% CHG	% to Total Plan Sales	%	%	$	%	%	(OPEN STORES)	PLAN ($000)	(OPEN STORES)
1	I TY											
2	LY											
3	PY											
4	II TY											
5	LY											
6	PY											
7	III TY											
8	LY											
9	PY											
10	IV TY											
11	LY											
12	PY											
13	V TY											
14	LY											
15	PY											
16	VI TY											
17	LY											
18	PY											
19	VII TY											
20	LY											
21	PY											
22	VIII TY											
23	LY											
24	PY											
25	IX TY											
26	LY											
27	PY											
28	X TY											
29	LY											
30	PY											
31	XI TY											
32	LY											
33	PY											
34	XII TY											
35	LY											
36	PY											
37	XIII TY											
38	LY											
39	PY											
40	XIV TY											
41	LY											
42	PY											
43	TOTAL TY											
44	LY											
45	PY											

Figure B-34: SUMMARY OF MERCHANDISE PLAN BY GROUP

SEASON'S EARNINGS PLAN BY MONTH

Form PR-2
MANAGEMENT

☐ Preliminary ☐ Final   Company _____   ☐ Spring ☐ Fall 19_____

($000)

LINE NO.				(1) FEB/AUG $	(2) %	(3) MAR/SEP $	(4) %	(5) APR/OCT $	(6) %	(7) MAY/NOV $	(8) %	(9) JUN/DEC $	(10) %	(11) JUL/JAN $	(12) %	(13) SEASON $	(14) %
1	SALES	RETAIL	PL														
2			LY														
3			PY														
4		COST	PL														
5			LY														
6		LEASED	PL														
7			LY														
8		TOTAL	PL														
9			LY														
10			PY														
11	SS SALES		PL														
12	GROSS MARGIN	RETAIL	PL														
13			LY														
14			PY														
15		COST	PL														
16			LY														
17		LEASED	PL														
18			LY														
19		TOTAL	PL														
20			LY														
21			PY														
22	OPERATING EXPENSE		PL														
23			LY														
24			PY														
25	INTEREST EXPENSE		PL														
26			LY														
27			PY														
28	OTHER INCOME		PL														
29			LY														
30			PY														
31	NET EARNINGS		PL														
32			LY														
33			PY														
34	EARNINGS INCREASE OVER LY		PL														
35			LY														
36			PY														
37	FLOW THROUGH %		PL														
38			LY														

NOTE: Sales %'s are to Last Year. G.M. %'s are on respective sales. All other %'s are to Total Sales.

fig. #B-35

Figure B-35: SEASON'S EARNINGS PLAN BY MONTH

PROFIT CONTRIBUTION OF GIVEN SPACE

	Current Products	Expansion With New Products	Difference (+)OR(-)
SALES			
VARIABLE COSTS			
CONTRIBUTION MARGIN			
IDENTIFIABLE FIXED COSTS			
PROFIT CONTRIBUTION TO JOINT SPACE			
JOINT SPACE & OTHER COSTS			
NET INCOME • • • • • • • • • • •			

Figure B-36: PROFIT CONTRIBUTION FOR DELETION OR ADDITION OF DEPARTMENT

SHOPPING RESULTS
Form No. 3-18 Rev. 4-81

STORE NO. _____ TIME _____ DATE _____

CHECKER'S NAME _____ Name Badge - (Yes or No) _____

CHECKER'S SIGNATURE _____

COURTESY

Did checker greet the customer? _____ Did checker say thank you? _____

ACCURACY (Answer Yes or No)

1. Did checker check bottom of the carriage first? _____

2. Did checker read then ring? _____

3. Did checker place receipt in customer's hand? _____

4. Did checker count change into customer's hand? _____

	GROCERY	MEAT	PRODUCE	OTHER	TAX	TOTAL	
AMOUNT							OVERAGE $
NO. OF ITEMS							SHORTAGE $
CHECKER TOTAL							

LIST OF ERRORS MADE

DEPARTMENT	ITEM	CORRECT PRICE	PRICE RUNG UP	+	−	REASON FOR ERROR
NUMBER OF ERRORS			TOTAL			

Rate of Re-Training _____   Cash Dept. Head Signature _____

172

Figure B-37: SHOPPING RESULTS

MaRLBOROUGH
FaRMS

Post Office Box 238

Marlborough

Tel. 203+228-0286

Connecticut 06447

ANNUAL PARTNER EVALUATION

Partner _____ Rated by _____

Date of Rating _____ For _____

Rate: S = Superior   A = Acceptable   F = Fair   U = Unacceptable

CONTRIBUTIONS TO MANAGEMENT TEAM _____

RELATIONS WITH SUBORDINATES _____

RELATIONS WITH CUSTOMERS _____

RELATIONS WITH SUPPLIERS _____

COMPLETION OF TASKS ON SCHEDULE _____

KNOWLEDGE IN SPECIALIZED AREAS:

    Production _____

    Data Processing _____

    Accounting _____

    Marketing _____

    New Products & Systems _____

    Systems _____

PRODUCTION OF NEW BUSINESS _____

UPGRADING OF OLD BUSINESS _____

RECEIVABLES OF NEW BUSINESS GENERATED _____

WRITING OR PUBLIC APPEARANCES _____

PARTICIPATION IN PROFESSIONAL ORGANIZATIONS _____

NEW CONTACTS GENERATED _____

PARTICIPATION IN COMMUNITY ORGANIZATIONS _____

OVERALL EVALUATION _____

COMMENTS: _____

_____

Figure B-38: ANNUAL PARTNER EVALUATION

P/N			JOB #	
NAME	REF.			
MATERIAL				
TOOLING				
SUB-CONTRACT			QUOTE	
LABOR	HOURS	$	BILLED	
MACHINE			TOTAL O.C.	
Engineering			COST LABOR	
Q.A.			COMM.	
TOTAL	@	$	PROFIT	
NOTES:			LOSS ( )	

	JOB. NO.	QUANTITY
PCS. ORDERED		
USED OR SHIPPED		
ALLOCATED TO OTHER JOBS		
INVENTORIED		
SCRAPPED		

Figure B-39: PROFIT ANALYSIS ON JOB ORDERS

BUDGETED INCOME STATEMENT

CONTRIBUTION APPROACH	(−)	(+)	PERCENT OF SALES	PERCENT OF TVC
SALES				
VARIABLE COSTS:				
Manufacturing Cost of Goods Sold				
Selling and Administrative Costs				
• TOTAL VARIABLE COSTS (TVC)				
→ CONTRIBUTION MARGIN				
FIXED COSTS:				
Plant Overhead Costs				
Selling and Administrative Costs				
• TOTAL FIXED COSTS (TFC)				
⊕ TARGET NET INCOME				

Figure B-40: CONTRIBUTION APPROACH TO BUDGETED INCOME STATEMENT TO QUANTITY EFFECTS OF SPECIAL PRICING

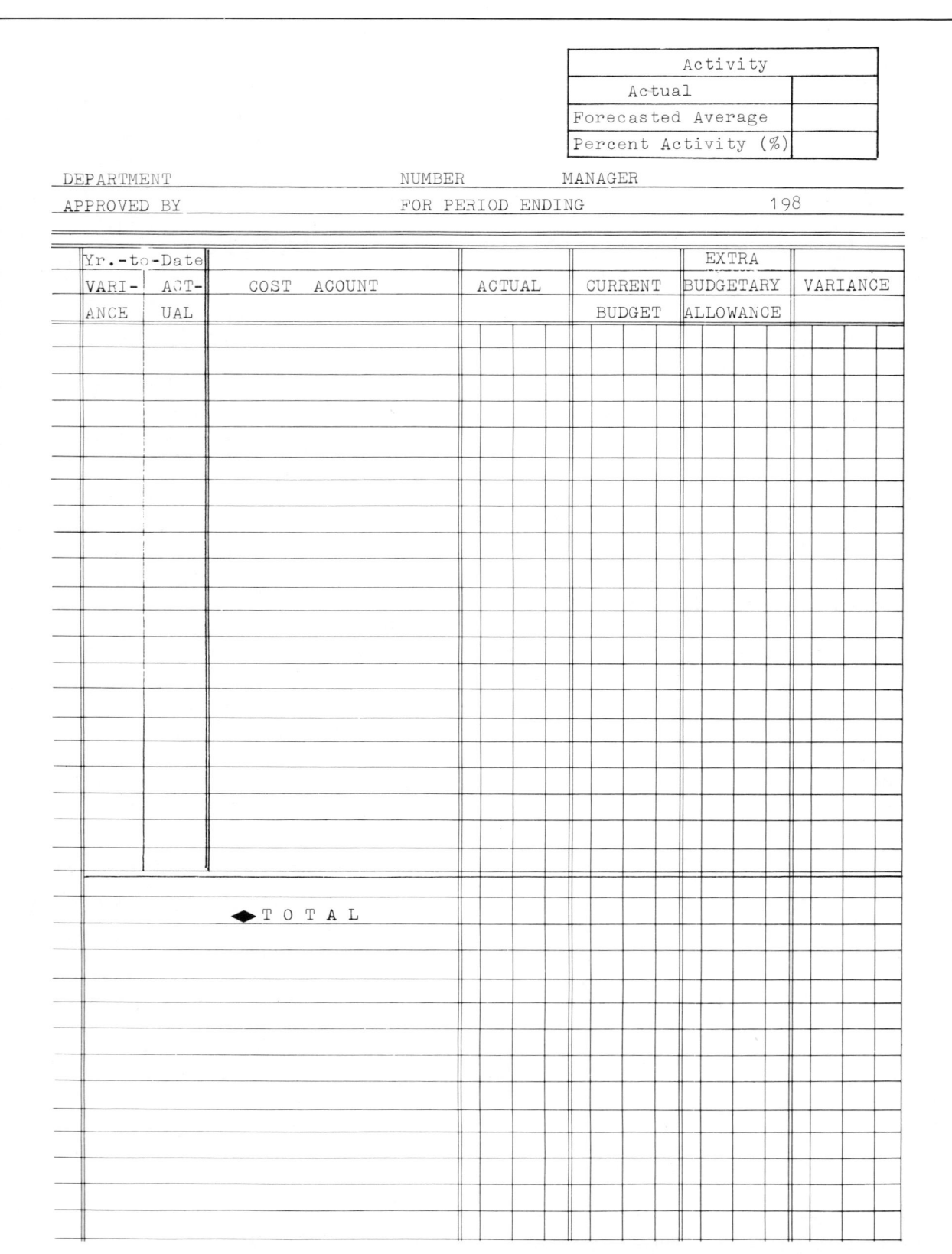

Figure B-41: PERFORMANCE-TO-BUDGET REPORT

MEMORANDUM

TO: M E C

FROM: Jerry Smith

DATE: October 10, 1974

SUBJECT: 1975 Profit Plan, Departmental
           Budget Package

Attached please find the 1975 Profit Plan budget package.

Each M E C level group has been broken down into the middle-management groups contained therein.

If and when the Finance Committee decision is reached on the C O L A, the effects will be factored into your departmental budget sheets by the Budget Department.

The current schedule for completion and return of this package is October 31, 1974.

If you have any questions, please contact your Finance Coordinator for assistance.

md

Jerry

Figure B-42: PROFIT PLAN—DEPARTMENTAL BUDGET PACKAGE
(Courtesy of Garden Way, Incorporated.)

"Guidelines to Completing the 1975 Profit Plan"

All department budgets should be based on the attached "1975 Profit Plan Parameters (Ex A)" and "1975 Fiscal Calender (Ex B)". Attached you will also find budget input forms showing, by department, the 1974 fiscal year-to-date (9 months through Aug.) actual expense plus space to record your budget by month for fiscal 1975.

Following are a few guidelines to assist you in completing your 1975 Budget.

1. *Exempt personnel:* Current weekly salary, plus planned merit increases, times the number of weeks shown on line 1 of the "1975 Profit Plan Parameters" for each month.

2. *Non-exempt personnel:* Current hourly rate, plus planned merit increases, times eight hours per day, times the number of working days shown on line 2 of the "1975 Profit Plan Parameters" for each month.

3. *Overtime:* Estimate the number of non-exempt overtime hours required each month, times the average *base* rate of the non-exempts in the department and *add* this to the amount calculated in item #2 above.

4. *Overtime Premium:* Equal to one-half the amount calculated in item #3.

5. *Holidays & Vacation: Do not* budget holiday or vacation pay for non-exempt employees; it will be charged to the M E C level through the fringe redistribution. Holiday and vacation pay for exempt employees is included in the base salary calculation as shown in item #1.

6. For the coming year we will be forecasting manpower requirements by pay grade, by month (see Ex C). With regards to this forecast as with the budgeting procedure, supervisors will be assigned to the next higher level of responsibility. We have also included in Ex C a form, "Supporting Comments," to be completed for each department, which will explain and support the manpower forecast.

Figure B-42 (continued)

7. *For Manufacturing Only:* With the installation of the Manufacturing Information System (M I S) it will be necessary to budget Manufacturing Direct and Indirect labor expense by "where used" and not (current policy) by employee assignment.

All indirect labor employees plus the indirect portion of the direct labor employee must be charged to one of the 100 series expense accounts shown below:

a. *Direct Labor:* For the 1975 Profit Plan we will be required to budget direct labor as only that labor required to *produce* the product and should not include any form of indirect labor such as:
   Break & wash up time
   Down time
   Set up time
   Administrative time, etc.

b. *Indirect Labor:* We will budget indirect labor by specific type; the categories are as follows:;

Expense A/C No.	Former ID No.	Description
XXX-151	11	Set Up
152	12	Plant Maintenance
153	13	Material Handling
154	14	Tooling Down Time
155	15	Machine Down Time
156	16	Job Preparation & Clean Up
157	17	Instruction
158	18 & 23	Management
159	19	Rework
160	20	Miscellaneous
161	21	Break & Wash Up
162	22	Service Parts
163	—	Electrical Maintenance
164	—	Machinery Maintenance
165	—	Machinery Relocation
166	—	Warehousing & Receiving
167	—	Quality Control

If additional account classifications are required, please contact Jerry Smith.

The above expense accounts, when budgeted, should be added to the departmental input sheets.

Figure B-42 (continued)

The following is the schedule we should like to follow in completing the 1975 Profit Plan:

Sept. 26:   R.W. Schwartz memo to M E C, Ex D.

Oct. 10:   Budget input package and detailed instructions for completing same.

Oct. 31:   Return completed departmental budgets to the Budget Department.

Nov. 13:   First complete draft of 1975 Profit Plan presented to M E C.

Dec. 14:   Final draft presented to M E C.

Dec. 5:   Final, M E C approved, 1975 Profit Plan presentation to the Board of Directors.

Don't forget, if you have questions, problems or whatever, please contact your Finance Coordinator; he will be available to work with you at any time.

Thanks,

Jerry

Figure B-42 (continued)

1975 PROFIT PLAN PARAMETERS

Item	Line	Dec	Jan	Feb	Mar	Apr	May	Jun	Jul	Aug	Sep	Oct	Nov
Weeks	1	4	4	5	4	4	5	4	4	5	4	4	5
Cum			8	13	17	21	26	30	34	39	43	47	52
Working Days	2	17	19	24	20	20	24	20	14	20	19	20	23
Cum		17	36	60	80	100	124	144	158	178	197	217	240
Holidays	3	3	1	1	—	—	1	—	1	—	1	—	2
Cum		3	4	5	5	5	6	6	7	7	8	8	10
Vacation Days	4	—	—	—	—	—	—	—	5	5	—	—	—
Cum		—	—	—	—	—	—	—	5	10	10	10	10
Units Produced	5	4,250	4,826	6,144	5,200	5,260	6,336	5,420	3,864	5,620	5,434	5,820	6,854
Cum		4,250	9,076	15,220	20,420	25,680	32,016	37,436	41,300	46,920	52,354	58,174	65,028
Production Per Day	6	250	254	256	260	263	264	271	276	281	286	291	298
Unit Orders Rec Cum	7						Not Available At This Time						
Orders Rec Cum	8												

181

Figure B-42 (continued)

1975
FISCAL CALENDAR
SECOND DRAFT

DEC

SU	MO	TU	WE	TH	FR	SA	#
1	2	3	4	5	6	7	5
8	9	10	11	12	13	14	6
15	16	17	18	19	20	21	7
22	(23)	(24)	(25)	26	27	28	8

JAN

SU	MO	TU	WE	TH	FR	SA	#
29	30	31	(1)	2	3	4	9
5	6	7	8.	9	10	11	10
12	13	14	15	16	17	18	11
19	20	21	22	23	24	25	12
							13

FEB

SU	MO	TU	WE	TH	FR	SA
26	27	28	29	30	31	1
2	3	4	5	6	7	8
9	10	11	12	13	14	15
16	(17)	18	19	20	21	22
23	24	25	26	27	28	1

MAR

#	SU	MO	TU	WE	TH	FR	SA
4	2	3	4	5	6	7	8
5	9	10	11	12	13	14	15
6	16	17	18	19	20	21	22
7	23	24	25	26	27	28	29

APR

#	SU	MO	TU	WE	TH	FR	SA
18	30	31	1	2	3	4	5
19	6	7	8	9	10	11	12
20	13	14	15	16	17	18	19
21	20	21	22	23	24	25	26

MAY

#	SU	MO	TU	WE	TH	FR	SA
22	27	28	29	30	1	2	3
23	4	5	6	7	8	9	10
24	11	12	13	14	15	16	17
25	18	19	20	21	22	23	24
26	25	(26)	27	28	29	30	31

JUNE

#	SU	MO	TU	WE	TH	FR	SA
27	1	2	3	4	5	6	7
28	8	9	10	11	12	13	14
29	15	16	17	18	19	20	21
30	22	23	24	25	26	27	28

JUL

#	SU	MO	TU	WE	TH	FR	SA
31	29	31	1	2	3	(4)	5
32	6	7	8	9	10	11	12
33	13	14	15	16	17	18	19
34	20	[21	22	23	24	25]	26

AUG

#	SU	MO	TU	WE	TH	FR	SA
35	27	[28	29	30	31	1]	2
36	3	4	5	6	7	8	9
37	10	11	12	13	14	15	16
38	17	18	19	21	21	22	23
39	24	25	26	27	28	29	30

SEP

#	SU	MO	TU	WE	TH	FR	SA
40	31	(1)	2	3	4	5	6
41	7	8	9	10	11	12	13
42	14	15	16	17	18	19	20
43	21	22	23	24	25	26	27

OCT

#	SU	MO	TU	WE	TH	FR	SA
44	28	29	30	1	2	3	4
45	5	6	7	8	9	10	11
46	12	13	14	15	16	17	18
47	19	20	21	22	23	24	25

NOV

#	SU	MO	TU	WE	TH	FR	SA
48	26	27	28	29	30	31	1
49	2	3	4	5	6	7	8
50	9	10	11	12	13	14	15
51	16	17	18	19	20	21	22
52	23	24	25	26	(27)	(28)	29

X - INVENTORY DATE*   ◯ - HOLIDAY   ☐ - PLANT SHUTDOWN

*The Corporate Services group will come up with the inventory dates.

PBD

Figure B-42 (continued)

GARDEN WAY

Manpower Needs Forecast - Fiscal 1975

Completed by: _____
Title: _____
Department: _____
Date: _____
Approved by: _____

Pay[1] Grade	Midpoint[2]	Current[3] Level	Months[4]											
			Dec	Jan	Feb	Mar	Apr	May	Jun	Jul	Aug	Sept	Oct	Nov
Total														

Instructions:

[1]Indicate non-exempt grades using Arabic numerals and exempt using Roman numerals.

[2]Use hourly rate for non-exempt and weekly rate for exempt personnel.

[3]Indicate the current number of employees in each pay grade. Count part-time people as ½ and temp. full-time as 1.

[4]Show your monthly staffing needs in each pay period.

Figure B-42 (continued)

1977 Profit Plan
PARAMETER REQUIREMENTS

RESP.

BAC	1.	Corporate Goals and Objectives for 1977. —Profit—Sales Growth—"Cause Activities"—Products—Personnel Dev.
BAC	2.	General Trends of our Goals and Objectives for 1978.
FIN. MKT.	3.	Price Changes for 1977, If a Change is to be Made.
MKT.	4.	Discount Changes for 1977, If a Change is to be Made.
BAC	5.	Backlog, *Target* in Weeks for 1977. (By Month if it Varies)
MKT	6.	Inquiries, by Month, for 1977.
BAC	7.	Probability of Unit Sales for 1977.

High ------------------------Units
Target----------------------Units
Low ------------------------Units

MKT	8.	Orders Received by Month for both Horse and Pony
MKT SALES	9.	Product Mix by Class of Customer, By Month for 1977, for each Product and also each Accessory which is Sold with the Product.
PROD	10.	Units Produced by Month and by Day for 1977 for both the Horse and the Pony.
MKT SALES	11.	Units Sold (Shipped or Delivered) *To Customers,* By Class of Customer, by Month, for both the Horse and the Pony. *By Location* (Troy, GWLC, Oregon DSC plus any other Outlets that We Expect to Open) for 1977.
MKT SALES	12.	Units Shipped from Troy to Other Outlets (GWLC & DSC's) by Month for both the Horse and the Pony for 1977.
CUST. SERV.	13.	Parts and Service Net Sales by Month for 1977.
MKT. SALES	14.	Net Sales of Non Garden Way Products from GWLC and DSC by Month for 1977. Also, the Cost of Sales (%) for these Non Garden Way Products.

Figure B-43: PROFIT PLAN—PARAMETER REQUIREMENTS
(Courtesy of Garden Way, Incorporated.)

RESP.

PRES.
BAC.

15. Capital and Major Expense Expenditure Dollar Limitations by Quarter for 1977.

PRES.
BAC.

16. Employment Ceiling (if any) for 1977 by Location.

These parameters should be completed and returned to the Financial Planning, Analysis and Review (FPAR) Group, no later than September 7, 1976 for inclusion in the budget package which will be distributed to all budgeting managers on September 13-15, 1976. Adherence to this time frame is necessary to insure completion of the 1977 Profit Plan on schedule. Thank you.

Figure B-43 (continued)

1977 PROFIT PLAN PARAMETERS

Sales Discounts

G.W. Products

Fiscal Month	Reg. Cust.	GWLC	DSC	Owner	Other				
Dec.									
Jan.									
Feb.									
Mar.									
Apr.									
May									
Jun.									
Jul.									
Aug.									
Sep.									
Oct.									
Nov.									
Total									

Item 4

Figure B-43 (continued)

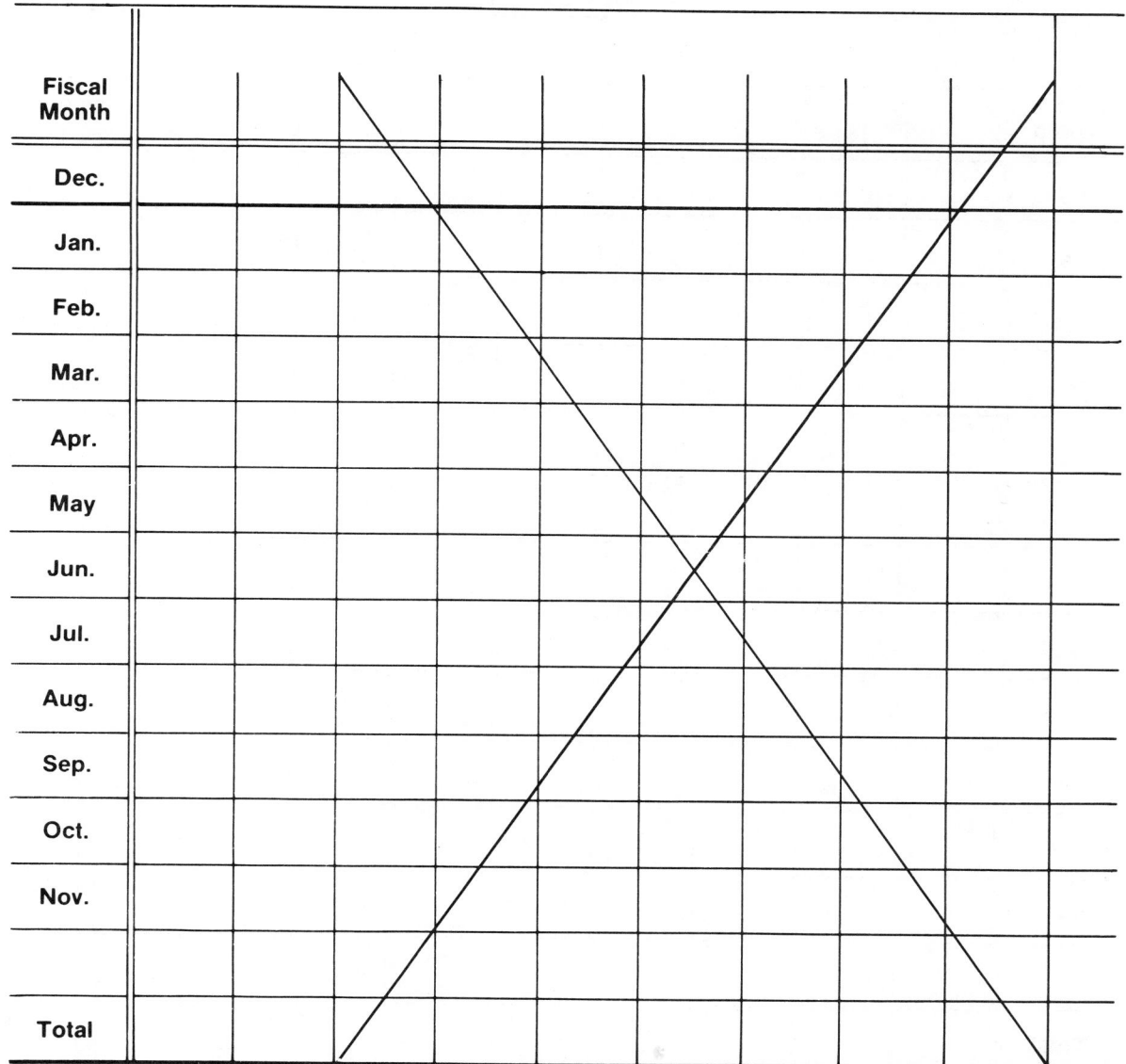

1977 PROFIT PLAN PARAMETERS

Backlog Target

in Weeks

Item 5

Figure B-43 (continued)

1977 PROFIT PLAN PARAMETERS

Total Inquires

Fiscal Month	Minimum					Target				
Dec.										
Jan.										
Feb.										
Mar.										
Apr.										
May										
Jun.										
Jul.										
Aug.										
Sep.										
Oct.										
Nov.										
Total										

Item 6

Figure B-43 (continued)

1977 PROFIT PLAN PARAMETERS

Horse Sales by Location

(Orders Received)

Fiscal Month	Minimum					Target			
	Troy	GWLC	DSC	Total		Troy	GWLC	DSC	Total
Dec.									
Jan.									
Feb.									
Mar.									
Apr.									
May									
Jun.									
Jul.									
Aug.									
Sep.									
Oct.									
Nov.									
Total									

Item 8 (1 of 2)

Figure B-43 (continued)

1977 PROFIT PLAN PARAMETERS

Pony Sales by Location

(Orders Received)

Fiscal Month	Minimum					Target				
	Troy	GWLC	DSC	Total		Troy	GWLC	DSC	Total	
Dec.										
Jan.										
Feb.										
Mar.										
Apr.										
May										
Jun.										
Jul.										
Aug.										
Sep.										
Oct.										
Nov.										
Total										

Item 8 (2 of 2)

Figure B-43 (continued)

1977 PROFIT PLAN PARAMETERS

Produce Mix - Units
Percent of Total Horse Units

Fiscal Month	4½	6	6 E.	7						Total	
Dec.										100	
Jan.										100	
Feb.										100	
Mar.										100	
Apr.										100	
May										100	
Jun.										100	
Jul.										100	
Aug.										100	
Sep.										100	
Oct.										100	
Nov.										100	
Total											

Item 9 (1 of 2)

Figure B-43 (continued)

1977 PROFIT PLAN PARAMETERS

Product Mix - Accessories
Percent of Total Horse Units

Fiscal Month	05 P.P.T. w/Hld.	07 P.P.T. w/o Hld.	09 C.T. w/Hld.	11 C.T. w/o Hld.	13 Furr. Att.	14 B.T. Tires	15 Dozer w/Att.	—	Carton	
Dec.										
Jan.										
Feb.										
Mar.										
Apr.										
May										
Jun.										
Jul.										
Aug.										
Sep.										
Oct.										
Nov.										
Total										

Item 9 (2 of 2)

Figure B-43 (continued)

1977 PROFIT PLAN PARAMETERS

Production Schedule

Fiscal Month	Minimum					Target			
	Horse	Pony		Total		Horse	Pony		Total
Dec.									
Jan.									
Feb.									
Mar.									
Apr.									
May									
Jun.									
Jul.									
Aug.									
Sep.									
Oct.									
Nov.									
Total									

Item 10

Figure B-43 (continued)

1977 PROFIT PLAN PARAMETERS

Units Shipped from Troy
To Other Locations

Fiscal Month	GWLC	DSC	Harris Seed	OTHER					Total
Dec.									
Jan.									
Feb.									
Mar.									
Apr.									
May									
Jun.									
Jul.									
Aug.									
Sep.									
Oct.									
Nov.									
Total									

Item 12

Figure B-43 (continued)

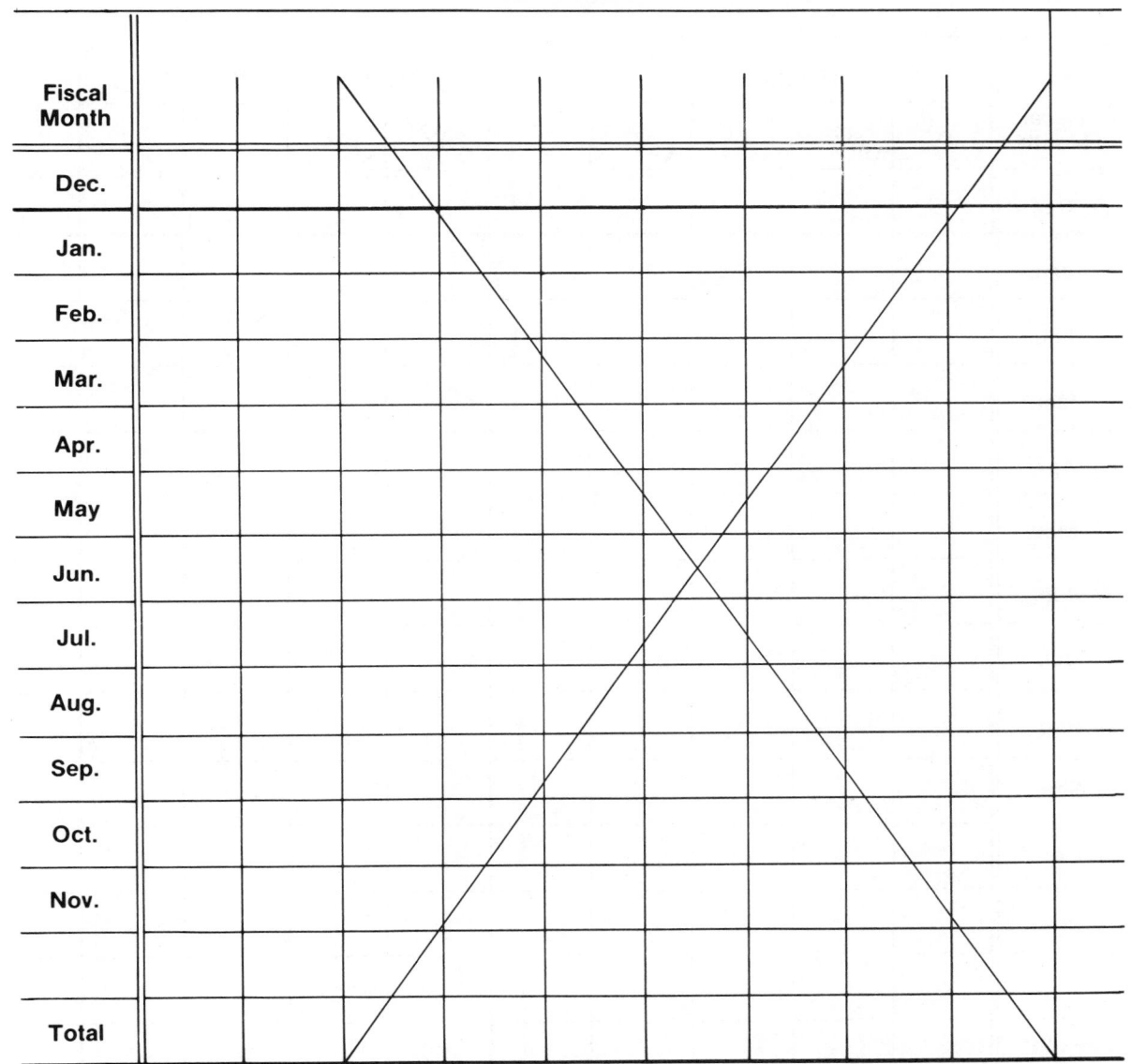

1977 PROFIT PLAN PARAMETERS

Parts & Service

Net Sales

Fiscal Month											
Dec.											
Jan.											
Feb.											
Mar.											
Apr.											
May											
Jun.											
Jul.											
Aug.											
Sep.											
Oct.											
Nov.											
Total											

Item 13

Figure B-43 (continued)

1977 PROFIT PLAN PARAMETERS

Non-G.W. Sales & Cost/Sales

Fiscal Month	Net Sales					Cost of Sales Percent				
	GWLC	DSC		Total		GWLC	DSC			
Dec.										
Jan.										
Feb.										
Mar.										
Apr.										
May										
Jun.										
Jul.										
Aug.										
Sep.										
Oct.										
Nov.										
Total										

Item 14

Figure B-43 (continued)

FORECAST

Year:	0	1	2	3	4	5
Units Sold (increase _____ % p.a.)						
Unit Price (increase _____ % p.a.)						
Turnover						
Materials (rising _____ % p.a.)						
Labor Productivity Index (assume _____ % p.a. increase)						
Number of Employees						
Average Pay per Employee (assume _____ % p.a. increase)						
Total Wage Bill						
TOTAL DIRECT COSTS						
Overhead (increase _____ % p.a.)						
PROFITS (Before Taxes)						
Taxes (@ _____ %)						
EARNINGS AFTER TAXES						

Period _____ to _____ Unit _____ By _____

ADDITIONAL ASSUMPTIONS

Figure B-44: FORECAST

Firm Name & Symbol: _____

	198A		198B		198C		198D	
(I) EST. EARNINGS ($)								
(II) EST. GROWTH RATE		%		%		%		%
(III) GROWTH FACTOR: 5 YEARS								
(IV) QUALITY FACTOR (PREM. + 0.10)								
(V) NONGROWTH P/E RATIO								
(VI) RECENT PRICE ($)								
(III) X (IV) X (V) = NORMAL GROWTH								

Figure B-45: NORMAL VALUE OF GROWTH STOCK

CO. NAME		Fiscal		Years		Ending:			
	198A	198B	198C	198D	198E	198F

	198A	198B	198C	198D	198E	198F
Analysis of Earning Power						
SALES (in millions)						
SALES--PERCENTAGE CHGE. PRIOR YR.						
SALES PERCENTAGE (usually 100%)						
COST OF GOODS SOLD						
GROSS PROFIT MARGIN						
OPERATING & ADMINISTRATIVE EXP.						
NET OPERATING PROFIT MARGIN						
PRE-TAX MARGIN						
TAXES						
NET PROFIT MARGIN (%)						
TAX RATE (%)						
TURNOVER: (times)						
Of Tangible Invested Capital						
EARNED ON INVESTED CAPITAL (%)						
EARNED ON COMMON STOCK EQUITY (%)						
Financial Factors						
EARNINGS PER SHARE:						
On _____ Shares						
Change in EPS from Prior Yr. (%)						
DIVIDENDS PER SHARE						
DIVIDEND PAYOUT RATIO (%)						
NET TANGIBLE ASSETS PER SHARE						
ANNUAL PRICE RANGE: (adjusted)						
High						
Low						
PRICE-EARNINGS RATIO:						
High						
Low						
LAST 12 MONTHS EARNINGS						
LAST CLOSING PRICE (date)						
P/E RATIO (last 12 mos. earnings)						
CURRENT PRICE/BOOK VALUE (%)						

Figure B-46: CORPORATE INVESTMENT ANALYSIS

FINANCIAL PLANNING FOR PROFIT AND COST CONTROL

SECTION C FORMS

Financial Planning
for Profit and
Cost Control

SECTION C

Financial Planning for Profit and Cost Control

Planning for profit prescribes financial planning—

- ◆ to achieve firm objectives;
- ◆ to finance the means to those goals;
- ◆ to control costs that accompany any plan of action;
- ◆ to find a cheaper path for implementing decisions;
- ◆ to increase profits of the department, plant, subsidiary, or group;
- ◆ to raise the long-term equity value of the corporation.

Overplanning may breed bureaucratization, higher planning costs and excessive accumulation of data. Underplanning suggests that additional resources devoted to financial planning will reduce risks and yield relatively greater return to investment. Whatever the plan, it must be understood at all levels and communicated to operating managers in language and format that clearly set forth corporate goals and strategy for achieving them, and, of course, commitment of adequate resources to bring the plan to fruition.

The beginning and end of liquidity and solvency is cash, or an appropriate substitute, so that much planning centers on cash flow projections. The Daily Cash Forecast (C-1) used by a multinational corporation tracks receipts and clearings, domestic as well as international movement of funds, on a daily basis. Nailed down in the analysis are compensating balances stipulated by various lending banks, the commercial paper inventory, other short-term or liquid investments, and borrowings. A forecast down to the last penny or pfennig is suspect; figures in this prototypic form are rounded off only to the nearest hundred thousand, stated in U.S. currency.

C-1

The Monthly Cash Forecast (C-2), simply presented, is readily understood. Estimated cash receipts added to the beginning cash balance yield cash available. Disbursements, or uses of cash, subtracted from available cash churn out the ending cash balance. The same basic configuration crops up in the next cash forecast form (C-3), modified to fit the needs of a shipping operation.

C-2

C-3

C-4   The next form, a Project Proposal and Three-Year Pro-Forma Cash Budget (C-4), abstracts cash flows related to a specific project. Thus, it furnishes an overview of the total investment proposal. The beginning of the period is usually characterized by investment outflows for machinery, fixtures and equipment, installation labor, raw materials, real estate purchase or lease, transaction costs, etc., while cash inflows normally occur after an investment has been made. For an ongoing project, outflows are associated with operations and maintenance and take place simultaneously with cash inflows. The difference between cash outflows and inflows yields the net change in cash, negative if outflows exceed inflows. To determine cash balances for each period, to beginning cash balances are added (appearing as either a negative or positive sum) net changes in cash. Such projections may be done for any period—monthly, quarterly, semiannually—and extended for as many years as reasonable. But the further out they are in time, the less meaning will monthly or quarterly results have because the greater chance of error nullifies finer details of monthly or quarterly projections.

C-5   Preparing cash flow projections prepares management to offset deficiencies in cash funds in some periods and to implement an adequate cash management plan during surplus periods to MINIMIZE COSTS, MAXIMIZE PROFITS. Too much borrowing, while safe, raises costs and adversely affects profits. Too much idle cash, also a safe position, lowers profit potential. The Monthly Cash Flow Projection (C-5), along with a profit and loss projection, break-even analysis, and adequate cost control data, represents an *important decision-making tool for increasing profits.* Projected data are then subsequently compared with actual data; and the correlation between cash flow and projected profits is analyzed to assist in future FINANCIAL PLANNING FOR BIGGER PROFITS AND SMALLER PER-UNIT COST.

C-6   *Cash inflows* emerge from sales planning and proper inventory management. The Monthly Sales and Stock Plan Report (C-6) compares actual with planned sales, and actual with planned inventories, during the current period, and against sales and inventory of a preceding period.

C-7   Another method used to bird-dog cash flows is the income statement (C-7):

   • First, determine operating profits.
   • Second, ascertain net cash flows.

Total available cash consists of the beginning cash balance plus receipts from receivables. From this subtract accounts payable, expenses, sales and administrative expenses, plus bank loans to be repaid. A negative result signals a cash shortage, requiring a bank loan.

C-8   A Cash Budget Forecast appears with instructions on the reverse side of the form (C-8). These are monthly projections. The form well suits a small firm operating on a cash basis; however, if accounts receivable are carried, enough time should be allowed for collection of receivables in order not to underestimate cash uses. At the same time, the firm may be buying acquired merchandise and supplies on terms shorter than it receives for goods sold. This difference must be accounted for and financed.

The Basis of a Cash Forecast form (C-9) applies well to a small manufacturing firm, in an easily understood format, for computing cash flows during the current month and forecast for the following three months. Carrying the analysis further, total variance between cash needs and collections and the target balance through the next date are calculated on the next form (C-10).

C-9

C-10

Because management must be sure that funds will become available as called for, and that sufficient working capital materializes to cover current demands, a financial plan or Six-Months' Working Capital Budget (C-11) costs a basic reference point of analysis. The availability at all times of enough, but not too much, working capital depends on detailed planning. *Planning expenditures* and *receipts* for each month comprehends accounts receivable and accounts payable turnover, seasonal tendencies and aberrations, and expected levels of sales activity.

C-11

The Worksheet for Calculating Receipts (C-12) on a seasonal basis reckons with end- and start-of-month inventories to gauge the inventory level change, sales, markdowns, employee discount, and shortages (shrinkage, spoilage, and theft) to yield total receipts according to plan and compared with last year. On this particular form, a worksheet, final consolidated results are later transmitted to corporate offices.

C-12

With service businesses that rely on contract renewals to maintain sales and revenue, a *preplanning tool* for estimating future sales is the Analysis of Contract Renewal Objectives (C-13). Data originates on the front line, from the representative(s) handling the account. The form obliges the representative to state his or her objectives, to condition his or her thinking in terms of growth, and also to call to the representative's attention possible problem areas in time to save, even increase, the value of a client's contract. Activity surrounding this form may seem a long way from the financial planning function, but without the representative's cooperation and input there would be fewer financial resources with which to plan. It requires a Weekly Statement (C-14) of revenue activity compared with the same week of the previous year, adjusted for special events; results are simply extrapolated for linear projection.

C-13

C-14

It is interesting to examine the Budgeting Procedure (C-15) employed by one firm. The nine-page procedural outline matches the preceding year's. Notice, first of all, that the firm does not use a zero-base-budgeting concept but uses *marginal analysis* instead. Analysis begins with a minimum level of 50,000 units assumed, and the budget is developed in terms of corporate objectives. The planning office requires four types of data input: manpower, fixed, direct input used to budget for the minimum level, and variable input to budget above the minimum level for the company to identify variable elements in the cost structure. Corporate planning has provided historical data essential for forward planning and has established a definite schedule for return of all information to the Budgeting Planning Group. Each department will append appropriate forms and supporting data, including major capital expenditures, and a manpower schedule.

C-15

C-16
The preceding organizer is an annual budget for the ensuing period; the next form is a *long-range profit plan* using selected operating data (C-16). The form makes due provision for:

(a)   actual data on the last three years;
(b)   the profit plan and estimated operating data for the current year;
(c)   the profit plan for the following two years;
(d)   projections of selected categories for three years beyond that.

Operating and other data are fractionalized into seven sections beginning with basic income statistics: sales, gross margin, profit before taxes. Assets are split into end-of-period data and year-to-date averages. Orders and backlog merits its own category with two entries: orders received (funded), and unfilled orders. Other data call for information on cash flow, capital appropriations and expenditures, manpower, space use, energy cost, depreciation, *inter alia*. The five pretax ratios listed are:

(a)   return on sales;
(b)   return on assets;
(c)   asset turnover;
(d)   collection period of accounts receivable;
(e)   production inventory turnover.

Cost conscious, profit minded. The last, but very important, category is GROWTH of projected sales and projected profits.

C-17
Form C-17 is actually a checklist of Parameter Requirements for the Annual Profit Plan. Its purpose is to assist individual managers in preparing an *annual profit plan*.

C-18
The Operating Plan Forecast, Profit and Loss Projection (C-18), a *valuable planning tool* during the financial planning stages, is a *key management tool* in CONTROLLING COSTS OF OPERATIONS. The forecast previews projected profits and losses month by month. Losses can be planned for (perhaps not consciously) just as easily as profits. Potential problem areas should be identified quickly and corrective action taken, given budget restraints.

This, of course, is not a cash flow analysis since cash flows and profits are not necessarily the same, but the monthly estimates needed for cash analysis can be taken from revenue and expense data appearing on this form. Notice that the left-hand column parades industry averages, which are useful in comparing the firm's performance with industry-wide averages. After operating estimates are developed for each period, and totaled, they can serve as target figures. Actual performance can be evaluated against target figures, or industry averages, or last year's performance. Data can also be used to identify product expansion or elimination decisions, whatever is necessary in PROFIT PLANNING.

C-19
Multiple-page form C-19 caters to Long-Range Planning by Earning Components. The 17 categories appear on pages two through four of the form; data are abstracted on the first page according to total owned retail stores, cost departments, leased departments,

and total company-wide actual and planned earnings. Data in each category begin with two years of actual figures followed by five-year projections of sales, gross margin, operating expense, other income, interest expense, and profits. All figures are stated both in dollar amounts and as percentages.

The same organization also makes long-range plans for generating an adequate return on equity (C-20). Columns (1) and (2) are for actual historical data; Columns (3) through (7) embrace projected figures. Equity participation is projected at a constant 53 percent of total capitalization; the income tax rate is assumed unchanged at 48 percent. Net income is obtained by multiplying earnings after interest times the inverse of the income tax rate.

C-20

The actual and long-range sales plan (C-21) proceeds store by store. Each store, or subsidiary, is responsible for its own five-year projections; data are then aggregated for the corporation. Actual figures on performance of the two most recent years plus forecast for the next five show up on the form.

C-21

The Preliminary and Final Earnings Plan (C-22) by store location derives from actual data for the current year and previous year and percent change in sales over the previous year. Other data include computations on gross margin (percent) by store, direct and allocated expenses, allocated interest, other income, and earnings. All data are stated in percentages for analytical and PROFIT-PLANNING purposes. The last two columns, important to FINANCIAL PLANNING, show data and changes on census figures, and store square footage. The latter is subdivided into square footage devoted to selling and merchandising and total building space. (Compare this one with the profit-planning form in Section B, Figure B-36.)

C-22

Data from the Earnings Plan (C-22) are valuable in developing a long-range earnings plan (C-23). Corporate financial planning dictates that information be developed on a store-by-store basis, on total square footage, and when the operations began. Actual inputs emerge for three prior years, plus the vital five-year projections of sales, gross margin, operating expenses, other income, interest expenses and anticipated profits before taxes.

C-23

A subset of this long-range plan is an interim earnings plan summary for the season (C-24) for new stores. The store manager, on the worksheet, plans for the season's sales, gross margin, expenses, and earnings before taxes. He also must anticipate return on investment for the first season and for the first full year's operation. This is a POWERFUL PLANNING TOOL for new managers. Being required to make a commitment to paper obligates store management to reveal considerable comprehension of local marketing requirements, careful use of financial resources, and a well-managed inventory plan. The written commitment also conditions store management to think in terms of their objectives and to strive harder to meet them.

C-24

C-25   Control of current and expected interest costs is pivotal for highly leveraged firms during transitional periods of business and economic cycles. This form (C-25) begins with actual figures on the three most recent years followed by interest-expense projections for the following five years. Analysis depends upon adequate estimates of investment by layer, that is, year by year, with after-tax average costs of capital indicated for previous years and projected for five years into the future. However, computing cost of funds involves considerable detail and knowledge of financial structure and capital markets. (For more on mathematical techniques to determine capital costs, see Robert P. Vichas, *Handbook of Financial Mathematics, Formulas, and Tables,* published by Prentice-Hall, Inc., Chapter 4.)

C-26   Besides interest expenses, another important aspect of FINANCIAL PLANNING FOR PROFITS is cost of labor. The annual Manpower Needs Forecast (C-26) projects number of full-time and part-time employees needed monthly and their average wage rate. Such forecasts will include temporary full-time as well as seasonal, part-time employees. The second page of the form (C-26), appended material, elicits further remarks and a statement of assumptions underlying the forecasted numbers. It also spotlights potential problem areas as well as the impact of technological change that may result in an altered labor-capital ratio.

C-27   For planning longer than one year, a Survey and Projections report (C-27) tabulates average number of employees by category, skill, or department five years ago and for the current year. Presumably, projections have already been anticipated for the next year so that the report projects demand two years from now and five years from now. This particular profile also analyzes changes in the total number of employees, in payroll expenses (see Section I for more on payroll forms for cost control), and net sales. The analyst also wants to establish equity, that is, owner participation, investment not only as a percent of total payroll but also by department or function. An interesting additional trend caught on this form are changes in fringe benefits as a percent of total payroll and information on absenteeism. Since absenteeism, like any other financial decision, must be financed by someone, the enterprise wants to know (1) just how much of a burden it has been carrying, and (2) what the probability is that this burden will be lesser or greater in future periods. The other point in financial planning centers on productivity.

C-28   Declining or increasing productivity affects the capital-labor mix, costs of operation, and profits. Computation of Marginal Product (C-28) refers to a physical product, rather than to a financial factor, but financial analysis emerges from actual output. The answer sought from these calculations is how much additional product will another unit of labor add to total production. Or the reverse, by laying off a certain number of workers, how much production will be lost. The *money value* of additional output gained or lost, a function of the price at which it is sold, is then calculated for application in financial planning.

Financial planning also depends upon a capital expenditures forecast for asset replacement and growth (more on this topic in Sections D and E). For large investments, a forecast is prepared for each project (C-29), which itemizes estimated project investment and costs by year(s) incurred. With this information management can determine project feasibiity in relationship to long-run financial plans and corporate objectives and availability of resources. All projects then entered in a forecast summary (C-30) are ranked according to desirability, return on investment, payback period, or whatever criterion is judged suitable for financial planning.

C-29

C-30

Of course, rate of return, payback period, etc., may not be apposite for accepting/rejecting investment projects. An Evaluation and Risk Analysis of Investment Projects (C-31) ranks investments according to the benefit-cost ratio, expected return and variance (the probability or chance that the rate of return will be something other than that forecasted). Covariations among projects considered are recorded in the right-hand columns. If variance arises, it may become appropriate to alter strategy, assumptions made in planning, or operational parameters. But the problem is that an adjustment in one may affect others so that adjustment continues until a new point is reached. If variance arises in the forecast, financial plans must be reexamined and readjusted.

C-31

Financial planning also may mean acquiring, selling, or issuing securities, preceded by an Industrial Security Financial Analysis (C-32). The security analysis includes historical information on income and expenses, capital structure, assets and liabilities, market values of the security, working capital, and ratio analysis. Some items may be omitted in some instances, and blank spaces are provided for additions of others.

C-32

Financing a capital project with a loan (C-33) is recorded on a two-part form—a data section and an analytical section. The upper section introduces the interest, discount, and tax rates, title of the project, total investment and total amount of loan, and depreciation method. The analytical section is for computing the present value of the cash outflows during the economic life of the project or investment.

C-33

Making loans means maintaining an Annual Loan History (C-34). The data card also provides for information on hazard insurance carried, payment of taxes and interest, and escrow balance. The Installment Loan History Report (C-35) registers details of the loan transaction, history of payments, and risk data on insurance carried. Since there are many sources of finance plans, some firms may make an Analysis of Alternative Financing Sources (C-36). In this form, all possible short-, medium-, and long-term sources are arrayed, and each is evaluated with respect to type and quality of financing plus availability.

C-34

C-35

C-36

Financial planning strokes not only profits but also control of costs. A specimen of this type of design is an Invoice Summary and Forecast (C-37). This particular paradigm relates to crude oil purchases. Outliving a profit plan means acquiring goods and services at the best prices by sending out Requests for Quotation (C-38) and then analyzing the Quotations (C-39) springing from the inquiries.

C-37

C-38
C-39

C-40   Submitting a Proposal (C-40) imposes an understanding of available resources and company objectives. Inventories, a use of investment funds, are managed properly when ordering and warehousing costs are minimized but sufficient materials and supplies are on hand to meet customer demands without delay and damage to profits. In a continuous process operation, materials and supplies are ordered on a schedule that avoids

C-41   production delays and profit leaks (C-41). In a jobbing plant, for example, a Purchase

C-42   Requisition (C-42) issued to the purchasing agent lists materials and subassemblies requested for a specific job, dates needed, and notation when the job has been promised. *Poor planning produces poor profit performance.*

C-43   Merchandise for resale demands the same careful inventory management (C-43) to maintain fast-moving, PROFITABLE STOCK on hand, and *mark down the money losers* to free that space for more profitable stock.

Safety stock time (C-44) is the additional time elapsed beyond the usual delivery time for stock. *Safety stock* is the additional stock on hand to cover such emergencies, shipping time, and other contingencies. Safety stock, in one sense, is a nonproductive employment of financial resources because it exceeds the required investment for normal conduct of business. In another sense, safety stock is an insurance premium paid so as not to drive customers away to competitors due to insufficient quantity and assortment of merchandise; it is a PROFIT SAFETY planning measure. The Annual Demand Safety

C-44   Stock Time Distribution (C-44) reduces divisional demand to a formula. Management first ranks, in descending order of demand, all inventory items. Items with highest demand, the money-makers, merit a larger safety stock than slow-movers. As a tool of financial planning and cost control, financial resources go where the money is and away from where it isn't.

C-45   To convert months of inventory on hand into money terms (C-45), the months of inventory on hand must relate to budgeted sales at cost. After cost and physical inventory figures are developed, actual conversion is uncomplicated. Corporate planners will incorporate planned inventory levels into the cash forecast described earlier in this section. Cash problems can be spread around; divisions may be requested to reduce

C-46   planned inventory levels to conserve cash. The Projected Purchases Worksheet (C-46) is a key element in making the financial plan flexible and viable. Finally, inventory management, cost control, and financial resource conservation depend on ordering just the correct amount of merchandise, minimizing the risk of overstocking and overinvestment, at the right time to coincide with cash flow projections, with sufficient

C-47   inventory on hand to *prevent stockouts* (C-47).

DAILY CASH FORECAST (U.S. ONLY)
(000,000)

Date: _____

Prepared By: _____

Date:	Monday	Tuesday	Wednesday	Thursday	Friday	This Week's Totals	
Receipts							
Clearings							
International							
Other							
" "							
" "							
Total							
Comp. Bals. — To (−)							
Comp. Bals. — From (+)							
Comm. Paper — Redem (−)							
Comm. Paper — Sale (+)							
Comm. Paper — Redem (−)							
Comm. Paper — Sale (+)							
Portfolio — Invest (−)							
Portfolio — Mature (+)							
Borrowings — Pay Back (−)							
Borrowings — Take Down (+)							
Net Effect							

Commercial Paper Recap:

Begin. of Week: _____

Net Change: _____

End of Week: _____

End of Week: _____

Portfolio Size:

Beginning of Week: _____

End of Week: _____

Borrowings Outstanding:

Beginning of Week: _____

End of Week: _____

_____

Figure C-1: DAILY CASH FORECAST AND ANALYSIS

MONTHLY CASH FORECAST

Cash Balance, Beginning $

Add: Cash Receipts (estimated):

    Collections on account $
    Other miscellaneous receipts   _____   _____

Cash Available

Less: Cash Disbursements:

    Rent
    Group insurance
    Other insurance
    Payroll
    Employer payroll taxes:
      FICA
      Federal UC tax
      State UC tax
    Property taxes
    Accounts payable to be paid
    Transfers to real estate partnership
    Federal income tax deposits required
      (1120)   _____   _____

Cash Balance, Ending $_____

Note: Projecting cash receipts should be relatively easy because the largest customers, G.E. and P.W.A., make payments on a regular cyclical basis. Also, the cash requirements forecast report prepared at month end by ADP would make forecasting payment of accounts payable easy.

Figure C-2: MONTHLY CASH FORECAST

SHIPPING COMPANY, LIMITED
Cash Forecast   **Millions of $**

Company/   Shipping Agency Account

Receipt from
Disbursement:
    Operating Expenses

Net for Month

Company, Limited

B.O.M.

    Receipts:
        Transportation
    Disbursements:
        Spot Charter

Net Receipts -

International Subsidiaries
Receipts:
    Transportation
Disbursements:
    Interest Expense
    Principal Payments

Net Receipts - Subsidiaries

Third Party
Receipts:
    Spot Charter
Disbursements:
    Operating Expenses
    Spot Charters
    Time Charters
    Miscellaneous

Net Receipts - Third Party

Net for Month

E.O.M.

Accounts Receivable
    Accumulated Invoices

SSR:tah

Figure C-3: CASH FORECAST FOR SUBSIDIARIES AND THIRD PARTIES

ACQUACULTURE DIV.

PROJECT PROPOSAL AND THREE-YEAR PRO FORMA CASH BUDGET (in thousands)

ITEMIZE CASH FLOWS	Beginning of Period			Year 1			Year 2			Year 3		
CASH INFLOWS:												
Cash Sales												
Receivables Collections												
Contributed Capital												
Debt (specify)												
Other Sources												
CASH RECEIVED												
CASH OUTFLOWS												
Inventories												
Raw Materials												
New Fixed Assets												
Used Machinery & Equipment												
Accounts Payable												
Labor Costs												
Administrative Costs												
Selling Costs												
Insurance Fees												
Hedging Costs												
Other Transaction Fees												
Dividends												
Local Taxes												
Other Expenses												
TOTAL CASH OUTFLOWS (−)												
+ Total Cash Inflows												
NET CHANGE IN CASH (difference)												
BEGINNING CASH BALANCES												
NET CHANGE (+ or −)												
ENDING CASH BALANCES												

Figure C-4: PROJECT PROPOSAL AND THREE-YEAR PRO-FORMA CASH BUDGET

INSTRUCTIONS ON REVERSE SIDE

MONTHLY CASH FLOW PROJECTION

NAME OF BUSINESS	ADDRESS	OWNER	TYPE OF BUSINESS	PREPARED BY	DATE

YEAR / MONTH	Pre-Start-up Position		1		2		3		4		5		6		7		8		9		10		11		12		TOTAL Columns 1–12		
	Estimate	Actual	Estimate	Actual	Estimate	Actual	Estimate	Actual	Estimate	Actual	Estimate	Actual	Estimate	Actual	Estimate	Actual	Estimate	Actual	Estimate	Actual	Estimate	Actual	Estimate	Actual	Estimate	Actual	Estimate	Actual	
1. CASH ON HAND (Beginning of month)																													1.
2. CASH RECEIPTS																													2.
(a) Cash Sales																													(a)
(b) Collections from Credit Accounts																													(b)
(c) Loan or Other Cash injection (Specify)																													(c)
3. TOTAL CASH RECEIPTS (2a+2b+2c=3)																													3.
4. TOTAL CASH AVAILABLE (Before cash out) (1+3)																													4.
5. CASH PAID OUT																													5.
(a) Purchases (Merchandise)																													(a)
(b) Gross Wages (Excludes withdrawals)																													(b)
(c) Payroll Expenses (Taxes, etc.)																													(c)
(d) Outside Services																													(d)
(e) Supplies (Office and operating)																													(e)
(f) Repairs and Maintenance																													(f)
(g) Advertising																													(g)
(h) Car, Delivery, and Travel																													(h)
(i) Accounting and Legal																													(i)
(j) Rent																													(j)
(k) Telephone																													(k)
(l) Utilities																													(l)
(m) Insurance																													(m)
(n) Taxes (Real estate, etc.)																													(n)
(o) Interest																													(o)
(p) Other Expenses (Specify each)																													(p)
(q) Miscellaneous (Unspecified)																													(q)
(r) Subtotal																													(r)
(s) Loan Principal Payment																													(s)
(t) Capital Purchases (Specify)																													(t)
(u) Other Start-up Costs																													(u)
(v) Reserve and/or Excrow (Specify)																													(v)
(w) Owner's Withdrawal																													(w)
6. TOTAL CASH PAID OUT (Total 5a thru 5w)																													6.
7. CASH POSITION (End of month) (4 minus 6)																													7.
ESSENTIAL OPERATING DATA (Non-cash flow information)																													
A. Sales Volume (Dollars)																													A.
B. Accounts Receivable (End of month)																													B.
C. Bad Debt (End of month)																													C.
D. Inventory on Hand (End of month)																													D.
E. Accounts Payable (End of month)																													E.
F. Depreciation																													F.

SBA FORM 1100 (8-75) REF: SOP 60 10 1

Figure C-5: MONTHLY CASH FLOW PROJECTION
(Courtesy of Small Business Administration.)

DEPARTMENT:								CLASSIFICATION:							
SALES				**STOCK**				**SALES**				**STOCK**			
week ending	last year	this year		last year	this year			week ending	last year	this year		last year	this year		
		planned	actual		planned	actual	on order			planned	actual		planned	actual	on order
cumulative to date								cumulative to date							
cumulative to date								cumulative to date							

Figure C-6: PLANNED AND ACTUAL MONTHLY SALES AND STOCK REPORT

P&L STATEMENT ADAPTED
TO SHOW CASH FLOW

Monthly Operations

Net sales $ _____

Less: Material used
    Direct labor
    Other mfging expense   _____
Cost of goods sold $ _____

Gross profit $ _____
Less: Sales expense   _____
    General and admin-
    istrative expense   _____

Operating profit $ _____

Cash Flow

Cash balance (beginning) $ _____
Receipts from receivables   _____
    Total available cash $ _____

Less Disbursements
    Trade payables   _____
    Direct labor   _____
    Other mfging expense   _____
    Sales expense   _____
    General and admini-
    istrative expense   _____
    Fixed asset additions   _____
    Bank loans to be repaid   _____
      Total disbursements $ _____

Indicated cash shortage $ _____
Bank loans to be obtained $ _____
Cash balance (ending) $ _____

Materials purchased $ _____
      Month-end position
Accounts receivable $ _____
Inventory $ _____
Accounts payable $ _____
Bank loans payable $ _____

Figure C-7: P&L STATEMENT ADAPTED TO SHOW MONTHLY CASH FLOW

Cash Budget Forecast

(Budget should be carried out to show retirement of bank debt)

MONTHLY SALES ....

Note Ref.		Month of	Month of	Month of	Month of	Month of	Month of
(1)	AVAILABLE CASH FUNDS						
(2)	Opening Cash Balance	......	......	......	......	......	......
(3)	Monthly Cash Collections	......	......	......	......	......	......
(4)	Miscellaneous Cash Collections	......	......	......	......	......	......
(A)	Total available cash funds	......	......	......	......	......	......
	DISBURSEMENTS						
(5)	Material Purchases	......	......	......	......	......	......
(5)	Payments to Subcontractors	......	......	......	......	......	......
(6)	Gross Payroll	......	......	......	......	......	......
(7)	Overhead	......	......	......	......	......	......
(8)	Executive Salaries of Partners' Withdrawals...........	......	......	......	......	......	......
(9)	Equipment Purchases	......	......	......	......	......	......
(10)	Contract Payments	......	......	......	......	......	......
(11)	Taxes (Employer's Share of Social Security, Property, etc.)	......	......	......	......	......	......
	....	......	......	......	......	......	......
(B)	Total Cash Disbursements	......	......	......	......	......	......
	MISCELLANEOUS						
(12)	Cash Over or Short	......	......	......	......	......	......
(13)	Bank Borrowings...........	......	......	......	......	......	......
(14)	Bank Loan Reductions...........	......	......	......	......	......	......
(15)	Cash Balance (Month End)	......	......	......	......	......	......
(16)	Cumulated Bank Debt...........	......	......	......	......	......	......

(See reverse for explanation)

Cash Budget Forecast

(Reverse Side)

NOTES

1. Period covered should be at most a calendar month or such shorter period as would more accurately reflect peak borrowing requirements.

2. Cash balance as per close of preceding month. New opening cash balance thereafter to be brought forward from the close of each previous period (i.e., from Item No. 15).

3. Adequate time lag should be allowed for collection of billings. Consideration should not be given to withholds until actually due.

4. Collections arising from other than normal billings.

5. Consideration should be given to actual *cash* required to pay for purchases of materials in accordance with suppliers' and/or subcontractors' credit terms.

6. Period's payroll requirements with the exception of executive salaries which should appear in Item No. 8. Entries under this heading should include employees' income tax and social security tax withholds.

7. Actual cash expenditures incident to factory, administrative, and other overhead except executive salaries which should appear in Item No. 8.

8. This should cover only actual cash payments on account of salaries and/or withdrawals. Entries under this heading should include income tax withholds.

9. Cash required for purchases of additional equipment.

10. Periodic payments on existing installment contracts such as equipment purchase contracts, deeds of trust, mortgages, and other such obligations.

11. Entries under this caption should appear only in periods when actual payment is to be made.

12. Enter excess of A over B in black; enter excess of B over A in red.

13. Enter only *actual* net borrowings in particular period required to cover cash shortage (Item No. 12) and to provide necessary working cash balance for opening of succeeding period.

14. Enter only actual net reduction in bank borrowings during period.

15. This is the period's closing cash balance after giving effect to net bank borrowings (Item No. 13) or reductions (Item No. 14). This balance is to be carried forward to the following period as Item No. 2.

16. This should include any bank borrowings outstanding at the beginning of the budget, plus or minus such subsequent borrowings or reductions as shown in Items Nos. 13 and 14. Headings may, of course, be altered to fit case under consideration.

Figure C-8: CASH BUDGET FORECAST
(Courtesy of California Bank.)

220

Basis of Cash Forecast (Page 1)

	August	September	October
Memo—Estimated net production based on production department backlog of unproduced quantities as of July 31, 19			
Funds to be provided from operations:			
Gross sales	.....	.....	.....
Less:			
Labor (30 percent based on April-June)	.....	.....	.....
Salaries and fixed expense	.....	.....	.....
Steel (40 percent based on April-June)	.....	.....	.....
Miscellaneous (20 percent based on April-June) ..	.....	.....	.....
Decrease in in-process inventory	.....	.....	.....
Total	.....	.....	.....
Balance (Profit before income taxes)	.....	.....	.....
Add back:			
Depreciation, provision for real estate taxes, and other reserve provisions	.....	.....	.....
Decrease in in-process inventory	.....	.....	.....
Total estimated funds provided from operations ..	.....	.....	.....
Add:			
Decrease in steel inventory (estimated on basis of purchasing and production department forecasts)	.....	.....	.....
Decrease in accounts receivable	.....	.....	.....
Increase in accrued payroll	.....	.....	.....
Total	.....	.....	.....
Deduct:			
Increase in accounts receivable (estimated)	.....	.....	.....
Federal income tax (quarterly installment)	.....	.....	.....
Equipment purchases per purchasing department ..	.....	.....	.....
Decrease in accrued payroll	.....	.....	.....
Total	.....	.....	.....
Estimated increase or decrease in cash balance	.....	.....	.....

Cash Forecast (Page 2)

	July		Forecast		
	Forecast	Actual	August	September	October
Forecast based on estimated production of					
Cash balance beginning of month					
Receipts:					
Accounts receivable	.....	.....	.....	.....	.....
Total	.....	.....	.....	.....	.....
Disbursements:					
Payroll:					
Hourly	.....	.....	.....	.....	.....
Salary	.....	.....	.....	.....	.....
Steel	.....	.....	.....	.....	.....
Miscellaneous supplies and expense items	.....	.....	.....	.....	.....
Equipment	.....	.....	.....	.....	.....
Federal income taxes (quarterly payment)	.....	.....	.....	.....	.....
Total	.....	.....	.....	.....	.....
Cash balance, end of month	.....	.....	.....	.....	.....
Less minimum balances	.....	.....	.....	.....	.....
Estimated amount of available cash	.....	.....	.....	.....	.....

Above forecast has been based on production department unproduced backlog as of July 31, 19 , and on the analysis shown on p. 1. The forecast for the months of August and September would normally be carried over from the previous forecast if there were no major changes with a footnote to explain any minor revisions required.

Figure C-9: BASIS OF CASH FORECAST

Seq. No.	Bank	3rd Qtr. Req'd MMDD's	Req'd Avg. Coll. Bal. MM	Total Variance MMDD's Y-T-D	Q-T-D MMDD's (Int'l & Subs. Accts.) (as of)	Estimated Balances MM (as of)	Actual MMDD's (as of)	Difference: MM Req'd by Qtr. End	Target Balance MM through (date)
0-4, 9					(/)	(/)	(/)		(/)
5					(/)	(/)	(/)		(/)
0					(/)	(/)	(/)		(/)
1					(/)	(/)	(/)		(/)
2					(/)	(/)	(/)		(/)
0, 8					(/)	(/)	(/)		(/)
0, 6					(/)	(/)	(/)		(/)
8					(/)	(/)	(/)		(/)
6					(/)	(/)	(/)		(/)
9					(/)	(/)	(/)		(/)
0-26					(/)	(/)	(/)		(/)
					(/)	(/)	(/)		(/)
					(/)	(/)	(/)		(/)
					(/)	(/)	(/)		(/)
					(/)	(/)	(/)		(/)
					(/)	(/)	(/)		(/)
					(/)	(/)	(/)		(/)
					(/)	(/)	(/)		(/)
					(/)	(/)	(/)		(/)

July 1 - September 30 = 92 Days   July 13, 19

Figure C-10: VARIANCE ANALYSIS

222

	January	February	March	April	May	June
Expected cash receipts:						
Cash sales						
Collections of receivables						
Miscellaneous sources						
Total cash receipts						
Expected cash payments:						
Material purchases						
Payroll						
Production overhead						
Selling and administration						
Income taxes						
Replacements						
Miscellaneous items						
Total cash payments						
Excess of receipts over expenditures						
Deficiency of receipts below expenditures						

Figure C-11: FORM FOR SIX-MONTHS' WORKING CAPITAL BUDGET
(From the book Cost Accounting for Small Manufacturers, 2nd Edition, by R. Lee Brummet and Jack C. Robertson. © 1972. Published by Small Business Administration.)

Form R-1
WORKSHEET

WORKSHEET FOR CALCULATING RECEIPTS

☐ Spring

☐ Fall   19_____

Company _____

		FEB/AUG		MAR/SEPT		APR/OCT		MAY/NOV		JUNE/DEC		JULY/JAN		SEASON	
		Plan	LY	Plan	LY	Plan	LY	Plan	LY	Plan	LY	Plan	LY	Plan	LY
1	EOM Stock — Total														
2	BOM Stock — Total														
3	Stock Level Change 1-2 (Show + or −)														
4	Sales														
5	Markdowns														
6	Employee Discount														
7	Shortage														
8	Calculated Receipts 3 + 4 + 5 + 6 + 7 = Total														

WORKSHEET ONLY — DO NOT RETURN TO CORPORATE OFFICE

Figure C-12: WORKSHEET FOR CALCULATING RECEIPTS

ANALYSIS OF CONTRACT RENEWAL OBJECTIVES

INSTRUCTIONS: Start with any month in which you have advance renewals of less than one-half of the contracts on your list. Next list and analyze all contracts to be renewed for that month and the following two months. Indicate what your renewal aims are, why, and how you intend to achieve them. Use a separate sheet for each customer.

MONTH _____ 19_____

Customer's name _____

Customer since _____

Present contract _____

Peak contract _____

Present usage _____

Peak usage _____

Method of operation _____

Immediate renewal objective _____

Long term renewal objective _____

Comments and plan of action:

Figure C-13: ANALYSIS OF CONTRACT RENEWAL OBJECTIONS

WEEKLY STATEMENT

THEATRE ....

TOWN .... WEEK # ....

FILM .... PLAYDATE .... TO ....

(All cash figures to be given to the nearest whole dollar.)

	Last Year	This Year
CANDY	....	....
TOTAL TO DATE	....	....
INCREASE/DECREASE*		
ADMISSIONS	....	....
TOTAL TO DATE	....	....
INCREASE/DECREASE*		
NET	....	....
TOTAL TO DATE	....	....
INCREASE/DECREASE*		

(*Cross one out.)

LIST HOLIDAYS OR OTHER EVENTS WHICH MAY HAVE AFFECTED YOUR THEATRE DURING THE WEEK.

....

....

....

....

REMARKS.

.... Manager.

Figure C-14: WEEKLY COMPARATIVE SALES ANALYSIS

1978 BUDGETING PROCEDURE

The procedure will be the same as last year.

For those of you who have forgotten or are still unsure of what we did, let's review the procedure again. We will budget for the necessities at a minimal level of 50,000 units. You will then be asked to develop a variable budget (based on one of the four parameters or independent variables) up to the target of 65,000 and beyond to the maximum level of 80,000 units for 1978.

We have four means of input to this system:

1. Manpower Input
2. Fixed Input
3. Variable Input
4. Direct Input

Manpower, Fixed and Direct Input will be used as the means to budget for the minimum level. The Variable Input should be used to budget above the minimum level. This will enable the company to identify the variable element in its cost structure.

The tools supplied to you for budgeting fiscal year 1978 include:

1. August 1977 Responsibility Reports.
2. 1978 Parameters (four: inquiries received; tiller orders received, units produced and parts orders received)
3. 9 Months - 1977 Departmental General Ledger
4. Manpower Input Worksheets
5. Major Expenditure Worksheets
6. 1978 Budget Input Worksheets
7. 1978 Profit Plan Schedule

Remember, all budget information is to be returned back to the Budgeting/Planning Group *no later than September 30th.* To expedite the budget preparation, two coordinators have been named. Jerry Smith will handle the Manufacturing Group while Susi Pensel will take care of the Marketing Group. If you need any additional assistance, please contact Bob Ostertag at Extension 2570.

Thanks and happy budgeting!

Figure C-15: BUDGETING PROCEDURE AND PLANNING

1978 FISCAL CALENDAR

240 Working Days

1st QUARTER 61 WKG DAYS

DECEMBER	JANUARY	FEBRUARY
19 Wkg Days	18 Wkg Days	24 Wkg Days

*	S	M	T	W	T	F	S
1 -	27	28	29	30	1	2	3
2 -	4	5	6	7	8	9	10
3 -	11	12	13	14	15	16	17
4 -	18	19	20	21	22	(23)	24

*	S	M	T	W	T	F	S
5 -	25	(26)	27	28	29	30	31
6-	1	(2)	3	4	5	6	7
7 -	8	9	10	11	12	13	14
8 -	15	16	17	18	19	20	21

*	S	M	T	W	T	F	S
9 -	22	23	24	25	26	27	28
10 -	29	30	31	1	2	3	4
11 -	5	6	7	8	9	10	11
12 -	12	13	14	15	16	17	18
13 -	19	(20)	21	22	23	24	25

2nd QUARTER 65 WKG DAYS

MARCH	APRIL	MAY
20 Wkg Days	20 Wkg Days	25 Wkg Days

*	S	M	T	W	T	F	S
14 -	26	27	28	1	2	3	4
15 -	5	6	7	8	9	10	11
16 -	12	13	14	15	16	17	18
17 -	19	20	21	22	23	24	25

*	S	M	T	W	T	F	S
18 -	26	27	28	29	30	31	1
19 -	2	3	4	5	6	7	8
20 -	9	10	11	12	13	14	15
21 -	16	17	18	19	20	21	22

*	S	M	T	W	T	F	S
22 -	23	24	25	26	27	28	29
23 -	30	1	2	3	4	5	6
24 -	7	8	9	10	11	12	13
25 -	14	15	16	17	18	19	20
26 -	21	22	23	24	25	26	27

3rd QUARTER 52 WKG DAYS

JUNE	JULY	AUGUST
19 Wkg Days	13 Wkg Days	20 Wkg Days

*	S	M	T	W	T	F	S
27 -	28	(29)	30	31	1	2	3
28 -	4	5	6	7	8	9	10
29 -	11	12	13	14	15	16	17
30 -	18	19	20	21	22	23	24

*	S	M	T	W	T	F	S
31 -	25	26	27	28	29	30	1
32 -	2	(3)	(4)	5	6	7	8
33 -	9	10	11	12	13	14	15
34 -	16	[17	18	19	20	21]	22

*	S	M	T	W	T	F	S
35 -	23	[24	25	26	27	28]	29
36 -	30	31	1	2	3	4	5
37 -	6	7	8	9	10	11	12
38 -	13	14	15	16	17	18	19
39 -	20	21	22	23	24	25	26

4th QUARTER 62 WKG DAYS

SEPTEMBER	OCTOBER	NOVEMBER
19 Wkg Days	20 Wkg Days	23 Wkg Days

*	S	M	T	W	T	F	S
40 -	27	28	29	30	31	1	2
41 -	3	(4)	5	6	7	8	9
42 -	10	11	12	13	14	15	16
43 -	17	18	19	20	21	22	23

*	S	M	T	W	T	F	S
44 -	24	25	26	27	28	29	30
45 -	1	2	3	4	5	6	7
46 -	8	9	10	11	12	13	14
47 -	15	16	17	18	19	20	21

*	S	M	T	W	T	F	S
48 -	22	23	24	25	26	27	28
49 -	29	30	31	1	2	3	4
50 -	5	6	7	8	9	10	11
51 -	12	13	14	15	16	17	18
52 -	19	20	21	22	(23)	(24)	25

* Week Number   [ ] Plant Shutdown   ( ) Holiday

THE FINANCE GROUP WILL DETERMINE THE INVENTORY DATES.

Figure C-15 (continued)

1978 PLANNING PARAMETERS

CODE NO	FIXED CODE	DEC	JAN	FEB	MAR	APR	MAY	JUN	JUL	AUG	SEP	OCT	NOV	TOTAL
1	MONTH	1	1	1	1	1	1	1	1	1	1	1	1	12
2	WEEK	4	4	5	4	4	5	4	4	5	4	4	5	52
3	DAY	19	18	24	20	20	25	19	13	20	19	20	23	52
4	HOUR	152	144	192	160	160	200	152	104	160	152	160	184	1,920

CODE NO	VARIABLE CODE	DEC	JAN	FEB	MAR	APR	MAY	JUN	JUL	AUG	SEP	OCT	NOV	TOTAL
1	INQUIRIES TARGET	12000	66000	60000	36000	24000	18000	12000	12000	12000	12000	24000	12000	300000
	INQUIRIES MINIMUM	10000	55000	50000	30000	20000	15000	10000	10000	10000	1000	20000	10000	250000
2	ORDERS REC. TARGET	4650	6010	6170	6790	4645	4000	6300	5850	4663	5935	5055	4833	64901
	ORDERS REC. MINIMUM	3582	4630	4753	5231	3579	3082	4854	4507	3592	4572	3894	3724	50000
3	PRODUCTION TARGET	4750	4500	6000	5000	5400	6750	5130	3510	5400	5130	5400	6210	63180
	PRODUCTION MINIMUM	3759	3561	4748	3957	4273	5341	4059	2777	4273	4059	4273	4920	50000
4	PTS ORDERS REC TARGET	6175	2755	5130	7790	13300	16340	8075	7125	6175	4940	11210	5985	95000
	PTS ORDERS REC MINIMUM	4550	2030	3780	5740	9799	12039	5950	5250	4550	3640	8260	4412	70000
5	2nd SHIFT 7½%													
6	3RD SHIFT 10%													

Figure C-15 (continued)

1978 PARAMETER DETAIL

ITEM	DEC	JAN	FEB	MAR	APR	MAY	JUN	JUL	AUG	SEP	OCT	NOV	TOTAL AVG
ORDERS RECEIVED													
Horse	3906	5108	5306	5771	3902	3360	5355	4972	4010	4689	4246	4060	54685
Pony	744	902	864	1019	743	640	945	878	653	1246	809	773	10216
TOTAL	4650	6010	6170	6790	4645	4000	6300	5850	4663	5935	5055	4833	64901
II. DISCOUNTS													
Customer	15%	10%	10%	10%	0%	0%	0%	20%	20%	20%	15%	15%	
Owner	20%	15%	15%	15%	5%	5%	5%	25%	25%	25%	20%	20%	
Dealer	34%	31%	25%	25%	25%	25%	30%	30%	30%	30%	34%	34%	
Parts	10%	10%	10%	10%	10%	10%	10%	10%	10%	10%	10%	10%	
III. PARTS ACTIVITY													
A. Sales													
T-B Parts	$ 28944	$30150	$ 50652	$127836	$130248	$235170	$145926	$ 95274	$ 82008	$ 62712	$142308	$ 74772	$1206000
Attach.	153984	51328	101052	104260	264660	247016	91428	115488	99448	83408	190876	101052	1604000
Old Tiller	1040	800	1800	2520	4840	6920	5760	4120	3640	1920	4320	2320	40000
TOTAL SALES $	$183968	$82278	$153504	$234616	$399748	$489106	$243114	$214882	$185096	$148040	$337504	$178144	$2850000
B. Orders Rec.	6175	2755	5130	7790	13300	16340	8075	7125	6175	4940	11210	5985	95000
IV. ATTACHMENTS-MIX													
HORSE													
PPT&H (1241)	3.4%	3.1%	3.7%	3.0%	3.5%	3.1%	4.0%	4.2%	3.9%	4.0%	3.5%	3.0%	3.5%
PP Only (1240)	.4%	.3%	.4%	.3%	.4%	.3%	.5%	.6%	.4%	.5%	.4%	.3%	.4%
CT&H (1243)	4.5%	5.0%	5.0%	5.5%	6.0%	6.0%	6.0%	5.8%	7.0%	6.5%	5.1%	5.0%	5.6%
CT Only (1242)	.5%	.5%	.5%	.7%	.8%	.8%	.6%	.9%	1.0%	1.3%	1.0%	.8%	.8%
Furr (1200)	1.4%	1.3%	1.4%	1.5%	1.6%	1.6%	1.6%	2.0%	1.4%	1.6%	1.6%	1.6%	1.5%
BTT	23.0%	24.0%	27.0%	33.0%	30.0%	32.0%	28.0%	31.0%	25.0%	30.0%	27.0%	25.0%	28.0%
DB&B (1343)	5.0%	4.8%	4.5%	4.0%	4.1%	4.0%	4.2%	4.5%	4.8%	5.2%	5.5%	5.0%	4.6%
BP (1419)	3.0%	3.0%	3.0%	4.0%	4.0%	4.5%	5.0%	5.0%	5.0%	6.0%	6.0%	6.0%	4.5%
H/F (1317)	46.0%	45.0%	45.0%	46.0%	47.0%	45.0%	46.0%	47.0%	45.0%	47.0%	46.0%	45.0%	46.0%
SP (1307)	1.5%	1.5%	1.5%	1.5%	1.5%	1.5%	1.5%	1.5%	1.5%	1.5%	1.5%	1.5%	1.5%
Chains (9146)	.4%	.4%	.4%	.4%	.4%	.4%	.4%	.4%	.4%	.4%	.4%	.4%	.4%
Carton	95.0%	95.0%	95.0%	95.0%	95.0%	95.0%	95.0%	95.0%	95.0%	95.0%	95.0%	95.0%	95.0%
PONY													
H/F (1356)	—	—	—	—	—	—	—	28.0%	26.0%	30.0%	26.0%	26.0%	27.0%
Carton	95.0%	95.0%	95.0%	95.0%	95.0%	95.0%	95.0%	95.0%	95.0%	95.0%	95.0%	95.0%	95.0%
V. PRODUCTION													
Horse	3990	3780	5040	4200	4536	5670	4309	2949	4536	4309	4536	5217	53072
Pony	760	720	960	800	864	1080	821	561	864	821	864	993	10108
TOTAL	4750	4500	6000	5000	5400	6750	5130	3510	5400	5130	5400	6210	63180

VI. TILLER-MIX

5 Std	12%
5 Elec	4%
6 Std	48%
6 Elec	15%
7 Kohler	21%
TOTAL	100%

Figure C-15 (continued)

1978 PROFIT PLAN SCHEDULE

BUDGETING/PLANNING GROUP SCHEDULE	ITEM	DUE DATE RETURN TO B.P. GROUP
8/23	A. 1978 Parameter Requirements	9/2
9/12	B. Aug. Responsibility Reports	
9/14-9/16	C. 1977 Parameters	
"	D. 9 mo's 1977 Dept. General Ledger	
"	E. Manpower Input Sheets	9/30
"	F. Major Expenditure Work Sheet	"
"	G. 1978 Budget Input Work Sheet	"
10/ 7	H. Manpower Printout #1	
"	I. Budget Worksheet Printout #1	
"	J. Budget Printout #1	
	K. Correction Input Sheets (H & I)	10/14
10/24	L. Manpower Printout #2	
"	M. Budget Worksheets Printout #2	
	N. Budget Printout #2	
10/31	O. Preliminary Package to Mgt.	
	P. Corrections as required	11/ 7
11/11	Q. Manpower Printout #3	
"	R. Budget Worksheet Printout #3	
"	S. Budget Printout #3	
11/14	T. Finalized Profit Plan	
	U. BOD corrections (if required)	11/16
11/21	V. Manpower Printout #4 (if required)	
"	W. Budget Worksheet Printout #4 (if required)	
"	X. Budget printout #4 (if required)	
11/25	Y. Load Computer	
12/ 5	Z. Finalized Profit Plan #2 (if required)	

Figure C-15 (continued)

MAJOR EXPENDITURES

1. All planned expenditures in excess of $200 should be included on this schedule, both capital and expense. Non-recurring expense items less than $200 should also be included.

2. All items should be identified by title with the amount being shown in the quarter (s) in which you expect it to be spent.

3. Each item in excess of $10,000 must be supported by an *attachment* justifying the expense. This should cover:
   A. °What° is being purchased?
   B. °Why° is it being purchased?
   C. Is this a °Cost Savings° project? If so, how much annually?
   D. What are the implications, if the planned purchase is not approved?

4. Major expenditure °expense° totals, by quarter, should be transferred to account #841 in the first month of that quarter. Exception: tooling, patterns and small tools should be transferred to their respective expense accounts.

Figure C-15 (continued)

MAJOR EXPENDITURES
CAPITAL & EXPENSE

DEPT. # _____

NAME _____

ITEM (Project No. Required)	1ST. QTR		2ND. QTR		3RD. QTR		4TH. QTR		TOTAL	
	CAP	EXP	CAP	EXP	CAP	EXP	CAP	EXP	CAP	EXP
TOTAL										
TRANSFER TOTAL EXPENSE TO A/C 841 IN MONTH SHOWN	/	841	/	841	/	841	/	841	/	/
	DEC		MAR		JUN		SEP			

Figure C-15 (continued)

MANPOWER SCHEDULE

1. Schedule by classification, all employees, by pay grade, for the *minimum* volume requirements.

2. This schedule should reflect all:
   A. Current employees
   B. New hires or transfers in
   C. Separations and/or transfers out
   D. Grade changes (promotions or otherwise)

3. All payroll costs will be budgeted at the midpoint of the employee's grade. Any additional budget required should be included on the budget worksheet.

Figure C-15 (continued)

BUDGET WORKSHEET

1. The Fixed and Direct Input should be used for budgeting to the minimum level. Variable Input should be used only for budgeting *above* the minimum level.

2. Fixed Input. Determine what timing sequence should be used. Show the fixed code. Show the fixed amount in whole dollars. This amount will be extended each month by the fixed code you have selected.

3. Variable Input. Determine which of the three (3) variable inputs affect your expense item. Show the variable code. Show the variable amount in cents ($1.25 as 1 25 or $10.25 as 10 25). This amount will be extended by the units *above* the minimum level each month.

4. Direct Input. Show the amount in whole dollars in the proper month.

5. Do not budget for:
   Fringe Account 330
   Depreciation Account 530
   Amortization Account 540
   Space Account 580

6. Shift. If your non-exempt workers are entitled to shift premium, show a Code 5 (second shift - 7½%) or a Code 6 (third shift - 10%) in the Variable Code column; *do not* show anything in the Variable Amount column.

Figure C-15 (continued)

1980 LONG RANGE PLAN

SELECTED OPERATING DATA
1976 – 1984

ITEM	ACTUAL 1976	ACTUAL 1977	1978	1979 PROFIT PLAN	1979 EST. AT	PROFIT PLAN 1980	PROFIT PLAN 1981	PROJECTIONS 1982	PROJECTIONS 1983	PROJECTIONS 1984
INCOME STATEMENT										
SALES										
PRODUCTION COST OF SALES										
GROSS MARGIN										
R&D (INCL B&P)										
PROFIT (BEFORE TAXES)										
ASSETS (END OF PERIOD)										
CURRENT ACCOUNTS RECEIVABLE										
PRODUCTION INVENTORIES										
GROSS INVENTORIES										
GROSS FIXED ASSETS										
NET FIXED ASSETS										
CUSTOMER PAYMENTS										
ASSETS EMPLOYED										
ASSETS (YTD AVERAGE)										
CURRENT ACCOUNTS RECEIVABLE										
PRODUCTION INVENTORIES										
GROSS INVENTORIES										
GROSS FIXED ASSETS										
NET FIXED ASSETS										
CUSTOMER PAYMENTS										
ASSETS EMPLOYED										
ORDERS & BACKLOG										
ORDERS RECEIVED (FUNDED)										
UNFILLED ORDERS										
OTHER DATA										
CASH FLOW										
SALES FOR ACCTS REC TURNOVER										
BID & PROPOSAL										
CAPITAL APPROPRIATIONS										
CAPITAL EXPENDITURES										
MANPOWER (YTD AVG.)										
SQUARE FOOTAGE (YTD AVG.)										
ENERGY COST										
DEPRECIATION										
SPARE PARTS ORDERS RECEIVED										
(INCLUDED IN TOTAL ORDERS RECEIVED ABOVE)										
PRETAX RATIOS										
RETURN ON SALES										
RETURN ON ASSETS										
ASSET TURNOVER										
COLLECTION PERIOD - CURRENT ACCOUNTS REC										
PRODUCTION INVENTORY TURNOVER										
GROWTH										
SALES – YEAR TO YEAR										
SALES – 3 YEAR RATE (ANNUALIZED)										
PROFIT – YEAR TO YEAR										
PROFIT – 3 YEAR RATE (ANNUALIZED)										

Figure C-16: SELECTED OPERATING DATA FOR LONG-RANGE PLANNING
(Courtesy of United Technologies.)

1978 PROFIT PLAN
PARAMETER REQUIREMENTS

RESPONSIBILITY	PARAMETER

President	1. *Fiscal Calendar 1978*
	   1. Holidays - number, when
	   b. Plant Shutdown
	   c. Month, Week, Days, Hours

Marketing	2. *Inquiries,* by month, for 1978 (target & minimum).

Marketing	3. *Order Analysis* - by month for 1978
	   a. Tillers - by
	     - Model (4P, 5P, 5E, 6S, 6E, 7K etc.)
	     - Customer Type (Mail order, Dealer, Owner, etc.)
	     - Location (Troy, DSC's, GWLC, etc.)
	   b. Parts and Service orders
	   c. Other - Two Way Cultivator, etc.

Marketing	4. *Probability of Unit Sales* for 1978
	   High ------------------------------Units 80,000
	   Target ----------------------------Units 60,000
	   Low ------------------------------Units 50,000

Marketing	5. *Sales Analysis* - by month for 1978
	   a. Tillers (Same as Orders #3-a)
	   b. Accessories as % of tiller sales
	   c. Parts and Service Net Sales
	   d. Other - Two Way Cultivator etc.
	     - Royalties

Marketing	6. *Selling Price Changes* for 1978 and when forecasted changes are to take place.
Marketing	7. *Discount Structure* for 1978 by customer type by month. Also by product line tillers, accessories, parts, etc.
Marketing	8. *Sales Incentives* such as coupons, give aways, etc. and when they are forecasted to be introduced.
Marketing	9. *Non Garden Way Products* sold from GWLC and DSC's. Net sales by month and Cost of Sales (5) for these products.
Manufacturing	10. *Units produced* - by month for 1978 a. Product Line - tillers (by model), accessories, service parts, etc.

Manufacturing	11. *Inventory Levels* - by location (GWLC, DSC's etc., by product line (horse, pony, accessories, service parts, etc) for:
	   a. Raw Material - Dollars Only
	   b. Work in Progress - Dollars Only
	   c. Finished Goods - Tiller Units, Dollars

President	12. *Payroll/Personnel*
	   a. Any forecasted COLA increases
	   b. 1978 mid-point for labor grades (exempt, non-exempt, and blue collar)

Finance/Marketing/ Manufacturing/ President	13. Organizational Chart for 1978

Figure C-17: PARAMETER REQUIREMENTS OF ANNUAL PROFIT PLAN
(Courtesy of Garden Way, Incorporated)

OPERATING PLAN FORECAST (Profit and Loss Projection)																				Name of Business
		Month 1			Month 2			Month 3			Month 4			Month 5			Month 6			
Revenue (sales)	Ind %	Estimate	Actual	%	Estimate	Actual	%	Estimate	Actual	%	Estimate	Actual	%	Estimate	Actual	%	Estimate	Actual	%	
Total Revenue (sales)																				
Cost of Sales																				
Total Cost of Sales																				
Gross Profit																				
Expenses																				
Salary expense: Sales people, office and other																				
Payroll Expenses (taxes, etc.)																				
Outside Services																				
Supplies (office and operating)																				
Repairs and Maintenance																				
Advertising																				
Car, Delivery and Travel																				
Accounting and Legal																				
Rent																				
Telephone																				
Utilities																				
Insurance																				
Taxes (real estate, etc)																				
Interest																				
Depreciation																				
Other Expenses (specify each)																				
Miscellaneous (unspecified)																				
Total Expenses																				
Net Profit																				

SBA FORM 1099 (8-75) REF: SOP 60 10 1

Figure C-18: OPERATING PLAN FORECAST
(Courtesy of Small Business Administration.)

For Period Ending																						
Month 7			Month 8			Month 9			Month 10			Month 11			Month 12			Totals				
Estimate	Actual	%	Estimate	Actual	%	Estimate	Actual	%	Estimate	Actual	%	Estimate	Actual	%	Estimate	Actual	%	Estimate	%	Actual	%

U.S. GOVERNMENT PRINTING OFFICE: 1975 O - 200-810

239

1979 LONG-RANGE PLANS
ACTUAL & PLANNED EARNINGS COMPONENTS BY
COMPANY _____

CATEGORY	YEAR	SALES		GROSS MARGIN		OPERATING EXPENSE		OTHER INCOME		INTEREST		EARNINGS	
		$000	%	$000	%	$000	%	$000	%	$000	%	$000	%
TOTAL OWNED RETAIL	1977												
	1978												
	1979												
	1980												
	1981												
	1982												
	1983												
COST DEPARTMENTS	1977												
	1978												
	1979												
	1980												
	1981												
	1982												
	1983												
LEASED DEPARTMENTS	1977												
	1978												
	1979												
	1980												
	1981												
	1982												
	1983												
TOTAL COMPANY	1977												
	1978												
	1979												
	1980												
	1981												
	1982												
	1983												

Figure C-19: LONG-RANGE PLANNING BY EARNINGS COMPONENTS

1979 LONG-RANGE PLANS
ACTUAL & PLANNED EARNINGS COMPONENTS BY

COMPANY _____

CATEGORY	YEAR	SALES $000	%	GROSS MARGIN $000	%	OPERATING EXPENSE $000	%	OTHER INCOME $000	%	INTEREST $000	%	EARNINGS $000	%
I. FASHION SEWING	1977												
	1978												
	1979												
	1980												
	1981												
	1982												
	1983												
II. SMALLWARES	1977												
	1978												
	1979												
	1980												
	1981												
	1982												
	1983												
III. FASHION ACCESSORIES	1977												
	1978												
	1979												
	1980												
	1981												
	1982												
	1983												
IV. READY-TO-WEAR	1977												
	1978												
	1979												
	1980												
	1981												
	1982												
	1983												
V. INTIMATE APPAREL	1977												
	1978												
	1979												
	1980												
	1981												
	1982												
	1983												

fig. #C-19

241

Figure C-19 (continued)

1979 LONG-RANGE PLANS
ACTUAL & PLANNED EARNINGS COMPONENTS BY

COMPANY _____

CATEGORY	YEAR	SALES		GROSS MARGIN		OPERATING EXPENSE		OTHER INCOME		INTEREST		EARNINGS	
		$000	%	$000	%	$000	%	$000	%	$000	%	$000	%
	1977												
	1978												
VI. CHILDREN'S	1979												
	1980												
	1981												
	1982												
	1983												
	1977												
	1978												
VII. MEN'S & BOYS'	1979												
	1980												
	1981												
	1982												
	1983												
	1977												
	1978												
VIII. FURNITURE, ETC.	1979												
	1980												
	1981												
	1982												
	1983												
	1977												
	1978												
IX. FASHION HOME FURN.	1979												
	1980												
	1981												
	1982												
	1983												
	1977												
	1978												
X. HOUSEWARES, ETC.	1979												
	1980												
	1981												
	1982												
	1983												

Figure C-19 (continued)

1979 LONG-RANGE PLANS
ACTUAL & PLANNED EARNINGS COMPONENTS BY

COMPANY _____

CATEGORY	YEAR	SALES		GROSS MARGIN		OPERATING EXPENSE		OTHER INCOME		INTEREST		EARNINGS	
		$000	%	$000	%	$000	%	$000	%	$000	%	$000	%
	1977												
	1978												
XI. MAJOR APPLIANCES	1979												
	1980												
	1981												
	1982												
	1983												
	1977												
	1978												
XII. MISCELLANEOUS	1979												
	1980												
	1981												
	1982												
	1983												
	1977												
	1978												
XIII. BUDGET STORE	1979												
	1980												
	1981												
	1982												
	1983												

Figure C-19 (continued)

19—LONG-RANGE PLANS
ACTUAL & PLANNED R.O.E. CALCULATION
COMPANY _____

WS-5

LINE NO		ACTUAL		LONG-RANGE PLANS				
		(1)	(2)	(3)	(4)	(5)	(6)	(7)
		1977	1978	1979	1980	1981	1982	1983
1	INVESTMENT							
2	CAPITALIZED LEASES							
3	TOTAL INVESTMENT (LINE 1 + LINE 2)							
4	EQUITY %	53.0	53.0	53.0	53.0	53.0	53.0	53.0
5	EQUITY (LINE 3 × LINE 8)							
6	EARNINGS AFTER INTEREST							
7	INCOME TAX COMPLEMENT	52.0	52.0	52.0	52.0	52.0	52.0	52.0
8	NET INCOME (LINE 6 × LINE 7)							
9	RETURN ON EQUITY (LINE 8 − LINE 5)							

Figure C-20: LONG-RANGE PLANNING OF RETURN ON EQUITY

1979 LONG RANGE PLANS
ACTUAL & PLAN STORE-FOR-STORE SALES CALCULATION

COMPANY _____

	(1)	(2)	(3)	(4)	(5)	(6)	(7)
ITEM	1977 ACTUAL	1978 ACTUAL	1979	1980	1981	1982	1983
1 GRAND TOTAL SALES IN CURRENT YEAR — $000							
A NAME:							
B NAME:							
C NAME:							
D NAME:							
E NAME:							
F NAME:							
G NAME:							
H NAME:							
I NAME:							
2 SALES IN ALL NEW STORES OPENED IN CURRENT YEAR (LINES A THRU I) — $000							
J NAME:							
K NAME:							
L NAME:							
M NAME:							
N NAME:							
O NAME:							
P NAME:							
Q NAME:							
R NAME:							
3 BEFORE ANNIVERSARY SALES OF NEW STORES OPENED IN PRIOR YR. (LINES J THRU R) — $000							
4 STORE-FOR-STORE SALES CURRENT YEAR (LINE 1 MINUS 2, MINUS 3) — $000							
5 PREVIOUS YEAR TOTAL SALES — $000*							
6 STORE-FOR-STORE % TY/LY (LINE 4 DIVIDED BY LINE 5)							

*IF A STORE IS CLOSED IN THE CURRENT YEAR, PREVIOUS YEAR SALES MUST BE REDUCED BY THE SALES ACHIEVED IN THAT STORE DURING THE PREVIOUS YEAR PERIOD COMPARABLE TO THE PERIOD THE STORE IS CLOSED IN THE CURRENT YEAR.

Figure C-21: LONG-RANGE SALES PROJECTIONS BY STORE

STORE LOCATION

☐ Preliminary   ☐ Spring

☐ Final   ☐ Fall   19 _____

Company _____

LINE NO.	(1) STORE LOCATION		(2) STORE OPENING MONTH/YEAR	(3) NET SALES $	(4) % CHG LY	(5) GROSS MARGIN %	(6) DIRECT EXPENSE $	(7) %
1		TY						
2		LY						
3		TY						
4		LY						
5		TY						
6		LY						
7		TY						
8		LY						
9		TY						
10		LY						
11		TY						
12		LY						
13		TY						
14		LY						
15		TY						
16		LY						
17		TY						
18		LY						
19		TY						
20		LY						
21		TY						
22		LY						
23		TY						
24		LY						
25		TY						
26		LY						
27	TOTAL ALL LOCATIONS	TY						
28		LY						

Rev: 3/78

METHOD OF INTEREST ALLOCATION: ☐ SALES   ☐ OTHER (SPECIFY) _____
    ☐ ASSET BASE

Figure C-22: EARNINGS PLAN BY STORE LOCATION

EARNINGS PLAN

Date Received by Corporate _____

(8) ALLOCATED EXPENSE %	(9) ALLOCATED INTEREST %	(10) OTHER INCOME %	(11) EARNINGS $	(12) %	(13) CENSUS 8101	(14) TOTAL	(15) SQUARE FOOTAGE SELLING	(16) TOTAL BLDG

WS-2

1979 LONG-RANGE PLANS
ACTUAL & PLANNED EARNINGS COMPONENTS BY LOCATION

COMPANY _____

STORE LOCATION	SQ FT 000	DATE OPENED	YEAR	SALES $000	%	GROSS MARGIN $000	%	OPERATING EXPENSE $000	%	OTHER INCOME $000	%	INTEREST $000	%	EARNINGS $000	%
			1976												
			1977												
			1978												
			1979												
			1980												
			1981												
			1982												
			1983												
			1976												
			1977												
			1978												
			1979												
			1980												
			1981												
			1982												
			1983												
			1976												
			1977												
			1978												
			1979												
			1980												
			1981												
			1982												
			1983												
			1976												
			1977												
			1978												
			1979												
			1980												
			1981												
			1982												
			1983												
			1976												
			1977												
			1978												
			1979												
			1980												
			1981												
			1982												
			1983												

Figure C-23: EARNINGS PROJECTIONS BY STORE LOCATION

248

SEASON'S EARNINGS PLAN SUMMARY

New Branch Store _____

Company _____

☐ Preliminary

☐ Final

☐ Spring

☐ Fall   19 _____

LINE		(1) PLAN $	(2) PLAN %	(3) SEASON ROI SUBMISSION $	(4) SEASON ROI SUBMISSION %	(5) 1ST YEAR ROI SUBMISSION $	(6) 1ST YEAR ROI SUBMISSION %
1	SALES SEASON						
2	GROSS MARGIN SEASON						
3	DIRECT OPERATING EXPENSE EXCL. PRE-OPENING SEASON						
4	OTHER INCOME SEASON						
5	EARNINGS BEFORE INTEREST AND TAXES SEASON						
6	PRE-OPENING EXPENSE SEASON						
7	ALLOCATED AND INTEREST EXPENSE SEASON						
8	NET EARNINGS BEFORE TAX SEASON						
9	STORE OPENING DATE	/ / DAY MONTH YEAR				/ / DAY MONTH YEAR	
10	SEASON SALES CONVERSION FACTOR						
11	MEMO: BASE SALES TRANSFER SALES						
13	TOTAL SALES						

DATE RECEIVED BY CORPORATE _____

Figure C-24: SEASON'S EARNINGS PLAN SUMMARY

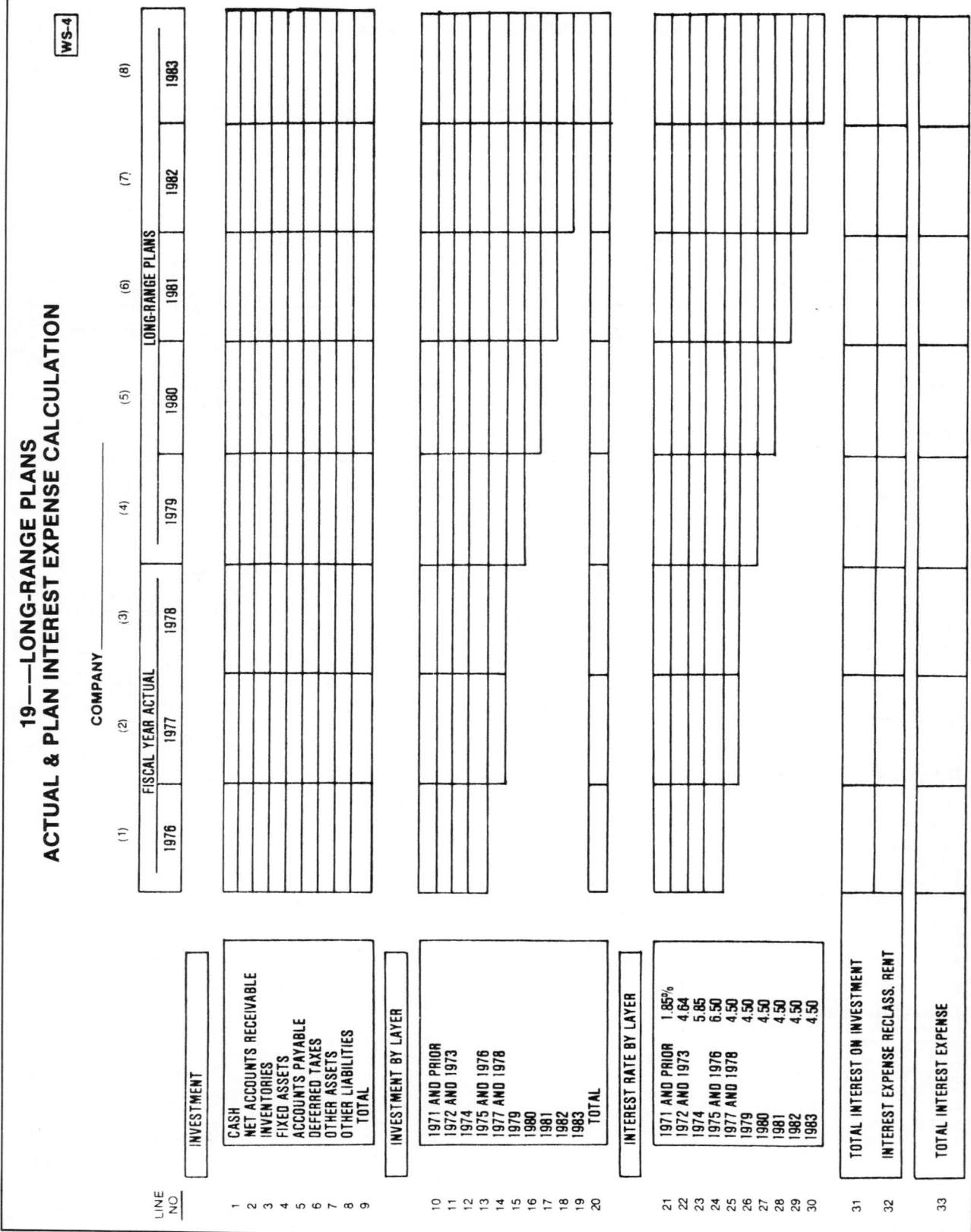

Figure C-25: LONG-RANGE PLANNING OF INTEREST EXPENSES

GARDEN WAY

Manpower Needs Forecast - Fiscal

Completed by: _____
Title: _____
Department: _____
Date: _____
Approved by: _____

Pay[1] Grade	Midpoint[2]	Current[3] Level	Dec	Jan	Feb	Mar	Apr	May	Jun	Jul	Aug	Sept	Oct	Nov
3	3.50	4	4	4	4	3	3	3	5	5	5	3	3	3
4	3.75	2	2	2	2	3	3	3	3	3	3	3	3	3
5	4.00	1	1	1	1	0	0	0	0	0	0	0	0	0
6	4.25	1½	1½	1½	1½	1½	1½	1½	1½	1½	1½	1½	1½	1½
VII	186.00	1	1	1	1	1	1	1	1	1	1	1	1	1
VIII	204.60	1	1	1	1	1	1	1	1	1	1	1	1	1
Total		10½	10½	10½	10½	9½	9½	9½	11½	11½	11½	9½	9½	9½

Months[4]

One part-time & one full-time employee.

Two temporary full-time people needed for the summer.

Instructions:

[1]Indicate non-exempt grades using Arabic numerals and exempt using Roman numerals.

[2]Use hourly rate for non-exempt and weekly rate for exempt personnel.

[3]Indicate the current number of employees in each pay grade. Count part-time people as ½ and temp. full-time as 1.

[4]Show your monthly staffing needs in each pay period.

Figure C-26: MANPOWER NEEDS FORECAST

251

GARDEN WAY

Manpower Needs Forecast - Fiscal

Supporting Comments

1. Comment on adequacy of your MP staffing:
   For the past 12 months _____

   _____

   _____

   Currently _____

   _____

   _____

2. What changes in objectives or business activity do you foresee for your department in the next fiscal year: _

   _____

   _____

   _____

   _____

3. What major assumptions have you made in making your estimates? _____

   _____

   _____

   _____

4. What are the possible technological impacts on your department? _____

   _____

   _____

5. What existing manpower skills are likely to increase the most in your department? _____

   _____

   _____

6. What new manpower skills are likely to be needed in your department? _____

   _____

7. What existing manpower skills are likely to be reduced or eliminated in your department? _____

   _____

   _____

8. *Special skill and professional requirements.* This section should be completed for all exempt positions and non-exempt positions in pay grade 7 or above.

   Use additional sheets if necessary.

Number Required	Position	Probable Recruitment from within Yes or No	Date Required
1.			
2.			
3.			
4.			

Figure C-26 (continued)

SURVEY and PROJECTIONS

	5 YEARS AGO		THIS YEAR		2 YEARS HENCE		5 YEARS HENCE	
● AVE. No. EMPLOYEES IN:								
• MANUFACTURING								
• ADM. & CLERICAL								
• SELLING & DISTRIBUTION								
• INTERNATIONAL								
• ALL OTHERS								
● AVE. TOTAL PAYROLL IN:								
• MANUFACTURING								
• ADM. & CLERICAL								
• SELLING & DISTRIBUTION								
• INTERNATIONAL								
• ALL OTHERS								
● PERCENT CHGE. IN No. EMPLOYEES								
● PERCENT CHGE. IN PAYROLL								
● NET SALES								
● EQUITY AT END OF PERIOD ____ AS % OF TOTAL PAYROLL:								
• MANUFACTURING								
• ADM. & CLERICAL								
• SELLING & DISTRIBUTION								
• INTERNATIONAL								
• ALL OTHERS								
● FRINGE BENEFITS AS % OF PAYROLL								
● AVE. No. DAYS ABSENT PER EMPLOYE								
● PAYROLL COST OF ABSENTEEISM ____ AND AS % OF TOTAL PAYROLL								

Figure C-27: SURVEY AND PROJECTIONS CHECKLIST

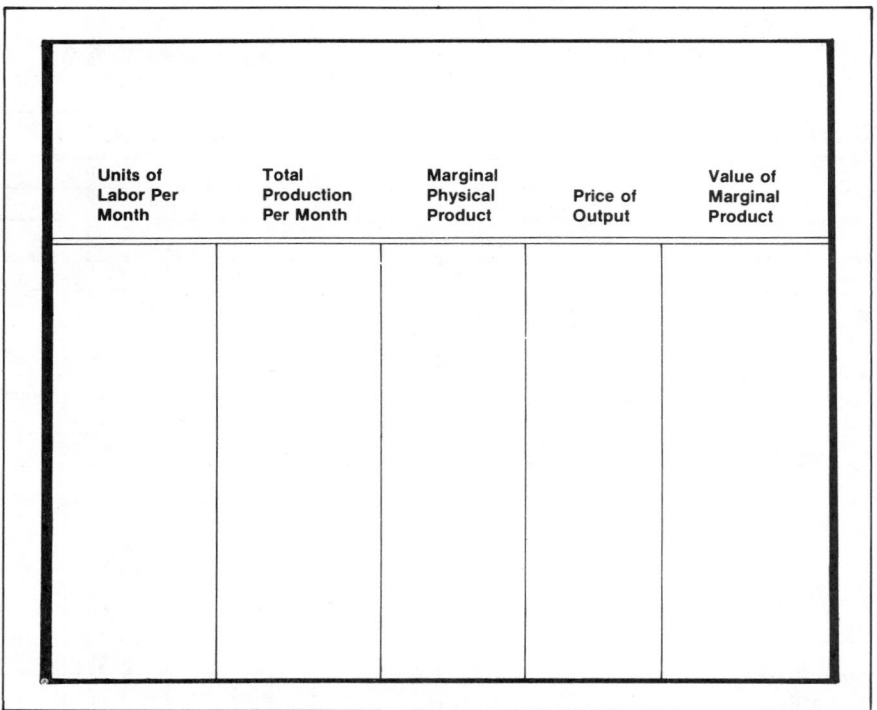

Units of Labor Per Month	Total Production Per Month	Marginal Physical Product	Price of Output	Value of Marginal Product

Figure C-28: COMPUTATIONS OF VALUE OF MARGINAL PRODUCT

CAPITAL EXPENDITURES PROJECT NO. _____

COMPANY _____ DATE _____

DIVISION _____ PLANT _____

TITLE

DISTRIBUTION OF COST	ESTIMATED COST	SCHEDULE OF EXPENDITURES BY YEARS	PRESENT-ESTIMATE
Investment			
Expense			
TOTAL ESTIMATED COST			
Date work scheduled to begin			
Estimated date of completion		Equipment available – 19___	

Additional capacity _____ New product _____ Betterment or replacement _____ | Essential ____ Desirable ____

DESCRIPTION OF PROJECT

PURPOSE AND NECESSITY (including estimated savings etc.)

Prepared by _____ Date _____

Figure C-29: CAPITAL EXPENDITURES FORECAST

(From the book Corporate Treasurer's and Controller's Handbook by L. Doris, Editor. © 1950 renewed 1978 by L. Doris, Editor. Published by Prentice-Hall, Inc., Englewood Cliffs, New Jersey 07632.)

CAPITAL EXPENDITURES FORECAST SUMMARY OF INDIVIDUAL PROJECTS

FORM _____

PREPARED BY _____

APPROVED _____

COMPANY _____

DIVISION _____

DATE _____

PROJECT NO	DESCRIPTIVE TITLE	ESSENTIAL OR DESIRABLE (E or D)	TOTAL ESTIMATED COST	DISTRIBUTION OF ESTIMATED COST		SCHEDULE OF ESTIMATED EXPENDITURES				
				INVESTMENT	EXPENSE	19 —	19 —	19 —	19 —	19 —

Figure C-30: CAPITAL EXPENDITURES FORECAST SUMMARY
(From the book Corporate Treasurer's and Controller's Handbook by L. Doris, Editor. © 1950 renewed 1978 by L. Doris, Editor. Published by Prentice-Hall, Inc., Englewood Cliffs, New Jersey 07632.)

EVALUATION AND RISK ANALYSIS OF INVESTMENT PROJECTS

Name of Project	Benefit-Cost Ratio	Expected Return	Expected Variance	Expected Capital Outlay	Cumulative Capital Outlay	COVARIANCE							
						1	2	3	4	5	6	7	
1													1
2													2
3													3
4													4
5													5
6													6
7													7

Figure C-31: EVALUATION RISK ANALYSIS OF INVESTMENT PROJECTS

257

FIRM:

FOR YEARS ENDING:

	198A	198B	198C	198D
GROSS SALES, REVENUE				
COST OF GOODS SOLD				
OPERATING EXPENSES				
OPERATING INCOME				
EARNINGS BEFORE INTEREST & TAXES				
FIXED CHARGES				
PRE-TAX EARNINGS MARGIN				
NET EARNINGS AFTER TAXES				
PREFERRED DIVIDEND REQUIREMENTS				
TOTAL ASSETS (LESS DEPR. RES.)				
INVESTED CAPITAL				
LONG TERM OBLIGATIONS				
PREFERRED STOCK (IF APPLICABLE)				
OWNERS' EQUITY				
CURRENT ASSETS				
CURRENT LIABILITIES				
NET WORKING CAPITAL				
PROPERTY ACCOUNT (GROSS)				
RES. DEPRECIATION & DEPLETION				
PROPERTY ACCOUNT (NET)				
INVENTORIES				
DEPRECIATION & DEPLETION EXPENSES				
MARKET VALUE:				
TOTAL INVESTMENT				
NET WORTH				
COMMON STOCK EQUITY				

A blank financial analysis worksheet form with the following row labels:

PERCENT BONDS IN INVESTED CAPITAL
PERCENT PREFERRED IN INVESTED CAP.
PERCENT COMMON IN INVESTED CAPITAL

WORKING CAPITAL PER $1,000 BOND

TIMES FIXED CHARGES EARNED:
    BEFORE TAXES
    AFTER TAXES
TIMES PREFERRED DIVIDENDS EARNED

PERCENT EARNED ON INVESTED CAPITAL

CURRENT RATIO
OPERATING RATIO
PCT. DEPR. EXP. ON PPTY. (GROSS)
PLANT TURNOVER (NET)
SALES-TO-FINAL INVENTORIES
RECEIVABLES TURNOVER

PCT. GROWTH IN SALES (OVER PREV.YR.
PERCENT PRE-TAX MARGIN
PCT. NET INCOME-TO-SALES
PCT. EARNED ON COMMON STK. EQUITY
SALES-TO-INVESTED CAPITAL
MANAGEMENT RATE OF RETURN
CASH FLOW-TO-DEBT
NET PROFITS ON WORKING CAPITAL

AVE. MARKET PRICE, COMMON STOCK
EARNINGS PER SHARE, COMMON STOCK
PCT. CHGE. IN EPS (OVER PRIOR YR.)
DIVIDEND PER SHARE, COMMON
DIVIDEND PAYOUT RATIO
DIVIDEND YIELD RATIO

Figure C-32: INDUSTRIAL SECURITY FINANCIAL ANALYSIS

FINANCING INVESTMENT WITH LOAN

Interest Rate _____ %   Method of Depreciation _____

Discount Rate _____ %   Total Amount of Loan $ _____

Tax Rate _____ %   Total Investment $ _____

Investment or Project _____

End of Year	Payments on Debt	Implied Interest Cost (_____%)	Savings on Interest (Tax _____%)	Depreciation	Savings on Depreciation (Tax _____%)	Total Tax Savings	Net Cash Outflow	Present Value of Cash Outflow (Discount _____%)

Figure C-33: ANALYSIS FOR FINANCING INVESTMENT WITH LOAN

ANNUAL LOAN HISTORY

*SEE REVERSE SIDE FOR TRANSACTION CODE EXPLANATION

| LOAN NUMBER | YEAR | | | | | | BEGINNING BALANCE | ESCROW | PRINCIPAL |

TRANSACTION CODE*	TRANSACTION DATE	DUE DATE	TRANSACTION AMOUNT	PRINCIPAL AMOUNT	ESCROW AMOUNT	INTEREST AMOUNT	OTHER AMOUNT	AFTER TRANSACTION	
								ESCROW BALANCE	PRINCIPAL BALANCE

YEAR	OTHER BALANCE	HAZARD INSURANCE	TAXES PAID	INTEREST PAID	LATE CHARGES	ESCROW BALANCE	LOAN BALANCE

LOAN NUMBER

STATEMENT DATE

ESCROW ANALYSIS

ESCROW ITEMS	CODE	ESTIMATED ANNUAL AMOUNTS	NEXT DUE	MOS. SINCE PAID	MONTHLY AMOUNT	ESCROW BALANCE REQUIRED	
						AFTER	PAYMENT

TOTALS →

PROJECTED ESCROW BALANCE AFTER YOUR   PAYMENT →

AMOUNT   ← TOTAL AMOUNT REQUIRED

ESCROW ADJUSTMENT

LOAN NUMBER

PRINCIPAL AND INTEREST PAYMENT	NEW MONTHLY ESCROW REQUIREMENT	1/12 ESCROW SHORTAGE	OTHER PAYMENT	NEW MONTHLY PAYMENT AMOUNT	YOUR NEW PAYMENT	CHANGE EFFECTIVE WITH PAYMENT DUE
+	+	+	=			

PLEASE MARK YOUR LOAN COUPON BOOK ACCORDINGLY

Figure C-34: MORTGAGE LOAN HISTORY REPORT
(Courtesy of Burroughs Corporation Office Products Group/Business Forms Division.)

261

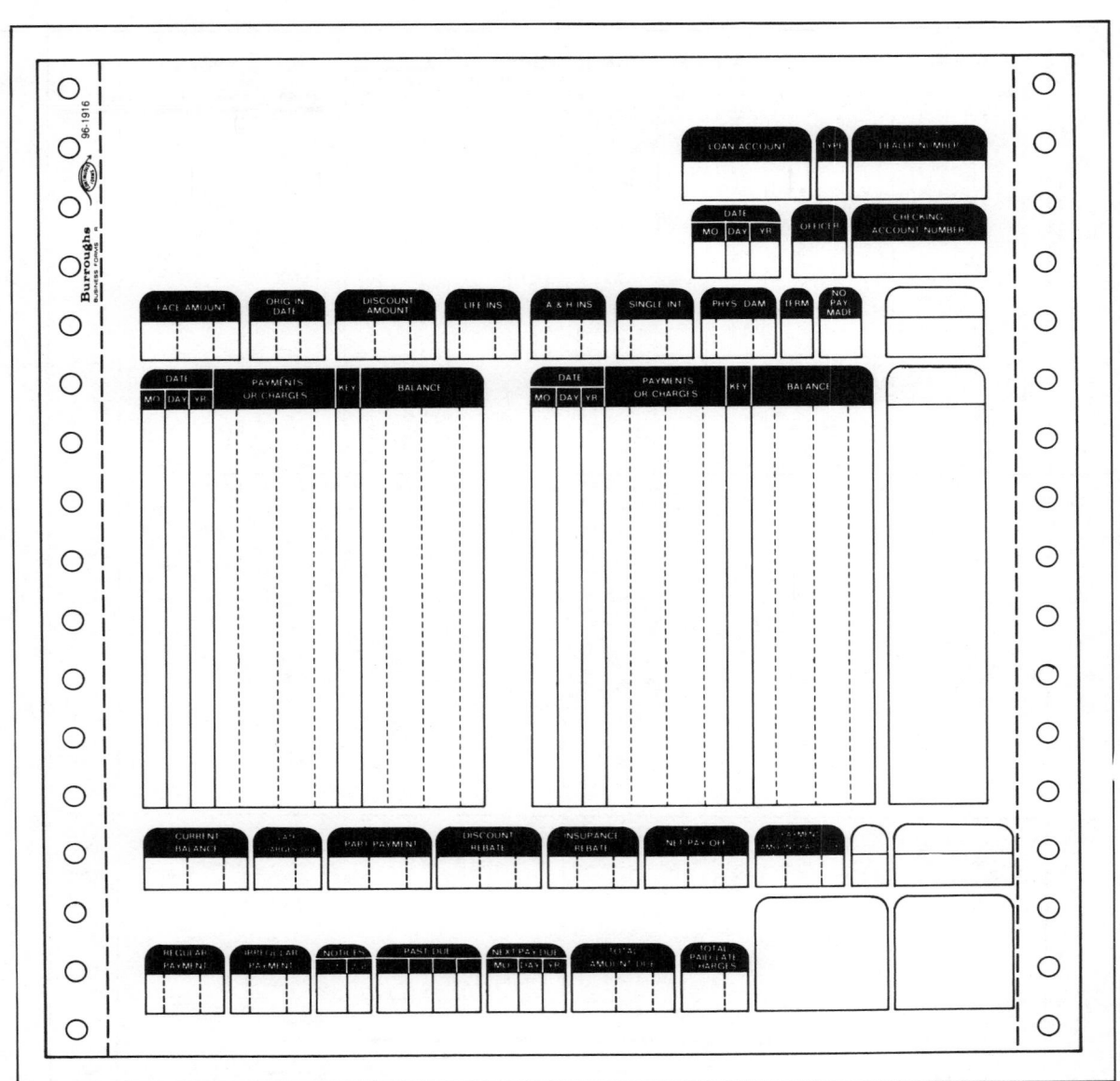

Figure C-35: INSTALLMENT LOAN HISTORY REPORT
(Courtesy of Burroughs Corporation Office Products Group/Business Forms Division.)

262

ANALYSIS OF ALTERNATIVE FINANCING SOURCES

SOURCES OF FUNDS	TIME FRAME ON USE	FORM OF FINANCING AVAILABLE	RISK TAKEN BY SOURCE	FACILITIES FOR MASS FINANCING	EXTENT OF MANAGEMENT COUNSEL	AVAILABILITY OF FUNDS
Intercompany	Medium	Debit	Shared	Limited		Variable
Suppliers	Short	Open Acc't	Med-High	Restricted	Some	Stable
Customers						
Employees	Short	Notes	High	Limited	None	Variable
Equity						
Debt Market	Long	Bonds	High	Substantial	Indirect	Cyclical
Life Ins. Cos.	Med-Long	Debt mostly	Moderate to Low	Substantial	Some	Steady
Development Corporations						
Int'l Lending Agencies						
Investment Cos.						
Pension Funds						
Commercial Banks						

Figure C-36: ANALYSIS OF ALTERNATIVE FINANCING SOURCES

INVOICE SUMMARY

Forecast Period _____

Receipts for Month of _____

Invoice In	To / From	Bbls	Lifting #	Date Lifted	Date Due	Amount Due
	Third Party /					

Figure C-37: INVOICE SUMMARY AND FORECAST

Request For Quotation
Inquiry Only
This Is Not An Order

To:

1 :

To:

2 :

To:

3 :

Summary Of Quotations				
Item	Quantity	No. 1	No. 2	No. 3
Other Information				
Delivery				
F.O.B.				
Terms				

Inquiry No.

Date

To Receive Consideration, Your Quotation Must
Be Received By

Please Quote Unit Price, Shipping Point, Terms, F.O.B. and delivery on the following:

Item	Quantity	Description and Delivery Required

Special Notice to Vendor

1. IF UNABLE TO QUOTE, PLEASE ADVISE AT ONCE AND RETURN BLUE PRINTS, SPECIFICATIONS, ETC.
2. SHOW ABOVE INQUIRY NUMBER ON ALL QUOTATIONS.
3. ITEMIZE ALL UNIT PRICES, DISCOUNTS, TERMS AND CHARGES. SHOW TAXES SEPARATELY, IF APPLICABLE.

4. ATTACH COMPLETE SPECIFICATIONS FOR ANY SUBSTITUTIONS OFFERED.
5. WE RESERVE THE RIGHT TO ACCEPT OR REJECT YOUR QUOTATION.
6. ALL QUOTATIONS SUBJECT TO ACCEPTANCE ON OUR USUAL PURCHASE ORDER FORM.

By _____

WilsonJones GRAYLINE FORM 44-152 4-PART © 1976 · PRINTED IN U.S.A.

Request
For Quotation 44-152

GrayLine SNAP-A-WAY FORM

Figure C-38: REQUEST FOR UNIT PRICE QUOTATION

Quotation

ELECTRO-METHODS, INCORPORATED
P. O. BOX 54   330 GOVERNORS HIGHWAY
SO. WINDSOR, CONNECTICUT 06074

DATE:

QUOTATION NO. ✱   874

YOUR INQUIRY NO.

In response to your inquiry, we submit the following quotation:

QUANTITY	DESCRIPTION	PRICE

TERMS:	F.O.B.	ESTIMATED SHIPPING DATE:

**We are a small business as defined by the Small Business Administration.
We are an Equal Opportunity Employer.**

By _____

Figure C-39: QUOTATION
(Courtesy of Electro-Methods, Inc., South Windsor, Connecticut.)

RAPIDFORMS® NO. 25103
PROPOSAL

REORDER FROM ~~REGENT~~ STANDARD FORMS, INC., INTERSTATE INDUSTRIAL PARK, BELLMAWR, N.J. 08030

Proposal

Page No. of Pages

BELLAIRE ALUMINUM PRODUCTS INC.
3945 14th ST. W.
BRADENTON, FLORIDA 33505
PHONE 746-2141

PROPOSAL SUBMITTED TO		PHONE	DATE
STREET		JOB NAME	
CITY, STATE AND ZIP CODE		JOB LOCATION	
ARCHITECT	DATE OF PLANS		JOB PHONE

We hereby submit specifications and estimates for:

SAMPLE FORM ONLY
REGENT STANDARD FORMS, INC

We Propose hereby to furnish material and labor — complete in accordance with above specifications, for the sum of:

________________ dollars ($ __________).

Payment to be made as follows:

All material is guaranteed to be as specified. All work to be completed in a workmanlike manner according to standard practices. Any alteration or deviation from above specifications involving extra costs will be executed only upon written orders, and will become an extra charge over and above the estimate. All agreements contingent upon strikes, accidents or delays beyond our control. Owner to carry fire, tornado and other necessary insurance. Our workers are fully covered by Workmen's Compensation Insurance.

Authorized Signature __________

Note: This proposal may be withdrawn by us if not accepted within __________ days.

Acceptance of Proposal — The above prices, specifications and conditions are satisfactory and are hereby accepted. You are authorized to do the work as specified. Payment will be made as outlined above.

Signature __________

Date of Acceptance: __________

Signature __________

FORM 2510 REGENT FORMS, BELLMAWR, N.J. 08030

Figure C-40: PROPOSAL AND ACCEPTANCE
(Courtesy of Regent Standard Forms, Inc., Bellmawr, New Jersey 08031.)

	STOCK NUMBER	DESCRIPTION	COST	SELLING PRICE	DATE		DATE		DATE		DATE		
					ON HAND	ORDERED	ON HAND	ORDERED	ON HAND	ORDERED	ON HAND	ORDERED	
1													1
2													2
3													3
4													4
5													5
6													6
7													7
8													8
9													9
10													10
11													11
12													12
13													13
14													14
15													15
16													16
17													17
18													18
19													19
20													20
21													21
22													22
23													23
24													24
25													25
26													26
27													27
28													28
29													29
30													30
31													31
32													32
33													33
34													34
35													35
36													36
37													37
38													38
39													39

Figure C-41: STOCK CONTROL AND PLANNING RECORD
(Copyright by Wilson Jones Company. All rights reserved. Forms may be obtained, subject to supply, from Wilson Jones Company, 6150 Touhy Avenue, Chicago, Illinois 60648.)

PURCHASE REQUISITION   NO. _____

PLEASE PURCHASE THE FOLLOWING   DATE _____
FOR DELIVERY NOT LATER THAN _____

QUANTITY	MATERIAL OR PART NUMBER	DESCRIPTION
		SIGNED _____

QUANTITY ON HAND _____   ORDER NO. _____

AVERAGE MONTHLY USAGE _____   DATE OF ORDER _____

DESIRED MAXIMUM _____

DESIRED MINIMUM _____   VENDOR _____

Figure C-42: PURCHASE REQUISITION
(From the book Cost Accounting for Small Manufacturers, 2nd Edition, by R. Lee Brummet and Jack C. Robertson, © 1972. Published by Small Business Administration.)

Inventory 44-292

GrayLine SNAP-A-WAY FORM

Inventory

Page No. _____

_____ 19 _____

Sheet No. _____

Department _____ Priced By _____ Checked By _____

Location _____ Extended By _____ Checked By _____

Called By _____ Entered By _____ Totalled By _____ Examined By _____

Quantity	Unit	Description/Stock Number	Price	Unit	Extension	Time In Stock	Marked Down Value		√
							Price	Extension	
		Brought Forward							
		Carried Forward							

Figure C-43: INVENTORY PRICING AND MARKDOWNS

ANNUAL DEMAND SAFETY STOCK TIME DISTRIBUTION

DIVISION ANNUAL DEMAND	NUMBER OF ITEMS	MINIMUM DEMAND IN LINES	ANNUAL DEMAND		SAFETY STOCK IN MONTHS
			LINES	DOLLARS	
A					
B					
C					
D					
E					
F					
G					
TOTAL					

Figure C-44: ANNUAL DEMAND SAFETY STOCK TIME DISTRIBUTION

A L E R I O N . S T A N D A R D S . C O .

INVENTORY CONVERSION

CONVERT _1.60_ MONTHS ON HAND TO INVENTORY DOLLARS FOR _May_

1.00	=	100% of _June_	forecasted sales at cost	$_85,000_
+ 0.60	=	_60_% of _July_	forecasted sales at cost	$_60,000_
+	=	___% of _____	forecasted sales at cost	$_____

_1.60_ = inventory for month of _May_ $_145,000_

CONVERT _1.65_ MONTHS ON HAND TO INVENTORY DOLLARS FOR _June_

1.00	=	100% of _July_	forecasted sales at cost	$_100,000_
+ 0.65	=	_65_% of _August_	forecasted sales at cost	$_55,000_

_1.65_ = inventory for month of _June_ $_155,000_

CONVERT _1.77_ MONTHS ON HAND TO INVENTORY DOLLARS FOR _July_

1.00	=	100% of _August_	forecasted sales at cost	$_85,000_
+ 0.77	=	_77_% of _September_	forecasted sales at cost	$_115,000_

_1.77_ = inventory for month of _July_ $_200,000_

COMMENTS:

Figure C-45: CONVERTING MONTHS ON HAND TO INVENTORY DOLLARS

WORKSHEET FOR IMO %
($000)

PR-16
WORKSHEET

☐ PRELIMINARY _____ DATE

☐ FINAL _____ DATE

TIES WITH PR-3 _____

DATED _____

☐ Spring
☐ Fall _____ 19 _____

Company _____

LINE	PLAN						LAST YEAR					
	MONTH			CUMULATIVE			MONTH			CUMULATIVE		
	COST (A)	RETAIL	%	COST (A)	RETAIL	%	COST	RETAIL	%	COST (A)	RETAIL	%
	(1)	(2)	(3)	(4)	(5)	(6)	(7)	(8)	(9)	(10)	(11)	(12)
BEG. INV. BEFORE DEDUCTION OF CASH DISCOUNT												
LESS: BEG. DISC RESERVE	( )			( )						( )		
BOS INVENTORY AND IMO INCL. CASH DISCOUNT												
FEBRUARY PURCHASES												
MARCH PURCHASES												
APRIL PURCHASES												
MAY PURCHASES												
JUNE PURCHASES												
JULY PURCHASES												
AUGUST PURCHASES												
SEPTEMBER PURCHASES												
OCTOBER PURCHASES												
NOVEMBER PURCHASES												
DECEMBER PURCHASES												
JANUARY PURCHASES												

(A) COST PURCHASES LESS PLANNED/ACTUAL CASH DISCOUNT TAKEN.

Rev: 2/79

DATE RECEIVED BY CORPORATE _____

Figure C-46: PROJECTED PURCHASES WORKSHEET

ALERION · STANDARDS · CO ·

Post Office Box 341266
Miami, Florida 33134 U.S.A.

INVENTORY DISTRIBUTION REQUIREMENTS PLANNING

	MARCH	APRIL	MAY	JUNE	JULY
REVIEW TIME					
LEAD TIME					
SAFETY STOCK TIME					
REORDER POINT TIME					
ON HAND					
ON ORDER					
DEMAND FORECASTED					
REORDER POINT					
CURRENT AVAILABLE					
PURCHASE ORDER					
PLANNED NEEDS					
SCHEDULED DELIVERY					

COMMENTS:

Figure C-47: INVENTORY DISTRIBUTION REQUIREMENTS PLANNING

ASSET ACQUISITIONS, LEASING, AND MERGERS FOR GROWTH

SECTION D FORMS

Asset Acquisitions, Leasing, and Mergers for Growth

Asset Acquisitions, Leasing, and Mergers for Growth

Organizations commonly state growth as an objective, perhaps the only objective, of the enterprise. Necessary to growth are cost controls, profit protection, and financial planning aimed at providing an orderly method for meeting growth objectives.

Growth reflects sustained increases in profits and value of the firm. Expansion, on the other hand, can result from equipment replacement, additional capacity, or acquisitions, which do not necessarily produce greater efficiencies, more profits per unit of input, or a rise in profits that occurs year after year. Growth is not simple expansion. But expansion is usually necessary to meet growth objectives; and that hangs on analysis of capital expenditures or acquisition of productive facilities.

Questions that any firm sooner or later must answer deal with replacement of existing equipment. When is the best time to replace? Should replacement be with technologically superior equipment that requires training employees for new skills or should the firm acquire equipment and processes similar to what is already existing? Should new equipment and facilities be purchased with an expenditure of surplus capital; should funds be borrowed and from where and how; or should equipment be leased, and, if so, for how long? Can a corporation, through acquisitions of or mergers with other firms, acquire the necessary production expertise and favorably shift the learning experience curve, or gain new markets, or neutralize competition; and what will be the synergistic effect of an acquisition or merger? Will the firm grow and increase profits?

The data base for answers to these questions derives from organized efforts to control costs, analyze profit decisions, and plan financial resource use. These are the inputs for asset acquisition, leasing, merger analysis, real estate transactions (Section E covers real estate) and accumulation of funds (see Section F for more on investment instruments) necessary to implement these decisions.

D-1   When should assets be replaced? In the form (D-1), the method of Analysis for Asset Replacement evaluates one possible system with another. Presumably each system spins on different capital-labor ratios in production of the same group of products. Or extending it, the analysis can include related products. Nevertheless, the final comparison is in *cash flow,* which reflects differences in costs and profits. Of course, data must be generated on net income and costs for input into this synoptic form.

D-2   Another approach (D-2) tackles the same problem, still comparing costs and annual revenues and profits, but it focuses on purchases of new equipment versus equipment now **D-3**   in use rather than including an examination of other alternatives. The next design (D-3) slightly varies the informational structure developed in the preceding form (D-2).

Both worksheets set forth the initial cash outflows. Both assume the usual flow in investment decisions; viz., that acquisition obliges use of funds when the investment materializes, and that income and profits generated from the investment will occur in future periods. Thus, the present outlay of funds is not discounted, the present value being equal to the actual amount, while future inflows are discounted according to the rate and time period applied to these flows. (Chapter 2 of the *Handbook of Financial Mathematics, Formulas, and Tables,* by Robert P. Vichas, published by Prentice-Hall, Inc., goes into considerable detail on present value computations with lucid examples.)

Tax adjustments, except for tax credits, do not arise in new equipment calculations, but a loss or gain in the sale of existing equipment will warrant adjustment to establish the total value of outflows of funds. The incremental approach is employed for revenue analysis. The analyst wants to know by how much REVENUES WILL INCREASE (not total revenues) with new equipment and/or how much COSTS ARE REDUCED in order to derive total return or benefits.

D-4   The Total Project Approach to Net Present Value (D-4), more appropriate in the capital budgeting process, takes into account a larger volume of outlays from the financial management and planning viewpoint. This technique, although similar to information preserved in the previous forms (D-2, D-3), is more akin to purposes of the system analysis (D-1). Capital budgeting marshals large commitments of funds whose PROFIT POTENTIAL extends well into an unforeseeable and uncertain future. The budgeting process should include:

- ◆ an appraisal of competition in order to forecast especially adverse effects on revenue and profits;
- ◆ an examination of effects on total costs of capital with large commitments of funds;
- ◆ an exposure of management problems which may erupt if too many projects are undertaken simultaneously.

These points do not appear on the financial profile but ought to form part of the total assay of investments.

For projects starting or ending within a given period under analysis, the Preliminary Capital Budget (D-5) relates to timing of implementation of selected projects within a definite period, such as the three-year period illustrated in the form. Horizontally, the form subsumes repairs and replacements, increased production, improvement in quality, administrative requirements, and employee safety and welfare on the job. Preliminary budgets are not final commitments; therefore, each proposal must be reviewed and defended and then considered within the context of total use of funds. Blanket authorization for smaller outlays does not dictate the more elaborate corporate review process; the bottom half of the form wraps up these relatively small outlays.

D-5

In reviewing the many replacement, new asset, and project proposals, management may rank them in a Prospective Investments Schedule (D-6) according to projected rate of return (or any other criterion selected). The enterprise may have a cutoff rate below which rates of return are unacceptable and investment proposals are discarded. Not all those at or above the cutoff rate necessarily will be accepted because of total resource constraints. Management may juggle investment decisions in order to MAXIMIZE RETURN to the enterprise because investments normally occur in indivisible chunks. Consequently, a high-return project may be dropped in favor of a lower-return one in order to most effectively employ total financial resources.

D-6

Long-range planning of capital allocations (D-7) may be approached on a store-by-store basis with capital expenditures listed for each location and major remodeling requirements for each retail center. This form begins with data on current and previous years with projections five years hence. Such investment decisions hinge partly on an analysis of space usage (D-8) in the recent past and forecasted needs five years forward.

D-7

D-8

Another input for capital budgeting decisions may include a Census Plan by Account (D-9). This six-page worksheet compares this year's performance of cost centers against last year's under 180 headings and subheadings for each subsidiary of the enterprise. Accumulation of such data is, of course, part of *cost control* (covered in Section A), but conclusions wrought from this information aid in *long-range financial planning* for GROWTH THROUGH ASSET ACQUISITIONS.

D-9

Accumulation of these cost data may result not in asset acquisitions but in a Capital Asset Dismantlement Report (D-10). The report shows reasons and authorization for disposition or dismantlement of equipment, financial history of the asset, how the asset was disposed of, and costs associated with disposition or dismantlement.

D-10

Equipment acquired or services requested is supported by a Request form (D-11). Note the amount of information required on this one-page form:

D-11

(a)   A control number.
(b)   Title of the request.

(c)   Requesting person, department, and location.
(d)   Brief description of the request.
(e)   Need for the equipment or service. (Notice emphasis on benefit, i.e., *cost saving,* with supporting documentation.)
(f)   Target date and *reason for* date selected.
(g)   Department head approval, data, and attached supporting data.

The next section of the form is completed by a technical or commercial subcommittee. The supporting details are attached; *cost analysis* summary data included on the form are:

(a)   one-time, nonrecurring costs;
(b)   equipment cost;
(c)   recurring costs—annual operating details.

The last section of the request is completed by a committee secretary. The reviewed request is either rejected, deferred, approved unconditionally, or approved with modification.

D-12

D-13

The Request for Funds (D-12), analogous to the preceding form (D-11), exacts a description of the investment and justification for expenditure, cost details, and a breakdown of cost information by category: Capital, Expense, and Accounting. The Request for Capital Expenditure (D-13) elicits details on material, labor, and other costs, with notations on the disposition of replaced assets. On the Request for Appropriation for Capital Expenditure form (D-14), reason for the expenditure, cost outlay and expense details, savings anticipated, estimated completion date and cash outlays required occupy the blank spaces.

D-14

In all of these forms (D-11 through D-14), the common requirement centers on *cost.* How much will it cost? And BENEFIT! Will acquisition of the new asset or investment in the project REDUCE COSTS, or INCREASE PROFITS, or if neither, then how else will it *benefit* the organization and CONTRIBUTE TOWARD MEETING OBJECTIVES? The other significant feature of the procedure and review process for developing better answers emanates from project approval assigned to levels within the enterprise. The purpose, of course, is to control capital expenditures—not to thwart them—but to achieve controlled growth by expending funds only on reviewed and approved projects and assets, by avoiding unnecessary or uncontrollable expenditures over the long run, by preventing avoidable extensions of the planned budget, by requiring adequate attention to benefit-cost analysis, and by applying the ancient principle that abundance is the result of restraint and *self-discipline.*

D-15

After a request for an expenditure has been approved, the authorization for expenditures follows, or a single form may combine Appropriation Request and Authority (D-15). The heading of this form allows for additional details on leasing (discussed next in this section) if the asset is not purchased. Further details identify the group or division and department, asset classification, amount of appropriation, *annual lease rate* and *lease duration, payback period* and *discounted rate of return.* Both division and corporate approval is required.

Although tentative corporate approval may be granted for plans of a general nature, action on the actual budgeted investment cannot proceed until an Authorization for Expenditure (D-16) receives appropriate *recommendations* at various levels before receiving *final approval* at the corporate level. The Authorization for Capital Expenditure (D-17), another example, highlights certain factors, with a TIME-SAVING *check-the-box system*. The entire process focuses on *control:* control of costs, profits, resource use, growth. Control means not to limit but to plan, to proceed with a reason and objective.

D-16

D-17

With go-ahead in hand, control is not tossed out with planning but follows each step of acquisition or production. A Purchase Requisition (D-18), issued to request materials or services related to the approved capital expenditure, signals the purchasing agent to buy parts and supplies of a specified quality at the best possible price. He or she may want to issue a Request for Quotation (D-19) in shopping for price and ability to perform. When satisfied with the results, a Purchase Order (D-20) follows, with terms and conditions of purchase stipulated.

D-18

D-19
D-20

Surveillance of company assets is perhaps the most important control procedure in the review and acquision stages. Two likely examples of forms are Property Ledger Control Sheet (D-21) and an Asset Record (D-22). The former lists several asets on each sheet; the latter lists a separate asset on each sheet. Generally, on such records will appear at least certain essential data:

D-21
D-22

(a) The asset description and assigned number of identification.
(b) Classification and other identification for repairs, replacement, guarantees, and internal control.
(c) Acquisition data for accounting and tax purposes: cost, date of acquisition, authorization number, economic life, freight costs, installation expenses, salvage value.
(d) Other data for investment credit and tax reduction: investment credit allowed, economic life and methods of depreciation, depreciation rate.
(e) Control information: location, department, building number, floor, and periodic physical verification.
(f) Costs, repairs, and betterments.
(g) Profit data: cost, salvage value, trade-in value, date asset became operative, i.e., income producing.
(h) Record of costs and repairs, depreciation reserves, and net asset book value on various dates.

Raising funds for asset acquisitions is another matter. (Investment instruments are treated in further detail in Section F.) It may mean selling your spouse's jewelry. To gain some idea of its value, the jewelry is first appraised (D-23). Of course, the jewelry may be one of the organization's assets, which is appraised periodically for insurance purposes.

D-23

It may be advantageous to refund an outstanding obligation to profit from market changes as well as acquire additional capital. Because refinancing is not a costless

D-24   operation, Refunding Calculations (D-24), to weigh net saving or net cost due to refunding, together with other planning tools, reinforce financial management decisions.

D-25   To record a security purchase or sale (D-25) for control purposes, on the form are listed both buyer and seller, issue name and date, coupon and maturity date, and the *yield-to maturity rate*. Also shown are the par value, accrued interest, discount or premium rate and amount, total cost, an assigned safekeeping cost, depository bank, and additional comments surrounding the transaction.

D-26
D-27   If capital is raised for ASSET ACQUISITION AND GROWTH through equity participation, common stock (D-26) is issued. Or short-term funds may be borrowed on a Promissory Note (D-27) as an interim measure. (Naturally, it is imprudent to finance fixed assets purchases with short-term funds; but short-term funds may be needed to supplement working capital due to the asset acquisition or to replace a temporary cash
D-28   drain.) Funds lent require adequate control and record-keeping (D-28), the same as handling and care of funds received.

D-29   An alternative to acquisition of assets is leasing. Before examining several forms relating to leasing, the Projection Film Report Form (D-29) actually refers to rentals; but notice that each rented asset, a film in this case, is subjected to an analysis of its condition, focus, defects, etc.—anything that may adversely affect profits. The other point analyzed is time, because *timing affects profits* through scheduling and customer satisfaction. Leasing requires no less attention than renting.

To lease or not centers not entirely on purchase versus lease questions because the alternative to leasing may well entail borrowing to acquire necessary assets. There are advantages to owning. There are advantages to leasing that may favor the latter by a wide margin. (For a discussion of the advantages of owning and leasing and the mathematics of comparing leasing with buying and borrowing, see the *Handbook of Financial Mathematics, Formulas, and Tables* by Robert P. Vichas, published by Prentice-Hall, Inc., Chapter 8, and for discounted cash flow methodology, Chapter 2.)

D-30   If a lessor earns a 28 percent return on investment and the borrowing rate to the prospective lessee is 14 percent, should not the potential lessee borrow and buy instead of lease in order to capture the rent, or difference, that would accrue to the lessor? The Lease or Buy (D-30) decision is not that simply arrived at. There are costs of ownership other than the cost of borrowed funds, and some of these costs depend upon laws which influence depreciation, investment credits, tax rates, and deductible expenses which alter profits. In the final analysis the effect on profits, not interest rate differentials alone, determines the net advantage (or disadvantage) of owning or leasing. The Lease-Borrow
D-31   Analysis (D-31) begins with two basic elements: time and applicable discount rate(s). Timing refers to inflow and outflows, the discount rate to opportunity costs. Other elements, including interest and tax rates, are then factored into the analysis.

Computations for Borrowing versus Leasing are modeled (D-32) with computation of the **D-32** present value of the tax shield from depreciation (Column 1). The example employs Sum-of-the-Years' Digits, but any appropriate depreciation method or rate applies. For computational purposes, the salvage value may equal book value, unless more precise market data are forecasted; the present values of these data appear in Column 2. The Net Present Value is the initial outlay plus present values of the salvage values minus present values of the tax shield. In this example probabilities are assigned on how long the asset may actually be used, periods less than the economic or lease life of the equipment. Columns 5 and 7 compare expected present values of buying versus leasing.

The next form, an Annual Profile for Buying versus Leasing Computations (D-33), **D-33** demonstrates Net Present Value analysis as a DECISION-MAKING TOOL. This example excludes explicit financing costs from the capital budgeting process. Lease payments and tax shield are discounted at a lower after-tax borrowing rate of the firm. Results balance the net present value of buying against the net present value of leasing flows. The net present value of buying is the sum of the present values of the asset's net after-tax cash operating profits plus the discounted after-tax salvage value minus original asset cost. The net present value of leasing flow is the present values of net after-tax cash operating profits minus after-tax present values of lease payments. The problem also may be approached by computation of the Present Values of Future Earnings (D-34). **D-34**

The Financial Benefits of a Non-Leveraged Lease Transaction to the Lessor format (D-35) examines the lease from the other end, the lessor, rather than the lessee. Under this **D-35** type of financial lease, the lessor uses its own funds entirely to purchase equipment for lease based upon availability of funds and projected rate of return. That is, the lessor engages in the same kind of investment planning and asset acquisition decisions, evidenced earlier in this section and in the preceding section, that any non-financial business enterprise cranks out. The form shown is one approach to decision-making from the lessor's viewpoint. The Financial Summary of Lease Results (D-36) computes **D-36** nominal and effective annualized rates of return on an after-tax basis.

Leasing does not substitute for under-capitalization. A lessor will churn out the same type of credit analysis (D-37) for leasing as it will for financing a purchase. Data from the five- **D-37** page Input Statement Control Sheet are subjected to computer analysis programmed for ratio analysis pertinent to the type and conditions of lease and industry within which the firm operates.

Both the Input Statement Control Sheet (D-37) and the Individual Leasing Record (D-38) **D-38** focus on motor carrier and truck leasing. The Individual Leasing Record records details on the type and use of equipment, acquisition costs, amount and length of lease, whether property is subject to investment credit, and economic life of the equipment. In this example, to place a specific piece of equipment under lease, the ILR form is completed, and the rental cost is tied to the prime lending rate so that over the lease period the cost of equipment is based on the average cost of funds for the period.

D-39
The lessor, in this instance, funds acquisitions through commercial paper issues. With the *leveraged financial lease,* contrasted with the non-leveraged lease, lessors borrow from third parties a substantial portion of the funds needed. A pandect of lease terms and transaction balances emerges in a Lease Obligation Computation (D-39), which supplies a continuous record of the loan balance, principal and interest.

Lawyer-consultant Richard Contino writes, "Capital equipment leasing is one of the most complex forms of financing in existence today. It involves sophisticated concepts often understood only by experts." A manager of a leasing company, in correspondence to this writer, states, "One objection to leasing that potential lessees often express is that the paperwork is complicated."

D-40
The Master Leasing Agreement (D-40) illustrated simplifies complex leasing matters. The procedure described grants the lessee a revolving line of credit that allows him to add and replace equipment as needed up to the maximum amount of credit granted. Since the rental rate floats with the prime rate, lessees can reduce down-side risks under a long-term lease when nominal interest rates are high and discourage long-term contracts.

Some *key elements* of a *lease* are:

- an unconditional promise to pay rents;
- the net lease to the lessor;
- hold harmless provisions;
- insurance protection;
- tax indemnity;
- termination values;
- casualty values;
- control of equipment sublease;
- true lease requirements (according to IRS rulings).

D-41
FINANCING GROWTH through issues of debt, common stock, mortgage obligations, or some other channel depends on comparative flotation costs (D-41). A referential analysis highlights transaction costs, likely acceptance of the issue (reflected in the discount or premium), and total net proceeds to the firm. For comparative purposes it seems more convenient to restate net proceeds and net costs on a per-unit basis, and issue transaction costs as a percentage of gross proceeds.

D-42
The Cost and Income Approaches for New Asset Acquisitions (D-42) are brought together in the illustrated nine-page form with lease analysis and option to purchase. Justification of expenses treated on the fifth page is followed by an explication of derivation of the overall capitalization rate. The mortgage-equity technique employed recognizes mortgage financing and equity yields. Assumptions are then stated. The last page condenses the results of valuation by various techniques—the Inwood technique, the mortgage-equity technique, and the income approach with figures rounded—all of which appear to produce approximately the same answer.

In merger and acquisition analysis, the main point is determination of the value of the firm. What's it worth? Using one of several acceptable approaches, each of which will yield a different answer, one determines the present value of future earnings (D-43) under varying assumptions of flows and discount rates. The going-business approach normally is more practical than one which relies on residual values of a defunct operation.

D-43

The first step in this approach calls for a forecast of earnings over some period, not a task taken lightly. The next is to estimate the residual value of the acquired firm after the payout period. The third step mandates a choice among several reasonable discount rates according to apparent financial risk, business risk, and inflation risk. The fourth is to calculate the present values of the forecasted income flows under the different discount rates assumed. From the total of present values subtract the amount of cash (if any) the buyer must advance at the time of acquisition to pay off obligations or for whatever reason. The final figures will signal a range of what may be a fair or reasonable price—at least one with which you can begin haggling.

Company cash flows (D-44), projected with and without the proposed acquisition, rank high in *decision-making* and *strategy formulation*. Computation of total cash drain and net cash available is a *useful analytical tool*. The form begins with sources of cash, viz., earnings after taxes plus depreciation and amortization. Uses of cash refer to any asset or equipment purchase that absorbs cash plus reduction of any liabilities. The cash position for each period equals the cash balance at the beginning of the period plus or minus the cash surplus or deficit for that same period.

D-44

Proposed acquisitions should fall within the enterprise's strategy for achieving its goals, preferably established by a written policy statement such as the one exhibited (D-45), with minimal financial criteria specifically set forth so that management will not waste time on undesirable acquisition prospects. Requirements other than financial ones, too, should be clearly understood. The illustrated Acquisition Criteria and Policy Checklist serves as ground rules when implementing corporate policy on external growth.

D-45

The last form in this series is a ten-page Acquisition Proposal (D-46) employed by a company that actively considered an acquisition candidate. The outline followed in the evaluation process was:

D-46

(a)   statement on minimal financial criteria;
(b)   description of activities of candidate and projections;
(c)   list of short-term advantages of acquisition;
(d)   list of long-term possibilities resulting from acquisition;
(e)   recommendation of the analyst;
(f)   appended material:
    (i)   assumptions used in calculations;
    (ii)   income projections by location;
    (iii)   company-wide five-year plan;
    (iv)   retail stores five-year plan;
    (v)   five-year cash flow analysis;
    (vi)   mail order division five-year plan.

ANALYSIS FOR ASSEST REPLACEMENT

BY: _____ DATE: _____

REMARKS: _____

	SYSTEM 1	SYSTEM 2	SYSTEM 3	SYSTEM 4
NET INCOME				
FOR 198A:				
ADD. TAXABLE INCOME OVER SYS.#1				
TAX LOSS				
NET TAXABLE INCOME (DIFFERENCE)				
EXTRA INCOME TAX OVER SYST. #1				
NET INCOME (DIFFERENCE)				
FOR 198B - 198A:				
ADD. TAXABLE INCOME OVER SYS. #1				
EXTRA INCOME TAX OVER SYSTEM #1				
NET INCOME (DIFFERENCE)				
COSTS				
DEPRECIATION				
PROPERTY TAXES				
RENTAL COSTS				
OTHER COSTS				
TOTAL				
CASH FLOW				
FOR 198A:				
NET INCOME DIFFERENTIAL				
DEPRECIATION DIFFERENTIAL				
TOTAL				
FOR 198B - 198A:				
NET INCOME DIFFERENTIAL				
DEPRECIATION DIFFERENTIAL				
TOTAL				

Figure D-1: ANALYSIS FOR ASSET REPLACEMENT

CALCULATIONS FOR ASSET REPLACEMENT

DEPT. _____ EQUIPMENT _____ NO. _____ BY _____ DATE _____

	AMOUNT BEFORE TAXES	AMOUNT AFTER TAXES	YEAR OCCURS	PRESENT VALUE FACTOR @ ____%	PRESENT VALUE
COSTS					
COST OF NEW EQUIPMENT					
SALVAGE VALUE OF OLD EQUIPMENT					
TAX (LOSS) GAIN ON SALE OF OLD EQUIPMENT					
PRESENT VALUE OF TOTAL COSTS (outflow of funds)					
ANNUAL RETURNS					
INCREASE IN SALES					
COST SAVINGS					
ANNUAL DEPRECIATION—NEW EQUIPMENT					
ANNUAL DEPRECIATION—OLD EQUIPMENT					
SALVAGE VALUE—OLD EQUIPMENT					
PRESENT VALUE OF TOTAL RETURNS (inflow of funds)					
PRESENT VALUE OF TOTAL COSTS MINUS TOTAL RETURNS					

Figure D-2: FORM FOR CALCULATIONS OF ASSET REPLACEMENT DECISIONS

REPLACEMENT DECISION

SUMMARY OF CALCULATIONS

	AMOUNT BEFORE TAX	AMOUNT AFTER TAX	YEAR(S) RECORDED	PRESENT VALUE FACTOR @ _____ %	PRESENT VALUES
Investment Outflows:					
New Equipment Purchase					
Residual Value of Old					
Tax Gain (Loss) on Sale					
PRESENT VALUE OF COSTS (Total Outflows)					
Annual Income (Inflows):					
Increase in Sales					
+ Cost Savings					
TOTAL BENEFITS					
Annual Depreciation (New)					
Annual Depreciation (Old)					
Salvage Value (New)					
PRESENT VALUE OF GAINS					
DIFFERENCE IN PRESENT VALUES					
ACTION RECOMMENDED:					

Figure D-3: REPLACEMENT DECISIONS ANALYSIS

	P V DISCOUNT FACTOR @			TOTAL PRESENT VALUE		
I. REPLACEMENT						
II. NONREPLACEMENT						
◆ I. R E P L A C E M E N T						
INITIAL INVESTMENT						
SALVAGE VALUE, END OF YEAR ___						
REPAIR/MAINTENANCE FOR ___ YEARS						
RECURRING CASH OPERATING COSTS						
→ PRESENT VALUE OF NET CASH OUTFLOWS						
◆ II. N O N R E P L A C E M E N T						
SALVAGE VALUE, END OF YEAR ___						
REPAIR/MAINTENANCE FOR ___ YEARS						
RECURRING CASH OPERATING COSTS						
OVERHAUL, END OF YEAR ___						
→ PRESENT VALUE OF NET CASH OUTFLOWS						
→ DIFFERENCE FAVORING REPLACE. (+)						

Figure D-4: TOTAL PROJECT APPROACH TO NET PRESENT VALUE

PRELIMINARY CAPITAL BUDGET

Unit _____

ITEMS	PROJECTED COSTS BY PERIOD					PROJECTED COSTS BY CATEGORY				
	Prior Year	This Year	Next Year	Second Year	Third Year	Additional Facilities	Replace-ments	Rehabil-itations	Repairs	Other Exp.
Required Capital Additions (Mktg.)										
Repairs and Replacements										
Capital Additions (Quality improve.)										
Investments (Cost-reduction req.)										
Administrative Requirements										
Expenditures for Safety/Health Imp.										
TOTAL OF ABOVE										

Items less than $ _____

Repairs and Replacements										
Capital Additions (Marketing)										
Capital Additions (Quality)										
Capital Additions (Cost-reduction)										
Administrative Requirements										
Safety/Health Improvement										
TOTAL OF ABOVE										
TOTAL OF ALL INVESTMENTS										

Figure D-5: PRELIMINARY CAPITAL BUDGET

PROSPECTIVE INVESTMENTS SCHEDULE

DATE OF PROPOSAL: 11/11/198?   CUTOFF RATE: 20%

RANKING METHOD: NPV   (in millions)

PREPARED BY: J Corcoran

NATURE OF PROJECT OR TITLE	AMOUNT OF FUNDS REQUIRED	CUMULA-TIVE TOTAL	RATE OF RETURN
1. Kanwa River Project	3.5	3.5	43%
2. Pleasantville Plant Expansion	1.8	5.3	31%
3. Energy Acquisition	10.1	15.4	28%
4. Office Bldg. (Cincinnati)	7.9	23.3	27%
5. Purchase of railway cars	2.0	25.3	23%
6. Purchase of Leased Space (N.Y.)	8.3	33.6	21%
7. Modernization of Auto Parts Div. Eq.	27.7	61.3	19%
8. Rhoden joint venture proposal	2.1	63.4	17%
9. Garden Center Marketing Program	0.3	63.7	11%
10. Installation of Pollution Control Eq.	2.6		06%
11. Purchase yacht, exec. & sales use.	1.1		06%

Figure D-6: PROSPECTIVE INVESTMENTS SCHEDULE

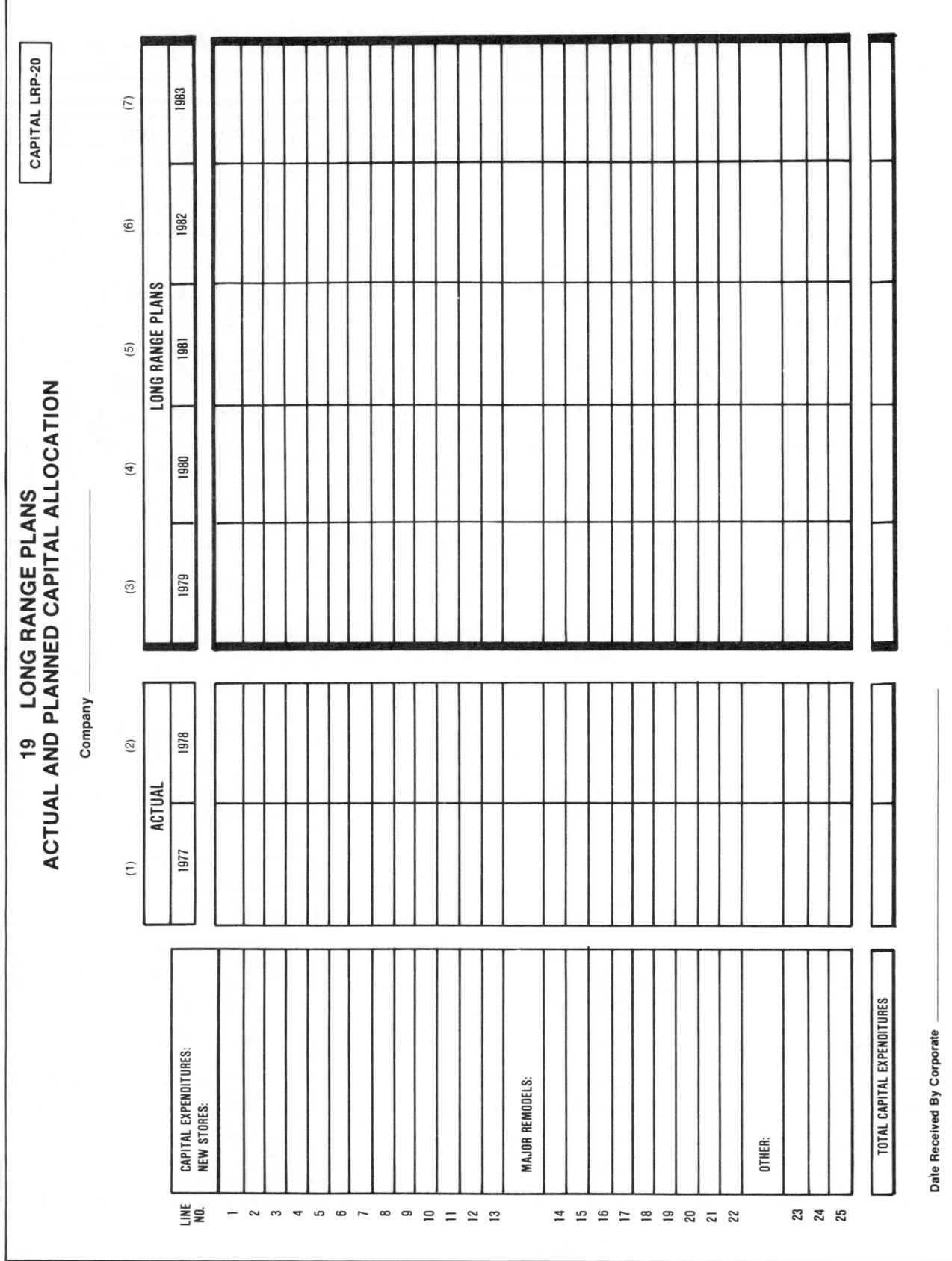

Figure D-7: ACTUAL AND PLANNED CAPITAL ALLOCATION

19 LONG RANGE PLANS
WORKSHEET FOR ANNUALIZED SQUARE FOOTAGE

WS-6

COMPANY _____

LINE NO.	STORE LOCATIONS	DATE OPEN/CLOSE	ANNUALIZED SQUARE FEET OF GROSS BUILDING AREA						
			1977 ACTUAL	1978 ACTUAL	1979	1980	1981	1982	1983
1	DOWNTOWN STORE								
2	WAREHOUSE STORE								
A	TOTAL DOWNTOWN AND WAREHOUSE STORE								
1									
2									
3									
4									
5									
6									
7									
8									
9									
10									
11									
12									
13									
14									
15									
16									
17									
18									
19									
20									
B	BRANCH STORES								
C	TOTAL COMPANY ANNUALIZED SQ. FT. (LINES A & B)								

Figure D-8: WORKSHEET FOR ANNUALIZED SQUARE-FOOTAGE USAGE

DETAIL CENSUS PLAN BY ACCOUNT

Company _____

☐ Spring

☐ Preliminary

☐ Fall   19 _____

☐ Final

		(1)	(2)	(3)	(4)		(5)	(6)
		PLAN			LY		B/(W) THAN LAST YEAR	
	EXPENSE CENTER	TY TOTAL	NEW STORES	EXISTING STORES	TOTAL		EXISTING STORES	TOTAL
1101	Gen. Manager & Assts.							
1103	Research Dept.							
	TOTAL 1100							
1151	Security							
1152	Shortage Control							
1153	Fitting Room Checkers							
1154	Employee Package Checkers							
	TOTAL 1150							
	GEN. MGMT. — TOTAL 1000							
2111	Controller & Assts.							
2112	General Accounting							
2114	Inventory Work							
	TOTAL 2110							
2151	Mail and Messengers							
	TOTAL 2151							
2252	Payroll Office							
	TOTAL 2250							
2301	Invoice Office, Excl. Whse							
2303	Accounts Payable							
	TOTAL 2300							
2501	Sales Audit							
	TOTAL 2500							
2601	Administration							
2602	Operations							
2603	Input (Central)							
2604	Input (Central)							
2605	Input (Central)							
2606	Input (Central)							
2607	Input (Central)							
2608	Input (Central)							

DATE RECEIVED BY CORPORATE _____

Figure D-9: DETAIL CENSUS PLAN BY ACCOUNT

DETAIL CENSUS PLAN BY ACCOUNT

Company _____

☐ Preliminary
☐ Final

☐ Spring
☐ Fall   19 _____

	EXPENSE CENTER	PLAN (1) TY TOTAL	PLAN (2) NEW STORES	PLAN (3) EXISTING STORES	LY (4) TOTAL	B/(W) THAN LAST YEAR (5) EXISTING STORES	B/(W) THAN LAST YEAR (6) TOTAL
2609	Input (Central)						
2610	Input (Central)						
	TOTAL 2600						
	CONTROL — TOTAL 2000						
3211	Charge Authorization						
	TOTAL 3210						
3221	Ac/Rec & File Maintenance						
	TOTAL 3220						
3231	Bill Adjustment						
	TOTAL 3230						
3311	Credit Mgrs. & Assts.						
3312	New Account Mgrs.						
3313	Credit Lobby						
3314	Credit Card Service Center						
	TOTAL 3310						
3321	Collections & P/L Accounts						
3322	Collection						
	TOTAL 3320						
3331	Cashier's Office						
3332	Mail Pay Bill Cashiers						
3333	Lay Away & COD						
	TOTAL 3330						
	CREDIT — TOTAL 3000						
4201	Publicity Dir. & Assts.						
4211	Artists, Photog. & Layout						
4212	Copywriters						
4213	Production						
4214	Publicity Cost Admin.						
	TOTAL 4200						

DATE RECEIVED BY CORPORATE _____

Figure D-9 (continued)

DETAIL CENSUS PLAN BY ACCOUNT

Company _____

☐ Spring

☐ Preliminary

☐ Fall   19 _____

☐ Final

	EXPENSE CENTER	PLAN			LY	B/(W) THAN LAST YEAR	
		(1) TY TOTAL	(2) NEW STORES	(3) EXISTING STORES	(4) TOTAL	(5) EXISTING STORES	(6) TOTAL
4241	Radio Advertising						
4242	Radio Copywriter						
	TOTAL 4240						
4251	Direct Mail						
	TOTAL 4250						
4261	Telev. Adv. Dir. & Assts.						
4262	Television Copywriters						
4263	Television Production						
	TOTAL 4260						
4301	Fashion Office						
4302	Special Events						
	TOTAL 4300						
4411	Display Mgr. & Assts.						
4412	Interiors & Windows						
4413	Craftsmen						
	TOTAL 4410						
4451	Sign Shop						
	TOTAL 4450						
4601	Eagle Stamp						
	TOTAL 4600						
	PUBLICITY — TOTAL 4000						
5111	Gen. Oper. Mgr. & Assts.						
5112	Planning						
5113	Warehouse Mgr. & Assts.						
	TOTAL 5100						
5201	Supply Purchase						
	TOTAL 5200						
5251	Print Shop						
	TOTAL 5250						

DATE RECEIVED BY CORPORATE _____

Figure D-9 (continued)

DETAIL CENSUS PLAN BY ACCOUNT

Company _____

☐ Preliminary

☐ Final

☐ Spring

☐ Fall   19 _____

	EXPENSE CENTER	(1) PLAN TY TOTAL	(2) PLAN NEW STORES	(3) PLAN EXISTING STORES	(4) LY TOTAL	(5) B/(W) THAN LAST YEAR EXISTING STORES	(6) B/(W) THAN LAST YEAR TOTAL
5501	Telephone Service						
	TOTAL 5500						
5701	Cleaning						
	TOTAL 5700						
5811	Maintenance Office						
5812	Carp., Painter & Plasters						
5813	General Maintenance						
	TOTAL 5810						
	OPERATIONS — TOTAL 5000						
6101	Pers., Empl., & Training						
6102	Special Trainee Account						
	TOTAL 6100						
6301	Medical Center						
6302	Employee Services						
	TOTAL 6300						
	PERSONNEL — TOTAL 6000						
7301	Receiving						
7303	Traffic Office						
7306	Return to Vendors						
7308	Freight Elevators						
7310	Checking & Marking						
	TOTAL 7300						
7501	Transfer Room						
7502	Drivers (Inc. Relay Drs.)						
	TOTAL 7500						
	MERCH. HANDLING — TOTAL 7000						
8051	Retail Dept. Managers						
8052	Cost Dept. Managers						
8053	Other Selling Supervision						
	TOTAL 8050						

DATE RECEIVED BY CORPORATE _____

Figure D-9 (continued)

DETAIL CENSUS PLAN BY ACCOUNT

Company _____

☐ Preliminary

☐ Final

☐ Spring

☐ Fall   19 _____

	EXPENSE CENTER	PLAN			LY	B/(W) THAN LAST YEAR	
		TY TOTAL	NEW STORES	EXISTING STORES	TOTAL	EXISTING STORES	TOTAL
8101	Retail Depts.						
8102	Cost Dept.s						
8103	Courtesy Shopper						
8104	Cosmetics						
8105	Vendor Sell. Credits						
8106	Commissions						
	TOTAL 8100						
8201	Stock Clerks						
	TOTAL 8200						
8251	Bridal Bureau						
8252	Personal Shoppers						
8253	Other Selling Services						
8254	General Adj. Bureau						
8255	Furniture Adj. Bureau						
8256	Exchange Desks						
8257	Customer Rtn. Goods Bm.						
8259	Customer Service - Misc.						
8260	Passenger Elevator Oper.						
	TOTAL 8250						
8341	Mail & Telephone Orders						
	TOTAL 8340						
8451	Free Customer Parking						
	TOTAL 8450						
8501	Pay Customer Parking						
	TOTAL 8500						
8672	Cashier Wrap & Pack						
8673	Package Collectors						
	TOTAL 8670						
8701	Supervisors & Assts.						
8702	Inside — Package						
8703	Pkg. Drivers & Helpers						
8704	Inside — Furniture						

Figure D-9 (continued)

300

DETAIL CENSUS PLAN BY ACCOUNT

Company _____

☐ Spring

☐ Preliminary

☐ Fall   19 _____

☐ Final

		(1)	(2)	(3)	(4)		(5)	(6)
		PLAN			LY		B/(W) THAN LAST YEAR	
EXPENSE CENTER		TY TOTAL	NEW STORES	EXISTING STORES	TOTAL		EXISTING STORES	TOTAL
8705	Furn. Drivers & Helpers							
8706	Parcel Post Clerks							
8707	Delivery — Br. Stores Only							
	TOTAL 8700							
8851	Truck & Garage Expense							
	TOTAL 8850							
	SELLING — TOTAL 8000							
9101	Merch. Mgrs. & Assts.							
9102	Fashion Coordinators							
9103	Comparison Shopping							
	TOTAL 9100							
9211	Buyers							
9212	Assistant Buyers							
9213	Executive Trainees							
	TOTAL 9210							
9301	Import Office							
	TOTAL 9300							
9401	Buyers Clericals							
9402	Unit Control Clerks							
9403	Merchandise Class Clerks							
	TOTAL 9400							
	MERCHANDISING — TOTAL 9000							
	GRAND TOTAL CENSUS							

DATE RECEIVED BY CORPORATE _____

Figure D-9 (continued)

CAPITAL ASSET

DISMANTLEMENT REPORT

DIVISION _____

DATE _____

REPORT NO.

DESCRIPTION:

Reasons and authorization for dismantlement or disposition:

HISTORY: Acquisition date   Depreciation record: Charged to date
         Asset No.   Remaining
         Original cost   Book value
         Replaced by Asset No.

DISPOSITION DATA: To whom sold
                  Value received
                  Date of receipt

DISPOSITION COSTS (itemize)

Accounting for disposition costs and salvage value:
    Acct No.
    Acct No.
    Acct No.
    Net Total

Accountant   Division Administrator

Figure D-10: CAPITAL ASSET DISMANTLEMENT REPORT

(From the book Corporate Treasurer's and Controller's Handbook by L. Doris, Editor. ©1950 renewed 1978 by L. Doris, Editor. Published by Prentice-Hall, Inc., Englewood Cliffs, New Jersey 07632.)

ADM3157 Rev. 8-76   **REQUEST FOR COMPUTER SERVICES AND/OR EQUIPMENT ACQUISITION**

COMPUTER SERVICES MANAGEMENT COMMITTEE (CSMC)

CONTROL NUMBER _____

SUBCOMMITTEE: ☐ TECHNICAL   ☐ COMMERCIAL

REQUESTING DEPARTMENT	LOCATION		DATE
SUBMITTED BY	TELE. EXT.	TITLE OF REQUEST	

BRIEF DESCRIPTION OF REQUEST   ☐ COMPUTER SERVICES AND/OR   ☐ EQUIPMENT ACQUISITION

BRIEF STATEMENT OF SCOPE, NEED AND BENEFIT (INCLUDING GROSS ANNUAL SAVINGS EXPECTED, APPEND DETAILED DOCUMENTATION)

COMPLETION TARGET DATE	REASON FOR DATE	
DEPARTMENT HEAD APPROVAL	DATE	☐ DETAIL ATTACHED

COMPLETED BY TECHNICAL OR COMMERCIAL SUBCOMMITTEE

COST ANALYSIS SUMMARY   ☐ DETAIL ATTACHED

NON-RECURRING COSTS – (SYSTEMS DEVELOPMENT, PROGRAMMING, ETC.) $ _____

EQUIPMENT - (COMPLETED BY EQUIPMENT ACQUISITION SUBCOMMITTEE): $ _____

TOTAL $ _____

ANNUAL OPERATING COSTS – RECURRING (COMPUTER TIME, USER PROCESSING, ETC.) $ _____

PREPARED BY	DATE	SUBCOMMITTEE CHAIRMAN APPROVAL	☐ REQUESTER NOTIFIED ☐ FORWARDED TO CSMC

COMPLETED BY SECRETARY – CSMC

REVIEW DATE	FORWARDED TO:	☐ SUBCOMMITTEE ☐ CSMC

DISPOSITION ACTION

☐ REJECT

☐ APPROVE

☐ APPROVE – REFER FOR FEASIBILITY STUDY AND/OR COST BENEFIT ANALYSIS

☐ APPROVE – IF MODIFICATION ACCEPTABLE

☐ APPROVE – DEFER IF ACCEPTABLE

SUBCOMMITTEE CHAIRMAN	DATE
CSMC CHAIRMAN	DATE
DATE REQUESTER NOTIFIED	

Figure D-11: REQUEST FOR COMPUTER SERVICES AND/OR EQUIPMENT ACQUISITION
(Courtesy of Northeast Utilities.)

◆ R E Q U E S T   F O R   F U N D S ◆

DIVISION	DEPARTMENT	SIC	BUDGET STATUS	PURPOSE CODE	APPROPRIATION NO.

DESCRIPTION OF EQUIPMENT OR PROJECT, COST DETAILS, JUSTIFICATION

Capital   ## Expense

ORIGINATED BY	DEPT. NO.	DATE	CONTROLLER REVIEW	DATE

ACCOUNT NOS.	AMOUNTS	ACCOUNT NOS.	AMOUNTS

DIVISION PRESIDENT	DATE	V.P. CORP. PLANNING	DATE

ENVIRONMENTAL REVIEW	DATE	FINAL CORPORATE APPROVAL	DATE

Accounting

APPROPRIATION TOTAL	APPROVED	DATE

Figure D-12: REQUEST FOR CAPITAL APPROPRIATION

REQUEST FOR CAPITAL EXPENDITURE

DIVISION _____

DATE _____

AUTHORIZATION NO. _____

ASSIGNED ASSET NO. _____

DESCRIPTION: (attach descriptive literature whenever possible)

Reasons for expenditure:

COST OF EXPENDITURE (attach any supplementary data)	ESTIMATED		ACTUAL	
Materials to be purchased: (include freight, duty, handling, and other appl. chgs.)				
Materials to be requisitioned from local inventory:				

Labor: Hrs. Estimated   Hrs. Actual
   Dismantling
   Construction
   Installation
   Contract				

Other Expense: (include designing, engineering, and overhead charges)				
Total expenditures:				
Disposition and net value of replaced or salvaged materials:				

Accounting disposition: Acct No.
                       Acct No.
                       Acct No.
                       Total Net Charges				

Approval requested:

Division Administrator   Chief Engineer

Approved: Date   Secretary

Completed   Date   Accountant

Figure D-13: REQUEST FOR CAPITAL EXPENDITURE
(From the book Corporate Treasurer's and Controller's Handbook by L. Doris, Editor. © 1950 renewed 1978 by L. Doris, Editor. Published by Prentice-Hall, Inc., Englewood Cliffs, New Jersey 07632.)

REQUEST FOR APPROPRIATION FOR CAPITAL EXPENDITURE

Division_____

Date_____

Request No._____

Description

Reason for expenditure

Cost – give supporting detail on separate sheets

	Estimated	Actual
Material to be purchased	_____	_____
Material from stock	_____	_____
Company labor	_____	_____
Contract labor	_____	_____
Other costs (describe)	_____	_____
Total	_____	_____

Estimated expenses

		Anticipated savings	
Depreciation	_____	Raw materials	_____
Insurance	_____	Operating labor	_____
Taxes	_____	Maintenance	_____
Interest	_____	Other (describe)	_____
Other (describe)	_____		_____
Total	_____	Total	_____

Estimated completion and cash requirements

Date	Percent complete	CASH REQUIREMENTS					
		Materials to be purchased	Materials from stock	Company labor	Contract labor	Other costs	Total

Approvals

Date Signature   Date Signature

Division head _____   Controller _____

Chief engineer_____   Appropriations_____
                                 Committee

Figure D-14: REQUEST FOR APPROPRIATION FOR CAPITAL EXPENDITURE
(From the book Business Finance Handbook by Lillian Doris, Editor, © 1953 by Prentice-Hall, Inc. Published by Prentice-Hall, Inc., Englewood Cliffs, New Jersey 07632.)

UNITED TECHNOLOGIES

APPROPRIATION REQUEST AND AUTHORITY

Subsidiary, Group, Division	Appropriation No.	Date
	Division Ref. No.	
Division/Dept.	Location	
Asset Classification	Product/Program	
Appropriation Amount	Budget Line Item	
Annual Lease Rate	Lease Duration	
Payback Period	Discounted Rate of Return	

Status	Line Item		Cash Flow Summary Year $(000)
Total Planned Appropriations			1
Appropriated To Date			2
This Appropriation	———————		3
Unappropriated Balance			4
			5
			6
			7
			8

ITEM NO.	QUANTITY	DESCRIPTION OF ASSET	ESTIMATED COST

Summary of Justification

Date	Division Approvals	Date	UTC Approvals
	Requested By		GROUP VICE PRESIDENT
			OPERATIONS ANALYSIS
			OTHER
			SR. VICE PRESIDENT FINANCE AND ADMIN.
	DIVISION CONTROLLER		PRESIDENT
	DIVISION PRESIDENT		CHAIRMAN/ EXECUTIVE COMMITTEE

UTC FORM 5036 REV. 1-77

Figure D-15: APPROPRIATION REQUEST AND AUTHORITY
(Courtesy of United Technologies.)

AUTHORIZATION FOR EXPENDITURE

BUDGET PROJECT
NO. _____

JOB NO. _____
AUTH NO. _____

COMPANY   DIVISION   PLANT

TITLE:

ESTIMATED COST		APPROPRIATION AVAILABLE	
		Amount heretofore approved in budget	
		Total expend authzd or requested, incl this auth	
EQUIPMENT	$	Balance not requested to date	
MATERIAL		Supplemental budget approval requested for this expenditure	

ESTIMATED COST		DISTRIBUTION OF EXPENDITURES			
LABOR					
HANDLING		INVESTMENT	$	%	a/c
TOTAL	$	EXPENSE	$	%	a/c

DESCRIPTION OF PROPOSED WORK:

PURPOSE AND NECESSITY FOR EXPENDITURE (including estimates of annual savings or other benefits):

	Date
Recommended by	Date
Recommended by	Date
Recommended by	Date
Authorized by	

Figure D-16: AUTHORIZATION FOR EXPENDITURE
(From the book Corporate Treasurer's and Controller's Handbook by L. Doris, Editor. © 1950 renewed 1978 by L. Doris, Editor. Published by Prentice-Hall, Inc., Englewood Cliffs, New Jersey 07632.)

AUTHORIZATION FOR CAPITAL EXPENDITURE

SUBSIDIARY _____ UNIT _____

DATE TRANSMITTTED _____ DATE APPROVED _____ CAP. EXP. NO. _____

CAPITAL EXPENDITURE REQUESTED:

Description:

Amount Requested $ _____   Amount Approved _____

Classification: **Priority:**   **Source:**

☐ Expansion   ☐ Essential   ☐ Purchase
☐ Replacement   ☐ Necessary   ☐ Construction
☐ Indirect Use   ☐ Desirable   ☐ Lease

JUSTIFICATION OF REQUEST:

☐ Profit Improvement   ☐ New Product   ☐ Tax Incentive
☐ Cost Reduction   ☐ Market Shares   ☐ Poss. Shortage
☐ Competition   ☐ Growth   ☐ Other

ESTIMATED COST DATE:

Basic Equipment	$ _____	In Plant:	
Buildings	$ _____	Engineering	$ _____
Land & Improvements	$ _____	Materials	$ _____
Satellite Equip.	$ _____	Labor	$ _____
Freight	$ _____	Equipment	$ _____
Taxes	$ _____	Overhead	$ _____
Installation	$ _____	Training	$ _____
Other Costs	$ _____	SUBTOTAL	$ _____
SUBTOTAL (Col. 1)	$ _____		
SUBTOTAL (Col. 2)	$ _____		
Miscellaneous	$ _____	Residual Value of	
TOTAL	$ _____	Old Equipment	$ _____

APPROVALS:

Originator _____ Date _____

Divisional President _____ Date _____

Exec. V.P.-Finance _____ Date _____

Corporate Planning _____ Date _____

Figure D-17: AUTHORIZATION FOR CAPITAL EXPENDITURE

PURCHASE REQUISITION

No. **7932**

Date _____

Purchasing Department
Please Purchase the Following Named Items

_____

INDICATE SOURCE OF SUPPLY IF KNOWN

Quantity	Number	Description

Purpose or Use _____

TO BE FILLED IN BY PURCHASING DEPT.
Date Ordered_____ Order No._____

When Wanted _____
From _____

For _____ Dept.
Approved _____

Figure D-18: PURCHASE REQUISITION
(Courtesy of Electro-Methods, Inc., South Windsor, Connecticut.)

ELECTRO-METHODS, INC.
P. O. Box 54 — 330 Governors Highway
So. Windsor, Connecticut 06074
Tel. 203 - 289-8661 — Twx 710-425-6016

Request for
Quotation

NUMBER	∗ 00542	DATE

The above number must appear on all quotations and related correspondence.
THIS IS NOT AN ORDER

QUOTE NOT LATER THAN	REQUISITION NO.	DATE OF REQUISITION	CHARGEABLE ACCOUNT NUMBER(S)	P. O. NUMBER

VENDOR	ITEM	SUMMARY OF QUOTATIONS BY QUANTITY
• • •		
• • •		
• • •		

DELIVERY REQUIREMENTS	DELIVERY PROMISED	TERMS	F.O.B.

ITEM	QUANTITY	DESCRIPTION	UNIT PRICE	AMOUNT

Buyer_____

REASON ORDER PLACED WITH SUCCESSFUL VENDOR	OTHER REASONS
Lowest Price Quality Best Del'y Service Only Source Best Design	
☐ ☐ ☐ ☐ ☐ ☐	

Figure D-19: REQUEST FOR QUOTATION
(Courtesy of Electro-Methods, Inc., South Windsor, Connecticut.)

ELECTRO-METHODS, INC.

E M inc

P.O. BOX 54, 330 GOVERNORS HIGHWAY, SOUTH WINDSOR, CONN. 06074

TEL. (203) 289-8661
TWX (710) 425-6016

VENDOR

DATE SHIPMENT REQUIRED AT ELECTRO-METHODS, INC.

NOTE

PLEASE ENTER OUR ORDER FOR THE FOLLOWING, SUBJECT TO INSTRUCTIONS HEREIN AND ALL TERMS AND CONDITIONS PRINTED ON THE REVERSE SIDE:

DATE OF ORDER	REQUISITION NO.	TERMS	F.O.B. SOUTH WINDSOR, CONN. OR	SHIP VIA	PREPAY ALL SHIPMENTS

ITEM	QUANTITY	PATTERN NO. PART NO.	DESCRIPTION OF MATERIALS AND OR SERVICES TO BE SUPPLIED	PRICE

IMPORTANT INSTRUCTIONS:

1 — PLEASE COMPLETE AND RETURN ACKNOWLEDGMENT PLY IMMEDIATELY CONFIRMING PRICE AND INDICATING EARLIEST SHIPPING DATE OF EACH ITEM.

2 — RENDER INVOICES PROMPTLY AND IN TRIPLICATE

3 — THIS ORDER IS SUBJECT TO THE TERMS AND CONDITIONS PRINTED ON THE REVERSE SIDE HEREOF, AND NO EXCEPTIONS WILL BE ALLOWED WITHOUT WRITTEN PERMISSION OF THE PURCHASING DEPARTMENT.

ELECTRO-METHODS, INC.

_____
PURCHASING

THE FOLLOWING ARMED SERVICES PROCUREMENT REGULATIONS APPLY:

☐ 7—103.21A

☐ 7—103.21B

☐ 7—104.33

☐ 7—104.41A

1. PRIORITY RATING _____ CERTIFIED FOR NATIONAL DEFENSE USE UNDER DMS REGULATION 1.

2. YOU ARE REQUIRED TO FOLLOW THE PROVISIONS OF DMS REG. 1 AND OF ALL OTHER APPLICABLE REGULATIONS AND ORDERS OF BDC IN OBTAINING CONTROLLED MATERIALS AND OTHER PRODUCTS AND MATERIALS NEEDED TO FILL THIS ORDER.

ORIGINAL PURCHASE ORDER — RETURN ACKNOWLEDGEMENT ATTACHED

Figure D-20: ORIGINAL PURCHASE ORDER
(Courtesy of Electro-Methods, Inc., South Windsor, Connecticut.)

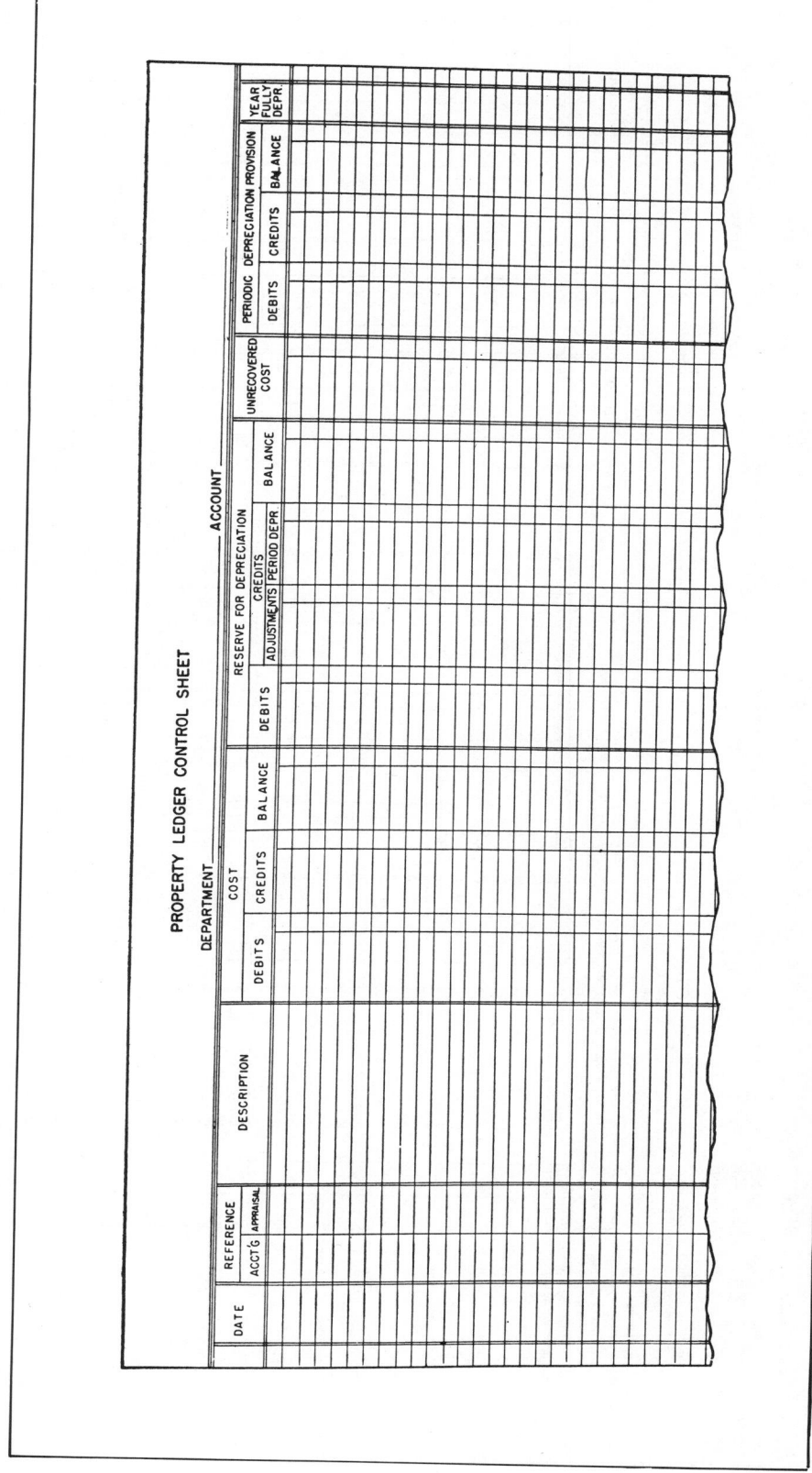

Figure D-21: PROPERTY LEDGER CONTROL SHEET

(From the book Corporate Treasurer's and Controller's Handbook by L. Doris, Editor. © 1950 renewed 1978 by L. Doris, Editor. Published by Prentice-Hall, Inc., Englewood Cliffs, New Jersey 07632.)

ASSET RECORD

SHEET NUMBER

ASSET NUMBER   DESCRIPTION OF ASSET

CLASS NUMBER   MADE BY
IDENTIFICATION
DATA—MFRS.
                                PURCHASED FROM   PURCHASE GUARANTEE

PLANT   CASH TRANSACTION   TRADE-IN TRANSACTION   DEPRECIATION

BUILDING   NET PRICE $ TOTAL COST $ ESTIMATED LIFE   TOTAL COST OR BASIS

FLOOR   FREIGHT $ NET BOOK VALUE $ CLASS LIFE   7% INVESTMENT CREDIT
                                AT TRADE-IN   DEPRECIATION
                                                          METHOD

DEPARTMENT   INSTALLATION $ TRADE-IN VALUE $ ADJUSTED BASIS
                                                          DEPRECIATION   20% 1ST YEAR
LOCATION   CASH DIFFERENCE $ RATE   ALLOWANCE
DATE PUT
INTO USE   BASIS   DEPRECIATION
                                                                                BASIS

REMARKS   TOTAL COST $ DEPRECIATION METHOD
             ESTIMATED   CHANGED TO
             SALVAGE VALUE $ NEW RATE   DATE

| ASSET, COST, BETTERMENTS, ETC. (Black Ink) REPAIRS, ETC. — MEMO. ONLY (Red Ink) | | | | | DEPRECIATION RESERVE | | | | NET ASSET |
MO	DAY	YR.	DEBITS	CREDITS	BALANCE	MO	DAY	YR.	DEBITS	CREDITS	BALANCE	VALUE

Wilson Jones
Form 602-28

Made in U.S.A

Figure D-22: ASSET RECORD

(Copyright by Wilson Jones Company. All rights reserved. Forms may be obtained, subject to supply, from
Wilson Jones Company, 6150 Touhy Avenue, Chicago, Illinois 60648.)

Appraisal

YOUR FIRM NAME HERE
A Line of Descriptive Advertising Here If You Wish
123 Main Street   Your Town, State and Zip
Phone 123-4567

TO WHOM IT MAY CONCERN:

This is to Certify that we are engaged in the jewelry business, appraising diamonds, watches, jewelry and precious stones of all descriptions.

We herewith Certify that we have this day carefully examined the following listed and described articles, the property of:

NAME_____

ADDRESS_____

We estimate the value as listed for insurance or other purposes at the current retail value, excluding Federal and other taxes. In making this Appraisal, we DO NOT agree to purchase or replace the articles.

DESCRIPTION	APPRAISED VALUE

The foregoing Appraisal is made with the understanding that the Appraiser assumes no liability with respect to any action that may be taken on the basis of this Appraisal.

_____   _____
APPRAISER   **DATE**

Figure D-23: JEWELRY APPRAISAL FORM

(Available from New England Business Service, Inc., North Main Street, Groton, Massachusetts 01450; 1-800-225-6380.

REFUNDING CALCULATIONS

INTEREST: OLD ISSUE _____ % NEW ISSUE _____ %
DISCOUNT RATE _____ % TAX RATE _____ %

	BEFORE TAXES	AFTER TAXES	NET SAVING
CASH OUTLAYS:			
PREMIUM AT $_____ per $1,000			
DUPLICATE INTEREST FOR CALL PER.			
REFUNDING EXPENSES			
CALL EXPENSE			
Less Tax Saving--------------------------			
TOTAL CASH OUTLAY ------------------------			
INTEREST CALCULATIONS:			
ANNUAL INTEREST-OLD ISSUE			
ANNUAL INTEREST-NEW ISSUE			
TOTAL AFTER TAX INTEREST (OLD)--------------			
TOTAL AFTER TAX INTEREST (NEW)--------------			
TOTAL DISCOUNTED INTEREST SAVED -------------------			
TOTAL AFTER TAX CASH OUTLAY ---------------------			
NET SAVING DUE TO REFUNDING ---------------------			

Figure D-24: REFUNDING CALCULATIONS

SECURITY PURCHASE OR SALE RECORD

Date _____

Bought From _____

Sold To _____

Issue Name _____

Coupon _____

Issue Date _____

Maturity Date _____

Maturity _____

Yield To Maturity _____

Par Value _____

Accrued Int. _____

Disc. or Prem.   Rate: _____ Amount: _____

Total Cost _____

Safekeeping Cost _____ 15.00 _____

No Check Amount _____

Depository Bank _____

Remarks: _____

_____

Form 819 Rev. 8-74 _____

Figure D-25: SECURITY PURCHASE OR SALE RECORD

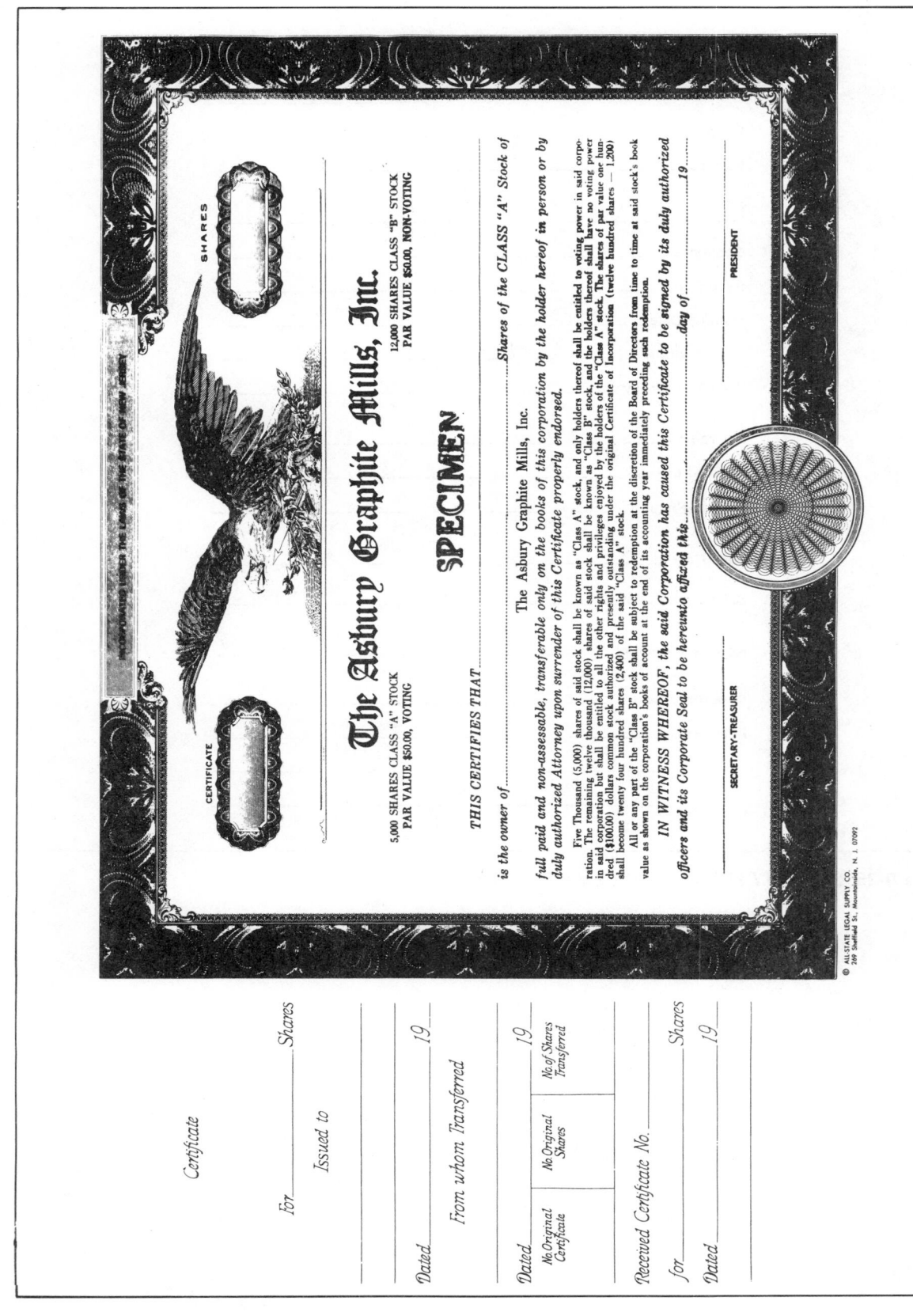

Figure D-26: CLASS "A" PAR VALUE (VOTING) STOCK CERTIFICATE
(Courtesy of All State Legal Supply Co., Mountainside, New Jersey 07092.)

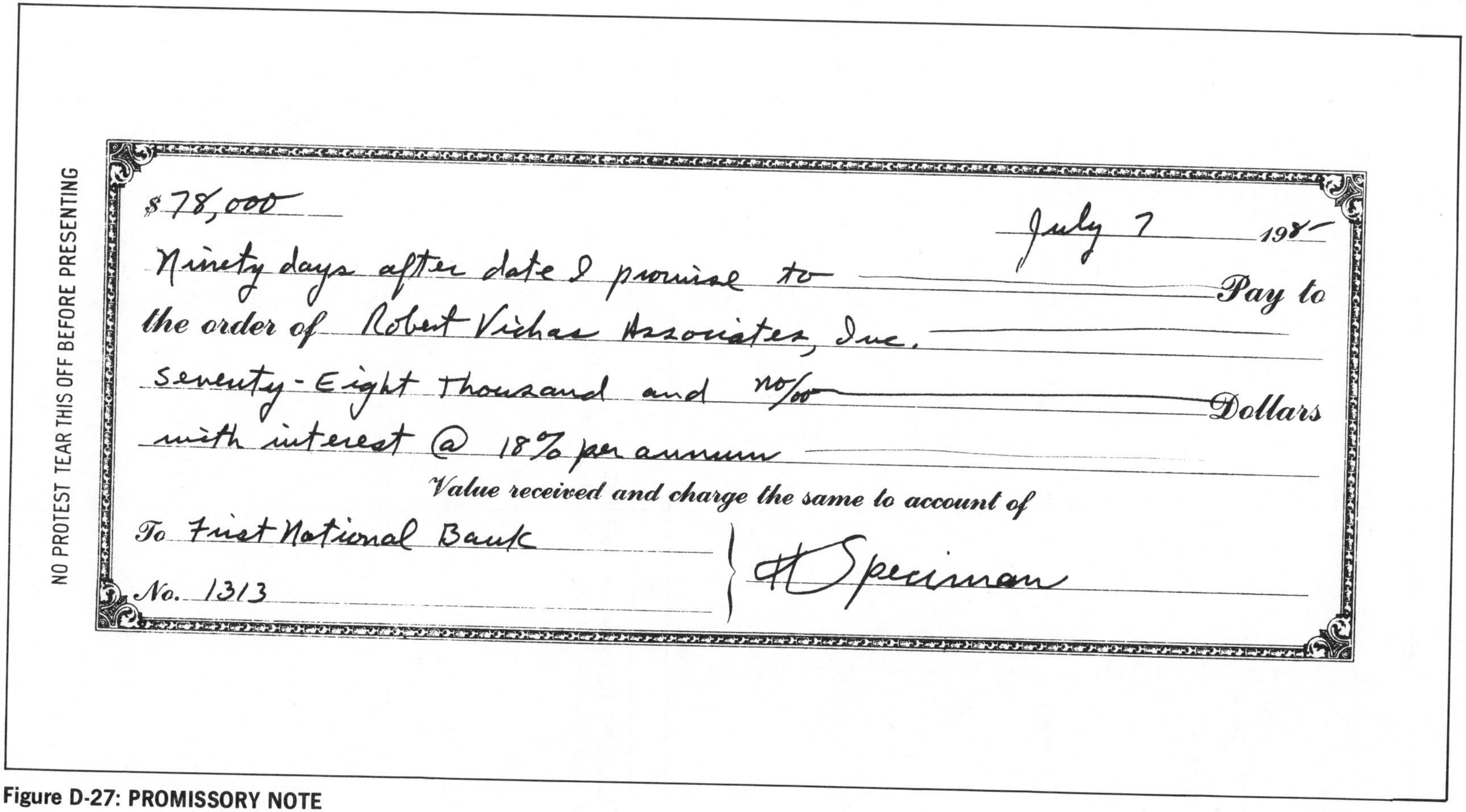

Figure D-27: PROMISSORY NOTE

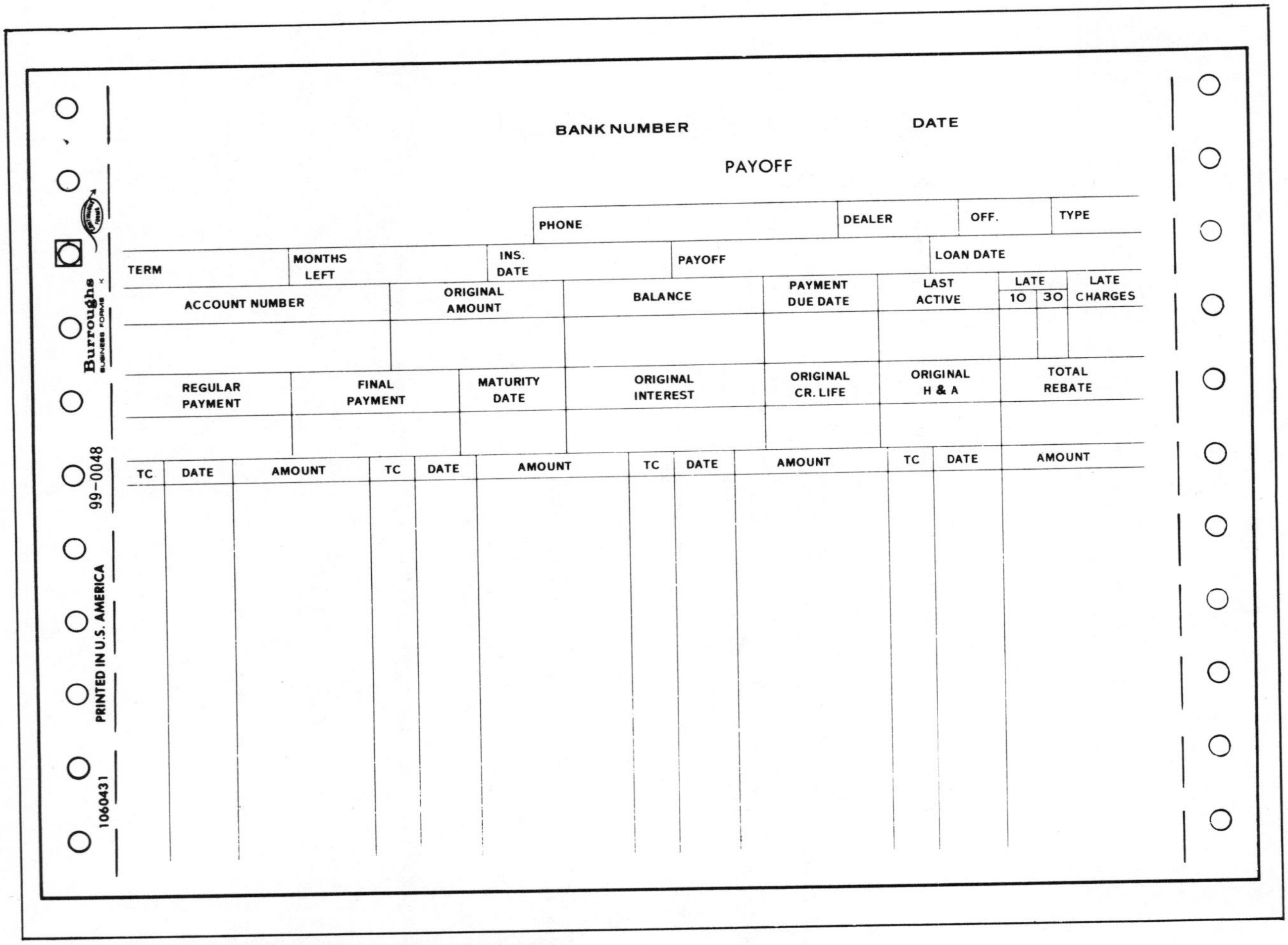

BANK NUMBER DATE

PAYOFF

PHONE	DEALER	OFF.	TYPE

TERM	MONTHS LEFT	INS. DATE	PAYOFF	LOAN DATE

ACCOUNT NUMBER	ORIGINAL AMOUNT	BALANCE	PAYMENT DUE DATE	LAST ACTIVE	LATE 10	LATE 30	LATE CHARGES

REGULAR PAYMENT	FINAL PAYMENT	MATURITY DATE	ORIGINAL INTEREST	ORIGINAL CR. LIFE	ORIGINAL H & A	TOTAL REBATE

TC	DATE	AMOUNT	TC	DATE	AMOUNT	TC	DATE	AMOUNT	TC	DATE	AMOUNT

Burroughs BUSINESS FORMS 99-0048 PRINTED IN U.S. AMERICA 1060431

Figure D-28: INSTALLMENT LOAN PAYOFF REPORT
(Courtesy of Burroughs Corporation Office Products Group/Business Forms Division.)

THEATRE CIRCUIT

PROJECTION FILM REPORT FORM

(Note: This report <u>MUST</u> be made out at <u>FIRST</u> showing of each new program)

Theatre _____ Town _____ Date of report _____

FEATURE_____ DISTRB. _____

B/W   Color   Reg.   Scope   Optical   Magnetic   No.
                                                        Reels

Please fill out following: (PLEASE BE ACCURATE)

Code: (F) Feature;   (CF) Co-Feature;   (C) Cartoon;   (N) Newsreel;

(S) Single;   (D) Double;   (FT) Featurette;   (TR) Trailer.

Subject	Code	Co.	SCHEDULE		ACTUAL	
			R-Time:	Began At:	R-Time	Began At:
				S		A

Compare 'actual' against 'schedule' - (S-A) +
DIFFERENCE: Show 'difference', plus or minus _____ or Min.

List any other shorts used below, trailers also, if more than one:

Title	Co.	Type	Running Time	
			Schedule	Actual

Condition of show: Describe in detail, such as condition of prints received, and any other details such as titled version, bad focus, no title, etc.

_____   _____
Manager signature   Projectionist signature

Projectionist,   One for Booth file, 3 to manager, Manager to keep second copy; third to West office; fourth to
Make 4 copies: New office.

Manager: Explain how * -'difference' was adjusted:

Figure D-29: PROJECTION FILM REPORT FOR NEW MOTION PICTURES

LEASE VS BORROWING Amount to Borrow $______ Interest ____% Method Depreciation ______ Tax Rate ____% Lease Payment $______ Semiannual Pay.$______

FOR:	198A 1st	198A 2nd	198B 1st	198B 2nd	198C 1st	198C 2nd	198D 1st	198D 2nd	198E 1st	198E 2nd	198F 1st	198F 2nd
A. Total Payment on Loan (semiannually)												
B. Interest Cost												
C. Loan Amortization												
D. Remaining Loan Balance												
E. Depreciation Expense												
F. Tax Deductible Expense (B) + (E)												
G. Tax Saving												
H. NET COST OF OWNING (A) - (G)												
I. LEASE COST AFTER TAX												
J. ADVANTAGE TO OWNING (I) - (H)												
K. Present Value (PV) Factor @ ____%												
L. PV OF ADVANTAGE OF OWNING (J) X (K)												

Figure D-30: COST COMPARISON OF BUYING VERSUS LEASING

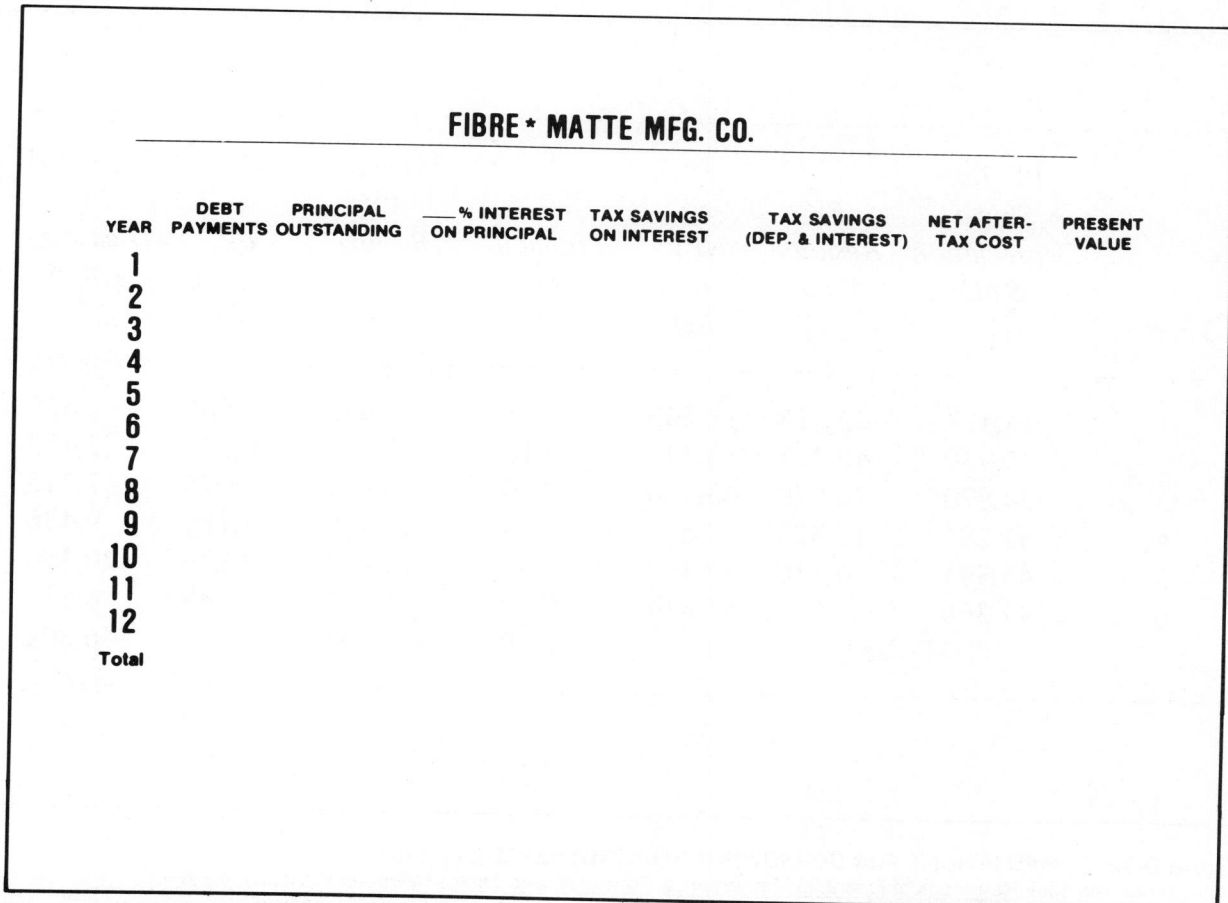

Figure D-31: LEASE-BORROW ANALYSIS

Year (t)	PV Tax Shield Depreciation SYD (1)	PV Residual Value (2)	NPV Costs (3)	Probabil- ities (4)	Expected PV (Buying) (3 × 4) (5)	PV Leasing (6)	Expected PV (Leasing) (4 × 6) (7)
1	14,423	72,115	18,462	0.05	923	12,500	625
2	25,980	46,228	32,792	0.10	3,279	24,519	2,452
3	34,870	26,670	43,460	0.20	8,692	36,076	7,215
4	41,281	12,822	50,897	0.20	10,179	47,189	9,438
5	45,391	4,110	55,499	0.35	19,425	57,874	20,256
6	47,366	0	57,634	0.10	5,763	68,148	6,815
TOTALS				1.00	$48,261		$46,801

Figure D-32: COMPUTATIONS FOR BORROWING (OWNING) VERSUS LEASING
(From the book Handbook of Financial Mathematics, Formulas, and Tables by Robert P. Vichas. © 1979.
Published by Prentice-Hall, Inc., Englewood Cliffs, New Jersey 07632.)

Year	Tax Saving on Depreciation $h(A)$ (1)	After-Tax Added Operating Costs $(1-h)K$ (2)	Salvage Value Net of Taxes $(1-h_v)(L-E)$ (3)	After-Tax Lease Payment $(1-h)s$ (4)	Present Value of $(1)-(2)+(3)$ @ 15% (5)	Present Value of (4) @ 4% (6)
1	0.50(15,000)	0.50(1,000)	—	0.50(13,500)	6,087	6,490
2	0.50(12,500)	0.50(1,000)	—	0.50(13,500)	4,348	6,241
3	0.50(10,000)	0.50(1,000)	—	0.50(13,500)	2,959	6,000
4	0.50(7,500)	0.50(1,000)	—	0.50(13,500)	1,858	5,770
5	0.50(5,000)	0.50(1,000)	—	0.50(13,500)	994	5,548
6	0.50(2,500)	0.50(1,000)	0.70(5,000)	0.50(13,500)	1,837	5,335
					$18,083	$35,384

$$\Delta NPV = 18,083 - 52,500 + 35,384 = +967$$

Figure D-33: ANNUAL PROFILE FOR BUY OR LEASE CALCULATIONS
(From the book <u>Handbook</u> <u>of</u> <u>Financial</u> <u>Mathematics,</u> <u>Formulas,</u> <u>and</u> <u>Tables</u> by Robert P. Vichas. © 1979.
Published by Prentice-Hall, Inc., Englewood Cliffs, New Jersey 07632.)

EXPECTED PRESENT VALUES OF LEASING VERSUS BUYING

ECONOMIC LIFE	PROBABILITIES	Buying		Leasing	
		PRESENT VALUE OF COSTS	EXPECTED PRESENT VALUES	PRESENT VALUE OF COSTS	EXPECTED PRESENT VALUES
1					
2					
3					
4					
5					
6					
7					
8					
9					

TYPE OF ASSET/EQUIPMENT _____

PURCHASE PRICE _____ MONTHLY LEASE (IF LEASED) _____

ASSUMED RATE _____ % LEASE RATE _____ % DATE NEEDED _____

Figure D-34: EXPECTED PRESENT VALUE OF LEASING VERSUS BUYING

TYPE OF EQUIPMENT:

ITEM				
CASH OUTFLOW:				
Management Fee				
Equipment Cost				
Lessor's Investment (equity + fee)				
Lease Payments:				
Number (months)				
Amount per Period				
Total Loan Amount				
At _____ %				
Number of Payments				
Amount of Each Payment				
Residual Value				
As percent of Investment				
Amount				
Cost to Lessee (%)				
Tax Rate (Cash Basis) (%)				
Investment Tax Credit				
Sinking Fund Rate (% after tax)				
Economic Life (years)				
Depreciation Life (years)				
Depreciation Method				
Lease Begins On:				

Figure D-35: FINANCIAL BENEFITS OF NON-LEVERAGED LEASE TRANSACTION TO LESSOR

FINANCIAL SUMMARY OF LEASE RESULTS

TYPE OF EQUIPMENT:

TYPE OF LEASE: RECOVERY PERIOD:

EFFECTIVE YIELD, ANNUAL COMPOUNDED:

ITEM			
NOMINAL ANNUAL YIELD AFTER TAX (%)			
EFFECTIVE ANN. YIELD AFTER TAX (%)			
CASH FLOW FROM:			
Asset Acquisition:			
Equity Investment			
Operations:			
Cash Receipts			
Residual Value			
Deferred Expenses			
CASH FLOW BEFORE:			
Debt Service:			
Interest & Principal			
Total Debt Service			
Taxes on Income			
NET FEDERAL TAXES ON INCOME			
CASH FLOW AFTER TAXES ON INCOME			

Figure D-36: FINANCIAL SUMMARY OF LEASE RESULTS

MOTOR CARRIER AND TRUCK LEASING
CREDIT INPUT STATEMENT CONTROL SHEET

Page 1 of 5

DATE: _____

CREDIT I D:

BANK I D: ____ ____

PREFIX ____ ____

NUMBER __ __ __ — __ __ __ __

_____
(COMPANY NAME)

DO NOT USE THIS SPACE:

INPUT AREA USE

INPUT DATE: _____

OPERATOR: _____

REMARKS:

REPORT PARAMETER INFORMATION

REPORT REQUESTS		use Y (yes)
BASE REPORT		
RATIO ANALYSIS		
CASH FLOW ANALYSIS		
COMMON STATEMENT		
ENDING DATE — REPORT PERIOD		MM/YY (DO NOT USE
		UNLESS REQUESTING ENDING
		REPORT PERIOD OTHER
		THAN LATEST DATE)

STATEMENT CONTROL INFORMATION

STATEMENT DATE						MM/DD/YY
STATEMENT PERIOD CODE						Y (yearly) M (monthly) P (periodic) 1 (1st quarter) 2 (2nd quarter) 3 (3rd quarter)
DATE STMENT SENT						MM/DD/YY
DATE STMENT RECVD						MM/DD/YY
STMENT DUE CODE						Y, Q, M, X, S
No. DAYS—Yrly Stmnt Due						use when "X" in 5
No. DAYS—Qtrly Stmnt Due						use when "X" in 5
INDUSTRY CATEGORY						1 (general) 2 (motor carriers) 3 (utilities) 4 (financial)
S I C NUMBER						4 digits
AUDIT TYPE						1 (certified) 2 (qualified) 3 (disclaimer) 4 (adverse)
AUDITOR NUMBER						5 (unaudited) 6 (management) 7 (restated) 8 (preliminary)
CONSOLIDATED STMT CODE						use 1 for subsidiary or affiliate
CONSOLIDATED REF. I D						if "1" in above, use parent company I D, if not, use zero.
TRUNCATION CODE						1 (thousands) 2 (millions)
ANALYST'S INITIALS						
STATEMENT TYPE						1 (consolidated) 2 (individual) 3 (combined) 4 (partnership)
CURRENCY CODE						5 (proprietorship) 6 (personal) 7 (consolidating) 8 ( )
EXCHANGE RATE						9 (pro-forma)

B-757 (rev. 3/79)

Figure D-37: AUTOMATED FINANCIAL STATEMENT ANALYSIS SPREAD SHEETS FOR MOTOR CARRIER AND TRUCK LEASING (Courtesy of the First National Bank of Boston.)

329

CREDIT I D:
PREFIX ___ ___
NUMBER ___ ___ ___ ___ ___ ___ ___

MOTOR CARRIER AND TRUCK LEASING
INPUT SHEET

*Value—one decimal point

ITEM #	DESCRIPTION	*VALUE Date	*VALUE Date	*VALUE Date	*VALUE Date	*VALUE Date	PROCESSING
	CURRENT ASSETS						
1	Cash (less Drafts Pbl)						
3	Short Term Investments						
4		*	*	*	*	*	Add to Item 45
5		*	*	*	*	*	Add to Item 45
8	A/R Customer						
9	A/R Interline						
10	A/R Affiliates						
14		*	*	*	*	*	Add to Item 18
17	A/R Other						
18	Gross Receivables						Sum of 8, 9, 10, 14, 17
19	Bad Debt Reserve						
21	Net Receivables						Item 18 Minus Item 19
22	Notes Receivable						
23	Parts & Supplies						
28		*	*	*	*	*	Add to Item 30
30	Total Inventory						Sum of 23 and 28
31	Tires & Tubes						
33	Taxes & Licenses						
35	Other Prepaids						
37	Total Prepaid Items						Sum of 31, 33, 35
39	Tax Refunds/CSVLI Pledged						
41		*	*	*	*	*	Add to Item 45
44	Other Current Assets						
45	Total Current Assets						Sum of 1, 3, 4, 5, 21, 22, 30, 37, 39, 41, 44
	FIXED ASSETS						
46	Carrier Operating Equip						
47	Depreciation						
49	Net Operating Equip.						Item 46, Minus Item 47
53	Other Operating Equip						
54	Depreciation						
56	Net Other Operating Equip.						Item 53 Minus Item 54
58		*	*	*	*	*	Add to Item 80
60	Intercompany Advances						
62	Investments in Affil/Sub						
64	Prepaid Interest						
66		*	*	*	*	*	Add to Item 80
67		*	*	*	*	*	Add to Item 80
68		*	*	*	*	*	Add to Item 80
69		*	*	*	*	*	Add to Item 80
70		*	*	*	*	*	Add to Item 80
71		*	*	*	*	*	Add to Item 80
79	Misc. Non-Current Assets						
80	Total Assets						Sum of 45, 49, 56, 58, thru 79

B-757

Figure D-37 (continued)

CREDIT I D:

PREFIX ___ ___

NUMBER __ __ __ __ — __ __ __

MOTOR CARRIER AND TRUCK LEASING
INPUT SHEET

*Value—one decimal point

ITEM #	DESCRIPTION	*VALUE Date	*VALUE Date	*VALUE Date	*VALUE Date	*VALUE Date	PROCESSING
	CURRENT LIABILITIES						
81	Notes Payable—Banks						
82							
85	Accounts Pbl & Accruals						Add to Item 105
86	A/P—Trade						
87	A/P—Interline						
88	A/P—Affil & Subs						
90	Total Accounts Payable						
91	Misc. Accruals & Resrvs						Sum of 86, 87, 88
92							
94	Current Income Tax Pbl						Add to Item 105
96	Other Term Debt—Cur.						
98							
99							Add to Item 105
101	Advances Payable						Add to Item 105
104	Other Current Liabs.						
105	Total Current Liabs.						Sum of 81, 82, 85, 90, 91 thru 104
106	Equipment Debt—Current						
107	Equipment Debt—Dfd.						
109	Other Term Debt—Dfd.						
112							
113							Add to Item 123
116	Deferred Credits						Add to Item 123
117							
118	Other Liabilities						Add to Item 123
123	Total Funded Debt						
125	Total Liabilities						Sum of 106 thru 118
126	Deferred Income Tax						Sum of 105 and 123
127	Minority Interest						
130							
	NET WORTH						
131	Subordinated Debt						
135	Preferred Stock						
137	Common Stock						
138	Capital Surplus						
139	Earned Surplus						
140							Add to Item 144
141							Add to Item 144
144	Total Net Worth						Sum of 131 thru 141
145	Intangibles						
146	Treasury Stock						
147							Subtract from 149
149	Tangible Net Worth						Item 144 Minus 145, 146, 147
150	Total Liabs & Equity						Sum of 125, 126, 127, 130 and 149 MUST equal 80

B-757

Figure D-37 (continued)

CREDIT I D:

PREFIX ___ ___

NUMBER ___ __ __ — __ __ __ ___

**MOTOR CARRIER AND TRUCK LEASING
INPUT SHEET**

Page 4 of 5

*Value—one decimal point

ITEM #	DESCRIPTION	*VALUE Date	*VALUE Date	*VALUE Date	*VALUE Date	*VALUE Date	PROCESSING
	OPERATING STATEMENT						
171	Operating Revenue						
175	Operating Exp (w/o Depr)						
177	Salaries—Officers						
178	Salaries & Wages						
179	Paid Time Off & Fringes						
180	Supplies						
181	Taxes & Licenses						
182	Insurance						
183	Communications & Utilities						
184	Building Rents						
185	Misc. Expenses						
190	Purchased Transport.						
191	Depreciation						
192	Depreciation Adj.						
193	Maintenance						
194	Terminal						
195	Traffic & Sales						
196	Insurance & Safety						
197	General & Admin.						
198	Amortization						
205		*	*	*	*	*	Add to Item 210
206		*	*	*	*	*	Add to Item 210
207		*	*	*	*	*	Add to Item 210
210	Total Operating Expenses						Sum of 175 thru 191 plus 193 thru 207 Minus 192
211	Net Operating Income						Item 171 Minus 210
214	Gain on Sale—Equip.						
215		*	*	*	*	*	Add to Item 221
216		*	*	*	*	*	Add to Item 221
217		*	*	*	*	*	Add to Item 221
220	Other Non-Optg. Inc						
221	Total Optg & Other Inc						Sum of 211 thru 220
222	Other Non-Optg Expenses						
223	Interest Expense						
225		*	*	*	*	*	Add to Item 226
226	Total Non-Optg Expenses						Sum of 222 thru 225
227	Profit Before Tax & Extr.						Item 221 Minus 226
229	Income Taxes Curr.						
230	Income Taxes Dfd.						
231	Extraordinary Gains						
232	Extraordinary Charges						
233	Minority Interest						
234	Equity in Earns of Subs						
235	Net Profit After Taxes						Sum of Items 227, 231, 234 Minus 229, 230, 232, 233
236	Preferred Dividends						
237	Common Dividends						
238	Capital Expenditures						
239	Adj. to Retained Earnings						
241	Shares Outstanding						
242	Dividends from Uncsl Sub.						

B-757

Figure D-37 (continued)

MOTOR CARRIER AND TRUCK LEASING
NOTES AND REMARKS

CREDIT ID:

PREFIX ⊔_⊔_⊔

NUMBER ⊔_⊔_⊔_⊔_–_⊔_⊔_⊔_⊔_⊔

STATEMENT DATE	ITEM #	SEQ #	NOTES AND REMARKS

B-757

Figure D-37 (continued)

INDIVIDUAL LEASING RECORD

DO NOT USE THIS SPACE

Effective Date of Lease

I.L.R. No.	☐ NEW ☐ USED		VENDOR

Make of Equipment	Model Year	Model	Engine No.	Serial (V.I.D.) No.

TYPE OF EQUIPMENT OR OTHER DETAILS

To be registered for highway use: Yes ☐ No ☐ | Location of Equipment | CITY | COUNTY | STATE

FOR FEDERAL USE TAX ON HIGHWAY MOTOR VEHICLES:			ACQUISITION COST			
NET WEIGHT	NO. OF AXLES	CATEGORY (Letter from Form 2290)	(1) Equipment $	(2) Body $	(3) Other Charges $	Acquisition Cost (1+2+3) $

Replacing Equipment No. ☐ New ILR ☐ Revising ☐ | Date of Original ILR or Last Revision

PERIOD IN MONTHS FOR FULL AMORTIZATION _____ | MONTHLY AMORTIZATION FIGURE $ _____

Monthly rent: For _____ months commencing the first day of _____ 19_____ equals the monthly amortization figure plus an amount computed as provided in the Leasing Agreement. Such rate is subject to periodic adjustments if so provided in the Leasing Agreement.

Unit to be fully amortized on last day of _____ 19_____.

Monthly rent for each month after fully amortized equals whichever of the following is provided in the Leasing Agreement:
A) _____ % of the original acquisition cost or B) $ _____ per month.

IF GENERAL ELECTION FOR INVESTMENT CREDIT IN FORCE, COMPLETE THIS SECTION

If property subject to investment credit? Yes _____ or No _____ (If yes, complete the following)

Date on which possession of this property is transferred to Lessee _____

If fair market value on such date is the same as acquisition cost check here ☐ or state fair market value on such date. $ _____

USEFUL LIFE CATEGORY (Check One)

3 YEARS OR MORE BUT LESS THAN 5 YEARS ☐	5 YEARS OR MORE BUT LESS THAN 7 YEARS ☐	7 YEARS OR MORE	LESS THAN 3 YEARS ☐ ☐

The undersigned Lessor hereby leases to the undersigned Lessee, and the Lessee acknowledges delivery to it in good condition of, the Equipment, with related equipment, described in the above Individual Leasing Record. The Lessee agrees to pay the rent set forth above. The covenants, terms and conditions of this lease are those appearing in the Leasing Agreement between the undersigned Lessor and Lessee dated _____ which covenants, terms and conditions are hereby incorporated by reference.

_____, Lessor _____, Lessee

By _____   By _____

Authorized Signature   Authorized Signature

I.L.R. SL 3/78

ORIGINAL
MAIL TO LESSOR

M MONTHLY 1
CHECK NO. _____ DATE OF CHECK _____ NO. OF I.L.R.s _____ AMOUNT $ _____

I.L.R. SL 3/78   COPY FOR LESSOR — MAIL TO LESSOR   2

I.L.R. SL 3/78   **COPY FOR BANK/ACCT. MAIL TO LESSOR**

I.L.R. SL 3/78   **COPY FOR LESSEE MAIL TO LESSOR**

I.L.R. SL 3/78   **COPY FOR LESSEE RETAIN THIS COPY**

I.L.R. SL 3/78   **COPY FOR LESSEE RETAIN THIS COPY**

Figure D-38: INDIVIDUAL LEASING RECORD
(Courtesy of Bankers Leasing Corporation, San Mateo, California.)

LEASE OBLIGATION COMPUTATION

SUMMARY OF LEASE TERMS

COST OF PROPERTY .... $ _____

LENGTH OF LEASE .... _____ (Years)

PERIODIC LEASE PAYMENT .... $ _____

ESTIMATED SALVAGE VALUE .... $ _____

INVESTMENT TAX CREDIT TO LESSOR .... $ _____

IMPLICIT RATE IN LEASE .... _____ (Percent)

Loan Balance

YEAR	BEGINNING MINIMUM LEASE PAYMENTS	ANTICIPATED SALVAGE VALUE	TOTAL	UNEARNED INCOME	BEGINNING LOAN BALANCE	PAYMENTS	
						PRINCIPAL	INTEREST
198A							
198B							
198C							
198D							
198E							
198F							
198G							

Figure D-39: LEASE OBLIGATION COMPUTATION AND LOAN BALANCE

MASTER LEASING AGREEMENT

Leasing Agreement as of the   day of   ,19   , by and between

BLC CORPORATION of San Mateo, California (herein called "Lessor") and

(herein called "Lessee").

In consideration of the mutual covenants hereinafter contained, Lessor and Lessee agree as follows:

1. *Definitions.* As herein used:

(a) "Equipment" means the following types of equipment owned or to be owned by the Lessor and leased by the Lessor to the Lessee or ordered by the Lessor for lease to the Lessee as provided herein:

(b) "Acquisition cost" of Equipment is an amount equal to the sum of the vendor's delivered price, dealer's delivery and handling charges, the cost of any original equipment which may be added, excise tax on the Equipment, any sales and use taxes, expenses of installation and freight, and other expenses required to effect delivery of the Equipment to the Lessee, less purchase discounts obtained.

(c) "Individual Leasing Record" is a record with respect to Equipment dated the date of the delivery of the Equipment to the Lessee and setting forth a full description of the Equipment, its acquisition cost, the location of the Equipment and such other details as the parties may desire. The signature of Lessee on an Individual Leasing Record shall constitute acknowledgment by Lessee that the Equipment has been delivered in good condition and accepted for lease by Lessee as of the date of the Individual Leasing Record. The Individual Leasing record shall contain a short form of lease to be executed by each of the parties reading substantially as follows:

"The undersigned Lessor hereby leases to the undersigned Lessee, and the Lessee acknowledges delivery to it in good condition of, the Equipment described above. The covenants, terms and conditions of this lease are those appearing in a Master Leasing Agreement between the undersigned Lessor and Lessee dated
19   , which covenants, terms and conditions are hereby incorporated by reference.

BLC CORPORATION, Lessor

By_____

_____ , Lessee

By _____ "

SEE PARAGRAPH 20 HEREOF FOR LESSOR'S DISCLAIMER OF WARRANTIES.

(A. Rev)   —1—

Figure D-40: MASTER LEASING AGREEMENT
(Courtesy of Bankers Leasing Corporation, San Mateo, California.)

(d) "Monthly amortization figure" for any Equipment for each full month during the lease of such Equipment is an amount equal to the acquisition cost of the Equipment divided by the number of months in the following schedule:

Type of Equipment	No. of Months

All other Equipment shall have a monthly amortization figure as approved by Lessor.

In determining the monthly amortization figure of Equipment, the anticipated useful life of such Equipment as it will be used by Lessee shall be considered, and upon request, the Lessee will furnish Lessor with information with respect thereto.

Monthly amortization shall be taken at the close of business of the last day of each full month of the lease of the Equipment until the amortized value of the Equipment has reached zero.

(e) The "aggregate amortization" of any Equipment is an amount equal to the sum total of the monthly amortization figures for each of the months for which rent for the Equipment has been paid.

(f) "Amortized value" of Equipment is the acquisition cost of the Equipment less its aggregate amortization.

(g) "Rent" for any Equipment for any month during the term of the lease of such Equipment will be the sum of the monthly amortization figure for such Equipment plus an amount computed by multiplying the following:

(1) The amortized value of such Equipment on the first day of such month, by

(2) A fraction having a numerator equal to the number of days in such month and a denominator of 360, by

(3) A Percentage equal to the sum of
percent (%) plus the higher of (i) the prime interest rate of The Chase Manhattan Bank on 90-day unsecured commercial loans on the fifteenth (15th) day of the preceding month, or (ii) the rate charged the Lessor on 90-day commercial paper issued by Lessor and sold by its commercial paper dealer on the fifteenth (15th) day of the preceding month or, if such paper has not been so sold on such date, the rate on such date quoted to Lessor on such paper by its commercial paper dealer. If, on any date referred to above, there shall be more than one such prime interest rate of The Chase Manhattan Bank in effect, or if more than one rate is charged or quoted to Lessor on such commercial paper then the last of such prime interest rates or the last of such commercial paper rates on such date shall be used. Upon

(A. Rev)

—2—

Figure D-40 (continued)

execution of this agreement, Lessor shall notify Lessee in writing of the then applicable percentage under this subsection (3). Thereafter, Lessor shall notify Lessee in writing of any change in such percentage. If the notice of change is given to the Lessee at least ten (10) days before the due date of a rent payment, the changed percentage shall be used in computing such rent payment. If such notice is given to Lessee less than ten (10) days before the due date of a rent payment, the changed percentage shall not be used in computing such rent payment, but an adjustment shall be made by Lessee in the next succeeding rent payment to give effect to the changed percentage for all previous months to which the changed percentage is applicable.

(h) Notwithstanding the foregoing subsection (g), when the aggregate amortization of any Equipment equals the acquisition cost of such Equipment, the monthly rent thereafter will be an amount equal to

2. *Agreement for Lease of Equipment.* Lessor shall lease to Lessee and Lessee shall lease from Lessor such Equipment as may be mutually agreed upon provided that the aggregate amortized value of Equipment leased by Lessor to Lessee hereunder shall not exceed $
All such leases shall be entered into in the manner and upon the terms and conditions set forth in this Master Leasing Agreement. Lessor and Lessee shall evidence their agreement to lease particular Equipment by signing and delivering to each other an Individual Leasing Record describing the Equipment. A request by the Lessee to the Lessor to acquire particular Equipment for lease hereunder shall obligate the Lessee to lease the Equipment from the Lessor upon delivery of the Equipment to the Lessee. Lessor and Lessee hereby declare that this Master Leasing Agreement is, and is intended to be, an agreement to lease, and that every Individual Leasing Record executed by the parties pursuant to this Master Leasing Agreement is a lease. The Lessor has or will have title to and will be the owner of the Equipment to be leased, and the Lessee does not hereby acquire any right, equity, title or interest in the Equipment, except the right, as Lessee, to use the same under the terms hereof. The parties agree to treat this Master Leasing Agreement as an agreement to lease and every Individual Leasing Record executed pursuant to this Master Leasing Agreement as a lease for all purposes, including without limitation, tax, accounting, regulatory or otherwise.

3. *Delivery.* Lessor shall not be liable to Lessee for any failure or delay in obtaining Equipment or making delivery thereof. Upon delivery of Equipment to Lessee and receipt by Lessor of vendor's invoice approved by Lessee together with an Individual Leasing Record with respect to the Equipment duly executed by Lessee and, if requested by Lessor, appropriate title papers for such Equipment, Lessor shall remit to the vendor a check for the total of the vendor's invoice for such Equipment, provided that the amount paid to the vendor by Lessor shall not exceed the acquisition cost of the Equipment. If the amount paid to the vendor by Lessor is less than the acquisition cost of the Equipment, to the extent that delivery costs or cost of additions to the Equipment have been met by Lessee, and do not exceed the acquisition cost, Lessor shall reimburse Lessee to the extent of such payment made by Lessee up to the amount of the acquisition cost.

4. *Lease Term.* The lease hereunder of Equipment shall be effective from the date of delivery of such Equipment, but, for convenience in computing amortization and rents, in all cases where delivery is made during the first through the fifteenth day of a month the lease term shall be deemed to commence on the first day of such month and in cases where delivery is made during the sixteenth through the last day of any month the lease term shall be deemed to commence on the first day of the next succeeding month. The lease term for each unit of Equipment shall be for a period beginning with the effective date thereof and ending one year after the last day of the month in which the effective date of the lease occurs. Thereafter, the lease term shall be extended from month to month until terminated, as provided in Sections 10, 11, 14, 15, 17 or 18 hereof. For further convenience in computing amortization and rents, any termination of a lease under Sections 10 or 11 hereof occurring during the first through the fifteenth day of any month shall be deemed to have occurred on the last day of the next preceding month and any such termination occurring during the sixteenth through the last day of any month shall be deemed to have occurred on the last day of said month. Notwithstanding the foregoing, at least the provisions of Section 9 and the first sentence of Section 11 of this Master Leasing Agreement shall apply as between Lessor and Lessee with respect to any Equipment from the time the Equipment is ordered by the Lessor pursuant to a request from the Lessee.

(A. Rev)   —3—

Figure D-40 (continued)

5. *Rent.* Lessee shall pay rent monthly in advance on the first day of each month. Reports from Lessee shall be rendered as close to such payment date as possible covering the computation of rent and other payments due hereunder for the month, adjustments to the preceding month's rent resulting from commencement or termination of the lease of any Equipment during such month and other appropriate items, if any.

6. *Use of Equipment.* Lessor and Lessee hereby acknowledge and agree that the Equipment leased hereunder shall at all times be the sole and exclusive property of Lessor, and Lessee shall have no right, title or property therein but only the right to use the same as herein provided. So long as Lessee is not in default in any obligation to the Lessor, Lessee may use the Equipment in the regular course of its business or the business of any subsidiary or affiliate of the Lessee and may permit others to use same for any lawful purpose. Such use shall be confined to the United States. Lessee shall promptly and duly execute, deliver, file and record all such documents, statements, filings and registrations, and take such further action as Lessor shall from time to time reasonably request in order to establish, perfect and maintain Lessor's title to and interest in the Equipment as against Lessee or any third party. Lessee shall notify Lessor in writing of any change in the principal location of any unit of Equipment. Notwithstanding the foregoing, no change of location shall be undertaken unless and until all such legal requirements shall have been met or obtained. At least once a year, or more frequently, if Lessor reasonably so requests, Lessee shall advise Lessor in writing where all Equipment leased hereunder as of such date is principally located. Lessee shall not use any Equipment or allow the same to be used for any unlawful purpose. Lessee shall use every reasonable precaution to prevent loss or damage to Equipment and to prevent injury to third persons or property of third persons. Lessee shall cooperate fully with Lessor and all insurance companies providing insurance under Section 8 hereof in the investigation and defense of any claims and suits. Lessee shall comply and shall cause all persons operating Equipment to comply with all insurance policy conditions and with all statutes, decrees, ordinances and regulations regarding acquiring, titling, registering, leasing, insuring, using, operating, and disposing of Equipment, and the licensing of operators thereof. Lessor or any authorized representative of Lessor may during reasonable business hours from time to time inspect Equipment wherever the same be located. Lessee shall not without prior written consent of Lessor sublease any Equipment nor permit, or suffer to exist, any lien or encumbrance other than those placed thereon by Lessor or by persons claiming only against Lessor and not against Lessee, nor shall Lessee assign any right or interest herein or in any Equipment, provided, however, that Lessee may sublet Equipment to any subsidiary or affiliate of Lessee, or to any contractor for use in performing work for Lessee, provided that such subletting shall in no way affect the obligations of Lessee hereunder, or the rights of Lessor hereunder. The Lessee shall register and title all automotive Equipment in the manner requested by Lessor. If requested by Lessor, Lessee shall cause one of its officers to hold in his custody and control all registration certificates and certificates of title covering automotive Equipment, as custodian for Lessor, and, if further requested by Lessor, Lessee shall cause such officer to certify annually in a written report to Lessor that all certificates of title required by applicable law and regulations have been obtained and are being held on behalf of Lessor. Lessee upon written request from Lessor, or if necessary or advisable under applicable law, shall attach to each unit of Equipment in a place designated by Lessor (or if no such place has been designated, in a prominent place), a sign, stencil, plaque or legend disclosing the ownership of Lessor and the interest of any mortgagee in the Equipment.

7. *Improvements and Repair of Equipment.* Lessee shall pay all costs, expenses, fees and charges incurred in connection with the use and operation of Equipment during the lease thereof. Lessee shall at all times, at its own expense, keep Equipment in first class condition and repair, and in good and efficient working order, reasonable wear and tear only excepted. This provision shall apply regardless of the cause of damage and all risks with respect thereto are assumed by Lessee. At its own expense, Lessee shall supply and replace all parts to the Equipment and shall supply the necessary power and other items required in the operation of the Equipment. In the case of motor vehicles or other automotive Equipment, Lessee shall supply and replace all items required in the operation of the automotive Equipment, including, without limitation, all parts, tires and tubes, gasoline, oil, and grease; shall put and keep such automotive Equipment or motor vehicles in condition to meet foreseeable climatic conditions; and shall arrange for the satisfactory garaging of such automotive Equipment. All improvements and additions to any of the Equipment shall become and remain the property

(A. Rev) —4—

Figure D-40 (continued)

of the Lessor, but two-way radio equipment, not owned by Lessor, shall remain the property of the Lessee or owner thereof.

8. *Insurance.* Lessee shall, at its own expense, with respect to Equipment maintain insurance insuring the respective interests of Lessor and Lessee and covering (a) physical damage to Equipment and (b) liability for personal injury, death and property damage resulting from the operation, ownership, use and possession of Equipment. All such insurance shall be in reputable companies satisfactory to Lessor. Policies covering physical damage risks shall be in an amount not less than the amortized value of Equipment and may not be subject to a deductible amount of more than $250. The Lessee shall maintain third-party liability coverage covering personal injury, death and property damage liability as a result of one accident in the amount of $5,000,000. Policies covering damage, destruction and loss of use of property of third persons may not be subject to a deductible of more than $250. Lessor shall be named insured and, with respect to physical damage coverage, a named loss payee in all insurance policies required under this Section. All such policies shall provide for at least ten (10) days' written notice to Lessor of any cancellation or material alteration of such policies. Lessee shall furnish Lessor certificates or other evidence satisfactory to Lessor or compliance by Lessee with the provisions hereof, but Lessor shall be under no duty to examine such certificates or to advise Lessee in the event its insurance is not in compliance herewith. Lessee covenants that it will not use or operate or permit the use or operation of any Equipment at any time when the insurance required by this Section is not in force with respect to such Equipment. Lessee's obligation to maintain insurance with respect to any Equipment shall commence on the actual day of delivery of the Equipment and shall continue until the Equipment is sold or the lease of the Equipment terminates, whichever is sooner. Lessee may itself insure such portions of the foregoing coverage as Lessor may approve in writing.

9. *Indemnity.*

1. Lessee agrees to indemnify and hold harmless the Lessor against any and all claims, demands and liabilities of whatsoever nature and all costs and expenses (including litigation expenses) relating to or in any way arising out of:

(a) the ordering, delivery, acquisition, title on acquisition, rejection, installation, possession, titling, registration, re-registration, custody by Lessee of title and registration documents, use, non-use, misuse, operation, transportation, repair, control or disposition of Equipment leased or requested by Lessee to be leased hereunder, except to the extent that such costs are included in the acquisition cost of such Equipment within the dollar limit provided in Section 2 hereof (or within any change of such limit agreed to in writing by Lessor and Lessee) and except for any general administrative or overhead expenses of Lessor;

(b) all recording and filing fees, stamp taxes and like expenses with respect to mortgages on the Equipment from the Lessor to any mortgagee;

(c) all costs, charges, damages or expenses for royalties and claims and expenses arising out of or necessitated by the assertion of any claim or demand based upon any infringement or alleged infringement of any patent or other right, by or in respect of any Equipment, provided, however, that Lessor will to the extent permissable make available to Lessee Lessor's rights under any similar indemnification arising by contract or operation of law from the manufacturer of Equipment;

(d) all federal, state, county, municipal, foreign or other fees and taxes of whatsoever nature, including but not limited to license, qualification, franchise, sales, use, gross receipts, ad valorem, business, property (real or personal), excise, motor vehicle, and occupation fees and taxes, and penalties and interest thereon, whether assessed, levied against or payable by Lessor or otherwise, with respect to Equipment or the acquisition, purchase, sale, rental, use, operation, control, ownership or disposition of Equipment or measured in any way by the value thereof or by the business of, investment in, or ownership by Lessor with respect thereto, excepting only net income taxes on the net income of the Lessor determined substantially in the same manner as net income is presently determined under the Federal Internal Revenue Code, and any excise, sales or use taxes included in the acquisiton cost of the Equipment;

(A. Rev) —5—

(e) any violation, or alleged violation, by Lessee of this Master Leasing Agreement or of any contracts or agreements to which Lessee is a party or by which it is bound, or any laws, rules, regulations, orders, writs, injunctions, decrees, consents, approvals, exemptions, authorizations, licenses and withholdings of objection, of any governmental or public body or authority and all other requirements having the force of law applicable at any time to Equipment or any action or transaction by Lessee with respect thereto or pursuant to this Master Leasing Agreement.

2. Lessee shall forthwith upon demand reimburse Lessor for any sum or sums expended with respect to any of the foregoing, or shall pay such amounts directly upon request from Lessor. Lessee shall be subrogated to Lessor's right in the affected transaction and shall have a right to determine the settlement of claims therein but in the best interests of Lessor. The foregoing indemnity in this section shall survive the expiration or earlier termination of this Master Leasing Agreement or any lease of Equipment hereunder.

10. *Termination of Leases of Equipment; Adjustment of Rent.* After the expiration of one year from the last day of the month in which the lease of any Equipment is effective, if such Equipment has become economically or otherwise obsolete or is no longer useful in the Lessee's business, and provided that the Lessee is not in default hereunder, Lessee may arrange for the termination of the lease of such Equipment in the manner and with the consequences hereinafter set forth. Lessee shall deliver written notice to Lessor signed by a vice president of Lessee. Such notice shall identify the Equipment the lease of which Lessee proposes to terminate, and constitute a certificate of Lessee that such Equipment has become economically or otherwise obsolete or is no longer useful in Lessee's business. After delivery of such notice, Lessee, on behalf of Lessor shall proceed directly with negotiating the sale of such Equipment to a third party unrelated to Lessor or Lessee and the Lessor shall execute and transmit to the Lessee all papers needed to effectuate the sale. Lessee shall cause the proceeds of sale of such Equipment to be transmitted promptly to the Lessor. In addition, Lessee shall pay to Lessor a termination rental payment equal to
percent (%) of the acquisition cost of any Equipment for which a lease is to be terminated. The lease of such Equipment and the Lessee's obligation to pay rent shall continue until such proceeds of sale and termination rental payment and additional rent, if any, are received by the Lessor, or Lessor's assignee, and shall thereupon terminate. If the net proceeds of sale of such Equipment are less than the amortized value of such Equipment at the time of the termination of the lease of such Equipment hereunder, the Lessee shall forthwith pay as additional rent an amount equal to such deficiency. If the net proceeds of sale of such Equipment are more than the amortized value of such Equipment at the time of the termination of the lease of such Equipment hereunder, the Lessor, in consideration of the Lessee's agreement hereunder to repair, maintain and insure the Equipment, shall as an adjustment of rent forthwith pay to Lessee or, at the option of Lessee, credit Lessee's account in an amount equal to the difference between said net proceeds of sale and said amortized value. If for any month funds are payable by Lessor to Lessee under this Section, the amount so payable may be deducted by Lessee from funds payable during the same month by Lessee for rent of Equipment.

11. *Loss or Destruction of the Equipment.* Lessee hereby assumes all risks of loss or damage to the Equipment howsoever the same may be caused. Lessee shall notify Lessor immediately of any loss or of any damage to any Equipment in an amount in excess of $1,000 and shall keep Lessor informed of all developments and correspondence regarding insurance rights and other rights and liabilities arising out of the loss or damage. In the event of total destruction of any of the Equipment or damage beyond repair or the commandeering, conversion or other such loss of any of the Equipment, or if the use thereof by the Lessee in its regular course of business is prevented by the act of any third person or persons, or any governmental instrumentality, for a period exceeding ninety (90) days, or if any of the Equipment is attached (other than on a claim against the Lessor but not the Lessee) or is seriously damaged and the attachment is not removed or the Equipment not repaired, as the case may be, in a period of ninety (90) days, then in any such event (a) Lessee shall promptly notify Lessor in writing of such fact, (b) within ten (10) days thereafter the Lessee shall pay to the Lessor, or Lessor's assignee, an amount equal to the amortized value of such Equipment at the time of payment, (c) the lease of such Equipment shall continue until such payment has been received by the Lessor, or Lessor's

(A. Rev)   —6—

assignee, and shall thereupon terminate, and (d) upon such payment all of Lessor's title to and rights in such Equipment and any insurance thereon shall automatically pass to the Lessee.

12. *Surrender of Equipment.* Upon the final termination of the lease as to any Equipment (other than a termination as provided for in Sections 10, 11, 14, 15, 17, or 18), Lessee shall surrender such Equipment to the Lessor at the Lessee's property where the Equipment is then located or at such other place as may be agreed upon. Lessee shall cooperate with Lessor in effecting removal of the Equipment from Lessee's property. Lessee shall pay the Lessor any amount by which the cost of removing and disposing of any Equipment exceeds the salvage value of the Equipment.

13. *Events of Default.* The following events of default by the Lessee shall give rise to rights on the part of the Lessor described in Section 14:

(a) Default in the payment of rent hereunder beyond the tenth (10th) day of the month for which the rent is due; or

(b) Default in the covenant of the Lessee in Section 8 hereof as to non-use of any Equipment as to which the required liability insurance is not in force; or

(c) Default in the payment or performance of any other liability, obligation, or covenant of the Lessee to the Lessor and the continuance of such default for thirty (30) days after written notice to the Lessee sent by registered or certified mail by the Lessor; or

(d) The termination of existence or business failure of, or an act of bankruptcy by, or the making of an assignment for the benefit of creditors by, the Lessee; or

(e) The institution of bankruptcy, reorganization, liquidation or receivership proceedings by or against the Lessee and, if instituted against the Lessee, its consent thereto or the pendency of such proceedings for thirty (30) days.

14. *Rights of Lessor upon Default of Lessee.* Upon the occurrence of any of the events of default described in Section 13 the Lessor may in its discretion do one or more of the following.

(a) Terminate the lease of any or all Equipment upon five (5) days' written notice to the Lessee sent by certified mail;

(b) Whether or not any lease is terminated, take immediate possession of any or all of the Equipment, including substituted parts, accessories or equipment and/or other equipment or property of the Lessor in the possession of the Lessee, wherever situated and for such purpose, enter upon any premises without liability for doing so;

(c) Whether or not any action has been taken under Sections 14 (a) or (b) above, the Lessor may sell any Equipment (with or without the concurrence or request of the Lessee) with the consequences set forth in Section 10 hereof;

(d) Hold, use or lease any Equipment as the Lessor in its sole discretion may decide, and continue to hold the Lessee liable for any deficiency between the rent received by the Lessor from others and the rent payable hereunder for the balance of the term of the lease of such Equipment;

(e) Invoke and exercise any other remedy or remedies available to Lessor by law or in equity.

If after default Lessee fails to deliver or converts the Equipment or the Equipment is destroyed, Lessee shall be liable to the Lessor for all unpaid rent to the date of such failure to deliver, conversion or destruction of such Equipment plus its amortized value at the time and all loss and damages sustained and all costs and expenses incurred by reason of the default. If after default Lessee delivers Equipment to Lessor or if Lessor repossesses Equipment, Lessee shall be liable for and the Lessor may recover from the Lessee all unpaid rent to the date of such delivery or repossession plus all loss and damages sustained and all costs and expenses incurred by reason of the default.

(A. Rev)   –7–

Figure D-40 (continued)   342

15. *Equipment To Be and Remain Personal Property.* It is the intention and understanding of both Lessor and Lessee that all Equipment shall be and at all times remain personal property. Lessee will obtain and record such instruments and take such steps as may be necessary to prevent any person from acquiring any rights in the Equipment paramount to the rights of the Lessor, by reason of such Equipment being deemed to be real property. If, notwithstanding the intention of the parties and the provisions of this Section 15, any person acquires or claims to have acquired any rights in any Equipment paramount to the rights of the Lessor, by reason of such Equipment being deemed to be real property, and such person seeks in any manner to interfere with the continued quiet enjoyment of the Equipment by the Lessee as contemplated by this Agreement, then the Lessee shall promptly notify the Lessor in writing of such fact (unless the basis for such interference is waived or eliminated to the satisfaction of the Lessor within a period of ninety (90) days from the date it is asserted) and the Lessee shall within ninety (90) days after such notice pay to the Lessor or Lessor's assignee an amount equal to the amortized value of the Equipment at the time of payment. The lease of the Equipment shall continue until such payment has been received and shall thereupon terminate; and upon such payment all of Lessor's title to and rights in such Equipment shall automatically pass to the Lessee.

16. *Miscellaneous.* This Agreement and all rights hereunder shall be governed by the laws of the State of   . Each of the parties hereto acknowledges that the other party shall not by act, delay, omission or otherwise be deemed to have waived any of its rights or remedies hereunder or under any other instrument given hereunder unless such waiver is given in writing and the same shall be binding to the extent therein provided and only upon the parties signing the same. A waiver of any one occasion shall not be construed as a waiver on any future occasion. No executory agreement shall be effective to change, modify or discharge, in whole or in part, this Master Leasing Agreement, or any other instrument given in connection herewith unless such agreement is in writing and signed by the party to be charged therewith. All rights, remedies and powers granted herein, or in any other instrument given in connection herewith, shall be cumulative and may be exercised singularly or cumulatively.

17. *Additional Right of Termination.* Either Lessor or Lessee may terminate this Master Leasing Agreement at any time with respect to any equipment not yet leased hereunder by giving at least sixty (60) days' notice in writing to the other party of such termination and setting forth in said notice the termination date. Provided, however, neither such notice nor termination shall affect any transactions entered into or rights created or obligations incurred prior to such termination. In the event of any such termination, Lessee shall arrange for and effect not later than two years from the termination date a termination of the lease of all Equipment hereunder and a sale of all Equipment in the manner and with the consequences as provided by Section 10 hereof. Notwithstanding the provisions of Section 4 hereof, the lease term for all Equipment, the lease of which is terminated under this Section, and the Lessee's obligation to pay rent shall continue until Lessor receives the proceeds of sale of such Equipment.

18. *Purchase of Equipment.* After the expiration of the amortization period of any Equipment leased hereunder, and provided that Lessee is not in default hereunder, Lessee may purchase such Equipment at its then fair market value. The lease of such Equipment and Lessee's obligation to pay rent therefor shall continue until the purchase price has been transmitted to Lessor and shall thereupon terminate. If the parties cannot agree on the fair market value of any such Equipment, they shall select a qualified independent appraiser to determine such value and his decision shall be final.

19. *Investment Tax Credit.* As permitted under Section 48(d) of the Federal Internal Revenue Code, Lessor shall elect to treat Lessee as having acquired the Equipment which is leased hereunder, if it qualifies for such election, for purposes of the investment credit provisions under Section 38 of the Federal Internal Revenue Code and Lessee shall consent to such election as to all Equipment leased hereunder and which qualifies for such election. Lessee shall provide Lessor with an annual summary statement as to all Equipment for Internal Revenue Service reporting purposes.

20. *DISCLAIMER OF WARRANTIES.* LESSEE AGREES AND ACKNOWLEDGES THAT ACCEPTANCE FOR LEASE OF THE EQUIPMENT SHALL CONSTITUTE LESSEE'S ACKNOWLEDGMENT AND AGREEMENT THAT LESSEE HAS FULLY INSPECTED SUCH

(A. Rev)   —8—

Figure D-40 (continued)

EQUIPMENT, AND THAT THE EQUIPMENT IS IN GOOD ORDER AND CONDITION AND IS OF THE MANUFACTURE, DESIGN, SPECIFICATIONS AND CAPACITY SELECTED BY LESSEE, THAT LESSEE IS SATISFIED THAT THE SAME IS SUITABLE FOR ITS PURPOSE, THAT LESSOR IS NOT A MANUFACTURER OR ENGAGED IN THE SALE OR DISTRIBUTION OF EQUIPMENT, THAT LESSOR HAS PURCHASED THE EQUIPMENT FROM VENDORS OF LESSEE'S CHOICE, AND THAT LESSOR HAS NOT MADE AND DOES NOT HEREBY MAKE ANY REPRESENTATION, EXPRESS WARRANTY, IMPLIED WARRANTY, OR COVENANT WHATSOEVER WITH RESPECT TO TITLE, MERCHANTABILITY, CONDITION, QUALITY, DURABILITY, SUITABILITY OR FITNESS OF THE EQUIPMENT IN ANY RESPECT OR IN CONNECTION WITH, OR FOR ANY PURPOSE OR USE OF LESSEE, OR ANY OTHER REPRESENTATION, WARRANTY OR COVENANT OF ANY KIND OR CHARACTER, EXPRESS OR IMPLIED, WITH RESPECT THERETO. Lessor shall, at Lessee's sole expense take all action reasonably requested by Lessee to make available to Lessee any rights of Lessor under any express or implied warranties of any manufacturer or vendor of the Equipment.

21. *Assignment by Lessor of Rights Under This Master Leasing Agreement and Mortgages of Equipment to an Assignee.* Lessee acknowledges notice that Lessor may finance its acquisition and ownership of the Equipment by borrowing and in that connection may, as security, grant to an assignee chattel mortgages on the Equipment, it being understood, however, that such chattel mortgages shall contain a provision to the effect that as long as Lessee is not in default hereunder or under any lease executed pursuant hereto, it shall be entitled to uninterrupted use of the Equipment on the terms herein provided. Lessee also acknowledges notice of the possible assignment by the Lessor to an assignee of the rents and all other sums due and to become due hereunder, all as security for obligations of the Lessor to the assignee. After such assignment the terms and provisions of this Master Leasing Agreement may not be altered, modified or waived without the written consent of such assignee. After such assignment and written notice thereof to the Lessee, the Lessee shall make payment of all rents and other payments due hereunder directly to the assignee, and such payments shall discharge the obligations of Lessee to Lessor hereunder to the extent of such payments. The assignment by the Lessor to the assignee of rights hereunder shall not transfer to the assignee the general title to Equipment or impose on the assignee any of the duties or obligations of the Lessor hereunder, but in all other respects the assignee shall have all the rights of the Lessor hereunder to the extent necessary to realize upon rents and other monies payable by the Lessee and to protect the assignee's security interest in Equipment resulting from the chattel mortgage.

IN WITNESS WHEREOF, Lessor and Lessee have duly executed this Master Leasing Agreement as of the day and year first above written.

Attest: _____   BLC CORPORATION, Lessor

                                                    By _____

Attest: _____   _____, Lessee

                                                    By _____

                                                                            (9-77)

(A. Rev)   —9—

Figure D-40 (continued)

COMPARATIVE FLOTATION COSTS

	DEBT	COMMON	OTHER
SIZE OF ISSUE			
NUMBER OF UNITS TO BE ISSUED			
UNDERWRITING COMMISSION			
REGISTRATION EXPENSES			
PRINTING & PREP. EXPENSES			
LEGAL FEES			
OTHER COSTS			
TOTAL ISSUE COSTS			
PREMIUM OR DISCOUNT (ANTICIPATED)			
NET PROCEEDS TO THE FIRM			
VALUE PER UNIT(E.G. SHARE)			
ISSUE COST PER UNIT			
PROCEEDS PER UNIT			
ANTICIPATED PREM. OR DISC. P/ UNIT			
NET PROCEEDS PER UNIT			
AS PERCENTAGE OF GROSS PROCEEDS:			
UNDERWRITING COMMISSION			
REGISTRATION EXPENSES			
PRINTING & PREP. EXPENSES			
LEGAL FEES			
OTHER COSTS			
TOTAL ISSUE COSTS			
PREMIUM (+) OR DISCOUNT (-)			
NET PROCEEDS TO FIRM			

Figure D-41: FLOTATION COST OF ALTERNATIVE EXTERNAL FUNDS

COST APPROACH

Source:

Marshall Valuation Service
Section 13, Pages 12, 13 & 14
Stores and Commercial Buildings
Excellent Retail, Class D

Section 17, Page 10
Silo

Section 66, Page 1
Site Improvements

Structure - (Except Greenhouse and Silo)

Building Data:

Area:	7,810± square feet
Average Story Height:	22 feet
Perimeter:	445± feet

Multipliers

Floor Area/Perimeter:	0.997
Story Height:	1.213
Current Cost:	1.14
Local Cost:	1.02

Base Cost: $30.17

Adjusted Base Cost:
    $30.17 x 0.997 x 1.213 x 1.14 x 1.02 = $42.43

Then:
    7,810± sq. ft. x $42.43 per sq. ft. = $331,378

Total Cost of Structure: $331,378

Greenhouse

    The greenhouse shall be a Lord and Burnham, standard 35' x 120', Blue Ribbon truss framed greenhouse.

Estimated Cost by Lord & Burnham: $ 77,720

Figure D-42: COST AND INCOME APPROACHES FOR NEW ASSET ACQUISITIONS
(Courtesy of Lexington Gardens Incorporated and Pepperidge Farm, Inc.)

COST APPROACH, continued

Silo

Silo Data:

Diameter:	50 feet
Height:	27.5 feet
Construction:	Wood

Multipliers

Current Cost:	1.04
Local Cost:	1.02
Wood Construction:	1.05

Base Cost: $15,714 (interpolated)

Adjusted Cost:
$15,714 x 1.04 x 1.02. x 1.05 = $17,503

Total Cost of Silo: $ 17,503

Figure D-42 (continued)

COST APPROACH, continued

Site Improvements

Paving and Base -
    45,600± sq. ft. @ $0.84/sq. ft. = $ 38,304
Curbing -
    2,500± ft. @ $3.94/ft. =   9,850
Walks* -   11,200
Storm Drains -
    8 catch basins @ $585 ea. =   4,680
    725± ft. 6" PVC @ $8.60/ft. =   6,235
Two Dry Wells (estimated) =   1,500
Fencing Gate and Stone Work* =   18,300
Signs* =   4,300
Plantings* =   24,700
Shade Racks* =   19,000
Retention Pond and Fill* =   9,700
Lighting (estimated) =   1,500
Shrub Sprinklers* =   3,400

Total Cost of Site Improvements: $152,669

* As per estimate supplied this office by the Clark Corporation and is
   considered reasonable.

Figure D-42 (continued)

COST APPROACH, continued

Summary

Cost of Structure:	$331,378
Cost of Greenhouse:	77,720
Cost of Silo:	17,503
Cost of Site Improvements:	152,669

Total Cost of Improvements: $579,270

This cost does not include several items (soft costs) such as interest during construction and other out of pocket costs. This typically ranges from 10% to 25%. Using a nominal 10%, then:

$579,270 x 1.10 =	$637,197
Add Estimated Land Value:	265,000

Value Indicated by Cost Approach, $902,197

                     rounded: $900,000

INCOME APPROACH

The rent for the subject proposal shall be $92,000 per year for the first ten years. The term of this lease may be extended at the option of Lexington Gardens, Incorporated for four additional terms of five years each. During option periods, if exercised, the basic annual rental shall be payable in the following amounts.

Term	Rental
1st five years option period:	$104,000
2nd five years option period:	$118,000
3rd five years option period:	$134,000
4th five years option period:	$152,000

Lexington Gardens, Incorporated has the option to purchase the subject property as follows:

Lease Elapsed Time	Purchase Price
4th through 10th years:	$ 938,000
1st five year option:	$1,052,000
2nd five year option:	$1,128,000
3rd five year option:	$1,202,000
4th five year option:	$1,282,000

Lexington Gardens, Incorporated shall be responsible for real estate taxes, interior and nonstructural repairs; maintenance of heating, cooling and electrical systems or components; maintenance of sidewalks, curbs, roadways and parking lots, including the removal of debris, snow, ice and obstructions considered unlawful; all charges for steam, gas, water, electricity, lights, heat, power and other services used in or about or supplied to the leased premises; and public liability insurance.

The landlord, Herbert T. Clark, III, shall be responsible for fire and hazard insurance and interior and exterior structural repairs; maintenance of all drainage and all water, gas, electricity and utility lines.

Then:

Gross Income*:		$92,000

Expenses

Management:	$ 920	
Reparis and Maintenance:	750	
Insurance:	1,102	
Reserve for Replacements:	1,000	
Total Expenses:		3,772
		$88,228

*   The appraiser made no allowance for vacancy and rent loss because the lease is guaranteed by Campbell Soup Company.

Figure D-42 (continued)

INCOME APPROACH continued

Justification of Expenses

Management - estimated at 1% to reflect the status of the tenant and a net lease.

Repairs and Maintenance - estimated for normal structural maintenance of a new building.

Insurance - based upon $0.10 per square foot of gross leasable area. Reflects the wood frame construction, type of use and the fact that the town does not have a full-time, paid fire department.

Reserve for Replacements - allows for eventual replacement of short-lived items, with consideration given to the responsibilities of the tenant.

Capitalization Process

The overall capitalization rate is derived for this property through the Mortgage-Equity Technique (Ellwood Method). This technique recognizes and gives effect to mortgage financing and equity yields. Net income before recapture and debt service is processed into value by the overall rate which includes the following considerations:

1. Terms of obtainable first mortgage: interest rates, amortization, mortgage loan-to-value ratio.

2. Equity position: typical length of ownership required to attract investment.

3. Estimated appreciation or depreciation of property values for ownership period.

The following mortgage terms are based upon conversations with several larger lending institutions.

Term of Mortgage:	25 years
Interest Rate:	12%
Loan-to-Value Ratio:	75%

INCOME APPROACH, continued

Capitalization Process, continued

A projected holding period of five years is used because of the purchase option. During this period of ownership, the average investor would seek a 10%* return on his equity. The appraiser assumes that the property will appreciate 10% over the holding period.

Value = Net Operating Income -:- Capitalization Rate

Where:

I = Net Operating Income
R = Capitalization Rate
R = Y - MC - Appreciation x Sinking Fund Factor
Y = Equity Yield (10%)
M = Loan-to-Value Ratio (75%)
C = Mortgage Coefficient

Then:

R = Y - MC-Appreciation x Sinking Fund Factor
R = 0.10 - (0.75 x - .019256)** - (0.10 x 0.163797)
R = 0.10 + 0.014442 - 0.016380
R = 0.098062, rounded to 9.8%

Net Operating Income = $88,228

Then:
$88,228 -:- 9.8% = $900,286

Value Indicated by Income Approach,
   Mortgage Equity Technique $900,286

* Typically, as the mortgage interest rate rises, the equity yield
   decreases and investors accept negative leverage to gain tax shelter.

   The equity yield reflects the investors risk, which for this property
   is reduced by rental increases during the option periods (typically,
   the rental decreases with the age of the improvements) and the
   guarantee of the lease by a highly rated national corporation.

** Ellwood Tables, Fourth Edition, Page 364.

INCOME APPROACH, continued

Inwood Technique

    The estimated market value can also be calculated using the Inwood Technique, since the lease is guaranteed by a nationally recognized corporation.

    The same mortgage terms and equity yield used in the Ellwood Method are used in the Inwood Technique as follows:

Mortgage	75% @ 12% =	0.090
Equity	25% @ 10% =	0.025
Discount Rate:		0.115, or 11.5%

Note: Although the lease is payable monthly in advance, the expenses would tend to be deferred, i.e. they would typically be paid during the year, or set up as a reserve during the year. This would result in a somewhat higher value, but is disregarded as not significant.

Net Operating Income = $88,228

Then:
    $88,228 -:- 12 = $7,352.33 per month.

    Present value factor for four years, payable monthly in advance is:

    38.330317 x 1.0095833 = 38.697648

Reversion factor for four years: 0.646994

Value of Income Stream =
    $7,352.33 x 38.697648 = $284,518

Value of Reversion =
    $938,000* x 0.646994 (reversion factor) =   606,880

Value Indicated by Income Approach,
    Inwood Technique: $891,398

* As per purchase option.

Figure D-42 (continued)

INCOME APPROACH, continued

Summary

Value Indicated by Income Approach,
    Inwood Technique: $891,398

Value Indicated by Income Approach,
    Mortgage Equity Technique: $900,286

Value Indicated by Income Approach, rounded: $900,000

Figure D-42 (continued)

PRESENT VALUES ᴏꜰ FUTURE EARNINGS

Yr.	Estimated Earnings (after taxes)	PV ____ %	PV ____ %	PV ____ %	PV ____ %
1					
2					
3					
4					
5					
6					
7					
8					
9					
10					
11					
	Subtotal				
	+ Residual Value				
	Subtotal				
	− Cash Advance				
	TOTAL				

Figure D-43: PRESENT VALUES OF FUTURE EARNINGS

COMPANY: _____ SIC: _____

DATE: _____ FORECAST: _____ TO _____

UNIT: _____ STATED IN: $000,ØØØ

	PRIOR YEAR	CURRENT YEAR	NEXT YEAR 198_	TWO YEARS 198_	THREE YEARS 198_
SOURCES OF CASH:					
Pre-Tax Profits					
Net Profit					
Depreciation					
NET CASH GENERATED					
USES OF CASH:					
Inventories (Increase)					
Receivables (Increase)					
Prepaids (Increase)					
TOTAL WORKING CAPITAL					
Fixtures & Equipment					
Leased Equipment					
Debt Repayments (L.T.)					
NET CASH DRAIN					
SURPLUS (DEFICIENCIES)					
SUMMARY CASH POSITION:					
Beginning Cash Balance					
Surplus (Deficiency)					
Ending Cash Balance					
CASH TRANSFERS					

Figure D-44: PROJECTED CASH FLOW OF BUSINESS UNIT

CONFIDENTIAL

MEMO

TO: R.G. McGovern
FROM: J.C. Griggs, II
DATE: January 9, 1978
SUBJECT: Acquisition Policy Statement for Pepperidge Farm, Inc.

In the decade from fiscal '78-'79 through fiscal '87-'88 it will be the internal objective of the management of Pepperidge Farm, Inc. to increase sales dollars at an annualized rate of 15.3%. This rate of growth will mean sales of $1.0 billion in fiscal '87-'88. See Table A.

Over the next decade this plan requires acquisitions outside our Bakery, Biscuit and Frozen Foods businesses totaling $101 million. This growth plan may also require acquisitions within our three basic businesses as well.

It is with these considerations in mind that the following Acquisition Policy Statement is submitted.

   I.   Minimal Financial Criteria:

Return on Investment	15% to 18%
Net Income on Net Sales	6% to 8%
Annual Sales Growth	10% to 15%

   II.   Other Requirements:

Strong management that will stay on
100% control
Minimum sales volume of $10.0 million within first five year plan
Superior quality reputation in its field
Products and management skills that are complimentary to the rest of our business
Enhancement of the Pepperidge Farm, Inc. reputation
Will not bleed Pepperidge Farm, Inc.
Payment of Interest Expense, Goodwill amortization and a 45% Dividend Rate

ta

Figure D-45: ACQUISITION POLICY CHECKLIST

ACQUISITION POLICY

1. Financial

   A. Return on Investment - 10%
   B. Risk of Investment
   C. Past Sales Growth
   D. Past Profit Growth
   E. Pooling of Interest Basis
   F. Future Sales and Profit Growth Prospects

2. Industry

   A. Potential to Grow - Sales and Profit
   B. Expertise in Industry
   C. A Growth Industry
   D. Competitive Position (Market Leadership)
   E. Markets Served
   F. Company Reputation
   G. Product Quality and Price
   H. Product Reputation
   I. Cyclicality

3. Feasibility

   A. Size of Company
   B. Owners Receptive
   C. Capable Management
   D. Location
   E. Labor Situation (Union ETC)
   F. Ethics
   G. Conflicts with us or Customers
   H. Price of Company

4. The Company

   A. Compatible Management
   B. % Utilization of Plant & Equipment
   C. Ability to Manufacture Products for us.
   D. Marketing Ability
   E. Research Capabilities
   F. Personnel Policies
   G. Distribution System
   H. Customers and Customer Relations
   I. Leases or other restrictions

Figure D-45 (continued)

TABLE A
($000)

Base Year Fiscal '77-'78 Sales of $240,000
Compounded Annual Growth Rate of 15.3%
Price Increases at 3.3% annually
Acquisitions in Bakery, Biscuit and Frozen are part of 10% growth
   of Existing Businesses

	Sales	Total Sales Increase $	3.3% Price	New Sales	10% Existing Businesses	2% New Ventures
77-78	240,000					
78-79	277,000	37,000	8,000	29,000	24,000	5,000
79-80	319,000	42,000	9,000	33,000	28,000	5,000
80-81	368,000	49,000	11,000	38,000	32,000	6,000
81-82	424,000	56,000	12,000	44,000	37,000	7,000
82-83	489,000	65,000	14,000	51,000	42,000	9,000
83-84	564,000	75,000	16,000	59,000	49,000	10,000
84-85	651,000	87,000	19,000	68,000	56,000	12,000
85-86	752,000	101,000	21,000	80,000	65,000	15,000
86-87	868,000	116,000	25,000	91,000	75,000	16,000
87-88	1,000,000	132,000	29,000	103,000	87,000	16,000

Figure D-45 (continued)

PEPPERIDGE FARM, INC.

TO: Executive Committee
FROM: J.C. Griggs, II
DATE: October 27, 1978
SUBJECT: Campbell Soup Co. Approved Acquisition Policy
                 Statement

A.   Requirements

      1)   Average earnings growth rate greater than 10%.
      2)   R.O.I. greater than 14%. Net profit to sales minimum of 4%.
      3)   Must be branded products with quality even if at higher prices.
      4)   Strong management that will stay on.
      5)   Sales volume over $50.0 million.
      6)   100% control with payment in Campbell stock or cash.

B.   Industries to be Considered

      —   Soft Drinks
      —   Soaps and Detergents
      —   Hospital Supplies and Equipment
      —   Flavorings, Spices, Food Additives
      —   Appliances and Specialized Machinery
      —   Food Processing
      —   China, Cookware and Tableware
      —   Plastic Materials and Rubber Products
      —   Recreational Products
           (Not leisure time in the entertainment field)

ta

Figure D-45 (continued)

PEPPERIDGE FARM, INC.

MEMO

TO: Executive Committee
FROM: J.C. Griggs, II
DATE: October 27, 1978
SUBJECT: Acquisition Policy Proposal for P.F. Inc.

If we are agreed that we must acquire businesses in order to achieve the 15.0% growth rate recommended by H.A. Shaub, then we must have a policy statement that will receive his approval.

Obviously, our P.F. policy cannot be too different from Campbell's approved policy.

In order to get the ball rolling, the writer would suggest the following:

1.   Net Income on Net Sales   6% - 8%
2.   Annual Sales Growth   10% - 15%
3.   Return on Investment   15% - 18%
4.   Strong management that will stay on
5.   100% control with payment in Campbell stock or cash
6.   Sales volume of at least $10.0 million within initial five year plan
7.   Superior quality reputation in its field
8.   Will not bleed P.F. Inc.

Campbell has listed industries they would consider. By definition, they have eliminated many others. Should P.F. also attempt to list those that would be of interest to us?

The writer suggests that this is the most critical and important subject that the Executive Committee has to come to grips with. It affects everything else we must do.

ta

Figure D-45 (continued)

MEMO

TO: R.G. McGovern
FROM: J.C. Griggs, II
DATE: December 30, 1977
SUBJECT: Acquisition Proposal for Williams-Sonoma, Inc.

I. The minimal financial criteria under the Pepperidge Farm, Inc. acquisition policy are:

— Return on Investment   15% to 18%
— Net Income on Net Sales   6% to 8%
— Annual Sales Growth   10% to 15%

Other requirements include:

— Strong management that will stay on
— 100% control
— Minimum sales volume of $10.0 million within first five year plan
— Superior quality reputation in its field
— Products and management skills that are complimentary to the rest of our business
— Enhancement of the Pepperidge Farm, Inc. reputation
— Will not bleed Pepperidge Farm, Inc.
— Payment of Interest Expense, Goodwill amortization and a 45% Dividend Rate

The Williams-Sonoma Company exceeds all our requirements in the five year plan. It is, therefore, a viable acquisition consideration.

A Five Year Plan is attached along with the Return on Investment calculations based on the format used by the Campbell Soup Company Strategic Planning Department.

II. Williams-Sonoma is a retailer of very high quality cookware and accessories through direct mail and four retail stores in California. In spite of its small ($5.0 million) base, the company has a national reputation in its category and has the potential of $20.0 sales within a five year period.

Cookware, cookbooks, kitchen and dining accessories and add-ons are virtually impossible to measure as a specific market. The Conference Board Guide to Consumer Markets 1977/1978 on page 165 breaks down the total $66.6 billion spent for housefurnishings and equipment in 1975. The tableware and utensils category was $5.9 billion in 1975, up from $2.37 billion in 1965.

Figure D-46: ACQUISITION POLICY

Acquisition Proposal for Williams-Sonoma, Inc.
Page 2

As a food related business it lends itself to association with Campbell and Pepperidge.

They are successful retailers and we need more of these skills in our corporation for future growth.

Their contacts with manufacturers here and abroad of the items they retail could lead us to other potential acquisitions in many areas if reverse integration is a strategy we wish to pursue.

Within ten years there could be 50 or more Williams-Sonoma retail outlets in major markets across the country providing us with a base for expanding into other retail lines; silverware, fine dinner place settings, cutlery, glassware, etc.

While a larger portion of the food dollar continues to go to "eating out" there is a very strong counter-activity among higher income women (and men) to become specialty or gourmet cooks at home. Superb dinners are difficult to find even in the most touted restaurants, and the prices are becoming astronomical. The home gourmet cook can serve these dinners at much less cost.

Cookbooks continue to sell second only to the Bible. Cooking classes and schools are increasingly popular. Williams-Sonoma has had James Beard on a retainer for several years and he has run cooking classes for them and they have been modestly profitable for the company.

III. Short Term Advantages

1. Provides both our mail order businesses with East Coast and West Coast warehouses.

2. Interchange of items between catalogs.

3. Exchange of house lists.

4. Retailing management skills.

5. Synergism between the management groups.

6. Add Godiva Boutique sections to Williams-Sonoma retail stores.

7. Immediate relationship with leading chefs, writers and food editors in the cooking field around the world.

Figure D-46 (continued)

Acquisition Proposal for Williams-Sonoma, Inc.
Page 3

    8. Add Williams-Sonoma outlets to Lexington Garden Centers.

    9. Put Williams-Sonoma catalogs in Pepperidge Farm Mail Order Buyers packs and vice-versa.

    10. European relationships through Delacre, Lazzaroni, Kambly, and other friends.

IV. Long Term Possibilities

    1. Base of 50 or more retail stores.

    2. Williams-Sonoma label on specialty and gourmet food products. S.S. Pierce left an unfilled void for a national label.

    3. Clothes starting with kitchen styles of elegant-informal.

    4. Wines - Importing, retailing and wholesale.

    5. Table linens, dining room furniture and accessories.

    6. Wholesaler. Sections in major department stores.

    7. Publish books.

    8. Institutional/Food Service tie-ins; cookware, products, recipes and skills.

V. The writer recommends that we pursue the possibility of acquiring this company without delay.

Figure D-46 (continued)

MEMO

TO: File
FROM: J.C. Griggs, II
DATE: January 6, 1978
SUBJECT: Financial Analysis of Williams-Sonoma
            Five Year Plan

The assumptions are attached along with the spread sheet.

1. Net Earnings (after Interest and Goodwill) increase to $1,401,000 in '82-'83. Percent net earnings increase to 7.2% before Interest but after Goodwill).

2. Net Sales increase from $4,530,000 projected for '77-'78 to $20,550,000 which is an average growth of 35.5%.

3. Asset Turns increase from 2.4 to 7.8 for a five year average of 4.5. Calculations based on continuing to lease present and future facilities.

4. Return on Investment averages 26.7% over the five year period. This allows about 10 points for a risk factor.

5. Dividends will be paid at 45% of Net Earnings after Interest.

6. No value has been placed on the existing House Lists.

ta

Figure D-46 (continued)

WILLIAMS-SONOMA
ASSUMPTIONS

(1)   Purchase price of $2,500,000.

(2)   Fixed assets of $18,000 Furniture and Fixtures $85,000 Leasehold Improvements.

(3)   Investment of $100,000 in Mail Order each year with average life of ten years.

(4)   Investment of $200,000 in new store Leasehold Improvements with a lease life of five years.

(5)   Working capital to increase at 50% of sales increase percentage.

(6)   Two new stores each year with stock valued at $75,000 each.

(7)   Net Income was reduced by $43,000 each year for amortization of goodwill on a 40 year basis. Goodwill was calculated as follows:

March 31, 1977	Balance Sheet Equity	$ 528,000
March 31, 1978	Projected Net Earnings	
	After Tax	261,000
		789,000
	Goodwill	1,711,000
Proposed Purchase Price		$2,500,000

(8)   Average investment was the sum of the beginning investment and the ending investment divided by two.

(9)   All figures are based on constant dollars.

(10)   Tax rate of 48%

Figure D-46 (continued)

RETAIL STORES

Date Opened		Net Sales ($000) '75-'76 Actual	Pre-Tax Operat. Income ($000) '75-'76 Actual	'76-'77 Actual	'77-'78 Projection		'78-'79 Plan Year I		'79-'80 II		'80-'81 III		'81-'82 IV		'82-'83 V	
4/58	San Francisco	587	109	805	940	188	1000	200	1100	220	1150	230	1200	240	1200	240
7/73	Beverly Hills	571	114	682	820	164	900	180	1000	200	1100	220	1150	230	1200	240
8/74	Palo Alto	192	15	254	305	61	365	73	440	88	530	106	600	120	700	140
8/77	Costa Mesa				200	-0-	400	20	560	56	730	110	840	168	1000	200
3/78	Dallas						200	-0-	400	20	560	56	730	110	875	175
4/78	Houston						200	-0-	400	20	560	56	730	110	875	175
8/78	#7						150	-0-	400	20	560	56	730	110	875	175
8/79	#8								200	-0-	400	20	560	56	730	110
8/79	#9								150	-0-	400	20	560	56	730	110
4/80	#10										200	-0-	400	20	560	56
8/80	#11										150	-0-	400	20	560	56
8/81	#12												200	-0-	400	20
8/81	#13												150	-0-	400	20
4/82	#14														200	-0-
8/82	#15														150	-0-
	Total Stores	1350	238	1741	2265	413	3215	473	4650	624	6340	874	8250	1240	10,455	1717

367

Figure D-46 (continued)

FIVE YEAR PLAN
TOTAL COMPANY

		Net Sales ($000)	% Sales Increase	Pre-Tax Profit ($000)	% to Sales	Net Income ($000)	%
Actual	74-75	1,105		93	8.4	55	5.0
Actual	75-76	2,329	110.8	179	7.7	105	4.5
Actual	76-77	3,319	42.5	182	5.5	101	3.0
Projection	77-78	4,530	36.5	458	10.1	238	5.3
I	78-79	6,500	43.5	604	9.3	314	4.8
II	79-80	9,250	42.3	900	9.7	468	5.1
III	80-81	12,550	35.7	1,371	10.9	713	5.7
IV	81-82	16,325	30.1	2,048	12.5	1,065	6.5
V	82-83	20,550	25.9	2,928	14.2	1,523	7.4

Notes

1. 48% Tax Rate

2. Net Income before interest deduction on Average Investment

Figure D-46 (continued)

FIVE YEAR PLAN

RETAIL STORES

		Net Sales ($000)	% Sales Increase	Pre-Tax profit ($000)	Pre-Tax Profit % to Sales
Actual	75-76	1,350		238	17.6%
Actual	76-77	1,741	+29.0		
Projection	77-78	2,265	+30.1	413	18.2%
I	78-79	3,215	+41.9	473	14.7%
II	79-80	4,650	+46.9	624	13.4%
III	80-81	6,340	+36.3	874	13.8%
IV	81-82	8,250	+30.1	1,240	15.0%
V	82-83	10,455	+26.7	1,717	16.4%

ASSUMPTIONS

1. Two new store openings per year - net. Plan April and August openings.

2. New stores:

	Sales Growth		Pre-Tax Operating Income
1st Year	$200,000	April	-0-
	$150,000	August	
2nd Year	$400,000		5%
3rd Year	+40% to $560,000		10%
4th Year	+30% to $730,000		15%
5th Year	+20% to $875,000		20%
Maximum	$1,200,000		20%

Figure D-46 (continued)

	Projected 77-78	78-79	79-80	80-81	81-82	82-83	Five Year Plan Totals	Average Five Years
Beginning Investment	238	2,500	2,867	3,122	3,041	2,878	14,408	2,882
Cash Inflow								
After Tax Earnings Before Int.		314	468	713	1,065	1,523	4,083	816
Int. after Tax (4¼% × line 22)		(106)	(114)	(127)	(129)	(122)	(598)	(120)
Net Earnings		208	354	586	936	1,401	3,485	696
Goodwill Deduction		(43)	(43)	(43)	(43)	(43)	(215)	(43)
Sub-Total		165	311	543	893	1,358	3,270	653
Depreciation		70	120	170	220	270	850	170
Total 6 & 9		278	474	756	1,156	1,671	4,335	866
Cash Expended								
Additions to Working Capital		251	270	273	272	271	1,337	267
Capital Expenditures		300	300	300	300	300	1,500	300
Dividends 45%		94	159	264	421	630	1,568	314
Total		645	729	837	993	1,201	4,405	881
Net Cash Generated 10 − 16		(367)	(255)	(81)	163	469	(71)	(14)
Ending Investment 1 + 18	2,500	2,867	3,122	3,041	2,878	2,409	14,479	2,896
Average Investment $\dfrac{1-20}{2}$		2,684	2,995	3,082	2,960	2,644	14,444	2,889
Net Sales	4,530	6,500	9,250	12,550	16,325	20,550	65,175	13,035
Asset Turns 24/22		2.42	3.09	4.07	5.52	7.77		4.51
% Net Earnings $\dfrac{4-7}{24}$		4.17	4.60	5.34	6.26	7.20		5.93
Return on Investment Before Interest and after Goodwill 26 + 28		10.1%	14.2%	21.7%	34.6%	56.0%		26.7%

Figure D-46 (continued)

FIVE YEAR PLAN

MAIL ORDER DIVISION

		Net Sales ($000)	% Sales Increase	Pre-Tax Profit	Pre-Tax Profit % to Sales
Actual	75-76	963		(61)	(6.3)
Actual	76-77	1,510	56.8	17	1.1
Projection	77-78	2,265	50.0	45	2.0
I	78-79	3,285	45.0	131	4.0
II	79-80	4,600	40.0	276	6.0
III	80-81	6,210	35.0	497	8.0
IV	81-82	8,075	30.0	808	10.0
V	82-83	10,095	25.0	1,211	12.0

Figure D-46 (continued)

REAL ESTATE FORMS FOR ACQUISITION, LEASING, PROFIT PROTECTION

SECTION E

Real Estate Forms for Acquisition, Leasing, Profit Protection

Figure   Page

Real Estate Forms for Acquisition, Leasing, Profit Protection

For most organizations real estate transactions, like asset acquisitions, are unavoidable. A supplier of materials or services, or a subcontractor, strives to PROTECT PROFITS AND MINIMIZE unplanned COSTS and LEGAL FEES. Real estate acquired or leased for production or investment purposes similarly necessitates forms especially geared to meet legal requirements for deeds, mortgages, settlement statements, etc.; and the purchase and sale of real estate and options produce another flurry of paperwork to satisfy and protect the various parties to the transactions. Management also becomes immersed in purchases, sales, leases, and rentals on behalf of certain employees and key personnel to facilitate intracompany personnel transfers. Consequently, the financial office may become enmeshed in rather low-level, individual transactions in distant geographical points.

The purpose of the first two forms is to put on notice others who may have an interest, direct or indirect, in a particular property and to PROTECT POTENTIAL PROFITS of a supplier of materials and/or services. Two examples, the California Preliminary Notice (E-1) and the Connecticut Notice of Intention to Claim Mechanic's Lien (E-2), represent geographic extremes, but both constitute a legal-based notice, when filed, and establish a basis for future claims. Notice that neither is a lien.

E-1
E-2

A Mechanic's Lien (E-3) is a legal right to a portion of a property by a supplier or contractor in order to assure payment for labor and materials. The priority and force of a lien, of course, varies from state to state. Some contractors, as a matter of routine, place mechanic's liens on all construction they participate in, which may have little more than nuisance value and may irritate customers as much as they protect profits. The nuisance of obtaining a Release of Attachment (E-4) may engender customer badwill and

E-3

E-4

E-5 adversely affect profits—a tradeoff that must rely on individual judgment of financial and marketing management. A Waiver of Mechanic's Lien (E-5) denotes that contractors, subcontractors, and material suppliers release and relinquish advantages of priority claims on a specific piece of property. Such a document, evidence of voluntary relinquishment, although increasing risk exposure for its signers, does decrease certain **E-6** risks to the lending agency. Notice of Subcontractor's Lien (E-6) parallels the purpose and content of the Notice of Intention to Claim a Mechanic's Lien (E-1, E-2); this form of intention is not available in every state. Of course, in this high-risk industry a **E-7** Subcontractor Agreement (E-7) is SOUND BUSINESS PRACTICE.

E-8 A Judgment Lien (E-8) derives from a debt confirmed by a decree of a court of law. An unsatisfied judgment may be protected by filing a lien against the debtor's property for the amount of adjudged obligation plus costs and legal interest (the rate allowed by the particular jurisdiction). When the debt is paid, the debtor may reasonably expect the **E-9** filing of the proper legal notice, a Satisfaction of Judgment (E-9), which releases his property from that particular encumbrance.

Acquisition of real estate requires financial planning (Section C) plus financing with **E-10** retained earnings, or bonds (Section F), or a Mortgage Note (E-10) secured by the property. Such a note stipulates the amount of the principal, interest rate, time sequence of payments, and such covenants as usually tend to protect the lender more than the mortgagor. And with the nascence of the HUD and federal and state disclosure laws, a **E-11** Disclosure Statement of Loan Secured by Real Property (E-11) must be completed. Such a statement requires the full names and addresses of borrowers and lenders, terms of payment and fees related to the loan contract, information on prepayment penalty, and disclosure on property and credit life insurance.

Other documents that may arise from mortgage transactions are:

E-12   (a)   Statutory Assignment of Mortgage (E-12). (In the example provided this form applies to individuals, partnership, or corporate assignment; an assignment transfers a right or interest.)
E-13   (b)   Partial Release of Mortgage (E-13), especially significant when a blanket mortage covers more than one property.
E-14   (c)   Notice of Lis Pendens, Mortgage Foreclosure (E-14), the result of a civil action to foreclose a mortgage and obtain possession of a mortgaged property. (A mortgage is another form of lien.)

E-15
E-16 Too, several forms relate to deeds. One is the Statutory Form Mortgage Deed for corporations or partnerships (E-15) or for individuals (E-16). With the exception of references to a corporation or individual (top left and last sentence), these two specimens are identical. A mortgaged deed is a deed by way of mortgage which has the effect of a mortgage on the property conveyed and establishes a lien on it. A Bond for Deed, such as **E-17** the four-page form (E-17) or the two-page, short form (E-18), is like a performance bond, **E-18** a registered agreement in which the sellers agree to consummate the transaction and deliver a good and sufficient warranty deed.

A Warranty Deed, like the sample long form for corporations or individuals (E-19), specifies that the sellers of property have a right to convey title on the described property; they bind themselves as well as their heirs, successors and assigns to *warrant* and define the conveyed property. Similarly, a Quit Claim Deed, for corporations or individuals (E-20), specifies that the sellers surrender all right, title, interest, claim, and demand to the property. The owner, by a quit claim deed, conveys his title or interests but makes no representation that the property is free from encumbrances except for those created by the owner himself.

E-19

E-20

That is, these various documents are for the PROTECTION OF business and individual ASSETS. However, the local government wants to protect its claim on the property of others and may require a Real Estate Conveyance Tax Statement (E-21). Unfortunately, this form, when filed, telegraphs to the world and to all other taxing authorities information on a private exchange.

E-21

Finally, to justify its existence, the U.S. Department of Housing and Urban Development requires completion of a Settlement Statement (E-22). Such documentation raises transaction costs, invades privacy, and provides information to other governmental agencies which have no direct reason to have interest in the matter.

E-22

Many companies accept the responsibility of personal home sales of transferred employees, and some subsidize losses resulting from house or condominium sales of key employees. Commonly, firms will utilize services of real estate brokers who keep prospect cards (E-23) on potential buyers. Typically, large real estate firms cross-reference these cards for INTERNAL CONTROL.

E-23

An Offer to Purchase (E-24) property possesses only limited legal force and becomes binding only when accepted by the buyer and seller and when specified conditions of sale are met. It tends to favor the buyer over the seller. But an Agreement to Buy (E-25) is stronger than an offer to purchase. A Purchase Agreement (E-26) briefly describes the property, terms and conditions of sale, the type of deed to be delivered, and penalties for default.

E-24

E-25
E-26

An attractive alternative to immediate purchase is a Real Estate Option (E-27). Usually the following conditions are established in the option agreement:

E-27

    (a)   a definite time within which the option must be exercised;
    (b)   the total purchase price, method of paying the price, and related contract provisions;
    (c)   the amount forfeited if the option is not exercised, and possibly the premium or cost for the option if exercised, i.e., any adjustments;
    (d)   how and where the option is to be exercised;
    (e)   provisions for assignment;
    (f)   any other conditions agreed to by both parties.

The advantage of an option is that it BUYS TIME, especially valuable when market or financial conditions are changing. The disadvantage is that it guarantees the loss of a specified sum (in most cases), if not exercised, and raises transactions costs if exercised.

E-28

E-29

Other paperwork will arise when dealing with a real estate broker. For example, an Exclusive Agency Listing (E-28) grants a specific real estate brokerage firm the right to sell and EARN A COMMISSION on the sale, exclusive of the owner's efforts and success of sale, effective for a specified time span; while an Open Listing Agreement (E-29) is less preferred by real estate brokers because it increases competition for sales and the inter-broker commission split.

E-30

E-31

The Notice of Showing (E-30) offers proof that a broker has shown a property to an identified client, and therefore, PROTECTS his or her right to a sales commission and his or her firm's PROFITS, and *builds public relations* by demonstrating that the brokerage firm is working hard to sell the property. Finally, the Instant Marketing of Commercial Brokers Information Form (E-31) is a medium for sharing information on client needs and inventory to INCREASE the opportunities for SALES AND PROFITS.

E-32

E-33
E-34

Of course, an open listing agreement may apply not only for sales but for leasing contracts (E-32) as well. The agreement establishes the amount of lease payment, time during which the agreement remains in effect, property description, terms of lease, and brokerage commission. Premises may be leased furnished or unfurnished (E-33), equipped or bare to the walls, and the lease agreement (E-34) should stipulate *all* conditions that both lessor and lessee have agreed to orally. If an agreement is well aired, the result may well be LOWER COSTS to the lessee and HIGHER PROFITS to the lessor.

E-35

E-36
E-37

E-38

For temporary needs of employees visiting for training purposes and programs and orientation sessions of short duration, renting may be preferred to leasing. Renting may require completion of a Rental Application (E-35), primarily a credit application and reference check (see Section H for more on credit control and analysis), and a rental agreement (E-36). And for those who overstay their lease, *sans* payment, a complaint and eviction proceedings (E-37) may not produce payment of rent in arrears, but it aids the lessor in regaining possession of the property. Finally, the broker, too, must meet his costs and PROFIT OBJECTIVES and send his statement (E-38) for commissions due on rentals.

CALIFORNIA PRELIMINARY NOTICE

YOUR ATTENTION IS DIRECTED TO **SECTIONS 3097** AND **3098 CALIFORNIA CIVIL CODE** WHICH REQUIRES US TO NOTIFY YOU, THAT IF BILLS ARE NOT PAID IN FULL FOR LABOR, SERVICES, EQUIPMENT OR MATERIALS FURNISHED, OR TO BE FURNISHED, THE IMPROVED PROPERTY (WHICH IS DESCRIBED HEREON) MAY BE SUBJECT TO MECHANICS' LIENS. (THIS STATEMENT IS APPLICABLE TO PRIVATE WORK ONLY.)

THIS IS NOT A LIEN. THIS IS NOT A REFLECTION ON THE INTEGRITY OF ANY CONTRACTOR OR SUBCONTRACTOR.

6217

TO:
OWNER
REPUTED OWNER
OR
PUBLIC AGENCY

DATED

YOU ARE HEREBY NOTIFIED

THAT THE UNDERSIGNED HAS FURNISHED OR WILL FURNISH LABOR, SERVICES, EQUIPMENT OR MATERIALS OF THE FOLLOWING DESCRIPTION.

FOR THE BUILDING, STRUCTURE OF OTHER WORK OF IMPROVEMENT LOCATED AT

THE NAME AND ADDRESS OF THE PERSON WHO CONTRACTED FOR THE PURCHASE OF SUCH LABOR, SERVICES, EQUIPMENT OR MATERIAL
IS:

TRUST FUNDS TO WHICH SUPPLEMENTAL FRINGE BENEFITS ARE PAYABLE

NAME

ADDRESS

NAME

ADDRESS

TO:
ORIGINAL
CONTRACTOR
OR
REPUTED
CONTRACTOR

NAME

ADDRESS

(MATERIAL MEN NOT REQUIRED TO FURNISH THE ABOVE)

NAME OF PERSON OR FIRM FURNISHING
LABOR, SERVICE EQUIPMENT OR MATERIAL

ADDRESS

BY _____ TITLE _____ DATE _____

TO:
CONSTRUCTION
LENDER
OR
REPUTED
CONSTRUCTION
LENDER

NOTICE
TO CONSTRUCTION LENDER ONLY

ESTIMATED TOTAL PRICE OF THE LABOR, SERVICES, EQUIPMENT OR MATERIALS DESCRIBED HEREON.

$ _____

LENDER'S COPY

ACKNOWLEDGMENT OF RECEIPT OF PRELIMINARY 20-DAY NOTICE
(SECTION 3097.1, CALIF. CIVIL CODE)

THIS ACKNOWLEDGES RECEIPT ON _____ (DATE) _____ OF COPY OF THIS PRELIMINARY 20-DAY NOTICE AT _____

(ADDRESS WHERE NOTICE RECEIVED)

DATE _____
(DATE THIS ACKNOWLEDGMENT IS EXECUTED)

(SIGNATURE OF PERSON ACKNOWLEDGING RECEIPT, WITH TITLE IF ACKNOWLEDGMENT IS MADE ON BEHALF OF ANOTHER PERSON)

6217

(ADDRESS OR DESCRIPTION OF JOB SITE)

UPON RECEIPT OF THIS NOTICE, PLEASE DETACH AND SIGN THIS ACKNOWLEDGMENT AND RETURN SAME TO SENDER.

REDIFORM 4S449 POLYPAK 4P449

LENDER'S COPY

Figure E-1: CALIFORNIA NOTICE PRELIMINARY TO MECHANIC'S LIEN
(Courtesy of Rediform Office Products, Paramus, New Jersey 07652.)

C67—NOTICE OF INTENTION TO CLAIM MECHANIC'S LIEN VST ©1976 by ALL-STATE LEGAL SUPPLY CO. 269 Sheffield St., Mountainside, N. J. 07092

TO

TAKE NOTICE that on , 19 , the undersigned commenced to furnish materials or render services for the construction, raising, removal or repairing of the building(s) on a lot of land owned by you, or the improvement of such lot or in the site development or subdivision of such lot or plot of land, situated in the city/town of . County of , Connecticut, bounded and described as follows:

being the property deeded to you by
on , 19 , by deed recorded in Vol. page ,
in the Land Records of

TAKE FURTHER NOTICE THAT THE UNDERSIGNED INTENDS TO CLAIM A MECHANIC'S LIEN THEREFOR on said land(s), lot or plot of land and building(s).

Dated at , this day of , 19

....

....

Figure E-2: NOTICE OF INTENTION TO CLAIM MECHANIC'S LIEN
(Copyright 1976 by All State Legal Supply Co., Mountainside, New Jersey 07092.)

A true and attested copy of Notice of Intention to Claim Mechanic's Lien.

....

An Indifferent Person

STATE OF CONNECTICUT

County of   ss: 19

On the above date, I left a true and attested copy of the within Notice of Intention to Claim Mechanic's Lien with and in the hands of, or at the usual place of abode of

at

The within is the original Notice of Intention to Claim Mechanic's Lien with my doings thereon endorsed.

Attest:

....

An Indifferent Person

On   19   , personally appeared the above named

an indifferent person, and made solemn oath to the truth of the foregoing return so made by him.

Before me,

.... Notary Public

Commissioner of the Superior Court

Figure E-2—Reverse Side

THIS IS TO CERTIFY THAT

of the Town of   County of   and State of Connecticut,
     heirs, successors and assigns, in accordance with a certain contract between   the
said
and
of the Town of   County of   and State of Connecticut
ha   a LIEN under the Statutes in such cases made and provided, on the following described premises and
to the dwelling house   and to other buildings standing
thereon, to the amount of   Dollars,
as nearly as the same can be ascertained.
    THE LIEN is for services rendered and materials furnished in the construction, erection, raising and
removal of said buildings

and for repairs done thereon, commencing the   day of   19
and ending the   day of   19   And the date of the
commencing   of   this   Lien   is   the   day   of   19
THE SAID PREMISES are situated in the Town of
County of   and State of Connecticut, recorded in the name of
         in the Land Records of the
Town of   in   Vol.   Page   , and   bounded   and
described as follows, viz.:

The name or names against whom this lien is being filed is/are

    THIS CERTIFICATE is made and filed within Sixty days from the time of ceasing to render services
and furnish material as aforesaid.

    IN WITNESS WHEREOF,
ha   hereunto set   hand this   day of   19

....

STATE OF CONNECTICUT   ss.   19
COUNTY OF

PERSONALLY APPEARED

signer   of the foregoing certificate, and made solemn oath to the truth of the same and that the amount
above named is justly due to the said
as nearly as the same can be ascertained, before me,

Received   19   At   M.   ....
                                  Notary Public — Justice of the Peace —
                                  Commissioner of the Superior Court

.... Town Clerk

Figure E-3: MECHANIC'S LIEN
(Courtesy of Mr. Gordon Ramsay, Cleaveland Legal Blank Service, Inc., E. Hartford, Connecticut.)

Release of Attachment—Mechanic's Lien   No. 154   Cleaveland Legal Blank Service, Inc.

Court

County

                              Vs.   19

THIS IS TO CERTIFY that a certain attachment mechanic's lien filed in the Town Clerk's
Office in the town of   , County of   and State of

Connecticut on the   day of   , 19   and recorded in Vol.   , Page   ,
in favor of

plaintiff claimant against

defendant owner , upon certain real estate situate in said town of
and more particularly described in said lien, is hereby released and wholly discharged, the debt thereby
secured having been fully satisfied.

        Dated at   this   day of   , 19   .

In the presence of

by .... Attorney of Record
and the authority subscribing the writ of attachment.
Plaintiff

State of Connecticut ⎫
                     ⎬ ss.
County of   ⎭

        Personally appeared

Signer   and Sealer   of the foregoing instrument, and acknowledged the same to be   free

act and deed, before me,

                                                    Notary Public
                                                    Justice of the Peace
                                        Commissioner of the Superior Court

Figure E-4: RELEASE OF ATTACHMENT—MECHANIC'S LIEN
   (Courtesy of Mr. Gordon Ramsay, Cleaveland Legal Blank Service, Inc., E. Hartford, Connecticut.)

To all whom it may concern: THIS CERTIFIES THAT

     We, the undersigned, contractors, sub contractors, material men, et cetra,

in consideration of One Dollar and other valuable considerations received to our full satisfaction of

of the Town of   County of   and State of Connecticut

have waived, relinquished and released and do hereby waive, relinquish and release all liens and claims of liens we now

have or may hereafter have upon a piece of land and all the buildings thereon standing, known as

situated in the Town of   , on the   side of

and bounded and described as follows, namely:

and more particularly described in a Deed from

to said   dated

and recorded in   Land Records volume   , page   for labor done or to be done

and materials furnished or to be furnished in the erection, construction or repair of said buildings.

Witness   hand   and   seal   this   day of   A. D. 19

....General Contractor	....Iron and Steel
....Block	....Lather
....Brick	....Lumber Dealer
Company furnishing same.	....Lumber for Inside Trim
....Carpenter	....Marble
....Cornice	....Mason
....Doors, Sash and Blinds	....Mason Supplies
....Electrician	*Company furnishing same.*
....Electric Fixtures	....Painter
Company furnishing same.	....Inside Painting and Decorating
....Elevator	....Paint and Decorator's Supplies
....Excavating Cellar	*Company furnishing same.*
....Cesspool and Stones for Same	....Plasterer
....Finished Floors	....Plumber
....Gas Piping	....Plumber's Supplies
....Grading	*Company furnishing same.*
....Hardware	....Sand and Stone
Company furnishing same.	....Stair Builder
....Heater and Radiators	....Tile
Company furnishing same.	
....Tinner and Roofer	....Walks
....Foundation	....Ready-Mix Concrete
....**Well Driller**	....Kitchen Cabinets

Figure E-5: WAIVER OF MECHANIC'S LIEN
(Courtesy of Mr. Gordon Ramsay, Cleaveland Legal Blank Service, Inc., E. Hartford, Connecticut.)

STATE OF CONNECTICUT

COUNTY OF   } ss.   19

                                             the owner of the premises herein described, being duly sworn, says that   he   ha   read the within and foregoing waiver of lien and the signatures thereto, and that the persons who have signed said waiver of lien are the only persons who are entitled to rights of lien against the property herein described.

Subscribed and sworn to, before me

....

                Notary Public

Lien Waiver

FROM

....

....

TO

....

....

Dated .... 19....

Received .... 19....

At .... M.

Recorded in ....

LAND RECORDS

Vol. .... Page ....

Town Clerk

Town Clerk:

After recording please return to:

Figure E-5 (continued)

Notice of Subcontractor's Lien   No. 146   Cleaveland Legal Blank Service, Inc.

To

                                             of

You are hereby notified that on the   day of   19

                                    of the Town of
State of Connecticut, commenced to furnish materials for and render services in the construction, raising, removal or
repairs of the building owned by you and located on land situated in the Town of
and bounded and described as follows:

that said materials and services were completed on the   day of   19   ,
and that   intend   to claim a lien therefore on said buildings and land in the amount of $,
which is justly due, as nearly as the same can be ascertained.

     IN WITNESS WHEREOF,

ha   hereunto set   hand and seal   this   day of   19

....

State of Connecticut
                               ss.   19
County of

    Personally appeared
who subscribed and swore to the truth of the foregoing notice of lien, and acknowledged that
executed the same before me.

                      ....
                      Notary Public   Justice of the Peace
                               Commissioner of the Superior Court

    And on the   day of   19   , I left a true and
attested copy of the foregoing notice of lien in the hands at the usual place of abode of the within named owner
of the premises.

                    Attest:..
                      Deputy Sheriff   Constable   An indifferent Person

Figure E-6: NOTICE OF SUBCONTRACTOR'S LIEN
(Courtesy of Mr. Gordon Ramsay, Cleaveland Legal Blank Service, Inc., E. Hartford, Connecticut.)

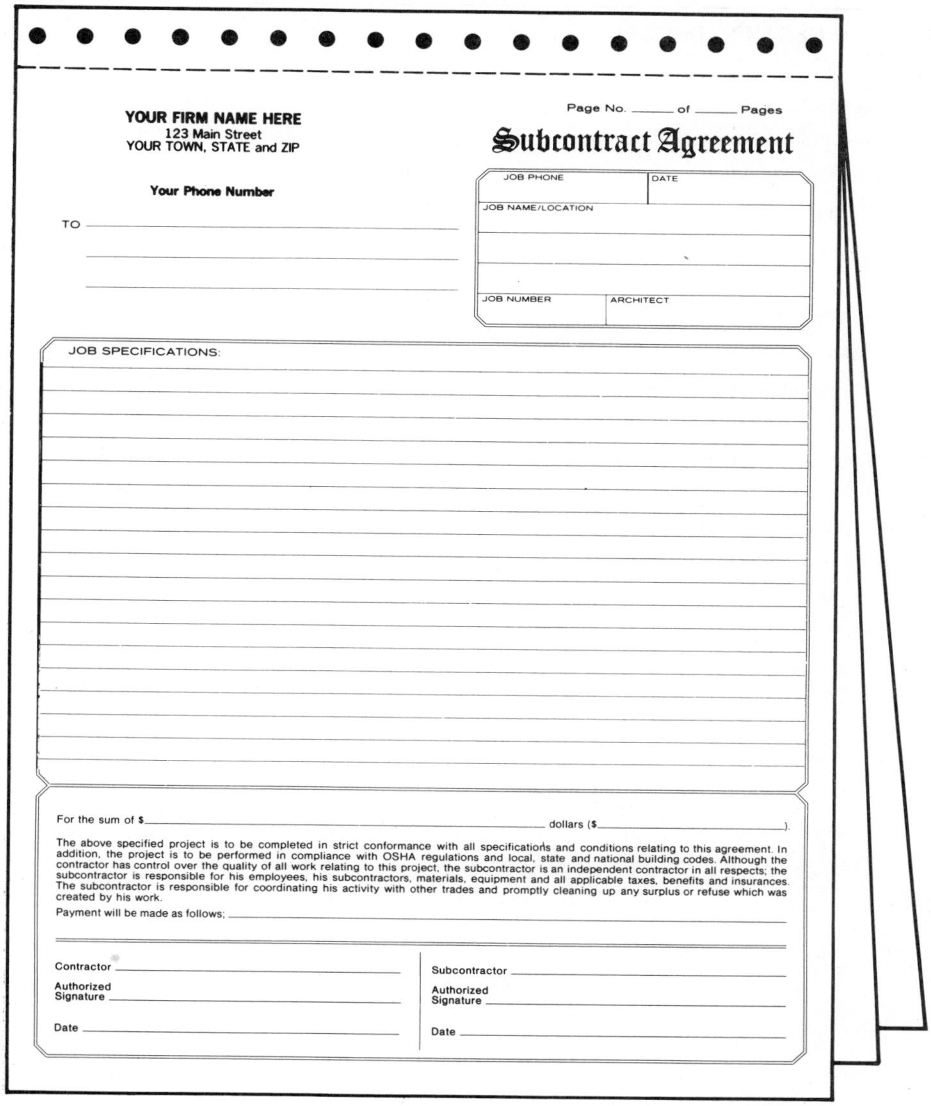

YOUR FIRM NAME HERE
123 Main Street
YOUR TOWN, STATE and ZIP

Your Phone Number

TO _____

_____

_____

Page No. _____ of _____ Pages

Subcontract Agreement

JOB PHONE	DATE
JOB NAME/LOCATION	
JOB NUMBER	ARCHITECT

JOB SPECIFICATIONS:

For the sum of $_____ dollars ($_____).

The above specified project is to be completed in strict conformance with all specifications and conditions relating to this agreement. In addition, the project is to be performed in compliance with OSHA regulations and local, state and national building codes. Although the contractor has control over the quality of all work relating to this project, the subcontractor is an independent contractor in all respects; the subcontractor is responsible for his employees, his subcontractors, materials, equipment and all applicable taxes, benefits and insurances. The subcontractor is responsible for coordinating his activity with other trades and promptly cleaning up any surplus or refuse which was created by his work.

Payment will be made as follows; _____

_____

Contractor _____   Subcontractor _____

Authorized
Signature _____   Authorized
Signature _____

Date _____   Date _____

Figure E-7: SUBCONTRACT AGREEMENT
(Available from New England Business Service, Inc., North Main Street, Groton, Massachusetts 01450; 1-800-225-6380.)

THIS IS TO CERTIFY, That

of the City/Town of   County of   State of
on the   day of   19   , in the Superior Court of Common Pleas.
Circuit Court,   Circuit holden at
in the County of   did obtain a judgment in   h   favor against

of the City/Town of   County of   State of
for the sum of   dollars
damages, and   dollars, costs of
suit, which judgment remains wholly unsatisfied; (on which judgment the sum of
                                                                            dollars is still due:)
and to secure said sum, and the lawful interest thereon, a judgment lien in favor of said
                                                                    is hereby placed
upon the following described real estate of said
situated in City/Town of   County of   to wit:

Recorded in Volume   , Page   , in the   Land Records;
pursuant to the statute in such case made and provided.
        This lien is filed within four months after said judgment was rendered and the same real estate
herein described was attached in said action on the   day of   19
Dated at   this   day of   19

                                                    by _____
                                                    Attorney for
Received for Record _____ at ___ M. Attest _____
                                                            Town Clerk

Figure E-8: JUDGMENT LIEN
(Courtesy of Mr. Gordon Ramsay, Cleaveland Legal Blank Service, Inc., E. Hartford, Connecticut.)

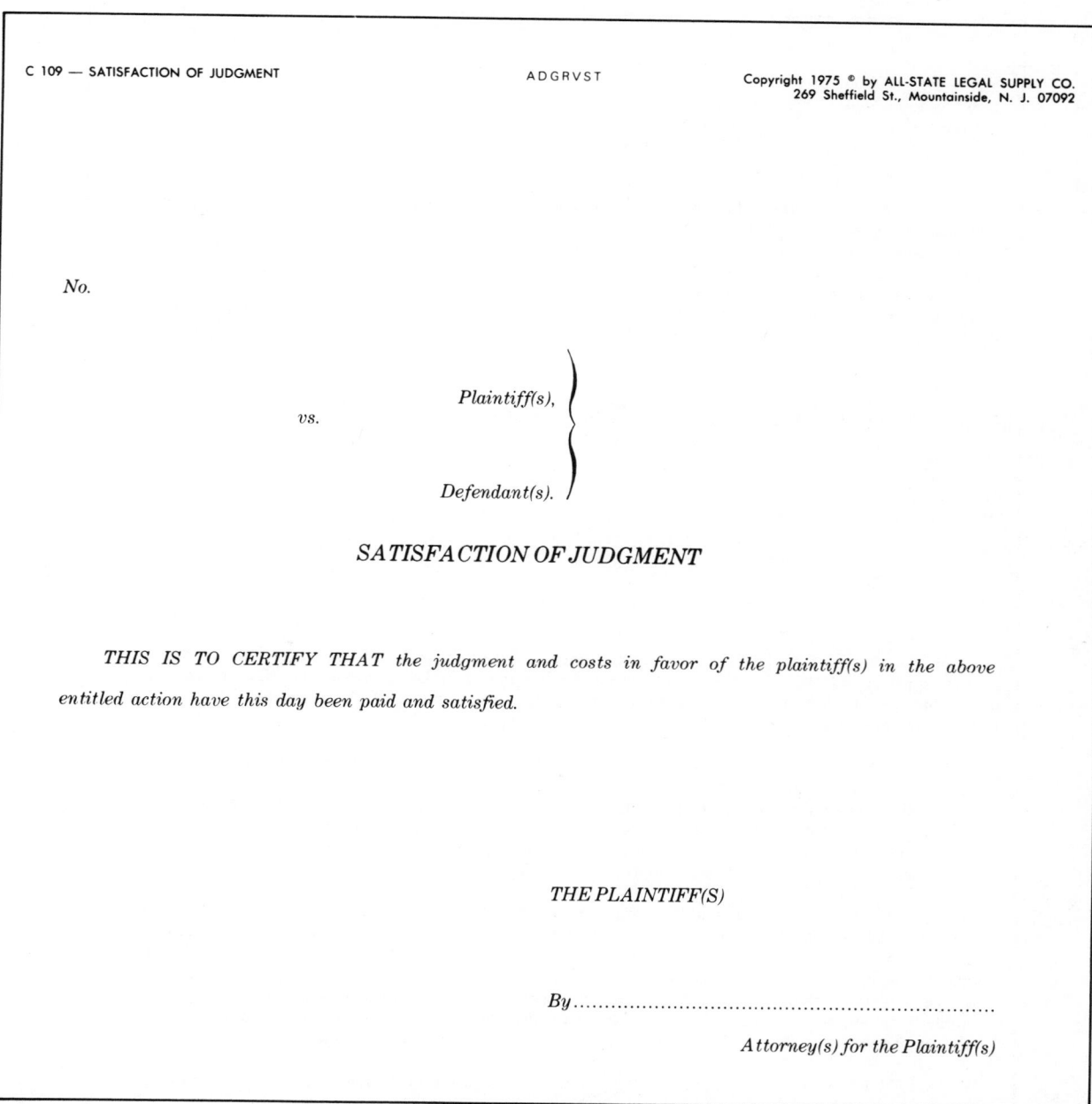

No.

Plaintiff(s),

vs.

Defendant(s).

SATISFACTION OF JUDGMENT

THIS IS TO CERTIFY THAT the judgment and costs in favor of the plaintiff(s) in the above entitled action have this day been paid and satisfied.

THE PLAINTIFF(S)

By ....

Attorney(s) for the Plaintiff(s)

Figure E-9: SATISFACTION OF JUDGMENT
(Copyright 1975 by All State Legal Supply Co., Mountainside, New Jersey 07092.)

MORTGAGE NOTE   No. 120S   Cleaveland Legal Blank Service, Inc.

$....................   19

FOR VALUE RECEIVED, the undersigned promise   to pay to the order of

at the   of the holder hereof, or at such other place as the holder   hereof shall designate in writing, the principal sum of

with interest from date on the unpaid balance at the rate of   percent per annum; together with all taxes assessed hereon against the holder   hereof;   and together with all costs of collection, including a reasonable attorney's fee, if this note shall be referred after default to an attorney-at-law for collection or if an action of foreclosure shall be instituted after default on this note or any mortgage securing this note.

The undersigned promise   to pay the said principal and interest as follows:

After   the undersigned reserve   the right to pay at any time the entire unpaid principal (plus interest accrued to the date of payment), and also reserve   the right to pay on the principal, on any day on which a principal payment is due. an amount equal to one or more of the principal payments next due.

If this note shall be secured by a mortgage, the undersigned agree   to pay all taxes and assessments on the mortgaged property; to keep the same free from mechanic's liens; to keep in a good state of repair all buildings or personal property mortgaged to secure this note; to keep the same insured against loss by fire or otherwise, in such forms of insurance as may be required by the holder hereof; and, if there shall be a prior mortgage or mortgages on the property mortgaged to secure this note, to perform all agreements contained in such prior mortgage or mortgages and the note or notes secured thereby.

If any payment due hereunder shall not have been paid within   days after the same is due, or if any other agreement of the maker   herein contained shall be in default and shall not have been fully performed within   days after the written notice of default has been mailed to any maker   hereof (addressed to the last known place of abode of any maker   hereof), or if title to said property is transferred, then the entire unpaid principal, with accrued interest, shall, at the option of the holder   hereof, become due and payable forthwith. Failure to exercise this option shall not constitute a waiver of the right to exercise the same in the event of any subsequent default.

If there shall be more than one maker of this note, the obligation of the undersigned shall be joint and several.

This note is secured by a mortgage   .... L..S.
on property located in the Town of
                        State of
Connecticut.   .... L..S.

Figure E-10: MORTGAGE NOTE
(Courtesy of Mr. Gordon Ramsay, Cleaveland Legal Blank Service, Inc., E. Hartford, Connecticut.)

RVST

ALL-STATE LEGAL SUPPLY CO
269 SHEFFIELD STREET, MOUNTAINSIDE, N.J. 07092

DISCLOSURE STATEMENT OF LOAN SECURED BY REAL PROPERTY
(DIRECT SECURED LOAN, EVIDENCED BY NOTE AND REAL PROPERTY MORTGAGE)

_____
(Date of Transaction)

_____
(Date Disclosures made to Borrowers)

BORROWERS: _____

| (Print FULL NAME) | (No., Street or R.F.D.) | (City) | (State) | (Zip) |

_____

| (Print FULL NAME) | (No., Street or R.F.D.) | (City) | (State) | (Zip) |

LENDER: _____

| (LENDER'S NAME) | (Mailing Address, including Zip) |

SUMMARY OF SECURED TRANSACTION (See Note and Real Property Mortgage, furnished, for COMPLETE DETAILS) Direct loan, secured by real property, by above LENDER to above BORROWERS, evidenced by **NOTE AND REAL PROP-ERTY MORTGAGE** (hereinafter termed "CONTRACT.") Loan is secured by security interest in real property owned by BORROWERS, which property is specifically described in said CONTRACT, upon terms and conditions stated therein. Said terms of said CONTRACT being incorporated herein by reference, executed copy having been furnished BORROWERS.

DISCLOSURES REQUIRED BY FEDERAL LAW

PAYMENT TERMS: Payable _____ after date; _or_ Payable in _____ equal monthly payments of $ _____ , commencing on _____ , 19____, and on the same day of the month thereafter. Further, if suit is instituted upon Borrower's _Default,_ to collect OUTSTAND-ING BALANCE or otherwise to enforce NOTE and REAL PROPERTY MORTGAGE; BORROWERS are liable for reasonable At-torneys' fees of LENDER. On default, BOR-ROWERS also are responsible for Foreclo-sure expenses, per CONTRACT.

BALLOON PAYMENT, if any, and condi-tions (if any) for refinancing same, if not paid when due:

$ _____ , _____

_____

_____

BASIC TERMS OF LOAN CONTRACT:

1. LOAN PROCEEDS: $ _____
2. OTHER CHARGES: (Total) . . . . $ _____
   - a. Premium, Property Ins. $ _____
   - b. Title Exam. Fees $ _____
   - c. Title Insurance $ _____
   - d. Property Survey Fees $ _____
   - e. Legal Fees, drafting documents $ _____
   - f. Escrow Deposit, for Taxes $ _____
   - g. Escrow Deposit, Insurance $ _____
   - h. Filing or Recording fees $ _____
   - i. Other _____ $ _____
3. AMOUNT FINANCED $ _____
4. FINANCE CHARGE $ _____
   - a. Non-refundable discount $ _____
   - b. Brokerage Fee $ _____
   - c. Other _____ $ _____
5. TOTAL OF PAYMENTS $ _____
6. **ANNUAL PERCENTAGE RATE** _____ %

LENDER will impose the following penalty charge for prepayment of the principal of the obligation, said penalty charge being computed in the method described hereunder. Further, conditions under which said prepayment penalty charge are disclosed below:

Method of computation of penalty: _____

Conditions, imposing penalty: _____

NOTE: In the space provided above, a description of any penalty charge made for prepayment of the principal, an explana-tion of the method of computing such penalty, and the conditions under which it may be imposed must be stated.

INSURANCE DISCLOSURES

PROPERTY INSURANCE, if written in connection with this Real Property Secured Transaction, may be obtained by BOR-ROWERS through any duly-licensed insurance Agent or Broker of their choice; subject only to LENDER'S right to refuse to accept any insurer offered by BORROWERS, _for reasonable cause._ If such insurance is procured by LENDER, with insur-ance premium therefor financed as part of this loan, the cost will be $ _____ , per annum, based upon current rates and classifications.

CREDIT LIFE AND/OR DISABILITY INSURANCE are _not_ required to obtain this loan, purchase of such through LENDER being voluntary on BORROWER'S part. No such credit insurance is provided unless _the Borrower to be insured under such Credit Insurance Policy_ signs the appropriate Statement below:

(a) The Premium (Cost) for Credit Life Insurance will be $ _____ , for the term of the credit.

(b) The Premium (Cost) for Credit Life & Disability Insurance will be $ _____ , for the term of the credit.

I DESIRE CREDIT LIFE AND DISABILITY INSURANCE   I DESIRE CREDIT LIFE INSURANCE ONLY

_____ (SEAL)   _____ (SEAL)
Date   (Signature of Customer)   ·Date   (Signature of Customer)

ACKNOWLEDGEMENT OF RECEIPT OF DISCLOSURES

The undersigned BORROWERS do herewith acknowledge receipt of the DISCLOSURES contained herein and in the NOTE and REAL PROPERTY MORTGAGE. They, further, acknowledge that at the time they received a copy of this Statement and of said NOTE and REAL PROPERTY MORTGAGE, forms were complete and filled-in and that all blanks in such forms were filled-in prior to their executing the same.

_____ (SEAL)
(WITNESS)   (Date Disclosures Received)   (Signature of Borrower)

_____ (SEAL)
(WITNESS)   (Date Disclosures Received)   (Signature of Borrower)

Figure E-11: DISCLOSURE STATEMENT OF LOAN SECURED BY REAL PROPERTY
(Courtesy of All State Legal Supply Co., Mountainside, New Jersey 07092.)

Corporation or Individual
STATUTORY ASSIGNMENT OF MORTGAGE   128SF

Cleaveland Legal Blank Service, Inc.
Hartford, Connecticut

of

for consideration paid, assign to

all interest in a mortgage from

to   dated

and recorded in Volume   at Page   of the

Connecticut Land Records.

Signed this   day of   , 19

Witnessed by:

....

....

STATE OF CONNECTICUT, ⎫
                                           ⎬ ss.   19
COUNTY OF   ⎭

    Personally Appeared
Signer(s) of the foregoing Instrument, and acknowledged the same to be
free act and deed, before me.

....
Notary Public / J. of Peace / Commissioner of Superior Court

STATE OF CONNECTICUT, ⎫
                                           ⎬ ss.   19
COUNTY OF   ⎭

    Personally Appeared
                                  , as aforesaid, Signer of the foregoing Instrument, and
acknowledged the same to be   free act and deed as such
              and the free act and deed of said corporation/partnership, before me.

....
Notary Public / J. of Peace / Commissioner of Superior Court

Figure E-12: STATUTORY ASSIGNMENT OF MORTGAGE
(Courtesy of Mr. Gordon Ramsay, Cleaveland Legal Blank Service, Inc., E. Hartford, Connecticut.)

 Cleaveland Legal Blank Service

Know All Men by These Presents,

THAT

for   ,
valuable considerations, do   hereby release and discharge from the lien and operation of a certain
mortgage from   Dollars and other good and
to
and recorded in the Land Records of the Town of   dated
and State of   in Vol.   County of
                                            , at Page   to which reference may be
had, all that certain piece or parcel of land, situated in said Town of
and being more particularly bounded and described as follows, to wit:

In Witness Whereof,

ha   hereunto set   hand   and seal   this   day of

Signed, Sealed and delivered in the presence of

.... [L. S.]

.... [L. S.]

STATE OF CONNECTICUT } ss.
COUNTY OF

On this   day of   19   , before me
                              , the undersigned officer, personally
appeared   known
to me (or satisfactorily proven) to be the person   whose name   is/are subscribed to the within
instrument and acknowledged that he/she/they executed the same for the purposes therein contained.
      In Witness Whereof I hereunto set my hand.

....
                    Notary Public — Commissioner of the Superior Court

STATE OF CONNECTICUT } ss.
COUNTY OF

On this   day of   19   , before me
                              , the undersigned officer, personally
appeared   who acknowledged
himself/herself to be the
                  , a corporation, and that   he   , as such
being authorized so to do, executed the foregoing instrument for the purposes therein contained, by
signing the name of the corporation by himself/herself as
      In Witness Whereof I hereunto set my hand.

....
                    Notary Public — Commissioner of the Superior Court

Figure E-13: PARTIAL RELEASE OF MORTGAGE
(Courtesy of Mr. Gordon Ramsay, Cleaveland Legal Blank Service, Inc., E. Hartford, Connecticut.)

Plaintiff(s)

vs.

Defendant(s)

NOTICE OF LIS PENDENS

NOTICE is hereby given of the pendency of a Civil Action between

as Plaintiff(s),

and

as Defendant(s),

brought by a Writ dated   , 19   and made returnable to the above-named Court to
be held at,   in the County of   on the
Tuesday of   19

The Civil Action is brought to Foreclose a Mortgage made by

to

dated   , 19   , and recorded in Volume   on Page   of
Land Records of the City/Town of   in the County of   and
State of Connecticut, and to obtain possession of the mortgaged premises.

The real estate affected by the Civil Action and upon which the aforementioned mortgage is a lien consists
of all that parcel(s) of land, with the building(s) and improvements thereon and the appurtenances belonging
thereto, situate in the City/Town of   , County of
and State of Connecticut, more particularly described as follows:

Dated at   , this   day of   , 19

The Plaintiff(s)

By --

Attorney(s) for Plaintiff(s)

Figure E-14: NOTICE OF MORTGAGE FORECLOSURE
(Copyright 1974 by All State Legal Supply Co., Mountainside, New Jersey 07092.)

(Corporation)   117SFC   Cleaveland Legal Blank Service, Inc.
                                                    Hartford, Connecticut

STATUTORY FORM MORTGAGE DEED

of
to secure payment of   dollars
with interest payable as provided in a certain promissory note dated
                                with final maturity on
grant   to
                                            of
with MORTGAGE COVENANTS

(Description and Encumbrances, if any and any additional provisions)

This mortgage is made upon the STATUTORY CONDITION

Signed this   day of   , 19
Witnessed by:

....

....

STATE OF CONNECTICUT, ⎱
                        ⎰ ss.   19
COUNTY OF   ⎰

    Personally Appeared
                        , as aforesaid, Signer of the foregoing Instrument, and
acknowledged the same to be   free act and deed as such
              and the free act and deed of said corporation/partnership, before me.

                            ....
                            Notary Public / J. of Peace / Commissioner of Superior Court

Figure E-15: STATUTORY FORM MORTGAGE DEED (CORPORATION)
(Courtesy of Mr. Gordon Ramsay, Cleaveland Legal Blank Service, Inc., E. Hartford, Connecticut.)

STATUTORY FORM MORTGAGE DEED

of

to secure payment of   dollars

with interest payable as provided in a certain promissory note dated

         with final maturity on

grant to

            of

with MORTGAGE COVENANTS

(Description and Encumbrances. if any and any additional provisions)

This mortgage is made upon the STATUTORY CONDITION

Signed this   day of   , 19

Witnessed by:

....

....

STATE OF CONNECTICUT, } ss.   19

COUNTY OF

  Personally Appeared

Signer(s) of the foregoing Instrument, and acknowledged the same to be

free act and deed, before me.

....
Notary Public / J. of Peace / Commissioner of Superior Court

Figure E-16: STATUTORY FORM MORTGAGE DEED (INDIVIDUAL)
(Courtesy of Mr. Gordon Ramsay, Cleaveland Legal Blank Service, Inc., E. Hartford, Connecticut.)

BOND FOR DEED D 108 Cleaveland Legal Blank Service, Inc. E. Hartford, Connecticut

THIS AGREEMENT MADE and concluded this day of 19 by and between

of

and

of

WITNESSETH, That the said in consideration of Dollars to paid by the said (the receipt whereof is hereby acknowledged) and in further consideration of the promises of the said

hereinafter contained, doth hereby promise and agree to and with the said that immediately upon the faithful performance of the said agreement hereinafter made, , the said

will on or before the day of 19 , make and deliver to the said

a good and sufficient Warranty Deed, containing the usual covenants in such deeds contained, of all that tract of land situate, lying and being in

IN CONSIDERATION WHEREOF the said doth hereby promise and agree to and with the said that will on or before the said day of 19 , pay to the said the further sum of dollars, in addition to the payment already made, being the balance of the purchase money hereby agreed upon for the said tract of land, in manner and form as follows, viz:

Figure E-17: BOND FOR DEED
(Courtesy of Mr. Gordon Ramsay, Cleaveland Legal Blank Service, Inc., E. Hartford, Connecticut.)

BECAUSE the anticipated damages are uncertain in amount and difficult to prove, because the parties hereto wish to liquidate said damages in advance, and because moneys paid in pursuance of this agreement are not greatly disproportionate to the damage reasonably to be anticipated in the event of breach, it is further agreed that if the said

shall fail to make the several payments, or any of them as herein before stated,   shall forfeit all claims to the premises described herein, and all moneys paid in pursuance of this agreement as liquidated damages.

IN TESTIMONY WHEREOF, we have hereunto set our hands and seals, and to a duplicate instrument of the same tenor and date, at
on the day and year first mentioned.

Signed, Sealed and Delivered in the presence of

....(L. S.)

....(L. S.)

....(L. S.)

....(L. S.)

STATE OF CONNECTICUT } ss.
COUNTY OF
          On this   day of   19   , before me
                              , the undersigned officer, personally
appeared
known to me (or satisfactorily proven) to be the person   whose name   is/are subscribed to the within instrument and acknowledged that he/she/they executed the same for the purposes therein contained.
          In Witness Whereof I hereunto set my hand.
                              ....
                              Notary Public — Commissioner of the Superior Court

STATE OF CONNECTICUT } ss.
COUNTY OF
          On this   day of   19   , before me
                              , the undersigned officer, personally
                                                  who acknowledged
appeared
himself/herself to be the   of
                              , a corporation, and that   he , as such
being authorized so to do, executed the foregoing instrument for the purposes therein contained, by signing the name of the corporation by himself/herself as
          In Witness Whereof I hereunto set my hand.

Grantees' Address   ....
....   *Notary Public — Commissioner of the Superior Court*

....

Figure E-17 (continued)

BOND FOR DEED   No. 109   Cleaveland Legal Blank Service, Hartford, Conn.

THIS AGREEMENT MADE and concluded this   day of   A.D. 19
by and between

of the Town of   County of   State of
and

of the Town of   County of   State of

WITNESSETH,   That the said   in consideration
of   Dollars to   paid by
the said   (the receipt whereof is
hereby acknowledged) and in further consideration of the promises of the said
                                        hereinafter contained, doth hereby promise and agree to and
with the said   that immediately
upon the faithful performance of the said
agreement hereinafter made,   , the said   will on or before
the   day of   19   , make and deliver to the said
          a good and sufficient Warranty Deed, containing the usual covenants in such deeds contained,
of all that tract of land situate, lying and being in

IN CONSIDERATION WHEREOF the said   doth hereby
promise and agree to and with the said
that   will on or before the said   day of   19   , pay to the
said   the further sum of
                          dollars, in addition to the payment already made, being the balance of the
purchase money hereby agreed upon for the said tract of land, in manner and form as follows, viz:

          And it is further agreed that if the said
shall fail to make the several payments, or any of them as herein before stated,   shall forfeit all claims
to the premises described herein, and all moneys paid in pursuance of this agreement.

          IN TESTIMONY WHEREOF, we have hereunto set our hands and seals, and to a duplicate instru-
ment of the same tenor and date, at   on the day and year first above mentioned.

Signed, Sealed and Delivered in the presence of,

....[L. S.]

....[L. S.]

....[L. S.]

Figure E-18: BOND FOR DEED—SHORT FORM
(Courtesy of Mr. Gordon Ramsay, Cleaveland Legal Blank Service, Inc., E. Hartford, Connecticut.)

STATE OF CONNECTICUT   } ss.
COUNTY OF   }

On this   day of   19   , before me
, the undersigned officer, personally

appeared
known to me (or satisfactorily proven) to be the person whose name is/are subscribed to
the within instrument and acknowledged that he/she/they executed the same for the purposes
therein contained.
In Witness Whereof I hereunto set my hand and official seal.

....
Notary Public — Commissioner of the
Superior Court

STATE OF CONNECTICUT   } ss.
COUNTY OF   }

On this   day of   19   , before me
, the undersigned officer, personally
who acknowledged

appeared
himself/herself to be the
of
, a corporation, and that   he, as such
being authorized so to do, executed the foregoing instrument for the purposes therein contained,
by signing the name of the corporation by himself as
In Witness Whereof I hereunto set my hand and official seal.

....
Notary Public — Commissioner of the
Superior Court

Bond for Deed

FROM

TO

Dated ....19 ....

Received ....19 ....
At............M.

Recorded in ....

Vol. ....   Page ....

LAND RECORDS

Town Clerk

Figure E-18—Reverse Side

C 24 — WARRANTY DEED — LONG FORM
Ind. or Corp.

A D G

To all People to Whom these Presents shall Come, Greeting:

Know Ye, *That*

for the consideration of *herein designated as the Grantors,*

received to the full satisfaction of the Grantors, from

do hereby give, grant, bargain, sell and convey to the Grantees *herein designated as the Grantees,*

To Have and to Hold *the premises hereby conveyed, with the appurtenances thereof, unto the Grantees and unto the Grantees' heirs, successors and assigns forever and to the Grantees' and their own proper use and behoof;* **and** *the Grantors do for themselves, their heirs, successors and assigns covenant with the Grantees, their heirs, successors and assigns that the Grantors are well seized of the premises as a good indefeasible estate in FEE SIMPLE; and have good right to grant and convey the same in manner and form as herein written and the same are free from all incumbrances whatsoever, except as herein stated.*

Figure E-19: WARRANTY DEED—LONG FORM (FOR INDIVIDUAL OR CORPORATION)
(Copyright 1978 by All State Legal Supply Co., Mountainside New Jersey 07092.)

And Furthermore, *the Grantors do by these presents bind themselves and their heirs, successors and assigns forever to WARRANT AND DEFEND the premises hereby conveyed to the Grantees and their heirs, successors and assigns against all claims and demands whatsoever, except as herein stated.*

In all references herein to any parties, persons, entities or corporations, the use of any particular gender or the plural or singular number is intended to include the appropriate gender or number as the text of the within instrument may require.

In Witness Whereof, *the Grantors have hereunto set their hands and seals, or if a corporation, it has caused these presents to be signed by its corporate officers and its corporate seal to be affixed hereto, this   day of   19*

Signed, Sealed and Delivered in the presence of
or Attested by

....

....

State of Connecticut
County of   } **ss.**

The foregoing instrument was acknowledged before me this   day of
19   , by

....

Commissioner of the Superior Court

Warranty Deed

TO

Dated   19

Received for Record   19

at   M.

Recorded in Vol.   Page

of

Land Records by

Town Clerk

Figure E-19—Reverse Side

C 30 B—QUIT CLAIM DEED
IND. OR CORP.

GRVST

To all People to Whom these Presents shall Come, Greeting:

Know Ye, *That*

herein designated as the Releasor,

for the consideration of

received to Releasor's full satisfaction from

herein designated as the Releasee,

does by these presents remise, release and forever Quit-Claim unto the said Releasee and to the Releasee's heirs, successors and assigns forever, all the right, title, interest, claim and demand whatsoever as the said Releasor has or ought to have in or to

Figure E-20: QUIT CLAIM DEED (FOR INDIVIDUAL OR CORPORATION)
(Copyright 1977 by All State Legal Supply Co., Mountainside, New Jersey 07092.)

To Have and to Hold the premises hereby remised, released and quit-claimed with all the appurtenances unto the said Releasee and to the Releasee's heirs, successors and assigns forever, so that neither the Releasor nor the Releasor's heirs, successors or assigns nor any other person claiming under or through the Releasor shall hereafter have any claim, right or title in or to the premises or any part thereof, but therefrom the Releasor and they are by these presents, forever barred and excluded.

In all references herein to any parties, persons, entities or corporations the use of any particular gender or the plural or singular number is intended to include the appropriate gender or number as the text of the within instrument may require.

In Witness Whereof, the Releasor has signed and sealed this instrument, or if a corporation, it has caused these presents to be signed by its corporate officers and its corporate seal to be hereto affixed this   day of   19   .

Signed, Sealed and Delivered in the presence of or Attested by

....

....

....

....

State of Connecticut
County of   } **ss.**

The foregoing instrument was acknowledged before me this   day of

19   , by

....
Commissioner of the Superior Court

Figure E-20—Reverse Side.

STATEMENT - REAL ESTATE CONVEYANCE TAX

Grantor: *Grantee:*

To Town Clerk of   *, Connecticut:*

The following information is submitted with reference to property located at

and in accordance with the Real Estate Conveyance Tax Law, Connecticut General Statutes § 12-494 et seq. § 12-504 et seq.

Check and insert applicable pertinent data:

☐ *Full purchase price, including assumed mortgage, etc.* $ _____
                 or
☐ *If a gift, or at nominal purchase price, insert actual (market) value of the property or interest conveyed* $ _____

☐ *Not subject to tax for following reason:*
   (Check appropriate reason)

      ☐ *Mortgage Deed*

      ☐ *Deed to or by the United States, State of Connecticut, any municipality or any agency, political subdivision or instrumentality thereof*

      ☐ *Strawman deed, deed which corrects, modifies, supplements or confirms a deed previously recorded*

      ☐ *Deed between husband and wife or parent and child - no consideration received*

      ☐ *Tax deed*

      ☐ *Deed releasing property which is security for a debt or other obligation*

      ☐ *Deed of partition*

      ☐ *Deed made pursuant to a merger of a corporation or a deed made by a subsidiary corporation to its parent corporation for no consideration other than the cancellation or surrender of this subsidiary's stock.*

Dated: *Signed* ....
                                       TYPE NAME OF GRANTOR OR REPRESENTATIVE BELOW LINE

RATE OF TAX —
Where purchase price or actual (market value) does not exceed $100.00 NO TAX.
Where such price or value exceeds $100.00 tax is 55¢ for each $500.00 or fractional part thereof.

Figure E-21: STATEMENT OF REAL ESTATE CONVEYANCE TAX
(Courtesy of All State Legal Supply Co., Mountainside, New Jersey 07092.)

HUD-1

Cleaveland Legal Blank Service, Inc.

FORM APPROVED OMB NO. 63-R-1501

A.

U.S. DEPARTMENT OF HOUSING AND URBAN DEVELOPMENT

SETTLEMENT STATEMENT

X 88 p. 1, Julius Blumberg, Inc., NYC 10013

B. TYPE OF LOAN

1. ☐ FHA 2. ☐ FMHA 3. ☐ CONV. UNINS.
4. ☐ VA 5. ☐ CONV. INS.

6. FILE NUMBER: 7. LOAN NUMBER:

8. MORTGAGE INSURANCE CASE NUMBER:

C. NOTE: This form is furnished to give you a statement of actual settlement costs. Amounts paid to and by the settlement agent are shown. Items marked *"(p.o.c.)"* were paid outside the closing; they are shown here for informational purposes and are not included in totals.

D. NAME OF BORROWER:

E. NAME OF SELLER:

F. NAME OF LENDER:

G. PROPERTY LOCATION:

H. SETTLEMENT AGENT:

PLACE OF SETTLEMENT

I. SETTLEMENT DATE:

J. SUMMARY OF BORROWER'S TRANSACTION		K. SUMMARY OF SELLER'S TRANSACTION	
100. GROSS AMOUNT DUE FROM BORROWER:		**400. GROSS AMOUNT DUE TO SELLER:**	
101. Contract sales price		401. Contract sales price	
102. Personal property		402. Personal property	
103. Settlement charges to borrower *(line 1400)*		403.	
104.		404.	
105.		405.	
Adjustments for items paid by seller in advance		*Adjustments for items paid by seller in advance*	
106. City/town taxes to		406. City/town taxes to	
107. County taxes to		407. County taxes to	
108. Assessments to		408. Assessments to	
109.		409.	
110.		410.	
111.		411.	
112.		412.	
120. GROSS AMOUNT DUE FROM BORROWER		**420. GROSS AMOUNT DUE TO SELLER**	
200. AMOUNTS PAID BY OR IN BEHALF OF BORROWER:		**500. REDUCTIONS IN AMOUNT DUE TO SELLER:**	
201. Deposit or earnest money		501. Excess deposit (see instructions)	
202. Principal amount of new loan(s)		502. Settlement charges to seller *(line 1400)*	
203. Existing loan(s) taken subject to		503. Existing loan(s) taken subject to	
204.		504. Payoff of first mortgage loan	
205.		505. Payoff of second mortgage loan	
206.		506.	
207.		507.	
208.		508.	
209.		509.	
Adjustments for items unpaid by seller:		*Adjustments for items unpaid by seller:*	
210. City/town taxes to		510. City/town taxes to	
211. County taxes to		511. County taxes to	
212. Assessments to		512. Assessments to	
213.		513.	
214.		514.	
215.		515.	
216.		516.	
217.		517.	
218.		518.	
219.		519.	
220. TOTAL PAID BY/FOR BORROWER		**520. TOTAL REDUCTION AMOUNT DUE SELLER**	
300. CASH AT SETTLEMENT FROM/TO BORROWER		**600. CASH AT SETTLEMENT TO/FROM SELLER**	
301. Gross amount due from borrower *(line 120)*		601. Gross amount due to seller *(line 420)*	
302. Less amounts paid by/for borrower *(line 220)*	( )	602. Less reductions in amt. due to seller *(line 520)*	( )
303. CASH (☐ FROM) (☐ TO) BORROWER		**603. CASH (☐ TO) (☐ FROM) SELLER**	

Figure E-22: SETTLEMENT STATEMENT
(Courtesy of Mr. Gordon Ramsay, Cleaveland Legal Blank Service, Inc., E. Hartford, Connecticut.)

L. SETTLEMENT CHARGES

		PAID FROM BORROWER'S FUNDS AT SETTLEMENT	PAID FROM SELLER'S FUNDS AT SETTLEMENT
700.	**TOTAL SALES/BROKER'S COMMISSION** based on price $ @ % =		
	Division of Commission (line 700) as follows:		
701.	$ to		
702.	$ to		
703.	Commission paid at Settlement		
704.			
	800. ITEMS PAYABLE IN CONNECTION WITH LOAN		
801.	Loan Origination Fee %		
802.	Loan Discount %		
803.	Appraisal Fee to		
804.	Credit Report to		
805.	Lender's Inspection Fee		
806.	Mortgage Insurance Application Fee to		
807.	Assumption Fee		
808.			
809.			
810.			
811.			
	900. ITEMS REQUIRED BY LENDER TO BE PAID IN ADVANCE		
901.	Interest from to @ $ /day		
902.	Mortgage Insurance Premium for months to		
903.	Hazard Insurance Premium for years to		
904.	years to		
905.			
1000.	**1000. RESERVES DEPOSITED WITH LENDER**		
1001.	Hazard insurance months @ $ per month		
1002.	Mortgage insurance months @ $ per month		
1003.	City property taxes months @ $ per month		
1004.	County property taxes months @ $ per month		
1005.	Annual assessments months @ $ per month		
1006.	months @ $ per month		
1007.	months @ $ per month		
1008.	months @ $ per month		
	1100. TITLE CHARGES		
1101.	Settlement or closing fee to		
1102.	Abstract or title search to		
1103.	Title examination to		
1104.	Title insurance binder to		
1105.	Document preparation to		
1106.	Notary fees to		
1107.	Attorney's fees to		
	(includes above items numbers; *)*		
1108.	Title insurance to		
	(includes above items numbers; *)*		
1109.	Lender's coverage $		
1110.	Owner's coverage $		
1111.			
1112.			
1113.			
	1200. GOVERNMENT RECORDING AND TRANSFER CHARGES		
1201.	Recording fees: Deed $; Mortgage $; Releases $		
1202.	City/county tax/stamps: Deed $; Mortgage $		
1203.	State tax/stamps: Deed $; Mortgage $		
1204.			
1205.			
	1300. ADDITIONAL SETTLEMENT CHARGES		
1301.	Survey to		
1302.	Pest inspection to		
1303.			
1304.			
1305.			
1400.	**TOTAL SETTLEMENT CHARGES** *(enter on lines 103, Section J and 502, Section K)*		

We, the undersigned, identified as Borrower in section D hereof and Seller in section E hereof, hereby acknowledge receipt of this completed Uniform Settlement Statement (pages 1 & 2) on   19

Borrower: Seller:

_____   _____

_____   _____

Figure E-22 (continued)

An important objective of RESPA is to provide real estate buyers with information about the costs of settlement services so that they may make informed judgments in evaluating settlement services. This objective would be thwarted if, as a matter of routine, borrowers waived their rights to receive completed settlement statements at or before settlement.

In the unusual situation where a charge to be paid by borrower or seller can not be ascertained at settlement the Regulations (Sec. 3500.10(c)) provide a waiver procedure. The form of waiver below is provided as a convenience and should be used with discretion and restraint.

W A I V E R

I, the undersigned, identified as the borrower on the reverse side hereof, hereby waive my right under the Real Estate Settlement Procedures Act and the Rules and Regulations promulgated thereunder to have the completed Uniform Settlement Statement delivered or mailed to me at or before settlement, with the understanding, however, that it is to be delivered or mailed to me as soon as practical after settlement.

Dated   19   Borrower:

....

....

Figure E-22 (continued)

CERTIFICATION OF MAILING BY PARTY CONDUCTING SETTLEMENT

It is hereby certified that a copy of the completed Uniform Settlement Statement (HUD-1, pages 1 and 2) was enclosed in a postpaid sealed envelope addressed to the Seller at the address set forth in section E of the Uniform Settlement Statement and deposited in an official depository under the exclusive care and custody of the United States Postal Service on this date, and a copy of same was enclosed in a postpaid sealed envelope addressed to the Borrower at the address set forth in section D of the Uniform Settlement Statement and deposited in an official depository under the exclusive care and custody of the United States Postal Service on this date.

Dated:.. ....

Print or type name beneath   Title

CERTIFICATION OF DELIVERY

I hereby certifiy that on   19   I delivered a copy of the within completed Uniform Settlement Statement to the Borrower identified in section D on the first page hereof and a copy to the Seller identified in section E on the first page hereof.

....

APPROVAL OF SETTLEMENT, DISBURSEMENTS AND DELIVERY OF DOCUMENTS

Each of the undersigned hereby approves the completed Uniform Settlement Statement and authorizes the disbursement of funds as indicated and the delivery of documents executed in connection with this transaction. It is understood that items charged on an estimated basis or in reliance upon third party statements will be adjusted to reflect actual amounts paid, by a refund or billing to the party charged in the completed Uniform Settlement Statement.

Dated:

BROKER(S)	SELLER	BORROWER/BUYER
....	....	....
....	....	....

Figure E-22 (continued)

PROSPECT CARD

Date .... Salesman ....

Name ....

Office Address .... Phone ....

Home Address .... Phone ....

Type ....Const. ....Section ....

Price ....Cash ....Lot ....

Rooms ....

Baths .... Garage ....

Family ....

Schools ....

Special Requirements ....

Recommended by ....

CLEAVELAND LEGAL BLANK SERVICE, HARTFORD, CONNECTICUT

No. 138G

Figure E-23: PROSPECT CARD
(Courtesy of Mr. Gordon Ramsay, Cleaveland Legal Blank Service, Inc., E. Hartford, Connecticut.)

OFFER TO PURCHASE

REALTOR ®

....
(Office Name & Address)

.... 19.........

I hereby submit an offer of $.................................

for land and buildings located on ....
....

owned by ....

Subject to the following conditions;

Obtaining a mortgage loan of $ .... at .... %, for .... years within .... working days.

Satisfactory report of builder's and termite inspection on or before ....

Closing to be on or before ....

Contracts to be signed by buyer on or before ....

Items to be included: ....

....

....

Items not to be included: ....

....

Seller's Attorney .... Buyer's Attorney ....

This offer to be accepted, or rejected and binder check returned, within .... days.,
subject to a mutually satisfactory contract.

Binder check in the amount of $.......................... attached.

Signed .... Date ....

Address ....

City & State ....

Accepted by ....

....

Figure E-24: OFFER TO PURCHASE

AGREEMENT TO BUY

Property of ....

Located ....

Consisting of ....

....

....

Total of purchase price $ .... bargained for on the following terms and conditions:

....

....

....

....

....

....

....

....

....

....

....

....

....

....

....

....

Unless otherwise stated in this agreement all adjustments of taxes, interest, insurance, water charges, rents, etc. are to be made as of the date of transfer, conveyance is to be made by Warrantee Deed, the same to be executed and delivered on or before the .... day of 19   .

The purchaser having paid the sum of $ .... receipt of which is hereby acknowledged, the same is to apply on the purchase price as first payment, conditional upon the acceptance of same by the owner. If rejected, said amount in full shall be returned to the said purchaser, the purchaser hereby accepting the above terms as binding.

.... 19 ....

Dated at ....

Signed .... Agent   Accepted by .... Owner

.... Address   .... Owner

.... Purchaser   .... Address

.... Purchaser

.... Address   Date of Acceptance ....

Cleaveland Legal Blank Service, Inc.
East Hartford, Connecticut 06108

No. 106C

Figure E-25: AGREEMENT TO BUY
(Courtesy of Mr. Gordon Ramsay, Cleaveland Legal Blank Service, Inc., E. Hartford, Connecticut.)

PURCHASE AGREEMENT

THIS AGREEMENT, made this _____ day
of _____, 19_____,
by and between: PURCHASER _____
ADDRESS _____
        Hereinafter called Purchaser, and

SELLER _____
ADDRESS _____
        Hereinafter called Seller. (Purchaser and Seller may refer to two or more persons).
        WITNESSETH: Seller agrees to sell and Purchaser agrees to purchase certain property known as:

NUMBER AND STREET _____
APPROXIMATE LOT SIZE _____ X _____ (more or less) AS APPEARS IN TOWN RECORDS
     Consisting of all the real property of the above owners at the above address, as of record appears,
  with buildings and improvements thereon and appurtenances thereto, in its present condition.
     Purchaser and Seller agree that the transfer will be closed by delivery of a warranty deed and
        closing will take place on or before_____ on which date OCCUPANCY will be granted.
     All adjustments of taxes, water rates, fuel oil, etc., will be made at time of closing.

TOTAL PURCHASE PRICE FOR SAID PROPERTY IS .... $ _____
          CASH DEPOSIT THIS DATE .... $ _____
         ADDITIONAL DEPOSIT, BY _____ .... $ _____
                         (DATE)
BALANCE IS TO BE PAID BY CASH OR CERTIFIED CHECK AT CLOSING, AS FOLLOWS:
           By Proceeds of_____ mortgage in the amount of $ _____
Interest rate not to exceed _____ % for a term not less than _____ yrs.

By assuming the existing mortgage of $ _____ Balance $ _____
of_____ _____% with an unexpired term of _____ approx. unpaid balance, with an interest rate
This agreement to buy is contingent upon the PURCHASER procuring a written mortgage commitment with terms and conditions as set forth
above by _____ 19_____ and PURCHASER agrees to make a mortgage application
immediately upon the signing of this dated contract. If the PURCHASER is unable to obtain a written mortgage commitment under the terms
stated above, all deposit money will be returned to PURCHASER.

It is hereby agreed that all deposit money is to be retained by the Listing BROKER unless otherwise agreed to by all of the parties hereto.

     SELLER agrees to convey the property by WARRANTY DEED free and clear of all encumbrances except taxes as adjusted, mortgages
     to be assumed, if any, building lines established, easements and restrictions of record, if any, and all provisions of any ordinance,
     municipal regulations or public or private law.

RISK OF LOSS: Risk of loss due to fire or other casualty until delivery of the deed shall be upon the SELLER.
     SELLER agrees to pay for termite and water test if required FHA or VA.
DEFAULT: If the PURCHASER defaults under this agreement and SELLER is not in default, all sums paid hereunder shall be paid over to and
retained by the SELLER as liquidated damages subject to any commission due to the Real Estate BROKER(S), and both parties shall be relieved
of further liability under this agreement.
     PURCHASER and SELLER agree that this AGREEMENT shall be binding upon their respective heirs, successors, assigns, executors,
     and administrators.

REAL ESTATE BROKER: The parties recognize _____
_____ as the sole real estate broker(s) in this transaction and as the
procuring cause for the sale. Seller agrees to pay the real estate commission to said broker(s).
     Other conditions (if any):

     The above are all the terms and conditions of the sale.
IN WITNESS WHEREOF THE UNDERSIGNED HAVE SET THEIR HANDS ON THE DAY AND YEAR FIRST MENTIONED ABOVE.
                           PURCHASER   SELLER

                         (SIGNATURE)   (SIGNATURE)

_____
    REAL ESTATE BROKER(S)   (SIGNATURE)   (SIGNATURE)

               206C   Cleaveland Legal Blank Service, Inc
                                            East Hartford, Connecticut 06108

Figure E-26: PURCHASE AGREEMENT
(Courtesy of Mr. Gordon Ramsay, Cleaveland Legal Blank Service, Inc., E. Hartford, Connecticut.)

Cleaveland Legal Blank Service Inc
31 Lewis Street. Hartford. Conn 06103

THIS AGREEMENT, made between

of   hereafter the Seller, and

              of

hereafter the Purchaser.

In consideration the sum of   paid by the Purchaser, the receipt whereof is hereby acknowledged, the Seller does hereby give and grant to the Purchaser, the exclusive right, privilege and option of purchasing, upon the terms and conditions hereinafter set forth, the real property situated in the Town of   , Connecticut and more particularly bounded and described as follows:

It is understood and agreed that this option is made and is to be exercised upon the following terms and conditions:

(1) This option must be exercised on or before the   day of   19   and, if not exercised, all rights hereunder shall expire at that time;

(2) This option is to be exercised by the Purchaser giving to the Seller written notice, either hand delivered or sent by certified mail by mailing, postmarked no later than midnight of the last day, return receipt requested, within the time set forth herein for the exercise of this option;

(3) The total purchase price for the said property shall be the sum of $, to be paid by the Purchaser, if this option is exercised as follows:
(Set forth here all the essential provisions of the contract of sale, showing not only the method of paying the purchase price, but also the encumbrances and other matters, subject to which title is to be taken, the adjustments to be made on closing and other matters of that nature or attach a copy of proposed Contract of Sale).

(4) Time is of the essence of this option; in the event that it is not exercised by the Purchaser, the sum of $, paid on the signing hereof, shall be retained by the Seller, free of all claims of the Purchaser and neither party shall have any further rights or claims against the other.

(5) In the event that this option is exercised, as herein provided, the parties hereto shall enter into a formal contract for the sale of said property, containing the terms and conditions herein set forth and providing for the closing of the title to such property on or before the   day of   , 19

(6) This option, and all rights hereunder, may be assigned by either party hereto and, if assigned by the Purchaser, any and all acts to be performed by him under this option or the contract to be entered into pursuant hereto, may be performed by such assignee, whether such assignment be made before or after the exercise of this option.

Signed by the Seller, this   day of   , 19

Signed and delivered in the Presence of:

....

....

Figure E-27: REAL ESTATE OPTION
(Courtesy of Mr. Gordon Ramsay, Cleaveland Legal Blank Service, Inc., E. Hartford, Connecticut.)

EXCLUSIVE AGENCY LISTING

This is an agreement between: Date.......................................

....agent and,

.... owner(s)

in regard to the sale of real property located at...
....

Agent agrees to actively attempt to sell the above premises using advertising media such as newspapers, signs, and/or any other ethical and recognized means of securing a sale. The Owner hereby authorizes the Agent to place FOR SALE or SOLD signs on the above premises for the duration of this contract.

For the time, effort and expense incurred by the agent to sell the above property, the owner(s) agree(s) to give the agent an exclusive agency to sell the property for

a period of .... days, through and including ...., 19.....,

at a rate of .... commission if sold at a price of $..........................., or at a price acceptable to the owner(s).

If the property is sold by anyone other than the owner(s) a commission will be due to the Agent. If the property is sold by the owner(s) to anyone other than people introduced to the property by the Agent, NO COMMISSION will be due.

Agent...   ....Owner

Address...   ....Owner

.... Address

No. 138 EAC   ....

Cleaveland Legal Blank Service, Inc., Hartford, Conn.

This agreement is subject to Sec. 53-35 of the General Statutes, as amended, (Public Accommodations Act).

Figure E-28: EXCLUSIVE AGENCY LISTING
(Courtesy of Mr. Gordon Ramsay, Cleaveland Legal Blank Service, Inc., E. Hartford, Connecticut.)

OPEN LISTING AGREEMENT

Date ....

.... owner(s)

....

of property located at ....

agree(s) to allow ....agent

to sell the above property. If an exclusive right to sell or exclusive agency is given to another agent, or property is sold or taken off the market, owner(s) agree(s) to notify this agent of such action in order to prevent further investment in time and money on the part of the agent.

This agreement is subject to Sec. 53-35 of the General Statutes as amended, (Public Accommodations Act).

SALE PRICE: ....   COMMISSION: ....

TERMS: ....

.... *Owner*

At .... *Owner*

.... *Agent*

Figure E-29: OPEN LISTING AGREEMENT

NOTICE OF SHOWING

DATE_____

PLEASE BE ADVISED THAT TODAY WE SUBMITTED TO:

_____

YOUR PROPERTY LISTED WITH THIS OFFICE LOCATED AT:

_____

PRICE QUOTED $_____   WE WILL ENDEAVOR TO INTEREST THIS PROSPECT FURTHER. IF THEY RETURN TO

EXAMINE SAME, OR CALL BY PHONE, PLEASE NOTIFY US AT ONCE, AS YOUR COOPERATION WILL GREATLY ASSIST IN

THE SALE OF YOUR PROPERTY.

NOTE: THIS NOTICE IS FOR YOUR INFORMATION. PLEASE KEEP IT FOR FUTURE
REFERENCE. A COPY IS ON FILE IN OUR OFFICE. IF ANY CHANGE HAS   BY_____
TAKEN PLACE SINCE YOUR PROPERTY HAS BEEN LISTED WITH THIS
OFFICE, WE WOULD APPRECIATE WORD FROM YOU AT ONCE.

Figure E-30: NOTICE OF SHOWING

COMMERCIAL BROKERS INFORMATION FORM

DATE:

INSTANT MARKETING

☐ ** PROPERTY WANTED   ☐ PROPERTY OFFERED

☐ FOR SALE   ☐ LEASE   ☐ BUILD TO SUIT   ☐ OTHER

(CHECK ONE)

RESIDENTIAL INCOME

— Apartments/Condominiums
— Motels
— Hotels
— Mobile Home Parks
— Rest and Nursing Homes

COMMERCIAL INCOME

— Service Stations
— Franchise Operations
— Office Buildings
— Professional Buildings (medical, etc.)
— Single Purpose (free standing theaters, bowling, restaurants, banks, etc.)
— Strip Stores
— Shopping Centers
— Multi-Purpose (includes combo residential-commercial)

LAND

— Farms
— Recreational
— Subdivision-Single Family
— Subdivision-Multiple Family
— Subdivision-Commercial
— Industrial
— Improved Lots (residential, commercial, industrial)
— Unzoned

INDUSTRIAL

— Warehouses
— Light Manufacturing (includes loft buildings)
— Heavy Manufacturing
— Industrial Parks

BUSINESS OPPORTUNITY

— Franchise Operation
— Food Business (bars, restaurants, ice cream parlors, etc.)
— Service Business (barber shop, beauty shop, TV repair, cleaners, laundromat, etc.)
— Retail Merchandising (grocery, drug, printing, dry goods, liquor stores, etc.)
— Automotive Services (service station, car wash, auto parts, auto dealerships, parking lots garages and repair shops, etc.)
— Public Accommodations & Recreation (theaters, bowling alleys, ski resorts, etc.)
— Public Accommodations (hotels, motels, etc.)
— Other Business Opportunities

TYPE OF LISTING (check one)

— EXCLUSIVE RIGHT
— SOLE AGENCY
— OPEN

PLEASE PRINT OR TYPE

LOCATION (optional): _____

BRIEF DESCRIPTION: _____

_____

_____

_____

_____

_____

*PRICE: $ _____ RENTAL OR SQ. FT. RATE: $ _____

*DATE AVAILABLE: _____ ZONING: _____

*COMMISSION: _____ SPLIT: _____ AVAILABLE FINANCING: _____

**PRICE RANGE: $ _____ AVAILABLE CASH: $ _____

**RATE OF RETURN REQUIRED: _____

REALTOR/ASSOCIATE: _____

AGENCY: _____ PHONE: _____

ADDRESS: _____
I certify that I have written authorization by the owner as per Public Act 175 & 73-29.

_____
Listing Agent's Signature

Figure E-31: COMMERCIAL BROKERS INFORMATION FORM

OPEN LISTING AGREEMENT
FOR LEASING

Date _____

_____ , owner of property

located at _____ ,

agrees to allow _____ the right to lease the above property and

such additional property as Landlord may decide to lease to a prospective tenant acceptable to the owner. If

an exclusive right to lease or exclusive agency is given to another agent, or property is leased or otherwise

taken off the market, owner agrees to notify this agent of such action in order to prevent further investment in

time and money on the part of the agent. This agreement will remain in effect until _____ ,

19____ unless terminated sooner by the owner for any of the above reasons.

This agreement is subject to Sec. 53-35 of the General Statutes as amended, (Public Accomodations Act).

Price: _____ (or such price as acceptable to owner.)

Leasing Commission: _____

Or, in the event that prospect should purchase at a price acceptable to owner:

Selling Commission: _____

Terms and/or Description _____

_____

_____

_____

_____

Owner _____

At _____ Owner _____

Agent _____

Figure E-32: OPEN LISTING AGREEMENT FOR LEASING

LEASE — FURNISHED OR UNFURNISHED

THIS LEASE, made the .... day of .... 19......,

between .... of ....

...., Lessor, and ....

.... of ...., Lessee,

WITNESSETH:

That the Lessor has rented to the Lessee, and that the Lessee has rented from the Lessor the premises described as follows:

With the appurtenances, together with the furniture and furnishings contained therein, if any, for the term commencing at

noon on ...., 19....., and ending at noon on ...., 19.....,

for the total rent of .... Dollars

($..), payable as follows:

THE LESSEE COVENANTS AND AGREES:

(1) To pay the rent punctually without demand

(2) To pay all charges for all utilities, including but not limited to fuel, water, telephone, gas and electric service;

(3) To keep, at his own expense, the lawn mowed and the grounds in good and neat order; to remove all garbage, ashes, refuse and waste from the premises during the term of this lease, and not to permit any accumulation of boxes, barrels, packages, waste paper or other refuse in or upon the premises.

(4) To make no alterations in the leased premises, to permit no waste or injury thereto, nor to the fixtures, trees, shrubbery or appurtenances thereon; and at his own expense, to make all repairs resulting from misuse or neglect and all minor repairs, but not including repairs which are necessary to comply with applicable building and housing codes materially affecting health and safety unless they are required because of acts of the Lessee. Minor repairs shall be defined as those repairs costing less

than $..

(5) To comply with all the laws of the State of Connecticut and the by-laws, rules and ordinances, including zoning regulations, of the Town within which the premises are situated, relating to health, nuisance, fire, highway and sidewalks, so far as the premises are concerned. The Lessee shall be liable for all fines, penalties, costs for violation of such laws, rules and ordinances with which Lessee has responsibility to comply by virtue of his occupancy of said premises.

(6) Except with the written consent of the Lessor, not to assign this lease, nor let or sublet the whole or any part of the premises, not to occupy or use the premises or permit them to be used or occupied for any purpose other than as a private residence for the Lessee and his family, nor to permit the premises to be used in any manner or for any purpose involving fire or

other hazard, nor to permit the premises to remain vacant or unoccupied for more than (..) days at one time without prior notice to the Lessor;

(7) To permit the Lessor, or others he may designate his agents, to show the premises to persons wishing to rent or pur-

chase during the last .... days of the term of this lease;

(8) At the termination of this lease, whether by lapse of time or by virtue of any express stipulation herein, to surrender the leased premises in as good state and condition as reasonable use and wear thereof will permit, damages by the elements excepted, the house and the premises to be left clean and in good order; and

(9) If this lease includes furniture and furnishings, to keep the same in good order and repair at his expense and also to pay for, replace or make good any and all damage or breakage to or loss of any furniture, furnishings, crockery, glass and other wares (excepting loss or damage by fire or hurricane) and to surrender and deliver up the furniture and furnishings at the expiration of the term of this lease in good condition, ordinary use and wear thereof excepted.

THE LESSOR COVENANTS AND AGREES:

(1) That he has good right to lease the premises as aforesaid;

(2) To deliver the premises to the Lessee in good condition; with all appliances and systems in good working order.

(3) That the Lessee, on paying the rent and performing the covenants aforesaid, shall and may hold the leased premises for the term herein set forth;

(4) That in case the dwelling house on the leased premises shall be partly damaged by fire or other causes (other than as a result of the fault or negligence of the Lessee), to such extent that the Lessee's enjoyment of the dwelling house is not substantially impaired, the same shall be repaired as speedily as possible at the expense of the Lessor;

(5) That in case the damage shall be so extensive as to substantially impair the Lessee's enjoyment of the leased premises, the Lessee may vacate all or any part of the dwelling unit rendered unusable by the fire or other casualty and the rent shall be proportionately adjusted; or the Lessee may immediately vacate the premises and notify the Landlord in writing within fourteen (14) days thereafter of his intention to terminate the rental agreement, in which case the rental agreement shall terminate as of the date of vacating;

Figure E-33: LEASE—FURNISHED OR UNFURNISHED

(6) That if any rent shall remain due and unpaid after the same shall have become due and payable or if there is any non-compliance with the covenants herein contained, this lease shall thereupon, at the option of the Lessor, by virtue of this express stipulation herein expire and terminate, and the Lessor shall give notice to the Lessee to quit possession or occupancy, and no waiver by the Lessor of any default shall impair any right of the Lessor in respect of any subsequent default. ....

It is agreed that this lease is made and procured through the agency and efforts of ....

....

and the Lessor agrees to pay such agent a commission which shall be due on the signing of the lease of ....

....

If the Lessee, his heirs, or assignee renews this lease, or continues to occupy the premises after the expiration of this lease, or if the relationship of Lessor and Lessee is renewed within one year between the Lessor and the Lessee, his heirs, or assignee, the Lessor agrees to pay the agent the commission as stated above.

It is further acknowledged and agreed that in the event that the Lessee or a member of his immediate family purchases the premises herein demised during any period of the Lessee's tenancy or within a period of time specified in a separate agreement after the termination of such tenancy, the Lessor has agreed by such separate agreement on Listing #..................................... to pay a sales commission to the agent.

Lessee will deposit with Lessor the sum of $... on .... to be held as security for the full and faithful performance by the Lessee of all the terms, repairs, covenants, and conditions of this lease upon the Lessee's part to be performed, which sum shall be returned to the Lessee with the interest due thereon as by law required and provided, within .... days after the expiration of the term herein, provided the Lessee has fully and faithfully carried out all of said terms, covenants and conditions on Lessee's part to be performed. In the event of a bona fide sale, subject to this Lease, Lessor shall have the right to transfer the security to the vendee for the benefit of the Lessee and the Lessor shall be considered released by the Lessee from all liability for the return of the security. Said security shall not be mortgaged, assigned, or encumbered by Lessee without the written consent of Lessor.

The Lessee agrees as part of the consideration of this lease to use the same Oil Company for oil delivery and care and maintenance of the furnace on the premises as is presently being used by the Lessor.

The Lessor agrees to provide the Lessee with a full tank of oil on the commencement date of this lease and the Lessee agrees to provide the Lessor with a full tank of oil on the expiration date of this lease.

The covenants and agreements herein contained shall inure to the benefits of, and shall be binding upon, the parties hereto and their heirs, successors and assigns.

....

....
has been engaged by the Lessor and is authorized to manage these premises in accordance with a separate agreement with the Lessor and the Lessee agrees to deal with said Managing Agent.

.... does not assume any responsibility for the management or up-keep of the premises or physical damage thereto.

Notice may be sent to the Lessee at the address of the premises and to the Lessor at ....

....

IN WITNESS WHEREOF, the parties hereto have hereunto set their hands and seals the day and date first above written.

Signed, Sealed and Delivered in the Presence of:

.... (L.S.)

.... (L.S.)
As to Lessor   Lessor

.... (L.S.)

.... (L.S.)
As to Lessee   Lessee

STATE OF CONNECTICUT } ss.:
COUNTY OF FAIRFIELD

Personally appeared

(Lessor), Signer and Sealer of the within instrument, and acknowledged the same to be his free act and deed, before me.

STATE OF CONNECTICUT } ss.:
COUNTY OF FAIRFIELD   ....
                                                                              Notary Public
Personally appeared   Commissioner of the Superior Court

(Lessee), Signer and Sealer of the within instrument, and acknowledged the same to be his free act and deed, before me.

....
Notary Public
Commissioner of the Superior Court

Figure E-33—Reverse Side

This Indenture

MADE BY AND BETWEEN

of the Town of   in the County of

and State of Connecticut, hereinafter called the LESSOR, and

of the Town of   in the County of

and State of   , hereinafter called the LESSEE

WITNESSETH, that the said Lessor, for and in consideration of the rents and covenants hereinafter reserved and contained, and to be paid, kept and fulfilled on the part of said Lessee, has let, and by these presents do grant, demise, and to farm let, unto the said Lessee

with the appurtenances, to have and to hold the same, for the term of

                           from the   day of   19

for the   rent of   Dollars, to be paid

in equal   payments at the   follows, to wit:

AND IT IS AGREED, That if any rent shall be in arrear and unpaid by the space of
days after the same shall be and become due and payable as aforesaid, or if default shall be made in any of the covenants herein contained and to be kept and fulfilled on the part of the said Lessee, then it shall be lawful for the said Lessor   at any time after such neglect or default, and without any previous demand or notice whatever, to re-enter and take possession of said leased premises, and such re-entry and taking possession shall

end and terminate this lease, and further that if the Lessee shall be declared insolvent or adjudicated a bankrupt the Lessor may terminate this lease and immediately take possession of said premises.

Figure E-34: LEASE
(Courtesy of Mr. Gordon Ramsay, Cleaveland Legal Blank Service, Inc., E. Hartford, Connecticut.)

And the said Lessee does covenant to pay to the said Lessor, the said yearly rents as hereinbefore specified, and further, that Lessee will not, during said term, assign or under-let said premises or any part thereof

without the permission in writing of the said Lessor, and will not occupy the said premises for any business deemed extra hazardous without the like consent. And the Lessee does hereby further agree to do no waste, to pay all water and gas charges, repair all broken window glass and all damage that may happen to gas and water pipes through the neglect or carelessness of Lessee or any of the occupants.

And the said Lessee does hereby further agree to comply with and conform to all the laws of the State of Connecticut, and the by-laws, rules and regulations of the City or Town within which the premises hereby leased are situated, relating to health, nuisance, fire, highways and side-walks, so far as the premises hereby leased are or may be concerned, and to save the Lessor harmless from all fines, penalties and costs for violation of or non-compliance with the same.

And the said Lessee does further agree that after default made in any of the covenants herein contained, the acceptance of rent or failure to re-enter by the Lessor shall not be held to be a waiver of right to terminate the lease, and said Lessor may re-enter and take possession of said premises the same as if no rent had been accepted after such default.

And at the expiration of the said term or other determination of this lease, the Lessee will quit and surrender the premises hereby demised in as good state and condition as reasonable use and wear thereof will permit, damages by the elements excepted, and the said Lessor shall have the right to enter said premises for the purpose of showing the same to applicants for hiring the same, at any time during the last month of said term.

And the said Lessee does covenant to and does hereby waive demand and notice of every kind and description whatever, which, were it not for said waiver, might otherwise be necessary in obtaining possession of said premises.

Figure E-34 (continued)

IN WITNESS WHEREOF, the parties have hereunto set their hands and seals and to a duplicate instrument of the same tenor and date, at

this .... day of .... 19 .

Signed, Sealed and Delivered in the presence of

....(L. S.)

....(L. S.)

....(L. S.)

....(L. S.)

....(L. S.)

STATE OF CONNECTICUT ⎫
                 ⎬ ss.
COUNTY OF ⎭

         On this .... day of .... 19 , before me

                                                   , the undersigned officer, personally appeared

known to me (or satisfactorily proven) to be the person whose name is/are subscribed to the within instrument and acknowledged that he/she/they executed the same for the purposes therein contained.

      In Witness Whereof I hereunto set my hand.

                                   ....
                                   Notary Public — Commissioner of the Superior Court

STATE OF CONNECTICUT ⎫
                 ⎬ ss.
COUNTY OF ⎭

         On this .... day of .... 19 , before me

                                              , the undersigned officer, personally
appeared   who acknowledged
himself/herself to be the

                                         of
                           , a corporation, and that he, as such
being authorized so to do, executed the foregoing instrument for the purposes therein contained, by signing the name of the corporation by himself herself as

      In Witness Whereof I hereunto set my hand.

                                   ....
                                   Notary Public — Commissioner of the Superior Court

In Consideration of the letting of the premises above described, and for the sum of one dollar,   do hereby become surety for the punctual payment of the rent, and performance of all and singular the covenant in the above indenture contained to be kept and performed by

                                                 Lessee therein named,
and if any default shall be made therein,   do hereby covenant and agree to pay unto
                        Lessor , in said indenture named, such sum or sums of moneys as will be sufficient to make up such deficiency and fully satisfy the conditions of said indenture, without requiring notice of any such default, or proof of demand being made.

      Given under   hand and seal at
this   day of   19

                                 ....(L. S.)

                                 ....(L. S.)

LEASE   No 101   Cleaveland Legal Blank Service, Inc.
Hartford, Connecticut

Figure E-34 (continued)

RENTAL APPLICATION   Form #41 R   Cleaveland Legal Blank Service, Inc.

Date ....

Social Sec. # ....

....
            Name in full

Age .... Marital Status ....

....
         Street and number

Home phone ....
Bus. phone ....

....
    City/Town   State   Zip Code

Wife's name .... No. of Dependent children ....

How long at present address .... Rent or own? ....

          Monthly rent or mortgage payment ....

Landlord or mortgage holder .... Address ....

Previous address .... How long ....

Present employer .... Position .... Annual Income ....

Address .... How long employed ....

        Previous employer .... How long ....

        Wife's employer .... How long ....

        Position .... Annual income ....

Other income: ....

Make and year of car .... Financed by ....

Bank .... ☐ Savings Account ☐ Checking Account ☐ Loan Account

Charge Accounts ....

Name of nearest relative not living with you ....

Premises Applied for

Apartment }
House   } at...

Number to Occupy.....................Adults........................Children........................Pets...............

Ages of Children..

Rent per Month $...Payment on Account.....................................

Term of Lease..Rent Begins...................Will Occupy.................

                    Signature..

Figure E-35: RENTAL APPLICATION
(Courtesy of Mr. Gordon Ramsay, Cleaveland Legal Blank Service, Inc., E. Hartford, Connecticut.)

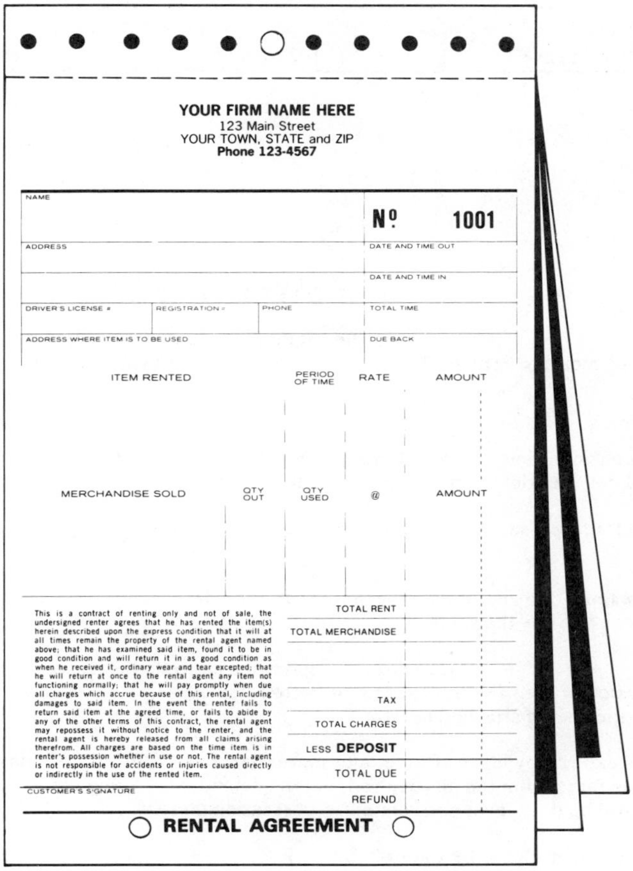

YOUR FIRM NAME HERE
123 Main Street
YOUR TOWN, STATE and ZIP
Phone 123-4567

NAME

Nº 1001

ADDRESS

DATE AND TIME OUT

DATE AND TIME IN

DRIVER'S LICENSE #

REGISTRATION #

PHONE

TOTAL TIME

ADDRESS WHERE ITEM IS TO BE USED

DUE BACK

ITEM RENTED	PERIOD OF TIME	RATE	AMOUNT

MERCHANDISE SOLD	QTY OUT	QTY USED	@	AMOUNT

This is a contract of renting only and not of sale, the undersigned renter agrees that he has rented the item(s) herein described upon the express condition that it will at all times remain the property of the rental agent named above; that he has examined said item, found it to be in good condition and will return it in as good condition as when he received it, ordinary wear and tear excepted; that he will return at once to the rental agent any item not functioning normally; that he will pay promptly when due all charges which accrue because of this rental, including damages to said item. In the event the renter fails to return said item at the agreed time, or fails to abide by any of the other terms of this contract, the rental agent may repossess it without notice to the renter, and the rental agent is hereby released from all claims arising therefrom. All charges are based on the time item is in renter's possession whether in use or not. The rental agent is not responsible for accidents or injuries caused directly or indirectly in the use of the rented item.

TOTAL RENT	
TOTAL MERCHANDISE	
TAX	
TOTAL CHARGES	
LESS **DEPOSIT**	
TOTAL DUE	
REFUND	

CUSTOMER'S SIGNATURE

RENTAL AGREEMENT

Figure E-35 RENTAL APPLICATION

(Available from New England Business Service, Inc., North Main Street, Groton, Massachusetts 01450; 1-800-225-6380.)

Ret.

              :   SUPERIOR COURT - G.A. #

       VS.   :

                         :

C O M P L A I N T

1. On   the plaintiff   leased to said defendant for the term of one month from said date for the monthly rent of $ payable in advance on said date, the following premises to wit:--

2. Then and there in consideration of said letting, the lessee   agreed to pay the said rent as aforesaid, and that   he   would not underlet the premises or any part thereof.

3. The lessee   entered into possession of said premises under said lease and ha   ever since continued to hold possession thereof.

4. Said monthly rent remained due and unpaid for more than nine days from said date of leasing and said defendant still neglect   and refuse   to pay the same.

5. On   the lessor   gave due notice to the lessee   in the manner prescribed by the statute, to quit possession of the said premises on or before   , and notice of termination of lease, a copy of said notice being attached hereto.

6. Though said lease has expired by lapse of time, and more than 5   days have elapsed since said notice was given, and the time therein limited has expired, yet the defendant   neglect   and refuse   to quit possession of said premises, but still hold   over and retain   possession thereof.

7. The defendant   owe   in all to the date of this writ $ to the plaintiff for the use and possession of said premises.

The Plaintiff Claims: Immediate possession of said premises and cost of suit.

Dated at   this   day of   A.D., 19

....

Commissioner of the Superior Court

Figure E-37: SUMMARY PROCESS ON PAROL LEASE
(Courtesy of Mr. Gordon Ramsay, Cleaveland Legal Blank Service, Inc., E. Hartford, Connecticut.)

```
┌─────────────────────────────────────────────────────────────────┐
│                                                                   │
│    ─────────────────────────────────────────────────────────     │
│                         NAME OF OFFICE                            │
│                                                                   │
│                                                                   │
│    ──────────────────────────      ──────────────────────────    │
│         SELLING  BROKER                        DATE               │
│                                                                   │
│                      STATEMENT                                    │
│                                                                   │
│   LISTING (NAME & # )  : ─────────────────────────────────────    │
│                                                                   │
│   ADDRESS            : ───────────────────────────────────────    │
│                                                                   │
│   RENTED/SOLD        : $ ──────────────────────────────────────   │
│                                                                   │
│   LISTING  COMMISSION : $ ─────────────────────────────────────   │
│                                                                   │
└─────────────────────────────────────────────────────────────────┘
```

Figure E-38: STATEMENT

SECTION F

INVESTMENT INSTRUMENTS AND NONRESIDENT CORPORATION REGISTRATION

SECTION F FORMS

Investment Instruments and Nonresident Corporation Registration

Investment Instruments and Nonresident Corporation Registration

Financial planning for profits and growth hinges not only on investments in new assets or real estate or existing companies but also on non-tangible or financial assets both for investment purposes (uses of capital) and for sources of funds to finance acquisitions and budget expansion into new geographical territories. This section focuses on short- and long-term securities, either as a source of or use for funds, control of these instruments, selected registration requirements for corporations advancing into new geographical areas domestically; while the following section looks into international operations.

The linking thread is cost control; and cost control exacts PROTECTION FROM LOSSES and pilfering, especially of negotiable instruments. The Checklist for Internal Control of Marketable Securities (F-1), a security measure, organizes a routine to keep close tabs on who has access to these valuable documents and to ensure a periodic update of the inventory of securities. The checklist probably should be reexamined quarterly and filed in at least two, physically separated, locations.

F-1

The Trustees' Account Ledger (F-2) is another type of control and record-keeping form for businesses that retain and transact in securities for other firms or individuals. Although this design was developed for *securities control* in an attorney's office, the format can be adapted to a wide range of applications. For example, with modification it can serve to chronicle hedging transactions of a concern, or report intracompany securities transactions, or, in addition to the Checklist (F-1), it tracks interim movements of securities. The far right column may best be utilized by stipulating a signature (not initials) for each exchange.

F-2

A petroleum company employs a fairly simple configuration on intracompany memos to report on Bank Balances and Investment Portfolio (F-3). These reports are filed monthly.

F-3

The reporter must indicate:

   (a)   opening and ending balances;
   (b)   the specific investment and its maturity date.

For *profit analysis* the rate of return is calculated on each investment each month. For *control purposes,* similar to preceding forms, the locations of these funds must appear at the bottom of the form. This particular design chalks up primarily short-term, liquid investments, used for worldwide reporting.

F-4   Of course, these compendious reports must be supported with official documents that confirm various deposits, such as the Confirmation of Deposit (F-4) in a Bahamas Bank. This is a multipurpose style for foreign credits and debits used by banks. Information recorded on various pages of this form includes the amount in foreign exchanges and in U.S. dollars, the maturity date and term of deposit, the rate and total interest paid.

   (a)   The first page is a credit for a time deposit.
   (b)   The second page is a debit memo showing amount due from foreign banks along with the preceding data.
   (c)   The fourth page is a credit memo on the maturity date showing income earned in investments but not collected.
   (d)   The sixth page relates to a request for cable service for instructions.
   (e)   The last page confirms acceptance of deposit and requires its return with an authorization signature.

That is, the form is designed for COST REDUCTION, by providing for inscription of duplicated information on all pages at one typing, and PROFIT CONTROL, by providing for close follow-up at all stages of the transactions. The next panel is an

F-5   example of two dividend checks (F-5).

F-6   A more sophisticated form, the Savings Transaction Journal and Trial Balance (F-6), delves into greater detail on individual transactions with data in a format acceptable to accounting. Notice on the left side the list of preprinted code numbers for credit and debit transactions, branch number, status of the account, and alert signals. Naturally, from the bank's viewpoint credits and debits mirror corporate accounts.

F-7
F-8   Short-term investments may include a Savings Certificate (F-7) in a Federal Savings and Loan Association, a Certificate of Deposit (F-8)—two forms are illustrated—or a
F-9   dividend Notice of Savings Certificate Earnings (F-9). A simpler method of tracing these
F-10   short-term investments (F-10) is employed by a midwest firm with worldwide interests. Because of its international investments, management requires reporting information on the currency of the account as well as the current exchange rate. Additional data from the right-hand columns are then transferred into the computer for storage and subsequent retrieval for PROFIT ANALYSIS and BUDGETING.

F-11
F-12   Business transactions also embrace various types of notes either issued or carried. The
F-13   first example is a Sight Draft (F-11). The second represents Series Notes (F-12). The third
F-14   is a Promissory Note (F-13). The fourth is a Warrant (F-14).

A *sight draft* is a commercial draft payable upon presentation. *Series notes* parallel serial bonds; all are issued on the same date but different maturity dates extend over a span of time. If the debtor defaults on any one note of the series, then the remaining notes may, at the option of the holder, become due at once. A *promissory note* is an unconditional written promise to pay a fixed sum of money on a fixed date. A *warrant* is evidence of indebtedness incurred by the corporation; it is redeemed for cash or check when presented to the drawee of the warrant.

In all of these instruments there are some common elements:

(a) Each is dated and signed.
(b) The payee (person to whom a promissory note or draft is payable) is named.
(c) The principal and interest rate are quoted.
(d) Due date is specified, except for the sight draft which is payable upon presentation.

From the lender's position, facts are maintained on all loans, the date and amount due, plus the interest rate with payments on principal and interest credited to each account (F-15).

F-15

At the beginning of this section it was suggested that the checklist (F-1) be filed in at least two separate places; the same holds true for other valuable documents which keep score on this activity and the documents themselves which require careful storage with a photocopy filed for reference. For example, if securities are held by an outside depository, five copies of the evidence would be made:

- ◆ The Custodian signs the original and a duplicate.
- ◆ The Treasurer signs the original.
- ◆ The original is sent to the Comptroller's office.
- ◆ The record copy and three other copies are held in the security record section.

With internal transactions, including notes and intracorporate transfers and advances, fewer copies are needed for security purposes; but an approved copy would be held by the Treasurer's office, a record copy for the Comptroller's office, and a transaction copy for the custodian.

For sale and delivery of securities, a form (F-16) in triplicate is adequate with one copy filed in the vault, another sent to the cashier, and one signed by the purchaser as a receipt of record which is subsequently filed. Each set contains:

F-16

(a) serial number;
(b) date;
(c) description of the transaction;
(d) spaces for approval, withdrawal, and receipt for securities;
(e) further details on the reverse side of the form.

Common stock represents equity participation in an enterprise, with residual rights to assets in the event of liquidation, and right to participate in the income stream when and if

F-17 dividends are issued. The Class "A" Common Stock Certificate (F-17) represents certain rights inferior to other classes of stock in order to gain exclusive voting power. The corporation maintains archives on shares of stock issued and outstanding (F-18), and adjusts for shares redeemed or canceled. The form accommodates data on:

(a) three classes of common stock plus treasury stock;
(b) details on issue date;
(c) number of shares issued;
(d) price of other consideration paid.

F-18 In addition to this macro record (in F-18), the corporation maintains a registry of
F-19 individual shareholder's activity (F-19), which dockets the certificate number, number of shares, class of stock, and date of purchase on one side of the ledger, with similar facts on the reverse side to report on transfers. Supplementary to those forms, a Record of Interest
F-20 or Dividends Earned (F-20) itemizes dividends paid on stock or interest paid on notes and bonds.

Three other documents relate to the transfer of stock besides the above form (F-18). The first is a Certification of the Corporate Resolution Granting Authority to Transfer
F-21 Securities (F-21). Names, titles and *specimen* signatures of duly elected corporate officers are listed and certified by two signatures:

(1) the Corporate Secretary, and,
(2) an official other than the Secretary.

Furthermore, the certifying officer's *signature must be guaranteed* by a firm with membership in a major stock exchange or a commercial bank.

F-22 The second is a Power of Attorney to Transfer Stock (F-22), which grants someone other than the owner the power to legally transfer or assign certain shares of stock. It is important that the stock certificate numbers be entered on this document, if a general power of attorney is not granted, in order to PROTECT the owner. But the power is
F-23 voided upon the death of the signer and owner of stock. The Stock Transfer Ledger (F-23) details from whom and to whom designated shares of stock have been transferred, including certificate number and specifics on whether some shares are still retained. The
F-24 third document is for the assignment and transfer of stock (F-24) with corresponding power of attorney.

F-25 For stock pledged as loan collateral for general business purposes, the displayed collateral demand loan agreement (F-25) documents which stock has been deposited with the bank as *security* on the front side with loan conditions spelled out. On the reverse there is lined space for inscribing additional activity and payments. The demand loan carries no specified maturity date; it is payable on demand of the bank. Interest due is billed at determined intervals. An alternative, a collateral time loan (F-26), has a fixed maturity date. Data on these types of loans are carried on a ledger card (F-27) which lists information on the stock held by the bank and on which from time to time the bank scores the market and *collateral value* of stock held. A similar file should be carried by the corporation to avoid unpleasant surprises.   **F-26**   **F-27**

Bonds as well as stocks require recordkeeping. A combination stock and bond register (F-28) substitutes for either investment instrument. Or if an organization issues a limited number of various securities it may well prefer to TRIM COSTS and maintain a joint register for stocks, bonds, and other securities (F-29).   **F-28**   **F-29**

A *bond,* a certificate of debt, represents a binding agreement between the issuing concern and the bondholder. For the organization it is a source of long-term funds; for the bondholder it is a financial asset. A bond bears a fixed interest (unless it is an income bond), comes in a variety of financial arrangements for PROFIT MAXIMIZATION and to induce investors to exchange savings for certificates, and usually is secured by a lien against specified corporate property.

A *debenture bond* (F-30) represents a concern's funded debt backed only by that concern's credit and not secured by a pledge of assets or mortgage of property. An *unsubordinated debenture bond* (F-31) is essentially identical to the debenture bond (F-30), except that claims of bondholders are subordinate to other obligees. In this illustration the caveat reads: "This Debenture is subject to and subordinate to the obligations, indebtedness and covenants of the company now existing or hereafter incurred or made in favor of any bank, banker, trust company or financial institution." Consequently, an investor carries greater risk (which does not necessarily reduce total risk to the issuer) and expects to be compensated for the additional burden with a higher interest rate (i.e., return on investment).   **F-30**   **F-31**

Convertible bonds may be converted into corporate stock within a certain time from issue and at a specified price. Since not all convertible bonds are equally attractive financially, they should be compared (F-32) in order to LOWER PORTFOLIO RISK and INCREASE RETURNS ON INVESTMENT. Although a nonprofit organization does not issue stock, it may issue bonds (F-33) such as the one depicted. Obligors maintain a bond register (F-34) to preserve data on interest, redemption, maturity, sinking fund, and other features not common to common stock but some of which appear in preferred stock emissions. And for the investor—individual, corporate, or nonprofit—he will want to consolidate security transactions for the year and chalk up gains and losses (F-35).   **F-32**   **F-33**   **F-34**   **F-35**

Companies expanding operations into new territories will first of all want to protect their trade style by filing a *trade name certificate* (F-36). In some states a trade style may be registered state-wide with the Secretary of State's Office; but Connecticut's state   **F-36** bureaucracy, for example, feels unduly burdened by having to keep track of several thousand domestic and foreign corporations, and relegates assumed name registration to the Town Clerk. However, a nonresident corporation will register with the appropriate state office (discussed at the end of this section).

F-37   But the selling of securities in any state requires a separate and additional application to register those securities (F-37). The illustrated Uniform Application, for those states which have adopted it, is easily understood, but with the stipulated attachments (Page 2, Question No. 8) the final package submitted may fill a good-sized box—which guarantees neither that the issuing corporation will invest the funds profitably nor that the investor will not lose his savings. The firm's officers will also sign a corporate resolution

F-38   (F-38) which initiates action for the firm to become involved in securities sales and complete the many required applications (F-37).

Notice, too, in Question 8(h) (in F-37), the requirement that the nonresident corporation consent to service of process. This acknowledgment of consent is accompanied by a

F-39   corporate resolution (F-39) to that effect. For nonresident corporations, this is an example of a form required for the appointment of an attorney for service of process (F-

F-40   40). Other states, such as Delaware, require the name of a resident agent for firms incorporated but not doing business in Delaware.

F-41   Like securities, the sale of franchises within a state also obliges registration, and some states have adopted a Uniform Franchise Registration Application (F-41). These, too, are lengthy and costly documents to complete, which consequently raises transaction costs to franchisees. A franchise is a right given by an organization to another to sell or distribute a product or service within an area for present compensation or future share of sales or profits. Most of the exhibited formularies consist of instructions rather than blanks to complete, accompanied by the requested supplementary documents and, naturally, the ever-present government fees.

F-42   Some states, like Texas, demand of nonresident corporations the completion and filing of an Anti-Trust Affidavit (F-42), which proclaims that within the previous year the corporation has not acted to lessen competition or in restraint of trade. This may seem strange for a state whose Railroad Commission for decades has restricted output of oil wells, to limit supply, restrain competition and sustain above-market rates for the products. Nevertheless, the affidavit is required.

F-43
F-44   A nonresident, or "foreign," corporation, whether for profit or not for profit, must apply
F-45   for a certificate of authority (F-43) to do business in states in which it has not
F-46   incorporated. The application and certificate of authority forms range from two-pagers
F-47   used in New Jersey (F-46) to four-pagers in Connecticut (F-44), Massachusetts (F-45),
F-48   Illinois (F-47), Wisconsin (F-48), Minnesota (F-49), or the eight-pager required in
F-49   Indiana (F-50).
F-50

Ohio requires an Application for License (F-51) for foreign corporations; the example shown is for corporations operating for profit. Florida requests a relatively modest filing fee for corporations applying for authorization to transact business in Florida (F-52).

    F-51

    F-52

In California, for a foreign corporation to qualify to transact intrastate business, a firm must file, in addition to the appropriate application, a statement of its principal offices and designation of an agent for process service with California (F-53); there is significant differential in required fees between stock and nonstock, nonprofit corporations.

    F-53

Of course, filing fees, license fees, franchise taxes, taxes on assets or in-state income, etc., vary substantially among the states. A sample Fee Schedule for new corporations (F-54) is reprinted. And there is the ritual of completing and filing an annual corporate report for profit and nonprofit corporations alike and the payment of the required fees, whether in Illinois (F-55) or Alaska (F-56).

    F-54

    F-55
    F-56

CHECKLIST FOR INTERNAL CONTROL OF MARKETABLE SECURITIES

By: Date:
Remarks:

1. Are securities kept in safe deposit vaults? _____
    (List below)

2. Does access require signatures or presence of two or more designated persons?
    _____ Who?

3. Is a record maintained of visits to safe deposit vaults? _____

4. Are securities not kept in a safe deposit vault under control of a corporate officer?_____
    Who? _____
    (Note exceptions)

5. Are all of the above mentioned securities (except bearer certificates) held in the corporate
    name? _____ (Note exceptions)

6. Are any securities pledged? _____ (List below)

7. Are any securities held for others or as collateral? _____
    (Attach separate list)

8. What is the date above securities were last inspected and checked against corporate records?
    _____ By _____ (Note discrepancies)

LIST OF SECURITIES

Description of Security	Bond or Certificate Number	Par or Face Value	No. Shares or Total Amount	Coupons Attached To Bonds	Location of Security

Figure F-1: CHECKLIST FOR INTERNAL CONTROL OF MARKETABLE SECURITIES

TRUSTEES' ACCOUNT LEDGER

CLIENT:_____
ADDRESS:_____
BUS. PHONE:_____ RES. PHONE:_____

BILLING ATTY._____
FEE BASIS:_____

ACCOUNT NO._____
FILE NO._____
SHEET NO._____

	DATE 19	EXPLANATION OF TRANSACTION	SOURCE OF FUNDS – PARTIES TO WHOM DISBURSED – NATURE OF DISBURSEMENTS	CODE NO. OR OTHER FILE NO.	CHECK NO. OR CHARGE NO.	CHARGES FEES, WITHDRAWALS OR DISBURSEMENTS	RECEIPTS FUNDS RECEIVED OR CREDITS	BALANCE DEBIT – (CREDIT)	
1									1
2									2
3									3
4									4
5									5
6									6
7									7
8									8
9									9
10									10
11									11
12									12
13									13
14									14
15									15
16									16
17									17
18									18
19									19
20									20
21									21

FORM TA 911 - B
COPYRIGHT 1973 BY ALL STATE LEGAL SUPPLY CO.
269 SHEFFIELD STREET, MOUNTAINSIDE, N. J. 07092

Figure F-2: TRUSTEES' ACCOUNT LEDGER
(Copyright 1973 by All State Legal Supply Co., Mountainside, New Jersey 07092.)

443

INTRACOMPANY CORRESPONDENCE

TO _____ DATE _____

OFFICE_____ FROM _____

_____ Bank Balances & Investment Portfolio _____ OFFICE _____
(USE THIS LINE FOR FILE REFERENCE OR SUBJECT)

For your records the following are the end of the month (   ) cash balances and investment portfolio as reported by
    and

	BALANCE	INVESTMENT	MATURITY	RATE (%)
_____	_____	_____	_____	_____
		_____	_____	_____
		_____	_____	_____
		_____	_____	_____
		_____	_____	_____
	_____	_____	_____	_____
		_____	_____	_____
		_____	_____	_____
		_____	_____	_____
		_____	_____	_____
		_____	_____	_____
_____	_____	_____	_____	_____
	_____	_____	_____	_____

The following balances are currently being maintained at

_____

_____

Figure F-3: BANK BALANCES AND INVESTMENT PORTFOLIO

NORTHWESTERN NATIONAL BANK OF MINNEAPOLIS
NASSAU BRANCH, DELTEC HOUSE
P.M.B. 29, NASSAU
BAHAMAS

REF # 14258

DATE_____

M
A
I
L

T
O

SAMPLE

WE CONFIRM HAVING MADE THE FOLLOWING DEPOSIT WITH YOU.

WE WILL DELIVER THROUGH:	WE WILL DELIVER TO:
ACCOUNT NUMBER:	

PRINCIPAL AMOUNT	VALUE DATE	RATE	INTEREST

U.S. DOLLAR AMOUNT	MATURITY DATE	NUMBER OF DAYS	PRINCIPAL AND INTEREST

Northwestern National Bank of Minneapolis

by SAMPLE

AN AUTHORIZED SIGNATURE

NORTHWESTERN NATIONAL BANK OF MINNEAPOLIS
NASSAU BRANCH, DELTEC HOUSE
P.M.B. 29, NASSAU
BAHAMAS

REF # 14258

DATE _____

CREDIT (VALUE DATE)

SAMPLE

ACCOUNT NUMBER:

PRINCIPAL AMOUNT	VALUE DATE	RATE	INTEREST

U.S. DOLLAR AMOUNT	MATURITY DATE	NUMBER OF DAYS	PRINCIPAL AND INTEREST

NW 893

Figure F-4: CONFIRMATION OF FOREIGN DEPOSIT
(Courtesy of Northwestern National Bank of Minneapolis.)

445

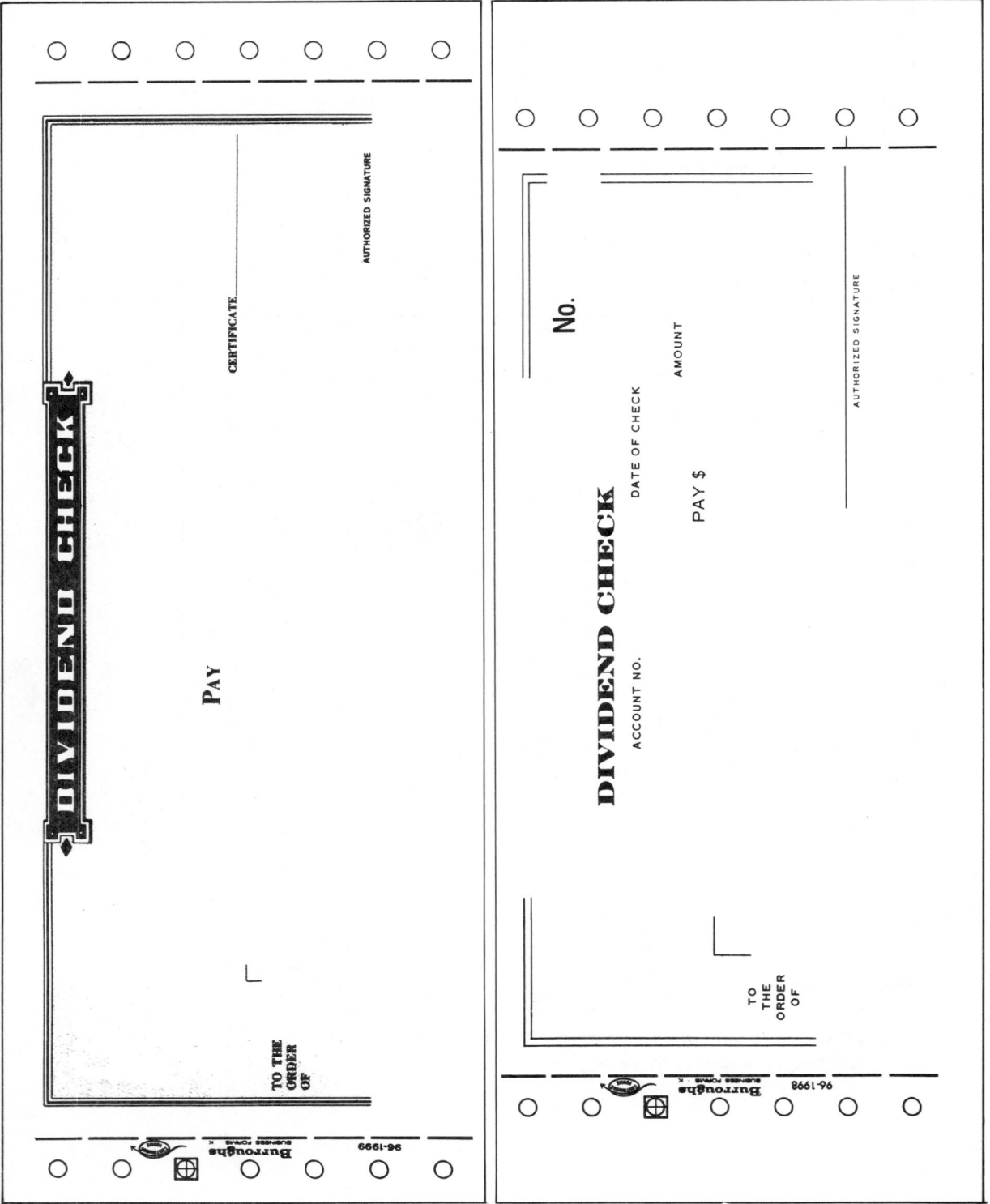

Figure F-5: DIVIDEND CHECKS (2)
(Courtesy of Burroughs Corporation Office Products Group/Business Forms Division.)

446

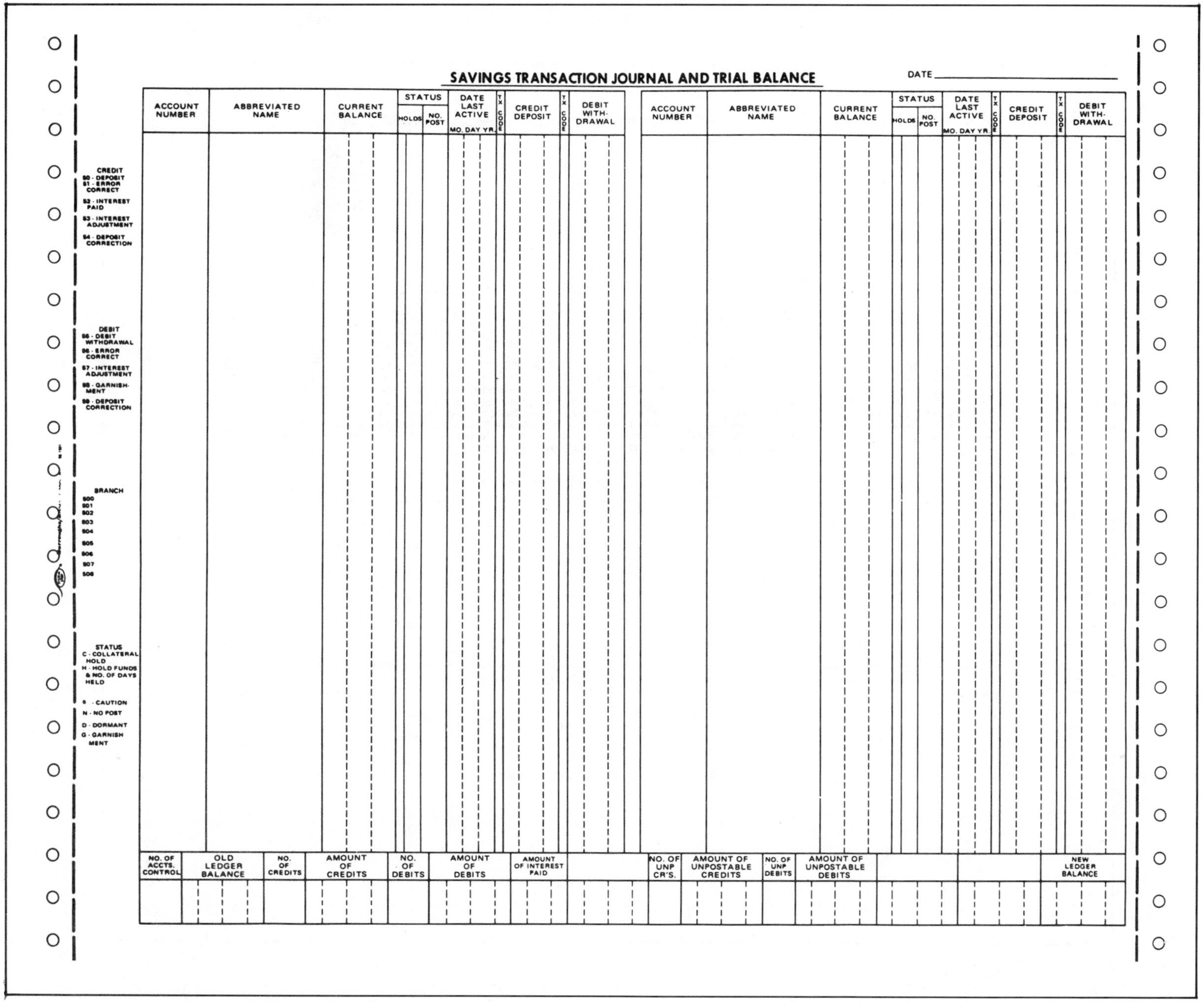

SAVINGS TRANSACTION JOURNAL AND TRIAL BALANCE

DATE ____________

ACCOUNT NUMBER	ABBREVIATED NAME	CURRENT BALANCE	STATUS HOLDS	STATUS NO. POST	DATE LAST ACTIVE MO. DAY YR.	TX CODE	CREDIT DEPOSIT	TX CODE	DEBIT WITH-DRAWAL	ACCOUNT NUMBER	ABBREVIATED NAME	CURRENT BALANCE	STATUS HOLDS	STATUS NO. POST	DATE LAST ACTIVE MO. DAY YR.	TX CODE	CREDIT DEPOSIT	TX CODE	DEBIT WITH-DRAWAL

NO. OF ACCTS. CONTROL	OLD LEDGER BALANCE	NO. OF CREDITS	AMOUNT OF CREDITS	NO. OF DEBITS	AMOUNT OF DEBITS	AMOUNT OF INTEREST PAID		NO. OF UNP CR'S.	AMOUNT OF UNPOSTABLE CREDITS	NO. OF UNP DEBITS	AMOUNT OF UNPOSTABLE DEBITS			NEW LEDGER BALANCE

CREDIT
50 - DEPOSIT
51 - ERROR CORRECT
52 - INTEREST PAID
53 - INTEREST ADJUSTMENT
54 - DEPOSIT CORRECTION

DEBIT
55 - DEBIT WITHDRAWAL
56 - ERROR CORRECT
57 - INTEREST ADJUSTMENT
58 - GARNISHMENT
59 - DEPOSIT CORRECTION

BRANCH
500
501
502
503
504
505
506
507
508

STATUS
C - COLLATERAL HOLD
H - HOLD FUNDS & NO. OF DAYS HELD
$ - CAUTION
N - NO POST
D - DORMANT
G - GARNISHMENT

Figure F-6: SAVINGS TRANSACTION JOURNAL AND TRIAL BALANCE
(Courtesy of Burroughs Corporation Office Products Group/Business Forms Division.)

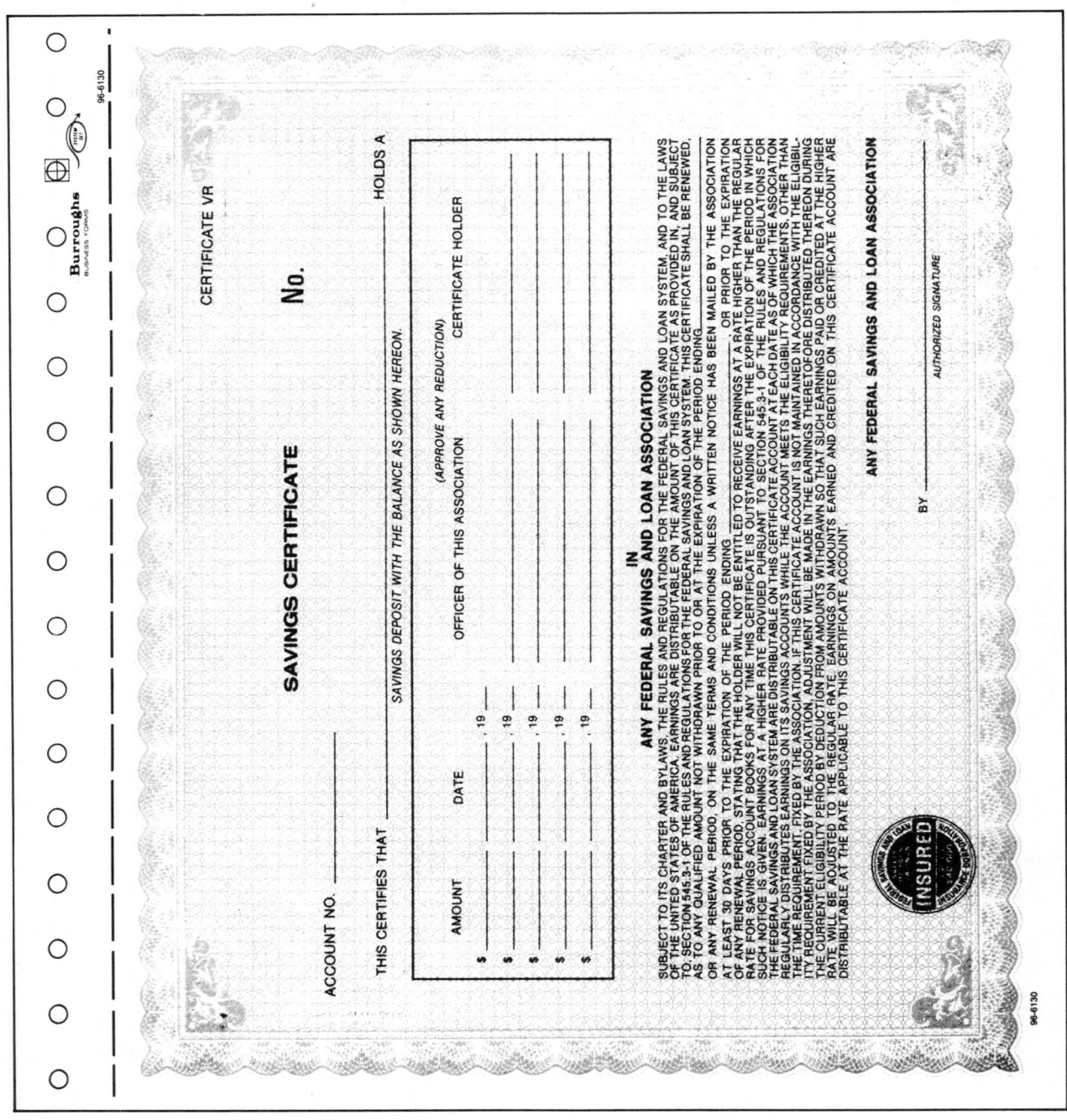

Figure F-7: FEDERAL SAVINGS AND LOAN SAVINGS CERTIFICATE
(Courtesy of Burroughs Corporation Office Products Group/Business Forms Division.)

448

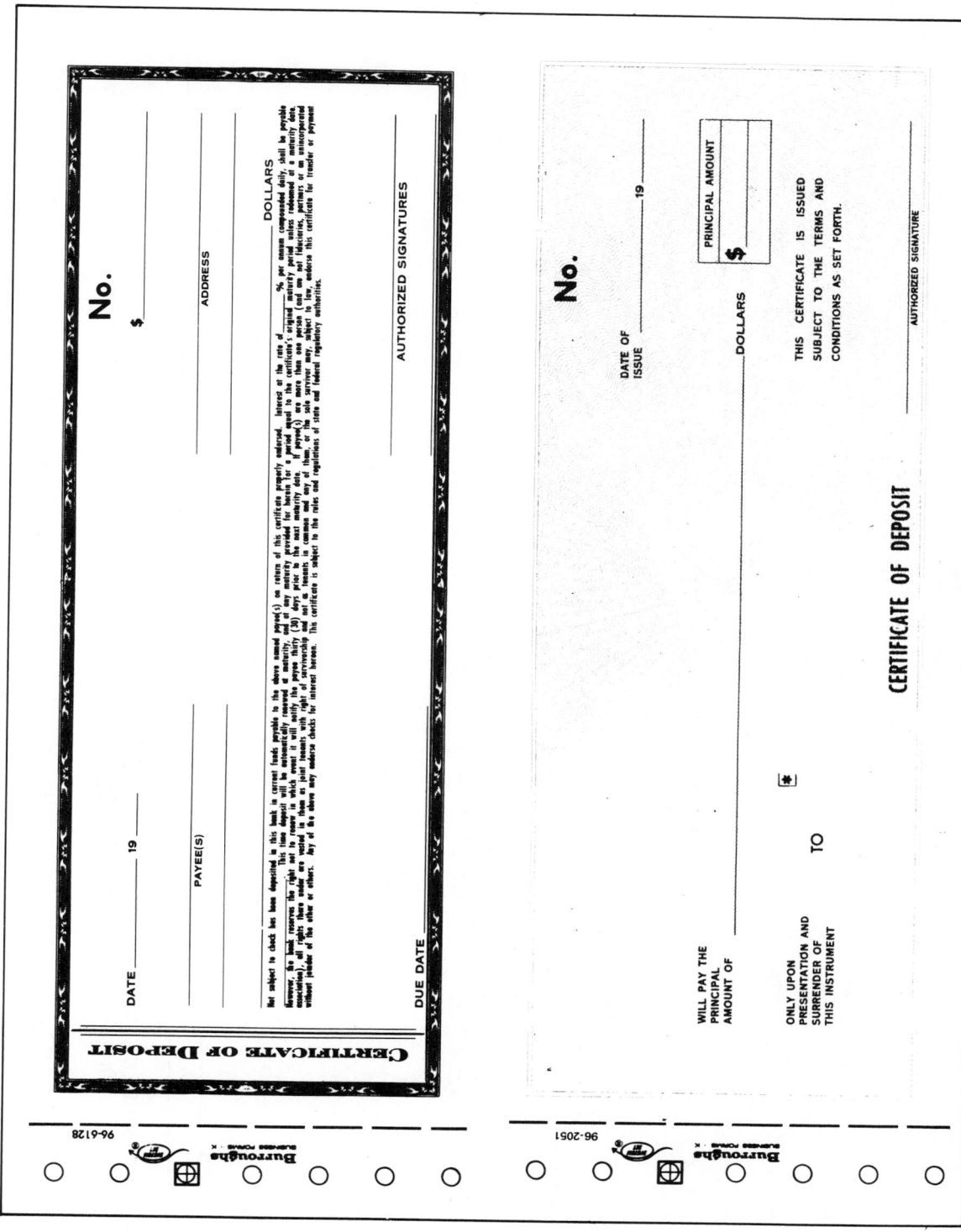

Figure F-8: CERTIFICATES OF DEPOSIT (2)
(Courtesy of Burroughs Corporation Office Products Group/Business Forms Division.)

449

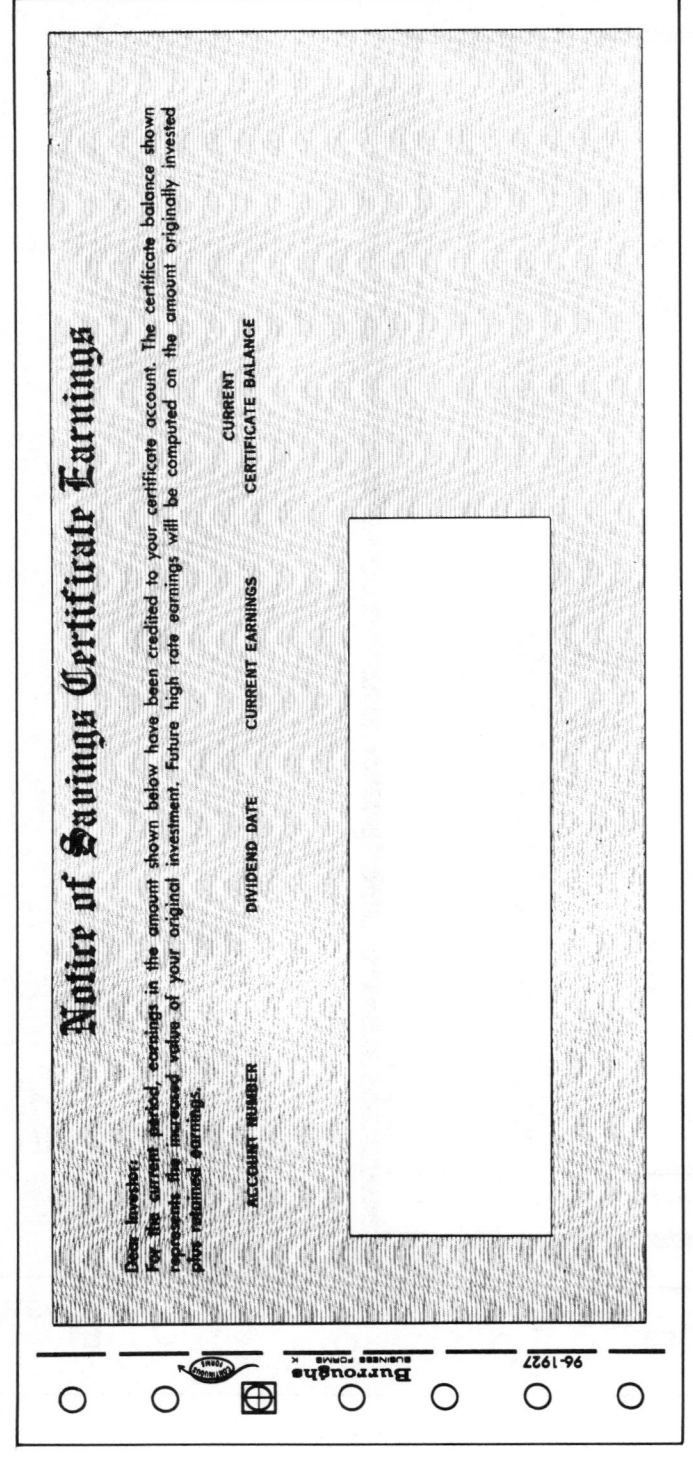

Figure F-9: NOTICE OF SAVINGS CERTIFICATE EARNINGS
(Courtesy of Burroughs Corporation Office Products Group/Business Forms Division.)

450

SHORT TERM INVESTMENTS

Bank _____

Month _____

Bank Location	Currency	Principal	Exchange Rate	Inv. Rate	From	To	# Days Card Col. 9-10	US$ Principal Card Col. 13-20	US$ Interest Card Col. 26-30

Figure F-10: RECORD OF SHORT-TERM DOMESTIC AND FOREIGN INVESTMENTS IN US $

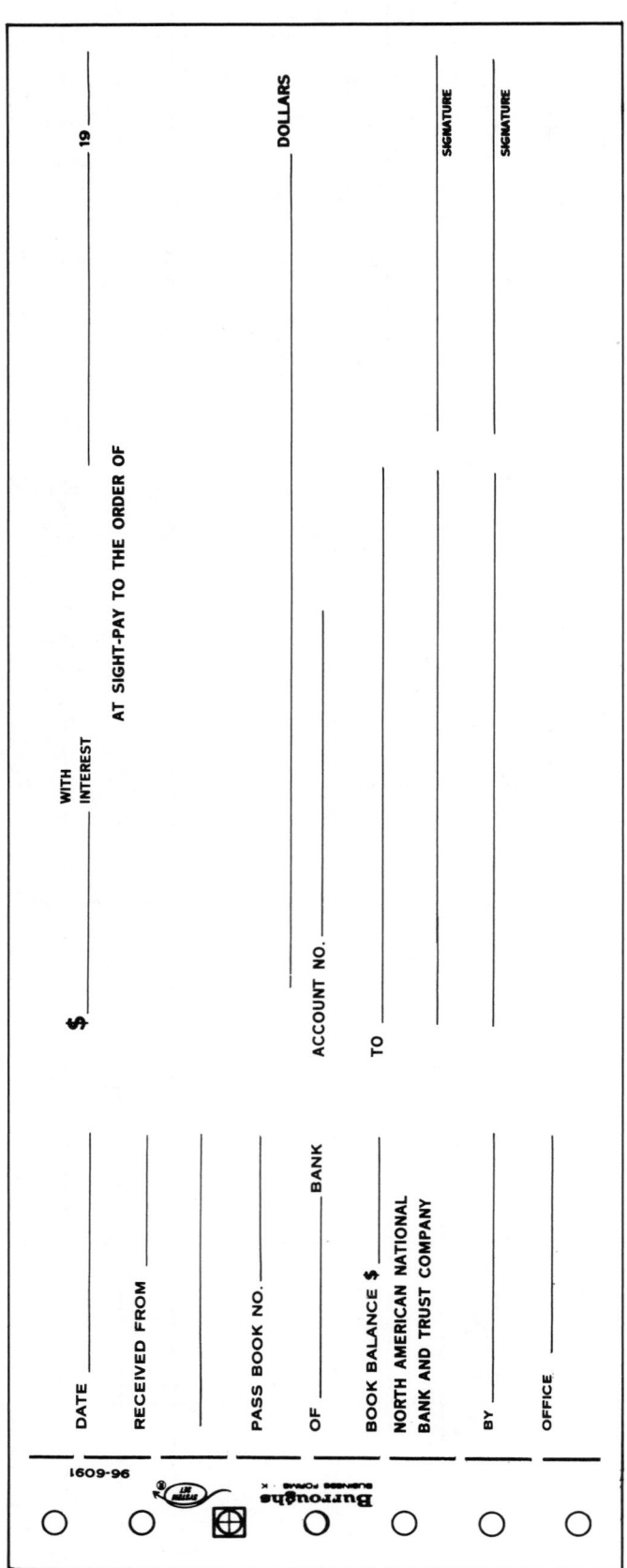

Figure F-11: SIGHT DRAFT
(Courtesy of Burroughs Corporation Office Products Group/Business Forms Division.)

$ _____ _____ _____ 19 ____

For value received _____ after date, the undersigned promise(s)

to pay to the order of _____

_____ Dollars

Payable at _____

with Interest @ _____ % per year from date hereof.

This is Note No._____ of a series of _____ notes. Upon default in payment of any one or more notes in this series, the remaining notes shall, at the option of the holder, immediately become due and payable without notice. Failure to exercise this option in any one or more instances shall not be considered a waiver of such option. Demand or presentment for payment, notice of nonpayment or dishonor, and protest or notice of protest are hereby expressly waived by all parties to this note, whether maker, endorser or otherwise. Holder may in the event of any default, charge all costs of collection including reasonable attorney fees.

Due Date _____ _____

Grace Period _____ _____

$ _____ _____ _____ 19 ____

For value received _____ after date, the undersigned promise(s)

to pay to the order of _____

_____ Dollars

Payable at _____

with Interest @ _____ % per year from date hereof.

This is Note No._____ of a series of _____ notes. Upon default in payment of any one or more notes in this series, the remaining notes shall, at the option of the holder, immediately become due and payable without notice. Failure to exercise this option in any one or more instances shall not be considered a waiver of such option. Demand or presentment for payment, notice of nonpayment or dishonor, and protest or notice of protest are hereby expressly waived by all parties to this note, whether maker, endorser or otherwise. Holder may in the event of any default, charge all costs of collection including reasonable attorney fees.

Due Date _____ _____

Grace Period _____ _____

$ _____ _____ _____ 19 ____

For value received _____ after date, the undersigned promise(s)

to pay to the order of _____

_____ Dollars

Payable at _____

with Interest @ _____ % per year from date hereof.

This is Note No._____ of a series of _____ notes. Upon default in payment of any one or more notes in this series, the remaining notes shall, at the option of the holder, immediately become due and payable without notice. Failure to exercise this option in any one or more instances shall not be considered a waiver of such option. Demand or presentment for payment, notice of nonpayment or dishonor, and protest or notice of protest are hereby expressly waived by all parties to this note, whether maker, endorser or otherwise. Holder may in the event of any default, charge all costs of collection including reasonable attorney fees.

Due Date _____ _____

Grace Period _____ _____

Figure F-12: SERIES NOTES
(Courtesy of All State Legal Supply Co., Mountainside, New Jersey 07092.)

NOTE

$ ....   , ..., 19..........

FOR VALUE RECEIVED .... after date, the undersigned promise (s)
....
to pay to ....
or order the sum of .... DOLLARS

in the following manner:

The sum of .... Dollars ....
after date, and a sum of .... Dollars each and every
.... thereafter until the entire amount of this note is fully paid and satisfied, with interest at
the rate of .... per annum.

Default in any one of the payments, after due, shall, at the option of the holder hereof, render the entire amount of this note remaining unpaid at that time immediately due and payable, with costs of collection, including a reasonable attorney's fee.

Each and every party to this instrument, either as maker, endorser, or otherwise, hereby waives presentment for payment, notice of dishonor, protest and notice of protest hereof; and also waives any and all defenses on the ground of any extensions or partial payments which may be accepted by the holder hereof before or after default.

....L. S.

....L. S.

Promissory Note   No. 126   Cleaveland Legal Blank Service, Inc.

Figure F-13: PROMISSORY NOTE
(Courtesy of Mr. Gordon Ramsay, Cleaveland Legal Blank Service, Inc., E. Hartford, Connecticut.)

Figure F-14: WARRANT

| ACCT. NUMBER _____ | | | | DEMAND COLLATERAL LOAN | | | | | | | | 96-6127 |

| NAME | | | | | | | | ADDRESS: | | | | |

INTEREST				INTEREST				PRINCIPAL			
DATE DUE	%	AMT. DUE	DATE PAID	DATE DUE	%	AMT. DUE	DATE PAID	DATE	LOAN	PAYMENTS	BALANCE

Figure F-15: DEMAND COLLATERAL LOAN CARD
(Courtesy of Burroughs Corporation Office Products Group/Business Forms Division.)

456

THE _____ COMPANY

SECURITY SALE OR WITHDRAWAL ORDER

COPY FOR

NUMBER

DATE

DESCRIPTION OF TRANSACTION

DELIVERY

MEMORANDA

APPROVED _____ SIGNED _____

SECURITIES WITHDRAWN FROM VAULT	SECURITIES RECEIVED _____
_____ DATE	DATE
	FOR _____
BY (1)_____ (2)_____	BY _____

Figure F-16: SECURITY SALE OR WITHDRAWAL ORDER

(From the book Corporate Treasurer's and Controller's Handbook by L. Doris, Editor. © 1950 renewed 1978 by L. Doris, Editor. Published by Prentice-Hall, Inc., Englewood Cliffs, New Jersey 07632.)

NUMBER	PIECES	SHARES OR DENOMINATION	TOTAL	NUMBER	PIECES	SHARES OR DENOMINATION	TOTAL

Figure F-16 (reverse side)

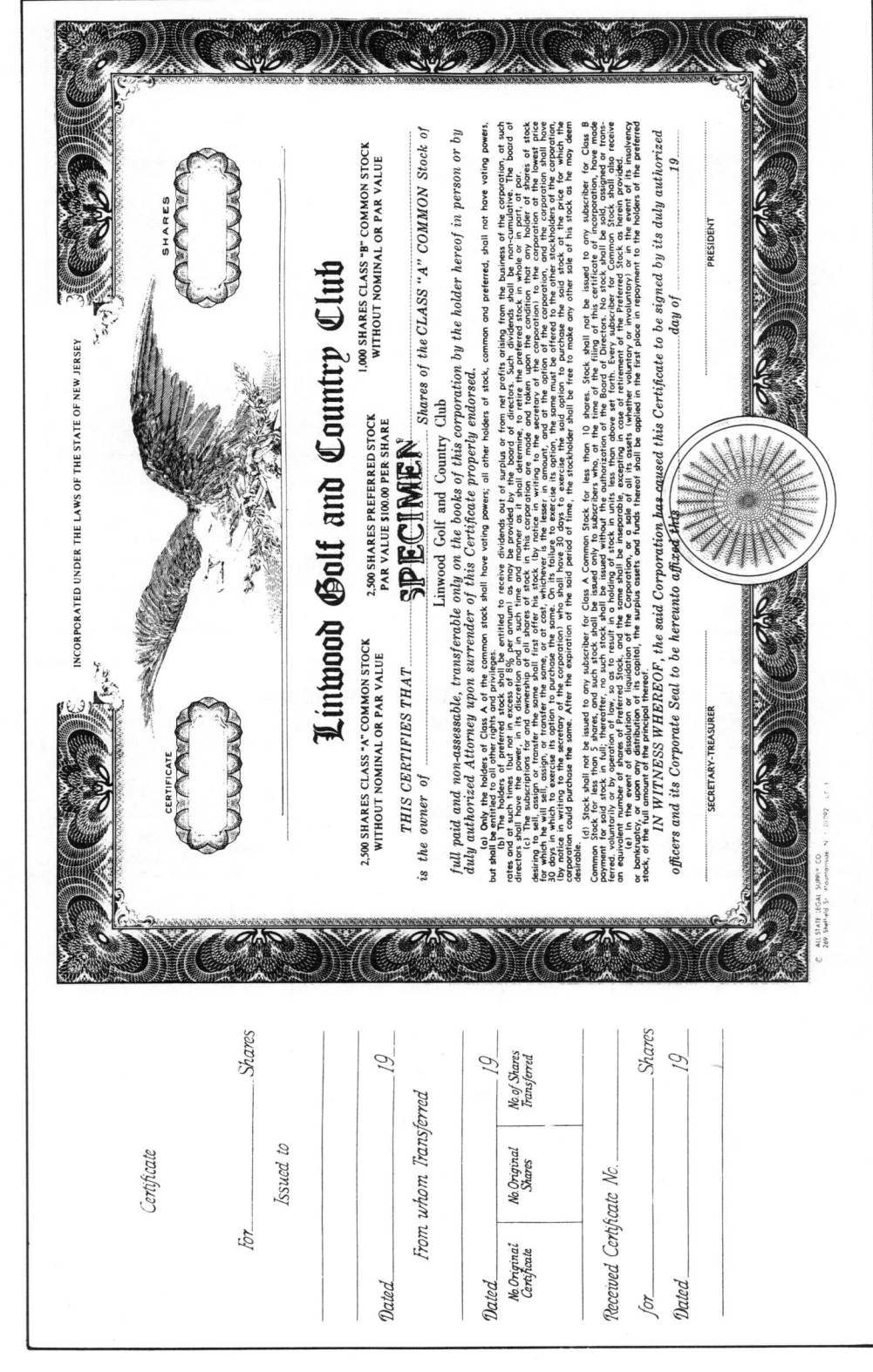

Figure F-17: CLASS "A" COMMON STOCK CERTIFICATE
(Copyright by All State Legal Supply Co., Mountainside, New Jersey 07092.)

....

(NAME OF CORPORATION)

REGISTER of SHARES of STOCK ISSUED and OUTSTANDING

TOTAL AUTHORIZED
CAPITAL STOCK

.... Class .... Par Value .... Class .... Par Value .... Class .... Par Value

	DATE of ISSUE	NUMBER of SHARES ISSUED	CONSIDERATION PAID		* CUMULATIVE TOTAL (By Class) OUTSTANDING			TREASURY STOCK	NUMBER of SHARES RETIRED REDEEMED OR CANCELLED
			CASH	PROPERTY or SERVICES	CLASS COMMON	CLASS	CLASS		
1									
2									
3									
4									
5									
6									
7									
8									
9									
10									
.									
12									
13									
14									
15									
16									
17									
18									
19									
20									
21									
22									
23									
24									
25									
26									
27									
?									
29									
30									
					Last figure in each column indicates grand total of that class issued and outstanding, to date of last entry.				Where shares have been retired, redeemed or cancelled, enter the number of shares here and reflect the reduced total of outstanding shares in the appropriate *cumulative total column.

Figure F-18: REGISTER OF STOCK ISSUED AND OUTSTANDING
(Copyright 1974 by All State Legal Supply Co., Mountainside, New Jersey 07092.)

INDIVIDUAL SHAREHOLDERS RECORD of SHAREHOLDINGS

(Each transaction involving a Certificate should be entered on a separate line)

Name of Shareholder _____ S. S. # _____

Address _____ Res. Phone _____

_____ Bus. Phone _____

	Cert. #	Number of Shares	Class of Stock	Date of Transaction						Total Shares Transf'd.	Cert. # Surrendered & Cancelled	New Cert. # Issued (if partial)	Cumulative Total of Shares Currently Owned
				Originally Acquired			Transferred						
				Mo	Day	Year	Mo	Day	Year				
1													
2													
3													
4													
5													
6													
7													
8													
9													
10													
11													
12													
13													
14													
15													
16													
17													
18													
19													
20													
21													
22													
23													
24													
25													
26													
27													
28													
29													
30													
31													
32													
33													

Form # UN-SR-1

Figure F-19: INDIVIDUAL SHAREHOLDERS RECORD OF STOCK TRANSACTIONS
(Copyright 1974 by All State Legal Supply Co., Mountainside, New Jersey 07092.)

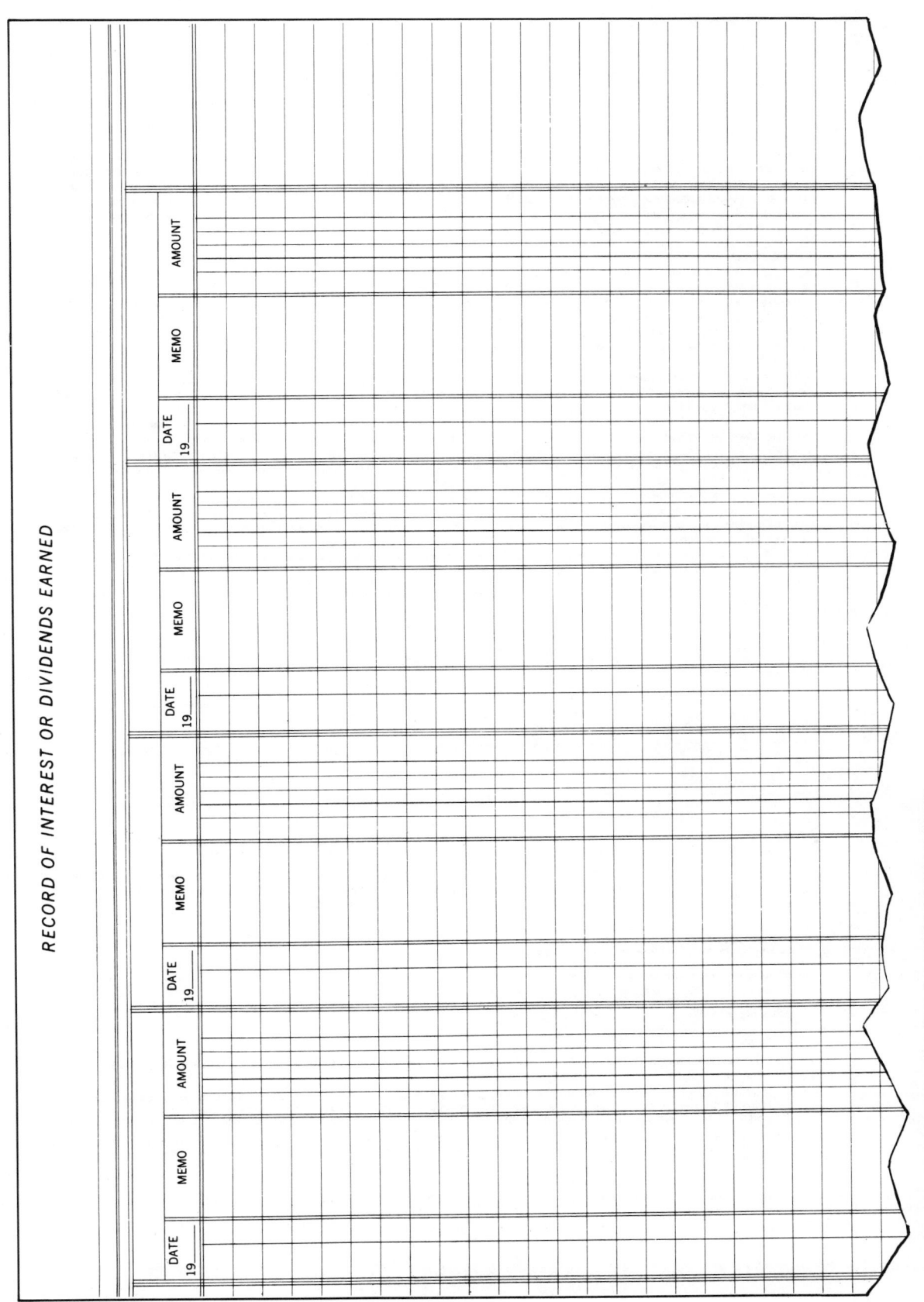

Figure F-20: RECORD OF INTEREST OR DIVIDENDS EARNED

CERTIFICATION
OF
CORPORATE RESOLUTION GRANTING AUTHORITY TO
TRANSFER SECURITIES

(1)   , Secretary of   , a
Corporation duly organized and existing under the laws of   and having its
principal place of business at   (herein called the "Corporation")
hereby certify that the following is a true copy of a resolution duly adopted by the Board of Directors (2) of the Corporation at a meeting thereof duly convened and held, on   , 197   , at which a quorum was
present and voting throughout and that such resolution is now in full force and effect and is in accordance with the provisions of the charter and by-laws of the Corporation.

RESOLVED:
    1. That any one/two of the following officers,
be and hereby is/are authorized and empowered to sell, assign, transfer or deliver any and all stocks, bonds, evidences of
interest and/or indebtedness, rights and options to acquire or to sell the same, and all other securities, corporate or otherwise, now or hereafter standing in the name of, or belonging to, this Corporation in any capacity, and to make, execute,
and deliver under the seal of the Corporation or otherwise, any and all written instruments necessary or proper to effectuate the authority hereby conferred.
    2. That The Bank of New York ("the Bank") be and hereby is authorized to honor the signatures of the above
noted persons without inquiry as to the circumstances or status of the purchaser, assignee, transferee or recipient, whether
or not such purchaser, assignee, transferee or recipient is an officer named herein, and whether or not such officer's signature is being honored.
    3. That the Secretary of the Corporation be and hereby is authorized and directed to certify to the Bank the names
and signatures of the present officers of the Corporation and the offices respectively held by them, and from time to time
hereafter, as changes in such offices are made, immediately to certify such changes and signatures to the Bank and the
Bank shall be fully protected and shall be indemnified and held harmless from any claims, demands, expenses (including
counsel fees), loss or damage resulting from, or arising out of, either honoring any signature so certified prior to its receipt
of a contrary certification or for refusing to honor any signature for which it has not received such a certification.
    4. That the Secretary of the Corporation be and is hereby authorized and directed to certify to the Bank that this
resolution has been duly adopted, is in full force and effect, and is in accordance with the provisions of the charter and by-
laws of the Corporation.
    5. That this resolution shall be and remain in effect until such time as the Bank receives a duly certified and adopted
resolution revoking the same.

    I further certify that the following are the names, offices, and signatures of the duly elected present officers of the
Corporation.

Name	Title	Specimen Signature
Name	Title	Specimen Signature
Name	Title	Specimen Signature
Name	Title	Specimen Signature

Secretary (3)

The undersigned hereby certifies that the foregoing instrument
has been signed by the Secretary and sealed with the seal of the
above-named Corporation.

To be signed by an official other than the secretary.   Title

(4) Witness my hand and the seal of the Corporation
on this   day of   197

(5) (Corporate seal)

Footnotes

1. The Certification must be made by the Secretary of the Corporation or a similar officer having custody of the
corporate records.

2. Resolutions passed by bodies other than the Board of Directors may under certain circumstances be acceptable. A
Resolution passed by any such other body, should, however, be supported by evidence of the authority of such body
to act in the premises. Such evidence might be in the form of a certified extract of the by-laws of the Corporation.

3. The Signature of the certifying officer must be guaranteed by a firm having membership in the New York or Midwest
Stock Exchange or a Commercial Bank or Trust Company having its principal office or a correspondent in the City
of New York.

4. This resolution must be dated.

5. Resolution must be certified under the Corporate Seal by an officer other than the one named to act.

1-620-0662 (1-78)

Figure F-21: CORPORATE RESOLUTION GRANTING AUTHORITY TO TRANSFER SECURITIES

POWER OF ATTORNEY TO TRANSFER STOCK GRVST

© 1979 ALL-STATE LEGAL SUPPLY CO
269 Sheffield St., Mountainside, N. J. 07092

Know All Men By These Presents, *that*

hereby constitute(s) and appoint(s)

to be *true and lawful attorney(s) for* *and in* *name(s) and behalf to sell, assign and transfer to*

PLEASE INSERT SOCIAL SECURITY OR OTHER TAXPAYER IDENTIFYING NUMBER OF ASSIGNEE

all or any part of the shares of *stock in the*

and standing in *name(s), represented by Certificate(s) number(s)*

and for that purpose to make and execute all necessary acts of Assignment and Transfer.

IN WITNESS WHEREOF, *have hereunto set* *hand(s) and seal(s) this*

day of *19*

Signed, sealed and delivered in the presence of ....

....

NOTE: The signature on this instrument must correspond exactly with the name(s) appearing on the stock certificate(s)

Figure F-22: POWER OF ATTORNEY TO TRANSFER STOCK
(Copyright 1979 by All State Legal Supply Co., Mountainside, New Jersey 07092.)

RECORD OF STOCK ISSUED

STOCK TRANSFER LEDGER

FORM # UN-511-2

Page No. ....

Copyright 1974 by ALL-STATE LEGAL SUPPLY CO.
269 Sheffield St., Mountainside, N.J. 07092

SHAREHOLDER	ADDRESS	DATE BECAME OWNER OF RECORD	SHARES ISSUED			FROM WHOM SHARES WERE TRANSFERRED — OR — IF ORIGINAL ISSUE ENTER AS SUCH	AMOUNT OF TAX (IF ANY)	TO WHOM SHARES ARE TRANSFERRED	DATE OF TRANS-FER	CERTIFICATE SURRENDERED		IF LESS THAN ALL SHARES ON CERTIFICATE ARE TRANSFERRED		
			CERT. #	CLASS OR SERIES	NO. OF SHARES	CONSIDER-ATION PAID (ORIG. ISSUE ONLY)					CERT. #	NO. OF SHARES	NO. OF SHARES TRANSF'D.	NEW CERT. #	SHARES RETAINED NO. OF SHARES

Figure F-23: STOCK TRANSFER LEDGER
(Copyright 1974 by All State Legal Supply Co., Mountainside, New Jersey 07092.)

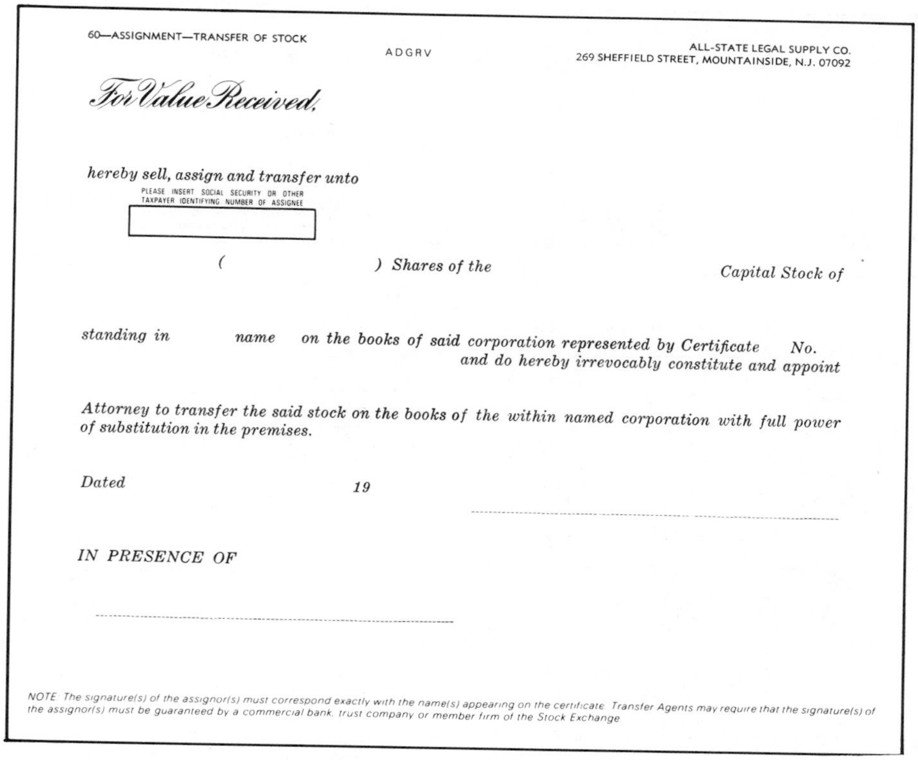
60—ASSIGNMENT—TRANSFER OF STOCK

ADGRV

ALL-STATE LEGAL SUPPLY CO.
269 SHEFFIELD STREET, MOUNTAINSIDE, N.J. 07092

For Value Received,

hereby sell, assign and transfer unto

PLEASE INSERT SOCIAL SECURITY OR OTHER TAXPAYER IDENTIFYING NUMBER OF ASSIGNEE

( ) Shares of the Capital Stock of

standing in name on the books of said corporation represented by Certificate No. and do hereby irrevocably constitute and appoint

Attorney to transfer the said stock on the books of the within named corporation with full power of substitution in the premises.

Dated 19

IN PRESENCE OF

NOTE: The signature(s) of the assignor(s) must correspond exactly with the name(s) appearing on the certificate. Transfer Agents may require that the signature(s) of the assignor(s) must be guaranteed by a commercial bank, trust company or member firm of the Stock Exchange.

Figure F-24: ASSIGNMENT AND TRANSFER OF STOCK
(Courtesy of All State Legal Supply Co., Mountainside New Jersey 07092.)

NON-PURPOSE "STOCK" COLLATERAL DEMAND LOAN

BOSTON, MASSACHUSETTS_____ 19_____ $_____

ON DEMAND, the undersigned (jointly and severally if more than one) promise(s) to pay to the order of

THE FIRST NATIONAL BANK OF BOSTON

at said Bank_____ Dollars,

with interest prior to maturity at _____% per annum, calculated on the basis of a 360-day year for the actual number of days elapsed, payable monthly in arrears, and with interest after maturity payable on demand at 12% per annum or, if higher, at a rate per annum which at all times shall be 4% above the lowest rate of interest being charged from time to time by said Bank for new 90-day unsecured loans to commercial borrowers, having deposited with said Bank as collateral for the payment and performance of all Obligations, the following property:_____

_____

_____

_____

_____

Should the holder at any time deem itself insecure, the undersigned shall deliver to the holder, forthwith upon demand, additional collateral in an amount and of a character satisfactory to the holder.

Upon the occurrence of any of the following events of default: (a) default in the payment or performance of any of the Obligations; (b) loss, theft, substantial damage, sale or encumbrance to or of any property constituting collateral hereunder or the making of any levy, seizure or attachment thereof or thereon or the failure to pay when due any tax thereon or, with respect to any insurance policy, any premium therefor; (c) default under any instrument constituting collateral hereunder; (d) death, dissolution, termination of existence, insolvency, business failure, appointment of a receiver of any part of the property of, assignment for the benefit of creditors by, or the commencement of any proceedings under any bankruptcy or insolvency laws by or against any Obligor; thereupon or at any time thereafter (such default not having been previously cured), at the option of the holder, all Obligations of the maker shall become immediately due and payable without notice or demand and the holder shall then have in any jurisdiction where enforcement hereof is sought, in addition to all other rights and remedies, the rights and remedies of a secured party under the Uniform Commercial Code of Massachusetts.

Any sums credited by or due from the holder to any Obligor and any property of any Obligor in which the holder has any security interest or which may be in the possession of the holder may at any time be treated or held as collateral for the payment or performance of the Obligations of such Obligor. Regardless of the adequacy of collateral, the holder may apply such sums or property or realizations upon any such security interest against said Obligations at any time in the case of a primary Obligor but only against matured Obligations in the case of a secondary Obligor.

The holder may at its option, whether or not this note is due, demand, sue for, collect or make any compromise or settlement it deems desirable with reference to collateral held hereunder. Right is expressly granted to the holder at its option to transfer at any time to itself or to its nominee any securities or documents pledged hereunder and to receive the income thereon and hold the same as security herefor, or apply it on the principal or interest due hereon or due on any liability secured hereby. The holder shall have no duty as to the collection or protection of collateral held hereunder or any income thereon, and shall not be bound to take any steps necessary to preserve any rights in collateral against prior parties.

No delay or omission on the part of the holder in exercising any right hereunder shall operate as a waiver of such right or of any other right under this note. No waiver of any right shall be effective unless in writing and signed by the holder nor shall a waiver on one occasion be construed as a bar to or waiver of any such right on any future occasion.

Each Obligor waives presentment, demand, notice, protest, and all other demands and notices in connection with the delivery, acceptance, performance, default or enforcement of this note or of any collateral hereunder, and assents to any extension or postponement of the time of payment or any other indulgence under this note or such collateral, to any substitution, exchange or release of collateral, and to the addition or release of any other party or person primarily or secondarily liable.

The undersigned will pay on demand all costs of collection and attorneys' fees paid or incurred by the holder in enforcing this note on default.

As herein used, 'Obligor' means any person primarily or secondarily liable hereunder or in respect hereto; 'Obligation' means any Obligation hereunder or otherwise of any Obligor to the holder whether direct or indirect, absolute or contingent, due or to become due, now existing or hereafter arising; and 'holder' means the payee or any endorsee of this note who is in possession of it, or the bearer hereof if this note is at the time payable to the bearer.

Address only:

(Number)   (Street)

(City)

C-418 (Rev. 11/75)   (State)   (Zip Code)

Signed by

Figure F-25: NON-PURPOSE STOCK COLLATERAL DEMAND LOAN
(Courtesy of The First National Bank of Boston.)

NON-PURPOSE "STOCK" COLLATERAL TIME LOAN

BOSTON, MASSACHUSETTS_____19_____ $_____

_____after date, the undersigned (jointly and severally if more than

one) promise(s) to pay to the order of _____

THE FIRST NATIONAL BANK OF BOSTON

at said Bank _____ Dollars

Interest or discount hereon shall be calculated on the basis of a 360-day year for the actual number of days elapsed.

Interest after maturity will be payable on demand at 12% per annum or, if higher, at a rate per annum which at all times shall be 4% above the lowest rate of interest being charged from time to time by said Bank for new 90-day unsecured loans to commercial borrowers. As collateral for the payment and performance of all obligations of the undersigned or any of us to the holder hereof, whether direct or indirect, absolute or contingent, due or to become due, now existing or hereafter arising (all herein called "Obligations"), there has been deposited with said Bank the following property: _____

_____

_____

Should the holder at any time deem itself insecure, the undersigned shall deliver to the holder, forthwith upon demand, additional collateral in an amount and of a character satisfactory to the holder.

Upon the occurrence of any of the following events of default: (a) default in the payment or performance of any of the Obligations; (b) loss, theft, substantial damage, sale or encumbrance to or of any property constituting collateral hereunder or the making of any levy, seizure or attachment thereof or thereon or the failure to pay when due any tax thereon or, with respect to any insurance policy, any premium therefor; (c) default under any instrument constituting collateral hereunder; (d) death, dissolution, termination of existence, insolvency, business failure, appointment of a receiver of any part of the property of, assignment for the benefit of creditors by, or the commencement of any proceedings under any bankruptcy or insolvency laws by or against any Obligor; thereupon or at any time thereafter (such default not having been previously cured), at the option of the holder, all Obligations of the maker shall become immediately due and payable without notice or demand and the holder shall then have in any jurisdiction where enforcement hereof is sought, in addition to all other rights and remedies, the rights and remedies of a secured party under the Uniform Commercial Code of Massachusetts.

Any sums credited by or due from the holder to any Obligor and any property of any Obligor in which the holder has any security interest or which may be in the possession of the holder may at any time be treated or held as collateral for the payment or performance of the Obligations of such Obligor. Regardless of the adequacy of collateral, the holder may apply such sums or property or realizations upon any such security interest against said Obligations at any time in the case of a primary Obligor but only against matured Obligations in the case of a secondary Obligor.

The holder may at its option, whether or not this note is due, demand, sue for, collect or make any compromise or settlement it deems desirable with reference to collateral held hereunder. Right is expressly granted to the holder at its option to transfer at any time to itself or to its nominee any securities or documents pledged hereunder and to receive the income thereon and hold the same as security herefor, or apply it on the principal or interest due hereon or due on any liability secured hereby. The holder shall have no duty as to the collection or protection of collateral held hereunder or any income thereon, and shall not be bound to take any steps necessary to preserve any rights in collateral against prior parties.

No delay or omission on the part of the holder in exercising any right hereunder shall operate as a waiver of such right or of any other right under this note. No waiver of any right shall be effective unless in writing and signed by the holder nor shall a waiver on one occasion be construed as a bar to or waiver of any such right on any future occasion.

Each Obligor waives presentment, demand, notice, protest, and all other demands and notices in connection with the delivery, acceptance, performance, default or enforcement of this note or of any collateral hereunder, and assents to any extension or postponement of the time of payment or any other indulgence under this note or such collateral, to any substitution, exchange or release of collateral, and to the addition or release of any other party or person primarily or secondarily liable.

The undersigned will pay on demand all costs of collection and attorneys' fees paid or incurred by the holder in enforcing this note on default.

As herein used, 'Obligor' means any person primarily or secondarily liable hereunder or in respect hereto; 'Obligation' means any Obligation hereunder or otherwise of any Obligor to the holder whether direct or indirect, absolute or contingent, due or to become due, now existing or hereafter arising; and 'holder' means the payee or any endorser of this note who is in possession of it, or the bearer hereof if the note is at the time payable to the bearer.

Address   (Number)   (Street)   *Signed*   _____

only   (City)   (State)   (Zip Code)   *by*   _____

C-119A (rev. 11/75)

Figure F-26: NON-PURPOSE STOCK COLLATERAL TIME LOAN
(Courtesy of The First National Bank of Boston.)

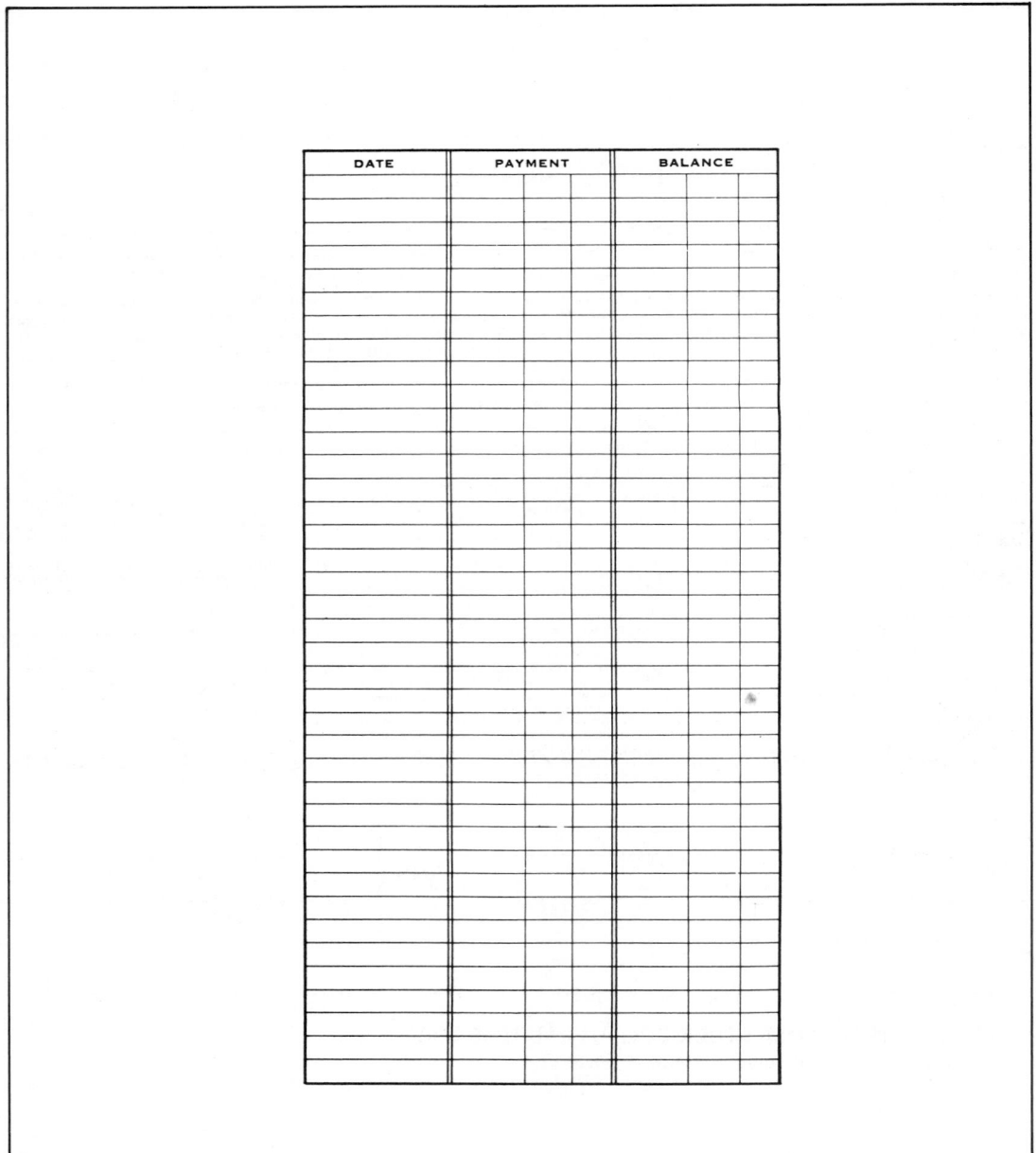

Figure F-26—Reverse Side

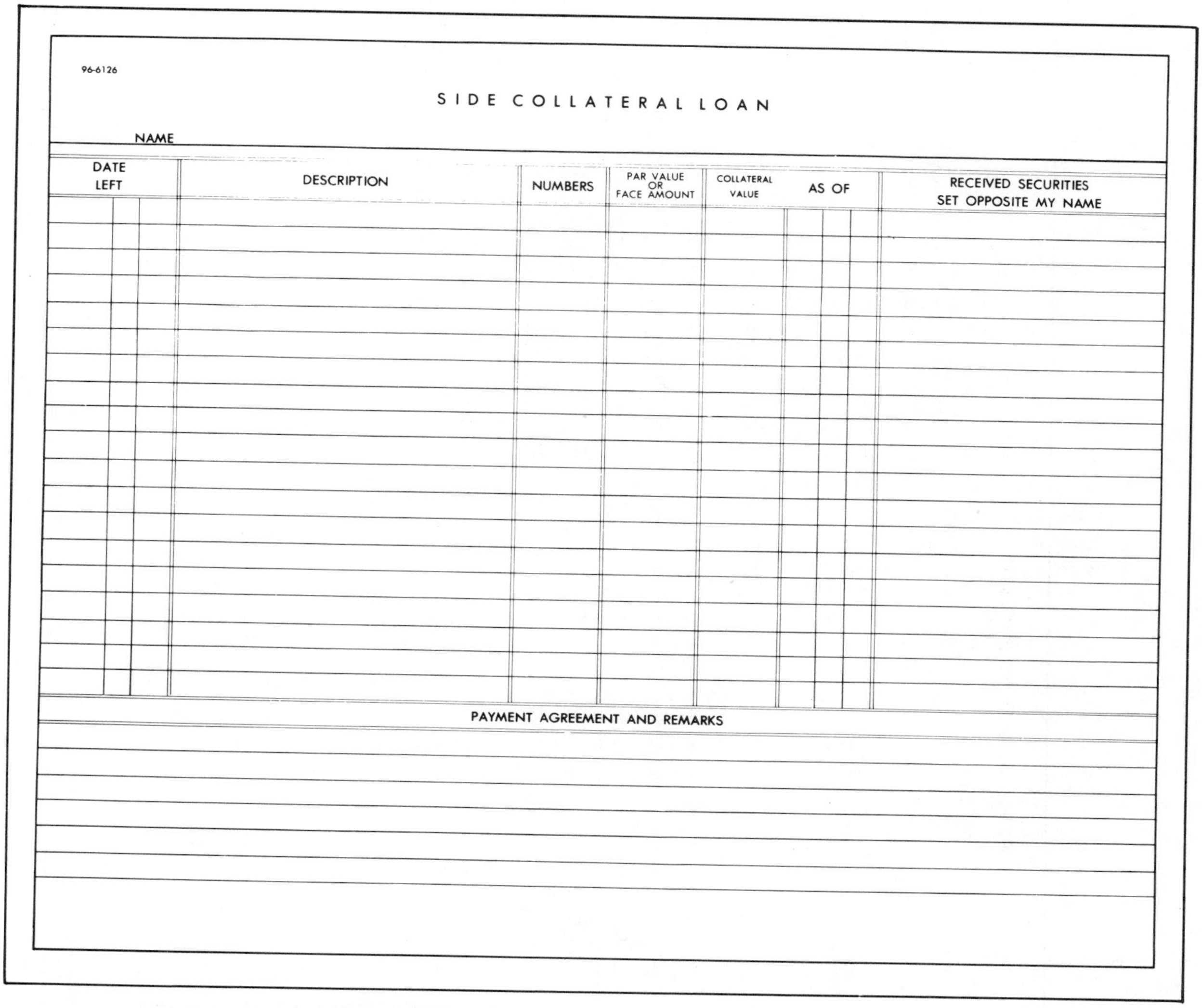

S I D E   C O L L A T E R A L   L O A N

NAME

DATE LEFT	DESCRIPTION	NUMBERS	PAR VALUE OR FACE AMOUNT	COLLATERAL VALUE	AS OF	RECEIVED SECURITIES SET OPPOSITE MY NAME

PAYMENT AGREEMENT AND REMARKS

Figure F-27: DEMAND COLLATERAL LOAN CARD
(Courtesy of Burroughs Corporation Office Products Group/Business Forms Division.)

STOCK AND BOND REGISTER

NAME _____

DESCRIPTION _____

DATE OF ISSUE _____   DATE OF MATURITY _____   INTEREST OR DIVIDEND _____   % PAYABLE _____   SEMI-ANNUALLY _____

DENOMINATION _____

WILSON JONES FORM 636-40	DATE 19__	OF WHOM PURCHASED	DATE 19__	SOLD TO	CERTIFICATE OR BOND NOS.	MATURITY	PAR VALUE	PRICE PAID	TOTAL COST	SOLD FOR	INTEREST OR DIVIDENDS EARNED	LOSS OR GAIN

Figure F-28: STOCK AND BOND REGISTER

(Copyright by Wilson Jones Company. All rights reserved. Forms may be obtained, subject to supply, from Wilson Jones Company, 6150 Touhy Avenue, Chicago, Illinois 60648.)

STOCKS — BONDS — SECURITIES

RECORDPLATE   EL MONTE, CA U.S.A. 648

COMPANY   CODE

DESCRIPTION
OF SECURITY

CALL PRICE   RATE, DIV.   PAYMENT
MATURITY   STOCK DIV.   DATES

BROKER   MARKET OR
                                                                EXCHANGE
CONVERSION   TAX
FEATURES   STATUS

DATE BOUGHT	NO. OF UNITS	CERTIFICATE NO.	PRICE	ACCRUED INT.	AMOUNT PAID		OTHER

DATE SOLD	NO. OF UNITS	CERTIFICATE NO.	PRICE	TAX	AMOUNT RECEIVED		PROFIT OR LOSS DESC.	AMOUNT

Figure F-29: RECORD OF STOCKS, BONDS, SECURITIES
(Courtesy of Rediform Office Products, Paramus, New Jersey 07652.)

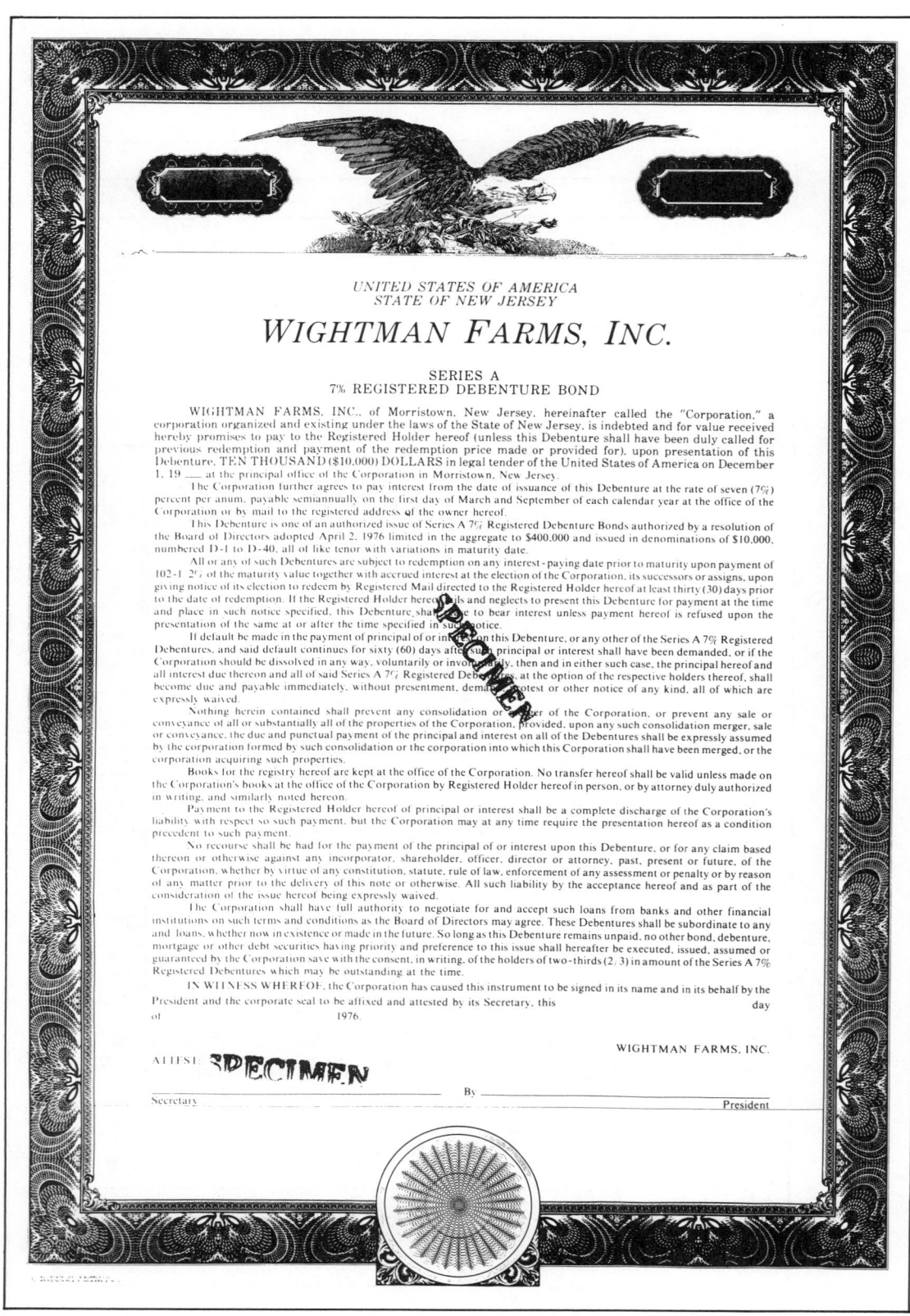

Figure F-30: 7% REGISTERED DEBENTURE BOND
(Copyright by All State Legal Supply Co., Mountainside, New Jersey 07092.)

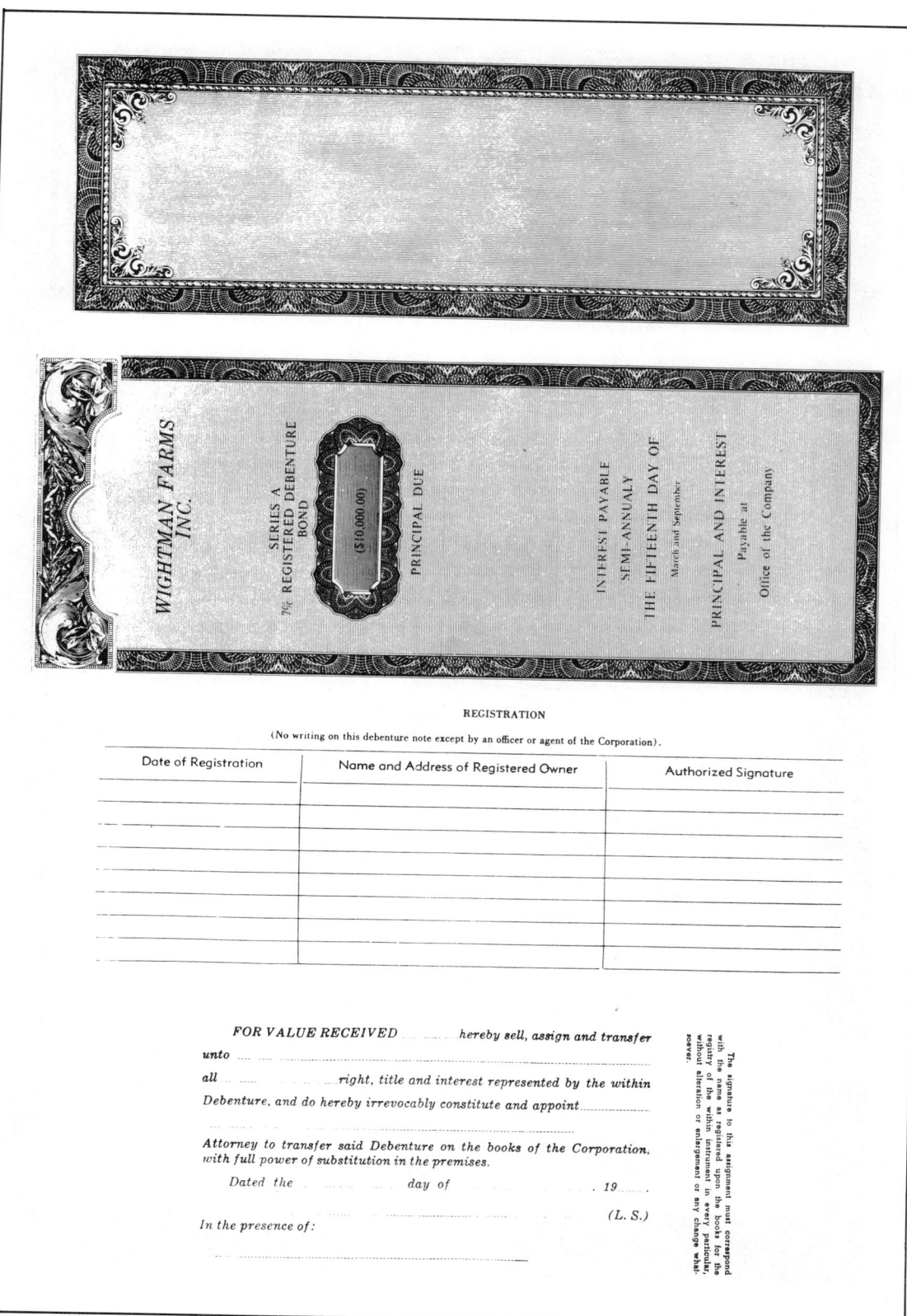

WIGHTMAN FARMS INC.

SERIES A
7% REGISTERED DEBENTURE BOND

($10,000.00)

PRINCIPAL DUE

INTEREST PAYABLE
SEMI-ANNUALLY
THE FIFTEENTH DAY OF
March and September

PRINCIPAL AND INTEREST
Payable at
Office of the Company

REGISTRATION

(No writing on this debenture note except by an officer or agent of the Corporation).

Date of Registration	Name and Address of Registered Owner	Authorized Signature

FOR VALUE RECEIVED .... hereby sell, assign and transfer

unto ....

all .... right, title and interest represented by the within

Debenture, and do hereby irrevocably constitute and appoint ....

....

Attorney to transfer said Debenture on the books of the Corporation,
with full power of substitution in the premises.

Dated the .... day of .... 19 ....

....
                                                          (L. S.)

In the presence of:

....

The signature to this assignment must correspond with the name as registered upon the books for the registry of the within instrument in every particular, without alteration or enlargement or any change whatsoever.

Figure F-30—Reverse Side

Figure F-31: SUBORDINATED DEBENTURE
(Copyright by All State Legal Supply Co., Mountainside, New Jersey 07092.)

474

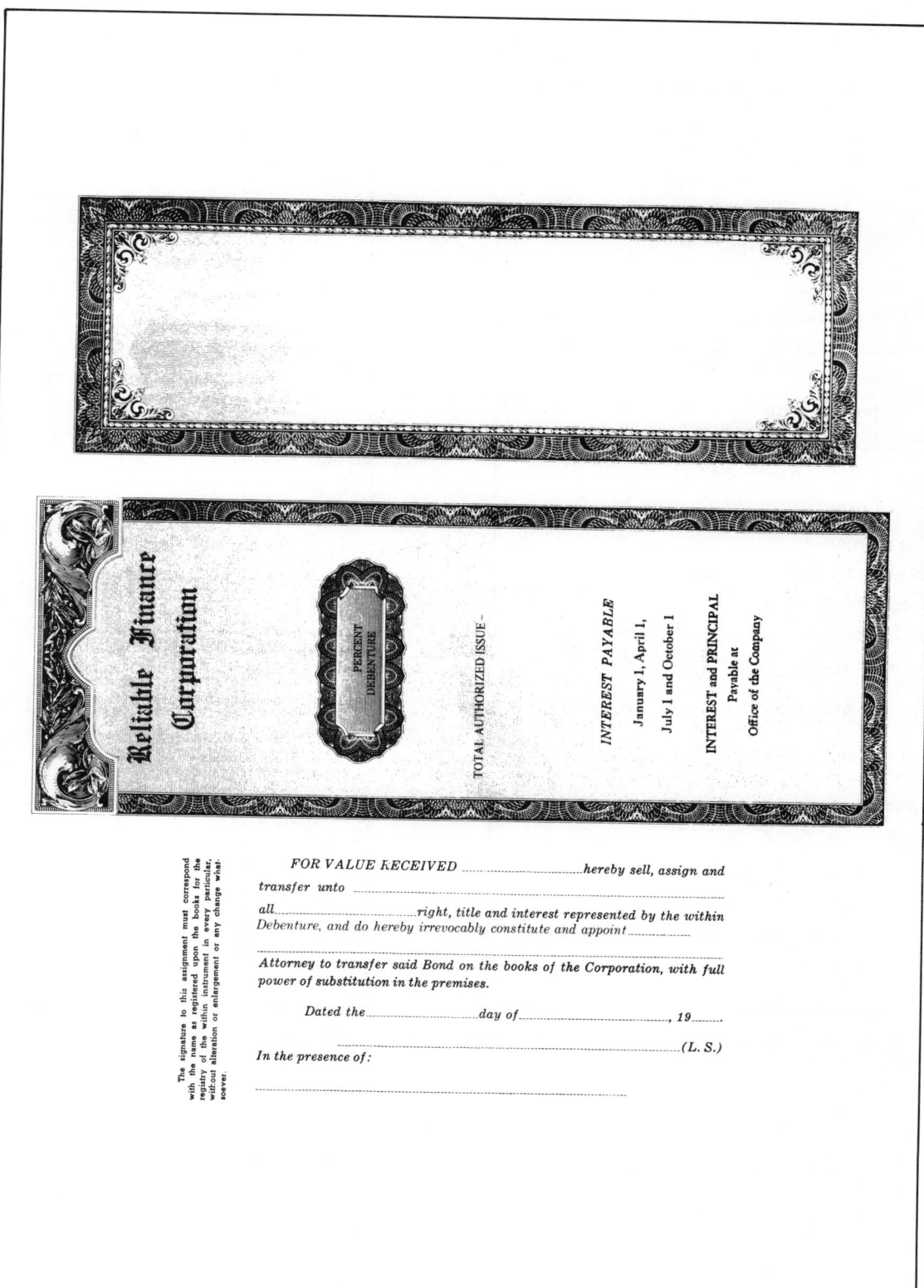

Figure F-31—Reverse Side

COMPARATIVE DATA ON CONVERTIBLE BONDS				
NAME OF FIRM: DUE DATE: BOND RATE:				
Factual				
Moody's rating				
Amount outstanding				
Conversion privilege expires on				
Call price				
Conversion price				
Conversion rate per $1,000 bond				
Market price at: (date)				
bond				
stock				
Yield to maturity				
Current yield:				
bond				
stock				
Analysis				
Conversion value (based on market price of common)				
Investment yield (%)				
Straight debt value				
Cost of conversion feature				
Market price premium over:				
conversion value				
straight debt value				

Figure F-32: FACTUAL AND ANALYTICAL INPUT FOR CONVERTIBLE BONDS

Figure F-33: BOND OF A NONPROFIT ORGANIZATION
(Copyright by All State Legal Supply Co., Mountainside, New Jersey 07092.)

BOND REGISTER

NAME OF BOND

RATING

AMOUNT $ RATE   %

DESCRIPTION OF BONDS

NUMBERS AND DENOMINATIONS

ISSUED BY   DATED

RATE OF INTEREST   %   NET RATE TO US   %   WHEN DUE

BONDS WHERE PAYABLE   INTEREST PAYABLE

INTEREST WHERE PAYABLE   REDEEMABLE

TRUSTEE

REMARKS

ANNUAL AMORTIZATION OF PREMIUM $

WILSON JONES FORM 637-40	DATE 19____	NUMBER	PRICE PER UNIT	BOUGHT OF/OR SOLD TO	AUDIT	POST. REF.	DEBIT	CREDIT	BALANCE

Figure F-34: BOND REGISTER

SALES SUMMARY OF GAINS AND LOSSES FOR YEAR

REDIFORM PARAMUS N J 07652 U.S.A. 649   © 1969

UNITS	SECURITY	BOUGHT			SOLD			P OR L. DESC.	PROFIT AMOUNT	LOSS AMOUNT
		DATE	PRICE	AMOUNT	DATE	PRICE	AMOUNT			

Figure F-35: ANNUAL SUMMARY OF SECURITY GAINS AND LOSSES
(Courtesy of Rediform Office Products, Paramus, New Jersey 07652.)

C 65 -- TRADE NAME CERTIFICATE | RVST | ALL-STATE LEGAL SUPPLY CO. 269 Sheffield St., Mountainside, N. J. 07092

Know all Men by these Presents,

The undersigned do hereby certify that h own conduct and transact the business of

under the assumed name of
and that the Post Office address of said business is

and that there are no other persons associated with the undersigned in the conduct of said business; and that the post office addresses given below are correct.

IN WITNESS WHEREOF, have hereunto set hand at
this day of 19

Name ....

Address ....

Name ....

Address ....

Name ....

Address ....

Name ....

Address ....

Name ....

Address ....

STATE OF CONNECTICUT, } ss.: Town of 19
COUNTY OF

Personally appeared

whose names are signed to the foregoing certificate and made oath to the truth of the same before me.

....
A Commissioner of the Superior Court

The above and foregoing is a true copy of the original certificate on file in the office of the Town Clerk of the Town of

Attest:

.... Town Clerk

Figure F-36: TRADE NAME CERTIFICATE
(Courtesy of All State Legal Supply Co., Mountainside, New Jersey 07092.)

FORM U-1

UNIFORM APPLICATION TO REGISTER SECURITIES

This form is to be used only where a registration statement covering the securities and offering described herein has been filed with the Securities and Exchange Commission.

Application to _____ of the State of _____

pursuant to Section _____ of the _____

1. Name and address of Issuer and principal office in this state:

2. Name, address and telephone number of correspondent to whom notices and communications regarding this application may be sent:

3. Name and address of applicant:

4. Registration or acceptance for filing is sought for the following described securities in the amounts indicated:

Description of Securities	Offering Price or Proposed Offering Price	Total Offering		Offering in This State	
		No. of Shares or Units	Amount	No. of Shares or Units	Amount
			$		$
Totals			$		$

Indicate the maximum commission to be charged: _____ %

5. Amount of filing and examination fees which are enclosed: $ _____ $ _____

6. A Registration Statement was filed with the Securities and Exchange Commission on _____

(date)

   and (became) (will become) effective on _____ .

(date)

7. (a) List the states in which it is proposed to offer the securities for sale to the public.

   (b) List the states, if any, in which the securities are eligible for sale to the public.

   (c) List the states, if any, which have refused, by order or otherwise, to authorize sale of the securities to the public, or have revoked or suspended the right to sell the securities, or in which an application has been withdrawn.

DO NOT WRITE BELOW THIS LINE

Figure F-37: UNIFORM APPLICATION TO REGISTER SECURITIES

8. Submitted herewith as a part of this application are the following documents (documents on file may be incorporated by reference):

    (a) One copy of the Registration Statement and two copies of Prospectus in the latest form on file under the Securities Act of 1933.

    (b) Underwriting Agreement, Agreement among Underwriters, and Selected Dealers Agreement.

    (c) Indenture.

    (d) Issuer's charter or articles of incorporation as amended to date.

    (e) Issuer's by-laws as amended to date.

    (f) Signed copy of opinion of counsel filed with Registration Statement pursuant to the Securities Act of 1933.

    (g) Specimen (type of security) _____ .

    (h) Consent to service of process accompanied by appropriate corporate resolution.

    (i) If an earning computation or similar requirement is required to be met in this state, attach a separate sheet as an exhibit showing compliance.

    (j) One copy of all advertising matter to be used in connection with the offering.

    (k) Others (list each):

9. The applicant hereby applies for registration or acceptance for filing of the above registered securities under the law cited above and in consideration thereof agrees so long as the registration remains in effect that it will:

    (a) Advise the above named state authority of any change prior to registration in this state in any of the information contained herein or in any of the documents submitted with or as a part of this application.

    (b) File with the above named state authority within two business days after filing with the Securities and Exchange Commission (i) any amendments other than delaying amendments to the federal registration statement, designating the changed, revised or added material or information by underlining the same; and (ii) the final prospectus, or any further amendments or supplements thereto.

    (c) Notify the above named state authority within two business days (i) upon the receipt of any stop order, denial, order to show cause, suspension or revocation order, injunction or restraining order, or similar order entered or issued by any state or other regulatory authority or by any court, concerning the securities covered by this application or other securities of the issuer currently being offered to the public; and (ii) upon the receipt of any notice of effectiveness of said registration by the Securities and Exchange Commission.

    (d) Notify the above named state authority at least two business days prior to the effectiveness of said registration with the Securities and Exchange Commission of (i) any request by the issuer or applicant to any other state or regulatory authority for permission to withdraw any application to register the securities described herein; and (ii) a list of all states in which applications have been filed where the issuer or applicant has received notice from the state authority that the application does not comply with state requirements and cannot or does not intend to comply with such requirements.

    (e) Furnish promptly all such additional information and documents in respect to the issuer or the securities covered by this application as may be requested by the above named state authority prior to registration or acceptance for filing.

Figure F-37 (continued)

FORM U-1
3

Date: _____

_____
Name of Applicant

By _____
(Name and Title)

STATE OF _____ }
COUNTY OF _____ } ss

The undersigned, _____ , being first duly sworn, deposes and says:

That he has executed the foregoing application for and on behalf of the applicant named therein; that he is _____ of such applicant and is fully authorized to execute and file such application; that he is familiar with such application; and that to the best of his knowledge, information and belief the statements made in such application are true and the documents submitted therewith are true copies of the originals thereof.

Subscribed and sworn to before me this _____ day of _____ , 19____.

_____
Name

_____
NOTARY PUBLIC

In and for the County of _____ .
State of _____ .
My Commission Expires: _____ .
(Notarial Seal)

- -

FOR AN ACKNOWLEDGMENT OF THE FILING OF THIS APPLICATION COMPLETE THE LEFT COLUMN BELOW

Name and address of correspondent

_____

_____

_____

Applicant

_____

Issuer

_____

State of _____

File Number _____

Date _____

Examiner _____

Telephone _____

Figure F-37 (continued)

FORM U-2A

1

UNIFORM FORM OF
CORPORATE RESOLUTION
OF

_____
(Name of Corporation)

RESOLVED, that it is desirable and in the best interest of this Corporation that its securities be qualified or registered for sale in various states; that the President or any Vice President and the Secretary or an Assistant Secretary hereby are authorized to determine the states in which appropriate action shall be taken to qualify or register for sale all or such part of the securities of this Corporation as said officers may deem advisable; that said officers are hereby authorized to perform on behalf of this Corporation any and all such acts as they may deem necessary or advisable in order to comply with the applicable laws of any such states, and in connection therewith to execute and file all requisite papers and documents, including, but not limited to, applications, reports, surety bonds, irrevocable consents and appointments of attorneys for service of process; and the execution by such officers of any such paper or document or the doing by them of any act in connection with the foregoing matters shall conclusively establish their authority therefor from this Corporation and the approval and ratification by this Corporation of the papers and documents so executed and the action so taken.

ADDITIONAL COPIES ON REQUEST
R. R. DONNELLEY & SONS COMPANY
CHICAGO · VICTORY 2-0272

(OVER)

Figure F-38: UNIFORM FORM OF CORPORATE RESOLUTION FOR SALE OF SECURITIES

FORM U-2A

2

CERTIFICATE

The undersigned hereby certifies that he is the _____

Secretary of _____, a corporation organized and existing under the laws of the State of _____;

that the foregoing is a true and correct copy of a resolution duly adopted at a meeting of the Board of Directors of said corporation held on the _____ day of _____, 19__, at which meeting a quorum was at all times present and acting; that the passage of said resolution was in all respects legal; and that said resolution is in full force and effect.

Dated this _____ day of _____, 19__.

_____
Secretary

(CORPORATE SEAL)

Figure F-38—Reverse Side

484

FORM U-2

UNIFORM CONSENT TO SERVICE OF PROCESS

KNOW ALL MEN BY THESE PRESENTS:

That the undersigned, _____ ,

(a corporation organized under the laws of the State of _____)

(a partnership) (an individual) (other _____) for the purpose of

complying with the laws of the State of _____ relating to either the registration

or sale of securities, hereby irrevocably appoints _____ , and the

successors in such office, its attorney in the State of _____ upon

whom may be served any notice, process or pleading in any action or proceeding against it arising

out of or in connection with the sale of securities or out of violation of the aforesaid laws of said

State; and the undersigned does hereby consent that any such action or proceeding against it may be

commenced in any court of competent jurisdiction and proper venue within said State by service of

process upon said officer with the same effect as if the undersigned was organized or created under

the laws of said State and had lawfully been served with process in said State.

It is requested that a copy of any notice, process or pleading served hereunder be mailed to:

_____
(Name and Address)

_____

Dated: _____ , 19____ .

_____

By _____

Title _____

By _____

(SEAL)

Title _____

(OVER)

Figure F-39: UNIFORM CONSENT TO SERVICE OF PROCESS

485

CORPORATE ACKNOWLEDGMENT

STATE OF _____ ⎱
COUNTY OF _____ ⎰ ss.

On this _____ day of _____ , 19__, before me _____ the undersigned officer, personally appeared _____ and _____ , known personally to me to be the _____ President and Secretary, respectively, of the above named corporation, and that they, as such officers, being authorized so to do, executed the foregoing instrument for the purposes therein contained, by signing the name of the corporation by themselves as such officers.

IN WITNESS WHEREOF I have hereunto set my hand and official seal.

_____
Notary Public

My Commission expires: _____

(NOTARIAL SEAL)

_____

INDIVIDUAL OR PARTNERSHIP ACKNOWLEDGMENT

STATE OF _____ ⎱
COUNTY OF _____ ⎰ ss.

On this _____ day of _____ , 19__, before me, _____ , the undersigned officer, personally appeared _____ to me personally known and known to me to be the same person(s) whose name(s) is (are) signed to the foregoing instrument, and acknowledged the execution thereof for the uses and purposes therein set forth.

IN WITHNESS WHEREOF I have hereunto set my hand and official seal.

_____
Notary Public

My Commission expires: _____

(NOTARIAL SEAL)

Figure F-39—Reverse Side

APPOINTMENT OF ATTORNEY FOR SERVICE OF PROCESS

FOREIGN CORPORATION

61-24 REV. 12-66

Complete either Section 1 or Section 2.

TO: The Secretary of the State of Connecticut

NAME OF CORPORATION	STATE OF INCORPORATION

SECTION 1

☐ The corporation appoints the Secretary of the State of Connecticut and his successors in office, to be its attorney upon whom all process, in any action or proceeding against it, may be served. The corporation agrees that any process against it which is served on the Secretary of the State shall be of the same legal force and validity as if served on the corporation, and that this appointment shall continue in force as long as any liability remains outstanding against the corporation in Connecticut.

SECTION 2

☐ The corporation appoints the natural person or corporation named below to be its attorney upon whom all process, in any action or proceeding against it, may be served. The corporation agrees that any process against it which is served on said attorney shall be of the same legal force and validity as if served on the corporation and that such appointment shall continue in force as long as any liability remains outstanding against the corporation in Connecticut.

(Fill in one only: A, B, or C.)

	NAME OF NATURAL PERSON WHO IS RESIDENT OF CONN.	BUSINESS ADDRESS
A		
		RESIDENCE ADDRESS
B	NAME OF CONNECTICUT CORPORATION	ADDRESS OF PRINCIPAL OFFICE IN CONN. (If none, enter address of appointee's statutory agent for service.)
C	NAME OF CORPORATION NOT ORG. UNDER LAWS OF CONN.°	ADDRESS OF PRINCIPAL OFFICE IN CONN. (If none, enter "Secretary of the State of Connecticut.")

*which has procured a Certificate of Authority to transact business or conduct affairs in this state.

ACCEPTANCE

NAME OF ATTORNEY FOR SERVICE OF PROCESS (Type or print)	SIGNED (Attorney for service of process)

AUTHORIZATION

NAME (President, or V-President, or Sec'y) (Type or print)	TITLE	SIGNED (Named officer)
Personally appeared the above officer and acknowledged the same to be his free act and deed, before me.	DATE	SIGNED (Notary Public)

Figure F-40: APPOINTMENT OF ATTORNEY FOR SERVICE OF PROCESS

UNIFORM FRANCHISE REGISTRATION APPLICATION

INSTRUCTIONS

The following instructions must be adhered to with respect to all applications for registration, registration renewal and amendment.

1. COMPLETION OF APPLICATION: An application for registration of the offer or sale of franchises shall include the following, all of which shall be verified by means of the prescribed signature page:

    A. Facing page.

    B. Supplemental information page(s).

    C. Salesmen disclosure form for all states except Washington.

    D. A copy of the proposed offering circular.

    The following shall be attached to the application:

    A. A second copy of the proposed offering circular.

    B. A cross reference sheet showing the location in the franchise agreement of the information required to be included in the application and in the offering circular. If any item calling for information is inapplicable or the answer thereto is in the negative and is omitted, a statement to that effect shall be made in the cross reference sheet.

    C. Two copies of any advertising to be used in connection with the offer or sale in this state of franchises.

    D. A consent to service of process.

2. DEFINITIONS:

    A. "Predecessor," for the purposes of the disclosure required by item 1 in the body of the offering circular, is defined as follows:

        A "predecessor" of a franchisor is (i) a person the major portion of whose assets have been acquired directly or indirectly by the franchisor, or (ii) a person from whom the franchisor acquired directly or indirectly the major portion of its assets.

-1-

Figure F-41: UNIFORM FRANCHISE REGISTRATION APPLICATION

B. "Franchise broker," for the purposes of the disclosure required by the cover page and item 2 in the body of the offering circular, is defined as follows:

A "franchise broker" is any person engaged in the business of representing a franchisor or subfranchisor in offering for sale or selling a franchise, except anyone whose identity and business experience is otherwise required to be disclosed at item 2 in the body of the offering circular.

3. DISCLOSURE: Each disclosure item should be either positively or negatively commented upon by use of a statement which fully incorporates the information required by the item.

4. SUBFRANCHISORS: When the person filing the application for registration is a subfranchisor, the application shall also include the same information concerning the subfranchisor as is required from the franchisor; the franchisor, as well as the subfranchisor, shall execute a signature page.

5. SIGNING OF APPLICATION: The application shall be signed by an officer or general partner of the applicant; however, it may be signed by another person holding a power of attorney for such purposes from the applicant. If signed on behalf of the applicant pursuant to such power of attorney, the application shall include as an additional exhibit a copy of said power of attorney or a copy of the corporate resolution authorizing the attorney to act.

6. MANUALLY SIGNED CONSENT OF ACCOUNTANT: All applications shall be accompanied by manually signed consent of the independent public accountant for the use of their audited financial statements as such statements appear in the offering circular.

7. APPLICATION TO AMEND THE REGISTRATION: An amendment to an application filed either before or after the effective date of registration shall contain only the information being amended identified by item number and shall be verified by means of the prescribed signature page. Each amendment shall be accompanied by a facing page in the form prescribed on which the applicant shall indicate that the filing is an amendment and the number of the amendment, if more than one.

8. NOTE: This Uniform Franchise Registration Application is an alternative means of complying with the state franchise investment laws. Because the Uniform Application form was designed to satisfy the varied requirements of a number of states, it may call for more information than any one state demands. Applicants should be aware that they may, if they wish, elect to file in each state the application form prescribed in that state, rather than the Uniform Application form.

Figure F-41 (continued)

B. Equipment, fixtures, other fixed assets, construction, remodelling, leasehold improvements and decorating costs, whether or not financed by contract, installment purchases, lease or otherwise.

C. Inventory required to commence operation.

D. Security deposits, other prepaid expenses and working capital required to commence operation.

E. Any other payments which the franchisee will be required to make in order to commence operations.

NOTE: The following statement shall be inserted in the offering circular at this point:

THERE ARE NO OTHER DIRECT OR INDIRECT PAYMENTS IN CONJUNCTION WITH THE PURCHASE OF THE FRANCHISE.

8. OBLIGATIONS OF FRANCHISEE TO PURCHASE OR LEASE FROM DESIGNATED SOURCES: State any obligations of the franchisee or subfranchisor, whether arising by terms of the franchise agreement or other device or practice, to purchase or lease from the franchisor or his designees, goods, services, supplies, fixtures, equipment, inventory or real estate relating to the establishment or operation of the franchise business. Regarding such obligations, state the following:

A. The goods, services, supplies, fixtures, equipment, inventory or real estate required to be purchased or leased from the franchisor or his designees.

B. Whether, and if so, the precise basis by which, the franchisor, its parent or persons affiliated with the franchisor will or may derive income based on or as a result of any such required purchases or leases.

C. To the extent known or estimable by the franchisor, the magnitude of such required purchases and leases in relation to all purchases and leases by the franchisee of goods and services which the franchisee will make or enter into (1) in the establishment and (2) in the operation of the franchise business.

9. OBLIGATIONS OF FRANCHISEE TO PURCHASE OR LEASE IN ACCORDANCE WITH SPECIFICATIONS OR FROM APPROVED SUPPLIERS: State any obligations of the franchisee or subfranchisor, whether arising by terms of the franchise agreement or other device or practice, to purchase or lease in accordance with specifications issued by the franchisor, or from suppliers approved by the franchisor, goods, services, supplies, fixtures, equipment, inventory or real estate relating to the establishment or operation of the franchise business. Regarding such obligations, state the following:

A. The goods, services, supplies, fixtures, equipment, inventory or real estate required to be purchased or leased in accordance with specifications or from suppliers approved by the franchisor.

B. The manner in which the franchisor issues and modifies specifications or grants and revokes approval to suppliers.

C. Whether, and for what categories of goods and services, the franchisor or persons affiliated with the franchisor are approved suppliers or the only approved suppliers.

Figure F-41 (continued)

D. Whether, and if so, the precise basis by which, the franchisor, its parent or persons affiliated with the franchisor may derive income from purchases made from it or from other approved suppliers, if this is the case.

10. FINANCING ARRANGEMENTS: State the terms and conditions of any financing arrangements offered directly or indirectly by the franchisor, its agent or affiliated company, including:

A. A description of any waiver of defenses or similar provisions in any note, contract or other instrument to be executed by the franchisee or subfranchisor.

B. A statement of any past or present practice or of any intent of the franchisor to sell, assign, or discount to a third party, in whole or in part, any note, contract or other instrument executed by the franchisee or subfranchisor.

C. A description of any payments received by the franchisor from any person for the placement of financing with such person.

11. OBLIGATIONS OF THE FRANCHISOR; OTHER SUPERVISION, ASSISTANCE OR SERVICES: Where applicable, describe the following:

A. The obligations to be met by the franchisor prior to the opening of the franchise business, citing by section and page the provisions of the franchise or related agreement requiring performance.

B. Other supervision, assistance or services to be provided by the franchisor prior to the opening of the franchise business although franchisor is not bound by the franchise or any related agreement to provide the same. As part of this disclosure franchisor must disclose that he is not so bound.

C. The obligations to be met by the franchisor during the operation of the franchise business, including, without limitation, the assistance to the franchisee in the operation of his business. Cite by section and page the provisions of the franchise or related agreement requiring performance.

D. Other supervision, assistance or services to be provided by the franchisor during the operation of the franchise business although franchisor is not bound by the franchise or any related agreement to provide the same. As part of this disclosure franchisor must disclose that he is not so bound.

E. The methods used by the franchisor to select the location for the franchisee's business.

F. The typical length of time between the signing of the franchise agreement or the first payment of any consideration for the franchise and the opening of the franchisee's business.

G. The training program of the franchisor, including:

(1) The location, duration and content of the training program;

Figure F-41 (continued)

(2) When the training program is to be conducted;

(3) The experience that the instructors have had with the franchisor;

(4) Any charges to be made to the franchisee and the extent to which the franchisee will be responsible for travel and living expenses of the person(s) who enroll in the training program;

(5) If the training program is not mandatory, the percentage of new franchisees that enrolled in the training program during the 12 months immediately preceding the date of the offering circular; and

(6) Whether any additional training programs and/or refresher courses are available to the franchisee and whether the franchisee will be required to attend the same.

12. EXCLUSIVE AREA OR TERRITORY: Describe any exclusive area or territory granted the franchisee and with respect to such area or territory state whether:

A. The franchisor has established or may establish another franchisee who will also be permitted to use the franchisor's trade name or trademark.

B. The franchisor has established or may establish a company-owned outlet using the franchisor's trade name or trademark.

C. The franchisor or its parent or affiliate has established or may establish other franchises or company-owned outlets selling or leasing similar products or services under a different trade name or trademark.

D. Continuation of the franchisee's areal or territorial exclusivity is dependent upon achievement of a certain sales volume, market penetration or other contingency and under what circumstances the franchisee's area or territory may be altered.

13. TRADEMARKS, SERVICE MARKS, TRADE NAMES, LOGOTYPES, AND COMMERCIAL SYMBOLS: Describe any trademarks, service marks, trade names, logotypes or other commercial symbols to be licensed to the franchisee including the following:

A. Whether the trademark, service mark, trade name, logotype or other commercial symbol is registered with the United States Patent Office and, if so, for each such registration state the registration date and number and whether or not the registration is on the principal or supplemental register.

B. Whether the trademark, service mark, trade name, logotype and other commercial symbol are registered in this state or the state in which the franchise business is to be located and the dates of such registrations.

C. A description of any presently effective determinations of the Patent Office, the trademark

-7-

Figure F-41 (continued)

administrator of this state or any court, any pending interference, opposition or cancellation proceeding and any pending material litigation involving such trademarks, service marks, trade names, logotypes or other commercial symbols and which is relevant to their use in this state or the state in which the franchise business is to be located.

D. A description of any agreements currently in effect which significantly limit the rights of the franchisor to use or license the use of such trademarks, service marks, trade names, logotypes or other commercial symbols in any manner material to the franchise.

E. Whether the franchisor is obligated by the franchise agreement or otherwise to protect any or all rights which the franchisee has to use such trademarks, service marks, trade names, logotypes or other commercial symbols and to protect the franchisee against claims of infringement or unfair competition with respect to the same.

F. Whether there are any infringing uses actually known to the franchisor which could materially affect the franchisee's use of such trademarks, service marks, trade names, logotypes or other commercial symbols in this state or state in which the franchise business is to be located.

14. PATENTS AND COPYRIGHTS: If the franchisor owns any rights in or to any patents or copyrights which are material to the franchise, describe such patents and copyrights, their relationship to the franchise and the terms and conditions under which the franchisee may use them, including their duration, whether the franchisor can and intends to renew any copyrights, and, to the extent relevant, the information required by Section 13 above with respect to such patents and copyrights.

15. OBLIGATION OF THE FRANCHISEE TO PARTICIPATE IN THE ACTUAL OPERATION OF THE FRANCHISE BUSINESS: State fully the obligation of the franchisee or the subfranchisor, whether arising by terms of the franchise agreement or other device or practice, to participate personally in the direct operation of the franchise business or whether the franchisor recommends participation in the same.

16. RESTRICTIONS ON GOODS AND SERVICES OFFERED BY FRANCHISEE: State any restriction or condition imposed by the franchisor, whether by terms of the franchise agreement or by other device or practice of the franchisor, whereby the franchisee is restricted as to the goods or services he may offer for sale, or limited in the customers to whom he may sell such goods or services.

17. RENEWAL, TERMINATION, REPURCHASE, MODIFICATION AND ASSIGNMENT OF THE FRANCHISE AGREEMENT AND RELATED INFORMATION: With respect to the franchise and any related agreements state the following:

A. The term and whether such term is affected by any agreement (including leases or subleases) other than the one from which such term arises.

B. The conditions under which the franchisee may renew or extend.

C. The conditions under which the franchisor may refuse to renew or extend.

-8-

Figure F-41 (continued)

D. The conditions under which the franchisee may terminate.

E. The conditions under which the franchisor may terminate.

F. The obligations (including lease or sublease obligations) of the franchisee after termination of the franchise by the franchisor and the obligations of the franchisee (including lease or sublease obligations) after termination of the franchise by the franchisee or the expiration of the franchise.

G. The franchisee's interest upon termination or refusal to renew or extend the franchise by the franchisor or by the franchisee.

H. The conditions under which the franchisor may repurchase, whether by right of first refusal or at the option of the franchisor. If the franchisor has the option to repurchase the franchise, state whether there will be an independent appraisal of the franchise, whether the repurchase price will be determined by a predetermined formula and whether there will be a recognition of goodwill or other intangibles associated therewith in the repurchase price to be given the franchisee.

I. The conditions under which the franchisee or its owners may sell or assign all or an interest in the ownership of the franchise or of the franchisee or in the assets of the franchise business.

J. The conditions under which the franchisor may sell or assign in whole or in part.

K. The conditions under which the franchisee may modify.

L. The conditions under which the franchisor may modify.

M. The rights of the franchisee's heirs or personal representative upon the death or incapacity of the franchisee.

N. The provisions of any covenant not to compete.

18. ARRANGEMENTS WITH PUBLIC FIGURES: State the following:

A. Any compensation or other benefit given or promised to a public figure arising, in whole or in part, from:

(1) the use of the public figure in the name or symbol of the franchise, or

(2) the endorsement or recommendation of the franchise by the public figure in advertisements.

B. Any right the franchisee may have to use the name of a public figure in his promotional efforts or advertising and any charges to be made to the franchisee in connection with such usage.

-9-

Figure F-41 (continued)

C. The extent to which such public figure is involved in the actual management or control of the franchisor.

D. The total investment of the public figure in the franchise operation.

19. ACTUAL, AVERAGE, PROJECTED OR FORECASTED FRANCHISEE SALES, PROFITS OR EARNINGS:

A. If the franchisor discloses to prospective franchisees the actual or average sales, profits or earnings of franchisees, an exact copy of the same shall be included in or as an exhibit to the offering circular. Such actual or average sales, profits or earnings shall contain the following legend in not less than 10-point boldface type:

THESE SALES, PROFITS OR EARNINGS ARE (AVERAGES) OF (A) SPECIFIC FRANCHISE(S) AND SHOULD NOT BE CONSIDERED AS THE ACTUAL OR POTENTIAL SALES, PROFITS OR EARNINGS THAT WILL BE REALIZED BY ANY OTHER FRANCHISE. THE FRANCHISOR DOES NOT REPRESENT THAT ANY FRANCHISEE CAN EXPECT TO ATTAIN THESE SALES, PROFITS OR EARNINGS.

B. Where projected or forecasted franchisee sales, profits or earnings are proposed to be used, an exact copy of the same shall be included in or as an exhibit to the offering circular. Such projected or forecasted sales, profits or earnings shall contain the following legend in not less than 10-point boldface type:

THESE PROJECTIONS (FORECASTS) OF SALES, PROFITS OR EARNINGS ARE MERELY ESTIMATES AND SHOULD NOT BE CONSIDERED AS THE ACTUAL OR POTENTIAL SALES, PROFITS OR EARNINGS THAT WILL BE REALIZED BY ANY SPECIFIC FRANCHISEE. THE FRANCHISOR DOES NOT REPRESENT THAT ANY FRANCHISEE CAN EXPECT TO ATTAIN THESE SALES, PROFITS OR EARNINGS.

C. With regard to Items 19. A. and B. above:

(1) The basis and assumptions for such actual, average, projected or forecasted sales, profits or earnings must be disclosed in detail;

(2) All actual, average, projected or forecasted sales, profits or earnings must be for or based upon a substantial number of franchisees in a concurrent equal period of time; provided, however, that any such representation is accompanied by a clear and conspicuous disclosure of the percentage of the total number of franchisees who have achieved such results; and further provided that if the sales, profits or earnings represented, projected or forecasted from were not made in the franchisor's fiscal year immediately preceding the date of the representation, the time period in which they were made must be clearly disclosed in immediate conjunction with such representation and with the same conspicuousness;

-10-

Figure F-41 (continued)

(3) All actual, average, projected or forecasted sales, profits or earnings must be prepared in accordance with generally accepted accounting principles and the amounts represented may not be in excess of sales, profits or earnings actually achieved by existing franchises;

(4) If franchises have not been in operation long enough to indicate what sales, profits or earnings may result, then the use of actual, average, projected or forecasted sales, profits or earnings is prohibited;

(5) Franchise locations upon which actual, average, projected or forecasted sales, profits or earnings are based must be identified by address, number of years of operation, whether substantially similar to the franchises offered, whether owner managed, whether such franchises received any services not generally available to other franchises and whether such sales, profits or earnings have been audited;

(6) All projections or forecasts of sales, profits or earnings shall include a statement of the extent to which such projections or forecasts relate to:

(a) Franchises of a type substantially similar to the franchises offered by this offering circular operating in the state where the franchise is to be located;

(b) Franchises of a substantially similar type throughout the United States;

(7) All projections and forecasts of sales, profits or earnings must include a break-even point insofar as sales and expenses and also must disclose other relevant financial ratios; and

(8) Franchisor shall include a statement that substantiation of all actual, average, projected or forecasted sales, profits or earnings will be made available to prospective franchisees upon reasonable demand.

20. INFORMATION REGARDING FRANCHISES OF THE FRANCHISOR: State the following as of the close of franchisor's most recent fiscal year:

A. The total number of franchises, exclusive of company owned or operated distribution outlets, of a type substantially similar to those offered herein and of that number, the number of such franchises which were operational as of the date of this offering circular.

-11-

Figure F-41 (continued)

B. The number of franchises in this state, exclusive of company owned or operated distribution outlets, of a type substantially similar to those offered herein and of that number, the number of such franchises which were operational as of the date of this offering circular.

C. The total number of franchises substantially similar to those offered herein for which a business is not yet operational although a franchise agreement has been signed.

D. The number of franchises in this state substantially similar to those offered herein for which a business is not yet operational although a franchise agreement has been signed.

E. The names, addresses and telephone numbers of all franchises under franchise agreements with the franchisor or its subfranchisor which are located in the state where the proposed franchise is to be located. To the extent that there are fewer than 10 such franchises located in said state, the list shall include at least the 10 such franchises which are most proximate to the location of the proposed franchise; and if fewer than 10 such franchises exist, the list shall identify all such franchises and include a statement to that effect.

In lieu of the above disclosure, the franchisor may attach to the offering circular a list of the names, addresses and telephone numbers of all its franchises under franchise agreements with the franchisor or its subfranchisors.

F. An estimate of the total number of franchises to be sold or granted during the one year period following the date of the offering circular.

G. An estimate of the number of franchises to be sold or granted in this state during the one year period following the date of the offering circular.

H. State the number of franchises in each of the following categories which within the three-year period immediately preceding the close of franchisor's most recent fiscal year have:

(1) been cancelled or terminated by the franchisor for:

(a) failure to comply with quality control standards; and

(b) other reasons;

(2) not been renewed by the franchisor;

(3) been reacquired through purchase by the franchisor; and

-12-

Figure F-41(continued)

497

(4) been otherwise reacquired by the franchisor.

21. FINANCIAL STATEMENTS: Financial statements shall be prepared in accordance with generally accepted accounting principles. Such financial statements shall be audited by an independent certified public accountant or, if permitted by the franchise law of a particular state, an independent public accountant. Unaudited statements may be used for interim periods.

A. The financial statements required to be filed by a franchisor shall include a balance sheet as of a date within 90 days prior to the date of the application and profit and loss statements for each of the three fiscal years preceding the date of the balance sheet and for the period, if any, between the close of the last of such fiscal years and the date of the balance sheet. The balance sheet as of a date within 90 days prior to the date of the application need not be audited. However, if this balance sheet is not audited, there shall be filed in addition an audited balance sheet as of the end of the franchisor's last fiscal year unless such last fiscal year ended within 90 days of the date of the application in which case there shall be filed an audited balance sheet as of the end of the franchisor's next preceeding fiscal year. The profit and loss statements shall be audited up to the date of the last audited balance sheet filed, if any.

B. Controlling company statements: Where state law permits, in lieu of the disclosure required by Item 21. A., complete financial statements of a company controlling the franchisor may be filed, but only if the unaudited financial statements of the franchisor are filed and the controlling company absolutely and unconditionally guarantees to assume the duties and obligations of the franchisor under the franchise agreement should the franchisor become unable to perform its duties and obligations.

C. Consolidated and separate statements:

(1) Where a franchisor owns, directly or beneficially, a controlling financial interest in any other corporation, the financial statements required to be filed should normally reflect on a consolidated basis the financial condition of the franchisor and each of its subsidiaries.

(2) A separate financial statement will normally be required for each substantial franchisor or subfranchisor related entity.

(3) A company controlling 80% or more of a franchisor shall normally be required to file its financial statements.

(4) Consolidated and separate financial statements shall be prepared in accordance with generally accepted accounting principles.

-13-

Figure F-41 (continued)

22. CONTRACTS: Attach a copy of all franchise and other contracts or agreements proposed for use or in use in this state, including, without limitation, all lease agreements, option agreements, and purchase agreements.

23. ACKNOWLEDGEMENT OF RECEIPT BY PROSPECTIVE FRANCHISEE: The last page of each offering circular shall contain a detachable document acknowledging receipt of the offering circular by the prospective franchisee.

Figure F-41 (continued)

REQUIREMENTS FOR PREPARATION
OF A UNIFORM FRANCHISE OFFERING CIRCULAR

COVER PAGE: The outside front cover of the offering circular shall contain the following information:

1. The title in boldface type: FRANCHISE OFFERING CIRCULAR FOR PROSPECTIVE FRANCHISEES REQUIRED BY THE STATE OF (name of state).

2. The name, type of business organization, principal business address and telephone number of the franchisor.

3. If different than 2. above, the name, principal business address and telephone number of the subfranchisor or franchise broker offering in this state the herein described franchise.

4. A sample of the primary business trademark, logotype, trade name, or commercial label or symbol used by the franchisor for marketing its products or services and under which the franchisee will conduct its business. (Place in upper left-hand corner of the cover page.)

5. A brief description of the franchise to be offered.

6. A summary of items 5 and 7 of the offering circular, to wit: Franchisee's Initial Franchise Fee or Other Payment and Franchisee's Initial Investment, respectively. (See page 4.)

7. Effective Date: (Leave blank until notified of effectiveness by state regulatory authority.)

8. The following statement in boldface type:

THIS OFFERING CIRCULAR IS PROVIDED FOR YOUR OWN PROTECTION AND CONTAINS A SUMMARY ONLY OF CERTAIN MATERIAL PROVISIONS OF THE FRANCHISE AGREEMENT. THIS OFFERING CIRCULAR AND ALL CONTRACTS OR AGREEMENTS SHOULD BE READ CAREFULLY IN THEIR ENTIRETY FOR AN UNDERSTANDING OF ALL RIGHTS AND OBLIGATIONS OF BOTH THE FRANCHISOR AND THE FRANCHISEE.

ALTHOUGH THESE FRANCHISES HAVE BEEN REGISTERED UNDER THE (name of law), REGISTRATION DOES NOT CONSTITUTE APPROVAL, RECOMMENDATION OR ENDORSEMENT BY THE (state regulatory authority) OR A FINDING BY THE (state regulatory authority) THAT THE INFORMATION PROVIDED HEREIN IS TRUE, COMPLETE, ACCURATE OR NOT MISLEADING. A FALSE, INCOMPLETE, INACCURATE OR MISLEADING STATEMENT MAY CONSTITUTE A VIOLATION OF BOTH FEDERAL AND STATE LAW, AND SHOULD BE REPORTED TO BOTH THE FEDERAL TRADE COMMISSION, WASHINGTON D. C. 20580 AND (name and address of state regulatory authority).

(name of law) MAKES IT UNLAWFUL TO OFFER OR SELL ANY FRANCHISE IN THIS STATE WHICH IS SUBJECT TO REGISTRATION WITHOUT FIRST PROVIDING TO THE PROSPECTIVE FRANCHISEE, AT LEAST (requisite time) PRIOR TO THE EXECUTION BY THE PROSPECTIVE FRANCHISEE OF ANY BINDING FRANCHISE OR OTHER AGREEMENT, OR AT LEAST (requisite time) PRIOR TO THE PAYMENT OF ANY CONSIDERATION BY THE FRANCHISEE, WHICHEVER OCCURS FIRST, A COPY OF THE OFFERING CIRCULAR, TOGETHER WITH A COPY OF ALL PROPOSED AGREEMENTS RELATING TO THE FRANCHISE.

-1-

Figure F-41 (continued)

9. The name and address of the franchisor's registered agent in this state authorized to receive service of process.

10. The name and address of the subfranchisor's or franchise broker's registered agent in this state authorized to receive service of process.

TABLE OF CONTENTS: Include a table of contents based on the requirements of this offering circular.

BODY OF OFFERING CIRCULAR: The offering circular shall contain the following information clearly and concisely stated in narrative form:

1. THE FRANCHISOR AND ANY PREDECESSORS: Set forth in summary form: (The disclosure regarding predecessors need only cover the 15 year period immediately preceeding the close of franchisor's most recent fiscal year.)

   A. The name of the franchisor and any predecessors thereto.

   B. The name under which the franchisor is currently doing or intends to do business.

   C. The franchisor's principal business address and the business address or addresses of any predecessors thereto.

   D. The business form of the franchisor whether corporate, partnership, or otherwise.

   E. A description of the franchisor's business and the franchises to be offered in this state.

   F. The prior business experience of the franchisor and any predecessors thereto including:

      (1) The length of time the franchisor has conducted a business of the type to be operated by the franchisee;

      (2) The length of time each predecessor conducted a business of the type to be operated by the franchisee;

      (3) The length of time the franchisor has offered franchises for such business;

      (4) The length of time each predecessor offered franchises for such business;

      (5) Whether the franchisor has offered franchises in other lines of business, including:

         (a) a description of such other lines of business;

         (b) the number of franchises sold in each other line of business;

-2-

Figure F-41 (continued)

              (c)   the length of time the franchisor
                    has offered each such franchise; and

      (6) Whether each predecessor offered franchises
           in other lines of business, including:

              (a)   a description of such other
                    lines of business;

              (b)   the number of franchises
                    sold in each other line of
                    business; and

              (c)   the length of time each
                    predecessor offered each such
                    franchise.

    2.   IDENTITY AND BUSINESS EXPERIENCE OF PERSONS AFFILIATED
WITH THE FRANCHISOR; FRANCHISE BROKERS: List by name and position
held the directors, trustees and/or general partners, as the case
may be, the principal officers (including the chief executive and
chief operating officer, financial, franchise marketing, training
and service officers) and other executives or subfranchisors who
will have management responsibility in connection with the operation
of the franchisor's business relating to the franchises offered by
this offering circular and all franchise brokers. With regard to
each person listed, state his principal occupations and employers
during the past five years.

    3. LITIGATION: State whether the franchisor, any person or
franchise broker identified in 2. above:

    A. Has any administrative, criminal or material civil
action (or a significant number of civil actions irrespective
of materiality) pending against him alleging a violation
of any franchise law, fraud, embezzlement, fraudulent
conversion, restraint of trade, unfair or deceptive
practices, misappropriation of property or comparable
allegations. If so, set forth the name of the person, the
court or other forum, nature, and current status of any
such pending action. Franchisor may include a summary
opinion of counsel as to any such action, but only if a
consent to use of such summary opinion is included as
part of this offering circular.

    B. Has during the 10 year period immediately preceding
the date of the offering circular been convicted of a felony
or pleaded nolo contendere to a felony charge or been held
liable in a civil action by final judgment or been the subject
of a material complaint or other legal proceeding if such felony,
civil action, complaint or other legal proceeding involved
violation of any franchise law, fraud, embezzlement, fraudulent
conversion, restraint of trade, unfair or deceptive practices,
misappropriation of property or comparable allegations. If so,
set forth the name of the person convicted, the court and date
of conviction or person against whom judgment was entered, penalty
or damages assessed in connection therewith and/or terms of
settlement.

    C. Is subject to any currently effective injunctive
or restrictive order or decree relating to the franchise or
under any federal, state or Canadian franchise, securities,
antitrust, trade regulation or trade practice law as a

-3-

Figure F-41 (continued)

result of a concluded or pending action or proceeding brought by a public agency. If so, set forth the name of the person so subject, the public agency and court, a summary of the allegations or facts found by the agency or court and the date, nature, terms and conditions of the order or decree.

4. BANKRUPTCY: State whether the franchisor or any predecessor, officer or general partner of the franchisor has during the 15 year period immediately preceding the date of the offering circular been adjudged bankrupt or reorganized due to insolvency or was a principal officer of any company or a general partner in any partnership that was adjudged bankrupt or reorganized due to insolvency during or within 1 year after the period that such officer or general partner of the franchisor held such position in such company or partnership, or whether any such bankruptcy or reorganization proceeding has been commenced. If so, set forth the name of the person or company adjudged bankrupt or reorganized or named in any such proceeding and the date thereof and any material facts or circumstances.

5. FRANCHISEE'S INITIAL FRANCHISE FEE OR OTHER INITIAL PAYMENT: Describe in detail the following:

A. The initial franchise fee or other initial payment for the franchise, if any, charged upon the signing of the franchise agreement, and whether payable in lump sum or installments. Set forth the manner in which the franchisor will use or apply such franchise fee or initial payment. State whether such fee or payment is refundable, and if so, under what conditions.

B. If an identical initial franchise fee or other initial payment is not charged in connection with each franchise agreement, state the method or formula by which such fee or payment is determined.

6. OTHER FEES: Describe in detail other recurring or isolated fees or payments, including but not limited to royalties, service fees, training fees, lease payments and advertising fees and charges that the franchisee is required to pay to the franchisor or persons affiliated with the franchisor or which the franchisor or such affiliated person imposes or collects in whole or in part on behalf of a third party. Include, if applicable, the formula used to compute such other fees and payments. State whether any such fee or payment is refundable, and if so, under what conditions.

7. FRANCHISEE'S INITIAL INVESTMENT: Describe in detail the following expenditures (which may be estimated or described by a low-high range, if not known exactly), stating for each to whom the payments are to be made, when such payments are to be determined, whether any payment is refundable, and if so, under what conditions and, if any part of the franchisee's initial investment in the franchise will or may be financed, an estimate of the loan repayments, including interest:

A. Real property, whether or not financed by contract, installment, purchase or lease. If neither estimable nor describable by a low-high range, describe the variable requirements, such as property, location and building size which make the real property expenditure neither estimable nor describable by a low-high range.

-4-

Figure F-41 (continued)

NOTICE

RE: ITEM 19 OF UNIFORM FRANCHISE OFFERING CIRCULAR – ACTUAL, AVERAGE, PROJECTED OR FORECASTED FRANCHISEE SALES, PROFITS OR EARNINGS.

Until such time as Item 19 of the Uniform Franchise Offering Circular is adopted by Administrative Rule by the Commissioner of Securities, all actual, average, projected or forecasted franchisee sales, profits or earnings must comport with the standards set forth in the Wisconsin Administrative Code at subsections SEC 34.02(1)(c) - (e), inclusive. The aforementioned subsections are set forth below:

WISCONSIN ADMINISTRATIVE CODE

SEC 34.02 <u>False, fraudulent and deceptive practices</u>. In connection with an offer to sell or sale of a franchise in this state, any person authorizing, aiding in, or causing such offer to sell or sale of franchises shall be deemed to be engaging in a "false, fraudulent or deceptive practice" within the meaning of section 553.58(1), Wis. Stats., and in a "fraudulent and prohibited practice" within the meaning of section 553.41, Wis. Stats., without limiting the authority of the Commissioner under sections 553.28 or 553.55, Wis. Stats., or the authority of the Department of Justice or of any District Attorney under section 553.54, Wis. Stats., if he:

(1) makes or causes to be made oral or written statements or representations with regard to:

(a) ...,

(b) ...,

(c) Industry wide total income representations or a portion thereof applicable to the prospective franchisee, whether actual or projected, for the product or service marketed by the franchisor when not accompanied by disclosure of the relationship, if any, of such representations to the franchisor's and its franchisee's actual income experiences.

(d) Projections of operations or of income or gross or net profits capable of being obtained by operation of the franchise by the franchisee without selecting representative data for the basis for use of the same under sections 553.22(3)(m) or 553.26(16), Wis. Stats., and without;

1. In the case of a franchise of a type substantially similar to other franchises sold by the franchisor a majority of which have been operational for greater than one year the disclosure, orally at the same time or clearly and conspicuously immediately adjacent to any such written representation, of the following:

-1-

Figure F-41 (continued)

"REPRESENTATIONS ARE BASED ON THE AVERAGE ACTUAL EARNINGS OR PROFITS OF ALL OUR FRANCHISEES IN OPERATION DURING AT LEAST A PORTION OF THE MOST RECENT FISCAL YEAR. THESE FIGURES SHOULD NOT BE CONSIDERED AS POTENTIAL EARNINGS OR REPRESENTATIONS OF PROFITS OF ANY SPECIFIC FRANCHISEE"; or

2. In the case of each franchise of a type substantially similar to the one being offered to the prospective franchisee and which has been operational for greater than one year the disclosure, orally at the same time or clearly and conspicuously immediately adjacent to any such written representation, of the following:

    a.   The name and address of the franchisee whose earnings or profits are being represented and the circumstances under which such earnings were made; and

    b.   The percentage of franchisees which the represented franchise equals; and

    c.   The average actual earnings or profits of all franchisor's substantially similar franchisees in operation during at least a portion of the most recent fiscal year together with the disclaimer called for in Wis. Adm. Code section SEC 34.02(1)(d)1.; and

    d.   THIS REPRESENTATION IS BASED ON ACTUAL EARNINGS OR PROFITS OF THE NAMED FRANCHISEE DURING THE PERIOD ABOVE STATED. THESE FIGURES SHOULD NOT BE CONSIDERED AS POTENTIAL EARNINGS OR EARNINGS CAPABLE OF BEING ATTAINED BY ANY OTHER FRANCHISEE.

3. In the case where there have been no franchisees of a type substantially similar to that offered and sold by the franchisor which were operational during the 12-month period preceding the date of such representation or where less than a majority thereof sold have become operational without disclosure, orally at the same time or clearly and conspicuously immediately adjacent to such written representation, of the following:

"ALL REPRESENTATIONS OF POTENTIAL EARNINGS OR PROFITS ARE MERELY ESTIMATES. NO FRANCHISES HAVE BEEN IN OPERATION LONG ENOUGH TO INDICATE WHAT, IF ANY, ACTUAL EARNINGS OR PROFITS MAY RESULT,"

(e) The actual income experiences of the franchisor or its franchisees without stating orally at the same time that certified audited financial statements are or are not available and if so, from what source or disclosing in writing immediately adjacent to such written figures the certified financial statements of the franchisor and its franchisees or a summary thereof, whether certified or unaudited, in the form required by Wis. Adm. Code, section SEC 35.05,

Register, October, 1972, No. 202

-2-

Figure F-41 (continued)

STATE OF WISCONSIN
OFFICE OF THE COMMISSIONER OF SECURITIES
FRANCHISE INVESTMENT DIVISION

Chapter 333, Laws of 1973
Secs. 178, 179 and 180
Amendments to Wis. Stat. ch. 553.72

Effective June 29, 1974

Wis. Stat. 553.72 of the statutes is amended to read:

553.72 FEES AND EXPENSES.

(1) The fee for filing an application for registration of the offer of franchises under s. 553.26 is $400.

(2) The fee for filing an application for renewal of a registration under s. 553.30 is $250.

(3) The fee for filing an amendment to the application filed under s. 553.31 is $100.

(4) The commissioner may by rule require the payment of prescribed fees for delinquent or materially deficient filings of information or documents required to be filed with the commissioner under this chapter.

(5) The expenses reasonably attributable to the examination of any matter arising under this chapter shall be charged to the applicant or registrant involved, but the expenses so charged shall not exceed such maximum amounts as the commissioner by rule prescribes.

Figure F-41 (continued)

I certify under penalty of law that I have read this application and the exhibits attached hereto and incorporated herein by reference, and know the contents thereof and that the statements therein are true and correct.

Executed at _____, _____, 19_____

_____

_____
(Signature(s) of Franchisor and/or Subfranchisor)

(SEAL)   By _____

                                Title _____

STATE OF _____)
)ss.
COUNTY OF _____)

    Personally appeared before me this _____ day of

_____ 19_____ the above-named _____

_____ (and) _____

to me known to be the person(s) who executed the foregoing

application (as _____ and _____

_____ respectively, of the above-named applicant) and

(each), being first duly sworn, stated upon oath that said

application, and all exhibits submitted herewith, are true and

correct.

                                _____

(Notary's Seal)   _____
                                              (Notary)

Figure F-41 (continued)

CORPORATE ACKNOWLEDGMENT

STATE OF _____)
)ss.
COUNTY OF _____)

On this _____ day of _____, 19_____, before me
_____ the undersigned officer, personally
   (Name of Notary)

appeared _____ and _____,

known personally to me to be the _____ President and

_____ Secretary, respectively, of the above named corporation,

and that they, as such officers, being authorized so to do, executed

the foregoing instrument for the purposes therein contained, by

signing the name of the corporation by themselves as such officers.

IN WITNESS WHEREOF I have hereunto set my hand and official

seal.

_____
Notary Public

(NOTARIAL SEAL)   My Commission expires: _____

_____

INDIVIDUAL OR PARTNERSHIP ACKNOWLEDGMENT

STATE OF _____)
)ss.
COUNTY OF _____)

On this _____ day of _____, 19_____, before

me, _____, the undersigned officer, personally

appeared _____ to me personally known and

known to me to be the same person(s) whose name(s) is (are) signed

to the foregoing instrument, and acknowledged the execution thereof

for the uses and purposes therein set forth.

IN WITNESS WHEREOF I have hereunto set my hand and official

seal.

_____
Notary Public

(NOTARIAL SEAL)   My Commission expires: _____

Figure F-41 (continued)

UNIFORM CONSENT TO SERVICE OF PROCESS

KNOW ALL MEN BY THESE PRESENTS:

That the undersigned, _____,

(a corporation organized under the laws of the State of _____)

(a partnership) (an individual) (_____), for the
                                    (other)

purpose of complying with the laws of the State of _____

relating to the registration, exemption from registration or sale

of franchises, hereby irrevocably appoints the _____
                                               (regulatory authority)

and the successors in such office, its attorney in the State of

_____ upon whom may be served any notice, process or

pleading in any action or proceeding against it arising out of or

in connection with the sale of franchises, or out of violation of

the aforesaid laws of said State; and the undersigned does hereby

consent that any such action or proceeding against it may be

commenced in any court of competent jurisdiction and proper venue

within said State by service of process upon said officer with

the same effect as if the undersigned was organized or created

under the laws of said State and had lawfully been served with

process in said State.

It is requested that a copy of any notice, process or pleading

served hereunder be mailed to:

_____
                  (Name and Address)

_____

Dated: _____, 19 _____.

                    _____
                    By _____
                        Title _____

(SEAL)

                    _____
                    By _____
                        Title _____

Figure F-41 (continued)

509

SALESMEN DISCLOSURE FORM

1. As required by this State's statute, list the persons who will engage in the offer or sale of franchises in this state and for each person list the following information:

   A. Name;

   B. Business address and telephone number;

   C. Home address and telephone number;

   D. Present employer;

   E. Present title;

   F. Social security number;

   G. Birthdate; and

   H. Employment or occupation during the past 5 years. For each such employment state the name of the employer, position held and beginning and ending dates for each such employment.

2. State whether any person identified in 1. above:

   A. Has any administrative, civil or criminal action pending against him alleging a violation of any franchise law, fraud, embezzlement, fraudulent conversion, restraint of trade, unfair or deceptive practices, misappropriation of property or any comparable allegations?

      YES _____   NO _____

   B. Has during the 10 year period immediately preceding the date of the offering circular:

      (1) been convicted of a felony or pleaded nolo contendere to a felony charge or been held liable in a civil action by final judgment if such felony or civil action involved a violation of any franchise law, fraud, embezzlement, fraudulent conversion, restraint of trade, unfair or deceptive practices, misappropriation of property or any comparable violations of law?

         YES _____   NO _____

      (2) entered into or been named in any consent judgment, decree, order or assurance under any federal or state franchise, securities, antitrust, monopoly, trade practice, or trade regulation law?

         YES _____   NO _____

-1-

Figure F-41 (continued)

(3) been subject to any order of any national securities association or national securities exchange (as defined in the Securities and Exchange Act of 1934) suspending or expelling such person from membership in such association or exchange.

YES _____   NO _____

C. With respect to each question above answered "YES" state:

(1) the name of each person or entity involved;

(2) the court, agency, association or exchange involved;

(3) a summary of the allegations;

(4) if applicable, the date of the conviction, judgment, decree, order or assurance; and

(5) the penalty imposed, damages assessed and nature thereof, terms and conditions of the judgment, decree, order or assurance.

-2-

Figure F-41 (continued)

UNIFORM FRANCHISE REGISTRATION APPLICATION

```
┌─────────────────────────────────┐
│          FILE NO.               │
│                                 │
└─────────────────────────────────┘
```
(Insert file number of previous
filings of Applicant, if any)

FEE: _____
      (To be enclosed by
      Applicant at time
      application is initially
      filed)

Date of Application: _____

APPLICATION FOR   (Check only one):

_____   REGISTRATION OF AN OFFER OR SALE OF FRANCHISES

_____   REGISTRATION RENEWAL STATEMENT OR ANNUAL REPORT

_____   POST-EFFECTIVE ⎫ AMENDMENT NUMBER _____ TO APPLICATION

                          ⎬ FILED UNDER SECTION _____

_____   PRE-EFFECTIVE ⎭ DATED _____

1.	Name of Franchisor.
	Name under which the Franchisor is doing or intends to do business.
2.	Franchisor's principal business address.
	Name and address of Franchisor's agent in the State of (Name of State) authorized to receive process.
3.	Name, address and telephone number of subfranchisors, if any, for this state.
4.	Name, address and telephone number of person to whom communications regarding this application should be directed.

Figure F-41 (continued)

SUPPLEMENTAL INFORMATION

1. List the following:

    A. The states in which this proposed registration
        is effective.

    B. The states in which this proposed registration
        is or will be shortly on file.

    C. The states, if any, which have refused, by
        order or otherwise, to register these franchises.

    D. The states, if any, which have revoked or
        suspended the right to offer these franchises.

    E. The states, if any, in which the proposed
        registration of these franchises has been
        withdrawn.

2. With respect to all franchises sought to be registered set
    forth, in budget form, the total projected financing required
    by franchisor to fulfill the franchisor's obligations to provide
    real estate, improvements, equipment, inventory, training and
    all other items included in the offering. Show separately the
    sources of all of the required funds including any proposed
    loans or contributions to capital.

Figure F-41 (continued)

STATE OF ....

COUNTY OF ....

Before me, the undersigned authority, on this day personally appeared ....

.... who being by me duly sworn, deposes and says:

That the .... is not a trust or organization in restraint of trade, in violation of the laws of Texas; that it has not, within twelve months next preceding the date of this affidavit, entered into any combination, contract, obligation or agreement to create nor which may tend to create or to carry out any restriction in trade or commerce or aids to commerce, nor to fix, maintain, increase or reduce the price of any merchandise, produce or commodity, or any article of commerce; nor to prevent or lessen competition in the manufacture, making, transportation, sale or purchase of any merchandise, produce or commodity, or any article of commerce, or in the preparation thereof for market; nor to fix or maintain any standard or figure whereby the price of same is or has been in any manner affected, controlled or established. That it has not, during said time, entered into, executed or carried out any contract, obligation or agreement with any person, corporation or association of persons not to sell or dispose of any commodity or articles of commerce below a common standard or figure, or to keep the price thereof at a fixed or graded figures, or to preclude a fair and unrestricted competition in the sale of any commodity or articles of commerce, or to regulate, fix or limit the output thereof, or to abstain from engaging in or continuing business or from the purchase or sale of any commodity or article of commerce partially or entirely within the State of Texas or any portion thereof.

Affiant further says that the above named corporation has not within twelve months next preceding the date of this affidavit, either directly or through the instrumentality of trustees or otherwise, acquired the shares or certificates of stocks or bonds, franchises or other rights or the physical properties or any part thereof of any other corporation or corporations for the purpose of preventing or lessening or which tends to affect or lessen competition. That it has not within said time entered into any agreements or understanding to refuse to buy from or sell to any other person, corporation, firm or association of persons any commodities or articles of commerce, nor entered into any agreement to boycott or threaten to refuse to buy from or sell to any person, firm or corporation or association of persons for the buying from or selling to any other person, firm, corporation or association of persons.

Affiant further says that no officer of the above named corporation has, within his knowledge, during the said twelve months, made on behalf of it or for its benefits, any such contract or agreement as is specified in this affidavit.

....

Sworn to and subscribed before me, this the .... day of .... A. D., 19 .

....

(SEAL)   Notary Public in and for ....

NOTE—The above affidavit must be subscribed and sworn to by the president or vice-president or secretary or treasurer or two of the directors of the corporation applying for permit.

Figure F-42: ANTI-TRUST AFFIDAVIT FOR TEXAS

INSTRUCTIONS FOR MAKING APPLICATION FOR CERTIFICATE OF
AUTHORITY BY FOREIGN CORPORATION

The following instruments should be furnished this office in connection with the application of a foreign corporation for a Certificate of Authority to transact business or conduct its affairs in the State of Texas:

1. Duplicate originals of the application for a Certificate of Authority. Both copies must have genuine signatures and Notary Seals.

2. Copy of charter and all amendments and supplements thereto, duly authenticated by the Secretary of State or appropriate State official of the parent State of the corporation.

3. Remittance of the statutory filing fee in the following sum in the form of a cashier's check, certified check, cash or post money order, payable to the Secretary of State of Texas:

    (a) $500.00, if corporation is organized for profit
    (b) $ 25.00, if Non-Profit corporation

4. Remittance of a cash trust deposit for payment of franchise taxes in the amount of $500.00 by a separate certified check, cashier's check, or a post money order, payable to the Comptroller of Public Accounts, as required by Article 12.06 of Chapter 12, Title 122a, Taxation-General, Vernon's Annotated Civil Statutes.

OR

If the corporation is Non-Profit and has been granted an exemption from payment of franchise taxes, a copy of a letter granting such exemption from the Comptroller of Public Accounts.

5. Anti-trust affidavit.

A franchise tax report is due within 90 days after expiration of one year from date Certificate of Authority is granted, unless the corporation obtains an exemption from the Comptroller of Public Accounts. The corporation must file its report with the Comptroller of Public Accounts and pay the franchise tax which may be due in order to maintain its right to do business in Texas.

The attached copies of the form promulgated by the Secretary of State are for your convenience, but the form is mandatory. It is recommended that the services of an attorney licensed in Texas be obtained prior to preparation of the application for the Certificate of Authority.

NOTE: A corporation for profit must send two $500.00 checks; total: $1,000.00.

Figure F-43: APPLICATION FOR CERTIFICATE OF AUTHORITY—TEXAS

APPLICATION FOR CERTIFICATE OF AUTHORITY

Pursuant to the provisions of Article 8.05 of the Texas Business Corporation Act, the undersigned corporation hereby applies for a Certificate of Authority to transact business in Texas:

1.   The name of the corporation is_____

_____

2.   If the name of the corporation does not contain the word "corporation", "company," "incorporated," or "limited" (or an abbreviation thereof), then the name of the corporation with the word or abbreviation which it elects to add thereto for use in Texas is: (or if the corporate name is not available in Texas, then specify the assumed name which the corporation elects to use in Texas and attach Assumed Name Certificate.)

_____

3.   It is incorporated under the laws of_____

4.   The date of its incorporation is_____ and the period

of its duration is_____. (State "Perpetual" or term of years).

5.   The address of its principal office in the state or country under the laws of which it is incorporated is

_____

_____

6.   The address of its proposed registered office in Texas is (a P.O. Box is not sufficient)_____

_____

and the name of its proposed registered agent in Texas at such address is

_____

_____

7.   The purpose or purposes of the corporation which it proposes to pursue in the transaction of business in Texas are:

8.   It is authorized to pursue such purpose or purposes in the state or country under the laws of which it is incorporated.

9.   The names and respective addresses of its directors are:

NAME   ADDRESS

_____   _____

_____   _____

_____   _____

_____   _____

_____   _____

Figure F-43 (continued)

10. The names and respective addresses of its officers are:

NAME   OFFICE   ADDRESS

_____   _____   _____

_____   _____   _____

_____   _____   _____

_____   _____   _____

_____   _____   _____

11. The aggregate number of shares which it has authority to issue, itemized by classes, par value of shares, shares without par value, and series, if any, within a class, is:

NUMBER OF SHARES	CLASS	SERIES	PAR VALUE PER SHARE OR STATEMENT THAT SHARES ARE WITHOUT PAR VALUE
_____	_____	_____	_____
_____	_____	_____	_____
_____	_____	_____	_____

12. The aggregate number of its issued shares, itemized by classes, par value of shares, shares without par value, and series, if any, within a class, is:

NUMBER OF SHARES	CLASS	SERIES	PAR VALUE PER SHARE OR STATEMENT THAT SHARES ARE WITHOUT PAR VALUE
_____	_____	_____	_____
_____	_____	_____	_____

13. The amount of its stated capital is $_____.
(See Texas Business Corporation Act, Article 1.02A (11) for definition of stated capital).

14. Consideration of the value of at least One Thousand Dollars ($1,000.00) has been paid for the issuance of its shares.

15. This Application is accompanied by a copy of its articles of incorporation and all amendments thereto, duly authenticated by the proper officer of the state or country under the laws of which it is incorporated.

_____

By_____

Its _____ President

and_____

Its _____ Secretary

STATE OF_____

COUNTY OF_____

I, the undersigned, a notary public, do certify that on this _____ day of
_____, 19____, personally appeared before me_____
_____ who being duly sworn, declared that he signed the foregoing document and that the statements therein contained are true.

(Notarial Seal)

_____
Notary Public

Figure F-43 (continued)

APPLICATION FOR CERTIFICATE OF AUTHORITY
FOREIGN CORPORATION
61-22 REV. 4-66

STATE OF CONNECTICUT
SECRETARY OF THE STATE

For office use only
ACCOUNT NO

INITIALS

Must be accompanied by:

1. An appointment of an attorney upon whom process may be served, and
2. A Certificate of Good Standing authenticated by appropriate officer of the state of incorporation.

TO: The Secretary of the State of Connecticut

Date

The corporation named below hereby applies for a Certificate of Authority to do business or conduct affairs in the State of Connecticut:

NAME OF CORPORATION	STATE OF INCORPORATION	DATE OF INCORPORATION	DURATION
ADDRESS OF PRINCIPAL OFFICE IN STATE OF INCORPORATION	ADDRESS OF EXECUTIVE OFFICES		
ADDRESS OF PROPOSED PRINCIPAL OFFICE IN CONNECTICUT			

DIRECTORS AND OFFICERS

Name	Title	Residence Address

THE CHARACTER OF THE BUSINESS WHICH THE CORPORATION INTENDS TO TRANSACT, OR THE AFFAIRS IT INTENDS TO CONDUCT, IN THE STATE OF CONNECTICUT IS

DESIGNATION OF SHARES*			NUMBER OF SHARES		
Class	Series	Par	Issued and Outstanding	Treasury	Authorized

(If a nonprofit corporation) No part of the corporation's income is distributable to its members, directors, or officers.

We hereby declare, under the ~~false statement~~ penalties of perjury, that the statements made in the foregoing application are true:

NAME OF PRESIDENT OR VICE PRESIDENT *(Print or type)*	NAME OF SECRETARY OR ASSISTANT SECRETARY *(Print or type)*
SIGNED *(President or Vice President)*	SIGNED *(Secretary or Assistant Secretary)*

*If a nonstock corporation, so state under "Designation of Shares".

FILING FEE	LICENSE FEE	CERTIFICATION FEE	TOTAL FEES
$	$	$	$

SIGNED *(For Secretary of the State)*

CERTIFIED COPY SENT ON *(Date)* | INITIALS

TO

CARD	LIST	PROOF

Figure F-44: APPLICATION FOR CERTIFICATE OF AUTHORITY—CONNECTICUT

FORM CD-FCC - 15M - 2/76

Commonwealth of Massachusetts

Secretary of the Commonwealth
1 ASHBURTON PLACE, BOSTON, MASS. 02108

FOREIGN CORPORATION CERTIFICATE

We, _____ , President/Vice President

and _____ , Clerk/Assistant Clerk or

Secretary/Assistant Secretary of

_____ , in compliance with the provisions

of General Laws, Chapter 181, Section 4, certify that:

1. The exact name of the corporation, including any words or abbreviations indicating incorporation or limited liability is:

2. The corporation is organized under the laws of:

3. The date of its organization is: _____
                                    (Month)   (Day)   (Year)

4. The location of its principal office is:

5. A brief description of the activities of the corporation within the Commonwealth of Massachusetts is as follows:

6. The location of its local office in the Commonwealth of Massachusetts, if any, is:

7. The name and address of its resident agent in the Commonwealth of Massachusetts, if any, is:

8. The date on which the corporation's fiscal year ends is: _____
                                                            (Month)   (Day)

Figure F-45: FOREIGN CORPORATION CERTIFICATE—MASSACHUSETTS

9. The names and residence addresses of its directors and the following officers are as follows:

                            NAMES   RESIDENCES

President

Treasurer

Clerk or
Secretary

Board of
Directors

10. Please indicate the fees which a Massachusetts corporation would be required to pay to register to do business in your State of incorporation:

The corporation hereby appoints the Secretary of the Commonwealth of Massachusetts and his successor in office to be its attorney in and for Massachusetts, upon whom all lawful process in any judicial or administrative proceeding in Massachusetts may be served so long as any liability incurred in the Commonwealth of Massachusetts while it was doing business in said Commonwealth shall remain outstanding.

IN WITNESS WHEREOF AND UNDER THE PENALTIES OF PERJURY, we hereto sign our names this _____ day of _____ , 19 ____

_____
President, Vice President

_____
Clerk/Assistant Clerk
or
Secretary/Assistant Secretary

Figure F-45 (continued)

THE COMMONWEALTH OF MASSACHUSETTS

FOREIGN CORPORATION CERTIFICATE
(General Laws, Chapter 181, Section 4)

I hereby approve the within Certificate and, the

filing fee in the amount of $ having been paid,

said Certificate is deemed to have been filed with me this

day of   , 19

Secretary of the Commonwealth

1 ASHBURTON PLACE, BOSTON, MASS. 02108

TO BE FILLED IN BY CORPORATION

Photo Copy of Certificate to be Sent

To:

_____

_____

_____

Copy Mailed

Figure F-45 (continued)

Form C-113
Rev. 7-9-74

APPLICATION FOR

CERTIFICATE OF AUTHORITY

OF

_____

(For Use by Foreign Corporations Only)

To: The Secretary of State   "FEDERAL EMPLOYER IDENTIFICATION NO."
State of New Jersey

Pursuant to the provisions of Section 14A:13-4, Corporations, General, of the New Jersey Statutes, the undersigned corporation hereby applies for authority to transact business in New Jersey, and for that purpose submits the following:

1. The name of the corporation is _____

_____ .

2. It is incorporated under the laws of _____ .

3. The date of its incorporation is _____ .

4. The period of its duration is _____ .

5. The address* of the main business or headquarters office of the corporation

is _____ .

(*State of incorporation, including zip code)

6. The address of the registered office of the corporation in New Jersey is

_____

(Include zip code)

and the name of its registered agent at such address is _____

_____ .

Said registered agent is an agent of the corporation upon whom process against the corporation may be served.

7. The business which the corporation is to transact in New Jersey is as follows:

8. The total number of shares of capital stock of the corporation is _____ .

9. The business that the corporation proposes to transact in New Jersey is a business that it is authorized to transact in its jurisdiction of incorporation.

10. Attached to this Application is a certificate attesting to the fact that the corporation is in good standing under the laws of the jurisdiction of its incorporation, executed by the proper official thereof and dated not earlier than 30 days prior to the date of the filing of this application.

It is not necessary to have filed a REGISTRATION OF A FOREIGN CORPORA-TION before applying for the CERTIFICATE OF AUTHORITY, but if you have done so please complete the following:

11. The name of the undersigned corporation is presently registered with the Secretary of State of New Jersey. That registration was initially filed on _____

(Date)

in accordance with the provisions of Section 14A:2-4, Corporations, General, of the New Jersey Statutes. The registration was renewed on _____

(Date or dates)

in accordance with the provisions of Section 14A:2-5, Corporations, General, of the New Jersey Statutes.

Figure F-46: APPLICATION FOR CERTIFICATE OF AUTHORITY—NEW JERSEY

In Witness Whereof, the undersigned corporation has caus-

ed this Application to be executed on its behalf by

its _____ * this _____

day of _____ , 19_____ .

_____

(Corporate name)

By _____ *

(Signature)

_____

(Print or Type Name and Title)

(*May be executed by the chairman of the board, or the president or a vice-president of the corporation.)

FOR USE BY FOREIGN CORPORATIONS ONLY

Fees for filing in Office of the Secretary of State, P.O. Box 1330, Trenton, N. J. 08625.

Filing Fee $165.00

NOTE: 1.   No recording fees will be assessed.
         2.   All checks drawn Out-of-State Banks must be certified.

TRANSACTION NO.: _____

FOLDER NO.:

FILED BY:
NAME:
ADDRESS:
CITY:
ZIP:

(Foreign Corporations Only)

APPLICATION FOR
CERTIFICATE OF AUTHORITY OF

Recorder's Initials

RECORDED AND FILED:

Figure F-46—Reverse Side

Form BCA—106 or 114
(FILE IN DUPLICATE)

Date Paid
License Fee $
Franchise Tax $
Filing Fee $
Penalty $
Clerk _____

_____

APPLICATION FOR { AMENDED
ORIGINAL **CERTIFICATE OF AUTHORITY OF FOREIGN CORPORATION**
REINSTATED

_____

_____, 19 _____

To Alan J. Dixon, Secretary of State, Springfield, Illinois:

_____ _____, a corporation organized

and existing under and by virtue of the laws of the State of _____hereby makes

application for a _____ certificate of authority to transact business in the State of Illinois and submits the following application pursuant to "The Business Corporation Act, " of Illinois:

First — The above corporation was duly incorporated under the laws of the State of _____

on the _____day of _____, A.D. 19 _____,

for a _____ duration.

Second — The location of the principal office as designated in the charter is _____

The locations of its principal places of business are:_____

_____

Third — The address of the proposed registered office of the State of Illinois will be located at

_____street in the city of _____

(_____), County of _____ , and the **name** of its **proposed register-**
(ZIP CODE)

ed agent in this State at such address is: _____

Fourth — The corporation is transacting business and qualified under the foreign corporation laws of the following states and countries other than Illinois:

Fifth — The names of its officers and directors and their addresses are as follows:

NAME	CITY and STATE	STREET and NUMBER
President		
Secretary		
Director		
Director		
Director		
Director		
Director		
Director		

Figure F-47: APPLICATION FOR CERTIFICATE OF AUTHORITY—ILLINOIS

Seventh—The number of shares which it has **authority to issue**, itemized by classes, par value of shares, shares without par value, and series, if any, within a class, is:

Class	Series (if any)	Number of Shares	Par value per share or statement that shares are without par value

Eighth—The number of its **issued shares**, itemized by classes, par value of shares, shares without par value, and series, if any, within a class, is:

Class	Series (if any)	Number of Shares	Par value per share or statement that shares are without par value

(NOTE: "Issued" shares, as used above, include (1) "outstanding" shares, and (2) all shares which have been issued and repurchased or redeemed by the corporation, but not cancelled of record in the home State.)

Ninth—The amount of stated capital and the amount of paid in surplus of the corporation as defined by "The Business Corporation Act" of Illinois, is:

Stated Capital $_____

(Note: If no Paid in Surplus, insert "None") Paid in Surplus $_____

Total $_____

Omit Articles Tenth through Fourteenth if an amended or reinstated application

*Tenth—Give an estimate of the total value of all the property of the corporation for the following year $_____

Eleventh—Give an estimate of the total value of all the property of the corporation for the following year that will be located in Illinois $_____

Twelfth—State the estimated total business of the corporation to be transacted by it everywhere for the following year $_____

Thirteenth—State the estimated annual business of the corporation to be transacted by it at or from places of business in the State of Illinois $_____

Fourteenth—
INTERROGATORIES:

(a) Is the corporation actually transacting business at the present time in the State where it was organized?

(b) From what office will the affairs of the corporation be managed?

(c) To what office or offices will all contracts with the corporation be forwarded for final acceptance?

(d) At what office or offices will the directors and stockholders meeting be held?

(e) The number of shares of all classes owned by residents of Illinois is:

(f) The number of shares of all classes owned by non-residents of Illinois is:

(g) Is the corporation transacting business in this State at this time?

(h) If your answer is in the affirmative, state the exact date on which it commenced to transact business in Illinois:

*PROPERTY as used in this application shall apply to all property of the corporation, real, personal, tangible, intangible, or mixed without qualification.

Figure F-47 (continued)

IN WITNESS WHEREOF, the undersigned corporation has caused this report to be executed in its name by its _____ President attested by its _____ Secretary, this _____ day of _____, A.D. 19____.

_____
(Exact Corporate Title)

Place
(Corporate Seal)
Here

By _____
President or Vice President

Attest:

_____
Secretary or Assistant Secretary

STATE OF _____

COUNTY OF _____ } ss.

I, _____, a Notary Public, do hereby certify that on the _____ day of _____, A.D. 19 ____, personally appeared before me _____, who declares that he is _____ President of the corporation, executing the foregoing document, and being first duly sworn, acknowledged that he signed the foregoing document in the capacity therein set forth and declared that the statements therein contained are true.

IN WITNESS WHEREOF, I have hereunto set my hand and seal the day and year before written.

Place
(Notarial Seal)
Here

_____
Notary Public

Form BCA–106 or 114

Box _____ File _____

APPLICATION FOR CERTIFICATE OF AUTHORITY OF FOREIGN CORPORATION

SECRETARY OF STATE CORPORATION DEPARTMENT TELEPHONE (217) 782-7880

NOTE: This form may be used in applying for either an original, an amended, or a reinstated certificate of authority. APPLICATIONS MUST BE ACCOMPANIED BY ONE COPY OF THE ARTICLES OF INCORPORATION AND ALL AMENDMENTS DULY AUTHENTICATED BY THE PROPER OFFICER OF THE STATE OR COUNTY WHEREIN IT IS INCORPORATED.

(File in Duplicate)

NEW APPLICATION
Filing Fee $75.00 plus license fee and franchise tax.

AMENDED APPLICATION
Filing Fee $25.00

REINSTATED APPLICATION
Filing Fee $100.00

Form BCA–106 or 114
Page 5   (05511—20M—3-78)

Figure F-47 (continued)

OFFICE OF THE SECRETARY OF STATE

APPLICATION FOR CERTIFICATE OF AUTHORITY OF FOREIGN CORPORATION

1. .... , a corporation,
(Use correct and complete corporate name)

hereby makes application for a .... certificate of authority to transact business in the State
of Wisconsin.   (Note E)

2. The corporation was incorporated under the laws of ....

on the .... day of .... , 19 ...., and is in good standing in its home state.

Duration of existence is ....

3. The address of its principal office in the state of incorporation is ....

....

4. The address of the proposed registered office in Wisconsin will be ....

.... street in the city of .... ,

Wisconsin .... , and the *name* of its *proposed registered agent in this State at such address is:*
              ZIP Code

....
(Note F)

5. The corporation is admitted or qualified to transact business in the following states, territories and countries:

6. Of the purposes authorized by its articles of incorporation, the corporation will NOT pursue the following in Wisconsin: (Note C)

7. Names and respective addresses of directors and principal officers:

TITLE	NAME	ADDRESS (Give street & number, City, State and ZIP code)
President	....	....
Vice Presidents ..	....	....
Secretary	....	....
Treasurer	....	....
Directors........	....	....
All directors must be shown	....	....
	....	....
	....	....
	....	....

8. The number of shares which it has *authority to issue,* itemized by classes, par value of shares, shares without par value, and series, if any, within a class, is:

Class	Series (if any)	Number of Shares	Par value per share or statement that shares are without par value

9. The number of its *issued shares,* itemized by classes, par value of shares, shares without par value, and series, if any, within a class, is:

Class	Series (if any)	Number of Shares	Par value per share or statement that shares are without par value

Figure F-48: APPLICATION FOR CERTIFICATE OF AUTHORITY—WISCONSIN

USE THE FOLLOWING ITEMS to compute the proportion of capital the corporation expects to have represented in Wisconsin in the coming year, using either calendar or fiscal year basis.

(Note: Start by entering items 10 (a) through 10 (g). Continue, and in sequence, first complete item 11, and next item 12, as each or both may be necessary, and post the resulting computations to the appropriate areas in item 10. Corporations having both Par Value and No Par Value shares issued will utilize both item 11 and item 12.)

		ESTIMATED	
10.	(a) Gross Business	$	
	(b) Plus Total Assets	$	
	(c) Total of line (a) and line (b)		$
	(d) Wisconsin Business	$	
	(e) Plus Wisconsin Assets	$	
	(f) Total of line (d) and line (e)		$

10. (g) Divide line (f) by line (c) and enter percentage .... %

(h)	Value of issued shares of PAR VALUE stock (From item 11(c))	$	
(i)	Value of issued shares of NO PAR VALUE stock (From item 12(g))	$	
(j)	Total of line (h) and line (i)		$
(k)	Multiply line (j) by line (g) and enter product	$	} ENTER THIS SUM IN ITEM 13

11. USE FOR PAR VALUE STOCK (Use this section to compute valuation of Par Value stock only)

(a)	Value of issued shares of Par Value stock, at Par	$	
(b)	Paid-in capital, in excess of Par, applicable to issued shares of Par Value stock	$	
(c)	Total of line (a) and line (b). Also enter this sum in item 10(h) above		$

12. USE FOR NO PAR VALUE STOCK (Use this section to compute valuation of No Par Value stock only)

(a)	Total Assets	$	
(b)	Deduct liabilities other than capital and surplus	$	
(c)	Total of line (a) minus line (b)		$
(d)	Deduct amount of line 10(h) above		$
(e)	Remainder of line (c) minus line (d)		$
(f)	Compute value of issued shares of No Par Value stock at $10 per share		$
(g)	Enter the greater of line (e) or line (f) here. Also enter this sum in line 10(i) above.		$

13. Proportion of paid-in capital represented in the State of Wisconsin, by its property located or to be acquired therein and by its business to be transacted therein, is $ .... (From item 10 (k). See Note D for fee information)

14. Has the corporation transacted business or acquired property in Wisconsin without holding a certificate of authority?

....
Yes or No

IN WITNESS WHEREOF, the undersigned corporation has caused this application to be executed in its name by its ....

.... President attested by its .... Secretary, this .... day of .... , A.D. 19.......

Place
Corporate Seal
Here

....
(Exact Corporate Title)

By ....
President

Attest:

....
Secretary

SEE REVERSE SIDE FOR INSTRUCTIONS AND SUGGESTIONS

Figure F-48 (continued)

APPLICATION OF FOREIGN CORPORATION FOR A CERTIFICATE OF AUTHORITY TO TRANSACT BUSINESS IN MINNESOTA

TO THE SECRETARY OF STATE,
State of Minnesota, St. Paul, Minn.

...., a corporation incorporated and

existing under the laws of the State of..., in compliance with Section 303.06

of the Minnesota Foreign Corporation Act, does hereby certify and set forth with respect to said

corporation:

(1) Its name is..and the (state)

(country) of organization is..

(2) It agrees to add..to its name for use in the State of

Minnesota so that the name of this corporation which it will use in the State of Minnesota is..............

.... (See instructions below.)

(3) The date of its incorporation was............................., 1........, and the period of its duration

is..

(4) The address of its principal office in the state or country of organization is..............................

.... (See instructions below.)

(5) The address of its proposed registered office in the State of Minnesota is..............................

.... (See instructions below); and the name of its

proposed resident agent in the State of Minnesota is..

whose address is identical with that of its proposed registered office above set forth.

(6) It irrevocably consents to service of process upon it as set forth in section 303.13 of the Minnesota
Foreign Corporation Act or any amendment thereto.

(7) The names and respective addresses of its officers and directors are as follows:

NAME	ADDRESS (See instructions below)	OFFICE

Figure F-49: APPLICATION OF FOREIGN CORPORATION TO TRANSACT BUSINESS IN MINNESOTA

(8) Its authorized aggregate number of shares having par value is..

of the par value of $........................per share and its authorized aggregate number of shares with-

out par value is.., which authorized shares are itemized by classes and
series as follows:

_____

_____

_____

_____

_____

_____

_____

(9) The issued or allotted aggregate number of its par value shares is..

of the par value of $........................per share and the issued or allotted aggregate number of its

shares without par value is.., which shares are itemized by classes and
series as follows:

_____

_____

_____

_____

_____

_____

_____

(10) The officers executing this application for a certificate of authority to transact business in the
State of Minnesota have been duly authorized so to do by its Board of Directors.
    IN WITNESS WHEREOF, Said corporation has caused this application to be executed by its........

President and its........................Secretary and its corporate seal to be hereunto affixed this

........................day of........................, A. D. 19........

AFFIX   _____

CORPORATE   _____, _____President.

SEAL   _____, _____Secretary.

STATE OF........................

County of........................   } ss.

    On this........................day of........................, A. D. 19........, before me personally appeared

_____ and _____,

to me personally known, who, being by me duly sworn, did say that they are respectively the........

President and........................Secretary of........................
that the seal affixed to the foregoing instrument is the corporate seal of said corporation, and that said
instrument was executed in behalf of said corporation by authority of its Board of Directors; that
they have read the foregoing application subscribed by them and know the contents thereof, and that

the same is true of their own knowledge; and said..

and ....acknowledged said instrument to be the free act and
deed of said corporation.

AFFIX   _____

NOTARIAL   Notary Public,........................County,

SEAL   State of........................

                             My commission expires........................

Figure F-49 (continued)

INSTRUCTIONS

Submit with this application, a copy of the articles of incorporation and amendments thereto, if any, with a certification by the proper officer of the state under the laws of which the corporation is organized.

Item (2)—If the name of the corporation ends with the word "Corporation" or the word "Incorporated" or the abbreviation "Inc." or contains the word "Company" or the abbreviation "Co." not immediately preceded by the word "and" or the character "&", this item may be disregarded by the applicant corporation; otherwise, the first blank in Item (2) must be filled in with the word "Incorporated" or the abbreviation "Inc." and the second blank must be filled in with the name of the applicant corporation with the added word or abbreviation which it agrees to use in the State of Minnesota. See Section 303.06, Subdivision 1 (2) of Minnesota Foreign Corporation Act.

Items (4), (5) and (7)—The addresses given must include the name of the post office, street and number, if any, or name of building and room or office number therein when customarily used as part of a mailing address.

Fees—Initial License Fee $125.00 (Sec. 303.07).

For filing application and issuing certificate $19.00 (Sec. 303.21 Subd. 2 (a).)

For remittance with certificate of authority to the county recorder of county of registered office in Minnesota $3.00 (Sec. 303.21, Subd. 1)—of Minnesota Foreign Corporation Act, Chapter 303 Minnesota Statutes.

Total fee $147.00

FOR RECORD BY THE SECRETARY OF STATE OF THE STATE OF MINNESOTA.

All fees and charges paid on..

Certificate issued and recorded, No. ....

Certificate transmitted with fee of $3.00 to county recorder,..

County, on..

....Clerk.

FOREIGN   CORPORATION

FILE NUMBER.................

Figure F-49 (continued)

Use White Paper—Size 8½ x 11 Inches—for Inserts

Filing Requirements—Present 2 Originally Executed
    Copies to Secretary of State.

Recording Requirements—None.

Other Requirements — a duly authenticated copy of the
Articles of Incorporation with all amendments thereto, as certified by the proper officer in the state wherein the Corporation is domiciled, must be submitted with and
accompany the Application.

Corporate Form No. 112 (July 1977)—Page One
APPLICATION FOR ADMISSION
Prescribed by the Secretary of State of Indiana

APPLICATION FOR ADMISSION

OF

_____ ,

A FOREIGN CORPORATION,
TO DO BUSINESS IN THE STATE OF INDIANA

The undersigned officers of the above _____ (State of domicile) corporation
(hereinafter referred to as the "Corporation"), which exists pursuant to the provisions of _____
_____ (statute pursuant to which the corporation exists),
as amended, desiring to effectuate the admittance of the Corporation to do business in the State of Indiana, certify
the following facts:

ARTICLE I
NAME

The name of the Corporation is:

_____

ARTICLE II
PRINCIPAL OFFICE

The location of its principal office or place of business outside the State of Indiana is _____
_____ ,

and the location of its proposed principal office or place of business in Indiana is _____
_____

(cf. Article XII).

Corporate Form No. 112 (July 1977)—Page Two

ARTICLE III
ADMISSION IN OTHER STATES

The Corporation has been admitted or is qualified to do business in the following states:

ARTICLE IV
CHARACTER OF BUSINESS

The character of business which the Corporation intends to carry on in Indiana is as follows:

Figure F-50: APPLICATION FOR ADMISSION TO DO BUSINESS IN INDIANA

ARTICLE V
AUTHORIZED SHARES

The Corporation is authorized to issue and has issued the following number of shares, respectively:

.... shares of .... without par value, of which ....
shares are presently issued and outstanding;

.... shares of .... with a par value of $ .... per share,
of which .... shares are presently issued and outstanding.

ARTICLE VI
STATEMENT OF TOTAL BUSINESS

Section 1. Fiscal Year. The fiscal year of the Corporation is from ....
to ...., both inclusive.

Section 2. Last Fiscal Year. The total amount of business transacted by the Corporation during its last complete fiscal year was $ ....

Section 3. Current Fiscal Year. The total amount of business to be transacted by the Corporation during its current fiscal year is estimated at approximately $ ....

Section 4. Next Fiscal Year. The total amount of business to be transacted by the Corporation during its next succeeding fiscal year is estimated at approximately $ ....

ARTICLE VII
STATEMENT OF INDIANA BUSINESS

The amount of business to be transacted by the Corporation at or from places of business in Indiana during the next succeeding fiscal years is estimated at approximately $ ....

Corporate Form No. 112 (July 1977)—Page Five

ARTICLE VIII
STATEMENT OF TOTAL TANGIBLE PROPERTY

Section 1. Last Fiscal Year. The total amount of tangible property employed by the Corporation during its last complete fiscal year was approximately $ ....

Section 2. Current Fiscal Year. The total amount of tangible property to be employed by the Corporation during its current fiscal year is estimated at approximately $ ....

Section 3. Next Fiscal Year. The total amount of tangible property to be employed by the Corporation during its next succeeding fiscal year is estimated at approximately $ ....

ARTICLE IX
STATEMENT OF INDIANA TANGIBLE PROPERTY

The amount of tangible property to be employed by the Corporation in the State of Indiana during its next succeeding fiscal year is estimated at approximately $ ....

ARTICLE X
CORPORATE OFFICERS

The names and post-office addresses of the officers of the Corporation are as follows:

Name	Office Held	Post-Office Address (Number, Street, and City)	State (and Zip Code)

Figure F-50 (continued)

ARTICLE XI
BOARD OF DIRECTORS

The names and post-office addresses of the Board of Directors of the Corporation are as follows:

Name	Post-Office Address	State
	(Number, Street, and City)	(and Zip Code)

ARTICLE XII
RESIDENT AGENT

The Resident Agent of the Corporation on whom service of legal process may be had in Indiana is

....
(Name)

and such agent's address is the same as the address of the principal office or place of business of the Corporation in Indiana, as given in Article II.

(Note: The Act requires that all corporations designate an individual or corporation resident in Indiana as Resident Agent; the Secretary of State may not be appointed as Resident Agent.)

Corporate Form No. 112 (July 1977)—Page Six

ARTICLE XIII
"INDIANA SHARES" FORMULA

Section 1. Calculation of Shares Represented in Indiana. The following calculation establishes the number of shares of the Corporation that will be represented in Indiana during the next succeeding fiscal year:

Clause (a) Insert figure from Article VII .... $_____

Clause (b) Insert figure from Article IX .... $_____

Clause (c) Add Clauses (a) and (b) .... $_____

Clause (d) Insert figure from Article VI, Section 4 .... $_____

Clause (e) Insert figure from Article VIII, Section 3 .... $_____

Clause (f) Add Clauses (d) and (e) .... $_____

Clause (g) Divide Clause (c) by Clause (f) .... _____

Clause (h) Set forth the number of authorized
shares of all classes presently issued
and outstanding from Article V .... _____

Clause (i) Multiply Clause (h) by Clause (g).
(Number of shares of the Corporation that will
be represented in Indiana during the next
succeeding fiscal year.) .... _____

Clause (j) Credit claimed as result of merger with
Indiana or previously qualified foreign
corporation (see Article XIV) — may
not exceed figure from Clause (i) .... _____

*Note—Special Instructions:
The purpose of Article XIII is to compute "Indiana Shares," as defined in IC 23-3-2-1(f) et sec., and thus determine the amount of fee due. It is imperative that this Section be fully completed.

Filing Fee Schedule

First 1,000 "Indiana Shares" or less .... (minimum fee) $30.00*

1,001 through 200,00 "Indiana Shares" .... 2¢ per share*

200,001 through 1,000,000 "Indiana Shares" .... 1¢ per shares*

Additional shares over 1,000,000 "Indiana Shares" .... 0.2¢ per share*

*Plus $6.00 Certificate of Admission fee

Figure F-50 (continued)

535

ARTICLES XIV
"INDIANA SHARES" CREDIT

Pursuant to IC 23-3-2-2(e) (as amended by Indiana Acts 1977, P.L. 76), foreign corporations which are the survivors of mergers or consolidations with Indiana corporations, or foreign corporations qualified to transact business in Indiana at the time of such merger or consolidation, may claim a credit for the aggregate of all shares of stock authorized the merging Indiana corporations and all "Indiana shares" paid by the merging foreign corporation(s) at the time of such merger or consolidation, provided that this Application for Admission is filed with the Secretary of State within thirty (30) calendar days of the filing of the Articles of Merger or Consolidation with the Secretary of State. This procedure does not operate to increase the presently qualifying corporation's "Indiana shares", per se, for future calculation in filing annual reports, but merely allows a credit for the shares previously paid by Indiana and foreign corporation parties to a merger into or consolidation with such corporation.

Section 1. Date of filing Articles of Merger or Consolidation _____
with the Secretary of State:

Section 2. Indiana or qualified foreign corporation parties to merger or consolidation:

Corporate Title	State of Domicile	Authorized Shares or "Indiana shares" paid
_____	_____	_____
_____	_____	_____
_____	_____	_____
_____	_____	_____
_____	_____	_____

Section 3. Total "Indiana Shares" Credit claimed
(aggregate of all authorized shares and "Indiana
shares" from Section 2.) . . . . _____ *

*NOTE: In transposing to Article XIII, Clause (j), this figure may not be greater than the figure reflected in Clause (i).

IN WITNESS WHEREOF, the undersigned officers of _____
execute this Application for Admission, and certify to the truth of the facts herein stated, this _____ day
of _____, 19____.

_____	_____
(Written Signature)	(Written Signature)
_____	_____
(Printed Name)	(Printed Name)
President or Vice-President	Secretary or Assistant Secretary

STATE OF _____)
) SS:
COUNTY OF _____)

I, the undersigned, a Notary Public duly commissioned to take acknowledgements and administer oaths in the State of _____, and the County of _____, certify that the abovesigned, respectively the _____ President and _____ Secretary of _____ personally appeared before me, acknowledged the execution of the foregoing Application for Admission, and swore or attested to the truth of the facts therein stated.

WITNESS my hand and Notarial Seal this _____ day of _____, 19____.

_____
(Written Signature)

_____
(Printed Name)

My Notarial Commission Expires: _____

Figure F-50 (continued)

C-200   Prescribed by
         ANTHONY J. CELEBREZZE, JR.
         Secretary of State   Approved by _____
FOREIGN CORPORATION — FOR PROFIT   Date _____
                                                     Fee _____

APPLICATION FOR LICENSE

TO THE SECRETARY OF STATE, COLUMBUS, OHIO

                                                     The Applicant, a foreign corporation
desiring to transact business in Ohio, pursuant to the provisions of Sections 1703.01 et seq., Revised Code of Ohio,
does hereby certify as follows:

*FIRST.   Its corporate name is _____

SECOND.   It is a corporation organized under the laws of _____

THIRD.   The complete address of its principal office is _____

               _____

FOURTH.   The name of the county and city, village or township in which the principal office within
               this State is to be located is _____

               _____

FIFTH.   It hereby constitutes and appoints _____ a
               resident of Ohio as its agent upon whom service of process may be had in the State of Ohio.
               The complete residence address of such person is _____

               _____

SIXTH.   It hereby consents irrevocably to the service of process on such person and his successors as
               long as the authority of such agents shall continue as provided by the Ohio Foreign
               Corporation Act, and to service of process on the Secretary of State in the event such person
               or persons cannot be found or in any of the other events whereby such service is authorized
               by the Ohio Foreign Corporation Act.

**SEVENTH.   The following is a brief summary of the corporate purposes to be exercised within Ohio:

               _____

               _____

               _____

               _____

               _____

               _____

EIGHTH.   The corporation has, has not *(strike out words not applicable)* had a prior license to transact
               business within the State of Ohio, issued on _____, 19_____ under
               # _____ .

NINTH.   This application is made, is not made *(strike out words not applicable)* to enable the
               corporation to prosecute or defend an action or suit the cause of which arose prior to this
               application.

Figure F-51: APPLICATION FOR LICENSE IN OHIO

TENTH.   The approximate date upon which the corporation began transacting business in Ohio is
_____

ELEVENTH.   The application is made to secure a temporary, permanent *(strike out word not applicable)* license.

TWELFTH.   THERE IS HEREWITH SUBMITTED A Certificate of Good Standing or subsistence, under the seal of the Secretary of State, or other proper official of the State under the laws of which the applicant is organized, dated not earlier than sixty days prior to the filing of this application, setting forth; (1) The exact Corporate Title; (2) The date of incorporation; (3) That the Corporation is in good standing or is a subsisting corporation.

THIRTEENTH.   The corporation has currently authorized a total of _____ shares and has _____ shares currently issued.

IN WITNESS WHEREOF, said _____ has caused this application to be executed by an executive officer duly authorized in the premises, this _____ day of _____, 19_____.

STATE OF _____
                                                                ss.
COUNTY OF _____

_____, being duly sworn, says that he is _____
                                                                                                    (Title)
_____ of the applicant and that the foregoing statements are true and correct according to his best knowledge and belief.

Sworn to before me and subscribed in my presence this _____ day of _____ ,
19____.

NOTARY PUBLIC _____

*If the name of the corporation is not available in Ohio and the corporation is unable to obtain consent to its use, it must insert the Trade Name under which it will do business in this State and must attach to this application a resolution of its board of directors, certified by its secretary or assistant secretary, stating that the corporation will transact business in this State only under the assumed name.

**The purpose(s) may not include any activity that could not be lawfully transacted by a domestic corporation. If the purpose is to carry on the practice of a profession, each shareholder must be licensed to practice that profession in this State.
(77 OAG 18)

Figure F-51 (continued)

Secretary of State

STATE OF FLORIDA
THE CAPITOL
TALLAHASSEE 32304

GEORGE FIRESTONE
SECRETARY OF STATE

D. W. McKINNON, DIRECTOR
DIVISION OF CORPORATIONS

The following requirements must be complied with to qualify:

1. A recent certified copy (WITHIN THE PAST 9 MONTHS) of your Articles of Incorporation and any amendments is required. The copy must be certified by the proper state official who has custody of the records pertaining to corporations in your state.

2. The certified copy must be a **positive copy** black print on white background and **completely legible** for microfilming.

3. Application for Authorization to Transact Business (CHA. 104) must be completed in its entirety.

4. Charter tax is determined by the number of authorized shares and their par value (if no par value shares, it is computed by number of shares only) represented in Florida (see 11 A-H of Application).

5. Schedule of fees is included to aid you in computation of charter tax.

6. Fees for qualification are:
   $30.00 **MINIMUM** charter tax
   $15.00 filing fee
   $ 3.00 registered agent.

7. Forward one check in the total amount—made payable to the Secretary of State.

Permits are no longer required to be issued upon qualification. You may request a certificate under seal for an additional $5.00.

Any further inquiries on this matter should be directed to the Division of Corporations at the above address or by calling (904) 488-9840.

FLORIDA — STATE OF THE ARTS

CHA. 104(a) REV 1/79

Figure F-52: APPLICATION FOR AUTHORIZATION TO TRANSACT BUSINESS IN FLORIDA

APPLICATION BY FOREIGN CORPORATION FOR AUTHORIZATION TO TRANSACT BUSINESS IN FLORIDA

1). _____
(NAME OF CORPORATION ADDING THE WORD "INCORPORATED", "COMPANY" OR "CORPORATION" IF NOT SO CONTAINED IN THE NAME AT PRESENT)

2). _____
(INCORPORATED UNDER LAWS OF)

3). _____ 4). _____
(DATE OF INCORPORATION)   (PERIOD OF DURATION)

5). _____
(ADDRESS OF PRINCIPAL OFFICE)

6). _____
(NAME OF FLORIDA REGISTERED AGENT)

_____
(STREET ADDRESS OF REGISTERED OFFICE)

_____
                                        FLORIDA
(CITY)   (ZIP CODE)

7). _____
(NATURE OF BUSINESS TO BE TRANSACTED IN FLORIDA)

8).   NAMES OF OFFICERS   SPECIFIC ADDRESS

_____ (P) _____

_____ (V) _____

_____ (S) _____

_____ (T) _____

        NAMES OF DIRECTORS   SPECIFIC ADDRESS

_____ (D) _____

_____ (D) _____

_____ (D) _____

_____ (D) _____

9). Acceptance by the Registered Agent: _____
                                        AGENT MUST SIGN ON THIS LINE

FLORIDA — STATE OF THE ARTS

(OVER)

Figure F-52 (continued)

10).

_____
(TOTAL AUTHORIZED SHARES (ITEMIZED BY CLASSES), PAR VALUE OF SHARES, AND SHARES
WITHOUT PAR VALUE).

_____

11). "VALUE" MAY BE DEFINED IN ANY TERMS CONSISTENT WITH GENERALLY
      ACCEPTED ACCOUNTING PRINCIPLES.

      A. ESTIMATED VALUE OF ALL PROPERTY OWNED BY THE
          CORPORATION FOR THE COMING YEAR, WHEREVER LOCATED $_____

      B. ESTIMATED GROSS AMOUNT OF BUSINESS TO BE TRANSACTED
          BY THE CORPORATION DURING THE COMING YEAR. $_____

      C. ESTIMATED VALUE OF ALL PROPERTY IN FLORIDA OWNED BY
          THE CORPORATION FOR THE COMING YEAR. $_____

      D. ESTIMATED GROSS AMOUNT OF BUSINESS TO BE TRANSACTED
          IN FLORIDA BY THE CORPORATION DURING THE COMING YEAR. $_____

      E. TOTAL OF "A" and "B". $_____

      F. TOTAL OF "C" and "D". $_____

      G. DIVIDE "F" by "E".   _____

      H. MULTIPLY "G" by TOTAL AUTHORIZED SHARES
          (AND THEIR PAR VALUE).   _____

      THE FLORIDA ALLOCATION FOR PURPOSES OF DETERMINING THE
      TAX ON AUTHORIZED CAPITAL STOCK WILL BE BASED ON THE TOTAL
      VALUE OF SHARES CALCULATED IN "H" ABOVE.

      _____   _____
      SECRETARY or ASSISTANT SECRETARY   PRESIDENT or VICE PRESIDENT

STATE OF
COUNTY OF

          THE FOREGOING INSTRUMENT WAS ACKNOWLEDGED BEFORE ME THIS _____ DAY

OF _____, 19 _____, BY _____
                                                      (NAME OF OFFICER)

_____ OF _____
        (TITLE OF OFFICER)   (NAME OF CORPORATION)

A _____ CORPORATION, ON BEHALF OF THE CORPORATION.
         (STATE OR COUNTRY)

(SEAL)   _____
                                                       NOTARY PUBLIC
       CHA. 104
       05/19/76

Figure F-52 (continued)

APPLICATION BY FOREIGN CORPORATION FOR AUTHORIZATION TO TRANSACT BUSINESS IN FLORIDA

1). _____

(NAME OF CORPORATION ADDING THE WORD "INCORPORATED", "COMPANY" OR "CORPORATION" IF NOT SO CONTAINED IN THE NAME AT PRESENT)

2). _____

(INCORPORATED UNDER LAWS OF)

3). _____ 4). _____

(DATE OF INCORPORATION)   (PERIOD OF DURATION)

5). _____

(ADDRESS OF PRINCIPAL OFFICE)

6). _____

(NAME OF FLORIDA REGISTERED AGENT)

_____

(STREET ADDRESS OF REGISTERED OFFICE)

_____FLORIDA_____

(CITY)   (ZIP CODE)

7). _____

(NATURE OF BUSINESS TO BE TRANSACTED IN FLORIDA)

8).   NAMES OF OFFICERS   SPECIFIC ADDRESS
    _____

    _____ (P) _____

    _____ (V) _____

    _____ (S) _____

    _____ (T) _____

       NAMES OF DIRECTORS   SPECIFIC ADDRESS
    _____

    _____ (D) _____

    _____ (D) _____

    _____ (D) _____

    _____ (D) _____

9). Acceptance by the Registered Agent: _____

                              AGENT MUST SIGN ON THIS LINE

FLORIDA — STATE OF THE ARTS

(OVER)

Figure F-52 (continued)

10).

_____
(TOTAL AUTHORIZED SHARES (ITEMIZED BY CLASSES), PAR VALUE OF SHARES, AND SHARES
WITHOUT PAR VALUE).

_____

11). "VALUE" MAY BE DEFINED IN ANY TERMS CONSISTENT WITH GENERALLY
ACCEPTED ACCOUNTING PRINCIPLES.

A.   ESTIMATED VALUE OF ALL PROPERTY OWNED BY THE
     CORPORATION FOR THE COMING YEAR, WHEREVER LOCATED $_____

B.   ESTIMATED GROSS AMOUNT OF BUSINESS TO BE TRANSACTED
     BY THE CORPORATION DURING THE COMING YEAR. $_____

C.   ESTIMATED VALUE OF ALL PROPERTY IN FLORIDA OWNED BY
     THE CORPORATION FOR THE COMING YEAR. $_____

D.   ESTIMATED GROSS AMOUNT OF BUSINESS TO BE TRANSACTED
     IN FLORIDA BY THE CORPORATION DURING THE COMING YEAR. $_____

E.   TOTAL OF "A" and "B". $_____

F.   TOTAL OF "C" and "D". $_____

G.   DIVIDE "F" by "E".   _____

H.   MULTIPLY "G" by TOTAL AUTHORIZED SHARES
     (AND THEIR PAR VALUE).   _____

THE FLORIDA ALLOCATION FOR PURPOSES OF DETERMINING THE
TAX ON AUTHORIZED CAPITAL STOCK WILL BE BASED ON THE TOTAL
VALUE OF SHARES CALCULATED IN "H" ABOVE.

_____   _____
SECRETARY or ASSISTANT SECRETARY   PRESIDENT or VICE PRESIDENT

STATE OF
COUNTY OF

          THE FOREGOING INSTRUMENT WAS ACKNOWLEDGED BEFORE ME THIS _____ DAY

OF _____, 19 _____, BY _____
                                        (NAME OF OFFICER)

_____ OF _____
   (TITLE OF OFFICER)   (NAME OF CORPORATION)

A _____ CORPORATION, ON BEHALF OF THE CORPORATION.
   (STATE OR COUNTRY)

(SEAL)
                                    _____
                                         NOTARY PUBLIC

CHA. 104
05/19/76

Figure F-52 (continued)

Office of the Secretary of State	1230 J Street	**CORPORATE DIVISION**	

Office of the Secretary of State

March Fong Eu

1230 J Street

Sacramento, California 95814

Requirements for Qualification of Foreign Corporations

To qualify for the transaction of intrastate business in the State of California a corporation organized under the laws of another state or country must file in the office of the Secretary of State of the State of California a signed statement setting forth the information prescribed by Section 2105, California Corporations Code, together with the designation of an agent for the service of process. A Statement and Designation form for compliance with these requirements is enclosed or may be obtained from the office of the Secretary of State.

Annexed to the Statement and Designation shall be a certificate by an authorized public official of the state or place of incorporation, to the effect that the corporation is an existing corporation in good standing in that state or place. IF A NONPROFIT CORPORATION IS TO BE QUALIFIED, the certificate must also indicate that the corporation is a nonstock, nonprofit corporation.

Upon the filing of such Statement and Designation, a Certificate of Qualification will be issued to the corporation.

The foregoing is applicable to both profit and nonprofit corporations.

Fees Are As Follows:

(a) STOCK or PROFIT CORPORATION: Filing of Statement; issuing Certificate of Qualification and Filing

Designation of Agent for Service of Process $350.00

Plus prepaid Franchise Tax 200.00

TOTAL $550.00

(b) NONPROFIT, NONSTOCK CORPORATION: Filing of Statement; issuing Certificate of Qualification;

and filing Designation of Agent for Service of Process . . . . $ 15.00

Plus prepaid Franchise Tax *(unless exemption granted)* 200.00

TOTAL $215.00

All foreign corporations doing business in California, other than those wholly exempted as hereinafter mentioned, are required to file tax returns annually and to pay a franchise tax on net taxable income derived from business done in California. The basic tax is $200.00 per year or 9 percent of the net taxable income, whichever is greater. Tax return forms, as well as more complete instructions, may be obtained from the Franchise Tax Board, Sacramento, California 95857.

THE FIRST ANNUAL MINIMUM FRANCHISE TAX OF $200 MUST BE PREPAID at the time of qualification (unless exemption therefrom be granted as hereinafter mentioned) and should be by check or money order REMITTED THROUGH THIS OFFICE at the time of qualification.

TAX EXEMPTION: If the corporation is a nonprofit corporation of one of the types enumerated in Article 1 of Chapter 4 of the Bank and Corporation Franchise Tax Law (See application form FTB 3500 accompanying these instructions) the accompanying tax exemption application, along with the required $10.00 application fee, may be submitted with the qualification papers in lieu of the minimum tax prepayment, but qualification will not be completed until the tax has been prepaid or exemption therefrom expressly granted by the Franchise Tax Board.

SEC/STATE Form LL-12

Figure F-53: STATEMENT AND DESIGNATION BY FOREIGN CORPORATIONS—CALIFORNIA

Statement and Designation

by

Foreign Corporation

_____

_____ ,

(Name of Corporation)

a corporation organized and existing under the laws of _____ ,

(Place or State of incorporation)

makes the following statements and designation:

1. The address of its principal executive office is _____

_____ .

(Insert complete address of principal executive office wherever located – Do not use Post Office Box)

2. The address of its principal office in the State of California is _____

_____ .

(Insert complete address of prnicipal office in California – Do not use Post Office Box.)

DESIGNATION OF AGENT FOR SERVICE OF PROCESS WITHIN THE STATE OF CALIFORNIA

3. *(Use this paragraph if the process agent is a natural person.)*

_____ ,

a natural person residing in the State of California, whose complete [ ] business [ ] residence address is

_____

_____ ,

(Do not use Post office box)

is designated as its agent upon whom process directed to the corporation may be served within the State of California in the manner provided by law.

NOTE: Either the business address or the residence address must be given. Indicate which by check mark in proper box.

FORM TO BE COMPLETED ON REVERSE SIDE

OVER

SEC/STATE Form LL-8

Figure F-53 (continued)

4. *(Use this paragraph if the process agent is a corporation. See instructions)*

_____ , a corporation

organized and existing under the laws of _____

is designated as agent upon whom process directed to the undersigned corporation may be served within the State of California, in the manner provided by law.

NOTE: Before it may be designated by any foreign corporation as its agent for service of process, a corporate agent must comply with Section 1505, California Corporations Code. (See instruction 2.)

5. The undersigned corporation hereby irrevocably consents to service of process directed to it upon the agent designated above, and to service of process on the Secretary of State of State of California if the agent so designated or the agent's successor is no longer authorized to act or cannot be found at the address given.

_____
(Name of Corporation)

_____
(Signature of corporate officer)

_____
(Typed name and title of officer signing)

INSTRUCTIONS:

1. There must be annexed to this statement, a certificate by an authorized public official of the state or place of incorporation of the corporation, to the effect that the corporation making the statement is an existing corporation in good standing in that state or place. IF A NONPROFIT CORPORATION IS TO BE QUALIFIED, the certificate must also indicate that the corporation is a nonstock, nonprofit corporation.

2. No domestic corporation may be designated as agent for service of process unless it has filed with the Secretary of State the certificate provided for by Section 1505, Corporations Code, and no foreign corporation may be designated unless it has qualified for the transaction of intrastate business in California and has filed with the Secretary of State of the State of California the certificate provided for by Section 1505, California Corporations Code. A domestic or foreign corporation must be currently authorized to engage in business in this State and be in good standing status on the records of the Secretary of State of the State of California, in order to file a certificate pursuant to this section.

NOTE: A CORPORATION CANNOT ACT FOR *ITSELF* AS AGENT FOR SERVICE OF PROCESS.

3. If a corporation is required to qualify under a D.B.A. (name other than the true corporate name) pursuant to Section 2106(b), Corporations Code, then in the first line of this statement set out the correct corporate name, followed by "which will do business in California as _____," setting forth the D.B.A. in the space indicated. The D.B.A. should not be set out in connection with the corporate name anywhere else in the statement.

4. If the corporation changes its name or if there are any changes in the information contained in this statement, then the corporation must file an Amended Statement and Designation. A form may be obtained from the Secretary of State.

Figure F-53 (continued)

ALAN J. DIXON
SECRETARY OF STATE

FEE SCHEDULE — NEW CORPORATIONS

Each new domestic and foreign business corporation is required to pay a filing fee, initial license fee and initial franchise tax at the time of issuance of Certificate of Incorporation or Authority.

The filing fee is $75.00.

The initial license fee is computed at the rate of 1/20th of 1% (50c per $1,000) in the amount of stated capital and paid-in surplus represented in Illinois, with minimum of 50c.

The initial franchise tax is assessed at the rate of 1/10th of 1% ($1.00 per $1,000) on the stated capital and paid-in surplus represented in this State with a minimum of $25.00 and a maximum of $1,000,000. The minimum initial franchise tax prorated according to the applicable month is as follows:

Jan.	$ 37.50	May	$ 29.17	Sept.	$ 20.83
Feb.	$ 35.42	June	$ 27.08	Oct.	$ 18.75
March	$ 33.33	July	$ 25.00	Nov.	$ 16.67
April	$ 31.25	Aug.	$ 22.92	Dec.	$ 14.58

The following is a schedule illustrating the fees required in instances where all of the property and business of the corporation is represented in this State.

Jan.	Feb.	Mar.	Apr.	May	June	July	Aug.	Sept.	Oct.	Nov.	Dec.
$113.00	$110.92	$108.83	$106.75	$1000.00 $104.67	$102.58	$100.50	$ 98.42	$ 96.33	$ 94.25	$ 92.17	$ 90.08
$117.50	$115.42	$113.33	$111.25	$10,000.00 $109.17	$107.08	$105.00	$102.92	$100.83	$ 98.75	$ 96.67	$ 94.58
$175.00	$170.84	$166.67	$162.50	$50,000.00 $158.34	$154.17	$150.00	$145.84	$141.67	$137.50	$133.33	$129.17
$275.00	$266.67	$258.34	$250.00	$100,000.00 $241.67	$233.34	$225.00	$216.67	$208.34	$200.00	$191.67	$183.34

Fees for corporations that represent they will issue in excess of $25,000 without further report to my office may be computed in the following manner:
Rate Per $1000.00, plus a $75.00 filing fee.

Jan.	Feb.	Mar.	Apr.	May	June	July	Aug.	Sept.	Oct.	Nov.	Dec.
$2.00	$1.9167	$1.8334	$1.750	$1.6667	$1.5834	$1.5000	$1.4167	$1.3334	$1.250	$1.1667	$1.0834

The fees set forth immediately above are also required in connection with a subsequent issuance of shares computed on a $1,000 basis; however, the fee for filing a Report of Issuance of Shares is only $1.00.

As of January 1, 1979, checks submitted with fees due must be from an Illinois attorney, a money order or a certified check. Checks from service companies are also acceptable.

Figure F-54: FEE SCHEDULE, NEW CORPORATIONS—ILLINOIS

THE BUSINESS CORPORATION ACT

FOR 19_____

ANNUAL REPORT

ALAN J. DIXON
SECRETARY OF STATE OF ILLINOIS

FILE NO _____

USE TYPEWRITER IN EXECUTING
THIS REPORT WHICH MUST BE
FILED PRIOR TO MARCH 1st.

FILING FEE $15.00

1.) CORPORATE NAME
    REGISTERED AGENT
    REGISTERED OFFICE
    CITY, STATE, ZIP CODE

2.) THE NAME AND OFFICIAL POSITION OF THE OFFICER EXECUTING THIS REPORT IS:

_____
(PRESIDENT, VICE PRESIDENT, SECRETARY, ASSISTANT SECRETARY, TREASURER, RECEIVER, ASSIGNEE, OR TRUSTEE.)

3.) THE ABOVE CORPORATION ORGANIZED UNDER THE LAWS OF THE STATE OF_____, PURSUANT TO THE
    PROVISIONS OF "THE BUSINESS CORPORATION ACT" OF THE STATE OF ILLINOIS, HEREBY MAKES THE FOLLOWING REPORT:

4.) THE NAMES AND RESPECTIVE ADDRESSES OF ITS OFFICERS AND DIRECTORS ARE: IF OFFICERS ARE DIRECTORS, SO STATE.

NAME	OFFICE	NUMBER AND STREET	CITY	STATE
	PRESIDENT			
	SECRETARY			
	TREASURER			
	DIRECTOR			
	DIRECTOR			
	DIRECTOR			

THE PRESIDENT AND SECRETARY CANNOT BE THE SAME INDIVIDUAL EXCEPT FOR SINGLE SHAREHOLDER CORPORATIONS ORGANIZED
UNDER THE MEDICAL CORPORATION ACT AND CERTAIN FOREIGN CORPORATIONS.

5.) THE FOLLOWING IS A BRIEF STATEMENT OF THE CHARACTER OF THE BUSINESS IN WHICH THE CORPORATION IS ACTUALLY ENGAGED:

6.) THE AGGREGATE NUMBER OF SHARES WHICH THE CORPORATION HAS AUTHORITY TO ISSUE (AS OF PRECEDING DECEMBER 31st)

    IS _____ITEMIZED AS FOLLOWS:

CLASS	SERIES (IF ANY)	NUMBER OF SHARES	PAR VALUE PER SHARE OR STATEMENT THAT SHARES ARE WITHOUT PAR VALUE

7.) THE AGGREGATE NUMBER OF ISSUED SHARES (AS OF PRECEDING DECEMBER 31st)

    IS _____ITEMIZED AS FOLLOWS:

CLASS	SERIES (IF ANY)	NUMBER OF SHARES	PAR VALUE PER SHARE OR STATEMENT THAT SHARES ARE WITHOUT PAR VALUE

8.) THE AMOUNT OF STATED CAPITAL AND PAID-IN SURPLUS
    AS OF DECEMBER 31st IS:

    STATED CAPITAL $_____

    PAID-IN SURPLUS $_____

READ INSTRUCTIONS ON BACK OF FLYER BEFORE FILLING IN.

    TOTAL $_____

↰ DO NOT DETACH ↱

PLEASE RETURN PRE-ADDRESSED FORM; OTHER ENCLOSED FORM FOR YOUR FILE

FILE NO _____

THE INFORMATION BELOW IS FOR THE PURPOSE OF COMPILING THE CERTIFIED LIST OF
CORPORATIONS REQUIRED BY SECTION 155 OF THE BUSINESS CORPORATION ACT.

PRESIDENT

SECRETARY

IF THE ABOVE OFFICERS' NAMES AND ADDRESSES ARE MISSING OR HAVE
CHANGED, ENTER ONLY THE ADDITIONS OR CORRECTIONS BELOW

PRESIDENT _____

| | NAME | NUMBER AND STREET | CITY | STATE |

SECRETARY _____

| | NAME | NUMBER AND STREET | CITY | STATE |

FOR INSTRUCTIONS SEE BACK OF FLYER

Figure F-55: CORPORATE ANNUAL REPORT—ILLINOIS

9.) DOES THE CORPORATION ELECT TO PAY A FRANCHISE TAX BASED UPON ITS ENTIRE STATED CAPITAL AND PAID-IN SURPLUS?

(IF ANSWERED IN THE NEGATIVE, COMPLETE PARAGRAPHS 10 THROUGH 15.)   ANSWER: _____

10.) THE TOTAL VALUE EXPRESSED IN DOLLARS OF ALL THE PROPERTY OF THE CORPORATION EVERYWHERE

LOCATED ON_____DAY OF_____ ,19 _____ $ _____

11.) THE TOTAL VALUE EXPRESSED IN DOLLARS OF ALL THE PROPERTY OF THE CORPORATION LOCATED IN

ILLINOIS ON _____DAY OF_____ ,19 _____ $ _____

12.) THE GROSS AMOUNT OF BUSINESS OF THE CORPORATION TRANSACTED EVERYWHERE DURING THE PAST

TWELVE MONTHS ENDING_____DAY OF_____ ,19 _____ $ _____

13.) THE GROSS AMOUNT OF BUSINESS OF THE CORPORATION TRANSACTED BY IT AT OR FROM PLACES OF
BUSINESS IN THE STATE OF ILLINOIS DURING THE PAST TWELVE MONTHS ENDING

_____DAY OF_____ ,19 _____ $ _____

14. GIVE THE LOCATION OF THE PRINCIPAL PLACES OF BUSINESS OF THE CORPORATION IN EACH STATE WHERE AUTHORIZED TO TRANS-
ACT BUSINESS AND THE AMOUNT OF BUSINESS TRANSACTED IN EACH STATE LAST YEAR:

15.) IF A FOREIGN CORPORATION, GIVE THE DATE OF INCORPORATION_____
AND THE PERIOD OF DURATION OR DATE OF EXPIRATION_____

16.) IF A FOREIGN CORPORATION, THE ADDRESS OF ITS PRINCIPAL OFFICE IN THE STATE OF ITS INCORPORATION IS:

_____   _____   _____
NUMBER AND STREET   CITY   STATE OR COUNTRY

IN WITNESS WHEREOF, THE UNDERSIGNED CORPORATION HAS CAUSED THIS REPORT TO BE EXECUTED IN ITS NAME BY ITS

_____ AND ITS CORPORATE SEAL TO BE HERETO AFFIXED THIS_____DAY
(PRESIDENT, VICE PRESIDENT, SECRETARY, ASSISTANT SECRETARY,
TREASURER, RECEIVER OR TRUSTEE)

OF_____A.D. 19_____

PLACE	_____
(CORPORATE SEAL)	EXACT CORPORATION NAME
HERE	BY_____
	(SIGNATURE OF PRESIDENT, VICE PRESIDENT, SECRETARY, ASSISTANT
	SECRETARY, TREASURER, RECEIVER OR TRUSTEE.)

STATE OF_____

COUNTY OF_____ } S.S.

I, _____ , A NOTARY PUBLIC, DO HEREBY CERTIFY THAT ON THE_____DAY
OF_____ A.D. 19 _____ , THE ABOVE OFFICER APPEARED BEFORE ME BEING FIRST DULY SWORN BY ME ACKNOWLEDGED
THAT HE SIGNED THE FOREGOING DOCUMENT IN THE CAPACITY THEREIN SET FORTH AND DECLARED THAT THE STATEMENTS THEREIN
CONTAINED ARE TRUE.

IN WITNESS WHEREOF, I HAVE HEREUNTO SET MY HAND AND SEAL THE DAY AND YEAR BEFORE WRITTEN.

PLACE
(NOTARIAL SEAL)
HERE   _____
                                             NOTARY PUBLIC

BCA 96-116

C-126

SPECIAL INSTRUCTIONS

* PARAGRAPH 1: IF THE INFORMATION IS PREPRINTED AND ANY PORTION DOES NOT AGREE WITH YOUR RECORDS, YOU MUST ACQUIRE AND FILE PRO-
PER FORMS FOR CORRECTIONS.

* PARAGRAPH 4: AN ILLINOIS CORPORATION MUST HAVE AT LEAST THREE DIRECTORS, EXCEPT THAT IF IT HAS LESS THAN THREE SHAREHOLDERS, THE
NUMBER MAY BE LESS THAN THREE, BUT NOT LESS THAN THE NUMBER OF SHAREHOLDERS.

* THE INFORMATION IN PARAGRAPHS 2 TO 5 INCLUSIVE, MUST BE GIVEN AS OF THE DATE OF THE EXECUTION OF THIS REPORT, THE INFORMATION IN PARA-
GRAPHS 6 TO 8 INCLUSIVE, MUST BE GIVEN AS OF DECEMBER 31ST. THE INFORMATION IN PARAGRAPHS 10 TO 15 INCLUSIVE, MUST BE GIVEN AS OF THE
CLOSE OF BUSINESS ON DECEMBER 31ST, OR AS OF THE END OF THE FISCAL YEAR NEXT PRECEDING DECEMBER 31ST IF THE CORPORATION IS ON A FISCAL
YEAR BASIS.

* THE AMOUNT OF THE STATED CAPITAL AND PAID-IN SURPLUS OF THE CORPORATION SET OUT IN PARAGRAPH 8 SHALL BE THE RESPECTIVE AMOUNTS
THEREOF AS DEFINED BY "THE BUSINESS CORPORATION ACT." THE PROPERTY REQUESTED IN PARAGRAPHS 10 AND 11 OF THIS REPORT SHALL INCLUDE
ALL PROPERTY OF THE CORPORATION, REAL, PERSONAL, TANGIBLE, INTANGIBLE, OR MIXED WITHOUT QUALIFICATION.

* IF PARAGRAPH 9 IS ANSWERED IN THE AFFIRMATIVE, PARAGRAPHS 10 TO 14, INCLUSIVE, NEED NOT BE ANSWERED. PARAGRAPHS 10 TO 14, INCLUSIVE, IF
ANSWERED, MUST BE ANSWERED AS OF DECEMBER 31ST OR AS OF THE END OF THE FISCAL YEAR.

* THE STATE OF ILLINOIS IS ENTITLED TO BASE ITS ANNUAL FRANCHISE TAX UPON ALL BUSINESS TRANSACTED BY A CORPORATION AT OR FROM PLACES
OF BUSINESS IN THIS STATE. THE FACT THAT THE GOODS MAY BE SHIPPED OUT OF THE STATE IS IMMATERIAL. IRRESPECTIVE OF THE MANNER OF DESIG-
NATION THEREOF BY THE LAWS UNDER WHICH A FOREIGN CORPORATION IS OR MAY BE ORGANIZED, THE STATED CAPITAL AND PAID-IN SURPLUS OF A
FOREIGN CORPORATION SHALL BE DETERMINED ON THE SAME BASIS AND IN THE SAME MANNER AS THE STATED CAPITAL AND PAID-IN SURPLUS OF A
DOMESTIC CORPORATION, FOR THE PURPOSE OF COMPUTING FEES, FRANCHISE TAXES AND OTHER CHARGES.

* UNLESS THIS REPORT IS FILED PRIOR TO MARCH 1ST, 10% MUST BE ADDED TO THE AMOUNT OF THE FRANCHISE TAX OTHERWISE DUE, AND THE CORPO-
RATION, IF DOMESTIC, IS ALSO SUBJECT TO DISSOLUTION; IF A FOREIGN CORPORATION, IT IS SUBJECT TO HAVING ITS AUTHORITY REVOKED AND TO A
FINE OF NOT EXCEEDING $500.00.

Figure F-55—Reverse Side

State of Alaska
Department of Commerce & Economic Development
Corporations
Pouch D
Juneau, Alaska 99811

 TO

Business
Sample

CORPORATION FRANCHISE TAX STATEMENT

CORPORATION ANNUAL REPORT

Dear Corporation Taxpayer:

Enclosed is your corporate franchise tax statement and the annual report form to be completed and returned to this office before February 1. The corporation franchise tax is $50.00 for domestic corporations and $100.00 for foreign corporations (incorporated outside the State of Alaska). Tax and report must be submitted together. Tax will not be accepted without completed report.

Please follow the instructions printed on the reverse side of the form. The instruction numbers coincide with the numbered spaces on the face of the annual report.

To avoid assessment of late filing fees and penalties please file timely and attach remittance as required. Thank you for your cooperation.

Corporations Section
Department of Commerce
and Economic Development
465-2530 or 465-2531

Enc: Corp. Franchise Tax Statement
and Annual Report Form

FORM 08-191 REV-2/78

Figure F-56: CORPORATION FRANCHISE TAX STATEMENT—ALASKA

AMOUNT DUE

If postmarked after February 1, a penalty of $25.00 is assessed on the tax plus a penalty on the annual report of 10% of the tax

Fee: Foreign - $100.00   Total fee after February 1: Foreign - $137.50
     Domestic - $ 50.00   Domestic - $ 82.50

YEAR	DATE	NO.	AMOUNT RECEIVED
		X 10754	

For Use By The Commissioner Only

RETURN WITH REMITTANCE TO

State of Alaska
Department of Commerce & Economic Development
CORPORATION SECTION
Pouch D
Juneau, Alaska 99811

MAKE CHECKS PAYABLE TO DEPARTMENT
OF COMMERCE & ECONOMIC DEVELOPMENT
TO ASSURE PROPER CREDIT, THIS NOTICE MUST BE RETURNED WITH
YOUR REMITTANCE. YOUR CANCELLED CHECK IS YOUR RECEIPT

- -

Do Not Detach For Office Use Only

STATE OF ALASKA
DEPARTMENT OF COMMERCE AND ECONOMIC DEVELOPMENT
CORPORATIONS SECTION
POUCH D - JUNEAU, ALASKA 99811

AUTHORITY: A.S. 10.05.699

(Type or print legibly)

NO. X 10754

ANNUAL REPORT

FOR YEAR ENDING DECEMBER 31, 19 _____

NAME OF CORPORATION _____   File No. _____

1. CORPORATION IS ORGANIZED UNDER THE LAWS OF THE STATE OR COUNTRY OF _____ .

2. ADDRESS OF PRINCIPAL CORPORATION OFFICE _____

3. REGISTERED AGENT _____
    (FILE CHANGE ON FORM 08-184)

4. REGISTERED OFFICE IN ALASKA _____
    (FILE CHANGE ON FORM 08-184)

5. CHARACTER OF BUSINESS IN WHICH CORPORATION IS ACTUALLY ENGAGED IN ALASKA _____

6. AGGREGATE NUMBER OF SHARES WHICH CORPORATION HAS AUTHORITY TO ISSUE, ITEMIZED BY CLASSES, PAR VALUE OF SHARES, SHARES WITHOUT PAR VALUE, AND SERIES, IF ANY, WITHIN A CLASS:

NUMBER OF SHARES	CLASS	SERIES	PAR VALUE PER SHARE

7. AGGREGATE NUMBER OF ISSUED SHARES, ITEMIZED BY CLASSES, PAR VALUE OF SHARES, SHARES WITHOUT PAR VALUE AND SERIES, IF ANY WITHIN A CLASS:

NUMBER OF SHARES	CLASS	SERIES	PAR VALUE PER SHARE

8. THE AMOUNT OF STATED CAPITAL AS OF THE CLOSE OF BUSINESS ON DECEMBER 31. $ _____

9. YOU MUST FURNISH THE NAMES AND ADDRESSES OF BOTH DIRECTORS AND OFFICERS. IF DIRECTORS AND OFFICERS ARE THE SAME PEOPLE WRITE IN "SAME" IN THE DIRECTORS AREA.

	NAME	COMPLETE ADDRESS
DIRECTORS	1.	
	2.	
	3.	
OFFICERS	1. PRES.	
	2. V. PRES.	
	3. SEC.	

10. ATTACH AS EXHIBIT "A" THE NAME AND ADDRESS OF EACH NONRESIDENT ALIEN AFFILIATE. IF YOU HAVE NONE, INDICATE IN THE SPACE PROVIDED. _____   (SEE REVERSE FOR EXPLANATION)

11. ATTACH AS EXHIBIT "B" A NAME AND ADDRESS OF EACH PERSON HAVING A DIRECT OWNERSHIP OR CONTROL OF AT LEAST 5 PER-CENT OF THE SHARES OR 5 PERCENT OF ANY CLASS OF SHARES AND THE PERCENTAGE OF SHARES OWNED BY THAT PERSON. EXHIBIT "B" SHALL COVER THE OWNERSHIP AS OF SEPTEMBER 30 OF THE REPORTING PERIOD. IF YOU HAVE NONE, INDICATE IN THE SPACE PROVIDED. _____

DATED _____ 19 _____

_____
CORPORATE SEAL

BY _____

TITLE _____

ATTESTED BY _____

FORM 08-191 REV.-2/78

Figure F-56 (continued)

The following applies to all Domestic and Foreign Corporations:

* ALASKA CORPORATION FRANCHISE TAX: As required by AS 10.05.717 and 765

Due: January 2 and is delinquent after February 1 of each year. If postmarked after February 1, a penalty of $25.00 is assessed on the tax plus a penalty on the annual report of 10% of the tax due.

Fee: Foreign - $100.00   Total late fee after February 1:   Foreign - $137.50
Domestic - $ 50.00   Domestic - $ 82.50

NOTICE: The Corporation Franchise Tax will not be accepted without the annual report.

Due: Between January 2 and February 1 the annual report must be filed with the DEPARTMENT OF COMMERCE AND ECONOMIC DEVELOPMENT. The reports and tax payments are made within the prescribed time if postmarked on or before the due date.

MAIL THE COMPLETED FORM TO THE CORPORATIONS SECTION
INSTRUCTIONS FOR FILING ANNUAL REPORTS
(Numbers correspond with report)

All items are required by law. THE REPORT MUST BE COMPLETE IN FULL OR IT WILL BE RETURNED UNFILED FOR COMPLETION. Annual Reports returned for completion must be postmarked April 1 or $7.50 late filing fee is assessed. AS 10.05.771

This form has been revised for use with the computer-based Corporation Data Systems. The pre-printed data (Item 1, 2, 3, 4, & 6) are as they appear on the corporate file.. Please verify these data. Note any changes or corrections on the form or as an attachment. Do not erase the pre-printed data. Some changes require filing additional forms or amendments.

2.   Domestic corporations must report the principal office address.

3. & 4. VERIFY THE AGENT AND OFFICE AS SHOWN. ALL CORPORATIONS MUST MAINTAIN A REGISTERED AGENT AND OFFICE IN THE STATE OF ALASKA. THE AGENT AND OFFICE ARE ORIGINALLY DESIGNATED IN THE ARTICLES OF INCORPORATION. ANY CHANGE MUST BE REPORTED TO THIS DEPARTMENT BY FILING A CHANGE OF REGISTERED AGENT AND/OR OFFICE. FORM 08-184 IS AVAILABLE FROM THIS OFFICE FOR THIS PURPOSE AND MUST BE SUBMITTED WITH THE APPROPRIATE FILING FEE.

5.   Be descriptive as to type of business, if inactive please note also.

6.   VERIFY NUMBER OF AUTHORIZED SHARES BY CLASS (COMMON PREFERRED). THIS NUMBER IS THE SAME AS THE AMOUNT AUTHORIZED IN THE ARTICLES OF INCORPORATION OR AMENDED ARTICLES. CHANGES MUST BE SUBMITTED BY AMENDMENT.

7.   THIS ITEM requires the report of all shares of authorized capital stock which have been issued to date.

8.   Stated Capital as defined by AS 10.05.825 (12). (A), (B) & (C).

9.   List all officers and directors giving their complete mailing addresses.   (The same individual cannot be President and Secretary.)   A corporation having less than three shareholders may have the same number of directors as shareholders. (AS10.05.177)

10.   AS 10.05.702 requires that the name and address of each affiliate which is a nonresident alien or a corporation whose place of incorporation is outside the United States and the percentage of outstanding shares controlled by each affiliate be listed in the annual report.

11.   AS 10.05.702(9) requires the report of names and addresses as described if shares are issued (see Item 7).

This report should be signed by two officers of the corporation or is signed by one officer and the corporate seal applied.

REMEMBER: 1. TYPE OR PRINT LEGIBLY.
2. BE SURE REPORT IS SIGNED AND TAX ATTACHED
3. BE SURE REPORT ARRIVES IN THIS OFFICE
   WITHIN PRESCRIBED FILING PERIOD.
4. NO COPIES OF ANNUAL REPORT ARE PROVIDED,
   PHOTOCOPY FOR YOUR FILE COPY.

It is mandatory that these requirements be met each year in the specified time for a corporation to be considered in good standing and avoid the department's initiating an action to involuntarily dissolve the corporation after six months delinquency.

Figure F-56: Reverse

INTERNATIONAL CASH AND CREDIT MANAGEMENT AND PROFIT PLANNING

SECTION

G

SECTION G FORMS

International Cash and Credit Management and Profit Planning

Figure   Page

International Cash and Credit Management and Profit Planning

Planning for profit in international operations, including foreign investments, deposits, and sales, spurs consideration of risk factors beyond those prevalent in predominately domestic activities or market exchanges stated and financed strictly in the domestic or home currency of an enterprise. In addition to commercial risks there are foreign exchange risks and government-inspired risks.

Commercial risks present problems of credit and collections; lack of the quality and quantity of information needed to make better credit decisions; delays, distance and transportation snags; misunderstandings arising from cultural differences; and cash management perplexities when dealing in other currencies.

Foreign exchange risks derive from the fact there are really two prices, instead of one, and two sets of risk, in a foreign transaction;

◆ One risk is price fluctuations of materials and final products which complicate profit planning.
◆ The other risk is price fluctuations in the relative values of currencies, i.e., foreign exchange risks.

Foreign exchange fluctuations in large part result from the differential rates at which various countries inflate currencies. Too, there may be political risks, war and threats of war, approval of new treaties adverse to an enterprise's operations, changes in tax rates or incentives, formation of a government corporation to compete directly in some industry ... and the list goes on—all of which renders profit planning a rather imprecise art. Forms in this section, rather than focus on political and governmental problems, bear upon international cash management, credit, and analysis.

The first form copes with control of the international movement of cash (G-1) within a transnational enterprise. Although the form is simple, considering the sums involved, it

G-1

G-2   chronicles the date of the transaction, from where and to where the funds flow, the amount, identification and CONTROL numbers FOR INTERNAL AUDIT, space for remarks appropriate to the matter, and signatures of the preparer of the memo and the approver of the transfer. The second form also refers to the transfer of funds (G-2) but is handled outside the firm. Used by an international banking organization, this form ticks off how funds are to be transferred and the priority for their transfer.

G-3   Transfers may occur in the same currency or may involve a spot purchase, sale, or swap of foreign exchanges (G-3). The *spot price* is the current market price; the exchange between currencies is completed shortly after the order for outright purchase or sale is entered. A *swap*, although more involved, aids in PROTECTION OF the VALUE of export sales or foreign investments and IMPROVES PROFIT PLANNING. The foreign currency swap is a fairly good hedge, although not a perfect one, against losses from adverse changes in the foreign exchange rate. One currency is swapped for another at a fixed ratio, the *swap rate,* and the exchange is reversed at some specified future date at the swap rate. The loss is the cost of inducing a financial house to mirror the transaction. (For the mathematics of swap arrangements, see Robert P. Vichas, *Handbook of Financial Mathematics, Formulas and Tables,* Prentice-Hall, Inc., 1979, Chapter 14.)

G-4   Besides spot and swap transactions, foreign currency may be bought or sold in the future, i.e., *forward* (G-4), which means that the exchange is consummated in the future (usually three months or six months, but any date can be agreed upon) at a future exchange price agreed upon today. Or there is *arbitrage,* which is the simultaneous buying and selling of foreign exchanges. There may be *time arbitrage, space arbitrage,* or *interest arbitrage.* Business firms would be concerned mainly with interest rate arbitrage, which relates to the flow of short-term funds. The purpose of arbitrage is to take advantage of *interest rate differentials. Covered-interest arbitrage* means that a lender of funds covers foreign exchange exposure in the forward market and shields the transaction against exchange rate shifts. (For a clear example of this type of transaction which uses futures contracts of the International Monetary Market, see Robert P. Vichas, *Getting Rich in Commodities, Currencies, or Coins,* Arlington House Press, 1975, Chapter 18.) Or foreign investment

G-5   instruments may be acquired (G-5) and not hedged.

G-6   Organizations involved in international sales usually rely on a bank to handle the associated financial exchange. Transfers rarely rely on mails but employ telex, cable, or Swift Payment Order (G-6), or SPO. "Swift" is a method of funds transfer that replaces cables and is used between banks.

G-7
G-8   Part of INTERNAL CONTROL OF CASH includes the confirmation slips received from financial institutions handling the foreign exchange transactions. The Confirmation of Foreign Exchange Purchases (G-7) and the Confirmation of Foreign Exchange Sale (G-8) are routine to banks and dealers who employ rather streamlined formats for even large exchanges. Actually there are six pages to each of these carboned forms. When the price differential between currencies is small, gross profit per unit of

currency exchanged is diminutive; but this orderly system of paperwork REDUCES OPERATING COSTS. Let's take a closer look at this controlled flow of paperwork:

- ◆ Credit Memo for Sale of Foreign Currency (G-9). **G-9**
- ◆ Debit Memo for Foreign Currency Sale (G-10). **G-10**
- ◆ Second Currency Purchase—Telex Memo (G-11). **G-11**
- ◆ Debit Memo, Exchange Risk—Purchases (Cross Deal) (G-12). **G-12**
- ◆ Debit Memo, Matured Risk (G-13). **G-13**

Each, of course, fulfills a specific function that helps CONTROL COSTS and PLAN FOR PROFITS. Generally, each contains the same minimal information:

- (a) date and reference number of the bank;
- (b) whether a forward or spot transaction;
- (c) sum of foreign currency involved;
- (d) the exchange rate on a specific date;
- (e) its equivalent value.

Specific instructions appear in bold type on each form, and on each sheet of multiple copies of a set of forms, to *minimize costs, maximize profits.*

Intracompany memos may well parallel the forms systems used by banks and exchange houses. For example, an international oil firm uses a simple memo to confirm its Eurodollar time deposits (G-14). Note the similarity with a previous form (G-5) and the one following (G-15). The memo highlights various dates: **G-14**

- (a) date that the deposit is confirmed;
- (b) date that the equivalent value in domestic (i.e., home country) currency is computed;
- (c) date that the deposit matures;
- (d) date that the authorization is signed.

For PROFIT PLANNING, the amount and yield are registered.

Not all are Eurodollar deposits. The Bahamas do a lively banking business, too. This Confirmation of a Time Deposit (G-15) reports on the same information as the previous form (G-14). There are six pages to the form, five of them perforated. The first two refer to credit and debit at value date; the next three to debit and credit at maturity date; and the last page confirms the deposit, which requests an authorized signature, and date, and return to the bank. **G-15**

Essentially, all forms linked with transfers of funds, foreign exchange transactions, and short-term investments carry about the same intelligence—i.e., date, reference number, principal amount, term of deposit or settlement date, interest rate and interest sum, and means of transfer—with minor variations to accommodate special needs. For example, although all of the following fulfill different purposes, note their similarity in structure:

- ◆ Confirmation of Placing—Bahamas (G-16). **G-16**
- ◆ Confirmation of Acceptance—Bahamas (G-17). **G-17**

G-18
G-19
G-20
G-21
G-22

◆ Time Deposit—Virgin Islands (G-18).
◆ Credit Memo, Fixed Deposit (G-19).
◆ Fixed Deposit Diary (G-20).
◆ Notice of Expiring Deposit (G-21).
◆ Confirmation Notice of Investment Transaction (G-22).

G-23

Another aspect of international operations bears upon credit and collections. Two important ways in which exports are financed, drafts and letters of credit, are portrayed. The first example is a draft and accompanying letter of instructions (G-23). A *draft* is a *bill of exchange,* which is an order to pay a definite sum to the order of an organization, person, or bearer, on a specified future date (for a time draft) or on demand (for a sight draft). A *clean draft* has no documents attached. With a *sight draft,* documents against payment, pragmatically payment occurs when goods arrive since documents tend to precede goods. In the illustration (G-23), documentation is required for payment.

G-24

The importer may finance purchases through his own bank and thereby substitutes the bank's credit for the firm's credit. (Letters of credit are discussed below.) A *time draft,* when accepted by the buyer's bank, becomes a *bank acceptance,* or a *time bill of exchange* (G-24), which may arise either from draft shipments or from letters of credit. The exporter draws a draft on an accepting bank and receives payment at sight by discounting the draft, although the importer may agree to pay the discount. The importer buys time by financing the transaction with his own commercial bank. A *banker's acceptance* is a negotiable money-market instrument because it is an unqualified promise by the accepting bank to pay the face amount of the draft at maturity. Prime banker's acceptances are traded in the money markets in denominations of $25,000 to $1,000,000. Maturities range up to six months.

G-25

A bank that collects a draft drawn by the exporter on the importer serves as the exporter's agent and is held responsible only for specific instructions received. Therefore, in order not to be remiss the exporter must instruct his bank carefully and adequately. Even in completing a form sent to the foreign bank to collect on a draft (G-25), it is the exporter's obligation to supply pertinent information not requested in the form. There are a number of essential points that must be furnished in the completion of any form:

(a) Description of the draft and shipping documents:

    (i) number of drafts, dates, and amounts;
    (ii) maturity date(s);
    (iii) names of drawer and drawee and drawer's number;
    (iv) number of bills of lading, invoices, consular invoices, packing lists, certificates of origin, and insurance certificates and other documents.

(b) Whether draft is to be paid or accepted by drawee (according to tenor) immediately upon presentation or to be held for arrival of merchandise.

(c) Whether foreign bank shall file protest for nonacceptance of the draft upon presentation.

(d) Instructions for notifying drawer when draft has not been paid.

(e) Amount of discount allowed (if any)—i.e., interest rebate—if draft is paid before maturity.

(f)   Who pays interest, collection charges, and stamp taxes, and whether such charges are to be waived if payment of them is refused.

(g)   Instructions on disposition of funds (such as forward, deposit, etc.), and in which currency payment is made, and whether advice is cabled, charges prepaid or collect.

(h)   Full instructions on the disposition of goods in case draft is dishonored.

(i)   Name of local representative with power of attorney or advisory power only.

The next form reflects the other side of the transaction, namely, a form cover letter to honor a sight draft drawn under a commercial letter of credit (G-26). Original shipping documents are attached, the nature of the merchandise indicated, and the shipping vessel and its shipping date named. Other data include the foreign exchange sum, exchange rate, and equivalent dollar amount, minus correspondent's charges and commission.

G-26

The next several forms deal with financing imports—*letters of credit.* Under a letter of credit, issued by the importer's bank on his behalf, the issuing bank agrees to honor drafts, up to a specified amount during some period, to cover the cost of imports. The bank's officer(s) signs the letter, names the beneficiary, and sends it to the seller. Terms, conditions, documentation required, and other details are spelled out in the letter and/or amendments. The letter of credit REDUCES RISK to the exporter since payment will be made, or guaranteed, by a bank of known financial standing to correspondents, the negotiating bank, paying bank, and confirming bank. Letters of credit may be irrevocable or revocable.

A confirmed, *irrevocable letter of credit,* the strongest commercial letter, may not be revoked by the issuing bank. A *revocable letter of credit* may be revoked by the bank should the credit worthiness of the importer deteriorate. A *documentary letter of credit* signifies that the issuing bank agrees to honor drafts only when accompanied by satisfactory bills of lading, invoices, and shipping documents.

The first form represented is an Application for Irrevocable Standby Letter of Credit (G-27). The importer agrees to a series of terms for a standby letter of credit. The importer agrees to pay on demand:

G-27

(a)   drafts presented to him;

(b)   the selling rate for cable services;

(c)   commissions and other charges;

(d)   collection or attorney fees.

Interest is payable on used and unused credit. The bank assumes no liability for imperfect or false documents, cable or message errors, or business interruptions. The agreement is assignable or transferable.

The next form is an Application for an Irrevocable Commercial Letter of Credit (G-28), which consists of a one-page form to complete and three and a half pages imposing conditions the importer must adhere to and fulfill, and stating exactly what services the bank will perform. These pages should be read carefully and *understood.*

G-28

G-29 The Irrevocable Letter of Credit (G-29) contains a definite promise by the issuing bank to honor drafts drawn by the beneficiary in accordance with terms and conditions established. This firm commitment by the bank may not be canceled prior to the letter's expiration date, which means that the exporter can engage in PROFIT PLANNING with a high degree of certainty. The credit may be reinforced by having the *notifying bank* in the exporter's country add its unqualified assurance that it will pay or accept drafts drawn by the exporter even if the foreign bank should refuse to honor them, which results in an

G-30 irrevocable confirmed letter of credit (G-30). This additional assurance greatly assists in MANAGEMENT OF CREDIT transactions.

Notice two *caveats* in this Letter of Credit Transmittal Advice.

◆ "As confirming bank, we will make payment after determining that all conditions of this credit have been met or after discrepancies have been waived by the issuing bank."

◆ "The original letter of credit or the originally signed operative cable and any amendments must accompany your documents when presented for negotiation."

It is extremely important that the exporter prepare documents with care and closely adhere to instructions in the irrevocable letter of credit to assure himself of future payment. In other words, CASH MANAGEMENT begins at the time of sale; otherwise there will be less cash to manage. However, many documents contain errors or discrepancies, or are incomplete. A minor discrepancy may be waived at the issuing bank's option, but usually documentation necessitates correction to conform with data in the letter of credit. The issuing bank may cable, at the exporter's expense, for an

G-31 amendment to the credit (G-31). That is, even an irrevocable letter of credit does not relieve the exporter of total financial risk in the transaction. It is the exporter's responsibility to meet documentation requirements or meet delay and further expenses in producing payment or even forego payment altogether. If an exporter must provide indemnity (i.e., furnish security or compensation for loss), he has sacrificed protection to profits.

G-32 The Form Cover Letter to advise the foreign bank of a letter of credit or amendment (G-
G-33 32) will be sent to the notifying bank, the correspondent bank of the issuing bank. The *notifying bank* advises the exporter of the existence of the letter of credit (G-33), to whom it sends the original, and the letter's terms, including the aggregate sum, expiration date, and disclaimer by the *advising bank* which states the advice "conveys no engagement by us." This example is a letter of credit irrevocable by the issuing bank but unconfirmed by the advising bank.

Thus far, you have seen representations of a letter of credit irrevocable by the issuing bank and confirmed by the advising bank, and irrevocable by the issuing bank but unconfirmed by the advising bank. The third type of commercial credit is a letter of credit

G-34 revocable by the issuing bank and unconfirmed by the advising bank (G-34). The letter of credit reduces certain risks to the exporter, but with the revocable letter of credit the order may be canceled at any time and payment refused even after shipment. On the other hand, revocable credit for the importer is easiest to obtain with little delay. The letter may be amended (G-35). Unamended conditions remain unchanged and unaffected.

G-35

Earlier a Documentary Letter of Credit (G-36) was mentioned. The form exhibited appears in the most current design. The trilingual format—English, Spanish, French—is practical and comprehensible almost anywhere in the world. Do notice that the middle section is entirely in English, which also would be true of attached documents. The essential point is that all attached documents must be complete, precise, and conform to the terms of the credit. Commercial documentary credits are revocable unless specifically stated to the contrary, but banks must examine all documents and papers with care to ascertain that on their face they appear to be in order.

G-36

If goods are shipped by ocean freight, a full set of *ocean bills of lading* in negotiable or transferable form and a certificate of insurance must be included. For air freight, an *air transportation waybill* (exhibited later in this section), air consignment note or receipt, and certificate of insurance must be included. Commercial invoices (see illustrations later in this section and in Section H) must be made out in the name of the applicant for credit (or other person as required in the credit) and signed. Payment may be refused if they have been made out for more than the credit amount. In addition, a special customs invoice (see the Canadian exhibit in this section) or a consular invoice, as well as other documents, such as a certificate of origin, may be called for. A Letter of Credit Checklist (G-37) pinpoints which documents are essential and, for the paying bank, which ones are not correct or contain discrepancies.

G-37

Although now assured of payment from the importer, the exporter still must prepare documents and pay for governmental controls. One is the Shipper's Export Declaration (G-38) for goods shipped from the United States. Before customs will clear merchandise for export, this declaration, in triplicate, must be completed and filed even for goods shipped between the American Continent and Puerto Rico and from the U.S. or Puerto Rico to American Samoa and the Virgin Islands. Of course, misrepresentation carries fines up to $10,000, and even a possible jail sentence, up to five years.

G-38

Unfortunately, the exporter must deal with not one but at least two governments and pay two or more sets of added bureaucratic costs. For example, Canada imposes an approved invoice form (G-39) for goods sold by an exporter (outside of Canada) prior to importation in order to REDUCE COSTS and gain most favored nation tariff rates. Required are:

G-39

    (a)   a certificate of origin;
    (b)   a certificate showing the fair market value;
    (c)   an accurate invoice;
    (d)   a statement that the exporter will not engage in either under- or over-invoicing by issuing a separate invoice;
    (e)   data on discounts, freight charges, production costs and profits, etc.

G-40
G-41   It may also be necessary to supply a Supplier's Statement of Non-Conforming Materials (G-40). But a simpler invoice (G-41) should do as well; it is really a duplicate invoice coupled with request for payment. Obviously, government complications raise costs and the price of the items to final consumers. The result: a decrease in total purchases; less rather than more foreign trade; overall, a lower material standard of living for everyone.

G-42   One shipping document that may crop up is an Air Waybill (G-42). The modeled form consists of 12 copies. Copy No. 12 is for the carrier, its destination accounting copy. Copy 11 is the invoice copy for the carrier; No. 10 the carrier information (invoice) copy. No. 9 is for the agent; No. 8 for the carrier (origin station copy); No. 7 for the second carrier; No. 6 for the third carrier; and No. 5 reserved for the destination airport. Copy No. 4 is the delivery receipt; original No. 2 for the consignee (person to whom articles are shipped); and original No. 1 for the issuing carrier.

G-43   The Shipper's Letter of Instruction for the Dispatch of Goods (G-43) spotlights data on shipping, value, insurance, and markings on packages, and those documents which should accompany the Air Waybill. A combination form combines the Export

G-44   Declaration with shipping instructions (G-44). This form is used for any single export shipment with a U.S. customs value of $250 or more.

Not all goods can be shipped under a general export license. Some require an Application
G-45   for Export License (G-45). The application may be rejected, or approved for a specific
G-46   number of months. If approved, an Export License (G-46) is issued. The license is very specific on who are the intermediate and ultimate consignees (receivers of goods), the quantity and unit price of goods shipped, and the country of ultimate destination. The
G-47   license may be amended by filing a Request for and Notice of Amendment Action (G-47). The amendment repeats the general details of the original export license plus the reason for amendment. Another form, Request to Dispose of Commodities or Technical Data
G-48   Previously Exported (G-48), requests authorization to reexport, sell, or make other disposition, and elicits the same essential details found on the previous forms. The last
G-49   form in this set is a request for a status report (G-49) on any of the above forms that had been filed with the Bureau of International Commerce, Office of Export Control, U.S. Department of Commerce.

Another alternative to international business is licensing or joint venture. The
G-50   Licensing/Joint Venture Proposal (G-50) is not a mandated license but a service of the Office of Export Development. The main purpose of this proposal is to acquire new products and technology from foreign companies under licensing or joint venture agreements. With foreign plant operations, COST CONTROL suggests at least an
G-51   annual review of comparative salaries (G-51).

An aspect of CASH MANAGEMENT and PROFIT PLANNING, analysis of income, derives from foreign short-term deposits and long-term investments. One further government-based issue is taxation. The Allocation Formula for Foreign Source Income

(G-52) is a formula application used to determine U.S. taxable income considered originating from operations in a foreign country attributable to foreign country transactions.

G-52

Another aspect centers on the determination of just what foreign operations are worth and whether they are profitable or not. This involves translation of financial statements into home country currency terms. The question naturally develops, in a changing market, as to which rate of exchange best describes the financial condition of subsidiaries stated in a foreign currency.

The first step is to ascertain the Applicable Rates for Foreign Statements Translations (G-53) as they relate to each item in the balance sheet, and then to apply them accordingly. Another important step consists of an analysis of the Foreign Currency Translation Exposure (G-54). The answer will depend upon particular assumptions employed and exchange rates used. Foreign currency translation exposure to risks of adverse rate changes must embrace both assets and borrowing, future commitments and expenses, and separate calculations for each currency involved. Finally, in projecting results, there should be some indication of the probability range of results and the most likely outcome of events. This particular form condenses considerable calculations and data gathering. To MINIMIZE RISKS, this report is updated monthly.

G-53

G-54

The Short-Term Borrowings form (G-55) furnishes further details on loans, the borrowing rate, and translated value, completed for each currency in which the multinational concern has made loans. For BETTER MANAGEMENT OF INTERNATIONAL FUNDS, all foreign exchange transactions are recorded (G-56); and Standard Exchange Rates Comparison (G-57), variance analysis, computation of net exposure and effective gains and losses are examined for BETTER PROFIT PLANNING.

G-55

G-56
G-57

Where business necessitates daily vigilance, the Input Form for Foreign Exchange Rates (G-58) provides easily read data on spot rates for a large number of foreign currencies. Forward rates, too, require analysis and projection of what those rates will be in the near future (G-59). Rates for Travel Pricing and acceptances are registered as early as 18 months ahead (G-60). Records are also maintained on international transfers and rates by currency (G-61). But Variance Analysis (G-62) on a weekly basis quickly pinpoints problem areas and the extent of foreign exchange exposure by category.

G-58

G-59
G-60
G-61
G-62

INTERNATIONAL CASH MOVEMENT

DATE: _____

LINE NUMBER
FOR INFO CASH
TRANSFER   _____

TRANSFER FROM:
(DISBURSEMENT)

_____

_____

_____

AMOUNT: _____

TRANSFER TO:
(RECEIPT)

TRANSACTION
CONTROL NUMBER: _____

_____

_____

_____

REMARKS: _____

_____

_____

_____

_____

Approved by _____   Prepared by _____

Form 42013 Rev. 6-78

Figure G-1: INTERNATIONAL CASH MOVEMENT MEMO

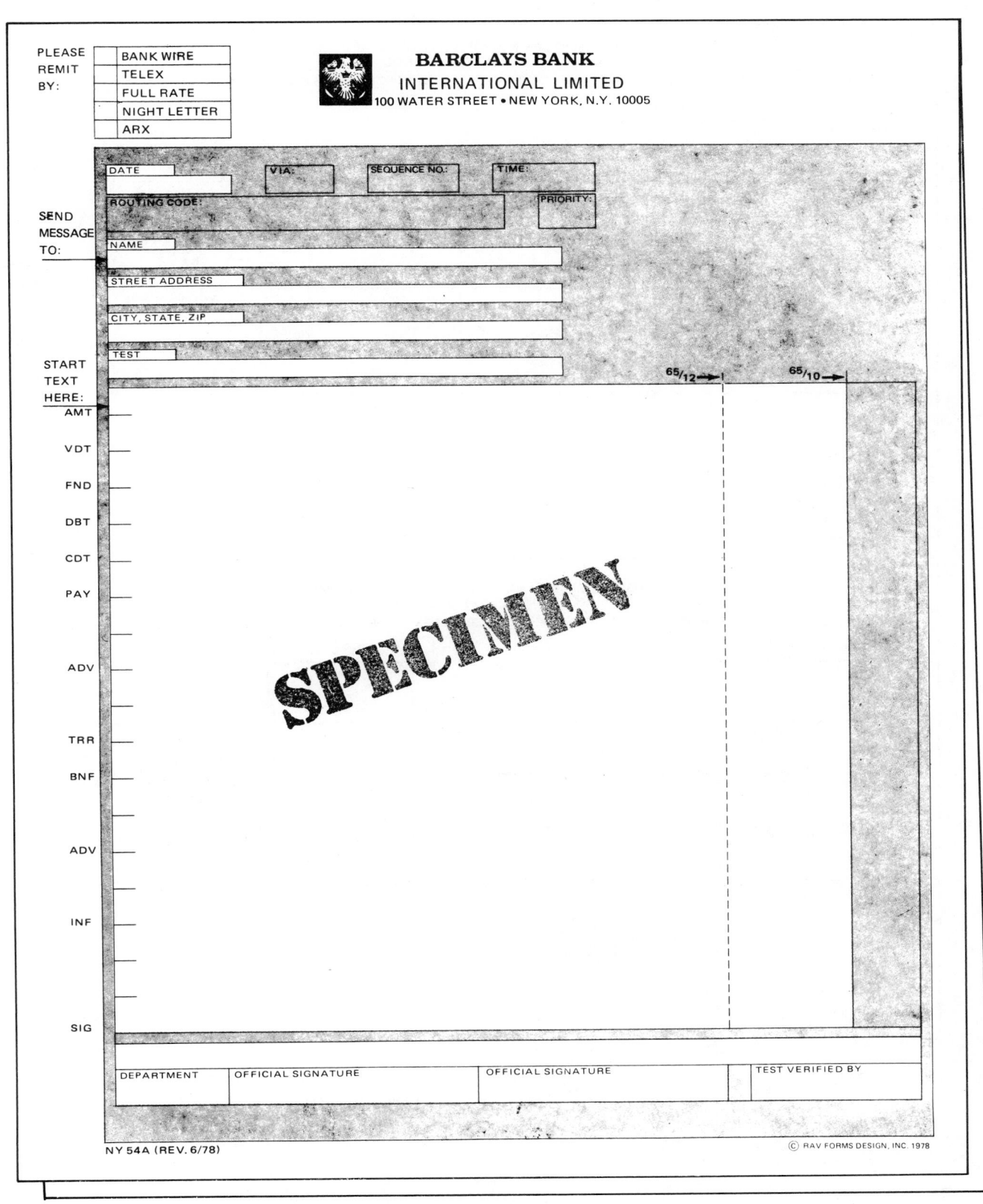

Figure G-2: PRIORITY REQUEST FOR TRANSFER OF FUNDS
(Courtesy of Barclays Bank International Limited.)

Sell

NORTHWESTERN NATIONAL BANK OF MINNEAPOLIS
FOREIGN EXCHANGE

☐ Outright ☐ Swap ☐ Option ☐ Dual Fgn Curr

Sold to - Customer | Cust. No. | Branch 01 | Date

Second Half of Swap Deal

[S]ell | Broker - Name | Phone | Telex

Value Date TO End Option Date

Value Date

SAMPLE

Foreign Currency - Name, Code | Foreign Amount | Rate | Over Ride ☐ YES ☐ NO

Rate | Over Ride ☐ YES ☐ NO

Counter Curr - or Other USD / | USD Amount - or Other | Base Rate - Dual Curr. | Fed F ☐ YES ☐ NO

USD Amount - or Other Curr.

Our Currency Nostro | Our Counter Currency Nostro (USD)

SAMPLE

FX Trader

Their Currency Nostro | Their Counter Currency Nostro (USD)

Comments

Cross Ref. No. 520322 | For A/C of | A/C No.

NW 291

ACCOUNTING

Purchase

NORTHWESTERN NATIONAL BANK OF MINNEAPOLIS
FOREIGN EXCHANGE

☐ Outright ☐ Swap ☐ Option ☐ Dual Fgn Curr

Purchased From - Customer | Cust. No. | Branch 01 | Date

Second Half of Swap Deal

[P]urch | Broker - Name | Phone | Telex

Value Date TO End Option Date

Value Date

SAMPLE

Foreign Currency - Name, Code | Foreign Amount | Rate | Over Ride ☐ YES ☐ NO

Rate | Over Ride ☐ YES ☐ NO

Counter Curr - or Other USD / | USD Amount - or Other | Base Rate - Dual Curr. | Fed F ☐ YES ☐ NO

USD Amount - or Other Curr.

Our Currency Nostro | Our Counter Currency Nostro (USD)

FX Trader

Their Currency Nostro | SAMPLE | Their Counter Currency Nostro (USD)

Comments

Cross Ref. No. 110275 | For A/C of | A/C No.

NW 292

ACCOUNTING

Figure G-3: BUY/SELL ORDERS FOR FOREIGN EXCHANGES, SWAP, OPTION
(Courtesy of Northwestern National Bank of Minneapolis.)

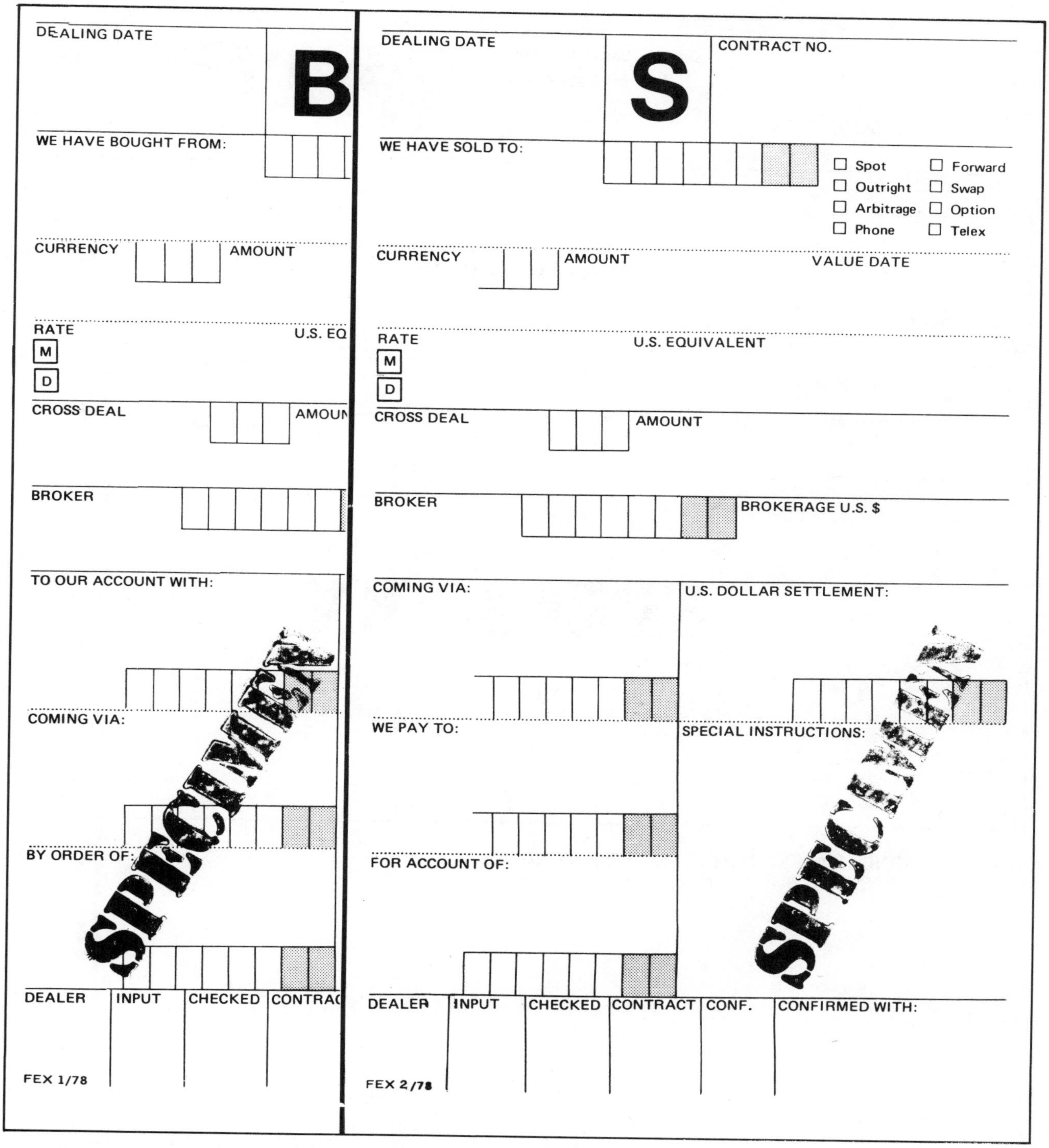
DEALING DATE
B
WE HAVE BOUGHT FROM:
CURRENCY
AMOUNT
RATE
U.S. EQ
M
D
CROSS DEAL
AMOUN
BROKER
TO OUR ACCOUNT WITH:
COMING VIA:
BY ORDER OF:
DEALER
INPUT
CHECKED
CONTRAC
FEX 1/78
SPECIMEN

DEALING DATE
S
CONTRACT NO.
WE HAVE SOLD TO:
☐ Spot
☐ Forward
☐ Outright
☐ Swap
☐ Arbitrage
☐ Option
☐ Phone
☐ Telex
CURRENCY
AMOUNT
VALUE DATE
RATE
U.S. EQUIVALENT
M
D
CROSS DEAL
AMOUNT
BROKER
BROKERAGE U.S. $
COMING VIA:
U.S. DOLLAR SETTLEMENT:
WE PAY TO:
SPECIAL INSTRUCTIONS:
FOR ACCOUNT OF:
DEALER
INPUT
CHECKED
CONTRACT
CONF.
CONFIRMED WITH:
FEX 2/78
SPECIMEN

Figure G-4: BUY AND SELL ORDERS FOR FOREIGN EXCHANGES
(Courtesy of Barclays Bank International Limited.)

Barclays Bank International Limited – New York
Money Market Cen SPECIMEN

Purchased

DEALING DATE: BROKER:

AMOUNT	SETTLEMENT	# OF DAYS	MATURITY	COUPON	YIELD

Barclays Bank International Limited – New York
Money Market Center

Sold

DEALING DATE: BROKER:

AMOUNT	SETTLEMENT	# OF DAYS	MATURITY	COUPON	YIELD

CUSTOMER	ISSUED	SETTLEMENT DATE

Delivery:

SPECIMEN

MM-1 (AG)

Figure G-5: MONEY MARKET CENTER SETTLEMENT NOTICE
(Courtesy of Barclays Bank International Limited.)

NW-635

MT
100 ☐☐☐
BLANK-REG. 01-URGENT

NORTHWESTERN NATIONAL BANK OF MINNEAPOLIS
INTERNATIONAL BANKING DEPARTMENT
MINNEAPOLIS, MINNESOTA 55480

DATE

(20) SPO   3258

RECEIVING BANK/SWIFT ADDRESS

TO

SAMPLE

(32A) | YY | MM | DD | CURR. CODE | AMOUNT |

RATE

PURCHASER NAME AND ADDRESS

| CABLE CHARGES | U.S. $ EQUIVALENT |

| COMMISSION | **TOTAL U.S. DOLLARS** |

AMOUNT IN WORDS

---

(50) ORDERING CUSTOMER

53
☐ A
☐ B
☐ C
☐ D
SENDER'S CORRESPONDENT BANK

57
☐ A
☐ B
☐ D
"ACCOUNT WITH" BANK

70 DETAILS OF PAYMENT

PAYMENT
☐ CHECK   ☐ CHARGE ACCOUNT (DESCRIBE)
☐ CASH

CODES
A — SWIFT ADDRESS
B — BRANCH OF SENDER/RECEIVER
C — BRANCH OF ORDERING BANK
D — FULL ADDRESS OF BANK/BRANCH/OFFICE

52 ORDERING BANK
☐ A
☐ B
☐ D

54 RECEIVER'S CORRESPONDENT OFFICE
B

(59) BENEFICIARY CUSTOMER (ACCOUNT NO. 1ST LINE)

71 ☐ BEN
☐ OUR

72 BANK TO BANK INFORMATION

NORTHWESTERN NATIONAL BANK
OF MINNEAPOLIS

BY

| PREPARED BY | AUTHORIZED BY | TEST KEY APPROVALS | MESSAGE I D NUMBER | INPUT BY | VERIFIED & REL. BY |

Figure G-6: SWIFT PAYMENT ORDER
(Courtesy of Northwestern National Bank of Minneapolis.)

CREDIT

DEBIT

CURRENCY (PURCHASE)

PURCHASE

BARCLAYS International

BARCLAYS BANK INTERNATIONAL LIMITED
100 WATER ST
NEW YORK, N. Y. 10005

Date	Our ref: P.
FORWARD	SPOT
ORDER	

We confirm having **BOUGHT** from you

Foreign Amount	Value date	Rate	Equivalent

to our credit with

via

In settlement

☐ please debit our account

☐ we credit your account

☐ we pay to

for your account

via

SPECIMEN

Authorised Signatories

AC 271

1

Figure G-7: CONFIRMATION OF FOREIGN EXCHANGE PURCHASE
(Courtesy of Barclays Bank International Limited.)

BARCLAYS International

Date	Our ref: S.
FORWARD	SPOT
ORDER	

BARCLAYS BANK INTERNATIONAL LIMITED
100 WATER ST.
NEW YORK, N. Y. 10005

SPECIMEN

We confirm having **SOLD** to you

Foreign Amount	Value date	Rate	Equivalent

to your credit with

via

In settlement

please credit our account

we debit your account

please remit to

for our account

via

Authorised Signatories

AC 270

1

Figure G-8: CONFIRMATION OF SALE OF FOREIGN EXCHANGE
(Courtesy of Barclays Bank International Limited.)

CREDIT

SALE

Date		Our ref: S.	**751120**
FORWARD		SPOT	
FAVOUR			

Head Office A/c-Nostro
Correspondents Nostro
Customers' Foreign Currency A/c

Foreign Amount	Value date	Rate	Equivalent

to pay

ACCOUNT

VOID

AC 270

2

Figure G-9: CREDIT MEMO FOR SALE OF FOREIGN CURRENCY
(Courtesy of Barclays Bank International Limited.)

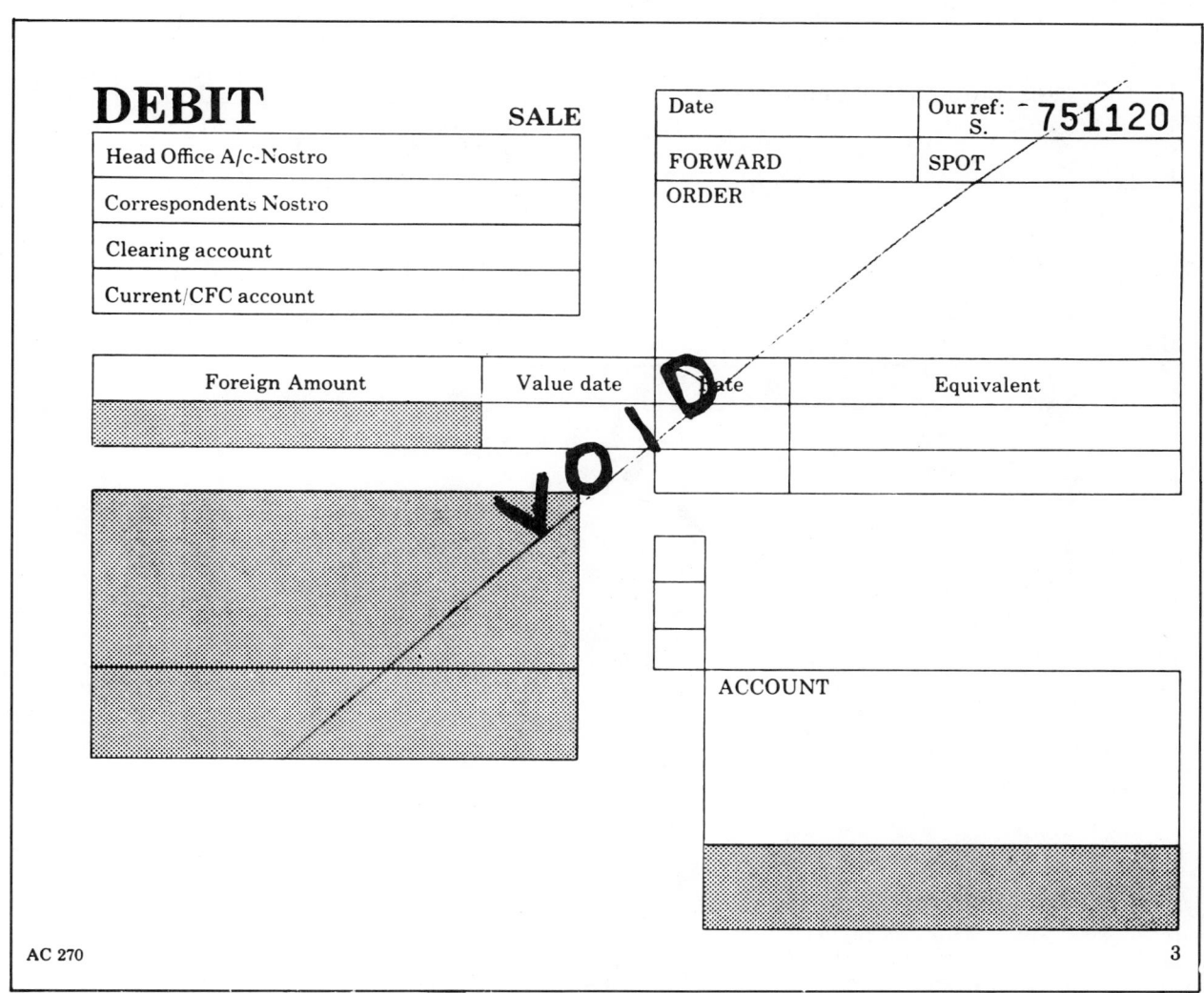

Figure G-10: DEBIT MEMO FOR FOREIGN CURRENCY SALE
(Courtesy of Barclays Bank International Limited.)

"2ND" CURRENCY (PURCHASE)

Date		Our ref: P.	30995
FORWARD		SPOT	
FAVOUR			

Foreign Amount	Value date	Rate	Equivalent

VOID

PAY
TELEX

PAY

for your account

TELEX TO

AC 271

6

Figure G-11: SECOND CURRENCY PURCHASE—TELEX MEMO
(Courtesy of Barclays Bank International Limited.)

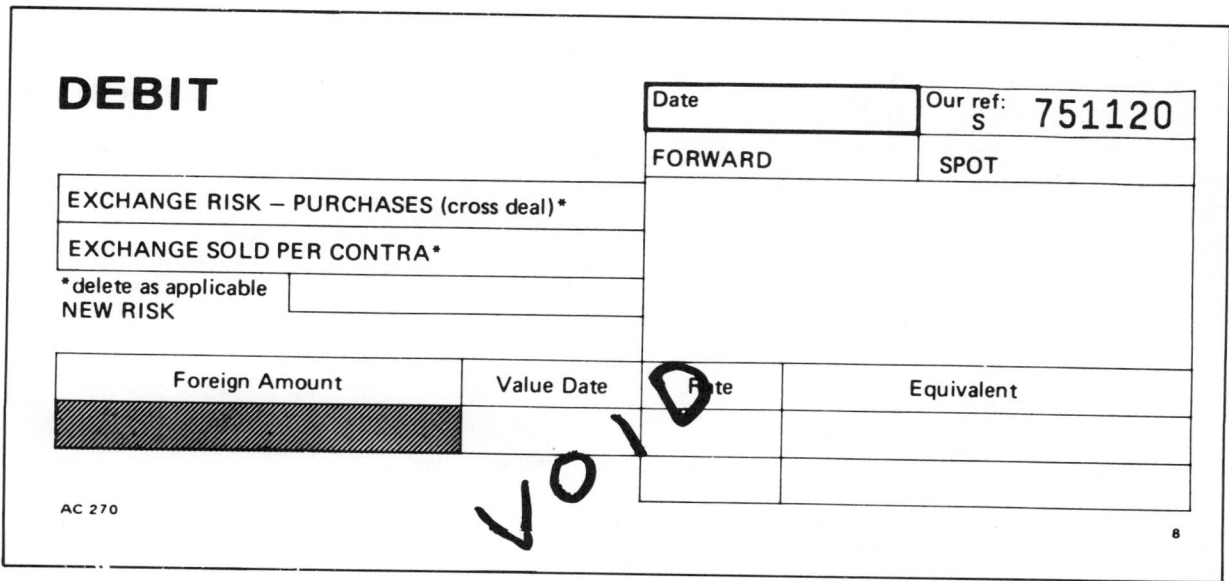

Figure G-12: DEBIT MEMO, EXCHANGE RISK—PURCHASES (Cross Deal)
(Courtesy of Barclays Bank International Limited.)

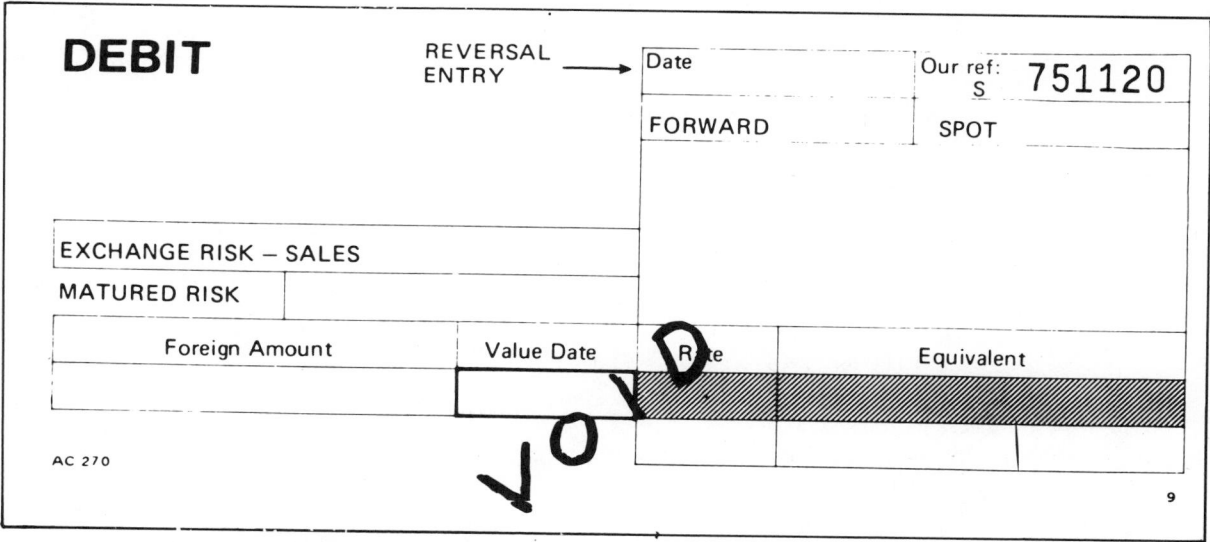

Figure G-13: DEBIT MEMO, MATURED RISK
(Courtesy of Barclays Bank International Limited.)

CONFIRMATION

Confirmation Date: _____

Value Date: _____

Attention: _____

Confirming call of: _____

PURCHASE:

Eurodollar Time Deposit

Amount: _____

Purchased: _____

Maturity: _____

Yield: _____

Branch: _____

Authorized Signature

_____

_____

Date: _____

Figure G-14: CONFIRMATION OF EURODOLLAR TIME DEPOSIT PURCHASE

BUSINESS FORMS & SYSTEMS INC.

NORTHWESTERN NATIONAL BANK OF MINNEAPOLIS
NASSAU BRANCH, DELTEC HOUSE
P.M.B. 29, NASSAU
BAHAMAS

REF # _____ 5530 _____

DATE _____

SAMPLE

WE CONFIRM HAVING ACCEPTED YOUR DEPOSIT
AS FOLLOWS:

PLEASE DELIVER TO:	MAIL TO:
ACCOUNT NUMBER	

PRINCIPAL AMOUNT	VALUE DATE	RATE	INTEREST
U.S. DOLLAR AMOUNT	MATURITY DATE	NUMBER OF DAYS	PRINCIPAL AND INTEREST

Northwestern National Bank of Minneapolis

by _____ **SAMPLE** _____
AN AUTHORIZED SIGNATURE

NORTHWESTERN NATIONAL BANK OF MINNEAPOLIS
NASSAU BRANCH, DELTEC HOUSE
P.M.B. 29, NASSAU
BAHAMAS

REF # _____ 5530 _____

CREDIT (VALUE DATE)

DATE _____

905 – 578 – 01 TIME DEPOSITS BANK	
ACCOUNT NUMBER:	

PRINCIPAL AMOUNT	VALUE DATE	RATE	INTEREST
U.S. DOLLAR AMOUNT	MATURITY DATE	NUMBER OF DAYS	PRINCIPAL AND INTEREST

NW 889

Figure G-15: CONFIRMATION OF TIME DEPOSIT—BAHAMAS
(Courtesy of Northwestern National Bank of Minneapolis.)

BARCLAYS International

Barclays Bank International Limited
BAY ST. NASSAU
BAHAMAS

Dealing date	Our ref: DP

To

SPECIMEN

We confirm having PLACED with you /

PRINCIPAL	DATES		INTEREST RATE
	From	To	At
			% pa

Interest will be calculated for

We shall pay to

	days	on	day basis
	Amount due		

for your account

via

At maturity please pay
PRINCIPAL + INTEREST

Broker

To

for our account

via

for our account

via

Authorised Signatories
AC272

→ CONFIRMATION

Authorised Signatories
AC272

Figure G-16: CONFIRMATION OF PLACING—BAHAMAS
(Courtesy of Barclays Bank International Limited.)

BARCLAYS International

Barclays Bank International Limited
BAY ST. NASSAU
BAHAMAS

Dealing date	Our ref: DA
To	

SPECIMEN

We confirm having ACCEPTED from you/

PRINCIPAL	DATES		INTEREST RATE
	From	To	At
			% pa

Interest will be calculated for

	days	on	day basis

Please pay to

for our account

via

Amount due

At maturity we shall pay
PRINCIPAL + INTEREST

Broker

To

for your account

via

Authorised Signatories
AC 273

To

for your account

via

Authorised Signatories
AC 273

➡ CONFIRMATION

Authorised Signatories
AC 273

Figure G-17: CONFIRMATION OF ACCEPTANCE—BAHAMAS
(Courtesy of Barclays Bank International Limited.)

10420

BARCLAYS International

Barclays Bank International Limited
CHARLOTTE AMALIE
ST. THOMAS
U.S. VIRGIN ISLANDS

Dealing date	Our ref: DA

To

SPECIMEN

We confirm having ACCEPTED from you/

PRINCIPAL	DATES		INTEREST RATE
	From	To	At % pa

Interest will be calculated for

Please pay to

	days	on	day basis

Amount due

for our account

via

At maturity we shall pay

PRINCIPAL + INTEREST

Broker

To

for your account

via

Authorised Signatories
AC 273

Broker

To

for your account

via

Authorised Signatories
AC 273

→ CONFIRMATION

for your account

via

Authorised Signatories
AC 273

Figure G-18: TIME DEPOSIT—VIRGIN ISLANDS
(Courtesy of Barclays Bank International Limited.)

582

CREDIT

FIXED DEPOSIT: 120

Nº

CARD CODE	TRAN CODE	GENERAL LEDGER ACCOUNT NUMBER		CENTRE NUMBER
1	2 3	4 5	11	
T C	6 0	1 3 0 1 7 0 0		2 3 3 4 0 0 0

DATE OF DEPOSIT

INTEREST RATE

% P.A.

PERIOD OF DEPOSIT

DAYS/MONTHS

EXPIRY DATE

AMOUNT
IN FIGURES

IN WORDS

DEPOSITOR'S NAME AND ADDRESS

SPECIMEN

FDR 1 (REV. 2-77) 2M AG

ACCOUNTANT.   MANAGER.

Figure G-19: CREDIT MEMO, FIXED DEPOSIT
(Courtesy of Barclays Bank International Limited.)

FIXED DEPOSITS DIARY

№ 0750

SPECIMEN

DATE OF DEPOSIT

INTEREST RATE

% P.A.

PERIOD OF DEPOSIT

DAYS/MONTHS

EXPIRY DATE

DEPOSITOR'S NAME AND ADDRESS

FDR 1 (REV. 2-77) 2M AG

AMOUNT
IN FIGURES

IN WORDS

TOTAL INTEREST PAYABLE _ _ _ _ _ _ _ _

PRINCIPAL _ _ _ _ _ _ _ _

Figure G-20: FIXED DEPOSIT DIARY
(Courtesy of Barclays Bank International Limited.)

Figure G-21: NOTICE OF EXPIRING INTEREST
(Courtesy of Barclays Bank International Limited.)

BARCLAYS International

Barclays Bank International Limited
100 Water Street, New York NY 10005
Telephone: (212) 530-0120
Telex: International 422778
      Domestic 126946

Dealing date	Our ref: DP
To	

SPECIMEN

We confirm having PLACED with you / sold to you

PRINCIPAL	DATES		INTEREST RATE	
	From	To	At	% pa

BARCLAYS International

Barclays Bank International Limited
100 Water Street, New York NY 10005
Telephone: (212) 530-0120
Telex: International 422778
      Domestic 126946

Dealing date	Our ref: DA
To	

SPECIMEN

We confirm having ACCEPTED from you/ purchased from you

PRINCIPAL	DATES		INTEREST RATE	
	From	To	At	% pa

Interest will be calculated for

Please pay to		days	on	day basis
	Amount due			
for our account	At maturity we shall pay			
via	PRINCIPAL + INTEREST			

Broker

To
for your account
via

Authorised Signatories

AC 273

1

Figure G-22: CONFIRMATION NOTICE OF INVESTMENT TRANSACTION
(Courtesy of Barclays Bank International Limited.)

**BARCLAYS BANK INTERNATIONAL LIMITED**
100 Water St., New York, N.Y. 10005
Telephone: (212) 530-0243
Cable Address: Barcladom
Domestic Telex: 12-6946, 12-8181, 710-581-5129
International Telex: 62-367 and 23-5537
Foreign Exchange Telex: 42-2778
Securities Telex: 42-2565

Gentlemen:

          DRAFT OF _____
          FOR _____
          DRAWN UNDER YOUR NO._____

          In consideration of your honoring the above described
draft notwithstanding the following:-

we hereby agree to repay to you on demand the amount of the draft
together with any expenses incurred in connection therewith,
provided that the documents which accompanied the draft are
returned to us, or you have been notified by the issuing bank
that the said documents have been returned to you or are being
held at your disposal.

          It is understood that you will communicate with the
issuing bank immediately and will inform us subsequently when
we may be released hereunder.

                    Yours faithfully,

                    Sub-Manager

                    For-Accountant

At sight of this SOLA of Exchange   ....19.........

Pay to the Order of   No....................................

....

the sum of...

....

....

....Value received

To ....

BE 1 (Revised 11/67)

Figure G-23: DRAFT AND ACCEPTANCE
(Courtesy of Barclays Bank International Limited.)

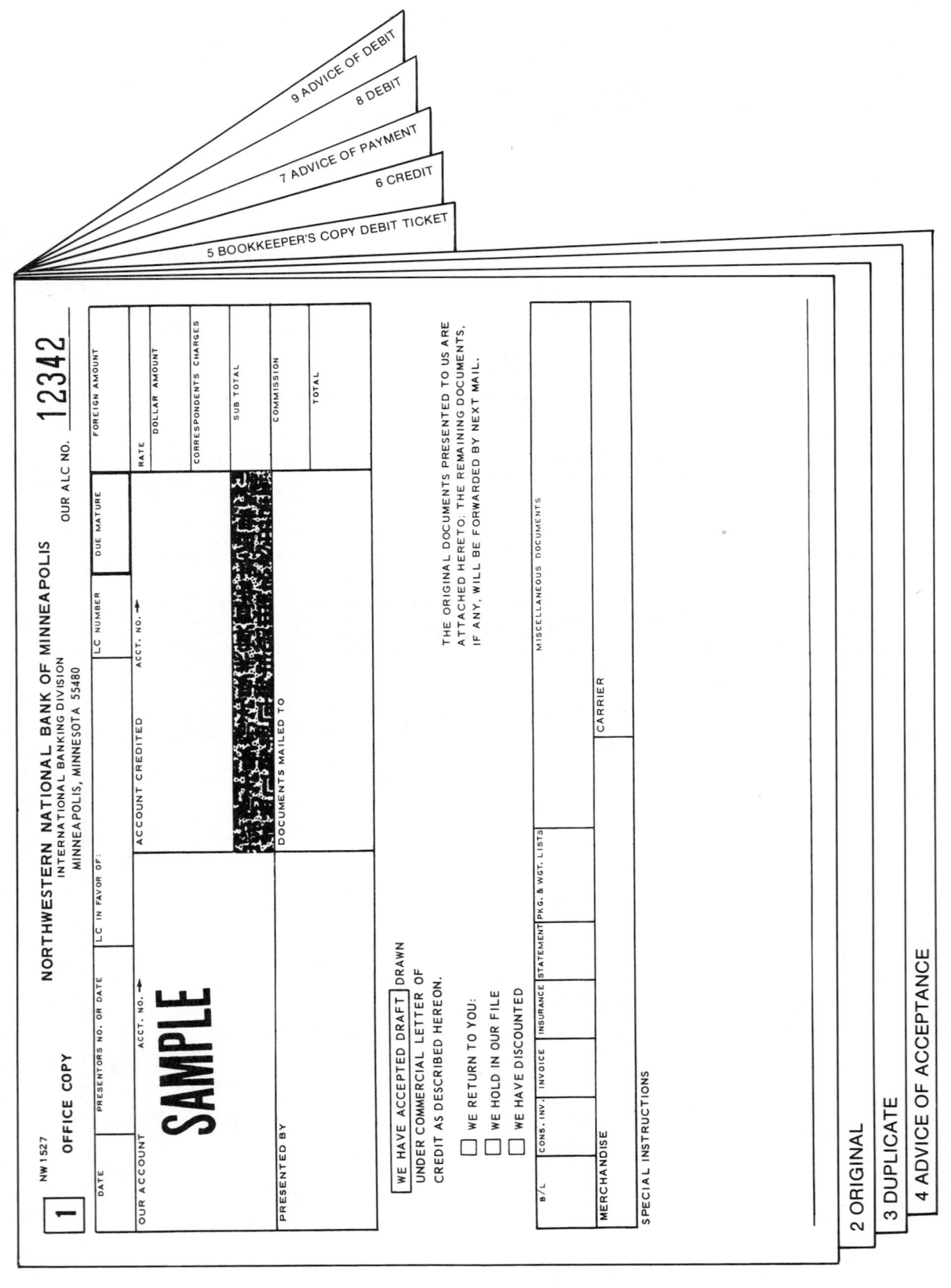

Figure G-24: COVER LETTER FOR ACCEPTANCE OF TIME DRAFT
(Courtesy of Northwestern National Bank of Minneapolis.)

A ACTION BUSINESS FORMS
535-6557 & Printing, Inc

NW 568

TO:

Northwestern National Bank of Minneapolis
International Banking Department
Seventh and Marquette
Minneapolis, Minnesota 55480
Telephone: 612-372-8078 Cable-NWNATLBANK MPS TELEX 29-0734

SAMPLE

ATTACH THIS COPY TO SHIPPING DOCUMENTS

DATE

REFERENCE NUMBER
FNX 55017

We enclose the following draft and documents for collection in accordance with the instructions shown below. Please accept this collection FOR ACCOUNT OF NORTHWESTERN NATIONAL BANK OF MINNEAPOLIS as if received directly from them and SEND PAYMENT, ALL REPORTS AND YOUR ACKNOWLEDGMENT TO THE BANK AT THE ABOVE ADDRESS MENTIONING THE REFERENCE NO. SHOWN ABOVE.

DATE OF DRAFT	DRAWERS NUMBER	TENOR	AMOUNT

DRAWER: DRAWEE:

BILLS OF LADING	P. P. RECEIPTS	INS. CERT'S.	INVOICES	CONSULAR INVOICES	PACKING LISTS	CERT'S. OF ORIGIN	OTHER DOCUMENTS

DELIVER DOCUMENTS AGAINST PAYMENT OR ACCEPTANCE ACCORDING TO TENOR OF DRAFT	PROTEST FOR NON-ACCEPTANCE	MERCHANDISE HAS BEEN CONSIGNED TO YOU
AIRMAIL NON-PAYMENT GIVING REASONS	PROTEST FOR NON-PAYMENT	—Collect from drawee all your charges including stamps, exchange, taxes, etc.
CABLE NON-PAYMENT GIVING REASONS	DO NOT PROTEST	—Plus Northwestern National Bank charge for each draft at 1/8%. (Minimum $5.00 Maximum $25.00)
AIRMAIL/ACCEPTANCE/NON-ACCEPTANCE	REMIT PROCEEDS BY AIRMAIL	
CABLE NON-ACCEPTANCE GIVING REASONS	ADVISE PAYMENT BY CABLE	
HOLD FOR ARRIVAL OF MERCHANDISE	CABLE PROCEEDS AT OUR EXPENSE	WAIVE CHARGES IF REFUSED
	CABLE PROCEEDS AT DRAWEE'S EXPENSE	DO NOT WAIVE CHARGES

IF EXCHANGE IS NOT IMMEDIATELY AVAILABLE AND IT IS NECESSARY TO PROVISIONALLY ACCEPT LOCAL CURRENCY PENDING AVAILABILITY OF U.S. DOLLAR EXCHANGE, OBTAIN FROM THE DRAWEES THEIR WRITTEN UNDERTAKING TO BE RESPONSIBLE FOR ANY EXCHANGE RISK.

ALLOW A DISCOUNT OF   IF PAID

COLLECT INTEREST AT THE RATE OF   % FROM
TO

IN CASE OF NEED REFER TO		WHO IS EMPOWERED BY US: TO ACT FULLY ON OUR BEHALF I. E. AUTHORIZE REDUCTIONS, EXTENSIONS, FREE DELIVERY, WAIVING OF PROTESTS ETC.	WHO MAY ASSIST IN OBTAINING ACCEPTANCE OR PAYMENT OF DRAFT, AS DRAWN, BUT IS NOT TO ALTER ITS TERMS IN ANY WAY.

SUBJECT TO UNIFORM RULES FOR COLLECTIONS (1978 REVISION), INTERNATIONAL CHAMBER OF COMMERCE, PUBLICATION NO. 322.

OTHER INSTRUCTIONS:

FROM _____

ADDRESS_____

SIGNED _____

SEE ALSO STANDING INSTRUCTIONS ON REVERSE SIDE

ALL CHARGES ARE THE RESPONSIBILITY OF THE PAYEE

Minneapolis, Minn., _____ 19____ No._____

_____ Pay to the order of

NORTHWESTERN NATIONAL BANK OF MINNEAPOLIS

_____ Dollars $_____

Value received and charge the same to account of

TO _____

Figure G-25: FORM SENT TO FOREIGN BANK TO COLLECT ON A DRAFT
(Courtesy of Northwestern National Bank of Minneapolis.)

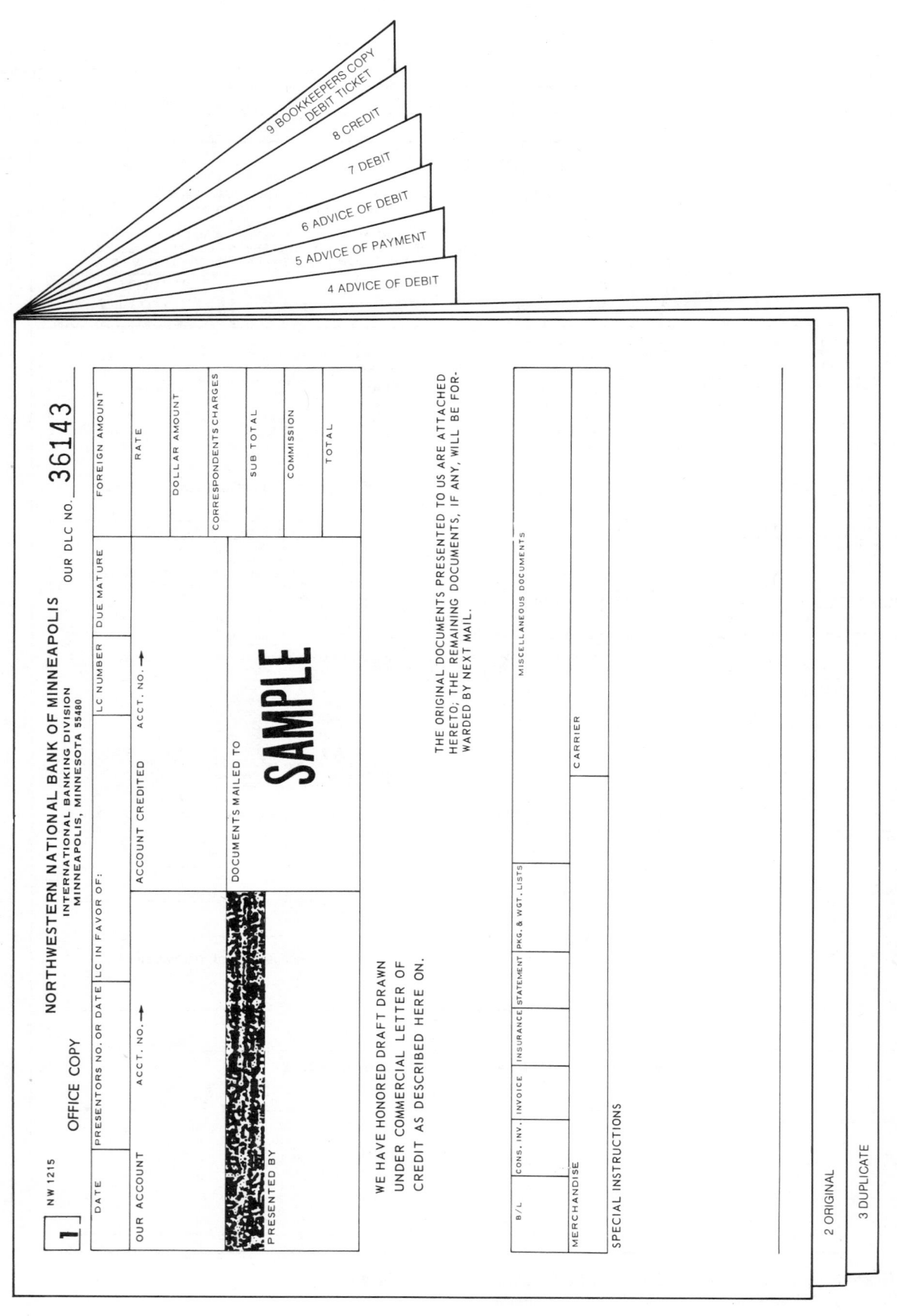

Figure G-26: COVER LETTER TO HONOR SIGHT DRAFT
(Courtesy of Northwestern National Bank of Minneapolis.)

APPLICATION FOR IRREVOCABLE STANDBY LETTER OF CREDIT

TO: NORTHWESTERN NATIONAL BANK OF MINNEAPOLIS
SEVENTH AND MARQUETTE
MINNEAPOLIS, MINNESOTA 55480

SAMPLE

PLEASE ISSUE AN IRREVOCABLE STANDBY LETTER OF CREDIT AS SET FORTH BELOW AND FORWARD TO YOUR CORRESPONDENT FOR DELIVERY TO THE BENEFICIARY BY:

☐ AIRMAIL ☐ AIRMAIL WITH SHORT PRELIMINARY CABLE ADVICE ☐ FULL CABLE

DATE

LC NUMBER

ADVISING BANK (IF BLANK CREDIT WILL BE SENT IN ACCORDANCE WITH BANK'S PRACTICE)	FOR ACCOUNT OF (APPLICANT)
ADDRESS	ADDRESS

IN FAVOR OF (BENEFICIARY)	AMOUNT
ADDRESS	DRAFTS MUST BE NEGOTIATED OR PRESENTED TO DRAWEE ON OR BEFORE
	EXPIRY DATE BELOW: (DATE) (EXPIRATION IN BENEFICIARY'S COUNTRY UNLESS OTHERWISE INDICATED)

AVAILABLE FOR DRAFTS AT SIGHT DRAWN ON YOU WHEN ACCOMPANIED BY (SPECIFY CERTIFICATES, DOCUMENTS OR OTHER WRITINGS REQUIRED):

THE CREDIT WILL BE SUBJECT TO THE UNIFORM CUSTOMS AND PRACTICE FOR DOCUMENTARY CREDITS OF THE INTERNATIONAL CHAMBER OF COMMERCE (1974 REVISION), I.C.C. PUBLICATION NO. 290 OR ANY SUCCESSOR PUBLICATION.

DATED THIS_____ DAY OF_____ 19_____

APPLICANT	CORRESPONDENT BANK
SAMPLE	AND BY_____
TITLE_____	**SAMPLE**
BY_____	AND BY_____
ITS_____	ITS_____

NI 4929

Figure G-27: APPLICATION FOR IRREVOCABLE STANDBY LETTER OF CREDIT
(Courtesy of Northwestern National Bank of Minneapolis.)

STANDBY LETTER OF CREDIT AGREEMENT

TO: Northwestern National Bank of Minneapolis
Seventh and Marquette
Minneapolis, Minnesota 55480

In consideration of your issuing from time to time, upon request by us (or any of us) but at your discretion in each instance, your Standby Letters of Credit (herein together called the "Credits"), we hereby agree as follows:

1. We agree to pay to you on demand, at your above address and in United States currency, the amount of each draft payable in United States currency and drawn under a Credit, or purporting to be so drawn.

2. We agree to pay to you on demand, at your above address and in United States currency, the equivalent (at your then selling rate for cable transfers to the place where and in the currency in which such draft or instrument is payable) of the amount of each draft payable in other than United States currency and drawn under a Credit, or purporting to be so drawn.

3. We agree to pay to you on demand a commission for each Credit at such rate or rates as you may from time to time establish, together with the amount of any and all charges and expenses paid or incurred by you or by any of your agents or correspondents in connection with any Credit.

4. All amounts payable by us under paragraphs 1 and 2 of this Agreement shall if unpaid bear interest from the date of demand; all other amounts payable by us under any provision of this Agreement, except this paragraph 4, shall if unpaid bear interest from the date you are first entitled to demand payment thereof, regardless of whether you actually do make demand. In all cases, such indebtedness shall bear interest at an annual rate equal to the highest rate or rates of interest payable by us (for periods of time such indebtedness is outstanding) pursuant to the provisions of any promissory note issued or endorsed by us and held by you, or, for periods of time during which no such promissory note is outstanding at (   ) and annual rate that shall be_____percent (%) per annum in excess of the prime rate of interest charged by you on 90-day unsecured loans to commercial borrowers of the highest credit rating and that shall change when and as said prime rate shall change. We agree to pay such interest to you on demand.

5. Except to the extent we may hereafter give you contrary instructions in writing:

    (a) your duty and that of your correspondents to examine certificates and other documents received by you or them under, or purporting to be under, any Credit, shall be fully discharged if you or they exercise reasonable care to ascertain that they appear on their face to be in accordance with the terms of such Credit;

    (b) your liabilities and responsibilities and those of your correspondents shall be strictly limited in accordance with the Uniform Customs and Practice for Documentary Credits of the International Chamber of Commerce (1974 Revision), I.C.C. Publication No. 290; and

    (c) you and your correspondents may receive and accept or pay as complying with the terms of a Credit any drafts, documents or certificates, otherwise in order, which may be signed by the administrator, executor, trustee in bankruptcy of or receiver of any of the property of (or any similar representative or trustee for), the person in whose name the Credit provides that any such drafts, documents or certificates must be drawn or issued.

6. You shall assume no liability or responsibility:

    (a) for the form, sufficiency, accuracy, genuineness, falsification or legal effect or any documents or certificates;

    (b) for the consequences arising out of any delay and/or loss in transit of any messages, letters or documents, or the delay, mutilation or other errors arising from the transmission of cables, telegrams or telex; or

    (c) for consequences arising out of the interruption of your business by acts of God, riots, civil commotions, insurrections, wars or other causes beyond your control or by any strikes or walkouts;

and none of the foregoing acts or things shall in any way affect or impair any of our obligations and any of your rights and powers specified in or arising under this Agreement. In furtherance and extension and not in limitation of the specific provisions set forth above, we agree that any action taken or omitted by you or by your correspondents under or in connection with the Credits, if taken or omitted with honesty in fact, shall be binding on us and shall not put you or your correspondents under any resulting liability to us. We further agree that we will indemnify you and your correspondents, and also your and their officers, employees and agents, and hold you and all of them harmless from and against each and every claim, demand, action or suit which may arise against you or them by reason of any action taken or omitted pursuant to this Agreement.

7. We agree to pay to you on demand any and all expenses, including reasonable attorneys' fees and legal expenses, incurred or paid by you in protecting or collecting our indebtedness to you under this Agreement or in protecting, exercising or enforcing any or all of your rights and remedies against us.

8. We further agree that:

    (a) This Agreement and your rights hereunder shall continue unimpaired and shall be binding upon us notwithstanding any delay, extension of time, increase in amount, renewal, compromise or other indulgence or modification granted or agreed to by you, with or without notice to or approval by us (or any of us) in respect of any of the Credits or any of our indebtedness to you under this Agreement.

    (b) You shall not be obligated to issue any Credits (or, having issued Credits, to issue further Credits) or in any other manner to extend any financial accommodation to us.

    (c) You shall not be deemed to have waived or released any of your rights or remedies (whether specified in or arising under this Agreement or otherwise available to you by law or agreement) unless you have signed a written waiver or release. Delay or failure to act on your part shall not constitute a waiver of or otherwise preclude enforcement of any of your rights and remedies. All of your rights and remedies shall be cumulative and may be exercised singularly or concurrently. You need not resort to any particular right or remedy before exercising or enforcing any other, and your resort to any right or remedy shall not preclude the exercise or enforcement of each other right and remedy.

    (d) This Agreement shall be governed by the laws of the State of Minnesota.

    (e) If any provision or clause of this Agreement or the application thereof to any person or circumstance is invalid, illegal or unenforceable in any respect, such invalidity, illegality or unenforceability shall not affect other provisions, clauses or applications of this Agreement which can be given effect, and this Agreement shall be construed as if the invalid or illegal or unenforceable provision, clause or application had never been contained herein.

    (f) If this Agreement is signed by or on behalf of several persons, it shall be construed and interpreted so as to establish in all instances the joint and several obligations of each of the undersigned and this Agreement shall be fully binding upon and enforceable against either, any or all of the undersigned. Each of us shall be deemed to be the agent of all the others, and except as expressly provided otherwise herein, you may act at the direction or request of any one or more of us and you may give a notice or notices (whether or not required to be given), to any one or more of us all as you may from time to time elect without notice to or approval by the others. You may terminate this Agreement with respect to, or release or discharge, any one or more of us without affecting or impairing the obligations of the rest of us, as to either past or future transactions. You may continue to act on the faith of this Agreement notwithstanding without limitation, the death, incompetence or dissolution of any of us or any change in the composition of any partnership or any other firm which may be a party hereto, until such time as you shall have received written notice that one or more of us desire this Agreement to be terminated. Such notice shall not affect in any way Credits theretofore issued or any rights with respect to indebtedness theretofore incurred under this Agreement or with respect to transactions theretofore initiated and shall be effective only as to any transactions initiated after the notice is given, and then only with respect to the obligations of those of us by which or as to which notice was given, and the rest of us shall remain obligated hereunder as if no such notice had been given.

    (g) This Agreement is without limitation as to duration or amount and shall be binding upon our respective heirs, legal representatives, successors and assigns and shall inure to the benefit of and be enforceable by you, your successors and assigns. You may assign or transfer this Agreement and you shall thereafter be forever relieved and fully discharged from any liability or responsibility with respect thereto, but you shall retain all of your rights and remedies specified in or arising under this Agreement with respect to any and all instruments and rights not so assigned or transferred.

    (h) Unless you agree otherwise, the Credit shall be subject to the Uniform Customs and Practice for Documentary Credits of the International Chamber of Commerce (1974 Revision) I.C.C. Publication No. 290, or the most recent revision thereof, but all of your rights arising under said Customs and Practice shall be in addition to, and not in limitation of, your rights under this Agreement.

We waive notice of your acceptance of this Agreement.

Figure G-27—Reverse Side

592

NORTHWESTERN NATIONAL BANK
OF MINNEAPOLIS

APPLICATION FOR IRREVOCABLE COMMERCIAL LETTER OF CREDIT

Please include an irrevocable commercial letter of credit substantially in accordance with this application and transmit it as indicated below (by check "X"). In issuing the Credit you are expressly authorized to make such changes from the terms herein below set forth as you, in your sole discretion, may deem advisable provided that no such changes shall vary the principal terms hereof.

DATE

☐ AIRMAIL   ☐ AIRMAIL WITH SHORT PRELIMINARY CABLE ADVICE   ☐ FULL CABLE

L C NUMBER

This part for bank use only unless you designate advising bank

SAMPLE

APPLICANT

BENEFICIARY

AMOUNT IN FIGURES

AMOUNT IN WORDS

EXPIRY DATE (IN BENEFICIARY'S COUNTRY UNLESS OTHERWISE INDICATED)

LATEST SHIP DATE

Available by drafts at _____ (tenor, i.e., "at sight", "30 days sight", etc.) for _____ % (100 or less) of invoice amount of merchandise drawn on you, or at your option; on your correspondent. Discount charges, if any are for account of the ☐ applicant ☐ beneficiary. Drafts must be accompanied by the following documents (in duplicate unless otherwise specified):

COMMERCIAL
☐ INVOICE IN

SPECIAL CUSTOMS
☐ INVOICE IN

PACKING
☐ LIST IN

WEIGHT/MEASUREMENT
☐ LIST IN

CERTIFICATE
☐ OF ORIGIN IN

SPECIFY IF FORM "A" IS REQUIRED
☐ YES   ☐ NO

☐ INSURANCE POLICY OR CERTIFICATE COVERING INVOICE VALUE AND INSURING AGAINST

INSURANCE COVERED BY THE BUYER/SELLER.
☐ We agree to keep insurance coverage in force until transaction is completed.

☐ War Risks   ☐ Marine Risks   ☐ All Risks   ☐ Other Risks As Follows:

FULL SET   CLEAN ON
☐ OF   BOARD
☐ Ocean ☐ Railway
☐ Inland (CHECK ONE)

BILLS OF LADING ISSUED TO ☐ Shippers order endorsed in blank,
☐ Order of

MARKED ☐ Collect
FREIGHT ☐ Prepaid

INDICATING
☐ O.C.P. MOVEMENT

NOTIFY
☐

INDICATING
☐ IN BOND TO

☐ AIRWAY BILL IN _____   CONSIGNED TO _____

COVERING SHIPMENT OF _____ MARKED FREIGHT ☐ Collect   ☐ Prepaid

(Please mention commodity only, omitting details as to grade, quality, etc.)

☐ C.I.F.   ☐ C & F   ☐ C & I   ☐ F.O.B.   NAME OF CITY OR PORT

OTHER DOCUMENTS OR INSTRUCTIONS:

_____

_____

_____

_____

_____

_____

☐ The documents must be presented for negotiation within _____ days after issuance date of Bill of Lading or prior to expiry date

Shipments from: _____ to _____

Partial Shipments ☐ Permitted   ☐ Prohibited
Transshipments ☐ Permitted   ☐ Prohibited

☐ Instruct Beneficiary to send one original Bill of Lading with Commercial Invoice, Special Customs Invoice, Packing List _____

Directly by airmail to:

_____

(Give complete name, address, and zip code)

Unless otherwise instructed, documents will be forwarded to us in one airmail by the negotiating bank. The credit will be subject to the Uniform Customs and Practice for Documentary Credits (1974 revision) the International Chamber of Commerce brochure No. 290.

NW 402B   **PLEASE DATE AND OFFICIALLY SIGN THE AGREEMENT ON THE REVERSE SIDE OF THIS APPLICATION.**

Figure G-28: APPLICATION FOR IRREVOCABLE COMMERCIAL LETTER OF CREDIT
(Courtesy of Northwestern National Bank of Minneapolis.)

In consideration of your issuing a Credit (hereinafter called the "Credit") substantially according to the Application appearing on the reverse side hereof, or as attached thereto and initialed by the undersigned (hereinafter called the "Applicant"), the Applicant hereby agrees as follows:

1. To pay you on demand, at your Head Office and in United States currency, the amount of each draft (whether SIGHT or TIME) which may be drawn IN UNITED STATES CURRENCY under the Credit, or purport to be so drawn; also, in any event and without demand, to effect such payment with respect to each such TIME draft sufficiently in advance of its maturity date to enable you to arrange (in the usual course of the mails) for cover to reach the place where such time draft is payable not later than ONE (1) business day prior to its maturity, it being understood that you will notify the Applicant of the amount and date of maturity of each such time draft.

2. To pay you on demand, at your Head Office and in United States currency, the equivalent (at your then selling rate for cable transfers to the place where and in the currency in which such draft is payable) of the amount of each draft (whether SIGHT or TIME) which may be drawn IN OTHER THAN UNITED STATES CURRENCY under the Credit, or purport to be so drawn; also, in any event and without demand, to effect such payment with respect to each TIME draft sufficiently in advance of its maturity date to enable you to arrange (in the usual course of the mails) for cover to reach the place where such time draft is payable not later than ONE (1) business day prior to its maturity, or, at your option, to provide you then with the amount of currency in which such time draft is payable in such form and manner as shall be acceptable to you, it being understood that (i) you will notify the applicant of the amount and date of maturity of each such time draft and (ii) the applicant will comply with any and all governmental exchange regulations now or hereafter applicable to any foreign exchange provided you pursuant to this paragraph, and will indemnify and hold you harmless from any failure so to comply.

3. In event of any U. S. Currency draft(s) being drawn by the Applicant on you whereby to refinance any obligation(s) set forth in "1" and "2" hereof and such draft(s) being accepted by you (at your option), the Applicant will pay you on demand, but in any event not later than ONE (1) business day prior to its maturity, the amount of each such acceptance. It is understood that each amount which may become due and payable to you under this agreement may, in your discretion and if not otherwise paid, be charged by you to any available funds then held by you for the account of the Applicant.

4. That, if the aforesaid Application requests the inclusion in the Credit of any provision for Clean Advance(s) to the beneficiary, you may place in the Credit such a provision in that respect as you may deem appropriate, under which any bank entitled to negotiate drafts under the Credit, acting in its discretion in each instance and upon the request and receipt in writing from the beneficiary, may make any one or more Clean Advances at any time on or prior to the date by which bills of exchange are to be negotiated under the Credit. The aggregate of such advance(s) shall in no event be more than the amount specified in the Application for Clean Advances, and in no event shall any such advance exceed the amount remaining available under the Credit at the time of the advance. While it is expected by the applicant that each such advance will be repaid to the bank(s) that made the advance(s) by the beneficiary from the proceeds of any draft(s) drawn under the Credit, should any such advance(s) not be thus repaid, the applicant will on demand pay you the amount(s) thereof as if such advance(s) were evidenced by draft(s) drawn under the Credit, together with interest on each such amount for the period that the same shall have been outstanding at such rate as you may find at the time of demand to be payable. It is understood that neither you nor any bank(s) which makes such advance(s) shall be obligated to inquire into the use that may be made thereof by the beneficiary and that you and each such bank shall be without liability for any wrongful use that may be made by the beneficiary of any funds so advanced.

5. To pay you on demand, with respect to the Credit, a commission at such rate as you may determine to be proper, and any and all such charges and expenses as may be paid or incurred by you in connection with the Credit, together with interest where chargeable.

6. That, except as instructions may be given you by the Applicant in writing expressly to the contrary with regard to, and prior to the opening of, the Credit: (a) you and/or any of your correspondents may receive and accept as "Bills of Lading" relative to the Credit any document(s) issued or purporting to be issued by or on behalf of any carrier which acknowledge(s) receipt of property for transportation, whatever the specific provisions of such document(s), the date of each such document shall be deemed the date of shipment of the property mentioned therein, and any such bill of lading issued by or on behalf of an ocean carrier may be accepted by you as an "Ocean bill of lading" whether or not the entire transportation is by water; (b) part shipment(s), and/or shipment(s) in excess of the quantity called for in the Credit, may be made and you may honor the relative drafts, the liability of the Applicant to reimburse you for payments made or obligations incurred on such drafts being limited to the amount of the Credit; (c) if the Credit specifies shipments in installments within stated periods, and the shipper fails to ship in any designated period, shipment of subsequent installments may nevertheless be made in their respective designated periods and you may honor the relative drafts; (d) you and/or any of your correspondents may receive and accept as documents of insurance under the Credit either insurance policies or insurance certificates which need not be for an amount of insurance greater than the amount paid by you under or relative to the Credit, and (e) you and/or any of your correspondents may receive, accept or pay as complying with the terms of the Credit, any drafts or other documents, otherwise in order, which may be signed by, or issued to, the administrator or executor of, or the trustee in bankruptcy or the receiver for any of the property of, the party in whose name the Credit provides that any drafts or other documents should be drawn or issued.

7. To procure promptly any essential import, export or other licenses for the import, export or shipping of any and all property shipped under or pursuant to or in connection with the Credit and to comply with any and all foreign and domestic governmental regulations in regard to the shipment of any and all such property or the financing thereof, and to furnish such certificates in that respect as you may at any time(s) require, and to keep the property covered by insurance satisfactory to you, issued by insurers acceptable to you, and to assign the policies or certificates of insurance to you, or to make the loss or adjustment, if any, payable to you, at your option, and to furnish you, if demanded, with evidence of acceptance by the insurers of such assignment.

8. That, as security for any and all obligations and/or liabilities of the Applicant hereunder, and also for any and all other obligations and/or liabilities, absolute or contingent, due or to become due, which are now, or may at any time(s) hereafter be owing by the Applicant to you, the Applicant hereby recognizes and admits your ownership in and unqualified right to the possession and disposal of any and all shipping documents, warehouse receipts, policies or certificates of insurance and other documents accompanying or relative to drafts drawn under the Credit and in and to any and all property shipped under or pursuant to or in connection with the Credit, or in any way relative thereto or to any of the drafts drawn thereunder (whether or not such documents, goods or other property be released to or upon the order of the Applicant on trust or bailee receipt or other security agreement), and in and to the proceeds of each and all of the foregoing, until such time as all the obligations and/or liabilities of the Applicant to you at any time existing under or pursuant to this Agreement, or the Credit herein referred to, or any other obligations or liabilities of the Applicant to you, now existing or hereafter arising, have been fully paid and discharged. That all or any of such property and/or documents, and the proceeds thereof, coming into your possession, or that of any of your correspondents, may be held and disposed of by you as hereinafter provided, it being understood that the receipt by you, or any of your correspondents, at any time, of other security of whatsoever nature, including cash, shall not be deemed a waiver of any of your rights or powers hereunder. Insofar as any property and/or documents, which may be held by you, or for your account, as collateral hereunder, may be released by you to or upon the order of the Applicant in trust, the Applicant will sign and deliver to you on demand such form(s) of trust receipt or other form(s) of security agreement and/or Statement(s) of Trust Receipt Financing and/or Financing Statement(s) as may be satisfactory to you, and will pay any relative filing fees, it being understood that your rights as specified herein or therein shall be in furtherance of and/or in addition to, but not in limitation of, your rights under any applicable law. Upon any transfer, sale, delivery, surrender or endorsement of any bill of lading, warehouse receipt or other documents at any time(s) held by you, or held for your account by and of your correspondents, relative to any draft(s) accepted by you in reliance hereon, the Applicant will indemnify and hold you harmless from and against each and every claim, demand, action or suit which may arise against you, or any such correspondent(s), by reason thereof.

SAMPLE

Figure G-28 (continued)

9. To pledge, and do(es) hereby pledge, to you as security for any and all the obligations and/or liabilities of the Applicant, hereinbefore or hereinafter referred to, now or hereafter existing any and all property of the Applicant now or at any time(s) hereafter in your possession or control, or that of any third party acting in your behalf, whether for the express purpose of being used by you as collateral security or for safekeeping or for any other or different purpose, including such property as may be in transit by mail or carrier to or from you, a lien and security interest being hereby given you upon any and all such property for the aggregate amount of any and all such obligations and/or liabilities; and the Applicant hereby authorizes you, at your option, at any time(s), whether or not the property then held by you as security hereunder is deemed by you to be adequate, to appropriate and apply upon any and all of the said obligations and/or liabilities, whether or not then due, any and all moneys now or hereafter with you on deposit or otherwise to the credit of or belonging to the Applicant and or, in your discretion, to hold any such monies as security for any such obligations or liabilities until the exact amount thereof, if any, shall have been definitely ascertained by you. Your rights and liens and security interest hereunder shall continue unimpaired, and the Applicant shall be and remain obligated in accordance with the terms and provisions hereof notwithstanding the release or substitution of any property which may be held as collateral hereunder at any time(s) or of any rights or interest therein, or any delay, extension of time, renewal, compromise or other indulgence granted by you in reference to any of the aforesaid obligations and/or liabilities, or any promissory note, draft, bill of exchange or other instrument given you in connection with any of the aforesaid obligations and/or liabilities, the Applicant hereby waiving notice of any such delay, extension, release, substitution, renewal, compromise or other indulgence, and hereby consenting to be bound thereby as fully and effectually as if the Applicant had expressly agreed thereto in advance.

10. At any time and from time to time, on demand, to deliver, convey, transfer, or assign to you, as security for any and all of the obligations and/or liabilities of the Applicant hereunder, and also for any and all other obligations and/or liabilities, absolute or contingent, due or to become due, which are now, or may at any time hereafter, be owing by the Applicant to you, additional security of a value and character satisfactory to you, or to make such cash payment(s) as you may require.

11. You are hereby authorized at your option and without any obligation to do so, to transfer to and/or register in the name(s) of your nominee(s) all or any part of the property which may be held by you as security at any time(s) hereunder, and to do so before or after the maturity of any of the said obligations and/or liabilities and with or without notice to the Applicant.

12. Upon the non-performance of any of the promises to pay herein above set forth, or upon the non-payment of any of the other obligations or liabilities above mentioned, or upon the failure of the Applicant forthwith, with or without notice, to furnish satisfactory additional collateral or to make payments on account as hereinbefore agreed, or to perform or comply with any of the other terms or provisions of this Agreement, or in the event of the failure in business, dissolution or termination of existence of the Applicant, or in case any petition in bankruptcy should be filed by or against the Applicant, or any proceedings in bankruptcy, or under any laws or regulations of any jurisdiction relating to the relief of debtors, should be commenced for the relief or readjustment of any indebtedness of the Applicant, either through reorganization, composition, extension or otherwise, or if the Applicant should make any assignment for the benefit of creditors to take advantage of any insolvency law, or if a receiver of any property of the Applicant should be appointed at any time, or in the event of any seizure, vesting or intervention by or under authority of a Government by which the management of the Applicant is displaced or its authority in the control of its business is curtailed, or if any funds or other property of the Applicant which may be in, or come into, your possession or control, or that of any third party acting in your behalf as aforesaid, should be attached or distrained or should be or become subject to any mandatory order of court or other legal process, then, or at any time after the happening of any such event, any or all of the aforesaid obligations and/or liabilities of the Applicant, shall, at your option, become due and payable immediately, without demand or notice; and full power and authority are hereby given you to sell, assign, and deliver all or any of the property hereinbefore referred to, at any broker's board, or at public or private sale, at your option, either for cash or on credit or for future delivery, without assumption of any credit risk, and without either demand, advertisement or notice of any kind, all of which are hereby expressly waived. At any sale hereunder, you may, in your discretion, purchase the whole or any part of the property sold, free from any right of redemption on the part of the Applicant, all such rights being also hereby waived and released. In event of any sale or other disposition of any of the property aforesaid, after deducting all costs or expenses of every kind for care, safekeeping, collection, sale, delivery or otherwise, you may apply the residue of the proceeds of the sale(s) or other disposition thereof, to the payment or reduction, either in whole or in part, of all or any of the aforesaid obligations and/or liabilities, whether or not then due, making proper allowance for interest on obligations or liabilities and return the overplus, if any, to the Applicant; all without prejudice to your rights as against the Applicant, with respect to any and all amounts which may be or remain unpaid on any of the aforesaid obligations and/or liabilities, at any time(s), provided, however, that where the provisions of the Uniform Commercial Code of any jurisdiction apply to such a default, you shall have in lieu of the foregoing all of the rights and remedies provided to a secured party by such Uniform Commercial Code as in effect at that time, and in addition to such rights and remedies, the Applicant further agrees that (1) in the event that notice is necessary, written notice mailed to the Applicant at the mailing address given above three days prior to the date of public sale of the property subject to the lien and security interest created herein or prior to the date after which private sale or any other disposition of said property will be made shall constitute reasonable notice, but notice given in any other reasonable manner or at any other reasonable time shall be sufficient, (2) in the event of sale or other disposition of such property, you may apply the proceeds of any such sale or disposition to the satisfaction of your reasonable attorneys' fees, legal expenses and other costs and expenses incurred in connection with your re-taking, holding, preparing for sale, and selling of the property, and (3) without including any other methods of sale, the sale of property shall have been made in a commercially reasonable manner if conducted in conformity with reasonable commercial practices of banks disposing of similar property, but in any event you may sell at your option on such terms as you may choose without assuming any credit risk and without any obligation to advertise.

13. That neither you nor any of your correspondents shall be responsible for: (a) the use which may be made of the Credit or for any acts or omissions of the beneficiary(ies) in connection therewith; (b) the existence, character, quality, quantity, condition, packing, value or delivery of the property purporting to be represented by documents; (c) any difference in character, quality, quantity, condition, or value of the property from that expressed in documents; (d) the validity, sufficiency or genuineness of documents, even if such documents should in fact prove to be in any or all respects invalid, insufficient, fraudulent or forged; (e) the time, place, manner or order in which shipment is made; (f) partial or incomplete shipment, or failure or omission to ship any or all of the property referred to in the Credit; (g) the character, adequacy, validity or genuineness of any insurance; (h) the solvency or responsibility of any insurer, or for any other risk connected with insurance; (i) any deviation from instructions, delay, default or fraud by the shipper and/or any other(s) in connection with the property or the shipping thereof; (j) the solvency, responsibility or relationship to the property of any party issuing any documents in connection with the property; (k) delay in arrival, or failure to arrive, of either the property or any of the documents relating thereto; (l) delay in giving, or failure to give, notice of arrival or any other notice; (m) any breach of contract between the shipper(s) or vendor(s) and the consignee(s) or buyer(s); (n) failure of any draft to bear any reference or adequate reference to the Credit, or failure of documents to accompany any draft at negotiation, or failure of any person to surrender or to take up the Credit or to send forward documents apart from drafts as required by the terms of the Credit, each of which provisions, if contained in the Credit itself, it is agreed may be waived by you, or (o) errors, omissions, interruptions or delays in transmission or delivery of any messages, by mail, cable, telegraph, wireless or otherwise, whether or not they may be in cipher. That you shall not be responsible for any act, error, neglect or default of any of your correspondents, and that the happening of any one or more of the contingencies referred to in the preceding sentence shall not affect, impair or prevent the vesting of any of your rights or powers hereunder. In furtherance and extension and not in limitation of the specific provisions hereinbefore set forth, it is hereby further agreed that any action, inaction or omission taken or suffered by you, or by any of your correspondents, under or in connection with the Credit or the relative drafts, documents or property, if in good faith, and in conformity with such foreign or domestic laws, customs or regulations as you or any of your correspondents may deem to be applicable thereto, shall be binding upon the Applicant and shall not place you or any of your correspondents under any resulting liability to the Applicant.

SAMPLE

Figure G-28 (continued)

14. The word "property" as used herein include goods and merchandise, as well as any and all documents relative thereto; also, securities, funds, choses in action, and any and all other forms of property, whether real, personal or mixed and any right or interest of the Applicant, therein or thereto.

15. That, in the event of any change or modification with respect to: (a) the amount or duration of the Credit; (b) the time or place of shipment of any relative property; (c) the drawing, negotiation, presentation, acceptance, or maturity of any drafts, acceptances or other documents, or (d) any of the other terms or provisions of the Credit, such being done at the request of the Applicant, this Agreement shall be binding upon the Applicant in all respects with regard to the Credit so changed or modified, inclusive of any action taken by you or any of your correspondents relative thereto.

16. That you may assign or transfer this Agreement, or any instrument(s) evidencing all or any of the aforesaid obligations and/or liabilities, and may deliver all or any of the property then held as security therefor, to the transferee(s), who shall thereupon become vested with all the powers and rights in respect thereto given you herein or in the instrument(s) transferred, and you shall thereafter be forever relieved and fully discharged from any liability or responsibility with respect thereto, but you shall retain all rights and powers hereby given with respect to any and all instruments(s), rights or property not so transferred.

17. No delay on your part in exercising any power of sale or any other rights or options hereunder, and no notice or demand, which may be given to or made upon the Applicant by you with respect to any power of sale or other right or option hereunder, shall constitute a waiver thereof, or limit or impair your right to take any action or to exercise any power of sale, or any other rights or options hereunder, without notice or demand, or prejudice your rights as against the Applicant in any respect.

18. That, except as otherwise expressly provided in this agreement or as you and the undersigned may otherwise expressly agree with regard to, and prior to your issuance of the Credit, the "Uniform Customs and Practice for Documentary Credits (1974 Revision), International Chamber of Commerce Brochure 290" shall in all respects be deemed a part hereof as fully as if incorporated herein and shall apply to the Credit.

Very truly yours,

SAMPLE

....
(SIGNATURE OF APPLICANT)

In consideration of the making of the foregoing Agreement by the Applicant, and of any action which may be taken under or pursuant thereto by Northwestern National Bank of Minneapolis (hereinafter called the "Bank") at any time(s), the undersigned hereby agrees with the Applicant and with the Bank to furnish to the Applicant, and/or its successors or assigns, as and when required from time to time, any and all such funds and collateral as may be necessary to fulfill the obligations undertaken by the Applicant in said Agreement and to indemnify and save harmless the Applicant, its successors or assigns, from all liabilities incurred by it or them under or by virtue of the said Agreement; also, to join with the Applicant, upon the request of the Bank, in the execution and delivery of any documents which may issue from the Applicant under the said Agreement. Furthermore, the undersigned hereby unconditionally guarantees to the Bank the due and punctual performance by the Applicant of each and all of the covenants and promises to be by the Applicant observed or performed by virtue of the terms of the said Agreement. Notice of the acceptance of this undertaking, and promptness in making any demand or claim hereunder, are hereby waived.

SAMPLE

....
(SIGNATURE OF CUSTOMER OF APPLICANT)

NOTE: To be signed for and on behalf of the APPLICANT and the CUSTOMER by such persons as have been duly authorized to enter into such Agreements as above.

Figure G-28 (continued)

Barclays Bank International Limited

date

IRREVOCABLE CREDIT No:-

To be quoted on all drafts and correspondence.

Beneficiary(ies)

Advised through

Accreditor

To be completed only if applicable

Our cable of

Advised through

Refers

Dear Sir(s)

In accordance with instructions received from
we hereby issue in your favour a Documentary Credit for
(say)
drawn on

available by your drafts

at
for the

invoice value, accompanied by the following documents:—

SPECIMEN

Covering the following goods:—

To be shipped from

to

not later than

Partshipment

Transhipment

The credit is available for

until

Drafts drawn hereunder must be marked "Drawn under Barclays Bank International Limited
branch, Credit number
".
We undertake that drafts and documents drawn under and in strict conformity with the terms of this credit will
be honoured upon presentation.

Yours faithfully,

Co-signed (Signature No.   )   Signed (Signature No.   )

CRE 202 (replacing CRE 83, 606 series)   W W Sprague & Co Ltd   PLEASE SEE REVERSE

Subject to Uniform Customs and Practice for Documentary Credits (1962 Revision,) I.C.C. Brochure 222

Figure G-29: IRREVOCABLE LETTER OF CREDIT
(Courtesy of Barclays Bank International Limited.)

DIRECTIONS TO NEGOTIATING/PAYING BANK

Please follow the instructions marked ☒

☐ A certificate that documents have been disposed of as required and that all terms of the credit have been complied with is to be attached to the First of Exchange.

☐ One set of documents is to be sent by airmail to

REIMBURSEMENT INSTRUCTIONS

☐ Debit our Hofex account in your books.

☐ Draw on our account with
quoting our Credit number

☐ Draw on us at sight in sterling at the rate ruling on the day of payment.

Where this form is in confirmation of a cable advice, this Credit is available only for any amount that has not already been availed of under such cabled advice and may not be availed of at all unless attached to our branch's or correspondent's notification of such cabled advice, the two jointly constituting evidence of the undrawn balance of the credit.

All drafts drawn under this credit must at the time of negotiation be endorsed on the bottom of this form by the negotiating bank, and the presentation of any draft shall be a warranty by the negotiating bank that such endorsement has been made.

This credit should be attached to any draft which exhausts the credit.

PARTICULARS OF DRAFTS NEGOTIATED UNDER THIS CREDIT

DATE	NAME OF NEGOTIATING BANK	AMOUNT IN WORDS	AMOUNT

Figure G-29—Reverse Side

NORTHWESTERN NATIONAL BANK
OF MINNEAPOLIS

International Department
7th and Marquette
Minneapolis, Minnesota 55480

LETTER OF CREDIT
TRANSMITTAL ADVICE

OUR LC ADVICE NO.	ISSUING BANK LC NO.	DATE ISSUED	ORIGINAL AMOUNT	ORIGINAL EXPIRATION	TODAY'S DATE

ISSUING BANK

SAMPLE

APPLICANT

BENEFICIARY

REIMBURSING BANK

MAIL
TO

At the request of the above issuing bank, we forward the following letter of credit instrument:

☐ PRELIMINARY CABLE

☐ OPERATIVE CABLE   ☐ MAIL CONFIRMATION OR FULL DETAILS OF PRELIMINARY CABLE   ☐ ORIGINAL LETTER OF CREDIT   ☐ AMENDMENT which becomes part of the credit and must be attached thereto.

☐ We will mail you details upon receipt from the issuing bank.

☐ This letter is solely an advice of a letter of credit opened by the issuing bank named above and conveys no engagement on our part.

As advising bank, we have assumed no obligation to honor drafts or demands for payment under this credit. If after examination of your documents, we determine that all terms and conditions have been complied with, we will make payment upon receipt of funds from the issuing bank or its U.S. agent.

☐ This credit contains reimbursement instructions for our bank, so we anticipate that we will be able to make payment promptly.

☐ We are not authorized to negotiate this credit. To expedite payment, we recommend you present documents directly to _____

☐ We confirm the attached credit/amendment and thereby undertake that all drafts and other demands for payment that conform to the credit will be honored by us.

As confirming bank, we will make payment after determining that all conditions of this credit have been met or after discrepancies have been waived by the issuing bank.

Please examine the enclosed carefully to be sure it does not vary from your contract with the buyer and to be certain you can comply with all the requirements. Note especially the description of merchandise since your invoice must correspond exactly. If necessary, please have the credit amended immediately to avoid delays in payment.

THE ORIGINAL LETTER OF CREDIT OR THE ORIGINALLY SIGNED OPERATIVE CABLE AND ANY AMENDMENTS MUST ACCOMPANY YOUR DOCUMENTS WHEN PRESENTED FOR NEGOTIATION.

When presenting documents, please indicate if we are to remit funds by cashiers check, credit your account with us or specify your account with our correspondent. If you have any questions, please call 372-8129.

AUTHORIZED SIGNATURE

AUTHORIZED SIGNATURE

SAMPLE

NW 995

CUSTOMER

FILE COPY

FOREIGN CORRESPONDENT BANK

DOMESTIC CORRESPONDENT BANK

Figure G-30: LETTER OF CREDIT TRANSMITTAL ADVICE
(Courtesy of Northwestern National Bank of Minneapolis.)

BARCLAYS International

Barclays Bank International Limited

IRREVOCABLE CREDIT No:-   Dated

Beneficiary(ies)	Advised through

Accreditor	To be completed only if applicable
	Our cable of
	Advised through
	Refers

Dear Sir(s),

     We advise that the above-mentioned credit has been amended as follows:-

SPECIMEN

All other terms and conditions remain unchanged.

Yours faithfully,

Signed (Signature No.   )   Countersigned (Signature No.   )

Barclays Bank International Limited
                       branch
                       date

OUR NUMBER	YOUR NUMBER

CRE 204   Perkins Bacon Ltd London

     Remarks

DEBIT ADVICE

In respect of our charges on this transaction

☐   We have debited your account as indicated

☐   Please let us have your remittance—

☐

MAIL TO

➤

FORMAT	ACCOUNT NUMBER
ADV	

CRE 204

Figure G-31: AMENDMENT TO IRREVOCABLE LETTER OF CREDIT
(Courtesy of Barclays Bank International Limited.)

SAMPLE

NORTHWESTERN NATIONAL BANK of Minneapolis

7th and Marquette Avenue • Minneapolis, Minnesota 55480
TELEPHONE (612) 372-8123
CABLE: Northwest Minneapolis
TELEX NO. 29-0734

International Banking Department

RE: Our LC Advice #_____

Gentlemen:

Enclosed are the original and one copy of the above
Letter of Credit/Amendment.

Please deliver the original to the beneficiary and retain
the copy for your files.

Sincerely,

Letter of Credit Division

Encs.

Figure G-32: FORM COVER LETTER FOR LETTER OF CREDIT ADVICE ON AMENDMENT
(Courtesy of Northwestern National Bank of Minneapolis.)

NORTHWESTERN NATIONAL BANK OF MINNEAPOLIS
INTERNATIONAL BANKING DEPARTMENT
Minneapolis, Minnesota 55480

SAMPLE

ADVICE OF
CORRESPONDENT'S IRREVOCABLE CREDIT

Advice No. _____
Date _____
$ _____

_____

_____

_____

Gentlemen:

We are instructed by _____

_____to advise you that they have opened their Irrevocable Credit

No. _____in your favor for account of _____

_____

up to but not exceeding the aggregate amount of _____

_____ available by your

draft on _____

at_____sight accompanied by:

Any draft drawn against this letter of credit must be marked: drawn as per_____

_____ credit No. _____dated _____

_____ engages with you that any drafts

drawn under and in compliance with the terms of this advice will be duly honored on delivery of documents as specified if presented at this office on or before_____ .

Documents must conform strictly with the terms of this credit. If you are unable to comply with its terms, please communicate with us and/or your customer promptly, with a view to having the conditions changed.

This letter is solely an advice of credit opened by_____

_____ and conveys no engagement by us.

Yours very truly,

Except so far as otherwise expressly stated, this Credit is subject to the "Uniform Customs & Practice for Documentary Credits (1974 Revision), International Chamber of Commerce, Publication 290."

NORTHWESTERN NATIONAL BANK OF MINNEAPOLIS

SAMPLE

AUTHORIZED SIGNATURE

BY _____

NW 466

BY _____

AUTHORIZED SIGNATURE

Figure G-33: ADVICE OF CORRESPONDENT'S IRREVOCABLE CREDIT
(Courtesy of Northwestern National Bank of Minneapolis.)

Barclays Bank International Limited

date

REVOCABLE CREDIT No. :-
To be quoted on all drafts and correspondence.

Beneficiary(ies)	Advised through

Accreditor	To be completed only if applicable
	Our cable of
	Advised through
	Refers

Dear Sir(s)

In accordance with instructions received from
we hereby issue in your favour a Documentary Credit for
(say)
drawn on   available by your drafts

at
for the   invoice value, accompanied by the following documents:–

Covering the following goods:–

To be shipped from   to

not later than

Partshipment   Transhipment

The credit is available for   until

Drafts drawn hereunder must be marked "Drawn under Barclays Bank International Limited
branch, Credit number   ".

We have no authority from our clients to confirm this credit or to guarantee acceptance/payment of drafts drawn
here against. This credit is therefore subject to cancellation without notice and the above particulars are for your guidance
only.

Yours faithfully,

Co-signed (Signature No.   )   Signed (Signature No.   )

CRE 203 (replacing CRE 89, 607 series)   W W Sprague & Co Ltd   PLEASE SEE REVERSE

Subject to Uniform Customs and Practice for Documentary Credits (1962 Revision,) I.C.C. Brochure 222

SPECIMEN

Figure G-34: REVOCABLE LETTER OF CREDIT
(Courtesy of Barclays Bank International Limited.)

603

DIRECTIONS TO NEGOTIATING/PAYING BANK

Please follow the instructions marked [X]

☐   A certificate that documents have been disposed of as required and that all terms of the credit have been complied with is to be attached to the First of Exchange.

☐   One set of documents is to be sent by airmail to

SPECIMEN

REIMBURSEMENT INSTRUCTIONS

☐   Debit our Hofex account in your books.

☐   Draw on our account with
quoting our Credit number

☐   Draw on us at sight in sterling at the rate ruling on the day of payment.

Where this form is in confirmation of a cable advice, this Credit is available only for any amount that has not already been availed of under such cabled advice and may not be availed of at all unless attached to our branch's or correspondent's notification of such cabled advice, the two jointly constituting evidence of the undrawn balance of the credit.

All drafts drawn under this credit must at the time of negotiation be endorsed on the bottom of this form by the negotiating bank, and the presentation of any draft shall be a warranty by the negotiating bank that such endorsement has been made.

This credit should be attached to any draft which exhausts the credit.

PARTICULARS OF DRAFTS NEGOTIATED UNDER THIS CREDIT

DATE	NAME OF NEGOTIATING BANK	AMOUNT IN WORDS	AMOUNT

Figure G-34—Reverse Side

NW 342 LETTER OF AMENDMENT   *NORTHWESTERN NATIONAL BANK OF MINNEAPOLIS*
INTERNATIONAL BANKING DEPARTMENT
Minneapolis, Minnesota 55480

RE   CREDIT NO. –
       ACCOUNT –   DATE

THE ABOVE LETTER OF CREDIT IS AMENDED AS FOLLOWS:

SAMPLE

ALL OTHER CONDITIONS REMAIN UNCHANGED

TO

                                                    AUTHORIZED SIGNATURE

                                                    # SAMPLE

                                                    AUTHORIZED SIGNATURE

MAIL
TO →

                                                    DATED

                         ☐ OUR CONFIRMATION COMMISSION
                         ☐ OUR AMENDMENT COMMISSION   _____
                         ☐ WE WILL BILL YOU
                         ☐ WE DEBIT YOUR ACCOUNT   L/C # _____

                                                    $

FILE FOLDER

CREDIT—GENERAL LEDGER

FILE COPY FOR L/C FOLDER

BOOKKEEPER'S TICKET

Figure G-35: LETTER OF AMENDMENT
(Courtesy of Northwestern National Bank of Minneapolis.)

NW 402

NORTHWESTERN NATIONAL BANK OF MINNEAPOLIS
7TH & MARQUETTE
MINNEAPOLIS, MINNESOTA 55480

Dirección cablegráfica Adresse télégraphique Cable address NWNATLBANK MPS	Nos. de télexes Nos. de telexs 29-0734 Telex numbers 29-0137	Lugar y fecha de expedición Minneapolis, Minn. Lieu d'émission et date Place and date of issue

Credito Documentario/Crédit Documentaire·Documentary Credit Irrévocable	Número de crédito Numéro du crédit Credit number del banco emisor del banco avisador de la banque émettrice **35820** de la banque notificatrice of issuing bank of advising bank

Banco avisador / Banque notificatrice / Advising bank	Ordenante / Donneur d'ordre - Applicant
Beneficiario / Bénéficiaire · Beneficiary	Importe / Montant / Amount

	Vencimiento Validité / Expiry
	Fecha / Date · Date para negociación en
	                       pour négociation à'
	                       for negotiation in

Estimado(s) Señor(es):   / M   / Dear Sir(s),

Por la presente expedimos este crédito documentario a su favor el cual es disponible mediante negociación de su giro
Nous émetions en votre faveur ce crédit documentaire qui est utilisable par négociation de votre traite ó
We hereby issue in your favour this documentary credit which is available by negotiation of your draft at

a cargo de
tirée sur
drawn on Northwestern National Bank of Minneapolis, Minneapolis, Minnesota

mostrando la cláusula: "Girado al amparo del crédito documentario No.   de (nombre del banco emisor)"
et portant la mention: "Tirée en vertu du crédit documentaire No.   **35820**   de (nom de la banque émettrice)"
bearing the clause: "Drawn under documentary credit No.   of (name of issuing bank)"

acompañando los siguientes documentos:
accompagnés des documents suivants:
accompanied by the following documents:

1. Full set of clean on board ocean bills of lading drawn to order of

     Notify

2. Signed commercial invoice in   covering:

     Special customs invoice in

     Packing list in

     Insurance covered by buyer/seller

SAMPLE

Expedición /Embarque de Expédition /Embarquement de Despatch /Shipment from a ó to	Embarques parciales Expéditions partielles Partial shipments	Transbordos Transbordements Transhipments

Condiciones especiales:
Conditions spéciales:
Special conditions:

Por la presente nos comprometemos con los girados y/o tenedores de buena fe que los giros emitidos y negociados de conformidad con los términos de este crédito serán debidamente honrados a su presentación y que los giros aceptados dentro de los términos de este crédito serán debidamente honrados a su vencimiento. El importe de cada giro debe ser endosado al reverso de este crédito por el banco negociador.
Nous garantissons aux tireurs et/ou porteurs de bonne foi que les traites émises et négociées en conformité avec les termes de ce crédit seront dûment honorées à présentation et que les traites acceptées conformément aux termes de ce crédit seront dûment honorées à leur échéance. Le montant de chaque traite doit etre inscrit au verso de ce crédit par la banque négociatrice.
We hereby engage with drawers and/or bona fide holders that drafts drawn and negotiated in conformity with the terms of this credit will be duly honoured on presentation and that drafts accepted within the terms of this credit will be duly honoured at maturity. The amounts of each draft must be endorsed on the reverse of this credit by the negotiating bank.
        Suyos atentamente / Vos dévoués / Yours faithfully,
        Northwestern National Bank of Minneapolis
 	
     _____
 	
Nombre y firma del banco emisor.
Nom et signature de la banque émettrice.
Name and signature of the issuing bank.
	Unless otherwise stated, the negotiating bank is to forward all original and duplicate documents to us by one registered airmail.
	
	Notificación del banco avisador
	Indications de la banque notificatrice
	Advising bank's notification
	Lugar, fecha, nombre y firma del banco avisador.
	Lieu, date, nom et signature de la banque notificatrice.
	Place, date, name and signature of the advising bank.
	
	SAMPLE

ESTE CREDITO ESTA SUJETO A LAS REGLAS Y USOS UNIFORMES RELATIVOS A LOS CREDITOS DOCUMENTARIOS (REVISION 1974) DE LA CAMARA INTERNACIONAL DE COMERCIO (PUBLICACION #290) SAUF STIPULATIONS PARTICULIERES EXPRESSEMENT DEFINES, CE CREDIT DOCUMENTAIRE EST SOUMIS AUX "REGLES ET USANCES UNIFORMES RELATIVOS AUX CREDITS DOCUMENTAIRES" (REVISION 1974) CHAMBRE DE COMMERCE INTERNATIONALE (PUBLICACION #290).
EXCEPT SO FAR AS OTHERWISE EXPRESSLY STATED, THIS DOCUMENTARY CREDIT IS SUBJECT TO THE "UNIFORM CUSTOMS AND PRACTICE FOR DOCUMENTARY CREDITS" (1974 REVISION) INTERNATIONAL CHAMBER OF COMMERCE (PUBLICATION #290).

COPY

COPY

COPY

COPY

COPY

Figure G-36: DOCUMENTARY LETTER OF CREDIT IN THREE LANGUAGES
(Courtesy of Northwestern National Bank of Minneapolis.)

LETTER OF CREDIT CHECK LIST

C = CORRECT	X = DISCREPANCY	N = NOT APPLICABLE

GENERAL CHECKING
- L/C is not overdrawn (money or goods). expired. late shipment.
- Draft and invoice amounts agree. and all documents presented are relative to each other.
- All specific terms and conditions of L/C are complied with.
- Special instructions have been followed.
- All documents required accounted for and cover letter O.K.
- Correspondent's charges correct and justified.
- Late Presentation. if specified. or within 21 days.
- Documents presented by extended expiration date in accordance with article 39.

SAMPLE

DRAFT
- Amount (figures and letters). currency. tenor. L/C No.. date (within expiry). interest clause (if any) per L/C.
- Drawee. Drawer. Payee. Endorser correct. draft signed and/or endorsed.
- No improper restrictive clauses.

OCEAN B/L
- Names and addresses of beneficiary. applicant. notify parties. flag and visa. if any. per L/C.
- Consigned to order or otherwise per L/C, and proper loading and discharge ports per L/C, not consolidated.
- It is signed: On Board notation dated and initialled or signed, or printed Shipped On Board or Shipped B/L.
- B/L issuance date or On Board date (when applicable) is within allowable time.
- Freight marked Collect or Prepaid per relative shipping terms; freight amount indicated if required. B/L doesn't show charter party. sailing vessel. issued by forwarder of consolidator. On Deck. or unclean. unless permitted by L/C.
- Marks and numbers quantities. general description. are as per commercial invoice and L/C and all corrections are initialled or signed by carrier or agent: no excess merchandise shipped.
- If transshipment prohibited. no transshipment; if allowed. through B/L covering all voyage.

AIR WAYBILL
- Names and addresses of beneficiary. applicant, notify parties, per L/C.
- Consigned per L/C and proper loading and discharge per L/C
- A/W/B issuance date is within allowable time.
- Freight marked Collect or Prepaid per relative shipping terms; flight number if required.
- It is signed; A/W/B not issued by a Forwarder: not unclean. no transshipment if prohibited by L/C.
- Marks and numbers. quantities. general description. are as per commercial invoice and L/C and all corrections are initialled or signed by carrier or his agent.

INS. POL. OR CERT.
- Policy or certificate: not acknowledgment or brokers cover unless allowed by L/C; riders or binders attached or duly cross-referenced.
- Signed. and if required. endorsed and/or countersigned.
- Covers proper value and risks per L/C. in currency of L/C.
- Not dated after B/L date. (Ref.: UCP Article 27) Issuance date and all corrections signed or initialled.
- Name of vessel, merchandise description. loading and discharge ports. marks and numbers. etc.. per commercial invoice. B/L and per L/C.

COMM. INV.
- Names and addresses of beneficiary and applicant and others per L/C.
- Description and corresponding amounts exactly per L/C: computations correct.
- Marks and numbers. shipping terms. order numbers. etc.. per L/C.
- All charges permitted per L/C terms. otherwise request special Accountee's permission.
- All merchandise shipped if partial shipments prohibited: invoicing in proportion with shipment if partial shipments allowed.
- All clauses. certification. visa. etc.. required are present and worded exactly as per L/C.

CONSULAR INV.
- Names and addresses. marks and numbers. order numbers. amounts not inconsistent with commercial invoice.
- Visaed and signed properly. no alteration except by Letter of Correction. filled out in all places indicated.
- Vessel name. ports. flag. and freight same as on B/L: insurance premium same as insurance document.
- All copies on official form except if allowed by L/C.

CERT. ORIG.
- Names and addresses per commercial invoice and per L/C.
- Issued by proper party and signed and showing description not inconsistent with commercial invoice and L/C; certified. legalized or notarized if required.

CERT. INSP.
- Names and addresses per commercial invoice and per L/C.
- Issued by proper party and signed and showing description relative to commercial invoice and L/C.
- Is in exact compliance with L/C and dated reasonably current.

P/L
- Names and addresses. marks and numbers. order numbers. etc.. same as relative per commercial invoice.
- All quantities and packaging not inconsistent with commercial invoice; contents of each package listed.

CUSTOMS INV.
- Names and addresses. marks and numbers. order numbers. amounts not inconsistent with other documents.
- Vessel name same as on B/L: signed Purchase Declaration unless no value samples.
- On official form. not tissue copies and contains any special wording required by L/C.

OTHER DOCUMENTS
- See details in Guide.

Date	LC No.	Drawing Amount	Initials	Computer Balance	Dated

NI 4334

Figure G-37: CHECKLIST FOR LETTER OF CREDIT
(Courtesy of Northwestern National Bank of Minneapolis.)

CLEAVELAND FORM NO. 614

FORM NO. U.S. DEPARTMENT OF COMMERCE – SESA, BUREAU OF THE CENSUS – DIBA, BUREAU OF EAST-WEST TRADE
7525-V
(12-10-73)

SHIPPER'S EXPORT DECLARATION
OF SHIPMENTS FROM THE UNITED STATES
Export Shipments Are Subject To Inspection By U.S. Customs Service and/or The Office of Export Control
READ CAREFULLY THE INSTRUCTIONS ON BACK TO AVOID DELAY AT SHIPPING POINT

Form Approved: O.M.B. No. 41-R0397

CONFIDENTIAL – For use solely for official purposes authorized by the Secretary of Commerce. Use for unauthorized purposes is not permitted (Title 15, Sec. 30.91 (a) C.F.R., Sec. 7(c) Export Administration Act of 1969, as amended, P.L. 91-184).

Authentication (When required)

Declarations Should be Typewritten or Prepared in Ink

DO NOT USE THIS AREA	DISTRICT	PORT	COUNTRY (For Customs use only)

File No. (For Customs use only)

1. FROM (U.S. port of export)

2. METHOD OF TRANSPORTATION (Check one):
☐ VESSEL (Incl. ferry) ☐ AIR ☐ OTHER (Specify) _____

2a. EXPORTING CARRIER (If vessel, give name of ship, flag and pier number. If air, give name of airline.)

3. EXPORTER (Principal or seller – licensee)   ADDRESS (Number, street, place, State)

4. AGENT OF EXPORTER (Forwarding agent)   ADDRESS (Number, street, place, State)

5. ULTIMATE CONSIGNEE   ADDRESS (Place, country)

6. INTERMEDIATE CONSIGNEE   ADDRESS (Place, country)

7. FOREIGN PORT OF UNLOADING (For vessel and air shipments only)

8. PLACE AND COUNTRY OF ULTIMATE DESTINATION (Not place of transshipment)

MARKS AND NOS.	NUMBERS AND KIND OF PACKAGES, DESCRIPTION OF COMMODITIES, EXPORT LICENSE NUMBER OR GENERAL LICENSE SYMBOL (Describe commodities in sufficient detail to permit verification of the Schedule B commodity numbers assigned. Do not use general terms.)	SHIPPING (Gross) WEIGHT IN POUNDS^a (REQUIRED FOR VESSEL AND AIR SHIPMENTS ONLY)	SPECIFY "D" OR "F"^b	SCHEDULE B COMMODITY NO. (Include Commodity Control List italicized digit, when required)	NET QUANTITY SCHEDULE B UNITS (State unit)	VALUE AT U.S. PORT OF EXPORT (Selling price or cost if not sold, including inland freight, insurance and other charges to U.S. port of export) (Nearest whole dollar, omit cents figures)
(9)	(10)	(11)	(12)	(13)	(14)	(15)

VALIDATED LICENSE NO. _____   OR GENERAL LICENSE SYMBOL _____

16. BILL OF LADING OR AIR WAYBILL NUMBER

17. DATE OF EXPORTATION (Not required for shipments by vessel)

18. THE UNDERSIGNED HEREBY AUTHORIZES _____
(Name and address – Number, street, place, State)
TO ACT AS FORWARDING AGENT FOR EXPORT CONTROL AND CUSTOMS PURPOSES.

EXPORTER _____ BY (DULY AUTHORIZED OFFICER OR EMPLOYEE) _____

▶ 19. I CERTIFY THAT ALL STATEMENTS MADE AND ALL INFORMATION CONTAINED IN THIS EXPORT DECLARATION ARE TRUE AND CORRECT. I AM AWARE OF THE PENALTIES PROVIDED FOR FALSE REPRESENTATION. (See paragraphs I (c) and (e) on reverse side.)

SIGNATURE _____ FOR _____
(Duly authorized officer or employee of exporter or named forwarding agent) (Name of corporation or firm, and capacity of signer, e.g., secretary, export manager, etc.)

ADDRESS _____

▶ Declaration should be made by duly authorized officer or employee of exporter or of forwarding agent named by exporter.

^a If shipping weight is not available for each Schedule B item listed in column (13) included in one or more packages, insert the approximate gross weight for each Schedule B item. The total of these estimated weights should equal the actual weight of the entire package or packages.

^b Designate foreign merchandise (reexports) with an "F" and exports of domestic merchandise produced in the United States or changed in condition in the United States with a "D." (See instructions on reverse side.)

LITHO IN U.S.A.

DO NOT USE THIS AREA

Figure G-38: SHIPPER'S EXPORT DECLARATION
(Courtesy of Mr. Gordon Ramsay, Cleaveland Legal Blank Service, Inc., E. Hartford, Connecticut.)

(M.A.)—FORM OF INVOICE APPROVED BY CANADIAN CUSTOMS (1959) FOR GOODS SOLD BY EXPORTER
PRIOR TO IMPORTATION, FOR ENTRY AT MOST FAVOURED NATION TARIFF RATES

(Place and Date) 19

Invoice of (General nature or class of merchandise) .... purchased

by .... of ....

from .... of ....

to be shipped from .... per ....

CUSTOMER'S ORDER NO. .... OUR ORDER NO. .... TERMS

Country of Origin	Marks and Numbers on Packages	QUANTITIES AND DESCRIPTION OF GOODS	Fair market value at time and place of shipment in currency of country of export (See clauses 5 to 8 of certificate of value hereon)	Selling price to the Purchaser in Canada (Specify currency of settlement)	
				@	Amount

* NOTE:
The following facts must be shown

Amount of: Freight, if any, prepaid and charged ....

Freight, if any, prepaid and not charged .... *

Freight, if any, allowed to be deducted by importer on settlement .... *

* If any freight is prepaid by the exporter and not charged, or is allowed to be deducted by the importer on settlement, a statement must be made on this invoice indicating whether or not the practice is consistent with the exporter's domestic market freight policy.

In cases where the vendor does not reside in the country of export or for other reasons the vendor is unable to sign the certificate both as to value and origin, a separate certificate of origin in prescribed form signed by the exporter in the country of export, bearing a full description of the goods and the marks and numbers of the packages, so that it may be identified with the shipment, will be accepted.

(M) I, the undersigned, do hereby certify as follows:

(1) That I am the .... of ....
    insert official capacity   name of exporter
    exporter of the goods described in the within invoice;
(2) That the said invoice is in all respects correct and true;
(3) That the said invoice contains a true and full statement showing the price actually paid or to be paid for the said goods, the actual quantity thereof and all charges thereon;
(4) That there is included in the said invoice the true value of all cartons, cases, crates, boxes and coverings of any kind and all charges and expenses incident to placing the said goods in condition packed ready for shipment to Canada;
(5) That the said invoice also exhibits the fair market value, at the time when and place from which the goods were shipped directly to Canada, of like goods when sold in the same or substantially the same quantities for home consumption in the ordinary course of trade under competitive conditions to purchasers located at that place with whom the vendor deals at arm's length and who are at the same or substantially the same trade level as the importer;
(6) That where like goods are not sold for home consumption in the circumstances described in the preceding section but where the goods shown on this invoice are similar to those sold for home consumption, the fair market value exhibited thereon is not less than the aggregate of
(a) the cost of production of the goods exported; and
(b) an amount that is the same percentage of the cost of production of the goods exported as the gross profit on the similar goods is of the cost of production of the similar goods;
(7) That the said fair market value is without
(a) any discount or deduction not shown, allowed and deducted on invoices covering sales for home consumption in the country of export in the ordinary course of trade;
(b) any deduction on account of any subsidy or drawback of Customs duty that has been allowed by the Government of any other country, or on account of any so-called royalty, rent or charge for use of any machine or goods of any description, that the seller or proprietor does or would usually charge thereon when the same are sold or leased or rented for use in the country of export; or
(c) any discount or deduction on account of the amount of consideration or money value of any special arrangement between any persons interested therein, because of the exportation or intended exportation of such goods, or the right to territorial limits for the sale or use thereof;
(8) That if the fair market value of the said goods described in this invoice is other than the value thereof as above specified, such fair market value has, to the best of my knowledge and belief, been fixed and determined under the authority of the Customs Act at the value exhibited in this invoice;
(9) That no different invoice of the goods mentioned in the said invoice has been or will be furnished to any one by me or on my behalf;
(10) That no arrangement or understanding affecting the purchase price of the said goods has been or will be made or entered into between the said exporter and purchaser or by any one on behalf of either of them other than as shown on the said invoice, either by way of discount, rebate, salary, compensation or in any other manner whatsoever;
(A) That each article on this invoice is bona fide the produce or manufacture of the country specified on the invoice as its Country of Origin;
    That such manufactured article on the invoice in its present form ready for export to Canada has been finished in such specified country of origin, and not less than

    one-half the cost of production of each such article has been produced through the industry of * ....

                                                                    (* Insert here name of country or countries)
entitled to the benefits of treaty or convention rates or the British Preferential Tariff.

Dated at ....
                                                                                    (Firm Name)

this .... day of ....
                                                                                    (Individual Signature and Title)

NOTE:—When invoicing goods which have been finished in a country specified on the invoice as its country of origin from materials originating in a country or countries entitled to the benefits of the Most Favoured Nation Tariff or the British Preferential Tariff, the names of the countries contributing to one-half the cost of production should be shown in the space provided in the certificate.
In the calculation of the cost of production for the purpose of determining the qualification for entry under the Most Favoured Nation Tariff none of the following items are to be included or considered, viz:—
1. Outside packages and expenses of packing thereinto.
2. Manufacturer's or exporter's profit or the profit or remuneration of any trader, broker, or other person dealing in the article in its finished manufactured condition.
3. Royalties.
4. Customs or excise duty or tax paid or payable on imported materials.
5. Carriage, insurance, etc., from place of production or manufacture to port of shipment.
6. Any other charges incurred or to be incurred subsequent to the completion of the manufacture of the goods.

FORM NO. 606

Figure G-39: INVOICE APPROVED BY CANADIAN CUSTOMS
(Courtesy of Mr. Gordon Ramsay, Cleaveland Legal Blank Service, Inc., E. Hartford, Connecticut.)

PRATT & WHITNEY AIRCRAFT OF CANADA LTD.

SUPPLIER STATEMENT OF NON-CONFORMING MATERIAL

AND P&WC INSPECTION WORK SHEET

P&WC 2881 (12-75)

REFERENCE NUMBER **72147**

PURCHASE ORDER		R/S NO.	SPLIT NO.	PACKING SLIP NO.	PART NUMBER			ENG CH	GRP NO.

INSPECTION COMPLETE ☐
INSPECTION INCOMPLETE ☐

INSP. DEPT.	ENG.	RAW MATERIAL CODE	RCC	PART TITLE
			SPD	

QTY REC'D	QTY INSP.	QTY MR.	HEAT BATCH OR HEAT CODE	BUYER		VENDOR CODE	VENDOR

ITEM NO.	IMS SEQ	B/P LOC	QTY	NON-CONFORMANCE (QUOTE SERIAL NUMBERS WHERE APPLICABLE)	P&WC MR DISPOSITION	MRD REF. NUMBER

◄— TOTAL NUMBER OF NON-CONFORMING PARTS

PWA OR P&WC SOURCE INSPECTOR	DATE D/M/Y	SUPPLIER QUALITY REPRESENTATIVE	DATE D/M/Y
P&WC QUALITY REVIEW	DATE D/M/Y	P&WC INSPECTOR	DATE D/M/Y

COPY 1

COPY 2

COPY 3

COPY 4

COPY 5

Figure G-40: SUPPLIER STATEMENT OF NON-CONFORMING MATERIAL
(Courtesy of Electro-Methods, Inc., South Windsor, Connecticut.)

610

/AiRBORNE

REMIT PAYMENT TO:
AIRBORNE FREIGHT CORPORATION
P.O. BOX 662
SEATTLE, WASHINGTON 98111

ORIGINATOR
INITIALS | STATION

INVOICE

NO. **9324705**

TRANSACTION TYPE

☐ IATA OUTBOUND   ☐ SPECIAL PICKUP/DELIVERY
☐ PICKUP/DELIVERY   ☐
☐ IATA INBOUND   ☐

| CUSTOMER REFERENCE NUMBER | DATE OF INVOICE | DATE OF SHIPMENT |

| WEIGHT | NO. OF PIECES | IATA NUMBER |
☐ LB.   ☐ KILO

| ORIGIN | DESTINATION |

| | LOCAL CURRENCY | U.S. DOLLARS |

CHARGES PER ATTACHED
NAME OF CARRIER_____ BILL NUMBER_____

PICKUP/DELIVERY_____

SPECIAL PICKUP/DELIVERY:
AUTHORIZED BY:_____

ADVANCED CHARGES —
AIRBORNE AIRBILL NUMBERS

OTHER_____ $
                               $
                               $

TOTAL OTHER CHARGES

PLEASE PAY THIS AMOUNT ➝

THIS IS YOUR INVOICE.
NO OTHER INVOICE
WILL BE RENDERED.
TERMS = NET 7 DAYS.

PLEASE RETURN DUPLICATE INVOICE
COPY WITH YOUR REMITTANCE

REFER TO THIS NUMBER WHEN REMITTING

NO. **9324705**

DUPLICATE INVOICE — RETURN WITH REMITTANCE

168 (6/79)

Figure G-41: DUPLICATE INVOICE AND REQUEST FOR PAYMENT
(Courtesy of Airborne Freight Corporation, Seattle, Washington.)

015- 67963755

	Airport of Departure	Execution date Day/Mth/Year	TC	CHGS Code	Cur'cy Code	for carrier use only

for carrier use only
Flight/Day | Flight/Day

015- 67963755

Airport of departure (address of first carrier) and requested routing | Airport of Destination | Flight/Day | Flight/Day

Booked

Routing and Destination

1 To | by first carrier | to | by | to | by

NOT NEGOTIABLE

AIR WAYBILL
(AIR CONSIGNMENT NOTE)
ISSUED BY
TRANS WORLD AIRLINES, INC.
KANSAS CITY, MISSOURI, U.S.A.
Member of International Air Transport Association

TWA
AIR FREIGHT
A WORLD-WIDE MARKETAIR SERVICE

2 Consignee's account number | Consignee's name and address

CUSTOMS DOCUMENT NOS.

3 Shipper's account number | Shipper's name and address

The shipper certifies that the particulars on the face hereof are correct. agrees to the CONDITIONS ON REVERSE HEREOF, accepts that carrier's liability is limited as stated in 4(c) on the reverse hereof and accepts such value unless a higher value for carriage is declared on the face hereof subject to an additional charge and that insofar as any part of the consignment contains restricted articles. such part is properly described by name and is in proper condition for carriage by air according to the International Air Transport Association's Restricted Articles Regulations.

SIGNATURE OF SHIPPER OR HIS AGENT

Carrier certifies goods described below were received for carriage subject to the Conditions on reverse hereof. the goods then being in apparent good order and condition except as noted hereon

4 Issuing carrier's agent, account no. | Issuing carrier's agent, name and city

EXECUTED ON (Date) at (Place)

TRANS WORLD AIRLINES, INC.

SIGNATURE OF ISSUING CARRIER OR ITS AGENT

Agent's IATA-Code

Copies 1. 2 and 3 of this Air Waybill are originals and have the same validity.

5 Currency | Declared value for carriage | Declared value for customs | Amount of insurance | INSURANCE-If shipper requests insurance in accordance with conditions on reverse hereof, indicate amount to be insured in figures in box marked 'amount of insurance'.

WEIGHT CHARGE AND VALUATION CHARGE
PREPAID | COLLECT
ALL OTHER CHARGES AT ORIGIN
PREPAID | COLLECT
Accounting information

6

No. of packages RCP	Actual gross weight	kg lb.	Rate class Commodity item no.	Chargeable weight	Rate/Charge	Total	Nature and quantity of goods (incl. dimensions or volume)

pre-paid

7 Prepaid weight charge | Prepaid valuation charge | Due carrier | Total other prepaid charges | Due agent | Total prepaid | For carrier's use only at destination

R Other charges (except weight charge and valuation charge) | Collect charges in destination currency

S | COD amount

T | Total charges

collect

8 Collect weight charge | Collect valuation charge | Due carrier | Total other collect charges | Due agent | COD amount | Total collect

9

Handling Information: These commodities licensed by the United States for ultimate destination...........................Diversion contrary to United States law prohibited.

AC-13 (3/78)
PRINTED IN U.S.A.

015- 67963755

Figure G-42: NON-NEGOTIABLE AIR WAYBILL
(Courtesy of Trans World Airlines, Inc.)

JAPAN AIR LINES

Member of International Air Transport Association

SHIPPER'S LETTER OF INSTRUCTION FOR DISPATCH OF GOODS

To: Japan Air Lines Co., Ltd. or its authorized agent

You are hereby requested and authorized upon receipt of the consignment to prepare and sign the Air Waybill and other necessary documents on our behalf and dispatch the consignment in accordance with your "Conditions of Contract".

The goods have been dispatch to JAL at _____ via _____ from _____
CITY   CARRIER   CITY

AIR CARRIAGE	To	FIRST CARRIER	For further instruction, phone
1. From (*U.S. Port of Export*)	To	CARRIER	

2a. Exporting Carrier
    JAPAN AIR LINES CO., LTD.

3. Exporter (*Principal or seller—licensee*)   Address (*Number, street, place, state*)

4. Agent of Exporter (*Forwarding agent*)   Address (*Number, street, place, state*)

5. Ultimate Consignee (*also notify party on AWB if item 6 is filled in*)   Address (*Place, country*)

6. Intermediate Consignee   Address (*Place, country*)

7. Foreign Port of Unloading   8. Place and Country of Ultimate Destination (*Not place of transshipment*)

INSURANCE	SHIPPER'S DECLARED VALUE		Charges on Air Waybill are payable by	
AMOUNT $ IF AMOUNT IS NOT INDICATED, SHIPMENT IS NOT INSURED.	FOR CUSTOMS $	FOR CARRIAGE $	☐ Shipper	☐ Consignee

9. MARK AND NOS.	10. NUMBER AND KIND OF PACKAGES, DESCRIPTION OF COMMODITIES, EXPORT LICENSE NUMBER	11. SHIPPING (GROSS) WEIGHT IN POUNDS	12. SPECIFY D OR F	13. SCHEDULE B COMMODITY NO.	14. NET QUANTITY IN SCHEDULE B UNITS	15. VALUE AT U.S. PORT OF EXPORT

These commodities licensed by U.S. for ultimate destination _____ Diversion contrary to U.S. law prohibited

Documents Attached to Accompany Air Waybill

☐ COMMERCIAL INVOICE   ☐ CONSULAR INVOICE   ☐ CERTIFICATE OF ORIGIN

☐ PACKING LIST   ☐ OTHER:

Special Instruction

SIGNATURE _____ DATE _____

- SPECIAL ATTENTION IS REQUIRED IN FILLING OUT THE NUMBERED COLUMNS, FROM 1 THROUGH 15, WHICH ARE IDENTICAL TO COLUMNS ON EXPORT DECLARATION.
- COLUMN 19 OF THE EXPORT DECLARATION MUST BE SIGNED IN INK.

PRINTED IN JAPAN   TS 50101

Figure G-43: SHIPPER'S LETTER OF INSTRUCTION FOR DISPATCH OF GOODS
(Courtesy of Japan Air Lines.)

U.S. DEPARTMENT OF COMMERCE
BUREAU OF THE CENSUS—BUREAU OF INTERNATIONAL PROGRAMS

SHIPPER'S EXPORT DECLARATION
OF SHIPMENTS FROM THE UNITED STATES

Export Shipments Are Subject To U.S. Customs Inspection

READ CAREFULLY THE INSTRUCTIONS ON BACK TO AVOID DELAY AT SHIPPING POINT

For shipments to foreign countries, the export declaration (a) must be presented to and authenticated by the Collector of Customs before the goods are placed on pier or dock or other place of loading for the purpose of exporting by water or air; (b) must be presented to and authenticated by the Collector prior to exportation where the goods are exported by other means.

Declarations Should Be Typewritten Or Prepared In Ink

CONFIDENTIAL For use solely for official purposes authorised by the Secretary of Commerce. Use for unauthorised purposes is not permitted. (Title 15, Sec. 30.5 (b) C.F.R.; 50 U.S.C. App., 2026c.)

Customs Authentication (For Customs use only.)

FILE NO. (For Customs use only.)

Do Not Use This Area	District	Port	Country (For customs use only)

1. FROM (U.S. Port of Export)   2. METHOD OF TRANSPORTATION (check one): ☐ Vessel (incl. ferry) ☒ Air ☐ Other (Specify)

2a. EXPORTING CARRIER (If vessel, give name of ship, flag and pier number. If air, give name of airline.)
AER LINGUS IRISH AIRLINES

3. EXPORTER (Principal or seller—licensee)   ADDRESS (Number, street, place, state)

4. AGENT OF EXPORTER (Forwarding agent)   ADDRESS (Number, street, place, state)

5. ULTIMATE CONSIGNEE   ADDRESS (Place, country)

6. INTERMEDIATE CONSIGNEE   ADDRESS (Place, country)

7. FOREIGN PORT OF UNLOADING (For vessel and air shipments only)   8. PLACE AND COUNTRY OF ULTIMATE DESTINATION (Not place of transshipment)

(9) MARKS AND NOS.	(10) NUMBER AND KIND OF PACKAGES, DESCRIPTION OF COMMODITIES, EXPORT LICENSE NUMBER, EXPIRATION DATE (OR GENERAL LICENSE SYMBOL) (Describe commodities in sufficient detail to permit verification of the Schedule B commodity numbers assigned. Do not use general terms. Insert required license information on line below description of each item)	(11) SHIPPING (Gross) WEIGHT IN POUNDS* (required for vessel and air shipments only)	(12) SPECIFY "D" OR "F"	(13) SCHEDULE B COMMODITY No.	(14) NET QUANTITY IN SCHEDULE B UNITS (State unit)	(15) VALUE AT U.S. PORT OF EXPORT (Selling price or cost if not sold, including inland freight, insurance and other charges to U.S. port of export) (Nearest whole dollar; omit cents figures)

These commodities licensed by the U.S. for ultimate destination.................................Diversion contrary to U.S. law prohibited.

16. WAYBILL OR MANIFEST NO. (of Exporting Carrier)   17. DATE OF EXPORTATION (Not required for shipments by vessel)

18. THE UNDERSIGNED HEREBY AUTHORIZES_____ (Name and address—Number, street, place, State)
TO ACT AS FORWARDING AGENT FOR EXPORT CONTROL AND CUSTOMS PURPOSES.
(DULY AUTHORIZED
EXPORTER_____ BY _____ OFFICER OR EMPLOYEE)

▶ 19. I CERTIFY THAT ALL STATEMENTS MADE AND ALL INFORMATION CONTAINED IN THIS EXPORT DECLARATION ARE TRUE AND CORRECT. I AM AWARE OF THE PENALTIES PROVIDED FOR FALSE REPRESENTATION. (See Paragraphs I (c), (e), on reverse side.)

Signature_____ (Duly authorized officer or employee of exporter or named forwarding agent)   For_____ (Name of corporation or firm, and capacity of signer; e.g., secretary, export manager, etc.)

Address_____

▶ Declaration should be made by duly authorized officer or employee of exporter or or forwarding agent named by exporter.
* If shipping weight is not available for each Schedule B item listed in column (13) included in one or more packages, insert the approximate gross weight for each Schedule B item. The total of these estimated weights should equal the actual weight of the entire package or packages.
▶ Designate foreign merchandise (reexports) with an "F" and exports of domestic merchandise produced in the United States or changed in condition in the United States with a "D." (See instructions on reverse side.)
CARRIERS, FORWARDERS AND EXPORTERS ARE REMINDED THAT IF A DESTINATION CONTROL STATEMENT IS REQUIRED ON A SHIPPER'S EXPORT DECLARATION COVERING A GIVEN SHIPMENT, SUCH STATEMENT MUST ALSO APPEAR ON ALL COPIES OF THE BILL OF LADING AND COMMERCIAL INVOICE. (See Comprehensive Export Schedule.)

Do Not Use This Area

6705

SHIPPING INSTRUCTIONS TO: _____

ROUTING VIA AerLingus Irish Airlines   Date_____

Received for Irish International Airlines

Prepaid ☐   Collect ☐   Goods Only ☐   Papers Only ☐   Both ☐

C.O.D. $_____   Remarks:_____

Insurance $_____   Thank You for Shipping by

Value for Carriage $_____   **Aer Lingus** Irish Airlines

NAJ 6705 - 8M - 4/77

SHIPPER — DETACH THIS PART FOR YOUR RECORDS

Figure G-44: EXPORT DECLARATION WITH SHIPPING INSTRUCTIONS
(Courtesy of Aer Lingus Irish Airlines.)

DO NOT DETACH THIS TOP PORTION FROM ORIGINAL, DUPLICATE, TRIPLICATE AND QUADRUPLICATE WHEN SUBMITTING APPLICATION

FORM DIB-622P(REV. 3-75)
(FORMERLY FC-419)   R.0735
Form Approved OMB No.

U.S. DEPARTMENT OF COMMERCE
DOMESTIC AND INTERNATIONAL
BUSINESS ADMINISTRATION
BUREAU OF EAST WEST TRADE
OFFICE OF EXPORT ADMINISTRATION
WASHINGTON, D.C. 20230

**APPLICATION FOR
EXPORT LICENSE**

DATE RECEIVED *(Leave Blank)*

CASE NO. *(Leave Blank)*

CONFIDENTIAL—Information furnished herewith is deemed confidential and will not be published or disclosed except in accordance with provision of Section 7(c) of the Export Administration Act of 1969, as amended.

DATE OF APPLICATION

APPLICANT'S TELEPHONE NO.

1. APPLICANT'S NAME

STREET ADDRESS

CITY, STATE, ZIP CODE

2. PURCHASER IN FOREIGN COUNTRY
(If same as ultimate consignee, state "SAME AS ITEM 3"; if same as intermediate consignee, state "SAME AS ITEM 4.")

NAME

STREET ADDRESS

CITY AND COUNTRY

3. ULTIMATE CONSIGNEE IN FOREIGN COUNTRY

NAME

STREET ADDRESS

CITY AND COUNTRY

4. INTERMEDIATE CONSIGNEE IN FOREIGN COUNTRY.
(If none, state "NONE;" if unknown, state "UNKNOWN.")

NAME

STREET ADDRESS

CITY AND COUNTRY

5. COUNTRY OF ULTIMATE DESTINATION

6. APPLICANT'S REFERENCE NUMBER

7. (a) QUANTITY TO BE SHIPPED

(b) COMMODITY DESCRIPTION AS GIVEN IN COMMODITY CONTROL LIST *(Include characteristics such as basic ingredients, composition, type, size, gauge, grade, horsepower, etc.)*

(c) EXPORT CONTROL COMMODITY NUMBER AND PROCESSING NUMBER

(d) TOTAL SELLING PRICE AND POINT OF DELIVERY
(Indicated F.O.B., F.A.S., C.I.F., etc.)

UNIT PRICE	TOTAL PRICE
	TOTAL

Figure G-45: APPLICATION FOR EXPORT LICENSE

615

8. FILL IN IF PERSON OTHER THAN APPLICANT IS AUTHORIZED TO RECEIVE LICENSE

NAME

STREET ADDRESS

CITY, STATE, ZIP CODE

9. IF APPLICANT IS NOT THE PRODUCER OF COMMODITY TO BE EXPORTED, GIVE NAME AND ADDRESS OF SUPPLIER.
(If unknown, state "UNKNOWN.")

10. END USE OF COMMODITIES COVERED BY THIS APPLICATION. DESCRIBE FULLY

11. IF APPLICANT IS NOT EXPORTING FOR HIS OWN ACCOUNT, GIVE NAME AND ADDRESS OF FOREIGN PRINCIPAL AND EXPLAIN FULLY

12. ADDITIONAL INFORMATION *(Attach separate sheet if more space is needed.)*

13. APPLICANT'S CERTIFICATION. — The undersigned applicant hereby makes application for a license to export and certifies as follows: That all statements herein, and in any documents or attachments submitted in support hereof, are true and correct to the best of his knowledge and belief; and that (a) he has read the instructions on the fifth copy of this application and is familiar with the U.S. Department of Commerce Export Administration Regulations; (b) this application conforms to such instructions and regulations; (c) unless Item 14 is completed, he negotiated with and secured the export order directly from the purchaser or ultimate consignee or through his or their agents abroad; (d) all parties to the export transaction, the exact commodities and quantities, or the exact technical data, and all other terms of the order and other facts of the export transaction are fully and accurately reflected herein; (e) documents and records evidencing the order and other facts of the export transaction to which this application relates will be retained by him for 2 years from whichever is later: the time of (i) the export from the United States, or (ii) any known reexport, transshipment, or diversion, or (iii) any other termination of the transaction, whether formally in writing or by any other means, and made available to the Department of Commerce upon demand; (f) any material or substantive changes in the terms of the order or other facts of the export transaction as reflected in this application or any certification made in connection therewith, whether the application is still under consideration or after a license has been granted, will be reported promptly by him to the Department of Commerce; and (g) if the license is granted, he will be strictly accountable for its use in accordance with the Department of Commerce Export Administration Regulations and all terms and conditions specified on the face of the license.

SIGN HERE IN INK

Type or Print _____ (Applicant *(Same as Item 1)*)

(Signature of person authorized to execute this application.)

Type or Print _____
(Name and title of person whose signature appears on the line to the left)

14. ORDER PARTY'S CERTIFICATION (See § 372.6 (c) of the *Export Administration Regulations*.) — The undersigned order party certifies to the truth and correctness of Item 13 (d) above, and that he has no information concerning the export transaction that is inconsistent with, or undisclosed by the application and agrees to comply with Items 13 (e) and 13 (f) above.

SIGN HERE IN INK

Type or Print _____ (Order Party)

(Signature of person authorized to sign for the Order Party)

Type or Print _____
(Name and title of person whose signature appears on the line to the left)

This license application and any license issued pursuant thereto are expressly subject to all rules and regulations of the Department of Commerce. Making any false statement or concealing any material fact in connection with this application or altering in any way the validated license issued, is punishable by imprisonment or fine, or both, and by denial of export privileges under the Export Administration Act of 1969, as amended, and any other Federal statutes.

FOR OFFICIAL USE ONLY

ACTION TAKEN	VALIDITY PERIOD	AUTHORITY	RATING		END USE CHECK	RE-EXPORT	DV	SUPPORT DOCUMENT	TECH. DATA	TYPE OF LICENSE
☐ APPROVED	MONTHS									
☐ REJECTED										
DOCUMENTATION										

_____ (Licensing officer)   (No.)   (Date)

_____ (Review officer)   (Date)

NOTE: Submit the first four copies of this application, Form DIB-622P (with top stub attached), to the Office of Export Administration, Room 1617M, Domestic and International Business Administration, U.S. Department of Commerce, Washington, D.C. 20230, retaining the quintuplicate copy of the form for your files. Remove the long carbon sheet from in front of the quintuplicate copy. Do *not* remove any other carbon sheets. See Special Instructions on back of quintuplicate. Reproduction of this form is permissible, providing that content, format, size, and color of paper and ink are the same.

ORIGINAL
0 E A FILE COPY

616

Figure G-45 (continued)

FORM DIB 628 (REV 3-75)

EXPORT LICENSE

U.S. DEPARTMENT OF COMMERCE
DOMESTIC AND INTERNATIONAL BUSINESS ADMINISTRATION
BUREAU OF EAST-WEST TRADE
OFFICE OF EXPORT ADMINISTRATION

Not approved unless the official validation stamp appears hereon.

VALIDATION

LICENSE NUMBER

License is hereby granted to the licensee named herein, upon the terms and provisions stated herein, to export from the United States the articles, materials, technical data, or supplies herein described. This license is granted in reliance on representations heretofore made by the licensee to obtain it and is expressly subject to all export control laws, regulations, rules, and orders. It is not transferable without written permission from the Office of Export Administration.

1. LICENSEE

2. PURCHASER

VOID

3. ULTIMATE CONSIGNEE IN FOREIGN COUNTRY

4. INTERMEDIATE CONSIGNEE

5. COUNTRY OF ULTIMATE DESTINATION

6. APPLICANT'S REFERENCE NO.

QUANTITY	DESCRIPTION OF COMMODITIES	EXPORT CONTROL COMMODITY NUMBER AND PROCESSING NUMBER	UNIT PRICE	TOTAL PRICE
	VOID			
			TOTAL	

NOTE:

- An Export License must be returned immediately to the Office of Export Administration, Room 1617M, Domestic and International Business Administration, U. S. Department of Commerce, Washington, D.C. 20230, (a) when it has been fully used, (b) when it has expired, or (c) when it has been determined that it will not be used or will no longer be used.

- Each shipment made against this license shall be entered on the reverse and licensee must sign prior to returning it.

- A Destination Control Statement is required to be shown on all bills of lading, air waybills, and commercial invoices. (See Export Administration Regulations §386.6.)

Figure G-46: EXPORT LICENSE

Form DIB 685P (Formerly IA-783)
(Revised 6-74)

U S DEPARTMENT OF COMMERCE
DOMESTIC AND INTERNATIONAL BUSINESS ADMINISTRATION
BUREAU OF EAST WEST TRADE
OFFICE OF EXPORT ADMINISTRATION

FORM APPROVED. OMB NO. 41-R1186.6.

REQUEST FOR AND NOTICE OF AMENDMENT ACTION

THIS SPACE FOR OFFICIAL USE ONLY

VALIDATION

1. CASE NO.	3. LICENSE NO.
2. APPLICANT'S REFERENCE NO.	4. EXPIRATION DATE OF LICENSE

☐ APPROVED   ☐ REJECTED

_____ _____
(Signature of licensing officer)   (Date)

REASON FOR REJECTION

5. RETURN COPY OF AMENDMENT NOTICE TO

6. NAME OF LICENSEE

13. AMEND LICENSE TO READ AS FOLLOWS:

7. COUNTRY OF ULTIMATE DESTINATION	8. DATES OF PREVIOUS EXTENSIONS (If any)

9. COMMODITY DESCRIPTION

10. EXPORT CONTROL COMMODITY NO.	11. PROCESSING NUMBER

12. FACTS NECESSITATING AMENDMENT

14. HAS THIS REQUEST BEEN PREVIOUSLY REJECTED OR IS IT PENDING IN ANY COMMERCE DEPARTMENT OFFICE?

IF YES, EXPLAIN ON SEPARATE SHEET. ☐ YES ☐ NO

15. SIGNATURE

_____
(Licensee)

BY _____
(Authorized agent)   (Title)   (Date)

ORIGINAL—Office of Export Administration---File Copy *(See instructions on reverse of triplicate)*

Figure G-47: REQUEST FOR AND NOTICE OF AMENDMENT ACTION

FORM DIB 69 P (8 74) (Formerly IA 45) (OMB No. 41-R1569 Approval Expires May 1976	U.S. DEPARTMENT OF COMMERCE DOMESTIC AND INTERNATIONAL BUSINESS ADMINISTRATION BUREAU OF EAST-WEST TRADE OFFICE OF EXPORT ADMINISTRATION WASHINGTON, D.C. 20230	CASE NO. (Leave Blank)

CONFIDENTIAL Information furnished herewith is deemed confidential and will not be published or disclosed except in accordance with Section of the Export Administration Act of 1969

REQUEST TO DISPOSE OF COMMODITIES OR TECHNICAL DATA PREVIOUSLY EXPORTED

1 DATE OF REQUEST

2(a). APPLICANT'S REF. NO.   2(b). APPLICANT'S TELEPHONE NO.

3. APPLICANT'S NAME

STREET

CITY, STATE, ZIP CODE

4. COMMODITIES OR TECHNICAL DATA PREVIOUSLY EXPORTED UNDER:

VALIDATED LICENSE NO. _____

(CASE NO. _____)

GENERAL LICENSE (Specify type) _____

5. NEW ULTIMATE CONSIGNEE

NAME

STREET

CITY AND COUNTRY

6. ORIGINAL ULTIMATE CONSIGNEE

NAME

STREET

CITY AND COUNTRY

7 I (WE) HEREBY REQUEST AUTHORIZATION TO: ☐ REEXPORT ☐ SELL
☐ OTHER (Specify) _____
THE FOLLOWING: (If this request is being submitted on behalf of another firm or individual, explain in Item 10 below.)

8.(a) QUANTITY	(b) DESCRIPTION OF COMMODITY OR TECHNICAL DATA	(c) EXPORT CONTROL COMMODITY NO. AND PROCESSING NO.	(d) DOLLAR VALUE

9 END USE OF COMMODITIES OR TECHNICAL DATA BY NEW ULTIMATE CONSIGNEE (Describe fully)

10. ADDITIONAL INFORMATION (Attach separate sheet if more space is needed)

11. APPLICANT'S CERTIFICATION - I(We) certify that the above statements are true to the best of my (our) knowledge and belief. If authorization is granted, I(We) will be strictly accountable for its use in accordance with the Export Administration Regulations and all terms and conditions specified on the authorization.

Type or Print _____ Applicant (Same as Item 3))

SIGN HERE IN INK _____ (Signature of person authorized to execute this request)

Type or Print _____ (Name and title of person whose signature appears on line to left)

FOR OFFICIAL USE ONLY

SPECIAL CONDITIONS

ACTION TAKEN	AUTHORITY	RATING	DV	TECH. DATA	
☐ APPROVED					
☐ REJECTED		END USE CHECK	RE-EX-PORT	SUPPORT. DOCUMENT	TYPE OF LICENSE
DOCUMENTATION					

(Licensing officer)   (No.)   (Date)

(Review officer)   (Date)

NOTE: Submit Form DIB-621P or FC-420 (Application Processing Card) and the first four copies of this request to the Office of Export Administration, Room 1617M, Domestic and International Business Administration, U.S. Department of Commerce, Washington, D.C. 20230 retaining the quadruplicate for your files. This form may be reproduced provided the content, format, size and color of paper and ink are the same.

ORIGINAL
O E A CASE FILE COPY

Figure G-48: REQUEST TO DISPOSE OF COMMODITIES PREVIOUSLY EXPORTED

FORM IA-743-A
(REV. 4-70)

U.S. DEPARTMENT OF COMMERCE
BUREAU OF INTERNATIONAL COMMERCE
OFFICE OF EXPORT CONTROL
WASHINGTON, D.C. 20230

REQUEST FOR, AND ADVICE ON, STATUS OF PENDING APPLICATION, AMENDMENT, OR REEXPORT REQUEST

INSTRUCTIONS—This page is to be filled out by applicant or applicant's agent. Please submit, in duplicate, to Office of Export Control (Attn: 854). One copy will be returned with the appropriate advice noted on the reverse side.

Requestors should allow the period of time set forth in §370.11(b) of the Export Control Regulations to expire before requesting advice on progress of an application, amendment, or reexport request. No action will be taken on earlier requests, unless an emergency exists and is explained. A status request should relate only to one application, amendment, or reexport request.

Name of Applicant Address (*Street, City, State, Zip Code*)

1. Date

2. Date of application, amendment, or reexport request (*Specify type*)

3. Requestor's Ref. No.

4. Case No. (*If known*)

5. Country of ultimate destination

6. Name of ultimate consignee

7. Commodity description

8. Export Control Commodity No.

8. Processing No.

10. Dollar value

11. Is telegraphic/telephonic reply desired at requestor's expense?

Telegraphic ☐ Yes ☐ No   Telephonic ☐ Yes ☐ No

Telephone No.   Area Code

12. Applicant's signature

13. Signature and address of authorized agent (*If not applicant*)

14. Remarks

Figure G-49: STATUS REQUEST ON REEXPORT REQUEST

FORM DIB-4036P (REV. 4-75)	**LICENSING/JOINT VENTURE PROPOSAL**	U.S. DEPARTMENT OF COMMERCE DOMESTIC AND INTERNATIONAL BUSINESS ADMINISTRATION BUREAU OF INTERNATIONAL COMMERCE

1. Name and address of company *(Street, City, State and Zip code)*

2. Year established

3. No. of employees

4. Sales last year $

5. Name and title of official to be contacted | Phone

6. Bank Reference

7. Products presently manufactured

(Kindly enclose brochures or data sheets describing these products)

8. Distribution system:
- ☐ international   ☐ nationwide   ☐ regional
- ☐ own sales force   ☐ reps   ☐ Other: _____

9. Foreign products which we might want to manufacture *(Please be specific, avoid broad terms such as "electronic products" or "light industrial machinery"):*

10. Type of arrangement desired: ☐ licensing   ☐ joint venture*

If a joint venture - we expect the following services and/or equity to be provided by the foreign participant

We will provide the following

(Kindly enclose copy of latest financial statement; annual report, if available; a prospectus; a brief history of company; and data on manufacturing facilities and distribution system.)

Additional information may be continued on reverse side of this form or provided on supplementary sheet numbered to correspond with items above.

Signature and title | Date

FORM DIB-4036P (REV. 4-75)   USCOMM-DC 45061-P75

Please return this completed form to: Office of Export Development/BIC (Room 4020)
Domestic and International Business Administration
U.S. Department of Commerce
Washington, D.C. 20230

Figure G-50: LICENSING/JOINT VENTURE PROPOSAL

ALL-AREAS ANNUAL SALARY DATA COMPARISONS

FOR: _____ DATE: _____

       (country or region)

Currency In Which Data Are Stated: _____

If Translated, State Exchange Rate Or Regional Adj. Ratio _____ As Of _____

	Large Firms	Medium Firms	Small Firms	Our Firm	Comments
			Trainees		
Minimum					
Maximum					
Median					
			1-2 Years Experience		
Minimum					
Maximum					
Median					
			Junior Level		
Minimum					
Maximum					
Median					
			Advanced Level		
Minimum					
Maximum					
Median					
			Senior Level		
Minimum					
Maximum					
Median					

Figure G-51: ALL-AREAS ANNUAL SALARY DATA COMPARISONS

ALLOCATION FORMULA FOR FOREIGN SOURCE INCOME

1. Gross sales in foreign country ....

2. Less: Related expenses ....

3. Taxable Income ....

4. Property in the U.S. ....

5. Property in foreign country ....

6. Asset Formula: $\qquad$ $4 \div (4 + 5) \times \frac{1}{2}(3) =$

7. Gross sales in U.S. ....

8. Gross sales in foreign country ....

9. Sales Formula: $\qquad$ $7 \div (7 + 8) \times \frac{1}{2}(3) =$

10. U.S. taxable income considered derived from U.S. sources
    attributable to foreign country transaction: $\qquad$ $(6) + (9) =$

11. U.S. taxable income considered derived from foreign country
    attributable to foreign country transactions: $\qquad$ $(3) - (10) =$

Figure G-52: ALLOCATION FORMULA FOR FOREIGN SOURCE INCOME

623

APPLICABLE RATES FOR FOREIGN STATEMENTS TRANSLATIONS		
	CURRENT RATE	HISTORICAL RATE
ASSETS		
Cash on hand and in bank (demand deposits)		
Time deposits		
Marketable securities carried at:		
cost		
current market price		
Accounts and notes receivable		
Allowance for doubtful accounts		
Inventories carried at:		
cost		
current replacement		
current selling price		
net realizable value		
contract price		
Prepaid expenses		
Refundable deposits		
Advances to unconsolidate subsidiaries		
Plant and equipment and fixtures		
Real estate		
Accumulated depreciation		
Life insurance, cash surrender value		
Patents, licenses, trademarks, formulas		
Goodwill		
Other intangible assets		
LIABILITIES		
Accounts and notes payable		
Overdrafts		
Accrued expenses		
Losses accrued (on contract commitments)		
Deferred income		
Bonds and other long term debt		
Unamortized premium or discount		
Convertible bonds payable		
Accrued pension obligations		
Other contingent obligations		

Figure G-53: APPLICABLE RATES FOR FOREIGN STATEMENTS TRANSLATIONS

(Local Currency 000's)

Prepared by _____

Date of Report _____

TREASURER'S OFFICE SCHEDULE 5
FOREIGN CURRENCY TRANSLATION EXPOSURE

Currency	CARD[1] Including Pipeline Excluding Borrowings	Travel	T/C	Fireman's Fund	Gross Exposure	Local Borrowing	Exposure after local borrowing	Forward Contracts	Net Exposure	Standard Rate	Net Exposure (U.S. $ Equiv)	CARD FORECAST Most[2] Likely	CARD FORECAST Range[3]	Card[4] Pipeline
	A	B	C	D	E	F	G	H	I	J	K	L	M	N
Data as of:														
Can. Dollar														
Br. Pound														
Fr. Franc														
Ital. Lira														
Belg. Franc														
D. Guilder														
Sw. Franc														
Jap. Yen														
German Mark														
Mex. Peso														
Aust. Dollar														
Sp. Peseta														
H.K. Dollar														

DISTRIBUTION:

1 Ongoing estimated position from last month's closing ledger position.
2 Most likely exposure (including pipeline) during next four weeks.
3 This is an acceptable deviation from most likely exposure level and not high-low extremes.
4 Pipeline same as in Column A.

Figure G-54: FOREIGN EXCHANGE TRANSLATION EXPOSURE (Courtesy of American Express Company.)

SHORT TERM BORROWINGS

Bank _____

Month _____

Bank Location	Currency	Principal	Exchange Rate	Bor. Rate	From	To	# Days Card Col. 9-10	US$ Principal Card Col. 13-20	US$ Expense Card Col. 26-30

Figure G-55: RECORD OF FOREIGN SHORT-TERM BORROWINGS

626

FOREIGN EXCHANGE TRANSACTIONS

DATE										
Bank of America										
Pittsburgh National										
1st Nat'l Bank of Chicago										
Harris Bank										
Chase										
Citibank										
Mellon Bank										
Morgan Guaranty Trust										
Manufacturers Hanover Trust										
Chemical Bank										
Toronto Dominion Bank										

Figure G-56: SUMMARY OF FOREIGN EXCHANGE TRANSACTIONS

STANDARD EXCHANGE RATES COMPARISON

		U.S. Dollar per Foreign Currency Unit			Foreign Currency Unit per U.S. Dollar			Variance %	Net Exposure	Effective Gain (Loss)
		Brown Bros.	Standard	Actual	Brown Bros.	Standard	Actual		$000's	$000's
1.	Argentina									
2.	Australia									
3.	Austria									
4.	Bahrain									
5.	Bangladesh									
6.	Belgium									
7.	Brazil									
8.	Britain									
9.	Canada									
10.	Denmark									
11.	Egypt									
12.	Finland									
13.	France									
14.	Greece									
15.	Hong Kong									
16.	India									
17.	Indonesia									
18.	Iran									
19.	Ireland									
20.	Israel									
21.	Italy									
22.	Japan									
23.	Korea									

Figure G-57: STANDARD EXCHANGE RATES COMPARISON
(Courtesy of American Express Company.)

STANDARD EXCHANGE RATES COMPARISON

		U.S. Dollar per Foreign Currency Unit			Foreign Currency Unit per U.S. Dollar			Var-iance %	Net Ex-posure $000's	Effec-tive Gain (Loss) $000's
		Brown Bros.	Stan-dard	Actual	Brown Bros.	Stan-dard	Actual			
24.	Lebanon									
25.	Malaysia									
26.	Mexico									
27.	Netherlands									
28.	New Zealand									
29.	Norway									
30.	Pakistan									
31.	Philippines									
32.	Portugal									
33.	Singapore									
34.	South Africa									
35.	Spain									
36.	Sweden									
37.	Switzerland									
38.	Taiwan									
39.	U.A.E. Dirham									
40.	Venezuela									
41.	West Germany									

Figure G-57 (continued)

American Express Company
Foreign Exchange Rates - Input Form
(Date)

LINE CODE	COUNTRY	CURRENCY	CODE	CURRENT DAY LOCAL CURRENCY TO U.S. DOLLARS	U.S. DOLLARS TO LOCAL CURRENCY
01	Australia	Dollar	BAXM	0	
02	Austria	Schilling	DNCO		0
03	Belgium-Comm'l	Franc	''		0
04	Belgium-Fin'l	Franc	''		0
05	Brazil	Cruzeiro	''		0
06	Canada	Dollar	TDBX		0
07	Canada Deferred	Dollar	''		0
08	China (Taiwan)	N.T. Dollar			0
09	Denmark	Krone	CMBX		0
10	Finland	Markka	DNCO		0
11	France	Franc	BAXX		0
12	Germany	D. Mark	''		0
13	Greece	Drachma	''		0
14	Hong Kong	Dollar	BAXX		0
15	India	Rupee	BAXM		0
16	Italy	Lire	BAXX		0
17	Jamaica	Dollar	''		0
18	Japan	Yen	BAXX		0
19	Lebanon	Pound	''		0
20	Malaysia	Ringget	BAXM		0
21	Mexico	Peso	CISF		0
22	Morocco	Dirham	''		0
23	Netherlands	Guilder	BAXX		0
24	New Zealand	Dollar	BAXM	0	
25	Norway	Krone	CMBX		0
26	Pakistan	Rupee	''		0
27	Philippines	Peso	''	0	
28	Portugal	Escudo	DNCO		0
29	Singapore	Dollar	CISX		0
30	South Africa	Rand	BAXM	0	
31	Spain	Peseta	DNCO		0
32	Sweden	Krona	CMBX		0
33	Switzerland	Franc	BAXX		0
34	United Kingdom	Pound	''	0	
35	U.S.S.R.	Ruble	''		0
36	Venezuela	Bolivar	BBH		0
37	Ireland	Pound	BAXX	0	

Figure G-58: FOREIGN EXCHANGE RATES—INPUT FORM
(Courtesy of American Express Company.)

630

FOREIGN EXCHANGE RATES
U.S. DOLLARS PER FOREIGN CURRENCY UNIT

DATE _____

Currency	A.E.I.B.C. Expected Rate At / /	1 Month Forward Market Rate	3 Month Forward Market Rate	BBH 3 Month Expected Rate
Canadian Dollar				
British Pound				
French Franc				
Italian Lira				
Belgian Franc				
Dutch Guilder				
Swiss Franc				
Japanese Yen				
W. German Mark				
Mexican Peso				
Australian Dollar				
Spanish Peseta				
Hong Kong Dollar				
Greek Drachma				
Indian Rupee				
Pakistan Rupee				
Taiwan Dollar				
Philippine Peso				
Singapore Dollar				
Austrian Schilling				
Bahrain Dinar	—	—	—	
Bangladesh Taka	—	—	—	
Brazilian Crusero	—	—	—	
Dubai Dirham	—	—	—	
Egyptian Pound	—	—	—	
Indonesia Rupiah	—	—	—	
Korean Won	—	—	—	
Danish Krone	—	—	—	

The above rates are due at the Comptroller's Office by Noon of the 7th workday of each month.

Figure G-59: FOREIGN EXCHANGE SPOT AND FORWARD RATES
(Courtesy of American Express Company.)

FOREIGN EXCHANGE RATES
FOR TRAVEL PRICING
as of
(U.S. Dollar per foreign currency unit)

Currency	3 Months	6 Months	9 Months	12 Months	15 Months	18 Months
Australian Dollar						
Austrian Schilling						
Belgian Franc						
British Pound						
Canadian Dollar						
Danish Krone						
Dutch Guilder						
Egyptian Pound						
French Franc						
Finnish Markka						
German Mark						
Greek Drachma						
Hong Kong Dollar						
Hungarian Forint						
Indian Rupee						
Israeli Pound						
Italian Lira						
Japanese Yen						
Jordanian Dinar						
Kenyan Schilling						
Mexican Peso						
Moroccan Dirham						
Norwegian Krone						

Figure G-60: FOREIGN EXCHANGE RATES FOR TRAVEL PRICING
(Courtesy of American Express Company.)

FOREIGN EXCHANGE RATES
FOR TRAVEL PRICING
as of
(U.S. Dollar per foreign currency unit)

Currency	3 Months	6 Months	9 Months	12 Months	15 Months	18 Months
Portuguese Escudo						
Russian Rouble						
Singapore Dollar						
South African Rand						
Spanish Peseta						
Swedish Krona						
Swiss Franc						
Turkish Lira						
Irish Pounds						

Prepared by: Treasurer's Office-International

Date:

Figure G-60 (Continued)

*U.S. Dollar　　**FOREIGN EXCHANGE ANALYSIS**　　T/C - Stanley 4173

CURRENCY		BANK CODE					
Canadian	$	TDBX					
Sterling	£ *	BAXX					
Deutsche Mark	DM	"					
Swiss Franc	SF	"					
Dutch Guilder	HFL	"					
French Franc	FF	"					
Japanese Yen	¥	"					
Italian Lira	LIT	"					
Hong Kong	HK	"					
Sweden	SK	CMBX					
Norway	NK	"					
Denmark	DK	"					
Belgian Franc/Com		DNCO					
" " Fin		"					
Finland	FMK	"					
Austrian Sch.	OSH	"					
Portugal	ESC	"					
Spain	PTSA	"					
Singapore		CISX					
Australian	$ *	BAXM					
New Zealand	*	"					
Malaysia		"					
India		"					
S.A. Rand	*	"					
Mexico		CISF					
Bolivar Venz.	*	—					
Greece		—					
Phillipines	*	—					
Ireland		BAXX					

Figure G-61: FOREIGN EXCHANGE ANALYSIS
(Courtesy of American Express Company.)

SCHEDULE 6

VARIANCE ANALYSIS

PRIOR WEEKLY ACTUAL VS. CURRENT WEEKLY ACTUAL EXPOSURE

(Local Currency 000's)   as of _____

Currency	NET EXPOSURE		Variance Longer/ (Shorter)	EXPLANATION OF VARIANCE						Total
	Prior Weekly Actual	Current Weekly Actual		(Inc)/Dec. Local Borrowing	(Inc)/Dec. in Forward Contracts	Inc/(Dec.) in Card Exposure	Inc/(Dec.) in Travel Exposure	Inc/(Dec.) in T/C Exposure	Inc/(Dec.) in FFIC Exposure	
	A	B	C	D	E	F	G	H	I	J
Canadian Dollar										
British Pound										
French Franc										
Italian Lira										
Belgian Franc										
Dutch Guilder										
Swiss Franc										
Japanese Yen										
W. German Mark										
Mexican Peso										
Aust. Dollar										
Spanish Peseta										
H.K. Dollar										

Distribution: Prepared by:

Date:
Frequency:

Figure G-62: VARIANCE ANALYSIS OF FOREIGN EXCHANGE EXPOSURE
(Courtesy of American Express Company.)

SECTION
H

CASH MANAGEMENT, CREDIT, COLLECTIONS–ANALYSIS AND CONTROL

SECTION H FORMS

Cash Management, Credit, Collections— Analysis and Control

639

Figure

Cash Management, Credit, Collections— Analysis and Control

Dun & Bradstreet, Inc. has often averred that a sale is incomplete until the money is collected. Assuming that the customer is satisfied, contract specs are met, and the seller fulfills any initial service agreement, even with payment assured, there is an intermediate step between credit and management of cash, namely, *adequate control procedures* during processing of receipts and prompt follow-through on problems and potential problems.

The first two exhibits are an organizer and a checklist. The Cash Management and Dividend Payout Procedures (H-1) clearly establish the profit orientation of the company and focus on EFFICIENT CASH MANAGEMENT. Obviously, bulging files are not encouraged, as evidenced by the S.C.R.A.P. legend, "Senseless Collection Reduces a Profit." Point number one of the guideline procedures states, "Efficient cash management benefits the consolidated profit and loss statement directly." The Treasurer recommends implementation of cash management procedures outlined under Point Five and dividend payout policy along the lines of Point Seven. The addendum to this policy statement is a corporate resolution of some years earlier that authorizes investment in various short-term securities, and implementation of the treasurer's recommendation.

H-1

Next, a cash (and check) control checklist (H-2) zeroes in on the question: How is incoming mail, with money in it, handled? Horizontally, departments, and individuals within the department, who handle the money are named in the heading. Mail flows vertically. The point is this: maintain an adequate internal system of checks and double-checks to avoid any critical gaps in mail and money handling and *plug up any potential profit leaks.*

H-2

H-3 Although modeled for the specific needs of an enterprise, an insurance company, the detail shown in the Office Cash Report (H-3) provides a good example that any *control-conscious organization* may modify to fit its own control requirements. The emphasis is not on saving time with a truncated report in this instance. Notice that a total of 83 items are printed on this cash report, including summary data, with blank spaces for addenda.

Handling substantial sums of money, in whatever form, requires care and caution rather than speed that may result in deletions or omissions or in unjustified brevity. Simplicity is preferred in financial communications, but not at the expense of losing funds. Control and PRESERVATION OF CASH and near-monies are objectives of forms of this type. They form a *crucial step* in cross-checking the internal flows of money, whether between branch office and home office or among departments.

Modifying this form for your own organization requires some time, but do your present forms (if any) provide for adequate control of this most valuable asset? Will benefits from faster transfer of funds, IMPROVED TURNOVER OF CASH, and better control over money outweigh costs of improving control and reporting procedures? Modifying this form may be a *real time-saver*. And with a detailed summary of transactions in hand, you can MANAGE CASH FLOW operations from a broader perspective.

H-4

H-5

H-6 The form for Tracking Daily Cash Movements (H-4) records the amount of funds transferred, from whom and to whom, the account name and number, the value date (i.e., date on which currency translation occurred) and today's date; it also provides space for special instructions. All such transfers require Confirmation (H-5), types of funds transferred, together with an authorized signature. Foreign exchange transactions, too, must be confirmed (H-6). Listed on the form are both buyer and seller, the currency involved, the dollar rate and value date, and authorized signature for CONTROL AND SAFETY.

H-7

H-8 With the Daily Cash Movements Report (H-7), a company with worldwide interests can scan all debit and credit funds transmitted among its various operating units and financial institutions holding these funds and liquid investments. Of course, information from this two-page form is entered in the computer for analysis to *maximize return* on and use of these resources. Finally, an analysis is made of Bank Balance Estimates (H-8) to calculate *float* and estimated bank balance.

H-9

H-10

H-11 With foreign short-term investments handled through a bank (also refer to section G for further details on international cash management), the firm will generate paperwork relating to acceptance and placing of funds (H-9), or credit and debit notices (H-10), or a credit memo on wire or phone transfer of domestic funds (H-11).

Another important step in *money management* is close surveillance of demand deposit accounts. The combination format statement of deposits and debits (H-12) provides: **H-12**

   (a)   a periodic summary of demand deposit transactions;
   (b)   details of activities for matching against internal records.

Such information figures in the analysis of PROFITABLE CASH MANAGEMENT to derive *optimal utilization* of periodic cash flows.

The money manager, or cash control department, may receive as many or more forms as it generates for internal and external application. Employees who handle these forms will want to become familiar with their purposes to distingush which forms clamor for *immediate attention.* Properly handled, these forms comprise part of the total system on MONEY CONTROL and furnish a means to locate errors, mishandling, fraud and theft. Examples of this genre include:

  ◆   Stop Payment Forms (two styles) on an already issued check (H-13).   **H-13**
  ◆   Overdraft Notices on insufficient funds (H-14).   **H-14**
  ◆   Insufficient Funds Notices for customers' checks not covered by funds (H-15).   **H-15**
  ◆   Returned Check Notice (H-16).   **H-16**
  ◆   Charge Advice (H-17).   **H-17**

The degree of action each requires at different times apparently ranges from routine to urgent. Common to all these forms are:

   (a)   the date;
   (b)   the amount of funds involved in the transaction;
   (c)   an account or identifying number;
   (d)   reason(s) for the debit or credit.
   (e)   name(s) or specific instructions.

But the Overdraft (H-14), Insufficient Funds (H-15), and Returned Check Notices (H-16) supply additional details that aid in posting information and cross-checking records internally. The titles of these forms, innocent enough in appearance and self-explanatory to anyone already familiar with them, obscure the extent of liability and responsibility of parties involved. These should be carefully observed, and an internal routine established for handling such contingencies. An uninformed clerk, through inaction, may aggravate what might have been handled routinely.

An additional step in control is prompt review of canceled checks. The review can provide an EARLY WARNING SIGNAL TO OFFSET ERRORS or catch misuse of an account. A high proportion of Americans have checking accounts (higher here than in any other country), but the number who have difficulty balancing a personal checking account seems equally high. How many of these persons become office personnel or business owners with responsibility for maintaining an orderly checking account is unknown. However, experience dictates the use of a simple check reconciliation

H-18 configuration (H-18) with easily understood instructions. This example illustrates an uncluttered and *streamlined format*. Of course, the design of a system will be a function of the type and complexity of an organization. But the approach should lean toward simplicity by partitioning the entire control procedure into manageable proportions. Simplicity often favors SAVING TIME through minimization of errors and time spent finding these errors.

The next several forms are simple enough, although they seem to add unnecessarily to the internal flow of paperwork. But they may be COST SAVING. In an inflationary or unsettled economy, *cost control* means more than simply holding down manufacturing and overhead costs. A good control system also helps to PREVENT UNPLANNED LEAKAGES in cash or credit flows.

H-19 ◆ Bank Deposit Memo (H-19).
H-20 ◆ Check Request (H-20).
H-21 ◆ Check Requisition (H-21).
H-22 ◆ Credit Memo for internal transfer of cash (H-22).
H-23 ◆ Debit Memo for internal transfer of cash (H-23).
H-24 ◆ Cash Letters (H-24).
H-25 ◆ Request to Increase/Decrease Federal Funds (H-25).
H-26 ◆ Confirmation of Interest (H-26).
H-27 ◆ Federal Reserve Debit Memo (H-27).

All serve to personalize the flow of paperwork and funds represented by these forms. Errors can be traced to specific persons, quickly and cheaply.

The form cash letter is another MONEY-SAVING EXAMPLE (H-24). Even if an executive spent only a brief 12 or 15 minutes writing each necessary letter, at $40,000 a year (salary and benefits), the letter would cost $5.00 in time spent alone. But when an $11,000-a-year employee spends five minutes addressing a form letter for mailing, the labor cost drops to one-tenth that figure.

Note that each of these forms requires a signature, or initials, or some method of identifying the person(s) behind the transaction. This personal identification relieves "the computer" of misplaced blame. Note that in addition to supplying the element of control, each instrument provides for specific instructions which facilitate entering the transactions for accounting purposes and subsequent auditing of accounts.

These forms model certain consanguineous features:

 • the date;
 • sum of money involved;
 • to whom payable;
 • to whom the amount is chargeable;
 • type of transaction;
 • purpose or special instructions;
 • the person handling the transaction.

Observe, also, that none of the structures, despite the size of the transaction, are complicated—MINIMIZING the possibility of ERRORS or *miscommunication*—yet still communicate adequately and clearly what they are supposed to and which purposes they serve. Titling the form in bold letters contributes to ease of RAPID IDENTIFICATION (color coding may help as well), filing, and retrieval.

Forms referring to the Federal Fund Market (H-25) or Federal Reserve Bank (H-27) illustrate SIMPLE HANDLING of routine multimillion dollar transactions; the complicated paperwork is reserved for petty cash transactions (H-28). (Also see accounting forms K-31 and K-32 for further application and safeguard of petty cash.)

H-28

Another TIME-SAVING LETTER SUBSTITUTE, the Remittance Advice (H-29), supplies identifying details on payments transmitted. It saves time by requiring only one typing of the address if windowed envelopes are used. It saves time by avoiding the need for an explanatory cover letter. It saves time by presenting all data in a uniform, clear-cut, unconfused manner so that the *recipient* SAVES TIME with a concise, deciphered message. It saves time by providing space for remarks for *additional* information not covered in the form and by eliminating the need for an *additional* letter or speed message.

H-29

Two other instruments for the transfer of funds are Sight Draft (H-30) and Warrant (H-31). A commercial draft is a written order of the drawer (firm drawing up the draft) which directs the drawee (usually a bank) to pay a named sum of funds to the order of a third party upon presentation of the instrument. The form is simple, but all legal elements must appear on the draft as they do in this example. The left-hand stub is a drawer's record of the transaction. A warrant evidences indebtedness of the firm; it is exchanged for cash or check when presented to the drawee.

H-30
H-31

The Authorization to Transfer Funds (H-32) relates to a hedging or speculative commodity or securities account with a brokerage firm, which allows the brokerage house to transfer funds among various accounts held in the same name without prior notice. Notice is given after completion of the transfer, however. Note, also, that there is no time limit in this agreement although any specific limiting clauses can be inserted. Restrictions may include the duration of the agreement, limits on the amount transferred among accounts, prior notice, etc., but the brokerage firm will resist changes that tend to weaken its privilege of offset.

H-32

The general form for an Irrevocable Letter of Credit (H-33) will vary in appearance among issuing banks (H-34), but will contain all the essentials seen in these examples. Directions are given directly on the form (H-33) for filling in the blanks. This particular format matches requirements established in the previous form (H-32); and a Letter of Credit substitutes for securities or other assets held as a security deposit by a brokerage firm. In this instance, a bank guarantees to pay any deficits, or obligations, up to a specific sum. The flexibility arising from use of bank credit (rather than depending upon the

H-33
H-34

credit rating of the business) is attractive for (1) firms hedging raw material purchases or sales of certain commodities to INCREASE PROFITS, (2) exporters and importers, or (3) expediting transactions that may otherwise require cash in advance in order to LOWER COSTS OF CREDIT.

H-35   When a bank accepts a draft drawn under a commercial letter of credit, it issues notice (H-35) to that effect. Observe that to SAVE TIME AND MONEY the bank employs a nine-page form—the top four are of half-page size, the bottom five of quarter-page size. The standardized form, and the procedure it encompasses, substitutes for expensive correspondence, contains required information that can be completed by any trained person, assures that each party to the transaction and each department within the organization will receive a copy. Destinations of the copies are:

- Number one—the Office Copy (yellow).
- Number two—the Original (white).
- Number three—a Duplicate (white).
- Number four—Advice of Acceptance (white).
- Number five—Bookkeeper's Copy, a *debit* ticket (green).
- Number six—a Credit ticket (white).
- Number seven—Advice of Payment (white).
- Number eight—Debit ticket (yellow).
- Number nine—Advice of Debit (blue).

H-36   Another means of securing transactions is with a Promissory Note (H-36); but the credit rating of the buyer, or issuer of the note, rather than that of the bank as in the Letter of Credit, must withstand scrutiny. The note itself provides prima facie evidence of an obligation and is valuable in court action only if the debtor organization has unencumbered assets. Being secured by collateral does not guarantee that a forced sale of assets will cover the debt, but possessing the Promissory Note may shield the financial officer of the creditor firm from criticism.

A Promissory Note must:

(a)   be in writing;
(b)   be signed by the maker;
(c)   contain an unconditional promise to pay a specific sum of money;
(d)   be payable on demand on a determinable future date;
(e)   be payable to the order of a specified party, or, in some cases, to the bearer.

Lacking any one of these requirements, the note is non-negotiable.

H-37   Unfortunately, in our statistics-based society, we place more faith in numbers than in the various other Cs of credit, of which character is not of the least importance. One measure of credit worthiness, especially of noncommercial applicants, is links to the local economy. The Application for Check Identification (H-37) helps to shed light on ties with employment, bank, and credit references, and assessment of character through occupation. More than one study has shown that persons in some occupations are better (worse) credit risks than others, despite significant differences in relative incomes. Of course, the creditor must, in some cases of marginal accounts, skirt the depths of business losses on one hand and the abyss of a discrimination suit on the other.

Another measure of credit confidence is the courtship between the debtor and other creditors. The Credit Inquiry (H-38), in whatever format, should suggest certain general items of information; a cover memo can take care of particulars not encompassed in the form itself.   **H-38**

Note the following elements of this form:

◆ The credit seeker is specifically identified by trade style (and/or corporate name) and address to avoid confusion with concerns of similar name. This is especially *crucial in cases of disputed accounts and litigation.*

◆ The length of time that trade experience has been reported denotes whether this is a new account or long established; it also helps to confirm stability of operations and consistency in other data reported.

◆ The largest amount of credit extended tells us whether this is a major supplier; e.g., a concern may normally discount small bills but run 90 days slow with a major, and accommodating, supplier.

◆ The amounts owing and past due signal something about the current condition of the debtor, and these amounts should be less than the largest amounts owing; otherwise there is a question of consistency in reporting figures.

◆ The payment record summarizes credit transactions and should be consistent with other data; e.g., an inquiry returned that shows the debtor taking discounts with an amount past due and a trend toward slowness reveals inconsistency.

Still another important source of preliminary or confirmatory credit information, especially for new accounts or new businesses, is the sales force, which in completing the Salesman's Credit Report (H-39) can furnish much information about an operation simply by being on the spot and observing. Not only can sales representatives aid the credit department, but by working together with it the representative can develop desirable customers through a Potential Customer Analysis (H-40), consistent with company sales and credit policies.   **H-39**   **H-40**

Credit information gathered from many internal and external sources is entered on a Credit Input Statement Control Sheet (H-41) for subsequent input into the computer and readback and printout of systematized data in desired formats for credit analysis and trend projections. (For examples of various statement and analytical outputs, see J-44 through J-47.) The control sheet exhibited for general industry requirements (H-41) may be supplanted with a specialized format such as the Utilities Credit Input Statement Control Sheet (H-42). The advantage of analysis by computer not only SAVES TIME, once the program has been written and tested, but also produces more data in less time for QUICKER CREDIT DECISIONS to *boost customer goodwill* and better assess the degree of risk assumed.   **H-41**   **H-42**

H-43   A Credit Folder (H-43), large enough to retain pertinent analytical data and information on each customer, may also contain basic account data on the outside of the folder for ready reference, the amount and type being a function of the procedure used and complexity of operations. Noncomputerized routines will favor the kind of detail exhibited in this design but will possibly favor quite different information with other systems.

H-44   Similarly, a Credit File Summary Card (H-44) provides an alternative source when computer terminals are available. EFFECTIVE CREDIT AND COLLECTION
H-45   ROUTINES also include a ledger Customer Sales and Payments (H-45). A record of
H-46   Charge Sales (H-46) registers the quantity of merchandise ordered, backordered, and shipped, its description and price, customer shipping data, and date account was billed.

H-47   Collection of accounts receivable begins *before* the account becomes past due, starting
H-48   with proper and prompt invoicing (H-47) and rendering of statements (H-48). The two examples shown are stubless, carbonless, and color coded. This design SAVES TIME because up to 20 percent of handling time is used in disposing of stubs and carbon papers, and SAVES MONEY because about one-fifth less storage space is needed.

H-49   Efficient handling of collection is also evidenced with this ten-page form letter of Bank Collection Instructions (H-49), distributed as follows: (i) Owner's file (blue); (ii) Original (white); (iii) Duplicate (green); (iv) Acknowledgment (white); (v) Tracer (pink); (vi) Control (white); (vii) Office Copy (yellow); (viii) Advice of Payment (white); (ix) Credit (pink, quarter-page); (x) Debit (blue, quarter-page).

H-50   But collection of accounts may require subroutines or further protection. A Subordination Agreement (H-50), as a condition to granting credit, requires other creditors to agree to place their claims in a lower or inferior status which, on one hand, increases risks to creditors, but, on the other, may decrease risks by keeping the firm viable long enough to pay off all creditors.

H-51   An Unlimited Guaranty (H-51) of payment and performance obligations is an unconditional contract by a third party, the Guarantor, who guarantees to the creditor that the customer will punctually pay (or perform) its obligations. *Unlimited guaranty* implies *all* indebtedness, obligations, and liabilities, as long as the guaranty is in force. If
H-52   the Guaranty is *limited* (H-52), the liability of the guarantor extends only to the assumed liability stated (in dollars) plus interest and costs. Either standing alone, or to reinforce
H-53   the preceding guarantees, collateral may be pledged (H-53) for the benefit of a borrower. The Agreement authorizes the lender to deal with the collateral as if the borrower were the absolute owner of it. When property is transferred or delivered to a creditor as
H-54   security for debt, the pledgor of collateral signs a Pledge Agreement (H-54).

For EFFECTIVE CONTROL, receivables should be analyzed (H-55) to determine age distribution of receivables, compared with a 150-day moving average (or other time span if more appropriate). Close vigilance provides an early signal of receivables moving away from norms or limits—a loss-control system that PROTECTS PROFITS. Further, for losses that will occur, provision should be made for charge-offs and recoveries of bad debts (H-56) as an aid in FINANCIAL PLANNING.

H-55

H-56

Delinquent accounts require prompt action, for the probability of collection diminishes rapidly after an account is 90 days old. A Reminder Statement (H-57) for overdue accounts may initiate the collection process, or a series of standardized Account Due Notices (H-58) may trigger the desired response. For an innovative approach to collection (H-59), try furnishing details of indebtedness before the debtor requests it. Eliminating unnecessary correspondence, this procedure SAVES TIME AND LETTER-WRITING EXPENSES and parries stall-type inquiries. Or experiment with this routine: rather than employing the telephone for collection, transmit an age analysis of the customer's obligations (H-60). If prepared in duplicate, one copy may routinely accompany the periodic statement, the others may be reserved for follow-up collection action.

H-57

H-58
H-59

H-60

Receivables collections sometimes develop from third-party sources of funds, or may indicate compromise through the acceptance of a note from the customer. A Demand Note (H-61) becomes due at the holder's option. An unsecured Time Note for a Corporate Customer (H-62) becomes due at maturity or on demand after default in payment or dissolution of the organization. For collateralized indebtedness, a Financing Statement (H-63) is presented to a filing officer for filing pursuant to the Uniform Commercial Code.

H-61
H-62

H-63

For the hard cases litigation may result in collection. An officer of the creditor signs the notarized Proof of Claim (H-64) for the amount of indebtedness plus interest. He must be sure to enter the precise corporate name to establish the debtor's correct corporate identity, available from records of the Secretary of State where incorporated or registered, to avoid expensive legal contests and entanglements. Two forms of evidence of debt, a Statutory Bond (H-65) and a Common Bond (H-66), bind the firm and its successors to specific obligations in the amounts stated in the documents.

H-64

H-65
H-66

As matters deteriorate, there may be a General Assignment (H-67) of the debtor's assets for the benefit of creditors, i.e., a transfer of assets by a debtor to an assignee in trust to apply against outstanding obligations. An insolvent debtor, one who is insufficiently liquid to pay off due obligations, may want to start anew and escape the tension and pressures surrounding insolvency. Legal relief is sought by filing a Petition for Voluntary Bankruptcy (H-68) in a U.S. District Court. Appended to the petition is a Statement of

H-67

H-68

H-69   Affairs for Bankrupt Engaged in Business (H-69), which enumerates all assets and liabilities of the petitioner. The bankrupt will want to list all debtors in correct amounts to safeguard against future claims; the creditor will want to verify that the amount listed for the firm is correct and possibly send a representative to bankruptcy proceedings. The other document, designed to protect creditors, is the Disclosure of Attorney Fees for the

H-70   Bankrupt (H-70), which must be filed by the attorney for the bankrupt. The purpose of this legal process is to liquidate the debtor's assets as quickly as feasible to settle with creditors (usually at a fractional amount of indebtedness) to allow the creditor to make new decisions or repeat past errors.

INTER-DEPT. CORRESPONDENCE — (General Office)
Remember S.C.R.A.P.! (Senseless Collection Reduces A Profit)

To: Mr. W.B. Murphy   **Date:** January 17, 1972

From: D.H. Springer

Subject: DIVIDENDS FROM PEPPERIDGE FARM

1. There are two considerations here — cash management on the one hand and investment in a subsidiary on the other. Efficient cash management benefits the consolidated profit and loss statement directly. The form which investment in a subsidiary takes and the payment of interest or dividends has no material direct impact on the consolidated profit and loss statement.

Cash Management

2. Judged by the criterion of interest cost of money, the most efficient way to manage our cash is to concentrate all cash in a single account. Short-term borrowing is minimized and, conversely, the investment of excess cash, when available, is maximized.

3. For all practical purposes, we do concentrate our domestic cash in a single account. Disbursements made by the plants and subsidiaries are covered by daily transfers of funds from our concentration account which are timed to take full advantage of float. The plants never have excess funds. The cash balances of domestic subsidiaries are controlled through management of their respective loan balances with the parent company and by adjustment of inter-company balances. When they need cash, loans are made; when cash balances exceed those required to compensate their banks for the activity in their accounts, transfers are made to the parent company and the loans are reduced.

4. Until the current fiscal year, Pepperidge Farm participated in the same system. There was always an outstanding loan balance, which was reduced from time to time as cash balances permitted. The loan balance now is zero, and a new mechanism is needed to manage Pepperidge Farm's cash.

5. If we were dealing with this matter solely as a question of cash management, we would propose the following:

   a. Invest Pepperidge Farm's daily excess balances of cash as deemed desirable. (See copy of Resolution dated April 26, 1961 attached.)

   b. Transfer cash balances in excess of Pepperidge Farm's needs for a week or more to Campbell. Evidence the transfer by a Campbell note bearing interest at the prime rate. On any occasion when Pepperidge Farm needs cash, transfer the funds from Campbell and reduce the Campbell note or evidence the transfer by a Pepperidge Farm note bearing interest at the prime rate, as the case may be.

   c. At least once each year declare a Pepperidge Farm dividend to Campbell in an amount equal to part or all of the current balance of Campbell notes to Pepperidge Farm.

Figure H-1: CASH MANAGEMENT AND DIVIDEND PAYOUT CRITERIA

6. Since the payment and receipt of interest or dividends between companies included in our consolidated financial statements are eliminated in the consolidation, neither has any material impact on the consolidated profit and loss statement. Centralized cash management does improve earnings by optimizing consolidated interest income (expense). Declaration of a dividend under this mechanism would not purport to serve any purpose other than to formalize the permanent transfer of the cash.

Investment in Pepperidge Farm

7. It may be that Pepperidge Farm should pay a dividend for reasons other than cash management. At least four possible approaches might be considered:

a. Declare a Pepperidge Farm dividend annually at least equal to the dividends paid on the Campbell shares exchanged for Pepperidge Farm shares. Currently that would amount to $1,179,462.92 ($1.10 × 1,072,239 shares).

b. Declare a Pepperidge Farm dividend annually for its share of the current Campbell dividend in proportion to its net worth at the end of the previous year. Such an approach would suggest a dividend of $1,816,558 this year.

$$\frac{\$25,713,000}{\$523,269,000} \times \$36,967,000 = \$1,816,558$$

c. Declare a Pepperidge Farm dividend at least equal to the consolidated earnings per share for the previous year on the Campbell shares exchanged for Pepperidge Farm shares. The indicated amount this year would be $2,144,478 ($2.00 × 1,072,239 shares).

d. Declare a Pepperidge Farm dividend annually for its share of the current Campbell dividend in proportion to its net income during the previous year. The amount of the dividend suggested by this method would be $2,953,294 this year.

$$\frac{\$5,369,000}{\$67,208,000} \times \$36,967,000 = \$2,953,294$$

8. None of these approaches would have any material impact on the consolidated profit and loss statement. The dividend would be paid in accordance with whatever approach is selected as most suitable if Pepperidge Farm has earned the indicated amount after taxes, even if it does not have cash available for the purpose. In such a circumstance, Pepperidge Farm would borrow the necessary funds from Campbell. The approach described in paragraph 7.b. appears most appropriate for declaring a dividend for purposes other than cash management. It is reasonable to expect that the net worth which Campbell shareholders have invested in Pepperidge Farm will produce its proportionate share of the dividends which they receive.

Figure H-1 (continued)

Mr. W.B. Murphy
January 17, 1972

Tax and Legal Consideration

9. There are no impediments under Connecticut law to Pepperidge Farm's declaring a dividend. The impact of various state taxes on the consolidated profit and loss statement is negligible, but it is unfavorable at the rate of about 0.14% after taxes. There are no Federal tax consequences.

Recommendation

10. <u>Cash Management.</u> Implement the procedures described in paragraphs 5.a. and 5.b.

11. <u>Dividend.</u>

    a. In fiscal 1971-72 declare a Pepperidge dividend equal to the dividends paid on the Campbell shares exchanged for Pepperidge Farm shares. See paragraph 7 a. The necessary funds will be available during the third fiscal quarter without borrowing.

    b. In subsequent years plan to declare a Pepperidge Farm dividend annually in accordance with the approach described in paragraph 7.b., if earned, even if it should be necessary for Pepperidge Farm to borrow from Campbell to do so.

                              Treasurer

DHS:nd
Attachment
cc: Mr. O.H. Curry
      Mr. R.G. McGovern
      Mr. W.L. Rudkin
      Mr. H.A. Shaub
      Mr. C.R. Stegmaier

Figure H-1 (continued)

PEPPERIDGE FARM, INCORPORATED

Board of Directors Resolution

April 26, 1961

★ ★ ★

AUTHORITY TO INVEST COMPANY FUNDS

RESOLVED, that the President, the Vice President - Operations, and the Treasurer, be and each of them hereby is individually authorized to purchase for the account of the Company, to the extent that funds are available, securities of the types named below having maturity dates not later than 24 months after the date of purchase, in such amounts as in his discretion may from time to time seem advisable:

Treasury Bills and other obligations of the United States Government;
Securities of United States Government Agencies (including Local Housing Authorities under the supervision of the Federal Housing and Home Finance Agency), whether guaranteed by the United States Government or not;
Securities of States and their Subdivisions and Instrumentalities;
Commercial Paper of Corporations (incorporated in the United States or in Canada) and Bankers Acceptances of Banks whose financial standing is in his opinion of the highest grade.

Figure H-1 (continued)

Transaction and Description of Steps	Corporate Secretarial Department		Treasurer's Department		Accounting Department
Incoming Mail	Corporate Secretary	Mail Clerk	Cashier	Clerk	Clerk
Receive		X			
Open and prepare duplicate list of checks and other valuable items ..	X				
Date- and time-stamp ..		X			
Identify or cross-reference checks, etc. to correspondence		X			
Deliver list and checks to cashier	X				
Receive list checks, verify and initial list			X		
Sort mail and deliver ..		X			
File duplicate list	X				
Prepare duplicate deposit slips			X		
Enter receipts in cash book				X	
Enter individual payments in accounts receivable ledger accounts					X

Figure H-2: FORMULA FOR ANALYZING CONTROL SYSTEM
(From the book Corporate Treasurer's and Controller's Handbook by L. Doris, Editor. © 1950 renewed 1978 by L. Doris, Editor. Published by Prentice-Hall, Inc., Englewood Cliffs, New Jersey 07632.)

OFFICE CASH REPORT

(Office)

OFFICE CODE

DATE

STATEMENT OF CONDITION		RECEIPTS (1)	DISBURSEMENTS (2)
Bank Balance	14		
Cash in Office	15		
ADV To Sub. Off	16		
Agents' Balances	19		
M.L. in Process	20		
ADV A/C Postage	21		
	23		
	24		
Notes (Inst. Bal.)	26		
ADV A/C Postage	27		
Total Debits	28		
Less Pending Items	29		
Net Due H.O.	30		
Previous Balance	31		
Transfer of Funds from H.O.	32		
	32A		
Deposit to H.O. Account	33		
Adjusters' Drafts—Casualty	34		
Adjusters' Drafts—Health			
Adjusters' Drafts—Group			
Group Claim Credit Memos	34A		
	35		
CHECKS AND DRAFTS FOR DEPOSIT IN HOME OFFICE	36		
Premiums Life Other	37		
" Life	38		
" Health	39		
U.S. COMMERCIAL / CANADA CASUALTY	40		
PERSONAL / PROPERTY	41		
" Surety	42		
Comms.—Life	43		
" Health	44		
U.S. COMMERCIAL / CANADA CASUALTY	45		
PERSONAL / PROPERTY	46		
" Surety	47		
Comm. Pd. through Accrual	48		
Ben. Plan.—Agts. Remitt.	49		
Field Issued Checks—H.O. Acct.	50		
Tax and Other Withholdings	51		
Collateral Asset	52		

Figure H-3: OFFICE CASH REPORT
(Courtesy of The Travelers Insurance Company.)

53	Installment Charges
54	Life Remittances
55	Cash Drawer Diff.
56	Agents' Diff.
57	Int. on Pol. Loans (Ded.)
58	Int. on Pol. Loans
59	Suspense Prem. Remitt.
60	Collateral Asset Held
61	Direct Billing Diff.
62	Policy Loans
63	Policy Loan Repayments
64	Salaries
65	Expenses
66	Cash Exchange Voucher–CLCS
67	Scrip–Budget Plan
68	EMAP Agree.
69	Scrip–E.S.S.
70	
71	Advance Acct. Travel
72	Budget Plan–Cash Remit. Voucher
73	Div. to Policyholders
74	Real Estate Suspense
75	Budget Diff.–SDG
76	Mort. Loan Suspense
77	Data Center–Cash Remitt. Vo.
78	Adjusters' Drafts–Group–Illinois
79	Group Claim Credit Memos–Illinois
80	Undeliverable Checks
81	Deposit VO. R R Group Conv.
82	Cash Exchange Voucher
83	Cash Exchange Voucher–Canada
84	Modified ADP Comm.-Canada
85	Asgd. Risk Instlmt. Charges
86	Personal Lines Vouchers
87	Medicare Voucher
88	Direct Billing Diff. C-P
89	Multi Line ADP Comm.–U.S.
90	Presto Transfer Vouchers
91	Premium Adjustment–LHFS
92	Commission Adjustment–LHFS
93	Casualty–Property Voucher
94	Life Voucher
95	Data Center Voucher
96	ADV. To AGTS-Career Life
97	ADV. To AGTS-Pers. Lines-Indy Co.
98	P.L. CPS Claim Credits
99	TOTALS

M-3151 REV. 12-78 PRINTED IN U.S.A.

Figure H-3: continued

```
                                    AMOUNT $_____

                    DAILY CASH MOVEMENTS

Transferred From: _____    Transferred To:  _____

Account Name:    _____    Account Name:    _____

Account Number: _____    Account Number:  _____

         Value Date: _____    Today's Date:    _____


                                       Spoke With:      _____
                                                       _____

Special Instructions: _____

         _____

         _____



         Form 224
```

Figure H-4: DAILY TRANSFER MEMO

```
                    C O N F I R M A T I O N


                                    Confirmation Date: _____

   Attention: _____          Value Date: _____

                                    Confirming Call Of: _____
   _____
   _____

   TRANSFER TO:        _____

                       _____

                       _____

                       _____



                                                        $_____

   _____
   _____

   TRANSFER FROM:      _____

                       _____

                       _____

                       _____


                                                        $_____
   _____
   _____

   Special Instructions _____

   _____

   _____

   Please send advice of this transaction to my attention at the above address.

   TRANSFER IN:   Fed Funds          ___      Authorized Signature

                  Available Funds    ___

                  Clearing House Funds ___     _____


                                             Date: _____
```

Figure H-5: CONFIRMATION OF TRANSFER OF FUNDS

CONFIRMATION

Foreign Exchange Transactions

Confirmation Date: _____

Attention: _____   Value Date: _____

Confirming Call Of: _____

===

BUYER: _____ agrees to purchase

_____ against the U.S. Dollar at a rate of

_____ for value _____ .

On the above value date please transfer the _____

as follows:

_____

_____

_____

===

SELLER: We shall transfer funds to the account of _____

_____ , account number _____

for the counter value of this purchase, U.S. $ _____

value _____ .

===

SPECIAL INSTRUCTIONS: _____

_____

===

It would be appreciated if you would forward advice of this
transaction to _____

_____ .

DATE: _____   _____
                                    Authorized Signature

Figure H-6: FOREIGN EXCHANGE TRANSACTIONS CONFIRMATION

Date: _____

DAILY CASH MOVEMENTS REPORT

Trans. Number	Line Number	Amount	Debit Party	Credit Party	Trans. Control Number

◀ { { TOTALS (**Note:** These totals should agree with those supplied by prior to execution "GO".)

Figure H-7: DAILY CASH MOVEMENTS REPORT

_____

Date

_____

Balance (+, −)   **Debits**   **Credits**

Clearings   _____   _____

      Total

Balance (+, −)   **Debits**   **Credits**

            Cks.   _____   **Dep.(s)-**   _____

            Cks.   _____   _____

Clearings

            B.E.   _____   _____

            CZBA _____   _____

            TZBA _____   _____

      Total

CONCENTRATION

Balance (+, −)   **Debits**   **Credits**

            B.E.   _____   **Dep.(s)-**   _____

            TM.   _____   _____

Clearings   **CO&G** _____   _____

            CM.   _____   _____

            CP.   _____   _____

      Total

REMARKS:

Figure H-7 (continued)

Bank Balance Estimate

Est. Book Balance	004	
A/P	022	
Dealer Assign.	036	
Oil & Gas	002	
Less: Good Funds Next Day		
Plus: Prior Day's N.Y. Transfers		
Today's N.Y. Transfers		_____
Subtotal		
Beginning Float		
Amount Disbursed Today		
Less: Amount Cleared Today		_____
Ending Float		
Subtotal		
Ending Float		
Estimated Bank Balance		

Figure H-8: BANK BALANCE ESTIMATE

```
┌─────────────────────────────────────────────────┐
│  FIXED      DEPOSIT  ~~~ING                       │
│  CALL              SPECIMEN                        │
├─────────────────────────────────────────────────┤
│  WE ACCEPT FROM                                   │
└─────────────────────────────────────────────────┘

┌─────────────────────────────────────────────────┐
│  FIXED         DEPOSIT │ DEALING                  │
│  CALL                  │ DATE                     │
│                        │                          │
├─────────────────────────────────────────────────┤
│  WE PLACE FROM                                    │
│                                                   │
│                                                   │
├─────────────────────────────────────────────────┤
│  CURRENCY         AMOUNT            RATE %         │
│                                                   │
├─────────────────────────────────────────────────┤
│  FROM:                    TO:                     │
│  _____           _____          │
│  NO. OF DAYS:             INTEREST:               │
│                                                   │
│  _____           _____          │
│  PHONE/TELEX/BROKER:                              │
├─────────────────────────────────────────────────┤
│                                    WILL PAY:      │
│         SPECIMEN                                  │
├─────────────────────────────────────────────────┤
│  AT MATURITY:                      WILL PAY:      │
│                                                   │
├─────────────────────────────────────────────────┤
│                                                   │
│                                                   │
│                                                   │
└─────────────────────────────────────────────────┘
```

Figure H-9: PLACEMENT AND ACCEPTANCE OF FUNDS FOR INVESTMENT
(Courtesy of Barclays Bank International Limited.)

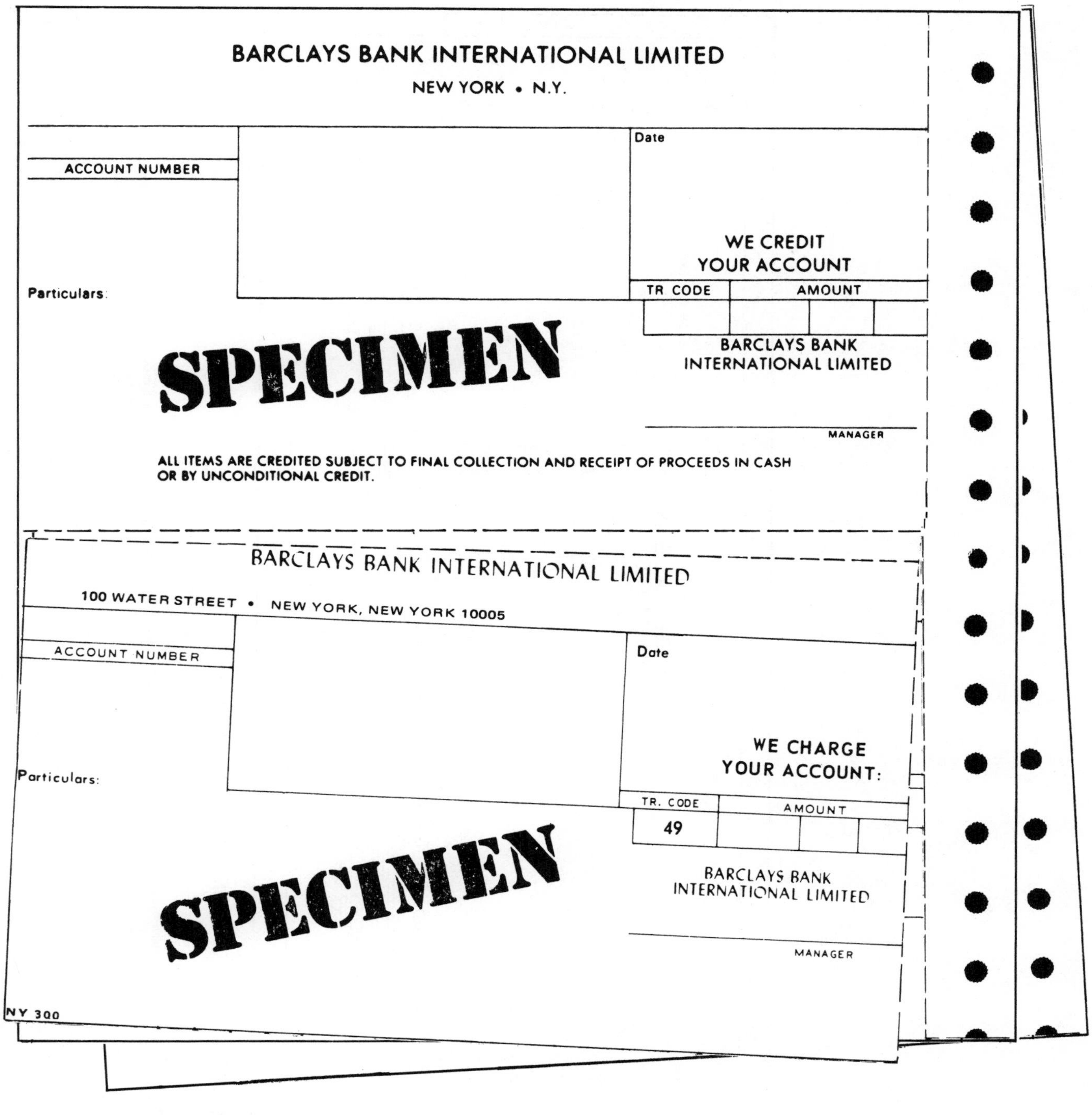
BARCLAYS BANK INTERNATIONAL LIMITED

NEW YORK • N.Y.

ACCOUNT NUMBER

Date

WE CREDIT
YOUR ACCOUNT

Particulars:

TR CODE	AMOUNT		

SPECIMEN

BARCLAYS BANK
INTERNATIONAL LIMITED

MANAGER

ALL ITEMS ARE CREDITED SUBJECT TO FINAL COLLECTION AND RECEIPT OF PROCEEDS IN CASH OR BY UNCONDITIONAL CREDIT.

BARCLAYS BANK INTERNATIONAL LIMITED

100 WATER STREET • NEW YORK, NEW YORK 10005

ACCOUNT NUMBER

Date

WE CHARGE
YOUR ACCOUNT:

Particulars:

TR. CODE	AMOUNT		
49			

SPECIMEN

BARCLAYS BANK
INTERNATIONAL LIMITED

MANAGER

NY 300

Figure H-10: CREDIT AND DEBIT NOTICES
(Courtesy of Barclays Bank International Limited.)

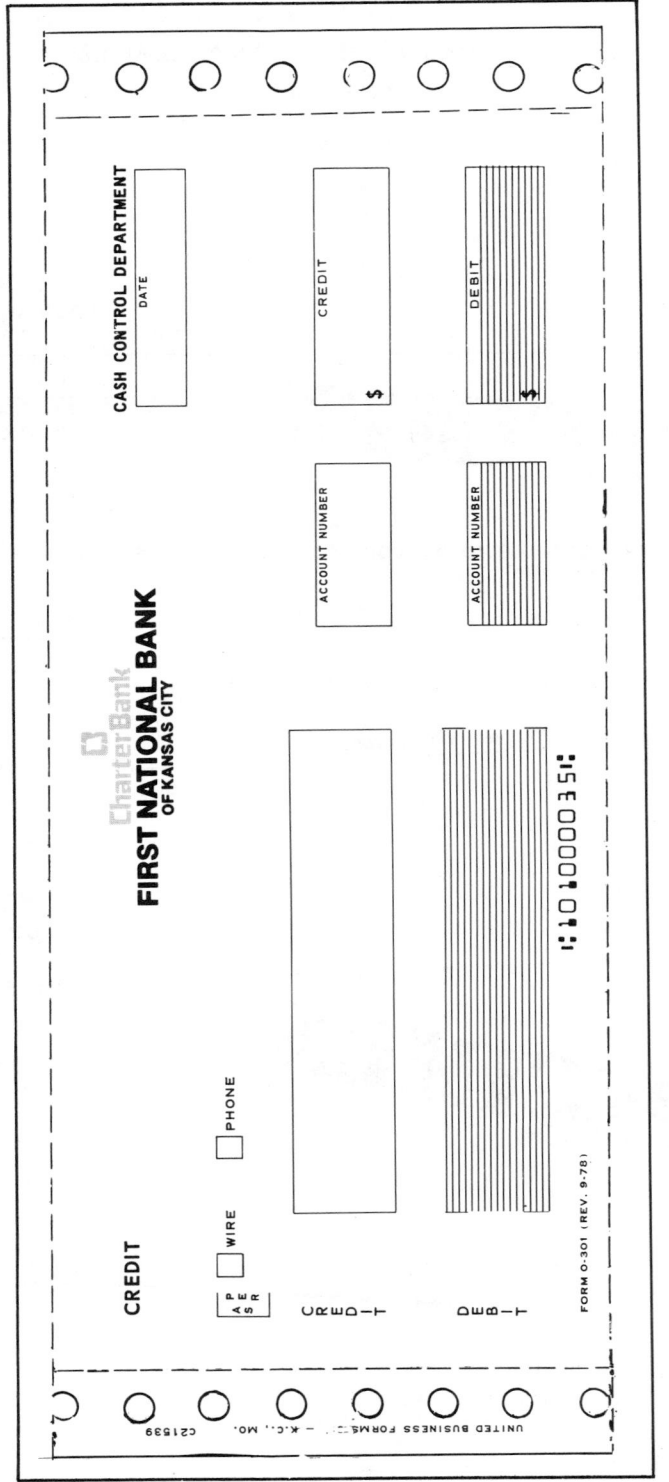

Figure H-11: CREDIT MEMO ON WIRE TRANSFER OF FUNDS
(Courtesy of First National Bank of Kansas City.)

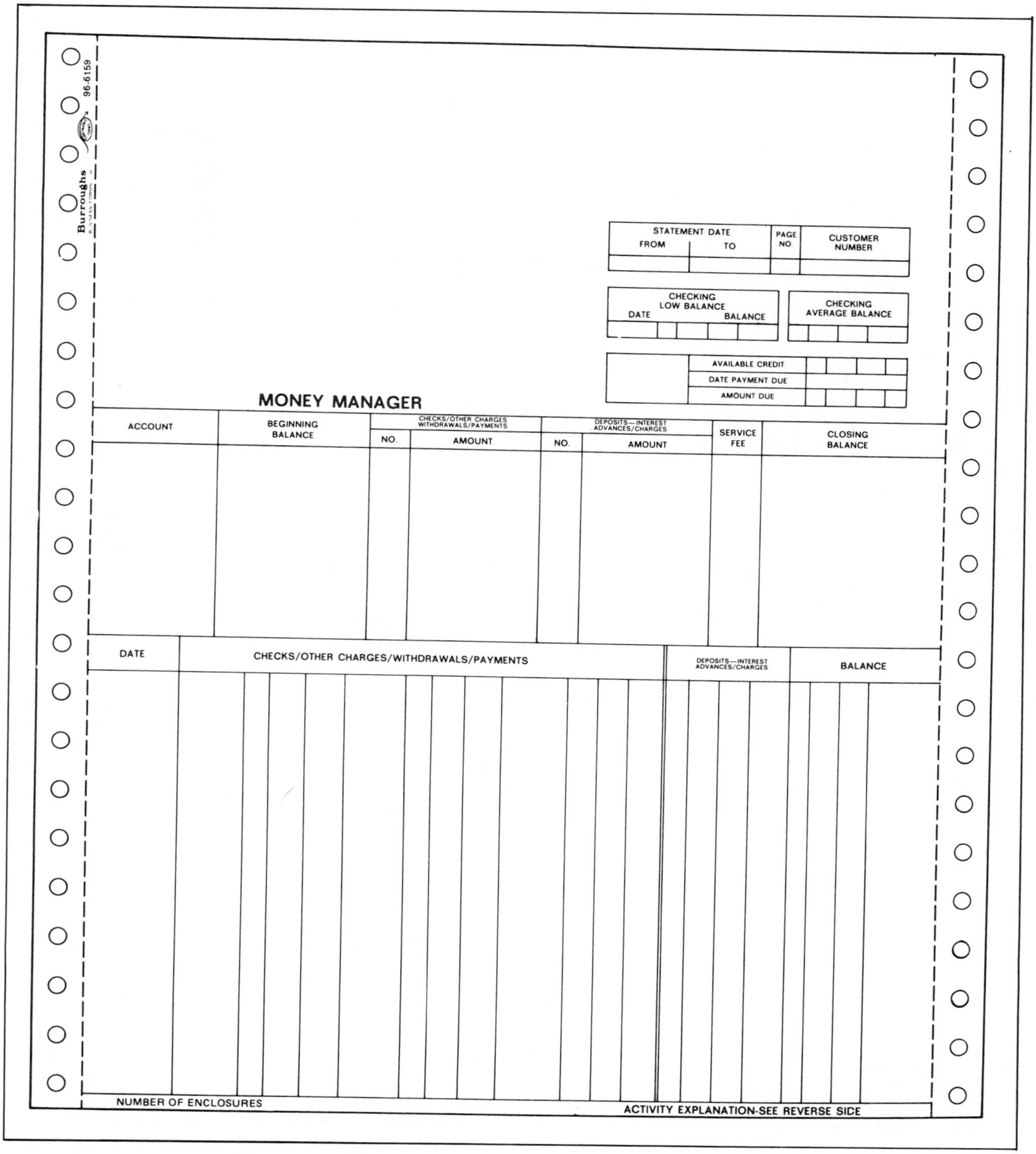

Burroughs 96-6159

STATEMENT DATE FROM | TO | PAGE NO. | CUSTOMER NUMBER

CHECKING LOW BALANCE DATE | BALANCE

CHECKING AVERAGE BALANCE

AVAILABLE CREDIT
DATE PAYMENT DUE
AMOUNT DUE

MONEY MANAGER

ACCOUNT	BEGINNING BALANCE	CHECKS/OTHER CHARGES WITHDRAWALS/PAYMENTS		DEPOSITS—INTEREST ADVANCES/CHARGES		SERVICE FEE	CLOSING BALANCE
		NO.	AMOUNT	NO.	AMOUNT		

DATE	CHECKS/OTHER CHARGES/WITHDRAWALS/PAYMENTS	DEPOSITS—INTEREST ADVANCES/CHARGES	BALANCE

NUMBER OF ENCLOSURES

ACTIVITY EXPLANATION-SEE REVERSE SIDE

Figure H-12: DEMAND DEPOSIT COMBINATION STATEMENT FOR MONEY MANAGERS
(Courtesy of Burroughs Corporation Office Products Group/Business Forms Division.)

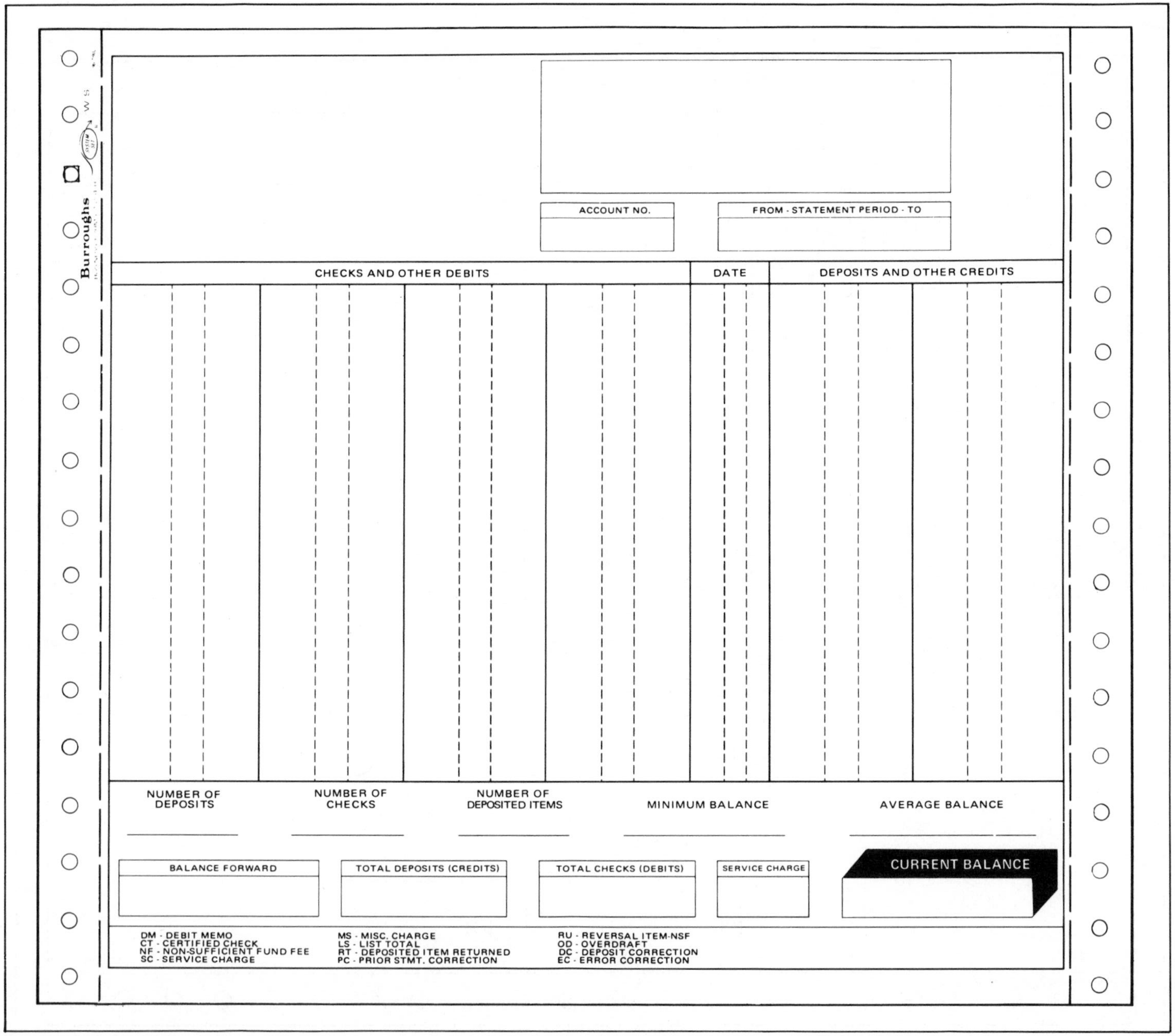

Figure H-12—Reverse Side

670

PLEASE STOP PAYMENT ON THE CHECK DESCRIBED BELOW

BRANCH NAME   DATE OF REQUEST   TELEPHONE NUMBER   ACCOUNT NUMBER

CHECK NUMBER   CHECK DATE   PAYEE   AMOUNT $

REASON FOR STOP-PAYMENT

☐ LOST   ☐ DISPUTE

DUPLICATE CHECK ISSUED?   NUMBER ☐ YES   ☐ NO

TIME RECEIVED   AM PM   RECEIVED BY

"This confirmation is our record of your stop payment order and reports our understanding of the order. If it is incorrect in any part, please advise us immediately as the bank will not be responsible for stopping the payment of any item unless accurately described in this stop payment confirmation. Acknowledgment is hereby made of the receipt of the notice of the expiration which takes effect SIX MONTHS from the date of this order.

The undersigned agrees to hold you harmless for all expenses and costs incurred by you on account of refusing payment on said item."

CUSTOMER SIGNATURE
PLEASE SIGN AND RETURN TO BANK

DETACH BEFORE SIGNING

Burroughs BUSINESS FORMS ®
96-6074

ACCOUNT NUMBER   RELEASE DATE   AMOUNT OF CHECK $

CHECK NUMBER _____   CHECK DATED _____   CHECK PAYABLE TO _____

TITLE OF ACCOUNT _____   ADDRESS _____   PHONE NO. _____

REASON FOR STOP PAYMENT _____   DUPLICATE ISSUED YES ☐ NO ☐

STOP
PAYMENT ORDER

If UNPAID, you are hereby authorized to stop payment on the check described above. In requesting you to stop payment of this negotiable instrument, the undersigned agrees to hold the bank harmless from any legal liability or cost which may be incurred by it on account or refusing payment thereof, and further agrees not to attempt to hold the bank liable should the check chance to be paid through inadvertence, oversight, accident, mistake or error, unless the undersigned is able to allege and prove actual damage by reason of such payment and in such event the liability should not exceed the amount of the check. Further, it is understood that this stop payment request does not become effective until the day following its receipt by the Bank and that this request is effective only until the release date shown above, but renewals may be made.

NOTE: No stop payment order or renewal shall be valid unless delivered in writing to the Bank and signed by a person authorized to sign checks or make withdrawals on or from an account.

THIS IS YOUR AUTHORITY TO CHARGE MY ACCOUNT $ _____

ISSUE DATE _____   TIME _____   SIGNATURE _____   RECEIVED BY _____

Burroughs BUSINESS FORMS ®
96-6075

Figure H-13: STOP PAYMENT FORMS (2)
(Courtesy of Burroughs Corporation Office Products Group/Business Forms Division.)

96-1987

Burroughs BUSINESS FORMS

OUR RECORDS INDICATE THAT WE HAVE PAID CHECK(S) IN EXCESS OF YOUR BALANCE AND HAVE OVERDRAWN YOUR ACCOUNT THE AMOUNT SHOWN BELOW. PLEASE MAKE YOUR DEPOSIT TO COVER.

ACCOUNT NUMBER	DATE	AMOUNT OVERDRAWN

96-1988

Burroughs BUSINESS FORMS

OVERDRAFT NOTICE

DATE	Account Number	Amount Overdrawn	No. of Checks	Total of Checks Paid	Unpaid Returned Check (s)	We Charge Your Account

We notify all customers at once when their account is overdrawn. This is done for your protection as well as our own. 1st - to protect against forgeries. 2nd - to protect against mistakes. 3rd - that you may know at once how your account stands. This notice should have prompt attention, and we trust you will appreciate our efforts to keep your account correct.

Figure H-14: OVERDRAFT NOTICES (2)

(Courtesy of Burroughs Corporation Office Products Group/Business Forms Division.)

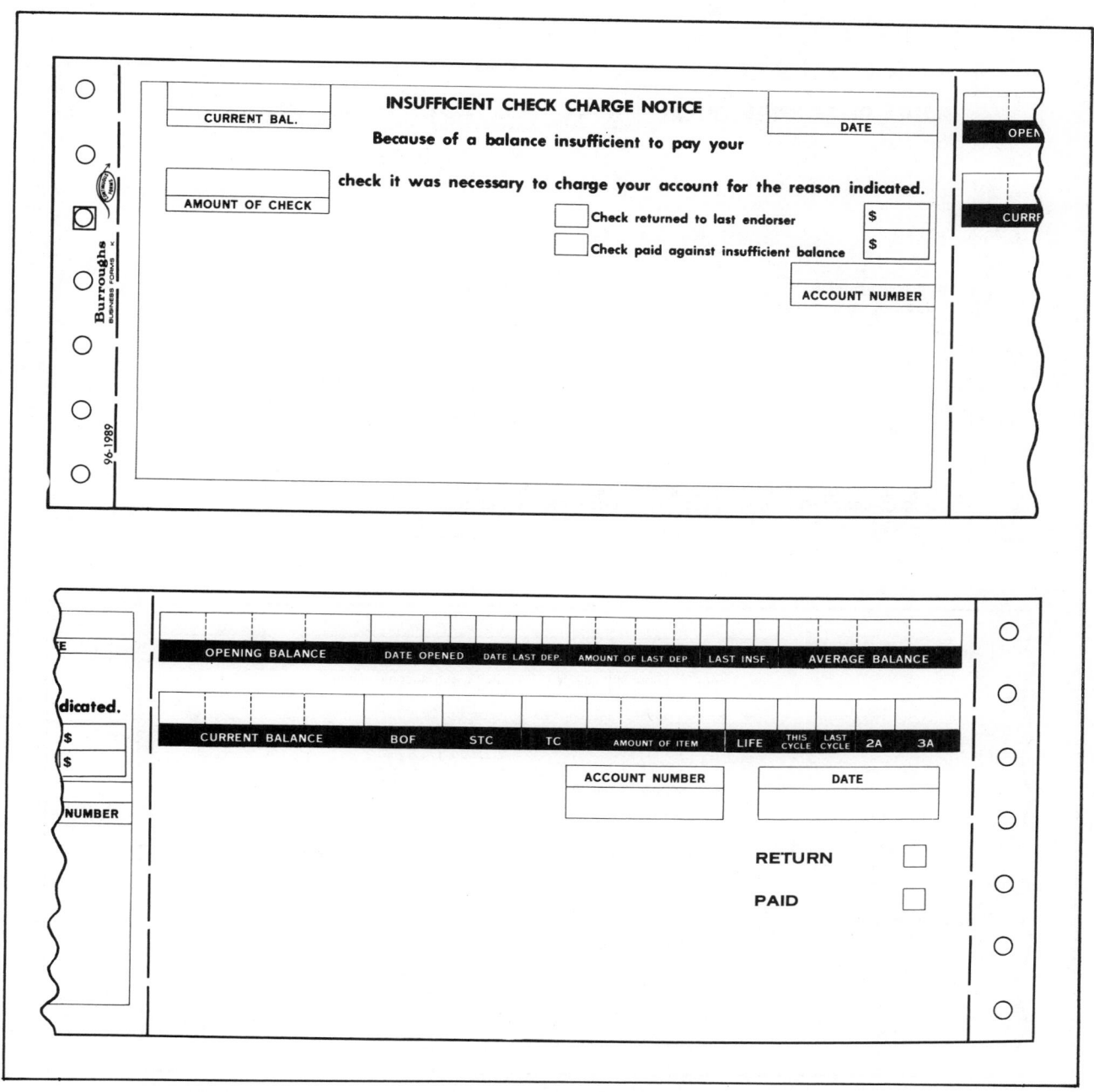

Figure H-15: INSUFFICIENT FUNDS NOTICES (2)
(Courtesy of Burroughs Corporation Office Products Group/Business Forms Division.)

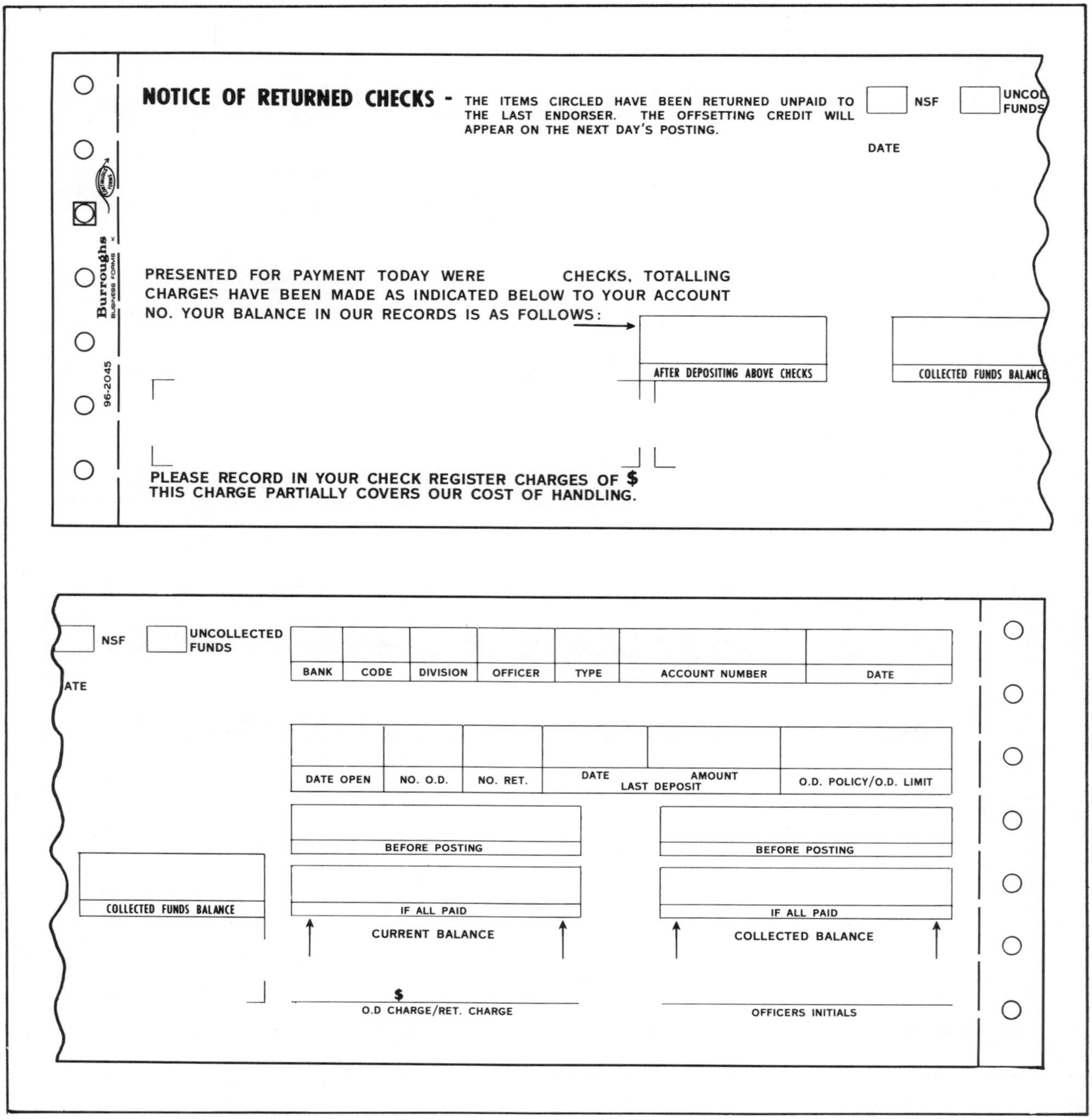

NOTICE OF RETURNED CHECKS -

THE ITEMS CIRCLED HAVE BEEN RETURNED UNPAID TO THE LAST ENDORSER. THE OFFSETTING CREDIT WILL APPEAR ON THE NEXT DAY'S POSTING.

NSF   UNCOL FUNDS

DATE

Burroughs
BUSINESS FORMS

96-2045

PRESENTED FOR PAYMENT TODAY WERE   CHECKS, TOTALLING
CHARGES HAVE BEEN MADE AS INDICATED BELOW TO YOUR ACCOUNT
NO. YOUR BALANCE IN OUR RECORDS IS AS FOLLOWS:

AFTER DEPOSITING ABOVE CHECKS

COLLECTED FUNDS BALANCE

PLEASE RECORD IN YOUR CHECK REGISTER CHARGES OF $
THIS CHARGE PARTIALLY COVERS OUR COST OF HANDLING.

NSF   UNCOLLECTED FUNDS

ATE

BANK	CODE	DIVISION	OFFICER	TYPE	ACCOUNT NUMBER	DATE

DATE OPEN	NO. O.D.	NO. RET.	DATE LAST DEPOSIT	AMOUNT	O.D. POLICY/O.D. LIMIT

BEFORE POSTING

BEFORE POSTING

COLLECTED FUNDS BALANCE

IF ALL PAID

IF ALL PAID

CURRENT BALANCE

COLLECTED BALANCE

$

O.D CHARGE/RET. CHARGE

OFFICERS INITIALS

Figure H-16: RETURNED CHECK NOTICE
(Courtesy of Burroughs Corporation Office Products Group/Business Forms Division.)

DATE_____**ACCOUNT NO.**_____ **ADVICE OF CHARGE**

According to our records your account was overdrawn today. Therefore it was necessary to:
☐ RETURN UNPAID THOSE ITEMS LISTED BELOW.
☐ PAY YOUR CHECK(S) CREATING AN OVERDRAFT.

$_____ payable to _____
$_____ payable to _____   per check has been charged. Please
$_____ payable to _____   make a deposit as soon as possible to cover
                                                                  this overdraft.
$_____ TOTAL CHARGED

NAME

96-6125 Burroughs BUSINESS FORMS

Figure H-17: CHARGE ADVICE
(Courtesy of Burroughs Corporation Office Products Group/Business Forms Division.)

675

For a change of name or address, please complete the form below.

NAME _____

ADDRESS _____

CITY _____ STATE _____ ZIP _____

SOCIAL SECURITY NO. _____ DATE ___/___/___

- *Clip and Return to Bank* -

HOW TO BALANCE YOUR ACCOUNT

1. Subtract from your check register any service, miscellaneous, or automatic charge(s) posted on this statement.

2. Mark (   ) your register after each check listed on front of statement.

3. Check off deposits shown on the statement against those shown in your check register

4. Complete the form at right.

5. The final "balance" in the form to the right should agree with your check register balance. If it does not, read "HINTS FOR FINDING DIFFERENCES" below

HINTS FOR FINDING DIFFERENCES

Recheck all additions and subtractions or corrections.

Verify the carryover balance from page to page in your check register.

Make sure you have subtracted the service or miscellaneous charge(s) from your check register balance.

NEW BALANCE (Transfer amount from other side)		$	
ADD: Deposits made since ending date on statement			
SUB-TOTAL		$	
Checks not listed on this or prior statements			
NUMBER	AMOUNT		
	$		
TOTAL CHECKS NOT LISTED ——→			
Subtract total checks not listed from sub-total above BALANCE		$	

This should agree with your check register balance.

96-1941

Figure H-18: CHECK RECONCILIATION FORMAT
(Courtesy of Burroughs Corporation Office Products Group/Business Forms Division.)

BANK DEPOSIT MEMO   .... 19 ....

Client ....   Client
                                                                                                  No. ....

Matter ....   File
                                                                                                  No. ....

Amount to be Deposited $ _____   CHECK ☐   CASH ☐

Credit to ....

....

SPECIAL INSTRUCTIONS ....

....

Deposit in ....
                                NAME OF BANK
Regular Acct. ☐   Attorney Acct. ☐   Trust Acct. ☐   Special Acct. ☐

....
PERSON MAKING DEPOSIT   ORIGINATING PARTY

BD - 16 — BANK DEPOSIT MEMO   © 1976 ALL-STATE LEGAL SUPPLY CO., 269 SHEFFIELD ST., MOUNTAINSIDE, N. J. 07092

Figure H-19: BANK DEPOSIT MEMO
(Copyright 1976 by All State Legal Supply Co., Mountainside, New Jersey 07092.)

CHECK REQUEST

AMOUNT $ ....   DATE .... 19 ....

☐ REGULAR ACCT. ....   ☐ TRUST ACCT. ....

PAYABLE TO ....

CHARGE TO ....

MATTER ....   FILE # ....

CHECK # ....   CHECK ISSUED .... 19 ....

PURPOSE ....

....

....
REQUESTED BY   APPROVED BY

CR4—CHECK REQUEST   © 1976 ALL-STATE LEGAL SUPPLY CO.
                                           269 SHEFFIELD STREET, MOUNTAINSIDE, N. J. 07092

Figure H-20: CHECK REQUEST
(Copyright 1976 by All State Legal Supply Co., Mountainside, New Jersey 07092.)

CHECK REQUISITION

CHECK NEEDED BY .... DATE REQUESTED .... 19..........
                    DATE   *TIME*

	BANK	*TYPE OF CHECK*	*CHARGE TO*
DRAW:	☐ Regular Acct.	☐ Regular	☐ Firm Expense
	☐ Trust Acct.	☐ Certified	☐ Client Expense

PAYEE .... $ ....

ADDRESS ....

IN PAYMENT OF ....

CHARGE TO .... CLIENT NO. ....

MATTER .... FILE NO. ....

DELIVER CHECK TO .... ☐ MAIL CHECK
                                                                        DIRECT TO ....

EXPLANATION/INSTRUCTIONS ....

REQUESTED BY	*APPROVED BY*

FOR RECORD KEEPING ONLY

Check No. .... Date Issued .... Acct. Charged .... Posted By ....

CR-3—CHECK REQUISITION   © 1976 ALL-STATE LEGAL SUPPLY CO., 269 SHEFFIELD ST., MOUNTAINSIDE, N. J. 07092

Figure H-21: CHECK REQUISITION
(Copyright 1976 by All State Legal Supply Co., Mountainside, New Jersey 07092.)

CREDIT — **INTERIOR TRANSFER**

FROM:

TO:

DESCRIPTION
RECEIVED:

DATE:		
100's		
50's		
20's		
10's		
5's		
2's		
1's		
SILVER		
MUTILATED		
TOTAL		

Burroughs Business Forms 96-6101

Figure H-22: INTERNAL CASH TRANSFER—CREDIT
(Courtesy of Burroughs Corporation Office Products Group/Business Forms Division.)

DEBIT — **INTERIOR TRANSFER**

FROM:

TO:

DESCRIPTION
RECEIVED:

DATE:		
100's		
50's		
20's		
10's		
5's		
2's		
1's		
SILVER		
MUTILATED		
TOTAL		

Burroughs Business Forms 96-6102

Figure H-23: INTERNAL CASH TRANSFER—DEBIT
(Courtesy of Burroughs Corporation Office Products Group/Business Forms Division.)

CASH LETTER FROM:

DATE _____

RUN 1 2 3 4 5 6 7 8 9 DN

TO:

WE ENCLOSE FOR CREDIT ITEMS HEREIN. WIRE (ADVISING NAME OF OUR ENDORSER) NON-PAYMENT OF ALL ITEMS $1,000 AND OVER EXCEPT ITEMS NOT PAID BECAUSE OF MISSING OR UNSATISFACTORY ENDORSEMENT. DO NOT PROTEST ITEMS OF $1,000 OR UNDER OR THOSE BEARING NO PROTEST OR SIMILAR AUTHORITY OF A PRECEDING ENDORSER.

Burroughs BUSINESS FORMS X

96-2031

For the Account of:

Date

THIS SPACE IS TO BE USED FOR RECAP OF TAPE TOTALS OR LISTING OF SINGLE ITEMS.

WIRE (GIVING NAME OF OUR ENDORSER) NON-PAYMENT OF ITEMS $1,000 AND OVER. EXCEPT THOSE UNPAID BECAUSE OF MISSING OR UNSATISFACTORY ENDORSEMENT. DO NOT PROTEST ITEMS $1,000 OR UNDER OR THOSE BEARING OUR NO PROTEST STAMP OR SIMILAR AUTHORITY OF A PRECEDING BANK ENDORSER.

Burroughs BUSINESS FORMS X

96-2032

Figure H-24: CASH LETTERS (2)
(Courtesy of Burroughs Corporation Office Products Group/Business Forms Division.)

NAME _____ ACCT. # _____

BANK
COMPANY _____

TYP FTR
AMOUNT _____

TEST

_____

SEND TO

DEBIT

YOUR ACCT.   OUR ACCT.

CREDIT

ADVISE   PHONE   WIRE

INFORMATION

INCREASE/DECREASE FED FUNDS

AMOUNT _____

BALANCE _____

Figure H-25: REQUEST TO INCREASE/DECREASE FEDERAL FUNDS
(Courtesy of First National Bank of Kansas City.)

CONFIRMATION and INTEREST ADVICE
Bank Wire CKSC; Telex SASNAK

First National Bank
of KANSAS CITY, MISSOURI
An Affiliate of First National Charter Corporation

CASH CONTROL DEPARTMENT
Kansas City, Missouri 64141
(816) 221-2800 Ext. 250

WE CONFIRM HAVING PURCHASED FEDERAL FUNDS FROM YOU AS DESCRIBED BELOW:

AMOUNT OF FUNDS	INTEREST RATE	NUMBER OF DAYS	PURCHASE DATE	REPAYMENT DATE
$				
SPECIAL INSTRUCTIONS:			AUTHORIZED BY VICE-PRESIDENT	

WE ARE CREDITING YOUR ACCOUNT

MAIL TO

ACCOUNT NUMBER	AMOUNT CREDITED
	$

FORM 0-302 REV. 3-77

UNITED BUSINESS FORMS CO. — K. C. MO.

Figure H-26: CONFIRMATION AND INTEREST ADVICE ON FEDERAL FUNDS PURCHASE
(Courtesy of First National Bank of Kansas City.)

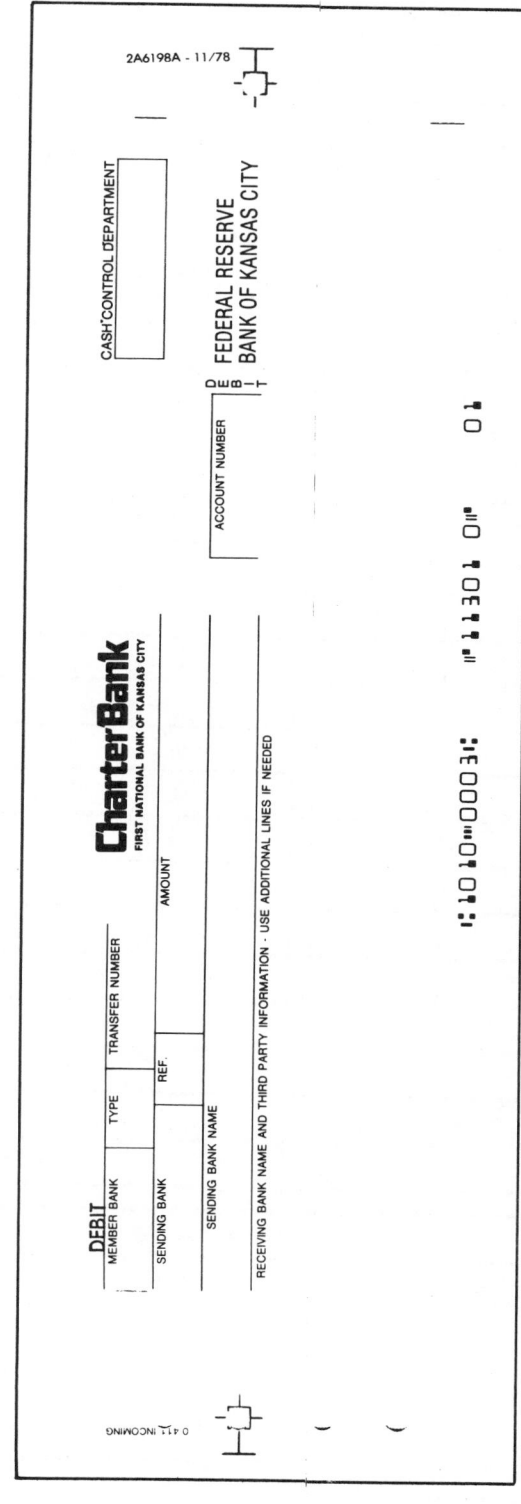

Figure H-27: FEDERAL RESERVE DEBIT MEMO—CASH CONTROL DEPARTMENT
(Courtesy of First National Bank of Kansas City.)

683

PRESENTING THE FINEST DOMESTIC AND FOREIGN FILMS

PETTY CASH REPORT

THEATRE:		WEEK ENDING:	
VENDOR	AMOUNT	EXPLANATION	For Office Use Only
1			
2			
3			
4			
5			
6			
7			
8			
9			
10			
11			
12			
	TOTAL		
MANAGER:		GEN. MANAGER:	

Please fill out completely and submit to the General Manager for approval.

Figure H-28: PETTY CASH REPORT BY VENDOR

Figure H-29: REMITTANCE ADVICE
(Courtesy of Rediform Office Products, Paramus, New Jersey 07652.)

REMITTANCE ADVICE

IN PAYMENT OF THE FOLLOWING:

TO

STREET & NO.

CITY   STATE   ZIP CODE

DATE

ENCLOSED IS OUR CHECK NO.

FOR THE SUM OF

| INVOICE DATE | INVOICE NO | AMOUNT OF INVOICE | DEDUCTIONS | | CASH DISCOUNT | | NET AMOUNT |
| | | | AMOUNT | NATURE | % | AMOUNT | |

REMARKS:

RECEIPT NOT NECESSARY

Rediform
9H 964

$
Due
Date
Favor of
Drawn on
No.
WILSON JONES CO. U.S.A.
SIGHT DRAFT
NO PROTEST TEAR THIS OFF BEFORE PRESENTING

$ 19
At days sight pay to
Dollars
Value received and charge the same to account of
To
No.

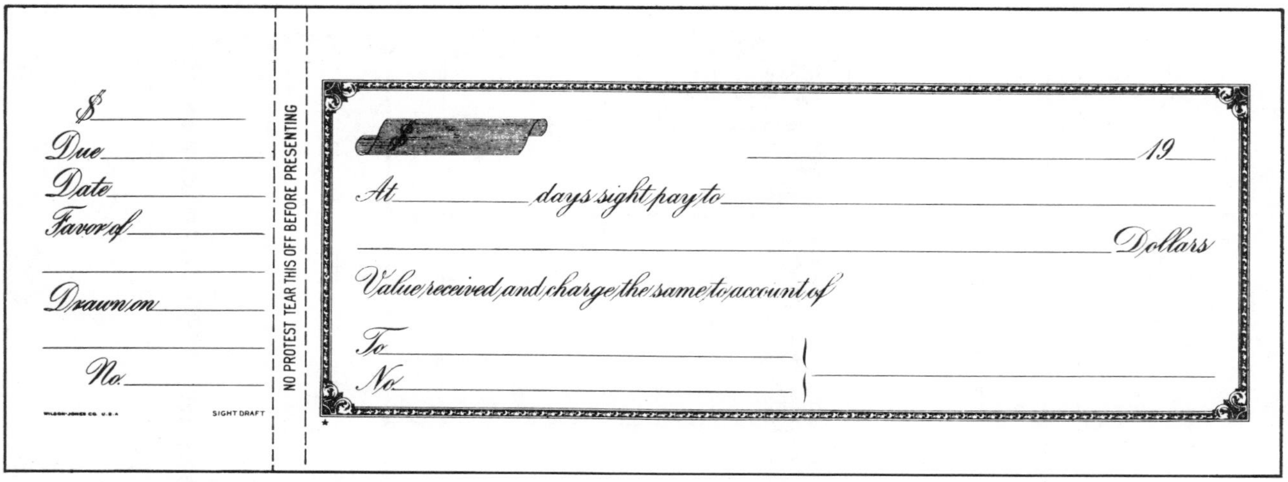

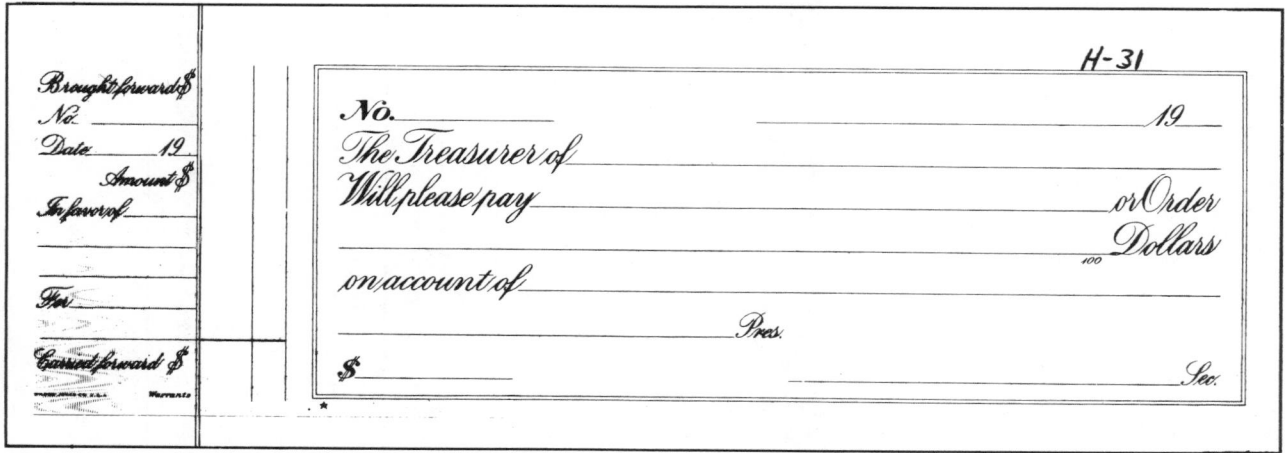

Figure H-30: SIGHT DRAFT—WITH STUB

Brought forward $
No.
Date 19
Amount $
In favor of
For
Carried forward $
Warrants

H-31
No. 19
The Treasurer of
Will please pay or Order
100 Dollars
on account of
Pres.
$ Sec.

Figure H-31: WARRANT—WITH STUB

AUTHORIZATION TO TRANSFER FUNDS

Account No. _____

Until further notice in writing, you are hereby authorized, at any time and from time-to-time, without prior notice to the undersigned, to transfer from (my/our) Regulated Commodity Account to any other account, held by you for (me/us) such excess funds, equities, securities, and/or other property as in your judgment may be required for margin, to avoid the calling of margin on open trades in commodities or securities, or to reduce any debit balance or to satisfy any such account in other security and/or commodity account.

You agree, however, that within a reasonable time after making any such transfer you will confirm the same in writing to the undersigned.

Customer's Signature _____

Title _____

Date _____

Signed at (city, state) _____

Figure H-32: AUTHORIZATION TO TRANSFER FUNDS

IRREVOCABLE LETTER OF CREDIT (A)

Customer's xx% Letter
of Credit

Issuing Bank: _____

At: _____

No. _____

This is an irrevocable Letter of Credit

To: _____*(Name and address of creditor)*_____

_____

_____

_____

_____

We hereby issue our irrevocable letter of credit in favor of

_____*(creditor)*_____ at the request of

_____*(correspondent bank, if applicable)*_____ for the account of

_____*(name of firm for whose account credit is issued)*___ in the amount of

_____*(in words)*_____ available at our

counters on or before _____*(expiration date)*_____, of your draft at

sight drawn on _____*(issuing bank)*_____ payable to

_____*(name of creditor)*_____ and stating on its

face "Drawn under Letter of Credit No. _____ issued by us"

accompanied by a statement signed by _____*(creditor)*_____

stating that the amount claimed represents the amount which

_____*(name of customer)*_____ owes to you in settle-

ment of its account.

We hereby agree to honor each draft drawn under and in compliance

with the terms of this credit, if duly presents (together with the

documents specified) at this office in _____*(city, state)*_____.

(Signed) _____

(Title) _____

Figure H-33: IRREVOCABLE LETTER OF CREDIT (A)

Barclays Bank International Limited
~~BARCLAYS BANK D.C.O.~~
INCORPORATED IN THE UNITED KINGDOM WITH LIMITED LIABILITY

....*Branch*

Date...

SPECIMEN

Dear Sir,

IRREVOCABLE CREDIT No. _____

OF _____

We are to-day informed by $\frac{\text{cable}}{\text{mail}}$ from

that they have established an Irrevocable Credit in your favour for account of

to the extent of £

(Say   )

available for your drafts on

at   to be accompanied by the following documents:

The expiry date of this credit is   19   which is the latest date
for

Kindly note that all drafts drawn under this Credit must be marked " Drawn under Irrevocable Credit
of   No.
dated   19   ''

undertake that all drafts
drawn under and in conformity with the terms of this Credit will meet with due honour provided that they are
marked as being so drawn.

We have no authority from our principals to confirm this credit and therefore this letter is solely an advice
of it and conveys no engagement by us. Any drafts negotiated by us under the credit will be subject to recourse
to yourselves

Where it is stated above that this Credit has been advised to us by cable it may be subject to alteration on
receipt of mail confirmation, in which case we shall advise you accordingly.

Yours faithfully,

CRE 78 (10/60)   *Accountant.*   *Manager.*

Figure H-34: IRREVOCABLE LETTER OF CREDIT (B)
(Courtesy of Barclays Bank International Limited.)

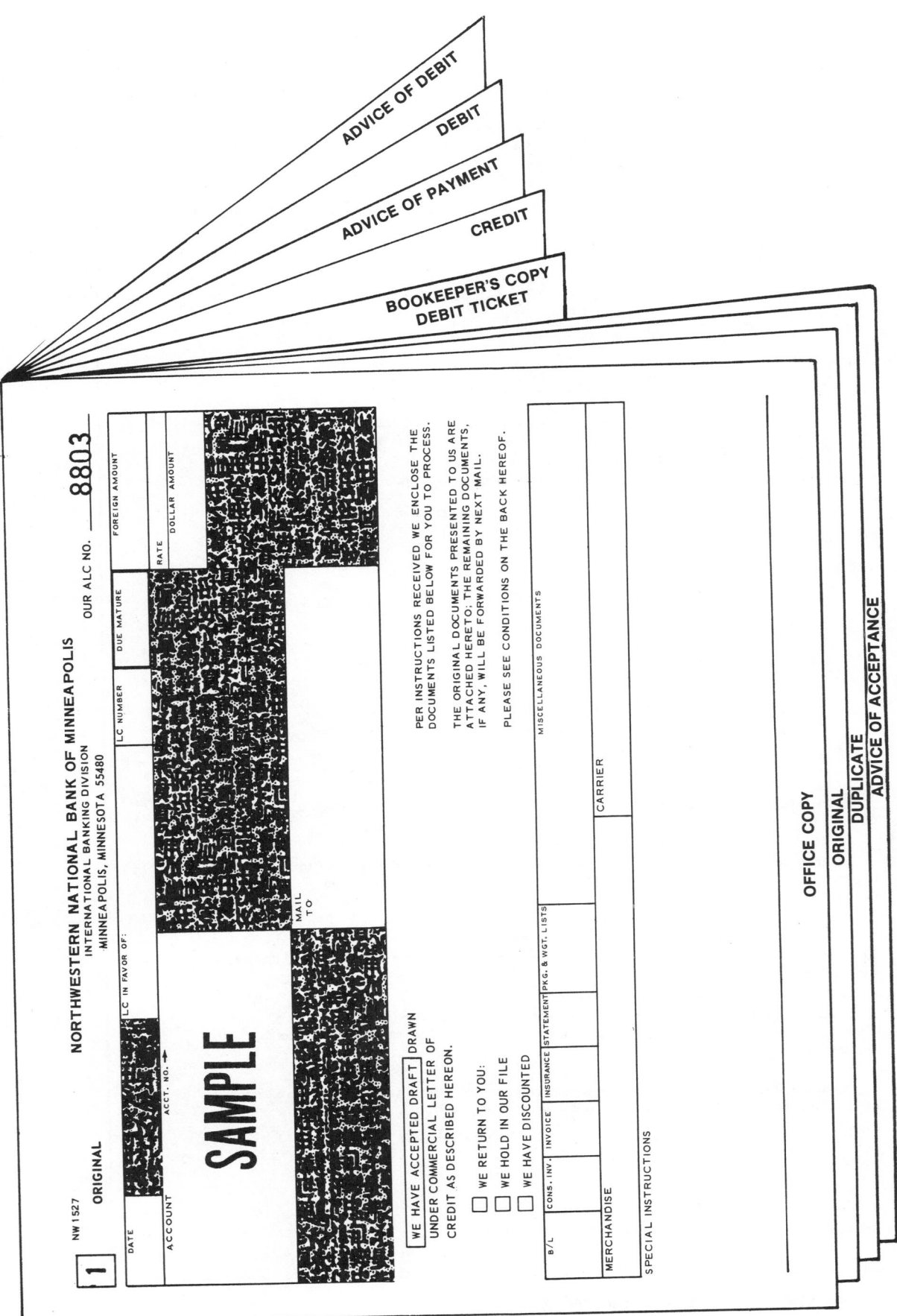

Figure H-35: ACCEPTANCE OF DRAFT DRAWN UNDER COMMERCIAL LETTER OF CREDIT
(Courtesy of Northwestern National Bank of Minneapolis)

690

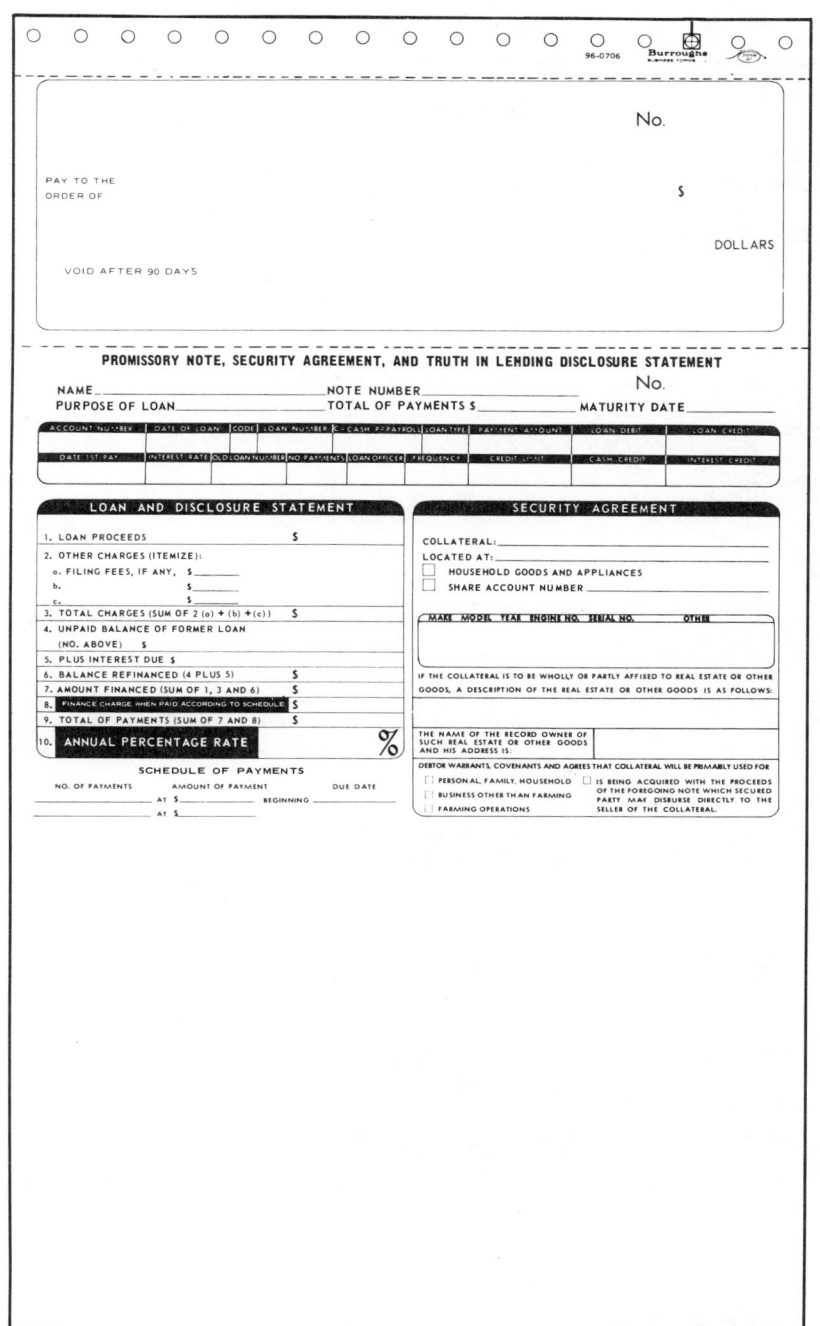

Figure H-36: PROMISSORY NOTE WITH TRUTH-IN-LENDING DISCLOSURE
(Courtesy of Burroughs Corporation Office Products Group/Business Forms Division.)

691

TED'S MARKET

APPLICATION FOR
CHECK IDENTIFICATION

I.D. NO. _____

NAME _____ DATE _____

WIFE'S NAME _____ PHONE NO. _____

ADDRESS _____

OCCUPATION _____ EMPLOYED BY _____

BUSINESS ADDRESS _____

YOUR BANK _____

CREDIT
REFERENCES 1. _____
REFERENCES 2. _____
REFERENCES 3. _____

THIS IS FOR PERSONAL CHECKS _____   Please be sure this signature is same
as will appear on check

THIS IS FOR PAYROLL CHECKS _____   MR. _____

MRS. _____

**TED'S MARKET
CUSTOMER I-D CARD**

ISSUED TO _____

I-D NUMBER _____

_____
HOLDER'S SIGNATURE

_____
ISSUED BY

EXPIRING DATE _____

Figure H-37: APPLICATION FOR CHECK IDENTIFICATION

CREDIT INQUIRY

Date_____

On_____

Street Address_____

City and State_____

_____

To_____

_____

_____

In order that we may consider opening a credit account with the above, we ask you in confidence to give us the following information:

✓ CHECK MANNER OF PAYMENT	
☐ Discounts	
☐ Prompt and Satisfactory	
☐ Prompt to_____days slow	
☐ Pays on account	
☐ Asks for more time	
☐ Slow but collectible	
☐ Slow and unsatisfactory	
☐ Accepts C. O. D.'s promptly	
☐ Settles by trade acceptance	
☐ Notes paid at maturity	
☐ Account secured	
☐ Collected by attorney	
☐ In hands of attorney	

Sold from_____ To_____

Terms_____

Largest amount owing recently $_____

Total amount now owing Notes included $_____

Amount past due . . . . . $_____

Recent trend toward   ☐ Promptness   ☐ Slowness

Makes unjust claims (State them)_____

_____

_____

Credit refused (State cause)_____

_____

_____

_____

_____

→If you have had no experience within a year, please check and return. ☐

Stamped addressed envelope is enclosed for your reply.

TOPS—form 3242
LITHO IN U.S.A.

We will be pleased to reciprocate in giving you any information we have regarding credits.
Yours truly,

_____

_____

_____

Figure H-38: CREDIT INQUIRY
(Courtesy of The Travelers Insurance Company.)

```
┌──────────────────────────────────────────────────────────────┐
│                                                                │
│                  SALESMAN'S CREDIT REPORT                      │
│                                                                │
│                                 Date......................     │
│                                                                │
│  Name of firm............................................... ·  │
│                                                                │
│  Address....................................................   │
│                                                                │
│           ..................................................   │
│                                                                │
│  Type of store or business..................................   │
│                                                                │
│  Names of principals.........................................  │
│                                                                │
│  Bank .......................................................  │
│                                                                │
│  References:  1.  ...........................................  │
│                                                                │
│               2.  ...........................................  │
│                                                                │
│               3.  ...........................................  │
│                                                                │
│               4.  ...........................................  │
│                                                                │
│  Brands carried:  ...........................................  │
│                                                                │
│           ..................................................   │
│                                                                │
│           ..................................................   │
│                                                                │
│  Check:                                                        │
│    Location:                 Excellent —  Satisfactory —  Poor —│
│    Competition:              Slight   —  Normal      —  Bad  —  │
│    Appearance of building:   Excellent —  Satisfactory —  Poor —│
│    Window display:           Excellent —  Satisfactory —  Poor —│
│    Layout:                   Excellent —  Satisfactory —  Poor —│
│    Counter display:          Excellent —  Satisfactory —  Poor —│
│    General interior appearance: Excellent — Satisfactory — Poor—│
│    Choice of merchandise:    Excellent —  Satisfactory —  Poor —│
│    Manager's sales personality: Excellent — Satisfactory — Poor—│
│    Character of employees:   Excellent —  Satisfactory —  Poor —│
│                                                                │
│  Remarks:...................................................   │
│                                                                │
│       ......................................................   │
│                                                                │
│       ......................................................   │
│                                                                │
│                    Signed ..................................   │
│                                                                │
└──────────────────────────────────────────────────────────────┘
```

Figure H-39: SALESMAN'S CREDIT REPORT
(From the book Corporate Treasurer's and Controller's Handbook by L. Doris, Editor. © 1950 renewed 1978 by L. Doris, Editor. Published by Prentice-Hall, Inc., Englewood Cliffs, New Jersey 07632.)

Line of Business: _____

Normal Selling Terms - Profit Margin	Objections Most Often Encountered and Responses That Work:
_____	
Average Collection Period:	
Average Sale Per Account Per Year:	
Type Account Sold and SIC Numbers	
_____	
Problem Accounts In the Trade: Slow Pay - Trending Poorly	Closing Techniques That Have Worked:
_____	

Controversial Accounts in the Trade,
  e.g., Questionable Future
       ″   Practices
    New Companies Starting or Moving In:	

_____	
Nearby Areas of Growth Retrogression	Approaches That Have Proved Effective:
_____	
Accounts That Caused Bad Debt Losses Recently:	
Added Sales Needed to Cover Cost of Service - (Cost of Service = Gross Profit % × Added Sales Needed)	
_____	

Prospects in This Line in My Territory:
  (Show hot ones with * plus Date you expect
  to close)	

Figure H-40: POTENTIAL CUSTOMER ANALYSIS

GENERAL INDUSTRY
CREDIT INPUT STATEMENT CONTROL SHEET

DATE: _____

CREDIT I.D.

BANK I D ____ __

PREFIX ____ __

NUMBER ____ __ __ __ __

(COMPANY NAME)

DO NOT USE THIS SPACE:

INPUT AREA USE

INPUT DATE: _____

OPERATOR: _____

REMARKS:

REPORT PARAMETER INFORMATION

REPORT REQUESTS		use Y (yes)
BASE REPORT		
RATIO ANALYSIS		
CASH FLOW ANALYSIS		
COMMON STATEMENT		
ENDING DATE — REPORT PERIOD		MM/YY (DO NOT USE UNLESS REQUESTING ENDING REPORT PERIOD OTHER THAN LATEST DATE)

STATEMENT CONTROL INFORMATION

STATEMENT DATE						MM/DD/YY
STATEMENT PERIOD CODE						Y (yearly) M (monthly) P (periodic) 1 (1st quarter) 2 (2nd quarter) 3 (3rd quarter)
DATE STMENT SENT						MM/DD/YY
DATE STMENT RECVD						MM/DD/YY
STMENT DUE CODE						Y, Q, M, X, S
No. DAYS—Yrly Stmnt Due						use when "X" in 5
No. DAYS—Qtrly Stmnt Due						use when "X" in 5
INDUSTRY CATEGORY						1 (general) 2 (motor carriers) 3 (utilities) 4 (financial)
S I C NUMBER						4 digits
AUDIT TYPE						1 (certified) 2 (qualified) 3 (disclaimer) 4 (adverse) 5 (unaudited) 6 (management) 7 (restated) 8 (preliminary)
AUDITOR NUMBER						
CONSOLIDATED STMT CODE						use 1 for subsidiary or affiliate
CONSOLIDATED REF. I D						If "1" in above, use parent company I D, if not, use zero.
TRUNCATION CODE						1 (thousands) 2 (millions)
ANALYST'S INITIALS						
STATEMENT TYPE						1 (consolidated) 2 (individual) 3 (combined) 4 (partnership) 5 (proprietorship) 6 (personal) 7 (consolidating) 8 ( ) 9 (pro-forma)
CURRENCY CODE						
EXCHANGE RATE						

B 764 rev 3-79

Figure H-41: AUTOMATED FINANCIAL STATEMENT ANALYSIS SPREAD SHEETS FOR GENERAL INDUSTRY
(Courtesy of The First National Bank of Boston.)

CREDIT I D _____

PREFIX ___ ___

NUMBER ___ ___ ___ ___ — ___ ___

(COMPANY NAME)

GENERAL INDUSTRY INPUT SHEET

**Value — one decimal point

ITEM #	DESCRIPTION	**VALUE Date	**VALUE Date	**VALUE Date	**VALUE Date	**VALUE Date	PROCESSING
	CURRENT ASSETS						
1	Cash						
3	Short Term Investment						
4							
5							add to item 33
7	Gross Receivables — Trade						add to item 33
9	Allowance for Bad Debts						
10	Net Receivables — Trade						
11	A/R 0 to 30 Days						
12	A/R 31 to 60 Days						
13	A/R 61 to 90 Days						
14	A/R 91 to 180 Days						
15	A/R 181 + Days						
17	Notes Receivables						
19							add to item 33
20							add to item 33
21	Raw Materials						
22	Work-In-Process						
23	Finished Goods						
24	Supplies & Misc. Invtry.						
25							add to item 28
26							add to item 28
27							add to item 28
28	Total Inventory						sum 21 thru 27
29							add to item 33
30							add to item 33
31	Other Current Assets						
33	Total Current Assets						sum 1 thru 5, 10, 17, 19, 20, 28 thru 31
	FIXED ASSETS						
34	Land						
35	Buildings						
36	Equipment						
37	Furniture & Fixtures						
39	Vehicles						
40	Leasehold Improvements						
41							
42	Misc. Fixed Assets						add to item 43
43	Gross Fixed Assets						sum 34 thru 42
44	Accum. Depreciation						
46	Net Fixed Assets						item 43 Minus 44
47							add to item 61
48							add to item 61
49							add to item 61
50							add to item 61
51	INV/ADV in Affil. & Subs.						
52							add to item 61
53							add to item 61
54	Prepaid & Dfd Expenses						
56							add to item 61
57	Other Assets						
59	Misc. Intangibles						
60	Goodwill						
61	Total Assets						sum 33, 46 thru 60

B 754 rev 3 79

Figure H-41 (continued)

CREDIT I D

PREFIX __ __

NUMBER __ __ __ ■

GENERAL INDUSTRY
INPUT SHEET

**Value one decimal point

ITEM #	DESCRIPTION	**VALUE Date	**VALUE Date	**VALUE Date	**VALUE Date	**VALUE Date	PROCESSING
	LIABILITIES						
63	Notes Payable—Banks						
64		*	*	*		*	add to item 78
65	Current Maturity of LTD						
67	Accounts Payable—Trade						
68	Notes Payable—Trade						
70	Accruals						
72	Income Taxes—Payable						
73	Due Affiliates						
74		*	*	*	*	*	add to item 78
75		*	*	*	*	*	add to item 78
76	Other Current Liabilities						
78	Total Current Liabilities						sum 63 thru 76
	NON CURRENT LIAB.						
79	Long Term Debt						
80		*	*	*	*	*	add to item 86
81		*	*	*	*	*	add to item 86
82		*	*	*	*	*	add to item 86
83	Reserves & Credits						
84		*	*	*	*	*	add to item 86
85	Other Liabilities						
86	Total Unsub. Liabilities						sum 78 thru 85
87	Subordinated Debt						
88		*	*	*	*	*	add to item 94
94	Total Liabilities						sum 86, 87, 88
95	Deferred Taxes						
96	Minority Interest						
	NET WORTH						
97		*	*	*	*	*	subtract from 108
98	Treasury Stock						
99		*	*	*	*	*	add to item 108
100	Capital—Preferred Stock						
101	Capital—Common Stock						
102	Paid—In Capital						
103	Retained Earnings						sum of 104 and 105
104	Restricted						
105	Unrestricted						
106		*	*	*	*	*	add to item 108
108	Net Worth (61 minus 94, 95, 96						sum of 99 thru 103, and 106 minus 97 and 98
109	Total Liabs. & Equity (= to 61)						sum of 94, 95, 96, and 108

B-754 (rev. 3/79)

Figure H-41 (continued)

COMPANY NAME

GENERAL INDUSTRY
INPUT SHEET

**Value — one decimal point

ITEM #	DESCRIPTION	**VALUE Date	**VALUE Date	**VALUE Date	**VALUE Date	**VALUE Date	PROCESSING
	OPERATING STATEMENT						
117	Net Sales Gross Income						
118							
120							add to item 122
121	Other Trade Revenue						add to item 122
122	Total Revenue						
123	Depreciation						sum of 117, 118, 120, and 121
124	Materials Used						
125	Direct Labor						
126	Factory Overhead						
127	Indirect Costs						
128	Freight In						
129	Other C. G. S.						
130							add to item 132
131	C.G.S. — Net of Depr						
132	Total C. G. S.						sum 123 thru 131
133	Gross Profits						item 122 Minus 132
134							add to item 137
135	Selling Expenses						
136	Gen. & Adm. Expenses						
137	Total S. G. & A. Expenses						sum of 134, 135, 136
138							add to item 145
139							add to item 145
140	Lease Expense						
141	Depreciation						
142	Amortization						
143	Other Operating Expenses						
145	Total Oper. Expenses						sum 137 thru 143
146	Operating Profit						item 133 Minus 145
147	Interest Expense						
148							subtract from item 153
149	Other Expenses						
150							add to item 153
151	Other Income						
153	Profit Before Taxes						sum of 146, 150, and 151 minus 147, 148, and 149
155	Income Tax						sum 156 and 157
156	Current Taxes						
157	Deferred Taxes						
158	Extraordinary Charges						
159	Extraordinary Gains						
160	Minority Interest						
161	Equity in Earnings of Subs						
162	Net Profit						sum of 153, 159, and 161 minus 155, 158, and 160
168	Preferred Dividends						
169	Common Dividends						
170	Reported Capital Expend.						
171	Adj to Retained Earnings						
172	Shares Outstanding						
173							
174	Dividends from Uncsl Sub						

B 754 rev 3 79

Figure H-41 (continued)

GENERAL INDUSTRY
NOTES AND REMARKS

CREDIT ID:
PREFIX
NUMBER

STATEMENT DATE | ITEM # | SEQ # | NOTES AND REMARKS

B-754 (rev. 3/79)

Figure H-41 (continued)

UTILITIES
CREDIT INPUT STATEMENT
CONTROL SHEET

CREDIT I D:

PREFIX ___ ___

NUMBER __ __ __ ▬ __ __ __ __

Page 1 of 5

DATE: _____

BATCH # _____

REPORT PARAMETER INFORMATION (Screen 01)

1 REPORT REQUESTS		use Y (yes) or N (no)
BASE REPORT		
RATIO ANALYSIS		
COMMON STATEMENT		
CASH FLOW ANALYSIS		
2 REPORT TYPE REQUEST		use Y (yearly) M (monthly) P (periodic) 1 (1st quarter) 2 (2nd quarter) 3 (3rd quarter)
3 ENDING DATE — REPORT PERIOD		MM/YY

STATEMENT CONTROL INFORMATION (Screen 02)

1 STATEMENT DATE						MM/DD/YY
2 STATEMENT PERIOD CODE						Y (yearly) M (monthly) P (periodic) 1 (1st quarter) 2 (2nd quarter) 3 (3rd quarter)
3 DATE STMENT SENT						MM/DD/YY
4 DATE STMENT RECVD						MM/DD/YY
5 STMENT DUE CODE						Y, Q, M, X, S
6 No. DAYS — Yrly Stmnt Due						use when "X" in 5
7 No. DAYS — Qtrly Stmnt Due						use when "X" in 5
8 INDUSTRY CATEGORY						1 (general) 2 (motor carriers) 3 (utilities) 4 (financial)
9 S I C NUMBER						4 digits
10 AUDIT TYPE						1 (certified) 2 (qualified) 3 (disclaimer) 4 (adverse) 5 (unaudited) 6 (management)
11 AUDITOR NUMBER						7 (restated) 8 (preliminary)
12 CONSOLIDATED STMT CODE						use 1 for subsidiary or affiliate
13 CONSOLIDATED REF. I D						if "1" in above, use parent company I D, if not, use zero.
14 TRUNCATION CODE						1 (thousands) 2 (millions)
15 STMNT REPLMNT CODE						"R" or Blank
16 ANALYST'S INITIALS						
17 COMPANY NAME						16 characters — use for all statement dates
18 STATEMENT TYPE						1 (consolidated) 2 (individual) 3 (combined) 4 (partnership) 5 (proprietorship) 6 (personal) 7 (consolidating) 9 (pro-forma)

B-761

Figure H-42: CREDIT INPUT STATEMENT CONTROL SHEET FOR UTILITIES
(Courtesy of The First National Bank of Boston.)

CREDIT I D:

PREFIX ___ ___ ___

NUMBER ___ ___ ___ ___ ___ ___

** Value—one decimal point

ITEM #	DESCRIPTION	**VALUE Date	**VALUE Date	**VALUE Date	**VALUE Date	**VALUE Date	PROCESSING
	ASSETS						
1	Cash						
3		*	*	*	*	*	add to item 45
4		*					add to item 45
6	Short Term Investments						
8	A/R Customers		*	*	*	*	
10		*	*	*	*	*	add to item 15
12		*	*	*	*	*	add to item 15
14	A/R Other						
15	Gorss Receivables						sum of 8, 10, 12, and 14
16	Allow for Bad Debts						
18	Net Receivables						item 15 Minus item 16
20		*	*	*	*	*	Add to item 45
22	Notes Receivables						
24	Unbilled Revenues						
25		*	*	*	*	*	add to item 45
26		*	*	*	*	*	add to item 45
27	Fuel						
28	Materials and Supplies						
30		*	*	*	*	*	add to item 34
31		*	*	*	*	*	add to item 34
33	Other Inventory						
34	Total Inventory						sum of 27, 28, 30, 31, and 33
37		*	*	*	*	*	add to item 45
38		*	*	*	*	*	add to item 45
39	Special Deposits						
40	Prepayments						
44	Other Current Assets						
45	Total Current Assets						sum of 1—6, 18, 20—26, 34—44
46	Land						
47	Utility Plant						
48	Accum. Depreciation						
49	Net Utility Plant						item 47 Minus item 48
50	Nuclear Fuel						
51	Accum. Depreciation						
52	Net Nuclear Fuel						item 50 Minus item 51
53	Non Utility Property						
54	Accum. Depreciation						
55	Net Non utility Prop						item 53 Minus item 54
58	Constn Work in Progrs						
59	Gross Property						sum 46, 47, 50, 53, and 58
60	Accum. Depreciation						sum 48, 51, and 54
61	Net Property						item 59 Minus item 60
62		*	*	*	*	*	add to item 80
63		*	*	*	*	*	add to item 80
64	Other Investments						
65		*	*	*	*	*	add to item 80
66	Fund Accounts						
67	Prepaid Expenses						
68	Unamortized Debt Expn						
69		*	*	*	*	*	add to item 73
70		*	*	*	*	*	add to item 73
71		*	*	*	*	*	add to item 73
72	Other Dfd Debits						
73	Total Deferred Debits						sum of 68 thru 72

B-761

Figure H-42 (continued)

CREDIT I D:

PREFIX __ __

NUMBER __ __ __ __ __ __ __ __

**Value—one decimal point

ITEM #	DESCRIPTION	**VALUE / Date	**VALUE / Date	**VALUE / Date	**VALUE / Date	**VALUE / Date	PROCESSING
74	Capital Stock Expense						
75	Capital Stock Discount						
76		*	*	*	*	*	add to item 80
77		*	*	*	*	*	add to item 80
78		*	*	*	*	*	add to item 80
79	Intangibles						
80	Total Assets						sum 45, 61—67, 73—79
	LIABILITIES						
81	Notes Payable—Banks						
82	Notes Payable—Other						
85	Accounts Payable						
87	Federal Taxes Accrued						
89		*	*	*	*	*	add to item 105
90	Interest Accruals						
91		*	*	*	*	*	add to item 105
93	Other Accruals						
94	Dividends Payable						
96	Customer Deposits						
98		*	*	*	*	*	add to item 105
99		*	*	*	*	*	add to item 105
101	Current Maturities Ltd.						
104	Other Current Liabs.						
105	Total Current Liabs.						sum 81 thru 104
106	Notes Payable Dfd.						
108	Mortgage Bonds						
110	Debentures						
111		*	*	*	*	*	add to item 113
113	Total Term Debt						sum 106 thru 111
116	Dfd Income Tax						
117	Dfd Tax Credits						
118		*	*	*	*	*	add to item 125
119		*	*	*	*	*	add to item 125
120		*	*	*	*	*	add to item 125
121	Other Dfd Credits						
122	Contrib in Aid of Constn						
123		*	*	*	*	*	add to item 125
124	Other Liabilities						
125	Total Liabilities						sum 105, 113, 116—124
126	Minority Interest						
127		*	*	*	*	*	add to item 150
	NET WORTH						
131	Treasury Stock						
133		*	*	*	*	*	subtract from item 146
135	Preferred Stock						
137	Common Stock						
138	Capital Surplus						
139	Earned Surplus						
140	Restricted						
141	Appropriated						
144		*	*	*	*	*	add to item 146
146	Total Capital Funds						sum 135—139, 144, Minus 131, 133
150	Liabilities & Capital Funds						sum 146, 125, 126, 127 Must equal 80

B-761

Figure H-42 (continued)

CREDIT I D:

PREFIX __ __ _

NUMBER __ __ __ — __ __ __ __ __

UTILITIES
INPUT SHEET

**Value—one decimal point

ITEM #	DESCRIPTION	**VALUE Date	**VALUE Date	**VALUE Date	**VALUE Date	**VALUE Date	PROCESSING
	OPERATING STATEMENT						
171	Operating Revenue—Elec.						
172	Operating Revenue—Gas						
173		*	*	*	*	*	add to item 177
176	Other Revenues						
177	Total Revenues						sum 171, 172, and 173
180	Fuel						
181	Purchased Power						
182		*	*	*	*	*	add to item 203
184	Other Operating Expenses						
186	Maintenance						
187	Depreciation						
188	Amortization						
189		*	*	*	*	*	add to item 203
190		*	*	*	*	*	add to item 203
193	Federal Inc. Tax—Net						sum of 194, 195 Minus 196
194	Fedl Inc. Tax—Cur						
195	Fedl Inc. Tax—Dfd						
196	Fedl Inc. Tax—Credit						
198	State Income Taxes						
199		*	*	*	*	*	add to item 202
201	Other Tax						
202	Total Taxes						sum of 193, 198, 199, 201
203	Total Operating Expenses						sum of 180-182, 184, 186-190, 202
204	Operating Income						item 177 Minus 203
206	Allowance for Funds						
207		*	*	*	*	*	add to item 214
208		*	*	*	*	*	add to item 214
210	Other Income—Net						
211		*	*	*	*	*	subtract from 214
213	Other Expenses—Net						
214	Income Before Interest						204, 206-208, 210 Minus 211, 213
216	Interest on LTD						
217	Interest on STD						
218		*	*	*	*	*	add to item 223
219	Other Interest Expense						
222	Amort of Debt Disc Exp						
223	Total Interest Expense						sum 216-219, 222
224	Inc Bfr Extrdnry Items						item 214 Minus item 223
226		*	*	*	*	*	Subtract from 235
228	Other Extrdnry Charges						
230		*	*	*	*	*	add to item 235
232	Other Extrdnry Credits						
233	Equity in Earns of Sub						
234	Minority Interest						subtract from 235
235	Net Income						224, 230, 232, 233 Minus 226, 228, 234
236	Preferred Dividends						
237	Balance for Common						item 235 Minus 236
238	Common Dividends						
239	Net Income After Dvdnds						item 237 Minus 238
240	Reported Capital Expend						
241	Adj to Retained Earns						
242	Shares Outstanding						
244	Dividends from Uncsl Sub						

B-761

Figure H-42 (continued)

CREDIT ID:
  PREFIX ⌊__⌋
  NUMBER ⌊__|__|__|__⌋—⌊__|__|__|__⌋

STATEMENT DATE	ITEM #	SEQ #	NOTES AND REMARKS
⌊__⌋/⌊__⌋/⌊__⌋	⌊__|__|__⌋	⌊__⌋	
	⌊__|__|__⌋	⌊__⌋	
	⌊__|__|__⌋	⌊__⌋	
⌊__⌋/⌊__⌋/⌊__⌋	⌊__|__|__⌋	⌊__⌋	
	⌊__|__|__⌋	⌊__⌋	
	⌊__|__|__⌋	⌊__⌋	
⌊__⌋/⌊__⌋/⌊__⌋	⌊__|__|__⌋	⌊__⌋	
	⌊__|__|__⌋	⌊__⌋	
	⌊__|__|__⌋	⌊__⌋	
⌊__⌋/⌊__⌋/⌊__⌋	⌊__|__|__⌋	⌊__⌋	
	⌊__|__|__⌋	⌊__⌋	
	⌊__|__|__⌋	⌊__⌋	
⌊__⌋/⌊__⌋/⌊__⌋	⌊__|__|__⌋	⌊__⌋	
	⌊__|__|__⌋	⌊__⌋	
	⌊__|__|__⌋	⌊__⌋	

B-761

Figure H-42 (continued)

CREDIT FOLDER

Corporate Name
or Trade Style _____   Proprietor(s) _____

Street _____   City _____   County _____   State _____

Subsidiary of (or)
Affiliated with _____   Rating _____   District Office _____

Account Guaranteed
By _____   Date _____   Warehouse _____

Address _____

Amount _____

CREDIT GUIDE	CLASS	Single Order Credit Limit	O. K.	DATE	Advice of Credit Guide Issued	CREDIT GUIDE	CLASS	Single Order Credit Limit	O. K.	DATE	Advice of Credit Guide Issued

Figure H-43: CREDIT FOLDER
(From the book Business Finance Handbook by Lillian Doris, Editor. © 1953 by Prentice-Hall, Inc.
Published by Prentice-Hall, Inc., Englewood Cliffs, New Jersey 07632.)

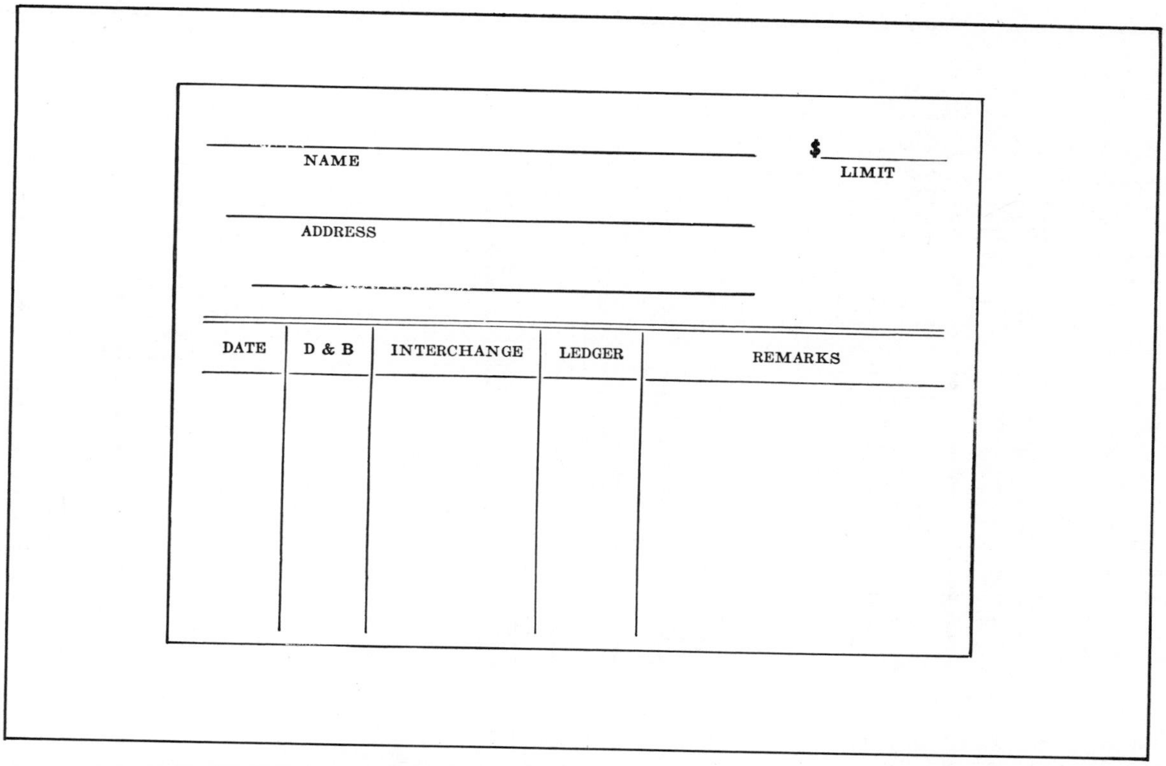
NAME

$ LIMIT

ADDRESS

DATE	D & B	INTERCHANGE	LEDGER	REMARKS

Figure H-44: CREDIT SUMMARY FILE CARD

(From the book Corporate Treasurer's and Controller's Handbook by L. Doris, Editor. © 1950 renewed 1978 by L. Doris, Editor. Published by Prentice-Hall, Inc., Englewood Cliffs, New Jersey 07632.)

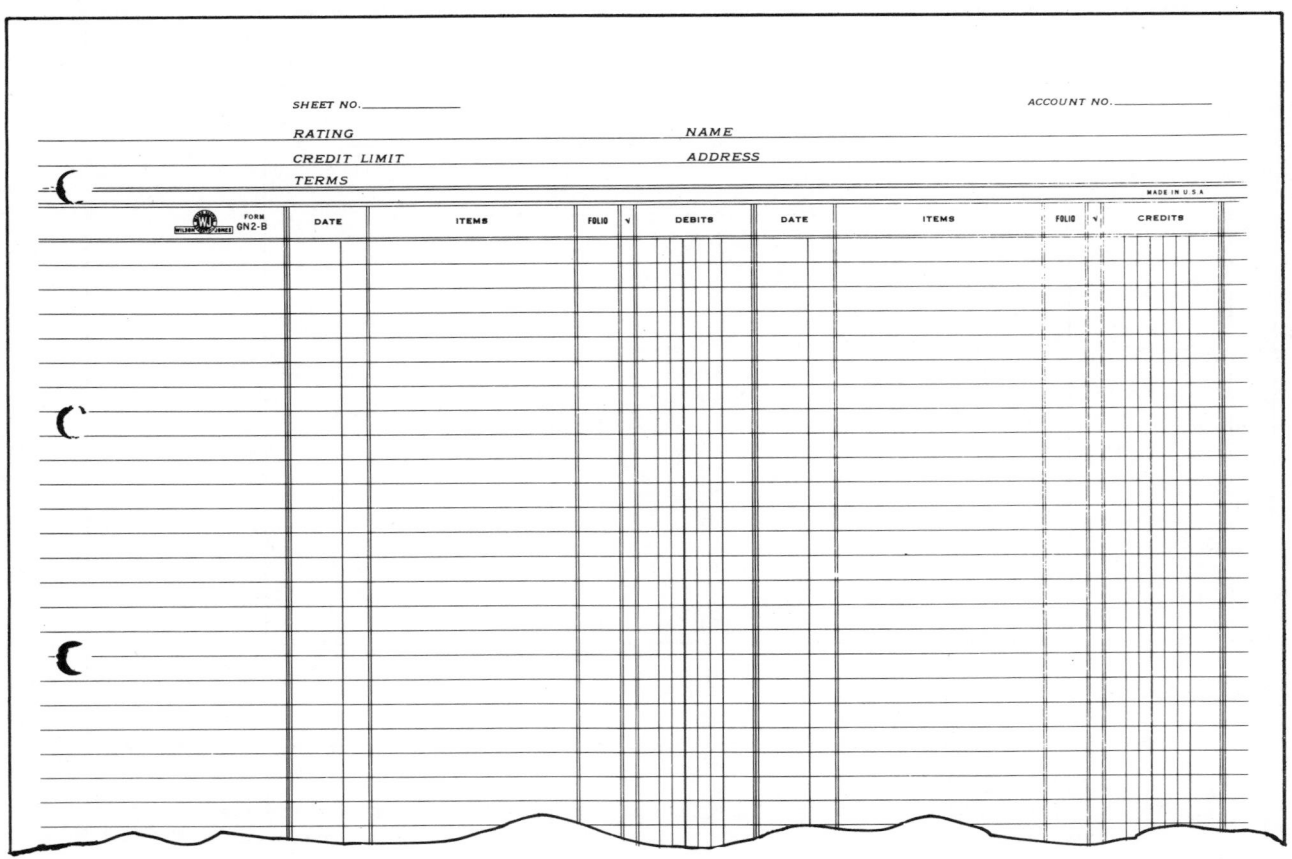

Figure H-45: CUSTOMER SALES AND PAYMENTS RECORD
(Copyright by Wilson Jones Company. All rights reserved. Forms may be obtained, subject to supply, from Wilson Jones Company, 6150 Touhy Avenue, Chicago, Illinois 60648.)

CHARGE SALES

SALESMAN		OUR NUMBER
TERMS		DATE
F. O. B.	Sold To_____	CUSTOMER'S NO.
WHEN SHIP	Address_____	DATE BILLED
HOW SHIP	Ship To_____	
	Address	

QUANTITY			DESCRIPTION	PRICE				
ORDERED	BACK ORD.	SHIPPED						

Rediform®
5H 36

Figure H-46: CHARGE SALES
(Courtesy of Rediform Office Products, Paramus, New Jersey 07652.)

INVOICE

NO.

DATE _____

SOLD TO _____

SHIPPED TO _____

YOUR ORDER NO.	OUR ORDER NO.	SALESMAN			
DATE SHIPPED	SHIPPED VIA	F.O.B.	TERMS		FOLD

QUANTITY ORDERED	QUANTITY SHIPPED	STOCK NUMBER/DESCRIPTION	PRICE	PER	AMOUNT

GrayLine "SNAP-A-WAY" FORM 44-402 4-PARTS
WILSON JONES COMPANY • © 1967 • PRINTED IN U.S.A.

ORIGINAL   874

GrayLine "SNAP-A-WAY" FORM 44-402 4-PARTS
WILSON JONES COMPANY • © 1967 • PRINTED IN U.S.A.

DUPLICATE   874

GrayLine "SNAP-A-WAY" FORM 44-402 4-PARTS
WILSON JONES COMPANY • © 1967 • PRINTED IN U.S.A.

TRIPLICATE   874

874

GrayLine "SNAP-A-WAY" FORM 44-402 4-PARTS
WILSON JONES COMPANY • © 1967 • PRINTED IN U.S.A.

QUADRUPLICATE

Figure H-47: INVOICE
(Copyright by Wilson Jones Company. All rights reserved. Forms may be obtained, subject to supply, from Wilson Jones Company, 6150 Touhy Avenue, Chicago, Illinois 60648.)

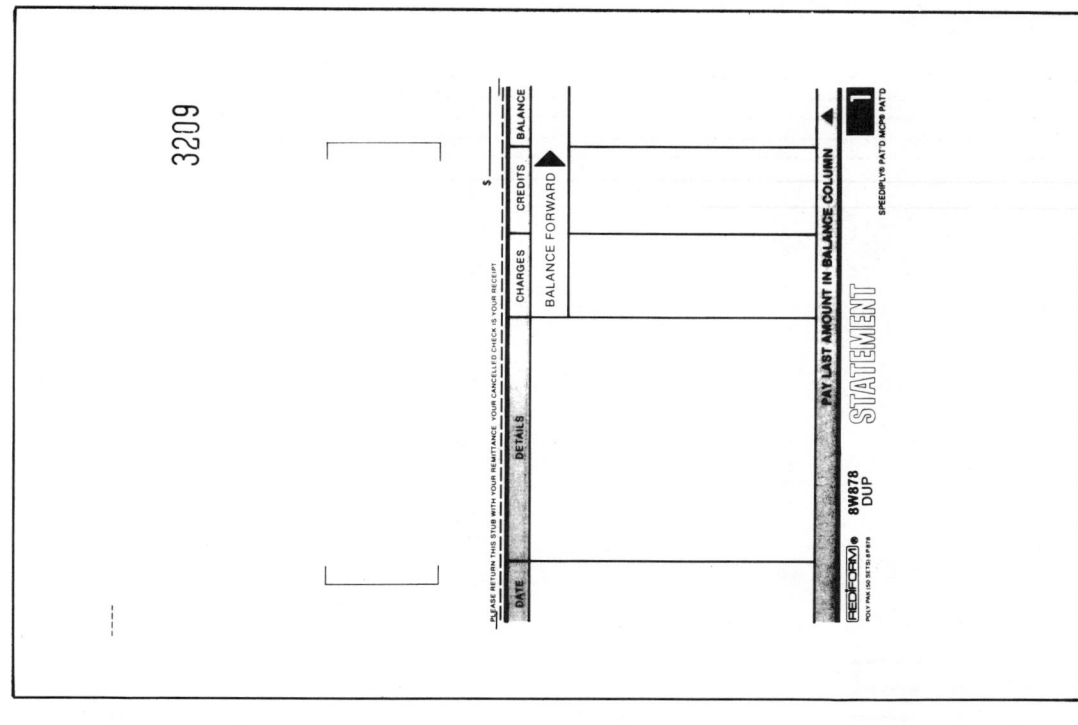

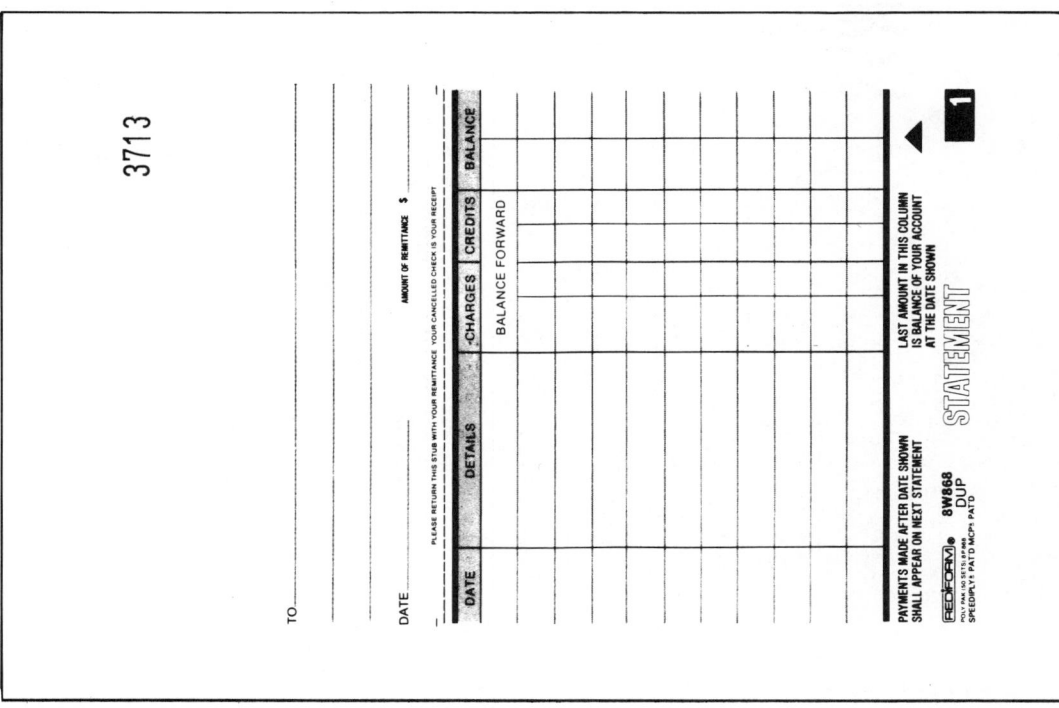

Figure H-48: STATEMENTS (2)

(Courtesy of Rediform Office Products, Paramus, New Jersey 07652.)

711

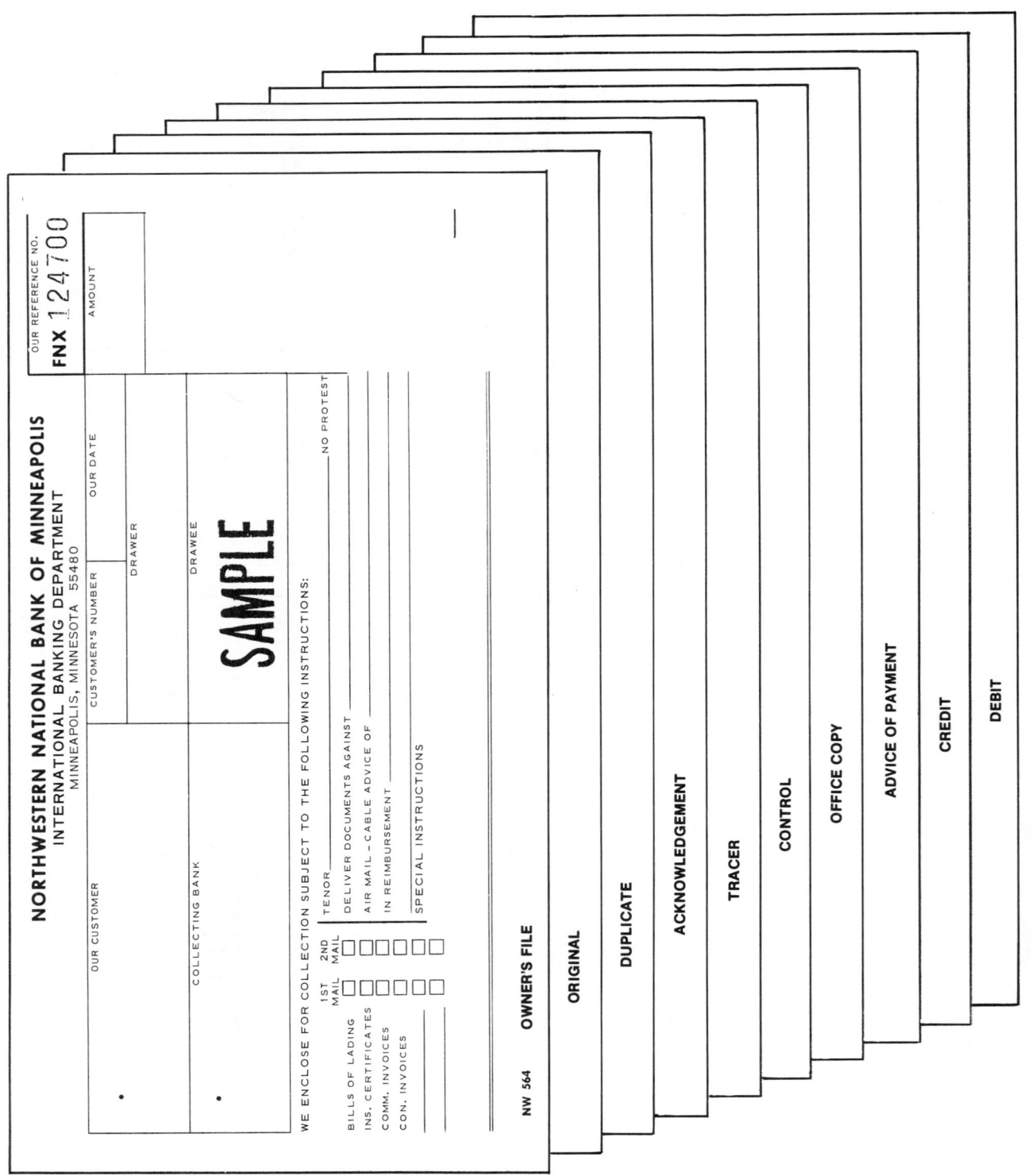

Figure H-49: BANK COLLECTION INSTRUCTIONS
(Courtesy of Northwestern National Bank of Minneapolis.)

SUBORDINATION AGREEMENT

WHEREAS .... a .... corporation having its principle place of business in ...., ...(herein called the "Borrower") is indebted to the amount indicated to each of the following:

.... $............................

.... $............................

.... $............................

(herein called the "Creditors" whether there be one or more than one), and

WHEREAS the Borrower and the Creditors have requested *The* FIRST NATIONAL BANK *of* BOSTON (herein called the "Bank") to grant financial accommodations to the Borrower, and the Bank has indicated that it is unwilling to do so unless the Borrower and the Creditors shall join in this agreement and the Creditors shall subordinate, to the extent and in the manner hereinafter set forth, the indebtedness hereinbefore referred to and also all other indebtedness (except for current or future salaries) of the Borrower to the Creditors, direct or indirect, absolute or contingent, due or to become due, now existing or hereafter arising (herein called the "Subordinated Debt") to all indebtedness of the Borrower to the Bank, direct or indirect, absolute or contingent, due or to become due, now existing or hereafter arising (herein called the "Bank Debt");

NOW, THEREFORE, in consideration of the premises and as an inducement to the Bank to grant financial accommodations to the Borrower, whether by loan or advance or extension of time for the payment of Bank Debt or otherwise, and in consideration of the granting thereof, the Borrower and the Creditors warrant to and covenant with the Bank as follows:

1. Until all Bank Debt shall have been paid in full, the Borrower shall not, directly or indirectly, make any payment of principal or interest on account of or transfer any collateral for any part of the Subordinated Debt, the Creditors shall not demand or accept from the Borrower or any other person any such payment or collateral nor cancel, set off or otherwise discharge any part of the Subordinated Debt and neither the Borrower nor the Creditors shall otherwise take or permit any action prejudicial to or inconsistent with the Bank's priority position over the Creditors created by this agreement.

2. To secure the performance of this agreement, the Creditors hereby assign, transfer and set over to the Bank the Subordinated Debt, whether evidenced by negotiable or non-negotiable instruments,

1

Figure H-50 (continued)

securities or other writings, book entries or otherwise, together with any collateral therefor, and have endorsed or assigned to the Bank and herewith deposit with it the following:

In the event such endorsement or assignment is omitted, the Bank is hereby irrevocably authorized to make the same. The Borrower and the Creditors shall make appropriate notations in their books to show the subordinate character of all Subordinated Debt which may now or hereafter be carried on open account.

3. The Creditors will not commence or join with any other creditor or creditors of the Borrower in commencing any bankruptcy, reorganization or insolvency proceedings against the Borrower. At any meeting of creditors of the Borrower or in the event of any proceeding, voluntary or involuntary, for the distribution, division or application of all or part of the assets of the Borrower or the proceeds thereof, whether such proceeding be for the liquidation, dissolution or winding up of the Borrower or its business, a receivership, insolvency or bankruptcy proceeding, an assignment for the benefit of creditors or a proceeding by or against the Borrower for relief under any bankruptcy, reorganization or insolvency law or any law relating to the relief of debtors, readjustment of indebtedness, reorganization, arrangement, composition or extension or otherwise, if all Bank Debt has not been paid in full at the time, the Bank is hereby irrevocably authorized at any such meeting or in any such proceeding:

(a) To enforce claims comprising Subordinated Debt either in its own name or the name or names of any Creditors, by proof of debt, proof of claim, suit or otherwise;

(b) To collect any assets of the Borrower distributed, divided or applied by way of dividend or payment, or any such securities issued, on account of Subordinated Debt and apply the same, or the proceeds of any realization upon the same that the Bank in its discretion elects to effect, to Bank Debt until all Bank Debt shall have been paid in full, rendering any surplus to the Creditors, pro rata;

(c) To vote claims comprising Subordinated Debt to accept or reject any plan of partial or complete liquidation, reorganization, arrangement, composition or extension; and

(d) To take generally any action in connection with any such meeting or proceeding which the Creditors might otherwise take.

4. Should any payment on account of or any collateral for any part of the Subordinated Debt be received by the Creditors, such payment or collateral shall be delivered forthwith to the Bank by the recipient for application to Bank Debt, in the form received except for the addition of any endorsement or assignment necessary to effect transfer of all rights therein to the Bank. The Bank is irrevocably authorized to supply any required endorsement or assignment which may have been omitted. Until so delivered any such payment or collateral shall be held by the recipient in trust for the Bank and shall not be commingled with other funds or property of the recipient.

2

Figure H-50 (continued)

5.   No part of the Subordinated Debt is evidenced by any instrument, security or other writing which has not previously been or is not concurrently being deposited with the Bank; the Creditors are the lawful owners of the Subordinated Debt and no part thereof has been assigned to or subordinated or subjected to any other security interest in favor of anyone other than the Bank. Until all Bank Debt has been paid in full, the Borrower shall not issue any instrument, security or other writing evidencing any part of the Subordinated Debt except at the request of and in the manner requested by the Bank; and the Creditors shall not assign or subordinate any part of the Subordinated Debt except to or in favor of the Bank.

6.   The Bank is hereby authorized to demand specific performance of this agreement, whether or not the Borrower shall have complied with the provisions hereof applicable to it, at any time when the Creditors shall have failed to comply with any provision hereof applicable to them. The Creditors hereby irrevocably waive any defense based on the adequacy of a remedy at law which might be asserted as a bar to the remedy of specific performance hereof in any action brought therefor by the Bank. The Creditors further waive presentment, notice and protest in connection with all negotiable instruments evidencing Bank Debt or Subordinated Debt to which they may be parties, notice of the acceptance of this agreement by the Bank, notice of any loan made, extension granted or other action taken in reliance hereon and all demands and notices of every kind in connection with this agreement, Bank Debt or Subordinated Debt; assent to any renewal, extension or postponement of the time of payment of Bank Debt or any other indulgence with respect thereto, to any substitution, exchange or release of collateral therefor and to the addition or release of any person primarily or secondarily liable thereon; and agree to the provisions of any instrument, security or other writing evidencing Bank Debt.

7.   The Borrower and the Creditors shall execute and deliver to the Bank such further instruments and shall take such further action as the Bank may at any time or times reasonably request in order to carry out the provisions and intent of this agreement.

8.   If all indebtedness of the Borrower to the Bank is at any time or times hereafter paid in full and thereafter the Borrower again becomes indebted to the Bank, the provisions of this agreement shall apply to such new indebtedness unless before the same is incurred the Creditors notify the Bank in writing to the contrary. If, in reliance upon this agreement, the Bank grants loans or extensions or takes other action, after the death or incapacity of or the termination of this agreement by the Creditors, but prior to the receipt by the Bank of written notice of such death, incapacity or termination, the Bank's rights shall be the same as they would have been had such death, incapacity or termination not occurred, and the Borrower and the Creditors shall indemnify the Bank and save it harmless from and against any loss, cost, liability or expense which it may have incurred or suffered by reason of any action so taken by it.

9.   If any warranty herein contained shall prove to have been materially false when made or in the event of a breach by the Borrower or the Creditors in the performance of any of the terms hereof, the Bank may, at its option, declare all Bank Debt to be forthwith due and payable, without presentment, demand, protest, or notice of any kind, notwithstanding any time or credit otherwise allowed.

10.   The rights granted to the Bank hereunder are solely for its protection and nothing herein contained shall impose on the Bank any duties with respect to any property of the Borrower or the Creditors received hereunder beyond reasonable care in its custody and preservation while in the Bank's possession. The Bank shall have no duty to preserve rights against prior parties in any instrument or chattel paper received hereunder.

11.   This agreement is intended to take effect as a sealed instrument, shall be binding upon the Borrower, the Creditors, their respective executors, administrators, other legal representatives, suc-

3

Figure H-50 (continued)

cessors and assigns, shall inure to the benefit of the Bank, its successors and assigns and shall be construed in accordance with the laws of the Commonwealth of Massachusetts. The obligations hereby undertaken by the Creditors shall be their joint and several obligations.

IN WITNESS WHEREOF, the parties hereto have caused this agreement to be duly executed this   day of   , 19

--   -- ⎤
                    Borrower   ⎥
                                                                                                 ⎥ Creditors
By--   -- ⎥
                                                                                                 ⎥
                                                    -- ⎦

4

Figure H-50: SUBORDINATION AGREEMENT
(Courtesy of The First National Bank of Boston.)

Guaranty
(UNLIMITED)

To: *The First National Bank of Boston*, including its overseas branches (the *"Bank"*):

1. *Guaranty of Payment and Performance of Obligations.* In consideration of the Bank's extending credit or otherwise in its discretion giving time, financial or banking facilities or accommodations to_____ _____(the *"Customer"*), the undersigned (the *"Guarantor"*) hereby unconditionally guarantees to the Bank that *(a)* the Customer will duly and punctually pay or perform, at the place specified therefor, or if no place is specified, at the Bank's Head Office or at the branch of the Bank where this Guaranty is given, all indebtedness, obligations and liabilities, direct or indirect, matured or unmatured, primary or secondary, certain or contingent, of the Customer to the Bank now or hereafter owing or incurred (including without limitation costs and expenses incurred by the Bank in attempting to collect or enforce any of the foregoing) which are chargeable to the Customer either by law or under the terms of the Bank's arrangements with the Customer, accrued in each case to the date of payment hereunder (collectively the *"Obligations"* and individually an *"Obligation"*); and *(b)* if there is an agreement evidencing or executed and delivered in connection with any Obligation, the Customer will perform in all other respects strictly in accordance with the terms thereof. This Guaranty is an absolute, unconditional and continuing guaranty of the full and punctual payment and performance by the Customer of the Obligations and not of their collectibility only and is in no way conditioned upon any requirement that the Bank first attempt to collect any of the Obligations from the Customer or resort to any security or other means of obtaining payment of any of the Obligations which the Bank now has or may acquire after the date hereof, or upon any other contingency whatsoever. Upon any default by the Customer in the full and punctual payment and performance of the Obligations, the liabilities and obligations of the Guarantor hereunder shall, at the option of the Bank, become forthwith due and payable to the Bank without demand or notice of any nature, all of which are expressly waived by the Guarantor. Payments by the Guarantor hereunder may be required by the Bank on any number of occasions.

2. *Guarantor's Further Agreements to Pay.* The Guarantor further agrees, as the principal obligor and not as a guarantor only, to pay to the Bank forthwith upon demand, in funds immediately available to the Bank, all costs and expenses (including court costs and legal expenses) incurred or expended by the Bank in connection with this Guaranty and the enforcement hereof, together with interest on amounts recoverable under this Guaranty from the time such amounts become due until payment at the usual rate charged by the Bank in similar circumstances, but in no event less than 12% per annum.

3. *Unlimited Liability of Guarantor.* The liability of the Guarantor hereunder shall be unlimited.

4. *Termination of Guaranty.* The obligations of the Guarantor under this Guaranty shall continue in full force and effect until the Bank shall have received from the Guarantor written notice of the Guarantor's intention to discontinue this Guaranty, notwithstanding any intermediate or temporary payment or settlement of the whole or any part of the Obligations. No such notice shall affect any rights acquired by the Bank hereunder prior to its receipt. In the event of any such discontinuance of this Guaranty or its termination in any other manner, all checks, drafts, notes, instruments (negotiable or otherwise) and writings drawn or made by or for the account of the Customer on the Bank or any of its agents purporting to be dated on or before the date such discontinuance or termination becomes known to the Bank, although presented to and paid or accepted by the Bank after that date, shall form part of the Obligations. No such notice shall be effective unless received and acknowledged by an officer of the Bank at its Head Office or at the branch of the Bank where this Guaranty is given.

5. *Security; Set-off.* The Guarantor grants to the Bank, as security for the full and punctual payment and performance of the Guarantor's obligations hereunder, a continuing lien on and security interest in all securities or other property belonging to the Guarantor now or hereafter held by the Bank and in all deposits and other sums credited by or due from the Bank to the Guarantor or subject to withdrawal by the Guarantor; and regardless of the adequacy of any collateral or other means of obtaining repayment of the Obligations, the Bank may at any time and without notice to the Guarantor set off the whole or any portion or portions of any or all such deposits and other sums against amounts payable under this Guaranty, whether or not any other person or persons could also withdraw money therefrom.

6. *Bank's Freedom to Deal with Customer and Other Parties.* The Bank shall be at liberty, without giving notice to or obtaining the assent of the Guarantor and without relieving the Guarantor of any liability hereunder, to deal with the Customer and with each other party who now is or after the date hereof becomes liable in any manner for any of the Obligations, in such manner as the Bank in its sole discretion deems fit, and to this end the Guarantor gives to the Bank full authority in its sole discretion to do any or all of the following things: *(a)* extend credit, make

Figure H-51: UNLIMITED GUARANTY AGREEMENT
(Courtesy of The First National Bank of Boston.)

loans and afford other financial accommodations to the Customer at such times, in such amounts and on such terms as the Bank may approve, *(b)* vary the terms and grant extensions or renewals of any present or future indebtedness or obligation to the Bank of the Customer or of any such other party, *(c)* grant time, waivers and other indulgences in respect thereto, *(d)* vary, exchange, release or discharge, wholly or partially, or delay in or abstain from perfecting and enforcing any security or guaranty or other means of obtaining payment of any of the Obligations which the Bank now has or acquires after the date hereof, *(e)* accept partial payments from the Customer or any such other party, *(f)* release or discharge, wholly or partially, any endorser or guarantor, and *(g)* compromise or make any settlement or other arrangement with the Customer or any such other party.

7. *Unenforceability of Obligations Against Customer; Invalidity of Security or Other Guaranties.* If for any reason the Customer has no legal existence or is under no legal obligation to discharge any of the Obligations undertaken or purported to be undertaken by it or on its behalf, or if any of the moneys included in the Obligations have become irrecoverable from the Customer by operation of law or for any other reason, this Guaranty shall nevertheless be binding on the Guarantor to the same extent as if the Guarantor at all times had been the principal debtor on all such Obligations. This Guaranty shall be in addition to any other guaranty or other security for the Obligations, and it shall not be prejudiced or rendered unenforceable by the invalidity of any such other guaranty or security.

8. *Waivers by Guarantor.* The Guarantor waives: notice of acceptance hereof, notice of any action taken or omitted by the Bank in reliance hereon, and any requirement that the Bank be diligent or prompt in making demands hereunder, giving notice of any default by the Customer or asserting any other right of the Bank hereunder. The Guarantor also irrevocably waives, to the fullest extent permitted by law, all defenses which at any time may be available in respect of the Guarantor's obligations hereunder by virtue of any homestead exemption, statute of limitations, valuation, stay, moratorium law or other similar law now or hereafter in effect.

9. *No Contest with Bank.* So long as any Obligation remains unpaid or undischarged, the Guarantor will not, by paying any sum recoverable hereunder (whether or not demanded by the Bank) or by any means or on any other ground, claim any set-off or counterclaim against the Customer in respect of any liability of the Guarantor to the Customer or, in proceedings under the Bankruptcy Act or insolvency proceedings of any nature, prove in competition with the Bank in respect of any payment hereunder or be entitled to have the benefit of any counterclaim or proof of claim or dividend or payment by or on behalf of the Customer or the benefit of any other security for any Obligation which, now or hereafter, the Bank may hold or in which it may have any share.

10. *Demands and Notices.* Any demand on or notice to the Guarantor shall be in writing and shall be effective when handed to the Guarantor or left at or mailed or sent by telegraph to the Guarantor's usual or last-known address.

11. *Amendments, Waivers Etc.* Except as otherwise provided in paragraph 4 of this Guaranty, no provision of this Guaranty can be changed, waived, discharged or terminated except by an instrument in writing signed by the Bank and the Guarantor expressly referring to the provision of this Guaranty to which such instrument relates; and no such waiver shall extend to, affect or impair any right with respect to any Obligation which is not expressly dealt with therein. No course of dealing or delay or omission on the part of the Bank in exercising any right shall operate as a waiver thereof or otherwise be prejudicial thereto.

12. *Miscellaneous Provisions.* This Guaranty is intended to take effect as a sealed instrument to be governed by and construed in accordance with the laws of the Commonwealth of Massachusetts and shall inure to the benefit of the Bank and its successors in title and assigns, and shall be binding on the Guarantor and the Guarantor's successors in title, assigns and legal representatives.

IN WITNESS WHEREOF, the Guarantor has executed this Guaranty or has caused this Guaranty to be executed on its behalf by an officer or other person thereunto duly authorized on the_____day of _____, 19_____.

_____   _____

By_____   _____
       Title

Note — A separate guaranty must be signed by each guarantor.

Figure H-51 (continued)

Certificate

The undersigned certifies to The First National Bank of Boston that:

1. He is the_____ (1)
of the Guarantor which executed the foregoing Guaranty and in that capacity has the authority to make this certificate on behalf of the Guarantor.

2. The Guarantor is a_____ (2),
validly organized or formed and existing in good standing and in the full enjoyment of its powers and franchises under the laws of _____ (3).

3. The execution and performance by the Guarantor of said Guaranty was, by appropriate corporate or other action, duly authorized and nothing which the Guarantor may be called upon to do as contemplated thereby will contravene any existing law, or rule or regulation thereunder, or any provision of its certificate of incorporation or by-laws or other document or documents evidencing its establishment or governing the conduct of its affairs of any agreement to which it is a party or by which it is bound.

IN WITNESS WHEREOF, the undersigned has made this certificate on behalf of the Guarantor this _____ day of _____,19_____.

_____

[Seal] (4)

---

(1) Insert title of person signing the certificate, i.e., Secretary, Clerk, trustee, partner, as the case may be.

(2) Insert type of business organization of Guarantor, i.e., corporation, business trust, partnership, as the case may be.

(3) Insert jurisdiction in which the Guarantor was formed.

(4) Impress corporate or common seal, if any.

Figure H-51 (continued)

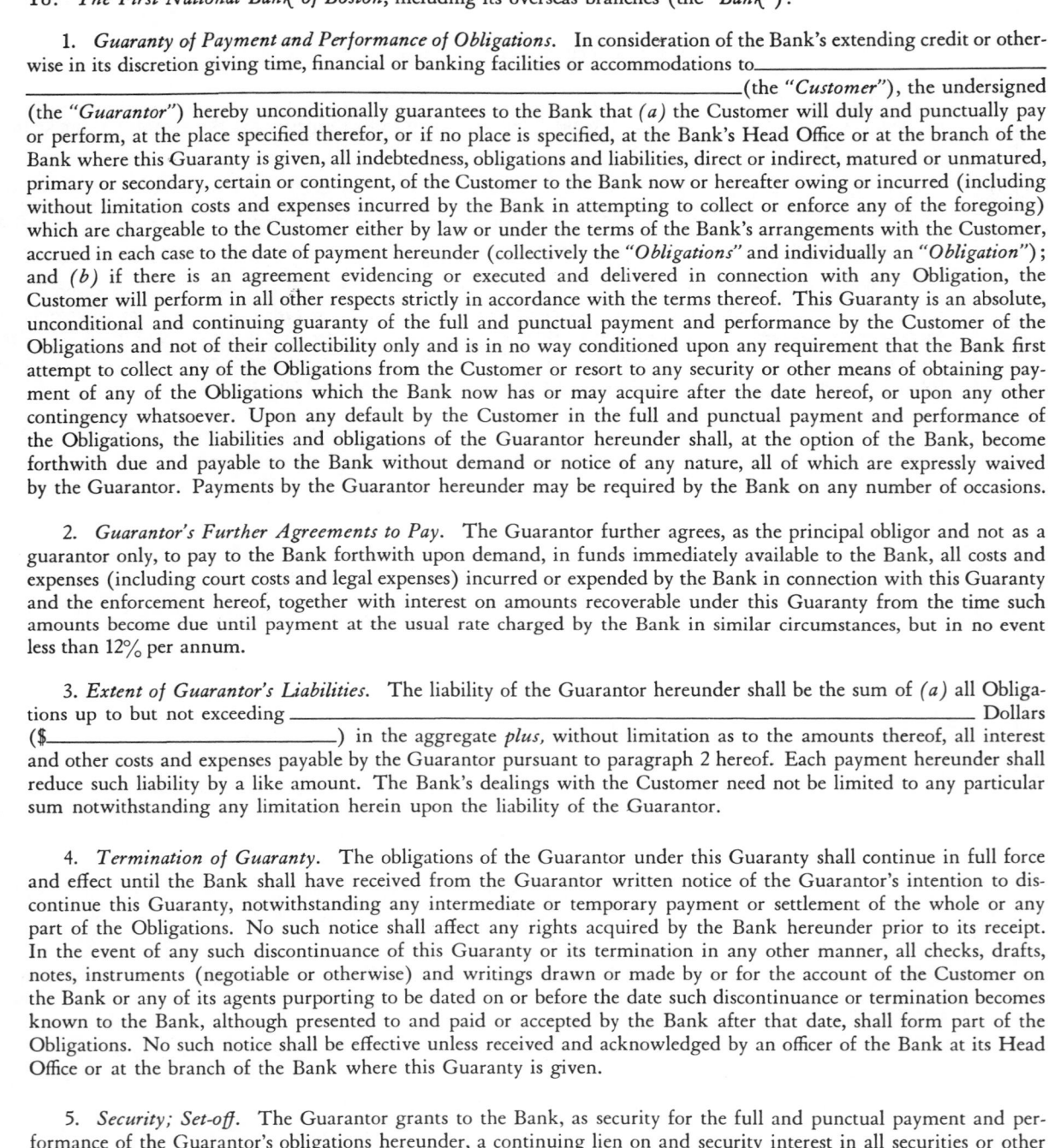

𝔊𝔲𝔞𝔯𝔞𝔫𝔱𝔶
(LIMITED)

To: *The First National Bank of Boston*, including its overseas branches (the *"Bank"*):

1. *Guaranty of Payment and Performance of Obligations.* In consideration of the Bank's extending credit or otherwise in its discretion giving time, financial or banking facilities or accommodations to⎯⎯⎯⎯⎯⎯⎯⎯⎯⎯⎯⎯⎯⎯⎯⎯⎯⎯⎯⎯⎯⎯⎯⎯⎯⎯⎯⎯⎯⎯⎯⎯⎯⎯(the *"Customer"*), the undersigned (the *"Guarantor"*) hereby unconditionally guarantees to the Bank that *(a)* the Customer will duly and punctually pay or perform, at the place specified therefor, or if no place is specified, at the Bank's Head Office or at the branch of the Bank where this Guaranty is given, all indebtedness, obligations and liabilities, direct or indirect, matured or unmatured, primary or secondary, certain or contingent, of the Customer to the Bank now or hereafter owing or incurred (including without limitation costs and expenses incurred by the Bank in attempting to collect or enforce any of the foregoing) which are chargeable to the Customer either by law or under the terms of the Bank's arrangements with the Customer, accrued in each case to the date of payment hereunder (collectively the *"Obligations"* and individually an *"Obligation"*); and *(b)* if there is an agreement evidencing or executed and delivered in connection with any Obligation, the Customer will perform in all other respects strictly in accordance with the terms thereof. This Guaranty is an absolute, unconditional and continuing guaranty of the full and punctual payment and performance by the Customer of the Obligations and not of their collectibility only and is in no way conditioned upon any requirement that the Bank first attempt to collect any of the Obligations from the Customer or resort to any security or other means of obtaining payment of any of the Obligations which the Bank now has or may acquire after the date hereof, or upon any other contingency whatsoever. Upon any default by the Customer in the full and punctual payment and performance of the Obligations, the liabilities and obligations of the Guarantor hereunder shall, at the option of the Bank, become forthwith due and payable to the Bank without demand or notice of any nature, all of which are expressly waived by the Guarantor. Payments by the Guarantor hereunder may be required by the Bank on any number of occasions.

2. *Guarantor's Further Agreements to Pay.* The Guarantor further agrees, as the principal obligor and not as a guarantor only, to pay to the Bank forthwith upon demand, in funds immediately available to the Bank, all costs and expenses (including court costs and legal expenses) incurred or expended by the Bank in connection with this Guaranty and the enforcement hereof, together with interest on amounts recoverable under this Guaranty from the time such amounts become due until payment at the usual rate charged by the Bank in similar circumstances, but in no event less than 12% per annum.

3. *Extent of Guarantor's Liabilities.* The liability of the Guarantor hereunder shall be the sum of *(a)* all Obligations up to but not exceeding ⎯⎯⎯⎯⎯⎯⎯⎯⎯⎯⎯⎯⎯⎯⎯⎯⎯⎯⎯⎯⎯⎯⎯⎯⎯⎯⎯⎯ Dollars ($⎯⎯⎯⎯⎯⎯⎯⎯⎯⎯⎯⎯⎯) in the aggregate *plus*, without limitation as to the amounts thereof, all interest and other costs and expenses payable by the Guarantor pursuant to paragraph 2 hereof. Each payment hereunder shall reduce such liability by a like amount. The Bank's dealings with the Customer need not be limited to any particular sum notwithstanding any limitation herein upon the liability of the Guarantor.

4. *Termination of Guaranty.* The obligations of the Guarantor under this Guaranty shall continue in full force and effect until the Bank shall have received from the Guarantor written notice of the Guarantor's intention to discontinue this Guaranty, notwithstanding any intermediate or temporary payment or settlement of the whole or any part of the Obligations. No such notice shall affect any rights acquired by the Bank hereunder prior to its receipt. In the event of any such discontinuance of this Guaranty or its termination in any other manner, all checks, drafts, notes, instruments (negotiable or otherwise) and writings drawn or made by or for the account of the Customer on the Bank or any of its agents purporting to be dated on or before the date such discontinuance or termination becomes known to the Bank, although presented to and paid or accepted by the Bank after that date, shall form part of the Obligations. No such notice shall be effective unless received and acknowledged by an officer of the Bank at its Head Office or at the branch of the Bank where this Guaranty is given.

5. *Security; Set-off.* The Guarantor grants to the Bank, as security for the full and punctual payment and performance of the Guarantor's obligations hereunder, a continuing lien on and security interest in all securities or other property belonging to the Guarantor now or hereafter held by the Bank and in all deposits and other sums credited by or due from the Bank to the Guarantor or subject to withdrawal by the Guarantor; and regardless of the adequacy of any collateral or other means of obtaining repayment of the Obligations, the Bank may at any time and without notice to the Guarantor set off the whole or any portion or portions of any or all such deposits and other sums against amounts payable under this Guaranty, whether or not any other person or persons could also withdraw money therefrom.

Figure H-52: LIMITED GUARANTY AGREEMENT
(Courtesy of The First National Bank of Boston.)

6. *Bank's Freedom to Deal with Customer and Other Parties.* The Bank shall be at liberty, without giving notice to or obtaining the assent of the Guarantor and without relieving the Guarantor of any liability hereunder, to deal with the Customer and with each other party who now is or after the date hereof becomes liable in any manner for any of the Obligations, in such manner as the Bank in its sole discretion deems fit, and to this end the Guarantor gives to the Bank full authority in its sole discretion to do any or all of the following things: *(a)* extend credit, make loans and afford other financial accommodations to the Customer at such times, in such amounts and on such terms as the Bank may approve, *(b)* vary the terms and grant extensions or renewals of any present or future indebtedness or obligation to the Bank of the Customer or of any such other party, *(c)* grant time, waivers and other indulgences in respect thereto, *(d)* vary, exchange, release or discharge, wholly or partially, or delay in or abstain from perfecting and enforcing any security or guaranty or other means of obtaining payment of any of the Obligations which the Bank now has or acquires after the date hereof, *(e)* accept partial payments from the Customer or any such other party, *(f)* release or discharge, wholly or partially, any endorser or guarantor, and *(g)* compromise or make any settlement or other arrangement with the Customer or any such other party.

7. *Unenforceability of Obligations Against Customer; Invalidity of Security or Other Guaranties.* If for any reason the Customer has no legal existence or is under no legal obligation to discharge any of the Obligations undertaken or purported to be undertaken by it or on its behalf, or if any of the moneys included in the Obligations have become irrecoverable from the Customer by operation of law or for any other reason, this Guaranty shall nevertheless be binding on the Guarantor to the same extent as if the Guarantor at all times had been the principal debtor on all such Obligations. This Guaranty shall be in addition to any other guaranty or other security for the Obligations, and it shall not be prejudiced or rendered unenforceable by the invalidity of any such other guaranty or security.

8. *Waivers by Guarantor.* The Guarantor waives: notice of acceptance hereof, notice of any action taken or omitted by the Bank in reliance hereon, and any requirement that the Bank be diligent or prompt in making demands hereunder, giving notice of any default by the Customer or asserting any other right of the Bank hereunder. The Guarantor also irrevocably waives, to the fullest extent permitted by law, all defenses which at any time may be available in respect of the Guarantor's obligations hereunder by virtue of any homestead exemption, statute of limitations, valuation, stay, moratorium law or other similar law now or hereafter in effect.

9. *No Contest with Bank.* So long as any Obligation remains unpaid or undischarged, the Guarantor will not, by paying any sum recoverable hereunder (whether or not demanded by the Bank) or by any means or on any other ground, claim any set-off or counterclaim against the Customer in respect of any liability of the Guarantor to the Customer or, in proceedings under the Bankruptcy Act or insolvency proceedings of any nature, prove in competition with the Bank in respect of any payment hereunder or be entitled to have the benefit of any counterclaim or proof of claim or dividend or payment by or on behalf of the Customer or the benefit of any other security for any Obligation which, now or hereafter, the Bank may hold or in which it may have any share.

10. *Demands and Notices.* Any demand on or notice to the Guarantor shall be in writing and shall be effective when handed to the Guarantor or left at or mailed or sent by telegraph to the Guarantor's usual or last-known address.

11. *Amendments, Waivers Etc.* Except as otherwise provided in paragraph 4 of this Guaranty, no provision of this Guaranty can be changed, waived, discharged or terminated except by an instrument in writing signed by the Bank and the Guarantor expressly referring to the provision of this Guaranty to which such instrument relates; and no such waiver shall extend to, affect or impair any right with respect to any Obligation which is not expressly dealt with therein. No course of dealing or delay or omission on the part of the Bank in exercising any right shall operate as a waiver thereof or otherwise be prejudicial thereto.

12. *Miscellaneous Provisions.* This Guaranty is intended to take effect as a sealed instrument to be governed by and construed in accordance with the laws of the Commonwealth of Massachusetts and shall inure to the benefit of the Bank and its successors in title and assigns, and shall be binding on the Guarantor and the Guarantor's successors in title, assigns and legal representatives.

IN WITNESS WHEREOF, the Guarantor has executed this Guaranty or has caused this Guaranty to be executed on its behalf by an officer or other person thereunto duly authorized on the_____day of _____, 19_____.

_____

By_____

Title

Note — A separate guaranty must be signed by each guarantor.

Figure H-52 (continued)

721

Certificate

The undersigned certifies to The First National Bank of Boston that:

1. He is the_____ (1)
of the Guarantor which executed the foregoing Guaranty and in that capacity has the authority to make this certificate on behalf of the Guarantor.

2. The Guarantor is a_____ (2),
validly organized or formed and existing in good standing and in the full enjoyment of its powers and franchises under the laws of _____ (3).

3. The execution and performance by the Guarantor of said Guaranty was, by appropriate corporate or other action, duly authorized and nothing which the Guarantor may be called upon to do as contemplated thereby will contravene any existing law, or rule or regulation thereunder, or any provision of its certificate of incorporation or by-laws or other document or documents evidencing its establishment or governing the conduct of its affairs of any agreement to which it is a party or by which it is bound.

IN WITNESS WHEREOF, the undersigned has made this certificate on behalf of the Guarantor this
_____ day of _____,19_____.

_____

[Seal] (4)

___

(1) Insert title of person signing the certificate, i.e., Secretary, Clerk, trustee, partner, as the case may be.

(2) Insert type of business organization of Guarantor, i.e., corporation, business trust, partnership, as the case may be.

(3) Insert jurisdiction in which the Guarantor was formed.

(4) Impress corporate or common seal, if any.

Figure H-52 (continued)

AGREEMENT AUTHORIZING PLEDGE OF COLLATERAL

(This agreement authorizes the Bank to deal with the undersigned's collateral as if it were owned by the Borrower.)

THE FIRST NATIONAL BANK OF BOSTON
BOSTON, MASSACHUSETTS 02110

...., 19.......

The undersigned hereby requests that you make a loan to — grant an extension of the time for the payment to you of present indebtedness of —..
(herein called the "Borrower") and authorizes the Borrower to deliver to and pledge with you the following property belonging to or standing in the name of the undersigned:

....

....

In consideration of your granting to the Borrower one or more such loans or extensions of time, the undersigned agrees that:

As herein used, "Obligations" shall include all obligations, direct or indirect, absolute or contingent, due or to become due, now existing or hereafter arising, of the Borrower or the undersigned to you which are incurred prior to the receipt by you of written notice of the termination of this agreement by the undersigned, or written notice of the death or incapacity of the undersigned. Notice of termination, death or incapacity as aforesaid shall not affect rights acquired by you prior to its receipt.

The above listed property and also all other property belonging to or standing in the name of the undersigned which is now held by you or may hereafter be delivered to you by the Borrower or the undersigned as security for any Obligation, together with all additions or accessions thereto (all of the foregoing being hereinafter called the "Collateral"), shall constitute security for all of the Obligations.

Right is expressly granted to you at your option to transfer at any time to yourself or to your nominee any securities constituting Collateral and to receive the income thereon and hold the same as security hereunder or apply it on the principal or interest due on any of the Obligations. You may, at your option, whether or not the Obligations are due, demand, sue for, collect or make any compromise or settlement you deem desirable with reference to the Collateral. You shall at all times have with respect to the Collateral, in addition to the rights and powers given you hereunder, all rights and powers given with respect to Collateral under any note or other evidence of any of the Obligations. You shall not be bound to take any steps necessary to preserve any rights in the Collateral against prior parties. You may deliver any of the Collateral to the Borrower at any time, the Borrower's receipt being sufficient acquittance to you for the same, and you may in general deal with the Collateral and proceeds thereof as if the Borrower were the absolute owner thereof. Regardless of the adequacy of the Collateral and any other security for the Obligations, any deposits or other sums at any time credited by or due from you to the undersigned may at any time be applied to or set off against any of the Obligations on which the undersigned is liable as a primary obligor and may at or after the maturity thereof be applied to or set off against any of the Obligations on which the undersigned is liable as a secondary obligor.

If any of the following defaults occur: (a) default in the payment or performance of any of the Obligations or of any liability or obligation to you of any indorser, guarantor or surety of or for any of the Obligations; (b) sale or encumbrance to or of any property constituting Collateral hereunder or the making of any levy, seizure or attachment thereof or thereon or the failure to pay when due any tax thereon or, with respect to any insurance policy, any premium therefor; (c) default under any instrument constituting Collateral hereunder; (d) death, dissolution, termination of existence, insolvency, business failure, appointment of a receiver of any part of the property of, assignment for the benefit of creditors by, or the commencement of any proceeding under any bankruptcy or insolvency laws by or against, any undersigned or any maker, indorser, guarantor or surety of or for any of the Obligations; (e) you deem yourself insecure by reason of a decline in value of the Collateral; thereupon or at any time thereafter (unless all existing defaults have been cured to your satisfaction), you may without notice or demand declare this agreement to be in default and shall thereafter have, in addition to all other rights and remedies, the rights and remedies of a secured party under the Uniform Commercial Code of Massachusetts. Unless the Collateral is perishable or threatens to decline speedily in value or is of a type customarily sold on a recognized market, you shall give to the undersigned at least five days' prior written notice of the time and place of any public sale thereof or of the time after which any private sale or any other intended disposition is to be made.

No delay or omission on your part in exercising any right hereunder shall operate as a waiver of such right or of any other right under this agreement. No waiver of any right shall be effective unless in writing and signed by you, and no waiver on one occasion shall be construed as a bar to or waiver of any such right on any other occasion.

The undersigned waives presentment, notice, protest, notice of acceptance of this agreement, notice of any loans made, extensions granted, collateral received or delivered or any other action taken in reliance hereon, all demands and notices in connection with the delivery, acceptance, performance, default, or enforcement of any note or other evidence of indebtedness for which any of the Collateral is pledged and all other demands and notices of any description, and assents to any extension or postponement of the time of payment or any other indulgence, to any substitution, exchange or release of collateral and to the addition or release of any party or person primarily or secondarily liable.

This agreement is intended to take effect as a sealed instrument and shall inure to the benefit of yourself and your successors and assigns and shall be binding upon the undersigned and any executor, administrator, or other legal representative of the undersigned. The Obligations of the undersigned under this agreement shall continue until all of the Obligations have been performed or paid in full. In the event that any of the Collateral or any deposit or other sum due from or credited by you is held or stands in the name of the undersigned and another or others jointly, you may deal with the same for all purposes as if it belonged to or stood in the name of the undersigned alone.

The undersigned acknowledges his understanding that this agreement, among other things, authorizes you to deal with the Collateral as if the Borrower were the absolute owner thereof.

....

COMMONWEALTH OF.. ⎱
                                                                                                            ⎰ ss.
COUNTY OF.. ⎰

On this..day of..., 19........

before me personally appeared..

....to me known to be the individual(s)
executing the foregoing agreement and acknowledged that the same was a free act and deed.

....
                                                                                                            Notary Public

(A separate agreement should be signed by each party with respect to property owned by him alone.
When property to be pledged is owned by more than one person, all owners should sign on one form.)

C-164

Figure H-53: AGREEMENT AUTHORIZING PLEDGE OF COLLATERAL BY A THIRD PARTY
(Courtesy of The First National Bank of Boston.)

PLEDGE AGREEMENT

(For use where pledgor delivers general collateral directly to Bank)

...............................19..........

THE FIRST NATIONAL BANK OF BOSTON
BOSTON, MASSACHUSETTS 02110

The undersigned hereby requests that you make a loan to — grant an extension of the time for the payment to you

of present indebtedness of — ....
(herein called the "Borrower"). In consideration of your granting to the Borrower one or more such loans or extensions of time, the undersigned herewith pledges with you the following property :

....

....

....

....

The above listed property and also all other property belonging to or standing in the name of the undersigned which is now or may hereafter be in your possession, together with all additions or accessions thereto (all of the foregoing being hereinafter called the "Collateral"), shall constitute security for any and all obligations, direct or indirect, absolute or contingent, due or to become due, now existing or hereafter arising, of the Borrower or the undersigned to you which are incurred prior to the receipt by you of written notice of the termination of this agreement by the undersigned, or written notice of the death of or incapacity of the undersigned, which notice of termination, death or incapacity shall not affect rights acquired by you prior to its receipt (all such obligations being hereinafter called the "Obligations").

Right is expressly granted to you at your option to transfer at any time to yourself or to your nominee any securities constituting Collateral and to receive the income thereon and hold the same as security hereunder or apply it on the principal or interest due on any of the Obligations. You may, at your option, whether or not the Obligations are due, demand, sue for, collect or make any compromise or settlement you deem desirable with reference to the Collateral. You shall not be bound to take any steps necessary to preserve any rights in the Collateral against prior parties. Regardless of the adequacy of the Collateral and any other security for the Obligations, any deposits or other sums at any time credited by or due from you to the undersigned may at any time be applied to or set off against any of the Obligations on which the undersigned is primarily liable and may at or after the maturity thereof be applied to or set off against any of the Obligations on which the undersigned is liable as a secondary obligor.

If any of the following defaults occur : (a) default in the payment or performance of any of the Obligations or of any liability or obligation to you of any indorser, guarantor or surety or for any of the Obligations; (b) sale or encumbrance to or of any property constituting Collateral hereunder or the making of any levy, seizure or attachment thereof or thereon or the failure to pay when due any tax thereon or, with respect to any insurance policy, any premium therefor; (c) default under any instrument constituting Collateral hereunder; (d) death, dissolution, termination of existence, insolvency, business failure, appointment of a receiver of any part of the property of, assignment for the benefit of creditors by, or the commencement of any proceeding under any bankruptcy or insolvency laws by or against, any undersigned or any maker, indorser, guarantor or surety of or for any of the Obligations; (e) you deem yourself insecure by reason of a decline in value of the Collateral; thereupon or at any time thereafter (unless all existing defaults have been cured to your satisfaction), you may without notice or demand declare this agreement to be in default and shall thereafter have, ii. addition to all other rights and remedies, the rights and remedies of a secured party under the Uniform Commercial Code of Massachusetts. Unless the Collateral is perishable or threatens to decline speedily in value or is of a type customarily sold on a recognized market, you shall give to the undersigned at least five days' prior written notice of the time and place of any public sale thereof or of the time after which any private sale or any other intended disposition is to be made.

No delay or omission on your part in exercising any right hereunder shall operate as a waiver of such right or of any other right under this agreement. No waiver of any right shall be effective unless in writing and signed by you, and no waiver on one occasion shall be construed as a bar to or waiver of any such right on any other occasion.

The undersigned waives presentment, notice, protest, notice of acceptance of this agreement, notice of any loans made, extensions granted, collateral received or delivered or any other action taken in reliance thereon, all demands and notices in connection with the delivery, acceptance, performance, default, or enforcement of any note or other evidence of indebtedness for which any of the Collateral is pledged and all other demands and notices of any description, and assents to any extension or postponement of the time of payment or any other indulgence, to any substitution, exchange or release of collateral and to the addition or release of any party or person primarily or secondarily liable.

This agreement is intended to take effect as a sealed instrument and shall inure to the benefit of yourself and your successors and assigns and shall be binding upon the undersigned and any executor, administrator, or other legal representative of the undersigned. The obligations of the undersigned under this agreement shall continue until all of the Obligations have been performed or paid in full. In the event that any of the Collateral or any deposit or other sum due from or credited by you is held or stands in the name of the undersigned and another or others jointly, you may deal with the same for all purposes as if it belonged to or stood in the name of the undersigned alone.

....

....

[A separate agreement should be signed by each pledgor with respect to property owned by him alone. When property to be pledged is owned by more than one person, all owners should sign on one form.]

C-337

Figure H-54: PLEDGE AGREEMENT
(Courtesy of The First National Bank of Boston.)

Month	Credit Sales ($00) (1)	EOM A/R ($00) (2)	150-day Moving Average (Daily Sales) (3)	EOM DSO (4)	Distribution, by Age, of Outstanding Receivables (in days)			
					0 – 30 (5)	30 – 60 (6)	60 – 90 (7)	90 – 120 (8)
(Year t – 1)								
July	810	1,443	45.4	31.8	17.4	6.1	6.2	2.1
Aug.	720	1,213	39.0	31.1	18.1	6.7	4.3	2.1
Sept.	900	1,313	33.4	39.3	25.8	7.2	4.5	1.8
Oct.	1,410	1,825	31.6	57.8	42.7	9.3	4.1	1.6
Nov.	1,770	2,348	37.4	62.7	45.4	11.9	4.2	1.3
Dec.	1,590	2,403	42.6	56.4	36.4	12.9	5.6	1.5
Jan.	1,470	2,335	47.6	49.1	30.5	10.2	6.3	2.1
Feb.	1,590	2,400	52.2	46.0	30.1	8.6	5.3	2.0
Mar.	1,830	2,650	55.0	48.2	32.7	8.6	4.5	2.3
Apr.	1,800	2,673	55.2	48.4	31.7	10.0	5.0	1.8
May	1,320	2,240	53.4	41.9	24.0	10.3	5.8	1.9
June	990	1,740	50.2	34.7	19.0	7.6	6.0	2.1
(Year t)								
July	1,050	1,615	46.6	34.7	21.5	6.2	4.5	2.5
Aug.	1,020	1,525	41.2	37.0	23.8	7.8	3.6	1.8
Sept.	1,110	1,593	36.6	43.5	29.1	8.3	4.6	1.5
Oct.	1,500	2,015	37.8	53.3	38.1	8.7	4.5	2.0
Nov.	1,740	2,380	42.8	55.6	39.5	10.4	4.3	1.4
Dec.	1,860	2,601	48.2	54.0	37.3	10.4	5.0	1.3
Jan.	1,710	2,585	52.8	49.0	31.3	10.6	5.3	1.8
Feb.	1,620	2,489	56.2	44.3	27.8	9.4	5.5	1.6
Mar.	1,800	2,616	58.2	44.9	29.6	8.7	4.9	1.7
Apr.	1,770	2,563	58.4	43.9	29.2	8.7	4.5	1.6
May	1,410	2,289	55.4	41.3	24.5	9.6	5.5	1.8
June	1,110	1,877	51.4	36.5	20.8	8.2	5.4	2.1

Sales for year t – 2, in reverse order, are: $900, $1,680, $1,740, $1,680.

Figure H-55: AGE DISTRIBUTION OF RECEIVABLES AND 150-DAY MOVING AVERAGE
(From the book Handbook of Financial Mathematics, Formulas, and Tables by Robert P. Vichas. © 1979. Published by Prentice-Hall, Inc., Englewood Cliffs, New Jersey 07632.)

| | PRELIMINARY | | **ESTIMATED ACCOUNTS RECEIVABLE BALANCES, PROVISION FOR P & L ACCOUNTS RESERVE ADJUSTMENT GROSS CHARGE-OFF, RECOVERIES AND NET CHARGE-OFF** | PR-13 WORKSHEET |
| | FINAL | | | |

($000's omitted)

☐ Spring
☐ Fall   19 _____

Company _____

SEASON		1 A/R BAL.	2 BAD DEBT RES. FACTOR	3 (1 × 2) PROV. FOR P&L A/Cs-RES. ADJ. (3320-16-21)	4 GROSS C/O (3320-16-20)	5 RECOVERIES (3320-16-22)	6 (4 − 5) NET C/O	7 (3 + 6) TOTAL BAD DEBT EXPENSE	8 CARRYING CHARGE INCOME
July/Jan	Est.								
	LY								
Feb/Aug	Plan								
	LY								
Mar/Sept	Plan								
	LY								
Apr/Oct	Plan								
	LY								
May/Nov*	Plan								
	LY								
June/Dec	Plan								
	LY								
July/Jan	Plan								
	LY								
Season TOTAL*	Plan								
	LY								

		PLAN		LY ACTUAL		PY ACTUAL		
CREDIT SALES		$000	%	$000	%	$000	%	

DATE RECEIVED
BY CORPORATE   _____

Figure H-56: ESTIMATED ACCOUNTS RECEIVABLE BALANCES AND RESERVE ADJUSTMENTS

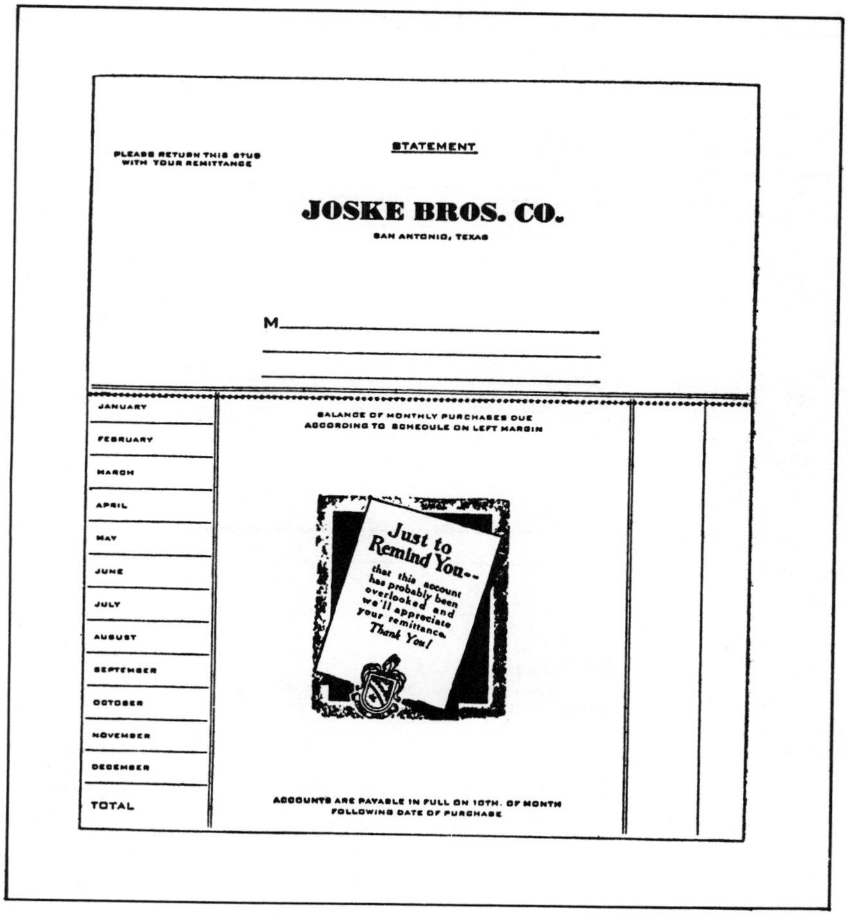

PLEASE RETURN THIS STUB
WITH YOUR REMITTANCE

STATEMENT

JOSKE BROS. CO.

SAN ANTONIO, TEXAS

M____________________

JANUARY	BALANCE OF MONTHLY PURCHASES DUE ACCORDING TO SCHEDULE ON LEFT MARGIN		
FEBRUARY			
MARCH			
APRIL	Just to Remind You-- that this account has probably been overlooked and we'll appreciate your remittance. Thank You!		
MAY			
JUNE			
JULY			
AUGUST			
SEPTEMBER			
OCTOBER			
NOVEMBER			
DECEMBER			
TOTAL	ACCOUNTS ARE PAYABLE IN FULL ON 10TH. OF MONTH FOLLOWING DATE OF PURCHASE		

Figure H-57: REMINDER STATEMENT

(From the book <u>Business Executive's Handbook</u>, 4th Edition, by Stanley M. Brown and Lillian Doris, Editors. © 1953 by Parker Publishing Company, Inc. Published by Parker Publishing Company, Inc., West Nyack, New York 10994.)

May we remind you that your account is *PAST DUE*.
Please forward your payment by return mail.

DUE DATE	AMOUNT	LATE CHARGE	TOTAL AMOUNT DUE

*The late charge shown applies when payment is over 10 days past due.

IF PAYMENT HAS BEEN MADE, PLEASE DISREGARD THIS REMINDER.

Burroughs BUSINESS FORMS
SYSTEM SET
96-6018

SECOND NOTICE

TO AVOID AN UNFAVORABLE REPORT ON YOUR CREDIT RECORD
WE SUGGEST AN IMMEDIATE PAYMENT OF THE AMOUNT DUE.

DUE DATE	AMOUNT	LATE CHARGE	TOTAL AMOUNT DUE

*The late charge shown applies when payment is over 10 days past due.

IF PAYMENT HAS BEEN MADE, PLEASE DISREGARD THIS REMINDER.

Burroughs BUSINESS FORMS
SYSTEM SET
96-6018

FINAL NOTICE

UNLESS PAYMENT IS RECEIVED BY RETURN MAIL IMMEDIATELY, ACTION WILL BE TAKEN.
IF FOR ANY REASON PAYMENT CANNOT BE MADE, CALL US.

DUE DATE	AMOUNT	LATE CHARGE	TOTAL AMOUNT DUE

*The late charge shown applies when payment is over 10 days past due.

IF PAYMENT HAS BEEN MADE, PLEASE DISREGARD THIS REMINDER.

Burroughs BUSINESS FORMS
SYSTEM SET
96-6018

Figure H-58: ACCOUNT DUE NOTICES (3)
(Courtesy of Burroughs Corporation Office Products Group/Business Forms Division.)

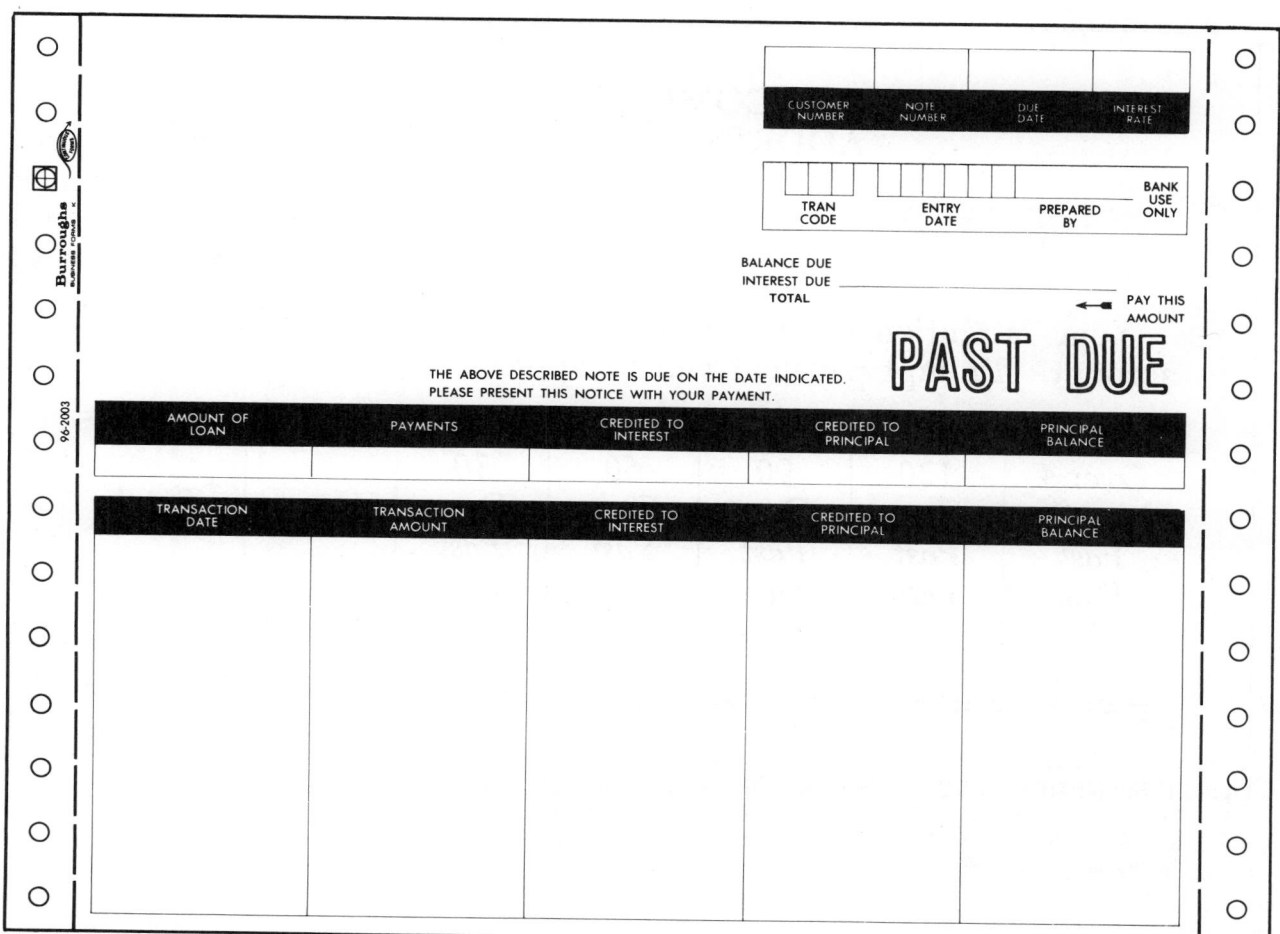

Figure H-59: PAST DUE NOTICE
(Courtesy of Burroughs Corporation Office Products Group/Business Forms Division.)

NAME OF COMPANY
ADDRESS

TERMS:
Accounts
payable in
full in 30
days.

. . . .

. . . .

Your attention is again called to the past-due portion of your account. Prompt payment will be appreciated.

Over 4 Months Past Due	120 Days Past Due	90 Days Past Due	60 Days Past Due	30 Days Past Due	Current	Total

Figure H-60: NOTICE TO CUSTOMER SHOWING AGE ANALYSIS OF ACCOUNT
(From the book Business Executive's Handbook, 4th Edition, by Stanley M. Brown and Lillian Doris, Editors. © 1953 by Parker Publishing Company, Inc. Published by Parker Publishing Company, Inc., West Nyack, New York 10994.)

BOSTON. MASSACHUSETTS . . . . 19 . . . . $ . . . .

ON DEMAND, the undersigned (jointly and severally if more than one) promise(s) to pay to the order of

THE FIRST NATIONAL BANK OF BOSTON   at said Bank

. . . . Dollars

with interest prior to maturity at   % per annum, calculated on the basis of a 360-day for the actual number of days elapsed, payable monthly in arrears, and with interest after maturity payable on demand at 12% per annum or, if higher, at a rate per annum which at all times shall be 4% above the lowest rate of interest being charged from time to time by said Bank for new 90-day unsecured loans to commercial borrowers.

This note and any or all other Obligations of the maker to the holder shall. at the holder's option. become immediately due and payable without notice or demand at any time after: (a) default in the payment or performance of any Obligation, or (b) death, dissolution, termination of existence, insolvency, business failure of or the commencement of any kind of insolvency proceedings by or against any Obligor. The undersigned will pay on demand all costs of collection and attorneys' fees paid or incurred by the holder in enforcing this note on default.

Any sums credited by or due from the holder to any Obligor and any property of any Obligor in which the holder has any security interest or which may be in the possession of the holder may at any time be treated or held as collateral security for the payment or performance of Obligations of such Obligor to the holder. Regardless of the adequacy of collateral, the holder may apply such sums or property or realizations upon any such security interest against said Obligations at any time in the case of any maker but only with respect to matured Obligations in the case of those secondarily liable. In addition to all other rights the holder shall have the rights and remedies of a secured party under the Uniform Commercial Code of Massachusetts in any jurisdiction in which enforcement is sought.

Every Obligor waives presentment, notice, protest and all other demands and notices and assents to any extension of the time of payment or any other indulgence, to any substitution, exchange or release of collateral and/or to the release of any other Obligor. As used herein "Obligor" means any person primarily or secondarily liable under or in respect hereto and "Obligation" means any obligation hereunder or otherwise of any Obligor to the holder whether direct or indirect, absolute or contingent, due or to become due. now existing or hereafter arising.

Address { . . . .   Signed by { . . . .

C-544 (Rev. 11/75)   . . . .

Figure H-61: DEMAND NOTE
(Courtesy of The First National Bank of Boston.)

BOSTON, MASSACHUSETTS, ... 19 . . . . . . $ . . . .

. . . . after date, the undersigned (jointly and severally, if more than one) promise(s) to pay to the order of   THE FIRST NATIONAL BANK OF BOSTON   at said Bank

. . . . Dollars.

. . . .

Interest or discount hereon shall be calculated on the basis of a 360-day year for the actual number of days elapsed. Interest after maturity will be payable on demand at twelve percent (12%) per annum or, if higher, at a rate per annum which at all times shall be four percent (4%) above the lowest rate of interest being charged from time to time by said Bank for new 90-day unsecured loans to commercial borrowers.

This note and any or all other Obligations of the maker to the holder shall, at the holder's option, become immediately due and payable without notice or demand at any time after: (a) default in the payment or performance of any Obligation, or (b) death, dissolution, termination of existence, insolvency, business failure or of the commencement of any kind of insolvency proceedings by or against any Obligor. The undersigned will pay on demand all costs of collection and attorneys' fees paid or incurred by the holder in enforcing this note on default.

Any sums credited by or due from the holder to any Obligor and any property of any Obligor in which the holder may have any security interest or which may be in the possession of the holder may at any time be treated or held as collateral security for the payment or performance of Obligations of such Obligor to the holder. Regardless of the adequacy of collateral, the holder may apply such sums or property or realizations upon any such security interest against said Obligations at any time in the case of any maker but only with respect to matured Obligations in the case of those secondarily liable. In addition to all other rights the holder shall have the rights and remedies of a secured party under the Uniform Commercial Code of Massachusetts in any jurisdiction in which enforcement is sought.

Every Obligor waives presentment, notice, protest and all other demands and notices and assents to any extension of the time of payment or any other indulgence, to any substitution, exchange or release of collateral and/or to the release of any other Obligor. As used herein "Obligor" means any person primarily or secondarily liable hereunder or in respect hereto and "Obligation" means any obligation hereunder or otherwise of any Obligor to the holder whether direct or indirect, absolute or contingent, due or to become due, now existing or hereafter arising.

Address only { . . . .   Signed by { . . . .

C543 (rev. 8/74)   { . . . .   { . . . .

Figure H-62: TIME NOTE FOR CORPORATE CUSTOMER
(Courtesy of The First National Bank of Boston.)

STANDARD FORM

UNIFORM COMMERCIAL CODE — FINANCING STATEMENT — FORM UCC-1

Filing fee — $5.00 + $1 for ea. add'l debtor.

No. 1214

CONNECTICUT

INSTRUCTIONS

1. PLEASE TYPE this form. Fold only along perforation for mailing.
2. Remove Secured Party and Debtor copies and send other 3 copies with interleaved carbon paper to the filing officer. Enclose filing fee.
3. If the space provided for any item(s) on the form is inadequate the item(s) should be continued on additional sheets, preferably 5" × 8" or 8" × 10". Only one copy of such additional sheets need be presented to the filing officer with a set of three copies of the financing statement. Long schedules of collateral, indentures, etc., may be on any size paper that is convenient for the secured party. Indicate the number of additional sheets attached.
4. If collateral is crops or goods which are or are to become fixtures, describe generally the real estate and give name of record owner.
5. When a copy of the security agreement is used as a financing statement, it is requested that it be accompanied by a completed but unsigned set of these forms, without extra fee.
6. At the time of original filing, filing officer should return third copy as an acknowledgement. At a later time, secured party may date and sign Termination Legend and use third copy as a Termination Statement.

This **FINANCING STATEMENT** is presented to a filing officer pursuant to the Uniform Commercial Code:

3. Maturity date (if any):

1. Debtor(s) (Last Name First) and address(es)

2. Secured Party(ies) and address(es)

For Filing Officer (Date, Time, Number, and Filing Office)

4. This financing statement covers the following types (or items) of property:

5. Assignee(s) of Secured Party and Address(es)

This statement is filed without the debtor's signature to perfect a security interest in collateral. (check ☒ if so)

☐ already subject to a security interest in another jurisdiction when it was brought into this state.

☐ which is proceeds of the original collateral described above in which a security interest was perfected:

Filed with: STATE OF CONNECTICUT, SECRETARY OF STATE, UNIFORM COMMERCIAL CODE DIV., STATE OFFICE BLDG., HARTFORD, CT. 06115

Check ☒ if covered: ☐ Proceeds of Collateral are also covered. ☐ Products of Collateral are also covered. No. of additional Sheets presented:

By: _____
Signature(s) of Debtor(s)

By: _____
Signature(s) of Secured Party(ies)

(1) Filing Officer Copy-Alphabetical   **STANDARD FORM - FORM UCC-1.**   (For Use in Most States)

Figure H-63: FINANCING STATEMENT—UNIFORM COMMERCIAL CODE

PROOF OF CLAIM IN LITIGATION

State of _____
County of _____ } ss

I, _____ , being first duly sworn, depose and state that:
I am _____ , of Alerion Standards Co., located at _____
_____ , a corporation incorporated under the laws of
the state of _____ , and that the attached bill of particulars is a
true and correct copy of the account due Alerion Standards Co., and against _____
_____ , and that the items debit and credit contained
therein, are to my personal knowledge true and correct, and that after allowing all just credits and set-offs, there is justly due and
unpaid thereon, the amount of $_____ , with legal interest to date.

Alerion Standards Co.

by _____

Title _____

Subscribed and sworn to before me this _____ day of _____ , 19_____ ,
as witness my hand and official seal

_____

_____

Amount of claim $_____

Amount of interest $_____

Total $_____

Figure H-64: PROOF OF CLAIM IN LITIGATION

Know All Men By These Presents:

THAT

of   as Principal, and

of   as Surety, are holden and firmly bound, jointly and severally

unto   of

in the penal sum of $, to which payment well and truly be made, we hereby bind ourselves, our heirs, executors, and administrators firmly by these presents.

The Condition of this obligation is such that, whereas the said

has brought an action, against the said   said action being returnable to the   Court for   County, on the first   day of   19   , demanding $ damages, the writ being dated at   on the   day of   19 and signed by   as   , and by direction of said writ an attachment has been placed upon the property of the said as follows:

Now Therefore, if the said   shall pay any judgment

that shall be recovered against   in said action not exceeding the amount of $ (the amount of damages demanded by said writ) or in default of such payment, shall pay to the officer having the execution issued on such judgment, on demand, the actual value of the interest not exempt from attachment and execution, of the said

in said attached property at the time of the attachment, not exceeding said amount of $ then this bond shall be void, but otherwise in full force and effect.

Dated at   this   day of   19

In presence of

....(L. S.)
                                                                        Principal

....(L. S.)
                                                                        Principal

....(L. S.)
                                                                        Surety

....(L. S.)
                                                                        Surety

Figure H-65: STATUTORY BOND
(Courtesy of All State Legal Supply Co., Mountainside, New Jersey 07092.)

......A. D., 19......

I, the undersigned, surety on the bond given in the above entitled matter, hereby certify that I am the owner of

real estate standing in my own name on the Land Records in the Town/City of......

......, Connecticut, and that in

my opinion, the fair market value thereof is $......

       The mortgages thereon are,   First, $......

                  Second, $......

    Other incumbrances, $......

                (Signed)......

                                      Surety.

           Address......

Subscribed and sworn to before me, this......day of......19......

......

Notary Public
Justice of the Peace
Commissioner of the Superior Court

Statutory Bond

TO

Figure H-65—Reverse Side

Know All Men By These Presents:

THAT

of   as Principal, and

of   as Surety, are holden and firmly bound, jointly and severally

unto   of

in the penal sum of $, to which payment well and truly be made, we hereby bind ourselves, our heirs, executors, and administrators firmly by these presents.

The Condition of this obligation is such that, whereas the said

has brought an action, against the said   said action

being returnable to the   Court for   County, on the

first   day of   19   , demanding $ damages, the writ being

dated at   on the   day of   19

and signed by   as   ,

and by direction of said writ an attachment has been placed upon the property of the said as follows :

Now Therefore, if the said   shall pay any judgment

that shall be recovered against   in said action not

exceeding the amount of $ (the amount of damages demanded by said writ) or in default

of such payment, shall pay to the officer having the execution issued on such judgment, on demand,

an amount not exceeding said amount of $ then this bond shall be void, but otherwise in full force and effect.

       Dated at   this   day of   19

       In presence of

....(L. S.)
                                                              Principal

....(L. S.)
                                                              Principal

....(L. S.)
                                                              Surety

....(L. S.)
                                                              Surety

Figure H-66: COMMON BOND
(Courtesy of All State Legal Supply Co., Mountainside, New Jersey 07092.)

....A. D., 19..........

I, the undersigned, surety on the bond given in the above entitled matter, hereby certify that I am the owner of

real estate standing in my own name on the Land Records in the Town/City of..

...., Connecticut, and that in

my opinion, the fair market value thereof is $..

        The mortgages thereon are,   First, $..

                        Second, $..

        Other incumbrances, $..

                       (Signed)..

                                                Surety.

            Address..

Subscribed and sworn to before me, this.................day of ....19........

....
Notary Public
Justice of the Peace
Commissioner of the Superior Court for
County

Common Bond

TO

Figure H-66—Reverse Side

Know All Men By These Presents:

That

herein designated as the Assignor, in consideration of

dollars,

the receipt whereof is hereby acknowledged, does hereby sell, assign and transfer to

herein designated as the Assignee,

all the right, title and interest of the Assignor in and to the following:

To Have and to Hold the same unto the Assignee and the Assignee's heirs, personal representatives, successors and assigns forever.

In all references herein to any parties, persons, entities or corporations the use of any particular gender or the plural or singular number is intended to include the appropriate gender or number as the text of the within instrument may require.

In Witness Whereof, the said Assignor, has signed and sealed this instrument or if a corporation has caused this instrument to be signed by its authorized corporate officers and its corporate seal to be hereto affixed, this   day of   19

Signed, Sealed and Delivered in the presence of
or attested by

....

....

State of Connecticut, County of   } ss.:

The foregoing instrument was acknowledged before me this   day of

19   , by

....

Commissioner of the Superior Court

Figure H-67: GENERAL ASSIGNMENT—INDIVIDUAL OR CORPORATION
(Copyright 1977 by All State Legal Supply Co., Mountainside, New Jersey 07092.)

PETITION FOR VOLUNTARY BANKRUPTCY

United States District Court

for the _____ District of _____

In re

_____ ,
Bankrupt (include here all names used by bankrupt within last 6 years)

Bankruptcy No. _____

VOLUNTARY PETITION

1. Petitioner's post-office address is _____ .

2. Petitioner has resided (or has had his domicile or has had his principal place of business) within this district for the preceding 6 months (or for a longer portion of the preceding 6 months than in any other district).

3. Petitioner is qualified to file this petition and is entitled to the benefits of the Bankruptcy Act as a voluntary bankrupt.

Wherefore petitioner prays for relief as a voluntary bankrupt under the Act.

Signed _____
Attorney for Petitioner

Address _____

_____
(Petitioner signs if not represented by attorney.)

_____ ,
Petitioner

VERIFICATION ON BEHALF OF A CORPORATION

State of _____

County of _____ , ss:

I, _____ , the president (or other officer or an authorized agent) of the corporation named as petitioner in the foregoing petition, do hereby swear that the statements contained therein are true according to the best of my knowledge, information, and belief, and that the filing of this petition on behalf of the corporation has been authorized.

_____

Subscribed and sworn to before me on _____ .

My Commission Expires:

_____ ,

_____
(Official Character)

(Unless further time is granted by the court pursuant to Rule 108, this petition must be accompanied by a schedule of the petitioner's debts and property, his claim for such exemptions as he may be entitled to, and a statement of his affairs. These additional statements shall be submitted on official forms, shall include the information about the petitioner's property and debts required by the Bankruptcy Rules and by the forms, and shall be verified under oath.)

on official forms, shall include the information about the petitioner's property and debts required by the Bankruptcy Rules and by the forms, and shall be verified under oath.)

on official forms, shall include the information about the petitioner's property and debts required by the Bankruptcy Rules and by the forms, and shall be verified under oath.)

on official forms, shall include the information about the petitioner's property and debts required by the Bankruptcy Rules and by the forms, and shall be verified under oath.)

Figure H-68: PETITION FOR VOLUNTARY BANKRUPTCY
(Courtesy of All State Legal Supply Co., Mountainside, New Jersey 07092.)

STATEMENT OF AFFAIRS FOR BANKRUPT ENGAGED IN BUSINESS

United States District Court

for the _____ District of _____

In re

_____ , } Bankruptcy No. _____

Bankrupt (Include here all names used by bankrupt within last 6 years).

STATEMENT OF AFFAIRS FOR BANKRUPT ENGAGED IN BUSINESS

(Each question should be answered or the failure to answer explained. If the answer is "none," this should be stated. If additional space is needed for the answer to any question, a separate sheet properly identified and made a part hereof, should be used and attached.

If the bankrupt is a partnership or a corporation, the questions shall be deemed to be addressed to, and shall be answered on behalf of, the partnership or corporation; and the statement shall be verified by a member of the partnership or by a duly authorized officer of the corporation.

The term, "original petition," as used in the following questions, shall mean the petition filed under Bankruptcy Rule 103, 104, or 105.)

1. Nature, location, and name of business.
a. Under what name and where do you carry on your business?

b. In what business are you engaged? (If business operations have been terminated, give the date of such termination.)

c. When did you commence such business?

d. Where else, and under what other names, have you carried on business within the 6 years immediately preceding the filing of the original petition herein? (Give street addresses, the names of any partners, joint adventurers, or other associates, the nature of the business, and the periods for which it was carried on.)

e. What is your employer identification number? Your social security number?

2. Books and records.
a. By whom, or under whose supervision, have your books of account and records been kept during the 2 years immediately preceding the filing of the original petition herein? (Give names, addresses, and periods of time.)

b. By whom have your books of account and records been audited during the 2 years immediately preceding the filing of the original petition herein? (Give names, addresses, and dates of audits.)

c. In whose possession are your books of account and records? (Give names and addresses.)

d. If any of these books or records are not available, explain.

e. Have any books of account or records relating to your affairs been destroyed, lost, or otherwise disposed of within the 2 years immediately preceding the filing of the original petition herein? (If so, give particulars, including date of destruction, loss, or disposition, and reason therefor.)

3. Financial statements.
Have you issued any written financial statements within the 2 years immediately preceding the filing of the original petition herein? (Give dates, and the names and addresses of the persons to whom issued, including mercantile and trade agencies.)

4. Inventories.
a. When was the last inventory of your property taken?

b. By whom, or under whose supervision, was this inventory taken?

c. What was the amount, in dollars, of the inventory? (State whether the inventory was taken at cost, market, or otherwise.)

d. When was the next prior inventory of your property taken?

e. By whom, or under whose supervision, was this inventory taken?

f. What was the amount, in dollars, of the inventory? (State whether the inventory was taken at cost, market, or otherwise.)

g. In whose possession are the records of the 2 inventories above referred to? (Give names and addresses.)

5. Income other than from operation of business.
What amount of income, other than from operation of your business, have you received during each of the 2 years immediately preceding the filing of the original petition herein? (Give particulars, including each source, and the amount received therefrom.)

OFFICIAL FORM 8 PAGE 1
OFFICIAL FORM 1973
GRAHAM-PIERCE LEGAL PRINTERS,
BOX 1866, EAST ST. LOUIS, ILL. 62208

Figure H-69: STATEMENT OF AFFAIRS OF BANKRUPT ENGAGED IN BUSINESS
(Courtesy of All State Legal Supply Co., Mountainside, New Jersey 07092.)

OFFICIAL FORM 8 PAGE 2
OFFICIAL FORM 1973
GRAHAM-PIERCE LEGAL PRINTERS,
BOX 1866, EAST ST. LOUIS, ILL. 62208

6. Tax returns and refunds.

a. In whose possession are copies of your federal and state income tax returns for the 3 years immediately preceding the filing of the original petition herein?

b. What tax refunds (Income or other) have you received during the 2 years immediately preceding the filing of the orignal petition herein?

c. To what tax refunds (income or other), if any, are you, or may you be, entitled? (Give particulars, including information as to any refund payable jointly to you and your spouse or any other person.)

7. Bank accounts and safe deposit boxes.

a. What bank accounts have you maintained, alone or together with any other person, and in your own or any other name, within the 2 years immediately preceding the filing of the original petition herein? (Give the name and address of each bank, the name in which the deposit was maintained, and the name and address of every person authorized to make withdrawals from such account.)

b. What safe deposit box or boxes or other depository or depositories have you kept or used for your securities, cash, or other valuables within the 2 years immediately preceding the filing of the original petition herein? (Give the name and address of the bank or other depository, the name in which each box or other depository was kept, the name and address of every person who had the right of access thereto, a description of the contents thereof, and, if the box has been surrendered, state when surrendered or, if transferred, when transferred and the name and address of the transferee.)

8. Property held for another person.

What property do you hold for any other person? (Give name and address of each person, and describe the property, the amount or value thereof and all writings relating thereto.)

9. Prior bankruptcy proceedings.

What proceedings under the Bankruptcy Act have previously been brought by or against you? (State the location of the bankruptcy court, the nature and number of proceeding, and whether a discharge was granted or refused, the proceeding was dismissed, or a composition, arrangement, or plan was confirmed.

10. Receiverships, general assignments, and other modes of liquidation.

a. Was any of your property, at the time of the filing of the original petition herein, in the hands of a receiver, trustee, or other liquidating agent? (If so, give a brief description of the property and the name and address of the receiver, trustee, or other agent, and, if the agent was appointed in a court proceeding, the name and location of the court and the nature of the proceeding.)

b. Have you made any assignment of your property for the benefit of your creditors, or any general settlement with your creditors, within the 2 years immediately preceding the filing of the original petition herein? (If so, give dates, the name and address of the assignee, and a brief statement of the terms of assignment or settlement.)

11. Property in hands of third person.

Is any other person holding anything of value in which you have an interest? (Give name and address, location and description of the property, and circumstances of the holding.)

12. Suits, executions, and attachments.

a. Were you a party to any suit pending at the time of the filing of the original petition herein? (If so, give the name and location of the court and the title and nature of the proceeding.)

b. Were you a party to any suit terminated within the year immediately preceding the filing of the original petition herein? (If so, give the name and location of the court, the title and nature of the proceeding, and the result.)

c. Has any of your property been attached, garnished, or seized under any legal or equitable process within the 4 months immediately preceding the filing of the original petition herein? (If so, describe the property seized or person garnished, and at whose suit.)

13. Payments on loans and installment purchases.

What repayments on loans in whole or in part, and what payments on installment purchases of goods and services, have you made during the year immediately preceding the filing of the original petition herein? (Give the names and addresses of the persons receiving payment, the amounts of the loans and of the purchase price of the goods and services, the dates of the original transactions, the amounts and dates of payments, and, if any of the payees are your relatives, the relationship; if the bankrupt is a partnership and any of the payees is or was a partner or a relative of a partner, state the relationship; if the bankrupt is a corporation and any of the payees is or was an officer, director, or stockholder, or a relative of an officer, director, or stockholder, state the relationship.)

14. Transfers of property.

a. Have you made any gifts, other than ordinary and usual presents to family members and charitable donation, during the year immediately preceding the filing of the original petition herein? (If so, give names and addresses of donees and dates, description, and value of gifts.)

b. Have you made any other transfer, absolute or for the purpose of security, or any other disposition which was not in the ordinary course of business during the year immediately preceding the filing of the original petition herein? (Give a description of the property, the date of the transfer or disposition, to whom transferred or how disposed of, and state whether the transferee is a relative, partner, shareholder, officer, or director, the consideration, if any, received for the property, and the disposition of such consideration.)

Figure H-69 (continued)

15. Accounts and other receivables.
Have you assigned, either absolutely or as security, any of your accounts or other receivables during the year immediately preceding the filing of the original petition herein? (If so, give names and addresses of assignees.)

16. Repossessions and returns.
Has any property been returned to, or repossessed by, the seller or by a secured party during the year immediately preceding the filing of the original petition herein? (If so, give particulars, including the name and address of the party getting the property and its description and value.)

17. Business leases.
If you are a tenant of business property, what are the name and address of your landlord, the amount of your rental, the date to which rent had been paid at the time of the filing of the original petition herein, and the amount of security held by the landlord?

18. Losses.
a. Have you suffered any losses from fire, theft, or gambling during the year immediately preceding the filing of the original petition herein? (If so, give particulars, including dates, names, and places, and the amounts of money or value and general description of property lost.)

b. Was the loss covered in whole or part by insurance? (If so, give particulars.)

19. Withdrawals.
a. If you are an individual proprietor of your business, what personal withdrawals of any kind have you made from the business during the year immediately preceding the filing of the original petition herein?

b. If the bankrupt is a partnership or corporation, what withdrawals, in any form (including compensation or loans), have been made by any member of the partnership, or by any officer, director, managing executive, or shareholder of the corporation, during the year immediately preceding the filing of the original petition herein? (Give the name and designation or relationship to the bankrupt of each person, the dates and amounts of withdrawals, and the nature or prupose thereof.)

20. Payments or transfers to attorneys.
a. Have you consulted an attorney during the year immediately preceding or since the filing of the original petition herein? (Give date, name, and address.)

b. Have you during the year immediately preceding or since the filing of the original petition herein paid any money or transferred any property to the attorney, or to any other person on his behalf? (If so, give particulars, including amount paid or value of property transferred and date of payment or transfer.)

c. Have you, either during the year immediately preceding or since the filing of the original petition herein, agreed to pay any money or transfer any property to an attorney at law, or to any other person on his behalf? (If so, give particulars, including amount and terms of obligation.)

(If the bankrupt is a partnership or corporation, the following additional questions should be answered.)

21. Members of partnership; officers, directors, managers, and principal stockholders of corporation.
a. What is the name and address of each member of the partnership, or the name, title, and address of each officer, director, and managing executive, and of each stockholder holding 25 per cent or more of the issued and outstanding stock, of the corporation?

b. During the year immediately preceding the filing of the original petition herein, has any member withdrawn from the partnership, or any officer, director, or managing executive of the corporation terminated his relationship, or any stockholder holding 25 per cent or more of the issued stock disposed of more than 50 per cent of his holdings? (If so, give name and address and reason for withdrawal, termination, or disposition, if known.)

c. Has any person acquired or disposed of 25 per cent or more of the stock of the corporation during the year immediately preceding the filing of the petition? (If so, give name and address and particulars.)

State of _____

County of_____, ss:

I, _____ , do hereby swear that I have read the answers contained in the foregoing statement of affairs and that they are true and complete to the best of my knowledge, information, and belief.

_____
Bankrupt.
Subscribed and sworn to before me on _____.

My commission expires: _____

_____
(Official character)

(Person verifying for partnership or corporation should indicate position or relationship to bankrupt.)

Figure H-69 (continued)

SCHEDULES
United States District Court

for the _____ District of _____

In re

_____ , Bankruptcy No._____

Bankrupt (include here all names used by bankrupt within last six years)

Schedule A—STATEMENT OF ALL DEBTS OF BANKRUPT

Schedules A-1, A-2, and A-3 must include all the claims against the bankrupt or his property as of the date of the filing of the petition by or against him.

Schedule A—1.—Creditors having priority.

Nature of claim	Name of creditor and complete mailing address including zip code. (If unknown, so state)	Specify when claim was incurred and the consideration therefor; when claim is contingent, unliquidated, disputed or subject to setoff, evidenced by a judgment, negotiable instrument, or other writing, or incurred as partner or joint contractor, so indicate; specify name of any partner or joint contractor on any debt	Amount of claim
a. Wages and commissions owing to workmen, servants, clerks, or traveling or city salesmen on salary or commission basis, whole or part time, whether or not selling exclusively for the bankrupt, not exceeding $600 to each, earned within 3 months before filing of petition			$
b. Taxes owing (itemize by type of tax and taxing authority) (1) To the United States (2) To any state (3) To any other taxing authority			
c. (1) Debts owing to any person, including United States, entitled to priority by laws of United States (itemize by type)			
(2) Rent owing to a landlord entitled to priority by laws of any state accrued within 3 months before filing of petition, for actual use and occupancy			
		Total	

FORM 6 - A - 1
OFFICIAL FORM 1973
GRAHAM-PIERCE LEGAL PRINTERS.
BOX 1866. EAST ST. LOUIS. ILL. 62208

Figure H-69 (continued)

Schedule A-2. — Creditors Holding Security

Name of creditor and complete mailing address including zip code. (If unknown, so state)	Description of security and date when obtained by creditor	Specify when claim was incurred and the consideration therefor; when claim is contingent, unliquidated, disputed, subject to setoff, evidenced by a judgment, negotiable instrument, or other writing, or incurred as partner or joint contractor, so indicate; specify name of any partner or joint contractor on any debt	Market value		Amount of claim without deduction of value of security	
			$		$	
		Total				

FORM 6 -   A-2
OFFICIAL FORM 1973
GRAHAM-PIERCE LEGAL PRINTERS.
BOX 1866, EAST ST. LOUIS, ILL. 62208

Figure H-69 (continued)

Schedule A-3.—CREDITORS HAVING UNSECURED
CLAIMS WITHOUT PRIORITY

Name of creditor (including last known holder of any negotiable instrument) and complete mailing address including zip code. (If unknown, so state)	Specify when claim was incurred and the consideration therefor; when claim is contingent, unliquidated, disputed, subject to setoff, evidenced by a judgment, negotiable instrument, or other writing, or incurred as partner or joint contractor, so indicate; specify name of any partner or joint contractor on any debt	Amount of claim
		$
	Total	

FORM 6 - A-3
OFFICIAL FORM 1973
GRAHAM-PIERCE LEGAL PRINTERS.
BOX 1866, EAST ST. LOUIS, ILL. 62208

Figure H-69 (continued)

Schedule B.—STATEMENT OF ALL PROPERTY OF BANKRUPT

Schedules B-1, B-2, B-3, and B-4 must include all property of the bankrupt as of the date of the filing of the petition by or against him.

Schedule B—1. — Real property.

Description and location of all real property in which bankrupt has an interest (including equitable and future interests, interests in estates by the entirety, community property, life estates, leaseholds, and rights and powers exercisable for his own benefit)	Nature of interest (specify all deeds and written instruments relating thereto)	Market value of bankrupt's interest without deduction for secured claims listed on Schedule A-2 or exemptions claimed in Schedule B-4	
		$	
		Total	

FORM 6. B-1
OFFICIAL FORM 1973
GRAHAM-PIERCE LEGAL PRINTERS,
BOX 1866, EAST ST. LOUIS, ILL. 62208

Figure H-69 (continued)

Schedule B—2. — Personal Property.

Type of property	Description and location	Market value of bankrupt's interest without deduction for secured claims listed on Schedule A-2 or exemptions claimed in Schedule B-4	
a Cash on hand			
b. Deposits of money with banking institutions, savings and loan associations, credit unions, public utility companies, landlords, and others		$	
c. Household goods, supplies, and furnishings			
d. Books, pictures, and other art objects; stamp. coin, and other collections			
e. Wearing apparel, jewelry, firearms, sports equipment, and other personal possessions			
f. Automobiles, trucks, trailers, and other vehicles			
g. Boats, motors, and their accessories			
h. Livestock, poultry, and other animals			
i. Farming supplies and implements			
j. Office equipment, furnishings, and supplies			
k. Machinery, fixtures, equipment, and supplies (other than those listed in Items j and l) used in business			
l. Inventory			
m. Tangible personal property of any other description			
n. Patents, copyrights, franchises, and other general intangibles (specify all documents and writings relating thereto)			
o. Government and corporate bonds and other negotiable and nonnegotiable instruments			
p. Other liquidated debts owing bankrupt or debtor			
q. Contingent and unliquidated claims of every nature, including counterclaims of the bankrupt or debtor (give estimated value of each)			
r. Interests in insurance policies (itemize surrender or refund values of each)			
s. Annuities			
t. Stocks and interest in incorporated and unincorporated companies (itemize separately)			
u. Interests in partnerships			
v. Equitable and future interest, life estates, and rights or power exercisable for the benefit of the bankrupt or debtor (specify all written instruments relating thereto)			

FORM 6.   B-2
OFFICIAL FORM 1973
GRAHAM-PIERCE LEGAL PRINTERS,
BOX 1866, EAST ST. LOUIS, ILL. 62208

Total

Figure H-69 (continued)

Schedule B—3 — Property not other wise scheduled.

Type of Property	Description and location	Market value of bankrupt's interest without deduction for secured claims listed in Schedule A-2 or exemptions claimed in Schedule B-4	
a. Property transferred under assignment for benefit of creditors, within 4 months prior to filing of petition [specify date of assignment, name and address of assignee, amount realized therefrom by the assignee, and disposition of proceeds so far as known to bankrupt]		$	
b. Property of any kind not otherwise scheduled			
		Total	

FORM 6, B-3
OFFICIAL FORM 1973
GRAHAM-PIERCE LEGAL PRINTERS.
BOX 1866. EAST ST LOUIS. ILL 62208

Figure H-69 (continued)

Schedule B—4. — Property claimed as exempt.

Type of property	Location, description, and so far as relevant to the claim of exemption, present use of property	Reference to statute creating the exemption	Value claimed exempt
			$
		Total	

OATH ON BEHALF OF CORPORATION TO SCHEDULES A AND B

State of _____

County of _____, ss.

I, _____ , the president (or other officer or an authorized agent) of the corporation named as bankrupt in this proceeding, do hereby swear that I have read the foregoing schedules, consisting of _____ sheets, and that they are a statement of all the debts and all the property of the corporation in accordance with the Bankruptcy Act, to the best of my knowledge, information, and belief.

Signed: _____

Subscribed and sworn to before me on _____.

My Commission Expires:

_____   _____,

_____   (Official character)

FORM 6,   B-4
OFFICIAL FORM 1973
GRAHAM-PIERCE LEGAL PRINTERS,
BOX 1866. EAST ST. LOUIS, ILL. 62208

Figure H-69 (continued)

SUMMARY OF DEBTS AND PROPERTY

(From the statements of the bankrupt in Schedules A and B)

Schedule	Debts and Property	Total
	DEBTS	
A-1/a	Wages having priority	
A-1/b(1)	Taxes owing United States	
A-1/b(2)	Taxes owing states	
A-1/b(3)	Taxes owing other taxing authorities	
A-1/c(1)	Debts having priority by laws of United States	
A-1/c(2)	Rent having priority under state law	
A-2	Secured claims	
A-3	Unsecured claims without priority	
	Schedule A total	
	PROPERTY	
B-1	Real property (total value)	
B-2/a	Cash on hand	
B-2/b	Deposits	
B-2/c	Household goods	
B-2/d	Books, pictures, and collections	
B-2/e	Wearing apparel and personal possessions	
B-2/f	Automobiles and other vehicles	
B-2/g	Boats, motors, and accessories	
B-2/h	Livestock and other animals	
B-2/i	Farming supplies and implements	
B-2/j	Office equipment and supplies	
B-2/k	Machinery, equipment, and supplies used in business	
B-2/l	Inventory	
B-2/m	Other tangible personal property	
B-2/n	Patents and other general intangibles	
B-2/o	Bonds and other instruments	
B-2/p	Other liquidated debts	
B-2/q	Contingent and unliquidated claims	
B-2/r	Interests in insurance policies	
B-2/s	Annuities	
B-2/t	Interests in corporations and unicorporated companies	
B-2/u	Interests in partnerships	
B-2/v	Equitable and future interests, rights, and powers in personality	
B-3/a	Property assigned for benefit of creditors	
B-3/b	Property not otherwise scheduled	
B-4	Property claimed as exempt . . . . $ _____	
	Schedule B total	

FORM 6—SUMMARY
OFFICIAL FORM 1973
GRAHAM-PIERCE LEGAL PRINTERS,
BOX 1866, EAST ST. LOUIS, ILL. 62208

Figure H-69 (continued)

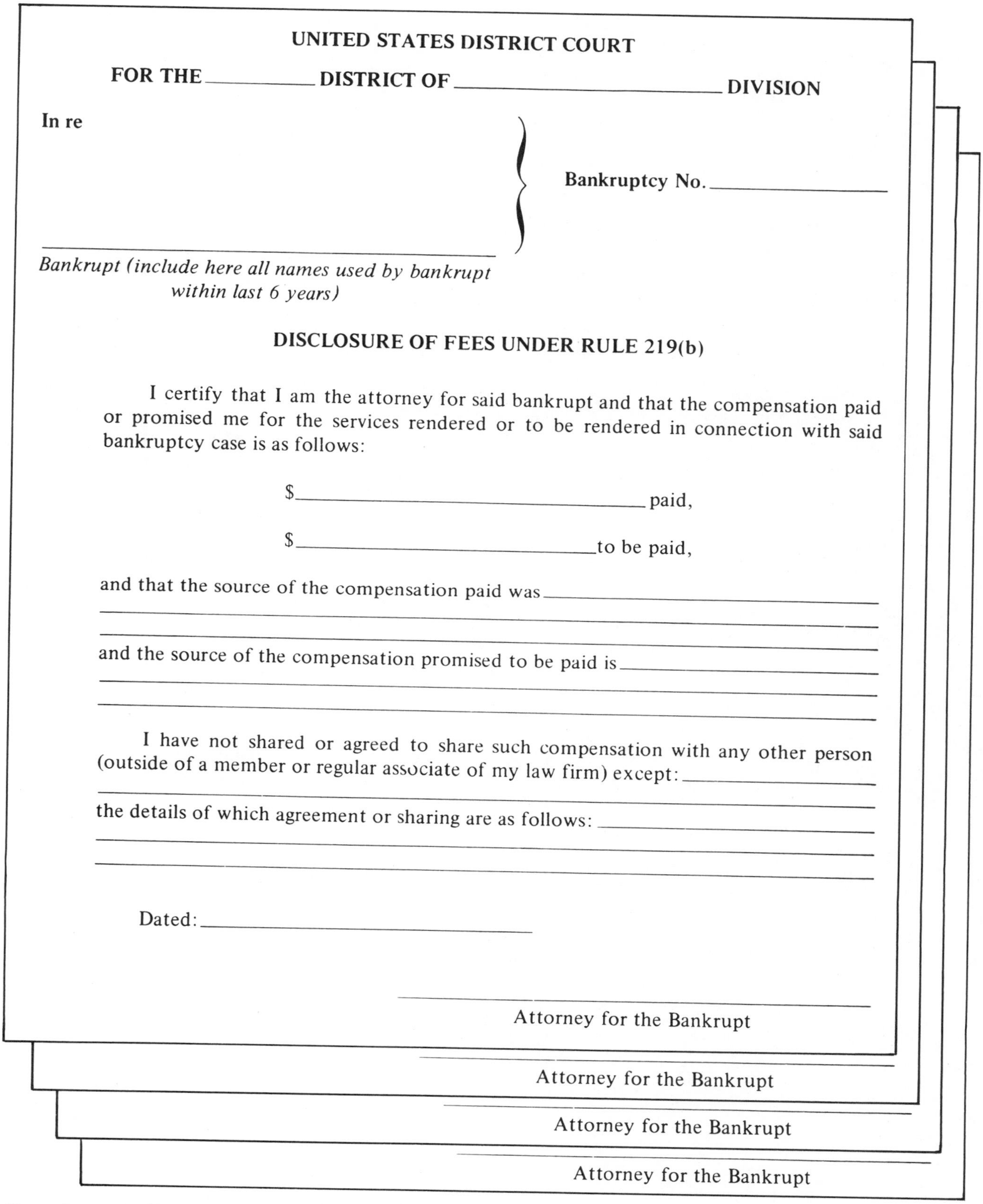

UNITED STATES DISTRICT COURT

FOR THE _____ DISTRICT OF _____ DIVISION

In re

}

Bankruptcy No. _____

_____

Bankrupt (include here all names used by bankrupt within last 6 years)

DISCLOSURE OF FEES UNDER RULE 219(b)

I certify that I am the attorney for said bankrupt and that the compensation paid or promised me for the services rendered or to be rendered in connection with said bankruptcy case is as follows:

$_____ paid,

$_____ to be paid,

and that the source of the compensation paid was _____
_____

and the source of the compensation promised to be paid is _____
_____
_____

I have not shared or agreed to share such compensation with any other person (outside of a member or regular associate of my law firm) except: _____
_____

the details of which agreement or sharing are as follows: _____
_____
_____

Dated: _____

_____
Attorney for the Bankrupt

_____
Attorney for the Bankrupt

_____
Attorney for the Bankrupt

_____
Attorney for the Bankrupt

Figure H-70: DISCLOSURE OF ATTORNEY FEES FOR THE BANKRUPT
(Courtesy of All State Legal Supply Co., Mountainside, New Jersey 07092.)

PAYROLL FORMS
FOR COST CONTROL,
ADMINISTRATION,
COMPLIANCE

SECTION

I

SECTION █ FORMS

Payroll Forms for Cost Control, Administration, Compliance

Payroll Forms for Cost Control, Administration, Compliance

Labor costs, ranging from 25 to 75 percent for most organizations, represent a major source of profit leaks, if not properly monitored and assigned. Employees who depend exclusively upon company generosity or benevolence for reasonable salary adjustments have less long-run job security than employees whose raises spring from productivity increases. Up to a point, productivity improvement derives from learning experiences and work organization, but beyond that point it arises from intensified application of capital equipment.

Despite dire predictions in the 1950s and early 1960s of technological unemployment, and replacement of jobs with machines, the productive sector of the American economy has absorbed a larger and larger work force; and real gross wages have risen due to expansion of capital investments. (It is no fault of industry that disposable incomes of workers have fallen due to higher local, state, and federal taxation plus decline of purchasing power due to inflation. It is admirable that the American people are willing to work harder and harder to support turgescent governmental expenditures, and a tribute to industry that makes it possible.)

In large part, forms in this section focus on CONTROL and MEASUREMENT OF LABOR COSTS and the administrative effort involved to maintain accurate records of costs and fringe benefits. Much of the paperwork is mandated by state and federal legislation ostensibly to protect employees, but it also raises the cost of doing business which must either be passed back to employees through slightly lower salaries or forward to final consumers (who are also employees somewhere) through higher prices.

Much payroll activity is routine but compels accuracy both in gathering data and in feeding it into the computer. Program efficiency and computer size affect the amount of hand labor and calculations imposed. Because there are frequent exceptions to payroll routines, the *possibility of profit leaks* abounds. The forms carry the payroll department story forward from time of hiring to termination, or disability, followed by other forms appropriately related to administration, compliance, and analysis.

I-1 The Cost Center Payroll Summary Form (I-1) separates regular salaries and wages from other payroll costs relating to overtime, paid vacations and sick leave and other compensated leaves of absence, by employee name (and number, which identifies the department or subunit). Data analysis blends physical (hours) and monetary (earnings) items—vertically by summaries of total costs in each category, horizontally by employee. This kind of consolidation is essential to cost analysis and control (Section A) and profit planning (Section B). For example, excessive absenteeism suggests further analysis of available data, and expenditures if practical, which may spark a change in hiring policy, training policy, compensation package, or selected dismissals. Similarly, excessive premium overtime adumbrates a POTENTIAL PROFIT LEAK begging resolution.

I-2 Payroll and Cost Analysis (I-2) approaches the issue of COST ANALYSIS horizontally by department or major function and vertically by salaries, overtime, fringe benefits, and expenses. That is, *payroll costs* are extended to embrace other direct expenses to better assess *labor costs*, prepare a *profit plan* (Section B), and compute *profit variance*. Horizontally the data may be extended into any number of subheadings, but the cost of additional details may rise geometrically if information was not initially entered in a cheaply retrievable form.

I-3 A weekly Time Record (I-3) accounts for number of hours worked and wage rate of each employee. This direct cost can then be charged against the particular job or production run. The payroll department will check this record against clock cards and weekly payroll for verification before passing it along for *cost analysis*. The In-and-Out Time Record (I-

I-4 4) permits considerably more detail on both actual hours worked, transferred from clock cards (not shown), if used, and authorized pay rates and deductions.

I-5 It is unlikely that a firm will allow the employee to decide overtime, for that invites a profit leak. One way to PLUG this PROFIT LEAK is to require an Overtime Permit (I-5) for all additional hours. The form is simple enough, yet it is an *effective brake,* because without the permit no overtime will be paid. Required on the form are:

    (a)   department number;
    (b)   employee name and clock number;
    (c)   number of overtime hours authorized;
    (d)   the job number (if applicable) or project identification;
    (e)   reason for the overtime;
    (f)   who requested overtime and who approved it, and the date.

Notice especially the additional space left for the reason. An accumulation of "reasons" may well give a clue to scheduling or organizational problems. But the space in the form may also be an EFFECTIVE COST CONTROLLER by discouraging indiscriminate awarding of overtime at higher wage rates.

The payroll department responds to a Payroll Change Notice (I-6) for changes in wage rates, transfers, and terminations. For future reference, the bottom portion abstracts the reason for termination notice and a truncated rating of the employee. The fact that this part of the profile requires only a minute encourages its completion.

I-6

Control of the use (or misuse) of payroll checks calls for a Payroll Checks Record (I-7) for each employee. Data on the form list the pay period, employee, gross amount, deductions, net earnings, and *check number*. Basic data on the employee appear in the card heading. The Payroll Record (I-8) does not elicit a check number but does provide space for total hours worked and wage rate.

I-7

I-8

Payroll records may be adapted to needs of specific organizations such as a theater projectionist payroll (I-9), which divides the work day into matinee or evening. For *control purposes*, notice that each theater's manager places one copy of the payroll report in the "Projection Booth File," retains another for his own file, and transmits a third copy to the home office for purposes of CONTROL AND ANALYSIS. From these data, a Master Payroll (I-10) emerges which compares actual payroll expenditure, by person, to the budgeted amount. Overtime must be explained and justified.

I-9

I-10

The weekly payroll record (I-11) for the department lists:

I-11

    (a) name of employee;
    (b) employee number and card or clock number;
    (c) number of hours worked;
    (d) authorized wage rate;
    (e) money totals of regular, overtime, and gross pay;
    (f) deductions;
    (g) net pay and check number.

The issued payroll check, with stub (I-12), supplies the same payroll information to the employee for his records and is a further control device on the payroll department—as well as an error-catcher.

I-12

For each individual a Cumulative Payroll Record (I-13) condenses information from periodic pay records, except check numbers. This information is consolidated monthly, with quarterly totals, for macro-payroll and labor cost analysis and a record of taxes paid by the organization (I-14).

I-13

I-14

The Job Work Order (I-15) exhibited exemplifies another approach to LABOR COST CONTROL and payroll department operations. In this instance, employees work mostly outside of the shop, without direct supervision, so that restraints against potential abuses rest with the customer. The employee can overcharge, although total hours cannot exceed the daily amount authorized, but the customer bears the cost so that materials, rather than labor, appear to be the major source of profit leak.

I-15

Consistent overcharging breeds bad customer relations, a profit leak; but management has some control over this through *comparative analysis*, i.e., comparison with similar jobs by other employees. The reverse side of this form calls for details on materials and labor, returned materials, cost of materials, and cost of labor. Travel costs are computed separately for each vehicle, with total number of miles indicated in each case. (A good idea in these days of high fuel and maintenance costs!) A block is also available for other direct costs. Then all costs are summarized, and profits or losses are recorded for later analysis.

I-16   When temporary employees are needed for a special project, seasonal or cyclical bulges, or as a cost-cutting strategy, the supervisor will complete a Temporary Contract Personnel Requisition (I-16) detailing when needed, why, and duties of the job. This request, signed by the supervisor or initiator, is subsequently approved by another person. The job may be advertised or placed with a private employment agency.

I-17   A Job Order Form (I-17) must specifically contain no suggestion of discrimination as to age, sex, religion, race, or national origin. But the form will contain basic data on position requisites, location, salary, and basic screening information. An employment agency will want to list additional information that will help pinpoint potential applicants and match employees to employer requirements as closely as possible. Despite the *caveat* on

I-18   discrimination, government agencies require at least summary data (I-18) on male-female composition of the workforce, and a horizontal recapitulation by race or national origin coupled with a vertical enumeration by job category.

I-19   Within the organization, the applicant screening process begins with an Application for Employment (I-19). This, along with the personal interview, is a primordial COST CONTROL DEVICE, although it is seldom considered in those terms. Unfortunately, the application centers more on governmental compliance than on eliciting the kind of information needed to screen out cost-unconscious applicants. The form exhibited is in a fairly standard format that complies with major laws and still provides sufficient information for initial assessment of an applicant.

I-20   Post-Hiring Information (I-20), equally important, is frequently overlooked. Notice the focus on COST SAVING: illness, injuries, and additional data that may eliminate some candidates on probation. For the payroll department there is information on deductions. Data from the application (I-19) and post-hiring record (I-20), together with other data solicited from the employee, are transferred to a Personnel Record (I-21). The remainder

I-21   of the front side of the card is devoted to service record information. The back side provides for an annual summary of wages, supervisor evaluation, and termination statistics. The experience chart grades the employee on a scale of 10 to 40.

I-22   Restaurant employees, for example, may fill out a time sheet (I-22) that calls not only for number of hours worked but also for adjustments, for tax purposes, on meals eaten at the establishment, lodging, and gratuities. Or the firm may prefer an Individual Payroll and Earnings Statement (I-23) for *simplified, low-cost recordkeeping* and payroll disbursement.

I-23

Paperwork for the payroll department does not end at this point, but it must guard against generating a volume that exceeds the resources and capability of the organization. Therefore, *payroll department efficiency* is no less significant to PROFIT MAXIMIZATION than shop efficiency. Some paperwork necessarily includes a Payroll Deductions form (I-24) to signal deductions and changes in deductions authorized; an application for health insurance (I-25) that lists basic information on the reverse side; a medical and dental insurance enrollment card (I-26) that records payouts on its reverse side; and a card authorizing Transfer Checking (I-27) so that deposits are made directly by the company to the employee's checking, savings, or investment account. Or part of the employee's wages may be directed to a credit union for deposit, which transaction is chronicled in a Credit Union Statement (I-28).

I-24
I-25
I-26
I-27

I-28

But this is not the end of it. If the company has a profit-sharing plan, at least annually each participating employee will receive a Statement of Employee's Interest in the Profit-Sharing Plan (I-29). Although the calculations may engage considerable labor time, the individual statement itself is simple. The inside address SAVES TIME AND MONEY; when folded, the heading, in a windowed envelope, substitutes for addressing the envelope. Another record, the Employer Retirement Fund (I-30), calls for monthly entries and annual totals expressed in amounts and in credits.

I-29

I-30

When there is a job-related accident or occupational disease, a comprehensive Accident or Occupation Disease Report (I-31) ensures that the employee will receive all payments or compensation he or she is entitled to and, at the same time, protects the employer from malingerers. The completed form complies with state regulations for insurance payments. It should also contain sufficient information to ascertain whether the accident or disease is chargeable to the firm. If it is, the firm, or its agent, must pay off fully and equitably. If it is not, the employee must look elsewhere for compensation. If disability is permanent, the employee files an Application for Disability Retirement (I-32). Supporting documents must accompany the application, and the company reserves the right to update the file periodically with current medical history.

I-31

I-32

Another MONEY-SAVER is the Hourly Employee Termination Checklist (I-33). Its purposes are to leave no threads dangling, to assure that the employee has been paid all salary due, and that he or she has returned all company property, whether the termination is voluntary or involuntary. If the employee files for state unemployment compensation, the employer must issue an Unemployment Notice (I-34), which is used in a determination of the validity of a claim for unemployment compensation benefits. The employer may also be required to transmit a Wage Statement (I-35), which enumerates, for the most current 26-week period, on a weekly basis, the total number of hours worked, wage rate, and total wages of the separated employee.

I-33

I-34

I-35

I-36
For PROFIT ANALYSIS and COST CONTROL, the information on a Job Ticket (I-36) includes the following:

    (a) department identification;
    (b) date and shift;
    (c) employee name and clock number;
    (d) account number;
    (e) order and part numbers and description;
    (f) number of pieces produced;
    (g) regular and overtime hours, pay rate, and earnings;
    (h) approval signature.

I-37
The Weekly Time and Distribution Report (I-37), an extension of the foregoing, inscribes essentially the same information but on a weekly basis.

I-38
The Labor Statement (I-38), a payroll distribution sheet by departments and operations, registers monthly and cumulative reports. Information listed in the form begins with data on raw materials and production costs. An analysis of employees, by job description category, indicates number of employees per function, PRODUCTIVITY, and *total labor cost* by function and for the entire operation. The last section of the form records the same information summarized by divisions.

I-39
Management can take advantage of data available from the payroll department in formats like the preceding or following three forms to aid in FINANCIAL PLANNING FOR PROFITS AND GROWTH. With the Production and Job Time Form (I-39), management can PINPOINT LABOR COSTS, IMPROVE INVENTORY MANAGEMENT, and ZERO IN ON LABOR PRODUCTIVITY. The left-hand block of information relates to inventory control data; the middle section ties down hours and times of production for inventory; the right-hand section pins down data on the parts or pieces manufactured.

I-40
Productivity is measured by analysis of information detailed in a Performance Level Report (I-40). This weekly record and quarterly compendium of each employee's production furnishes a basis for pay raises and promotion, measurement of employee productivity, some indication of supervisory performance, and input on departmental evaluation.

I-41
Which leads to the Department Performance Report (I-41). *Office productivity* is as important to *profits* as is *shop productivity*, and failure to CONTROL CLERICAL COSTS may develop into a major profit leak. Of course, materializing workload performance standards will initially require considerable observation and analysis; these may be achieved via sampling techniques. It is not only employee effectiveness being measured by the performance report but the supervisor's and departmental or functional manager's as well. With all employees working together, in a cooperative atmosphere, productivity—and profits—should rise.

COST CENTER PAYROLL SUMMARY FORM

COST CENTER SUMMARY   198____   FOR MONTH ENDING _____

EMPLOYEE NAME NUMBER	SALARY RATE	TOTAL HOURS	REG. HOURS	STRAIGHT OVERTIME	PREM. OVRTM	SICK LEAVE	COMP. LEAVE	HOLIDAY	OTHER ABSENCES	EARNINGS

COST CENTER HOURS

COST CENTER TOTAL SUM

TOTAL ADJUSTMENTS

TOTAL HOURS & EARNINGS

Figure I-1: COST CENTER PAYROLL SUMMARY FORM

PAYROLL AND COST ANALYSIS

	OFFICE MANAGEMENT		SALES		PRODUCTION		GENERAL MGMT	
	Monthly	Annual	Monthly	Annual	Monthly	Annual	Monthly	Annual
Salaries & Wages								
Overtime								
Benefits & Bonuses								
TOTAL COMPENSATION								
Travel/Entertainm't								
Meetings/Conferences								
Telephone (LD)								
Advertising Exp.								
Subscriptions								
Special Services								
Employee Relations								
Legal Fees								
Other Expenses								
Miscellaneous								
TOTAL								

Figure I-2: PAYROLL AND COST ANALYSIS

TIME RECORD

TIME RECORD FOR WEEK ENDING _____

NAME OF EMPLOYEE	HOURLY RATE	ORDER NO.___		ORDER NO.___		ORDER NO.___		ORDER NO.___		ORDER NO.___		OVERHEAD		TOTALS	
		HRS.	COST	HRS.	COST	HRS.	COST	HRS.	COST	HRS.	COST	HRS.	COST	HRS.	COST
TOTALS															

Figure I-3: TIME RECORD

(From the book Cost Accounting for Small Manufacturers by R. Lee Brummet and Jack C. Robertson. © 1972. Published by Small Business Administration.)

IN-AND-OUT TIME RECORD

Week Ending _____ 19 _____

NAME OF EMPLOYEE		MON.	TUE.	WED.	THU.	FRI.	SAT.	SUN.	TOTAL HOURS WEEKLY	BASE RATE	TOTAL STRAIGHT TIME EARNINGS	TOTAL OVERTIME EARNINGS	DEDUC-TIONS	NET WAGE
	IN													
	OUT													
	IN													
	OUT													
	IN													
	OUT													
TOTAL DAILY HOURS														
	IN													
	OUT													
	IN													
	OUT													
	IN													
	OUT													
TOTAL DAILY HOURS														
	IN													
	OUT													
	IN													
	OUT													
	IN													
	OUT													
TOTAL DAILY HOURS														
	IN													
	OUT													
	IN													
	OUT													
	IN													
	OUT													
TOTAL DAILY HOURS														
	IN													
	OUT													
	IN													
	OUT													
	IN													
	OUT													
TOTAL DAILY HOURS														
	IN													
	OUT													
	IN													
	OUT													
	IN													
	OUT													
TOTAL DAILY HOURS														
	IN													
	OUT													
	IN													
	OUT													
	IN													
	OUT													
TOTAL DAILY HOURS														

Figure I-4: IN-AND-OUT TIME RECORD
(Courtesy of Litton Office Products.)

OVERTIME PERMIT

A copy of this Permit must be sent to timekeeper. Overtime will not be paid for unless approved.

Dept._____ Date_____

Name_____ Clock No._____

Is Authorized to Work_____Hours Overtime

On Job No._____For_____

Reason_____

_____

_____

Requested by_____

Approved by_____

STANDARD FORM 505
REGENT STANDARD FORMS, INC., PENNSAUKEN, N. J. 08109

Figure I-5: OVERTIME PERMIT
(Courtesy of Regent Standard Forms, Inc., Bellmawr, New Jersey 08031.)

PAY ROLL CHANGE NOTICE

PLEASE
(Check ✔)

☐ Enter on Pay Roll   Date_____

☐ Change Rate

☐ Transfer To_____ Entered_____

☐ Pay Off & Remove From Pay Roll   Time Dept.

Name_____ S.S.A/C No._____

Dept._____ Shift_____ Clock No._____

Date Effective_____ Hour_____ A. M. / P. M.

Old Rate_____Per_____New Rate_____Per_____

Remarks_____

_____

RECORD   ☐ Discharged   ☐ Left   ☐ Laid Off   Would You Re-Employ? Yes ☐ No ☐

	Excellent	Good	Fair	Poor	
Ability					Approved
Conduct					
Attendance					Foreman
Production					Supt.

STANDARD FORM 503
REGENT STANDARD FORMS, INC., BELLMAWR, N.J. 08031

Figure I-6: PAYROLL CHANGE NOTICE
(Courtesy of Regent Standard Forms, Inc., Bellmawr, New Jersey 08031.)

TIME WK'D	DATE PAY PERIOD ENDING	TO THE ORDER OF	GROSS AMOUNT	INCOME TAX	SOC. SEC.				DEDUCTIONS			← DEDUCTION AMOUNTS NET AMOUNT	CHECK NUMBER

NAME _____

STREET _____

CITY _____   YEAR _____

CLOCK NUMBER _____

SOC. SEC. NUMBER _____

PHONE NO. _____

DEPT. _____

DATE STARTED _____
DATE LEFT _____

MARITAL STATUS □ M.   □ F.
NO. OF EXEMPT.

RECORD OF PAY RATE CHANGES
DATE | RATE

FORM NO. RLW-15

PRINTED IN U.S.A.

□ 1ST & 2ND QUARTER
□ 3RD & 4TH QUARTER

Figure I-7: PAYROLL CHECKS RECORD
(Courtesy of Regent Standard Forms, Inc., Bellmawr, New Jersey 08031.)

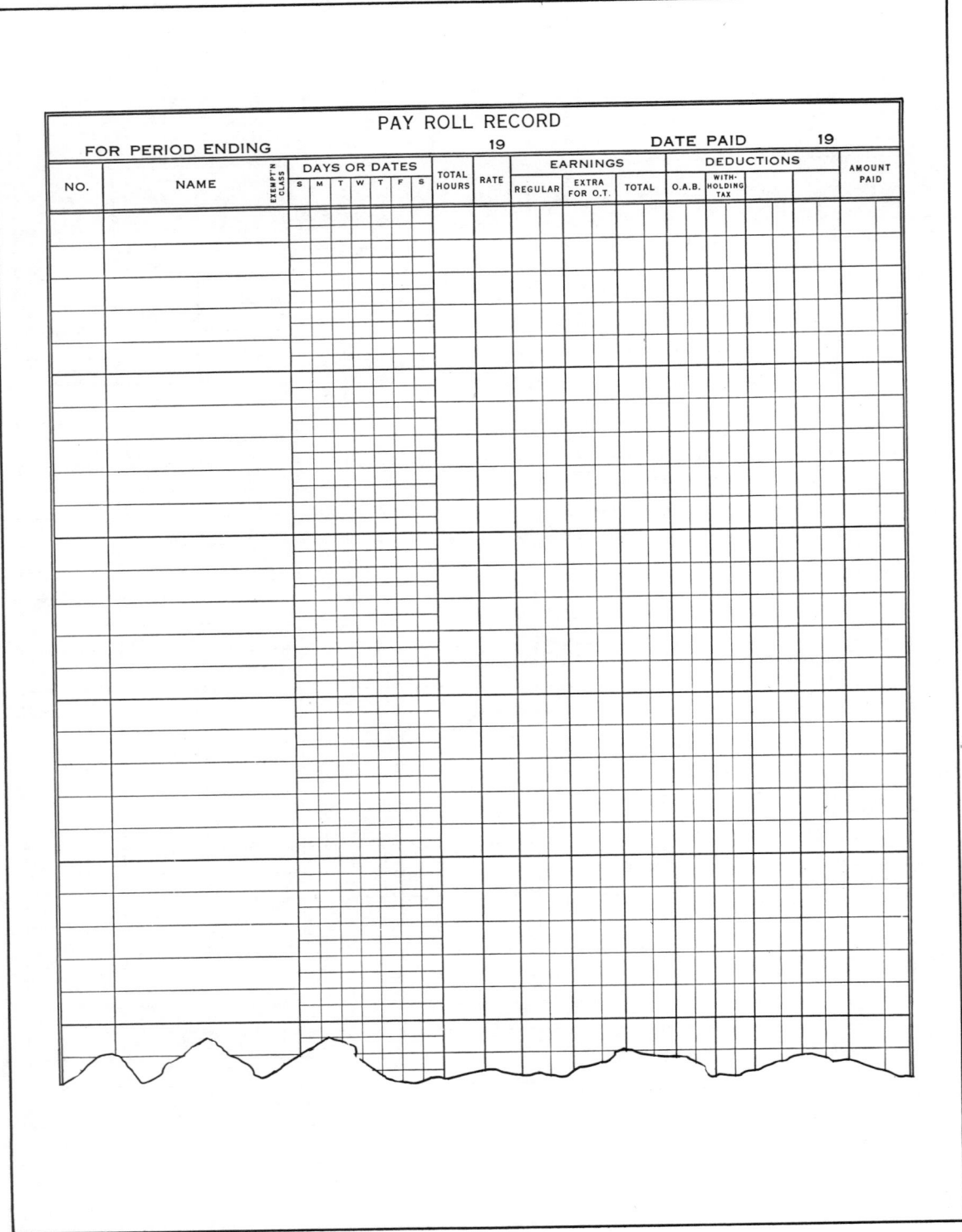

Figure I-8: PAYROLL RECORD
(Courtesy of Litton Office Products.)

THEATRE CIRCUIT

PROJECTIONIST PAYROLL

THEATRE..................... TOWN....................... FROM............. TO.............

Dt	Day	Operator	From	To	Total	Pay	Overtime
	WEDNESDAY Matinee						
	Evening						
	THURSDAY Matinee						
	Evening						
	FRIDAY Matinee						
	Evening						
	SATURDAY Matinee						
	Evening						
	SUNDAY Matinee						
	Evening						
	MONDAY Matinee						
	Evening						
	TUESDAY Matinee						
	Evening						

Overtime Reasons...

....

OPERATOR	TOTAL HRS.	REG. PAY	OVER.PAY.	GROSS.
TOTALS				

Base Allotment$..........

Projectionist......................... Manager....................................

Copies to Home Office, Manager and Projection Booth File.

Figure I-9: PROJECTIONIST PAYROLL FORM

MASTER PAYROLL

Theatre Number

THEATRE _____

TOWN _____

WEEK ENDING _____

BUDGET	POSITION	EMPLOYEE NAME	MS	E	HOURS	RATE	REG. PAY	OVER PAY	GROSS	FICA	F.I.T.	OTHER	NET PAY

OVERTIME EXPLANATION

BUDGET PAY			REGULAR PAY	OVERTIME PAY	GROSS PAY	F.I.C.A. SOCIAL SECURITY	F.I.T. INCOME TAX	OTHER DED.	NET PAY

Figure I-10: MASTER PAYROLL

Line no.	Name of employee	Empl. no.	Card no.	Hrs. worked	Reg. rate	Totals			Deductions						Net pay	Check no.
						Reg.	OT	Gross wages	Income taxes	FICA	Group ins.	Union dues	Other	Total		
1																
2																
3																
4																
5																
6																
7																
8																
9																
10																
TOTALS																

Payroll for week ended _____

Department _____

Page _____

Figure I-11: WEEKLY PAYROLL FORM

(From the book Cost Accounting for Small Manufacturers by R. Lee Brummet and Jack C. Robertson. © 1972. Published by Small Business Administration.)

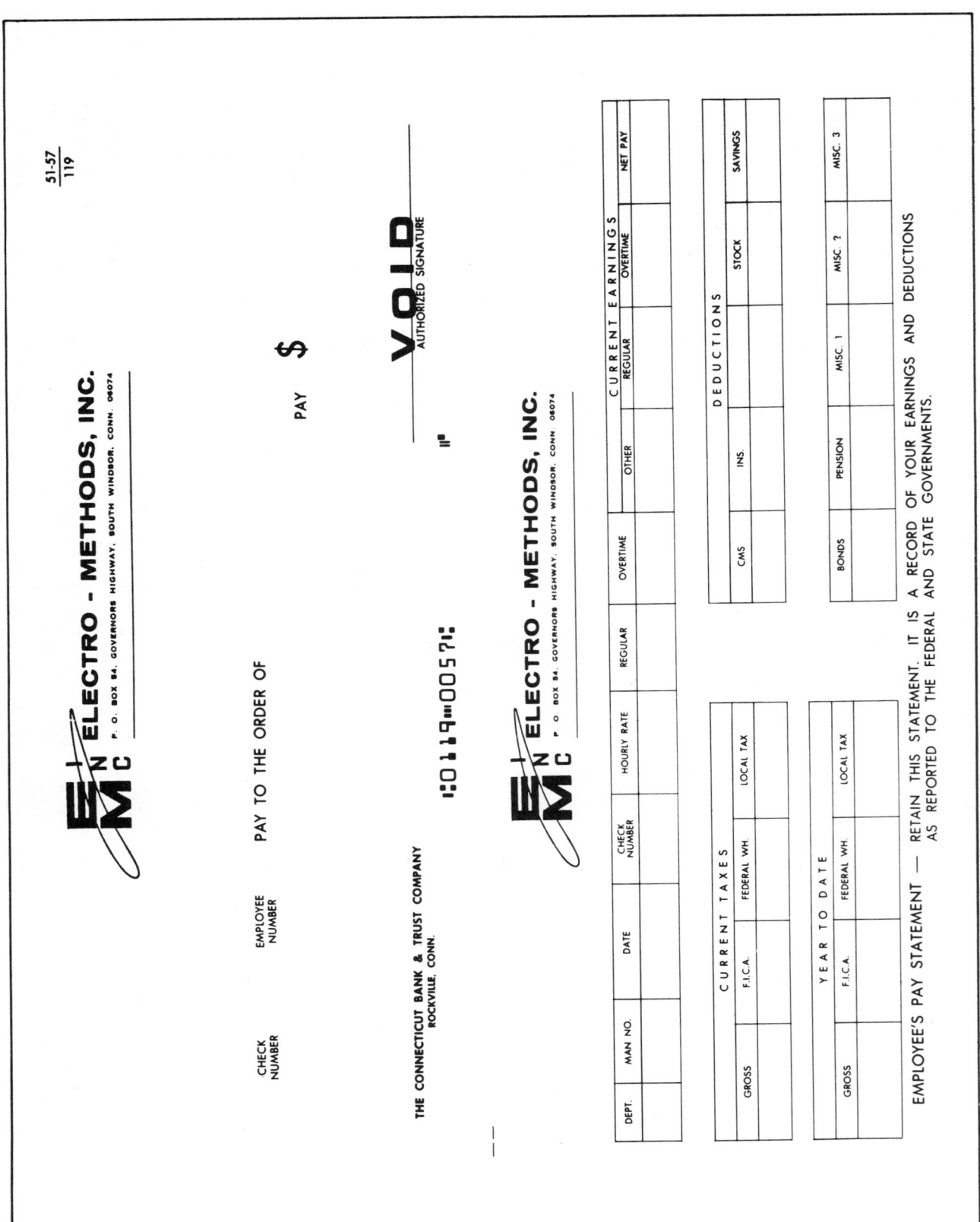

Figure I-12: PAYROLL CHECK AND EMPLOYEE'S PAY STATEMENT
(Courtesy of Electro-Methods, Inc., South Windsor, Connecticut.)

QTR.	EARN-INGS	DEDUCTIONS					NET PAID
		F.O.A.	WITH HLD'G	LO-CAL			
1st							
2nd							
3rd							
4th							
Tot							

NAME _____ EXEMPTIONS ____
ADDRESS _____ TEL. _____
S.S. NO. _____CLOCK NO.___SEX___SINGLE___MARRIED___
DATE BORN___DATE EMPLOYED___HRS. PER DAY___PER WK.___
POSITION_____DATE TERMINATED_____REMARKS_____
RATE: DATE_____ $ _____PER_____DATE_____ $_____PER____

FIRST QUARTER — 19 _____

RRPS FORM EF-12

PAY PERIOD	REGULAR TIME		OVER-TIME		TOTAL EARNINGS	NON-TAXABLE	AMT. TAXABLE	DEDUCTIONS						NET EARNINGS	
	TIME	RATE	HRS.	RATE		SICK PAY ETC.		F.O.A.	WITH-HOLDING	LO-CAL				AMOUNT	DATE PAID
TOTAL QTR.															

SECOND QUARTER — 19 _____

REDI-RECORD PAYROLL SYSTEMS INC. OCEANSIDE, N.Y.

PAY PERIOD	REGULAR TIME		OVER-TIME		TOTAL EARNINGS	NON-TAXABLE	AMT. TAXABLE	DEDUCTIONS						NET EARNINGS	
	TIME	RATE	HRS.	RATE		SICK PAY ETC.		F.O.A.	WITH-HOLDING	LO-CAL				AMOUNT	DATE PAID
TOTAL QTR.															
TOTAL 6 MOS.															

Figure I-13: CUMULATIVE PAYROLL FORM FOR INDIVIDUAL
(Courtesy of Litton Office Supplies.)

RECAPITULATION GROSS PAYROLL AND TAXES PAID

MONTH	TOTAL GROSS PAYROLL	TAXABLE PAYROLL F.I.C.A. MEDICARE	TAXABLE PAYROLL STATE U.C.	RECORD OF TAXES PAID						
				F.I.C.A. MEDICARE AMOUNT	DATE PAID	FEDERAL WITHHOLDING TAX AMOUNT	DATE PAID	STATE UNEMP. COMP. AMOUNT	DATE PAID	
JANUARY										
FEBRUARY										
MARCH										
TOTAL 1st QTR.										
APRIL										
MAY										
JUNE										
TOTAL 2nd QTR.										
TOTAL TO DATE										
JULY										
AUGUST										
SEPTEMBER										
TOTAL 3rd QTR.										
TOTAL TO DATE										
OCTOBER										
NOVEMBER										
DECEMBER										
TOTAL 4th QTR.										
TOTAL for YEAR										

S-K FORMS COMPANY
919 WALNUT STREET   PHILADELPHIA, PA. 19107
RECAPITULATION B

Figure I-14: RECAPITULATION GROSS PAYROLL AND TAXES PAID
(Courtesy of Litton Office Supplies.)

**RAPIDFORMS®** NO. 8545

JOB WORK ORDER

REORDER FROM REGENT STANDARD FORMS, INC.
INTERSTATE INDUSTRIAL PARK, BELLMAWR, N.J. 08031

JOB WORK ORDER

MOYLAN PUMP SERVICE
Box 306
Eastland, Texas 76443
817/629-2244

BILL TO		PHONE
ADDRESS		CUSTOMER ORDER NO.
CITY		ORDER TAKEN BY
JOB NAME AND LOCATION		DATE ORDERED
JOB PHONE	☐ DAY WORK ☐ CONTRACT ☐ EXTRA	DATE PROMISED ☐ A.M. ☐ P.M.

☐ No one home   ☐ Total amount due   ☐ Total billing to be mailed after completion of work

DESCRIPTION OF WORK:

_____
_____
_____
_____
_____
_____
_____
_____
_____
_____
_____
_____
_____

HOURS	LABOR	AMOUNT			
	@		TOTAL MATERIALS		
	@		TOTAL LABOR		
	@				
	@		SUB TOTAL		
I hereby acknowledge the satisfactory completion of the above described work:	TOTAL LABOR		TAX		
SIGNATURE		DATE COMPLETED / /	TOTAL		

FORM 8545. REGENT FORMS. BELLMAWR. N.J. 08031

Figure I-15: JOB WORK ORDER
(Courtesy of Regent Standard Forms, Inc., Bellmawr, New Jersey 08031.)

JOB COST RECORD

CUSTOMER'S ORDER NO.

MATERIAL RECORD

REQ. NO.	DESCRIPTION	PRICE	COST

LABOR RECORD

DATE	EMP.	HOURS	RATE	COST

TOTAL LABOR COST

TRAVEL EXPENSES

DATE	VEHICLE	MILES	RATE	COST

TOTAL TRAVEL COST

MISC. COSTS

	TOTAL	
	LESS RETURNED MATERIALS	
	COST OF MATERIALS	

OTHER DIRECT COSTS

REQ. NO.	DESCRIPTION	PRICE	COST
	SUB-CONTRACTORS		
	SPECIAL EQUIPMENT		
	OTHER		
	TOTAL DIRECT COSTS		

COST RECORD

TOTAL MATERIAL COST	
TOTAL LABOR COST	
TOTAL DIRECT COST	
TOTAL TRAVEL COST	
TAX / INSURANCE	
PERMITS / MISC. COSTS	
TOTAL COST	

PROFIT OR LOSS RECORD

TOTAL SELLING PRICE	
LESS TOTAL COST	
GROSS PROFIT	
LESS OVERHEAD COSTS % OF SELLING PRICE	
NET PROFIT (LOSS)	

(Before writing on this side, detach this sheet or place a writing plate between this sheet and carbon on the other side.)

Figure I-15—Reverse Side

REQUISITION

CONTRACT LABOR

JOB TITLE

SUPERVISOR   DEPARTMENT   SEX

UNIT   DEPT. NO.   EXT.

DATES NEEDED

SHIFT HOURS

REASON

JOB DUTIES

SIGNED BY   TITLE   DATE

APPROVED BY   TITLE   DATE

NO. INT.	W	B	H	AI	O	ADVERTISED

Figure I-16: TEMPORARY CONTRACT PERSONNEL REQUISITION

Job Order No. _____ Office Code _____ Counselor Code _____

Date _____ Fee _____ Exclusive _____ Time _____

Advertising _____ Wonderlic _____ Received by — Letter [ ] W.C. [ ] E.C. [ ]

In Person [ ]

Firm _____		Position _____
Address _____		Age _____
Phone _____	Contact _____	Job Location _____
Product _____	Hours _____	Industry _____
Interview Starts _____	Job Starts _____	Salary _____ Comm. _____
No. of Employees — Female _____	Male _____	Draw _____ Travel _____
		Car Nec. _____ Car Furn. _____
Labor Contract	Labor Dispute	Union Member	Fringe Benefits _____	Expenses _____ Mileage _____
Yes [ ] No [ ]	Yes [ ] No [ ]	Yes [ ] No [ ]		Education _____
				Degree _____
				Experience _____

DESCRIPTION:

Figure I-17: JOB ORDER FORM

778

JOB CATEGORY ANALYSIS

Hires for April

Job Categories	Total	Male						Female				
	Sum A-K	White B	Black C	S/A D	Asian E	Ind. F	White G	Black H	S/A I	Asian J	Ind. K
Officials & Managers												
Professionals												
Technicians												
Sales Workers												
Office & Clerical												
Craftsmen (Skilled)												
Operatives (Semi-Skilled)												
Laborers (Unskilled)												
Service Workers												
TOTAL:												

Figure I-18: JOB CATEGORY ANALYSIS
(Courtesy of Electro-Methods, Inc., South Windsor, Connecticut.)

application for employment

We are an equal opportunity employer, dedicated to a policy of non-discrimination in employment on any basis including race, creed, color, age, sex, religion or national origin.´

PERSONAL INFORMATION

Date _____   Social Security Number _____

Name _____
               Last   First   Middle

Present Address _____
               Street   City   State   Zip

Permanent Address _____
               Street   City   State   Zip

Phone No. _____   Height _____   Weight _____

State Name and Department of Any Relatives, Other Than Spouse, Already Employed By This Company _____

Referred By _____

(Vertical right margin: Last / First / Middle)

EMPLOYMENT DESIRED

Position _____   Date You Can Start _____   Salary Desired _____

Are You Employed Now? _____   If So May We Inquire of Your Present Employer _____

Ever Applied to this Company Before? _____   Where _____   When _____

EDUCATION

	Name and Location of School	Circle Last Year Completed	Did You Graduate?	Subjects Studied and Degree(s) Received
Grammar School			☐ Yes ☐ No	
High School		1 2 3 4	☐ Yes ☐ No	
College		1 2 3 4	☐ Yes ☐ No	
Trade, Business or Correspondence School		1 2 3 4	☐ Yes ☐ No	

Subjects of Special Study or Research Work _____

What Foreign Languages Do You Speak Fluently? _____

Read _____   Write _____

Activities Other Than Religious (Civic, Athletic, etc.) _____
EXCLUDE ORGANIZATIONS, THE NAME OR CHARACTER OF WHICH INDICATES THE RACE, CREED, COLOR OR NATIONAL ORIGIN OF ITS MEMBERS.

Form M660-26NR   Printed in U.S.A.
©1977 Wilson Jones Company

(Continued on Other Side)

APPLICATION FOR EMPLOYMENT

Figure I-19: APPLICATION FOR EMPLOYMENT
(Copyright 1977 by Wilson Jones Company. All rights reserved. Forms may be obtained, subject to supply, from Wilson Jones Company, 6150 Touhy Avenue, Chicago, Illinois 60648.)

FORMER EMPLOYERS List Below Last Four Employers, Starting With Last One First

Date Month and Year	Name and Address of Employer	Salary	Position	Reason for Leaving
From				
To				
From				
To				
From				
To				
From				
To				

REFERENCES: Give Below the Names of Three Persons Not Related To You, Whom You Have Known At Least One Year.

	Name	Address	Business	Years Acquainted
1				
2				
3				

PHYSICAL RECORD: Do you have any physical condition which may limit your ability to perform the job applied for?

In Case of Emergency Notify

Name   Address   Phone No.

I authorize investigation of all statements contained in this application. I understand that misrepresentation or omission of facts called for is cause for dismissal. Further, I understand and agree that my employment is for no definite period and may, regardless of the date of payment of my wages and salary, be terminated at any time without any previous notice.

Date   Signature

DO NOT WRITE BELOW THIS LINE

Interviewed By   Date

REMARKS:

Neatness		Character	
Personality		Ability	

Hired   For Dept.   Position   Will Report   Salary Wages

Approved: 1.   2.   3.

Employment Manager   Dept. Head   General Manager

Figure I-19 (continued)

POST HIRING INFORMATION

LAST NAME	FIRST NAME	MIDDLE	DATE

SOCIAL SECURITY NO.	SEX ☐ MALE ☐ FEMALE	HEIGHT FEET INCHES	WEIGHT LBS.

PRESENT ADDRESS		PHONE

CITY	STATE	ZIP	NAME OF SPOUSE

EMPLOYEE: READ THIS INTRODUCTION CAREFULLY BEFORE ANSWERING ANY QUESTIONS IN THIS BLOCKED-OFF AREA. The Civil Rights Act of 1964 prohibits discrimination in employment practice because of race, color, religion, sex or national origin. P.L. 90-202 prohibits discrimination on the basis of age with respect to individuals who are at least 40 but less than 70 years of age. The laws of some States also prohibit some or all of the above types of discriminations as well as some additional types such as discrimination against the physically handicapped.

DO NOT ANSWER ANY QUESTION CONTAINED IN THIS BLOCKED-OFF AREA UNLESS THE EMPLOYER HAS CHECKED THE BOX NEXT TO THE QUESTION, thereby indicating that the requested information is needed for national security laws, a bona fide occupational qualification, business necessity or other legally permissible reasons including administration of Employee Benefit Programs.

☐ How long have you lived at present address? _____

☐ Previous address _____ How long did you live there? _____
No.   Street   City   State   Zip

☐ Marital Status: Single _____ Married _____ Engaged _____ Separated _____ Divorced _____ Widowed _____

☐ Date of Marriage _____ ☐ Number of dependents including yourself _____ ☐ Are you a citizen of the U.S.A.? _____

☐ BIRTHDATE: _____

☐ Indicate dates you attended school:

Elementary _____ High School _____ College _____
From   To   From   To   From   To

Other (Specify type of school) _____
From   To

☐ Have you ever been bonded? _____ If yes, on what jobs? _____

☐ Have you had a major illness in the past 5 years? _____ If yes, describe _____

_____

☐ Have you received compensation for injuries? _____ If yes, describe _____

_____

Employer may list other bona fide occupational questions on lines below:

☐ _____

☐ _____

DO NOT WRITE BELOW THIS LINE

PAYROLL DATA

FEDERAL WITHHOLDING:	EXEMPTIONS CLAIMED							
	ADDITIONAL AMOUNT WITHHELD							

INSURANCE	DATE ELIGIBLE	DATE JOINED	DATE WITHDRAWN
UNION STATUS			
PENSION PLAN			
CREDIT UNION			

INSURANCE	DATE ELIGIBLE	DATE JOINED	DATE WITHDRAWN
LIFE			
MEDICAL—SELF			
DEP.			
MAJ. MED.—SELF			
DEP.			

FORM 243 REGENT STANDARD FORMS, INC., BELLMAWR, N.J. 08031

Figure I-20: POST-HIRING INFORMATION AND PAYROLL DATA
(Courtesy of Regent Standard Forms, Inc., Bellmawr, New Jersey 08031.)

PERSONNEL RECORD — VR-70 FAULTLESS FORM

NUMBER	NAME				CA	SE	CO	JA	CH	X	MALE	FEM.	S M D W	1	2	3	4	5	10	15	20	25	30	35	+
							RACE				MARITAL			YEARS OF SERVICE											

ADDRESS		TELEPHONE NO.	EDUCATION	SCHOOL	YRS.	GRAD.	NAME OF COURSE OR SPECIAL TRAINING
				COMMON SCHOOL			
				HIGH SCHOOL			
				COLLEGE			
NOTIFY		RELATIONSHIP		TECHNICAL			
				BUSINESS			
				CORRESPONDENCE			

ORIGIN / PERSONAL DATA / IDENTIFICATION

DATE OF BIRTH		OWNS HOME	RENTS		SING.	MAR.	DIV.	WID.	HEIGHT	WEIGHT	COMP.
PLACE OF BIRTH		NO. OF CHILDREN							VISION	HEARING	DEFECTS
NATURALIZED		REMARKS:							SIGNATURE		
NATIONALITY		CHURCH		CLUB							

SERVICE RECORD

DATE	RATE	PER	DEPT.	OCCUPATION	REMARKS	TERMINATION DATE	REASON

PTD IN U.S.A.

Figure I-21: PERSONNEL RECORD
(Courtesy of Litton Office Products.)

NAME

YEAR	EARNINGS DAYS	AMOUNT	EXPERIENCE OCCUPATION	TIME	TALENTS AND HOBBIES EXPERIENCED IN	INTERESTS	TERMINATION REASON	
							DECREASING FORCE	
							DISCHARGE	
							OTHER POSITION	
							DISSATISFIED WAGES	
							" WORK	
							SICKNESS	
							SKILL	
							EXCELLENT	
							AVERAGE	
							POOR	

	DATE			DATE		REMARKS	CHARACTER	
	PERSONAL APPEARANCE						RELIABLE	
	HABITS						UNRELIABLE	
	HEALTH						AGITATOR	
	INITIATIVE						INSUBORDINATE	
	INTELLIGENCE						**PRODUCTION**	
	LOYALTY						FAST	
	DEVELOPMENT						MEDIUM	
	TRADE ABILITY						SLOW	
	ABILITY TO DIRECT						**DISPOSITION**	
	SELF CONTROL						TROUBLESOME	
	COOPERATION						AVERAGE	
	FAIR AVERAGE						GOOD	
	BY						RE-EMPLOY	YES NO

EXPERIENCE CHART

1	2	3	4	5	6	7	8	9	10	11	12	13	14	15	16	17	18	19	20	21	22	23	24	25	26	27	28	29	30	31	32	33	34	35	36	37	38	39	40

FAULTLESS FORM

Figure I-21—Reverse Side

Name _____ Position _____

Week Ended _____ 19 _____

DAY	A. M.		P. M.		NIGHT		TOTAL HOURS
	In	Out	In	Out	In	Out	
Monday							
Tuesday							
Wednesday							
Thursday							
Friday							
Saturday							
Sunday							
TOTAL							

Hourly Rate_____for_____hours $_____

    Allowances:

Meals per week:_____Light Meals at 35¢ $_____

(*Maximum allowance*)_____Full Meals at 60¢ $_____
(*$1.80 per day*)

Gratuities: _____¢ ea. hr. for_____hrs. $_____

Lodging: $_____

    Total Allowances $_____

Net Wages after allowances but before S. S.
and withholding taxes deducted. $_____

    Deductions:

      Social Security & O. A. B. $_____

      Withholding Tax $_____

    Total Deductions $_____

Net Amount Due Employee $_____

I hereby attest that as a service employee I have received in gratuities during this pay period not less than ☐ $2.00 a day (part time) or ☐ $10.00 a week (full time) and acknowledge that the amount specified above as gratuities, not to exceed 45 cents per hour, has been received by me and applied as part of the Minimum Fair Wage of $1.85 an hour.

I certify that the time and hours shown above are true and correct.

Signed..

—PLIMPTON'S—

Figure I-22: PAYROLL RECORD FOR RESTAURANTS
(Courtesy of Litton Office Products.)

Wilson Jones

Individual Payroll and Earnings Record

With Quarterly Summary Forms

This Individual Payroll and Earnings Record provides a complete, convenient method for keeping all data required for compiling State and Federal reports under the Wage and Hour, Social Security, Unemployment Compensation, and Withholding Tax Laws. A table is provided on the back of the cover of the book for summarizing the necessary data for report purposes.

Each book serves as a payroll and earnings record for one employee for a period of one year and with the permanent copies intact, can easily be preserved for the period required by law.

Each form, in duplicate, is for a weekly payroll period and provides space for time worked, rate, gross earnings, deductions, net pay, and the Employee's signature. One copy is for the Employee, thereby furnishing him with the necessary statement of his earnings. The other copy, which remains in this book, is for the Employer's permanent record.

Special Features in This Book—

1. Convenient duplicate form for complete record of time worked, deductions, net pay, and Employee's signature.
2. Quarterly summary table for earnings and deductions for use in compiling State and Federal reports.
3. Carbon paper.
4. When completed, this book can be filed and conveniently preserved for the required four year period.

Individual Payroll and Earnings Statement

Employer's Name _____

Date _____ 19____

Employee's Name _____

Employee's Number _____

Salary for Period Beginning _____ Ending _____

EARNINGS

	S	M	T	W	T	F	S	Total Hours	Rate Per Hour		Total
REGULAR HOURS WORKED										$	
OVER TIME										$	
NON-CASH COMPENSATION (Meals, Room, Etc.)									(A)	$	
OTHER CASH COMPENSATION (Commissions, Etc.)										$	
TOTAL WAGES (or Salary if on Weekly, Semi-Monthly or Monthly Basis)										$	
TIPS REPORTED RECEIVED BY EMPLOYEE									(B)	$	
TOTAL EARNINGS—Including Tips										$	

TAX DEDUCTIONS

F.I.C.A.	$	
Federal Income Tax Withheld	$	
State Income Tax Withheld	$	
	$	
	$	
LESS TOTAL TAX DEDUCTIONS		$
NET EARNINGS AFTER TAX DEDUCTIONS		$

OTHER DEDUCTIONS

NON-CASH COMPENSATION (Line A Above)	$	
TIPS REPORTED RECEIVED BY EMPLOYEE (Line B Above)	$	
LESS TOTAL OTHER DEDUCTIONS		$
	NET AMOUNT PAID EMPLOYEE	$

☐ PAID IN CASH   ☐ PAID BY CHECK NO. _____

I certify this statement is correct and I have received the above stated amount

Employee's Signature _____

Wilson Jones
GRAYLINE FORM S6052

Employee's Copy

PRINTED IN U.S.A

Employee's Signature _____

Wilson Jones
GRAYLINE FORM S6052

Permanent Copy

PRINTED IN U.S.A

Figure I-23: INDIVIDUAL PAYROLL AND EARNINGS RECORD

PAYROLL DEDUCTIONS

Period Ending_____ Soc. Sec. No._____

Name_____

Earnings_____ $_____

Fed. Ins. Cont. Act_____ _____

Fed. Withholding Tax_____ _____

State Withholding Tax_____ _____ _____

_____ _____

_____ _____

_____ _____ _____

                                    Total Deductions _____
                                    Net Earnings $

Employer_____
EFFICIENCY® LINE NO. 50 AN **AMPAD** PRODUCT

Figure I-24: PAYROLL DEDUCTIONS
(Courtesy of Litton Office Products.)

Figure I-25: BLUE CROSS APPLICATION
(Courtesy of Electro-Methods, Inc., South Windsor, Connecticut.)

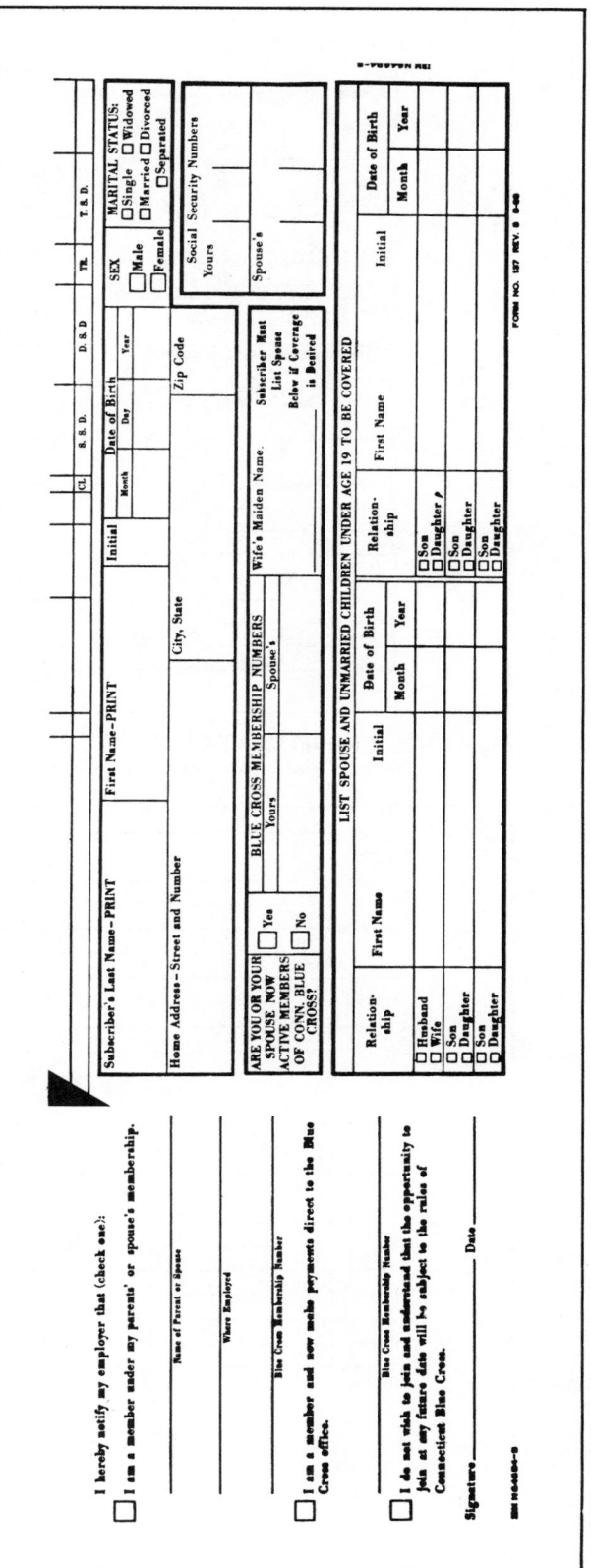

Figure I-25—Reverse Side:

1. DO NOT COMPLETE SHADED AREAS.
2. PLEASE TYPE OR PRINT PLAINLY.

4. FIRST CARBON COPY TO DENTAL CLAIM OFFICE. (If applicable)
   SECOND CARBON COPY FOR YOUR FILES.

3. CARD MUST BE DATED AND SIGNED.

1B1820

| □ NEW ENROLLMENT □ REINSTATEMENT | Emp. I.D. No. | Reinst. Code | Override | Bill Date | D/TIC |

| Account No. | Employee's Last Name | | Initials | Social Security No. | Date Mo. Day Yr. of Birth | S E X | □ M □ F |

| Date Perm. Mo. Day Yr. Employed or Rehired | Who are your eligible dependents? □ None ☑ Spouse □ One Child □ Two or More Children SPOUSE'S Date of Birth Mo.___ Day___ Year___ | Do you wish dep. benefits? Medical □ Yes □ No Dental □ Yes □ No |
| BF   *Beneficiary and Relationship | | Do you wish supplemental benefits? □ Yes □ No |

In lieu of CG Medical Coverage, I am participating in □ HMO_____ □ Armed Forces Program
□ Another Group Insurance Plan

| Name of Employer | Div.-Class-Location | Occupation | Earnings | □ Wk. □ Mo. □ Yr. |

**Provisions on reverse side accepted

DATE _____ SIGNATURE_____

Sub.	Class	Coverage		Effective Date Mo. Day Yr.	Amount	Cert.	Rdr.	Adj. Date Mo. Day Yr.	Adj. Code	Sched. or Ex. Cd.	New Bus.
			LIFE								
			D&D								
			DI								
			LTD								
			MED-E								
			MED-D								
			DENT-E								
			DENT-D								

ENROLLMENT CARD

Figure I-26: ENROLLMENT CARD
(Courtesy of Electro-Methods, Inc., South Windsor, Connecticut.)

LIFE	Date				
	Amt.				
	Date				
	Amt.				
	Date				
	Amt.				
D&D	Date				
	Amt.				
	Date				
	Amt.				
DI	Date				
	Amt.				
LTD	Date				
	Amt.				
MED-E	Date				
	Cov.				
MED	Date				
	Cov.				
DENT-E	Date				
	Cov.				
DENT	Date				
	Cov.				

*Unless otherwise provided where two or more beneficiaries are named, the proceeds shall be paid in equal shares to the named beneficiaries, if surviving the insured, or to the survivor or survivors. If no beneficiary survives, payment shall be made in accordance with the terms of the policy. This designation revokes any and all previous designations. The right to further change the beneficiary is reserved unto the insured.

**I accept the insurance provided by my employer's group insurance plan and authorize deductions from my earnings of the required contributions, if any, toward the cost of the insurance. This authorization applies only if employee contributions are required.

GF3024   Cat. #229757   CONNECTICUT GENERAL LIFE INSURANCE COMPANY

Figure I-26—Reverse Side

788

CBT PERSONAL SERVICE SUMMARY THESE ACCOUNTS ARE ACCEPTED SUBJECT TO THE CONDITIONS ON THE REVERSE SIDE.

1. NAME	SOCIAL SECURITY NO.	DATE OF BIRTH

2. NAME	DATE OF BIRTH	HOME PHONE	BUSINESS PHONE

3. ADDRESS (NO. STREET)	HOW LONG ___ YRS.	EMPLOYED BY

4. ADDRESS (CITY & STATE)	ZIP CODE	IDENTIFICATION OR BANK REFERENCE

5.

6. CHECK BOXES (I Have / Please Open)

1. PERSONAL CHECKING	☐ ☐	5. JET TRANSFER (Telephone)	☐ ☐	9. TRANSFER CHECKING	☐ ☐	13. JET BANKING CARD	☐ ☐
2. REG. SAVINGS (STMT)	☐ ☐	6. CREDIT CARD	☐ ☐	10. NOW ACCOUNT	☐ ☐	14. SAFE DEPOSIT BOX	☐ ☐
3. REG. SAVINGS (PSBK)	☐ ☐	7. OPEN END	☐ ☐	11. INVESTMENT SAVINGS	☐ ☐	15. PSBK. TO STMT.	☐ ☐
4. COMBINED STATEMENT	☐ ☐	8. CASH RESERVE	☐ ☐	12. PREMIUM SAVINGS	☐ ☐	OTHER	☐ ☐

I (WE) AUTHORIZE THE COMBINING OF ACCOUNTS SHOWN IN RENDERING A MONTHLY STATEMENT ☐YES ☐NO

I (WE) AUTHORIZE TRANSFER CHECKING ☐YES ☐NO

RECEIPT OF AGREEMENTS GOVERNING SAVINGS, CHECKING AND NOW ACCOUNTS SHOWN IS ACKNOWLEDGED.

SIGNATURE

SIGNATURE

FOR BANK USE

TYPE OF ACCOUNT	J / S	ACCOUNT NUMBER	COMBINE WITH EXISTING ACCOUNT NO.	BRANCH NO.
				EMP. NO.
				DATE
				NAME

DEPOSIT CONTRACT

Items received for deposit or collection are accepted on the following terms and conditions. The Bank acts only as depositor's collecting agent and assumes no responsibility beyond its exercise of due care. All items are credited subject to final payment and to receipt of proceeds of final payment in cash or solvent credits by the Bank at its own office. The Bank may forward items to correspondents and shall not be liable for default or negligence of correspondents selected with due care nor for losses in transit and each correspondent shall not be liable except for its own negligence. Items and their proceeds may be handled by any Federal Reserve Bank in accordance with applicable Federal Reserve rules, and by the Bank or any correspondent, in accordance with any common bank usage, with any practice or procedure that a Federal Reserve Bank may use or permit another bank to use, or with any other lawful means. The Bank may charge back, at any time prior to midnight on its business day next following the day of receipt, any item drawn on the Bank which is ascertained to be drawn against insufficient funds or otherwise not good or payable. An item received after the Bank's regular afternoon closing hour shall be deemed received the next business day.

It is agreed that this account shall be subject to service and maintenance charges heretofore adopted by the Bank and now in effect, and to such charges and changes in existing charges as shall become effective upon the posting of notice in the main office of the Bank or upon giving depositor not less than 10 days written notice mailed to his last known address.

All charges provided for herein may be deducted from this account and the Bank shall not be liable for dishonoring checks, drafts, acceptances, or other instruments for the payment of money because of insufficient funds resulting from from the deduction of such charges.

If "Open End" privileges have been granted by the Bank, the Bank may pay checks, drafts, acceptances or other instruments for the payment of money drawn against otherwise insufficient funds by making additions to the account in such amounts (in multiples of $50.00 each) as the Bank shall deem appropriate and charging such additions, together with any **FINANCE CHARGE** thereon, to the Credit Card balance of the depositor, or , in the case of a joint account, the depositors or any of them in the Bank's sole discretion. The Bank may cancel such privileges at any time. Any **FINANCE CHARGE** shall be assessed in accordance with the terms and conditions regarding Cash Transactions as contained in the Bank's Credit Card Customer Agreement, as amended from time to time.

To the extent permissable by law and/or regulation, the Bank is hereby given a lien and right of set-off upon and as to all deposits in this account or in course of deposit against any indebtedness of the depositors or any of them to the Bank, direct or contingent, however arising, whether secured or unsecured. Depositor agrees that in the event it becomes necessary to engage counsel to collect any overdraft existing, for whatever reason, in the account, depositor will pay all costs of collection, including reasonable attorneys fees.

The Bank may, on behalf of itself and depositor, waive demand, notice and protest, on all paper received or purchased for deposit or collection.

Upon presentation, the Bank may refuse payment of and return as unpaid to the presenting party any and all paper when, at the opening of business on the day of presentment, there is not a sufficient balance of collected funds to pay such paper.

The Bank reserves the right to post all deposits, including deposits of cash and of items drawn on it, not later than midnight of its next business day after their receipt by the Bank during regular banking hours, and shall not be liable for damages for nonpayment of any presented item resulting from the exercise of this right. Bank reserves the right to terminate the account without notice at any time that it shall deem the continuation of the account relationship not to be in its best interest.

In case the Bank is requested to stop payment on a check, draft, acceptance, or other instrument for the payment of money, it is expected to use all diligent care in stopping same but the Bank will not be responsible in case the check, draft, acceptance, or other instrument is paid through inadvertence or accident. Any written request for stop payment shall remain in effect for six (6) months unless such request is renewed in writing. Oral requests for stop payment shall remain in effect for fourteen (14) calendar days unless confirmed in writing within that period.

Unless otherwise instructed the Bank is authorized to forward by ordinary mail statements of this account together with all cancelled checks, drafts, acceptances, and other instruments for the payment of money to depositor's last-known address and such deposit in the mail shall constitute delivery.

As to any savings account, whether or not "Negotiable Order of Withdrawal" privileges have been granted by the Bank with respect to such account, the Bank reserves the right, in accordance with applicable statutes, to withhold payments for three (3) months after application for withdrawal is made or withdrawal order is presented.

JOINT ACCOUNTS — The account, if it is in two or more names, shall be owned by the depositors as joint tenants, any one or more of whom may withdraw, transfer, dispose of, and instruct as to all or any part of the balance of the account, all without any responsibility or liability on the part of the Bank for the use or disposition which may be made of funds withdrawn or transferred, including (without limitation) any such funds as may be paid or transferred to or deposited with the Bank to the individual account(s) of any one or more of the depositors. The Bank is authorized to credit to the account funds or instruments belonging or payable to the depositors, or any of them. If "Open End" privileges are in effect as to the account, fund transfers and any **FINANCE CHARGE** may be charged to the Credit Card balance(s) of the depositors or any of them in the Bank's sole discretion. Each depositor appoints each other depositor his attorney with power to deposit in the account moneys or paper of any of them and for that purpose to endorse any paper payable to any of the depositors or to them jointly. In the event of the death of any of the joint tenants, the amount on deposit to the credit of the account at the time of such death shall belong to the survivor(s), subject to the provisions hereof and any applicable legal requirements. Each surviving depositor agrees to notify the Bank immediately upon the death of any other depositor. All obligations and liabilities of the "depositor" hereunder shall be the joint and several responsibility of each joint depositor.

Figure I-27: TRANSFER CHECKING

CREDIT UNION STATEMENT

TRANSACTION DATE	MEMO NUMBER	TRANSACTION	TRANSACTION AMOUNT	SHARES OR PRINCIPAL	FEES OR INTEREST	SHARE OR LOAN BALANCE

ACCOUNT NO.	
SOC. SEC. NO.	
YR-TO-DATE DIV.	YR-TO-DATE INTEREST

OPG 99-0889

Burroughs

TDS-40   1077

Figure I-28: CREDIT UNION STATEMENT
(Courtesy of Burroughs Corporation Office Products Group/Business Forms Division.)

STATEMENT OF EMPLOYEE'S INTEREST IN PROFIT SHARING PLAN

_____ 198 _____

_____

_____

_____

Dear

For the year ended _____ , your total earnings,
for calculations in the Profit Sharing Plan, were $ _____ .
The number of years of continuous participation were _____ .
The number of units allocated to your account were _____ .

At the start of the year, your account was
valued at: $ _____

Your share of this year's contribution is: $ _____

Your share of sums forfeited from terminating
employees is: $ _____

Your share of investment profits (losses)
of the fund is: $ _____

The gross value of your account is: $ _____

The percent of vested (nonforfeitable)
interest in the Fund is: _____ %

The amount of your vested (nonforfeitable)
interest in the Fund is: $ _____

Yours sincerely,

By _____

Figure I-29: STATEMENT OF EMPLOYEE'S INTEREST IN PROFIT-SHARING PLAN

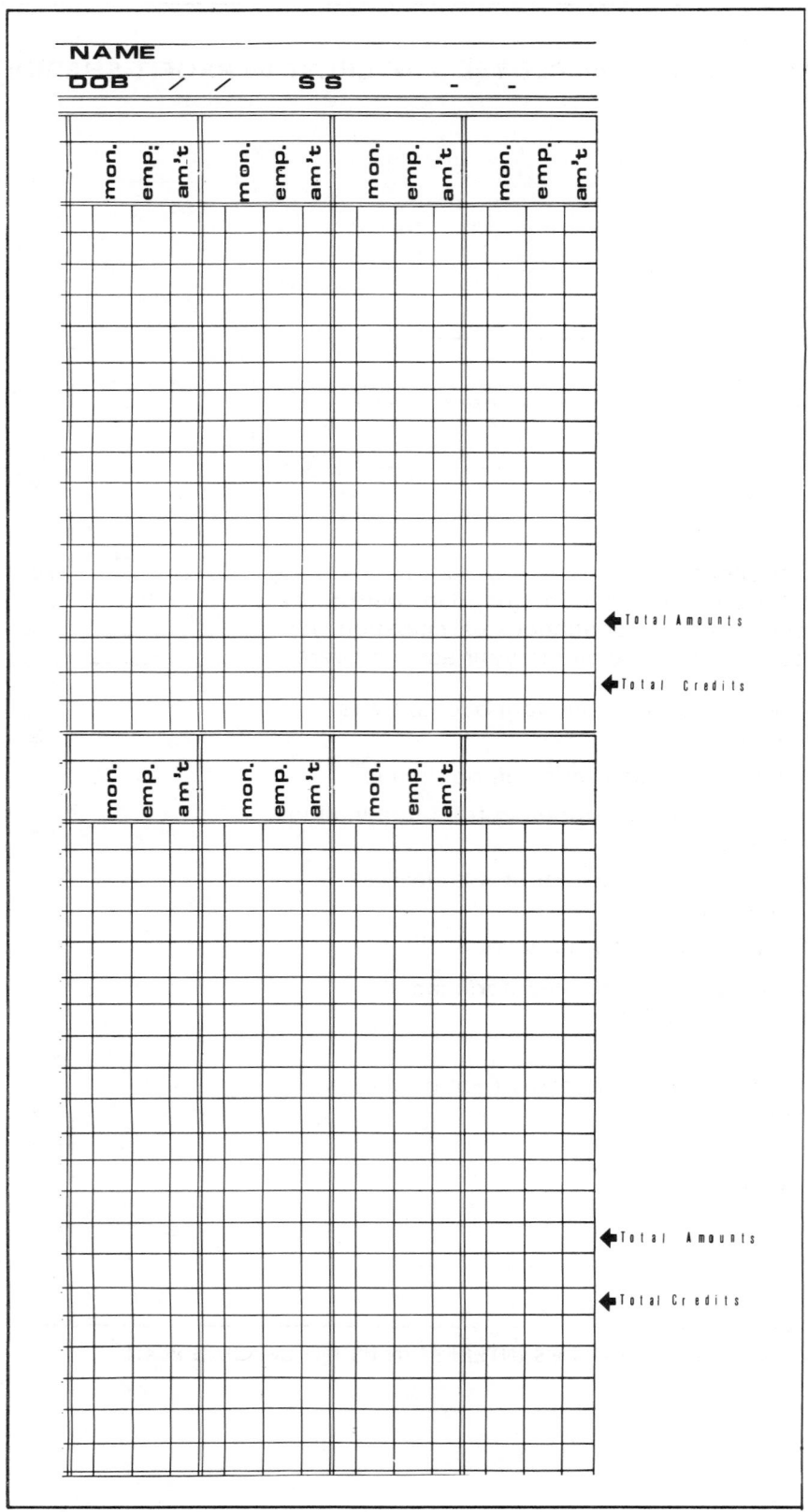

Figure I-30: EMPLOYER RETIREMENT FUND

Case No. ....
(for office use only)

Approved
19
By ....

REPORT OF ACCIDENT OR OCCUPATIONAL DISEASE TO AN EMPLOYEE

TO BE FILLED OUT IN DETAIL BY DIVISION HEAD
FORWARD IMMEDIATELY TO:

Date of Report .... Date of Accident ....

DEPARTMENT REPORTING ....

SECTION OR DIVISION .... LOCATION ....

DIVISION HEAD FILING REPORT ....
(not injured person) Title ....

Injured person's name ....

Address in full ....

Date of Birth: .... Sex ....
month day year

Occupation .... Title ....

Date of Employment ....

Was injury caused by the wilful and serious misconduct of injured or by his intoxication? .... If so, explain: ....

....

....

....

....

Did injury arise out of and in the course of injured person's employment? (Yes or No) ....

Is this an old injury aggravated by present employment? (Yes or No) .... If so, explain: When, Where and if injury was compensible ....

....

....

....

....

Give name of attending physician, for old injury ....

Has injured returned to work? .... If so, when? ....

Give name of nearest relative and where (He or She) can be contacted Phone No. ....

Name .... Address ....

Has this person been notified? (Yes or No) .... When? ....

Figure I-31: ACCIDENT OR OCCUPATIONAL DISEASE REPORT

2 ## ACCIDENT OR CAUSE OF INJURY

Date of accident .... Hour .... M Date Stopped Work .... 19........

Place where accident occurred ....

City or Town ....

Did accident occur on State Property? (Yes or No) .... Private Property? (Yes or No) ....

If so, state what part of premises, establishment or buildings ....

....

Cause of injury ....

....

If caused by machinery or instrument, state name and type of same ....

If falling accident, state what caused fall ....

....

How did accident happen? Report in detail ....

....

....

....

....

....

....

....

Witnesses of accident:
Names   Where employed.

....

....

....

Name and address of attending Physician:

....

If taken to hospital, give name ....

Also state type of transportation and name of person or firm supplying same ....

....

[Signed] Name ....

Title ....

Figure I-31 (continued)

REPORT OF OCCUPATIONAL DISEASE

Name of Disease ....

Date of the first manifestation of a symptom of occupational disease ....

Nature of Disease ....

....

....

....

Previous condition of health ....

Was employee examined at the time of employment? (Yes or No) ....

If so; give date of examination .... By whom ....

Give date of examination just prior to first manifestation ....

Has employee ever received compensation previously for this disease? (Yes or No) ....

If so; give date of its first manifestation of a symptom ....

Give name of attending physician ....

Give name of employer at that time ....

Remarks by person filing Report ....

....

....

....

....

COMPENSATION STATUS

Able to work after Accident or Occupational Disease? (Yes or No) ....

Date removed from payroll .... Date Returned ....

Weekly wages for preceding 26 weeks ....

Weekly wages for preceding 26 weeks if employed in an institution:

    (a) Amount of cash received weekly: ....

    (b) Amount of cash weekly maintenance ....

        Total wages: ....

                [Signed] Name ....

                        Title ....

Figure I-31 (continued)

4

STATEMENT OF CLAIMANT
(Third Party)

What is your name .... Occupation ....

Address ....

Married or Single .... If married, name of husband or wife ....

In what company do you carry your insurance? ....

Kind of insurance carried ....

Place of accident .... Date and Time ....

Make of Auto .... Type .... Year .... License No. .... State ....

Name of Owner .... Age ...... Address ....

Name of Driver .... Age ...... Address ....

Names, Ages and Addresses of Occupants ....

....

Were you or anyone riding in your car injured ....

Names and Addresses of injured ....

Nature and Extent of injuries ....

....

....

Name and Address of Attending Doctor ....

Were there any witnesses to accident (Give names and addresses) ....

....

How did accident happen? Give full account stating speed and direction of each car ....

....

....

....

....

....

Nature of damage to your car ....

Amount for which you are making claim ....

Witness to: Signature of
Signature ....   Claimant ....

Dated .... 19........

Figure I-31 (continued)

APPLICATION FOR DISABILITY RETIREMENT

(PLEASE PRINT)

NAME _____ SOCIAL SECURITY NO. _____

ADDRESS _____ CITY _____ STATE _____ ZIP ____

DATE OF BIRTH _____ LAST EMPLOYER _____

NAME OF UNION _____ LOCAL NO. _____

NAME, ADDRESS, RELATIONSHIP OF NEAREST RELATIVE:

_____
    Name   Address   Relationship

NAME, ADDRESS OF DOCTOR:

_____
    Name   Address   Phone

CHECK ONE:

1)   My total disability is due to my participation in the Armed Forces and is a service-oriented disability: _____ Yes _____ No

2)   My total disability is due to an industrial accident which occurred during my regular schedule: _____ Yes _____ No.

3)   I am presently receiving $_____ monthly compensation due to an industrial accident.

I have been continuously and totally disabled for a period of six months and am applying for Disability Retirement Benefits. I understand that I may be required to prove, by medical examination not more than twice a year, my continuous disability. I also agree to notify the Administrative Office of the Ward Retirement Fund of any change in my medical or employment status. The foregoing statements are true to the best of my knowledge. I understand that a false statement will disqualify me for disability benefits. I hereby authorize all physicians and hospitals to furnish the Ward Employer Retirement Fund all information in their possession with reference to my personal history and physical condition.

SIGNATURE OF EMPLOYEE (MEMBER) _____ DATE _____

Attached:

(a)   Letter from my doctor describing and certifying the effective date of my total and permanent disability.

(b)   Birth certificate or proof of birth date.

ADMINISTRATIVE USE ONLY

Past Service Credits _____ Current Service Credits _____ Total _____

Monthly Disability Benefits $ _____ Beginning _____

Administrative Office: BY _____ Date _____

APPROVED BY THE WARD EMPLOYER RETIREMENT FUND COMMITTEE

By _____ Date _____

By _____ Date _____

Figure I-32: APPLICATION FOR DISABILITY RETIREMENT

HOURLY TERMINATION CHECK LIST

NAME _____

FORWARDING ADDRESS _____

_____

DIVISION _____ DEPARTMENT _____

UNIT _____ DEPT. NO. _____ EMPLOYEE NO. _____

SUPERVISOR _____ TELEPHONE _____

EFFECTIVE TERMINATION DATE _____

VACATION PAY DUE	$ _____
SICK LEAVE ATTENDANCE PAY DUE	$ _____
CHANGE OF STATUS FORM	_____
TERMINATION INTERVIEW FORM	_____
VACATION CARD	_____
HISTORY CARD	_____
REVIEW REMINDER	_____
FOLDER	_____
LOCATOR CARD	_____
ADDRESS CARD	_____
CREDIT UNION	_____
CAFETERIA	_____
COMPANY STORE PURCHASES	_____
RETIREMENT PLANS	_____
INFORMATION CARD	_____
IDENTIFICATION CARD	_____
SECURITY CLEARANCE	_____
UNIFORMS	_____
IDENTIFICATION OR SECURITY BADGE	_____
_____	_____
_____	_____

TERMINATION INTERVIEW

DATE	_____
TIME	_____
BY (INTERVIEWER)	_____
CHECK(S)	_____

Figure I-33: HOURLY EMPLOYEE TERMINATION CHECKLIST

1. UNEMPLOYMENT NOTICE UC-61 (Rev. 10-77)	4. COMPANY NAME, STREET, TOWN, STATE and ZIP CODE	5. EMPLOYEE'S NAME
2. CONN. REGISTRATION NO.		6. EMPLOYEE'S SOCIAL SECURITY NO.
3. CLOCK NUMBER		7. DATE LAST WORKED / 8. RETURN TO WORK DATE (only if definite)

9. Did employee work sometime in each of the four calendar weeks prior to the week in which he last worked? YES ☐   NO ☐
If "NO," enter Saturday week ending dates of the last 5 weeks during which the employee worked for you during the two-month period prior to the Date Last Worked. (Work during any part of a week constitutes work during that week). If answer above is "YES" omit dates.

1. _____   2. _____
3. _____   4. _____   5. _____

10. REASON FOR UNEMPLOYMENT
1. ☐ Laid off for lack of work
2. ☐ Left work voluntarily
3. ☐ Discharged for repeated willful misconduct or felonious conduct
4. ☐ Discharged for willful misconduct
5. ☐ Other Reasons

11. WAGES — Wages for last week of work from Sunday to Date Last Worked (If less than full week) | No. of Hours | WAGES $

12. Will any payment be made or has any payment been made which is not wages for work actually performed? Yes ☐   No ☐

13. TYPE OF PAYMENT (If yes above)
1. Severance 2. Vacation
3. Holiday 4. Other

14. LAST DATE COVERED BY PAYMENT

TYPE	No. of Hours/Days Covered	AMOUNT	DATES COVERED

15. I certify that the information contained in this notice is true and correct.
Signature and title of Official   DATE   Office Use   Clmt. Stmt. Yes ☐

☐ REQUEST FOR UNEMPLOYMENT NOTICE — The bearer states that he was recently separated from your employ and that he did not receive an Unemployment Notice, Form UC—61, or that he subsequently lost or mislaid it. In order not to delay a decision on the validity of a claim for unemployment benefits which he has filed, we request that you complete the other side of this form and give it to the claimant now so that he may present it at our office.

IMPORTANT INSTRUCTIONS TO EMPLOYER

Fill out form clearly and completely showing your CORRECT CONNECTICUT REGISTRATION NUMBER and employee's CORRECT SOCIAL SECURITY NUMBER. An incorrect registration number may result in improper charges to your experience account. Give this copy to the separated worker at the time of separation regardless of the reason for separation. If this is impossible, this copy must be mailed to the worker's last known address. Do not send a copy to this agency.

WAGES FOR LESS THAN A FULL WEEK (Item 11)

Enter wages for work performed for the calendar week Sunday through Saturday which includes the last date worked if less than a full week. Do not delay issuing form if payroll records are not available; partial wages will be requested by our local office if claim is filed.

EXPLANATION OF PAYMENTS OTHER THAN WAGES (Item 12)

These cover separation wages, wages in lieu of notice, vacation pay, holiday pay, bonus or any other payment other than wages paid employee for work actually performed up to and including the last day worked. Employee's wages for the last week or weeks worked for you, payment for which was received subsequent to the date of separation, are not to be included.

CLOCK NO. (Optional)

For employers desiring clock no., store location, etc. on charge forms to assist in locating employee records. (Maximum 6 digits)

IMPORTANT INSTRUCTIONS TO EMPLOYEE

Check this form carefully. An improperly completed form may cause delay in the payment of unemployment benefits to you. The effective date of your claim depends upon the date YOU first report to the Unemployment Compensation Office. To protect your benefits you should report AS SOON AS POSSIBLE after being separated from your employer. Bring this form with you.
UC—61 (Rev. 10-77)

ADMINISTRATOR
Unemployment Compensation Act

Figure I-34: UNEMPLOYMENT NOTICE

WAGE STATEMENT

Policy No. .... Claim No. ....

Employer .... Electro-Methods, Inc. ....

Employee .... Henry Duda ....

Date of Acc. .... 07-25-79 .... Stopped Work ....

If Returned to Work: Date ....

WEEK NO.	WEEK ENDING	HRS. WORKED	RATE	TOTAL WAGE	WEEK NO.	WEEK ENDING	HRS. WORKED	RATE	TOTAL WAGE
1	7-28-79	30.00		173.25	14	4-28-79	55.20		329.70
2	7-21-79	40.00		231.00	15	4-21-79	55.20		329.70
3	7-14-79	50.00		288.75	16	4-14-79	38.00		278.25
4	7-07-79	45.20		313.95	17	4-7-79	45.20		250.95
5	6-30-79	10.00		57.75	18	3-31-79	58.20		353.33
6	6-23-79	50.00		288.75	19	3-24-79	58.00		351.75
7	6-16-79	50.00		288.75	20	3-17-79	50.00		288.75
8	6-9-79	55.00		328.13	21	3-10-79	55.00		328.13
9	6-2-79	45.00		312.38	22	3-3-79	58.00		351.75
10	5-26-79	48.00		273.00	23	2-24-79	55.00		328.13
11	5-19-79	55.00		328.13	24	2-17-79	55.00		312.50
12	5-12-79	50.00		288.75	25	2-10-79	55.20		314.00
13	5-5-79	38.00		215.25	26	2-3-79	58.60		339.50
								TOTAL	7,544.28

Was this employee given free rent, lodging, board, tips, bonus or other allowance in addition to the above earnings?

_____ If yes, state weekly value thereof $ _____

Describe: _____

I certify that the above is true and correct:

Signed this _____ day of _____ , 19 _____ _____
(Name of Employer)

By _____

Form 720-158 (Ed. 1/76) Printed in U.S.A.
(Replaces CX 12006 Ed. Jan. 56)

PLEASE RETURN PROMPTLY

Figure I-35: WAGE STATEMENT

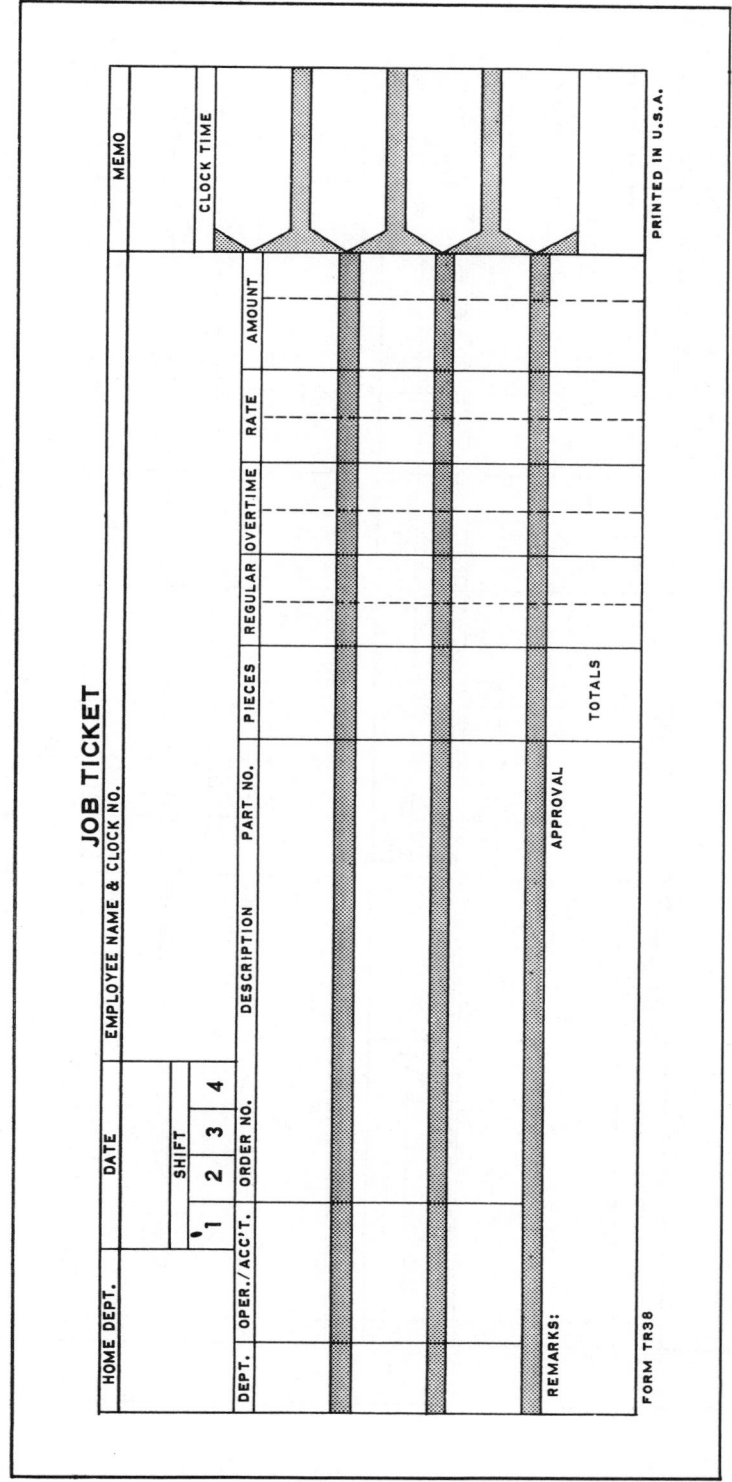

Figure I-36: JOB TICKET
(Courtesy of Regent Standard Forms, Inc., Bellmawr, New Jersey 08031.)

801

WEEKLY TIME AND DISTRIBUTION REPORT

EMPLOYEE NAME AND NUMBER

WEEK ENDING

JOB CLASS.

SHIFT √

| 1 | 2 | 3 |

PROJECT OR DEPT.

TYPE OF WORK

JOB NO. OR DESCRIPTION	ACCOUNT	SUB. ACCT.	HOURS WORKED BY DAYS							TOTAL HOURS	RATE	AMOUNT
			1	2	3	4	5	6	7			
1												
2												
3												

JOB NO. OR DESCRIPTION	ACCOUNT	SUB. ACCT.								T.O.T. HRS.	RATE	AMOUNT
			1	2	3	4	5	6	7			
4												
5												
6												

GROSS PAY

EMPLOYEE

SUPERVISOR	WEEK ENDING	PROJECT OR DEPT.	F.I.C.A.	WITH. TAX	A	B	C	D	E	NET PAY

FORM TR 58

PRINTED IN U.S.A.

Figure I-37: WEEKLY TIME AND DISTRIBUTION REPORT
(Courtesy of Regent Standard Forms, Inc., Bellmawr, New Jersey 08031.)

LABOR STATEMENT

_____ REFINERY   _____ PERIOD

MONTH					YEAR-TO-DATE			
				POUNDS RAWS MELTED				
				DAYS OPERATED				
				AVERAGE MELT PER DAY				
				DAYS IN PERIOD				
				AVERAGE MELT PER DAY				
MEN	PER 100 LBS. HOURS	PER 100 LBS. CENTS	AMOUNT	DEPARTMENT	MEN	PER 100 LBS. HOURS	PER 100 LBS. CENTS	AMOUNT
				1 RAW SUGAR WAREHOUSING				
				2 " " WEIGHERS & SAMPL'S				
				3 " " DUMPING				
				4 WASH BOX				
				5 RAW SUGAR CENTRIFUGALS				
				6 SWEETLAND PRESSES				
				7 VALLEZ PRESSES				
				8 KILNS & FILTERS				
				9 SUGAR BOILERS				
				10 REFINED SUGAR CENTRIFUGALS				
				11 GRANULATORS & BINS				

MEN	PER 100 LBS. HOURS	PER 100 LBS. CENTS	AMOUNT	DEPARTMENT	MEN	PER 100 LBS. HOURS	PER 100 LBS. CENTS	AMOUNT
				34 OFFICE EMPLOYEES				
				35 PERSONNEL & EMPLOYMENT				
				36 SUPTS. & ASSTS.				
				37 DRAFTSMEN				
				38 CHEMISTS & LABORATORY EMP.				
				39 PLANT ADMINISTRATION				
				GRAND TOTAL				

MEN	PER 100 LBS. HOURS	PER 100 LBS. CENTS	AMOUNT	DIVISIONS	MEN	PER 100 LBS. HOURS	PER 100 LBS. CENTS	AMOUNT
				REFINING				
				SHIPPING & WAREHOUSE REFINED				
				REPAIRS				
				PACKING BULK SUGARS				
				PACKING SMALL PACKAGES				
				GRAND TOTAL				

Figure I-38: LABOR STATEMENT
(From the book Corporate Treasurer's and Controller's Handbook by L. Doris, Editor. © 1950 renewed 1978 by L. Doris, Editor. Published by Prentice-Hall, Inc., Englewood Cliffs, New Jersey 07632.)

NAME			HOURS	TIME	Lot	Pieces	Lot	Pieces
Date	Clock No.							
S S	Account No.							
Bin No.	Part No.							
Day	Average	Unusual						
Night								
TOTAL PIECES								
				Total Hours				

Figure I-39: PRODUCTION AND JOB TIME FORM

PERFORMANCE REPORT

EMPLOYEE NAME		NUMBER	SHIFT	UNIT

DEPARTMENT	SUPERVISOR	LEVEL	DATE	RATING

PREVIOUS REPORT	ACTUAL HOURS	STANDARD HOURS	% UNIT PERFORMANCE	RATING

WEEK ENDING	ACTUAL HOURS	STANDARD HOURS	PCT. UNIT PERFORMANCE	WORK LOAD (UNITS)	COMMENTS
QUARTER TOTALS					
YEAR TO DATE					

Figure I-40: EMPLOYEE PERFORMANCE LEVEL REPORT

DEPARTMENT PERFORMANCE REPORT

Unit	Department	Supervisor	Date

Number Employees	Total Payroll $	Quarter	Percent Change	Previous Rating	Current Rating

WORK LOAD DATA

WORK LOAD DATA	NUMBER OF UNITS	WORK LOAD DATA	NUMBER OF UNITS
Number of Units Filed		Number of Sales Tickets	
Number Payroll Entries		Number of Statements	
Number Claims Processed			

CATEGORY	EMPLOYED	(+) OVER-TIME	VACA-TION	ABSENCES	OTHER	TOTAL ACTUAL	REQUIRED	EFFEC-TIVITY (%)	DOLLAR VARIANCE
Acctg. Clerks									
Book-keepers									
Sales									
File									
TOTALS									

Figure I-41: DEPARTMENT PERFORMANCE REPORT

806

ACCOUNTING FOR CONTROL, ANALYSIS, AND PROFITABILITY

SECTION J FORMS

Accounting for Control, Analysis, and Profitability

SECTION J

Accounting for Control, Analysis, and Profitability

In keeping with the dominant theme of this handbook, *cost control, profit analysis, and financial planning,* examples selected for this section continue to nourish these MONEY-SAVING, MONEY-MAKING, MONEY-PLANNING IDEAS. Forms in this section roughly fit into eight subgroups: (1) customer billing, sales and inventory control; (2) shipping and delivery; (3) accounts receivable and cash control; (4) miscellaneous, minor and travel expenses; (5) payroll and labor cost analysis; (6) financial statement analysis; (7) budgeting and source and use of funds analysis; (8) net worth and owners' equity computations.

The first subset of forms focuses on invoicing, customer billing, purchases, sales and inventory control. Beginning with a Customer Record Card (J-1) for each individual customer, a record is kept on the following; **J-1**

    (a)   customer name and address;
    (b)   credit terms and credit limit;
    (c)   customer account number and entry sheet number;
    (d)   space for special shipping, special requirements, etc.;
    (e)   date, item, whether debit or credit, and balance.

Similarly, a Client's Account Ledger (J-2), for professional services, underscores essentially the same data with additional space for check or charge number, and explanation of each transaction for future reference. **J-2**

A TIME-SAVING SYSTEM for professional offices, adaptable to other concerns as well, the Client Journal (J-3) reports on basic data found in the preceding forms (J-1, J-2), with additional details important to billing and profitability analysis. Note the "Special Billing Instructions" in the heading, for on-the-spot reference. All services rendered are carefully designated; time to a tenth of an hour is calculated for each employee or professional. The client is billed according to the hourly rate assigned to each task. As a **J-3**

J-4   further TIME SAVER, this information, instead of being transcribed directly into the journal, can be typed onto adhesive labels (J-4) for transfer to the journal on each labor entry required. Non-billable time is coded according to letters printed in the heading, and entered.

J-5   Pricing services and products invites frequent analysis and review. In the above instances, clients were billed according to time actually spent by each non-professional and professional working on a particular matter; but the issue of identifying the hourly rate was not raised. For materials, labor, and subcontract work, a Pricing Sheet (J-5) demonstrates another method for approaching the same problem.

J-6   Final pricing, of a good or service, depends neither on time nor on costs but on demand for that particular grade of service or good matched against the available supply of it. While some attorneys, for example, can wring barely $15 or $20 per hour out of a client, a few can persuade clients to pay them that much for only a few minutes of time. Similarly, a low-cost good may command exceedingly high prices, in a free market, while a high-cost good may be a low-profit item. Whatever the price and the PROFIT, a contract, whether for wedding photos (J-6) or computer services, lets the buyer know what the price will be and lets the seller PLAN FOR PROFITS.

J-7   Within the organization, a Purchase Requisition (J-7) encourages cost control and sound inventory management. A purchase order is issued (more on this in Section A), one copy
J-8   of which is transmitted to *cost accounting* (J-8), ever vigilant for cost and profit leaks. To
J-9   avoid double payment of sales tax, another cost and profit leak, a Resale Certificate (J-9) completed by the buyer of parts, merchandise, or labor service, is forwarded to the seller for his files. If the ordered parts and goods are not forthcoming, to minimize production
J-10   scheduling problems the buyer sends a Purchase Order Follow-Up (J-10). If the original purchase order has been made out in multiple copies, one goes to cost accounting (J-8), and another is retained for follow-up (J-10)—an efficient system that RAISES LABOR PRODUCTIVITY, SALARIES, AND PROFITS.

J-11   For a real TIME SAVER, a multipurpose form is used for invoicing, back orders, and commissions (J-11). Note, too, that both packing slip and invoice numbers are the same. Each part is numbered and described; unit price and amount are shown. Where a simpler
J-12   invoicing system suffices, the Speed Invoice (J-12) may be just the MONEY-SAVING ticket.

J-13   The next several forms relate to shipping, freight bills, bills of lading, merchandise claim, and delivery records. The Freight Bill (J-13) conveys the following:

(a)   information on the carrier of freight;
(b)   name and address of shipper;
(c)   the name and address of the consignee;
(d)   merchandise description: quantity, type, weight;

(e)   shipping rate and whether shipping charges are prepaid or collect;
(f)   signature acknowledging receipt of merchandise in good condition;
(g)   total amount due (payable within seven days).

The Shipping Order and Freight Bill (J-14) contains the same information as in the above form (J-13) with additional data on shipping instructions.	**J-14**
J-13

A *bill of lading,* a document used by railroad and motor carriers, acknowledges receipt of goods for transportation to a specified destination. A contract between the shipper and the carrier, it provides for proper delivery of goods under stipulated conditions and regulations. Bills of lading are usually prepared by the shipper on one of the types of blank forms illustrated, and at least in triplicate:

◆ Uniform Straight Bill of Lading (J-15). Notice the proviso that if the shipment is to be delivered to the consignee without recourse to the consignor, then either freight charges must be prepaid or merchandise will not be released without payment of freight costs.	**J-15**

◆ Straight Bill of Lading—Short Form (J-16). A straight bill of lading, made out to the consignee, is not negotiable under law.	**J-16**

◆ Uniform Order Bill of Lading (J-17). Order bills essentially are of two types: those made out to the order of the consignee; those made out to the order of the shipper, and endorsed either in blank or to a named consignee. This bill is used for domestic shipments only and has been adopted by carriers in Official, Southern, Western, and Illinois classification.	**J-17**

◆ Railroad Bill of Lading (J-18). Actually a uniform straight bill of lading used by railroads for domestic shipments, it is not negotiable.	**J-18**

◆ Motor Carrier's Bill of Lading (J-19). Similarly to above documents, this is used for domestic transport of goods.	**J-19**

Delivery in California requires a Weighmaster's Certificate of Weight and Measure (J-20), which certifies that described merchandise has been weighed, measured or counted by a Public Weighmaster. The weighmaster's signature is the official word on the accuracy of weight and content. Rather specific details appear on the vehicle, driver, commodity, and shipper.	**J-20**

On the Delivery Receipt for Air Freight (J-21) are the Airbill Number, delivery information and charges—prepaid or collect—plus other data found on the various bills of lading. The delivery receipt is part of the Airbill set. The *airbill* represents the contract between the shipper and the carrier; it is non-negotiable. (For an example of an Air Waybill, see G-42.) For all claims, except overcharges, the forwarder must receive complaints in writing within 240 days, and concealed damage must be reported within 14 days of receipt for nonperishables and two days for perishables. Air freight charges are based on actual or dimensional weight, whichever works out to be greater. Merchandise received, subject to inspection by the buyer, in unsuitable or incomplete condition or not measuring up to specifications, is subject to adjustment. The consignee files a Merchandise Claim (J-22) which shows the invoice number, date, and amount, and reference data on the merchandise.	**J-21**

J-22

Delivery records are important cost control documents. Receiving department control forms were illustrated earlier (Section A). The following two records refer to sales and delivery people outside of the business office, at the point of purchase or pick-up. The **J-23** Delivery Record (J-23) logs in the following:

    (a)   consignee and full address;
    (b)   weight and number of packages;
    (c)   whether C.O.D.;
    (d)   full signature of the person receiving the merchandise;
    (e)   data on the route, driver, vehicle, and carrier.

J-24 The other control delivery form (J-24) certifies fuel oil delivery. Actual delivery is controlled automatically as it leaves the tanker so that every gallon is accounted for. The beginning and ending meter readings are stamped on the delivery receipt. The customer must sign for the delivered fuel oil as a further check against employees and to forestall later complaints.

The next several forms focus on cash control and receivables. (For further forms on cash management, see Sections G and H.) It is important to have developed an adequate control system on cash handling (cash being interpreted as cash or checks). The Cash **J-25** Control Review (J-25) lists 15 questions for INTERNAL AUDIT of CASH CONTROL PROCEDURES. If you are omitting some steps in this procedure, and have profit leaks, perhaps this is the place to begin a reexamination of your office work flow, separation of responsibilities, and built-in safety checks.

J-26 The Cash Report (J-26), too, is a system for trailing funds between and within the office. The statement of condition condenses cash flow activities for the period. The rest of the form communicates individual cash receipt and cash disbursement items. The Duplicate **J-27** Deposit (J-27) on the left-hand side itemizes deposits in the usual way: bills, coins, and checks. The form also keeps tabs on the name of the firm from whom cash was received and which corresponding account was debited or credited. Accounts receivable and sales discounts are the two most usual categories; the third, right-hand column is for all other items, which summon individual explanations. Checks received are treated in the same manner as cash. Total cash and checks deposited must match accounts to which these sums correspond.

Similarly, accounts receivable are balanced against specific types of expenses and time, by employee, that apply to a specific job. In this instance, a different form emerges for **J-28** each customer (J-28). The staff member charges the customer for a specified number of hours translated into money amounts. All other expenses are itemized. The balance is billed to the customer, minus any credits.

J-29 Daily transactions are recorded in a Journal (J-29). This form applies to bank transactions, or, modified, fits other types of businesses. The left-hand side imparts account identification, viz., account number, abbreviated name, and current balance.

The next column, "Remarks," signals any special treatment of the account. Four columns post debits, another posts credits, and the last posts special charges. A summary of all transactions appears at the bottom of the journal.

International money transfers, usually handled through banks, command specific instructions for disposition of funds (J-30). But within the office, even petty cash receipts (J-31) and disbursements (J-32) mandate control against profit leaks. In some offices, petty cash is more than petty, inviting problems and losses. The Cash Control Review (J-25) pinpoints *petty cash control*. Question No. 7 asks whether petty cash funds are maintained at a reasonable level. The above forms (J-31, J-32) respond to Control Question No. 9. Other forms, here and elsewhere in this volume, correspond to other questions in the Control Review. Debit (J-33) and Credit (J-34) Tickets monitor general ledger account flows.

J-30
J-31
J-32

J-33
J-34

Like cash, expenses, too, must be watched and controlled. For example, long-distance telephone charges necessitate a Telephone Toll Call Record (J-35) not only to verify telephone bills but also to account for these costs. For bulk mail, of course, a Postage Record (J-36) of individual mail-outs would not make sense; however, for individual pieces requiring certification, or a significant quantity of correspondence—contracts, proposals, reports, etc.—to a single destination, the form provides a *record on costs* as it relates to specific accounts and on mail actually sent and when. These forms help to plug profit leaks and develop back-up records of calls made or mail sent that may be important in later disputes. Another *profit leak plugger,* the Travel Expense Report (J-37), should be a routine matter covered in cost control, and if not in cost control, then certainly in accounting for expenses for tax purposes.

J-35

J-36

J-37

Accounting for payroll and labor costs springs from an individual record of hours worked, gross earnings, and deductions withheld (J-38) for later forwarding to the appropriate taxing agency or other disposition. Good accounting suggests that the net amount paid and the check number should be disclosed for later verification. This form also calls for other information on the individual in the heading; while the next form (J-39), a similar record-keeping system, is a weekly payroll summary for all employees. Only individual names appear in the appropriate space with no other additional personal data on the employee as in the preceding individual payroll record (J-38).

J-38

J-39

The Payroll Summary Record (J-40) is a compendium of data drawn from the weekly report for monthly recapitulation by total amount, not by individual, and quarterly summaries. Data on the payroll check stub (J-41) should match that in the employee's records, and in the Payroll and Disbursements Journal (J-42). Finally, an analysis of employee work distribution will result in cost standards, or Distribution of Office Staff Hours (J-43), that help PINPOINT PROFIT LEAKS within the organization.

J-40

J-41
J-42

J-43

Whether for internal or external purposes, financial analysis begins with basic financial data for the current year and for several preceding years for comparative purposes. The

J-44   first set of data (J-44) covers the five most recent years of the base report:

◆ Page 1 of the consolidated report is a five-year comparative statement of the firm's financial condition, a list of its assets and liabilities, tangible net worth, and net working capital.

◆ Page 2 is a comparative income statement showing calculations of gross profit, operating profit, profit before taxes, and net profit, plus a reconciliation of net worth for the four most recent years.

◆ Page 3 is a four-year summary of changes in financial position—sources and uses of working capital—and changes in working capital analysis.

◆ Page 4 summarizes financial information, with a few basic liquidity and operating ratios and other pertinent facts. Notes on matters affecting the financial data appear at the bottom of the page.

J-45   The proximate two-page form (J-45) restates data from financial and income statements for the five-year period in percentages. Assets are stated as a percentage of total assets, liabilities, and capital, and net worth as a percentage of total liabilities and equity. All figures in the income statement are expressed in terms of net sales, with net sales being the base number.

J-46   The next analytical step is a Flow of Funds Analysis (J-46). The first page of this format treats four-year figures on operating inflows and outflows and trade and operations financing inflows and outflows. The second page, covering the same most recent four-year span, reports on external financing inflows and outflows and discretionary funds outflow, and gives a summary of changes and cash needs funded internally. The following

J-47   step is a Ratio Analysis (J-47). In the example, four categories of ratios are highlighted: liquidity, leverage, interest coverage, and operating performance.

J-48   Last is a Trend Analysis (J-48). We know where the firm has been. Now where is it going, financially? The underlying assumption is that tomorrow will change little from yesterday—sometimes a dangerous assumption to make (which is why people, not computers, make better final decisions). Some items analyzed are sales growth, cost of goods sold, receivables, inventories and other selected assets, accounts payable and tax liabilities, depreciation, dividend payouts, and income tax rate. Two figures appear: (1) an unweighted average of the past five years; (2) a weighted average which weights most recent years most heavily on the assumption that the near term future will be most like the recent past.

J-49   Budgeting funds always involve capital expenditures, but sometimes expenses, such as insurance, are overlooked. The Insurance Budget Report (J-49) covers casualty, fire and other destruction, and liability at all locations and on all equipment. Adequate insurance PROTECTS COMPANY ASSETS.

J-50   Budgeting focuses on uses of funds, but sources of funds, either internal or external, finance these uses. An examination of Sources and Uses of Funds (J-50) is important in profitability probes. Loans are one source, and as part of routine auditing, loan records are periodically verified (J-51). If overdraft loans are a source of short-term funds, the lending agency will maintain a Daily Trial Balance (J-52) of these transactions, accounting for loan balance and interest, tracking transactions and past due data, and noting credit limits and credit availability.

J-51
J-52

From the borrower's side, vigilance is kept on insurance coverage, loans, collateral pledged, and tax information. The Checklist for Internal Reporting (J-53) poses 15 pertinent questions on these matters, which invite not just a simple "yes" or "no" response but appended documents (or copies) which support the audit. Tax reports and payments may be followed with a Record for Corporate Returns and Declarations of Estimated Taxes (J-54); a separate page for each return and taxing authority chronicles the tax return from initial filing to amendments to examination.

J-53

J-54

The last three forms deal with equity. The first is a Reconciliation of Net Worth (J-55). Net worth reconciliation also appeared in the illustrated financial statement set (J-44, page 2). The second relates to computations and four-year summary of Stockholders' Equity plus financial reserves (J-56). The third is a Stockholders' Ledger (J-57), which records transfers of stockholders' equity, certificate numbers, and number of shares. Nonstock organizations, on the other hand, may have acquired nonprofit status.

J-55

J-56
J-57

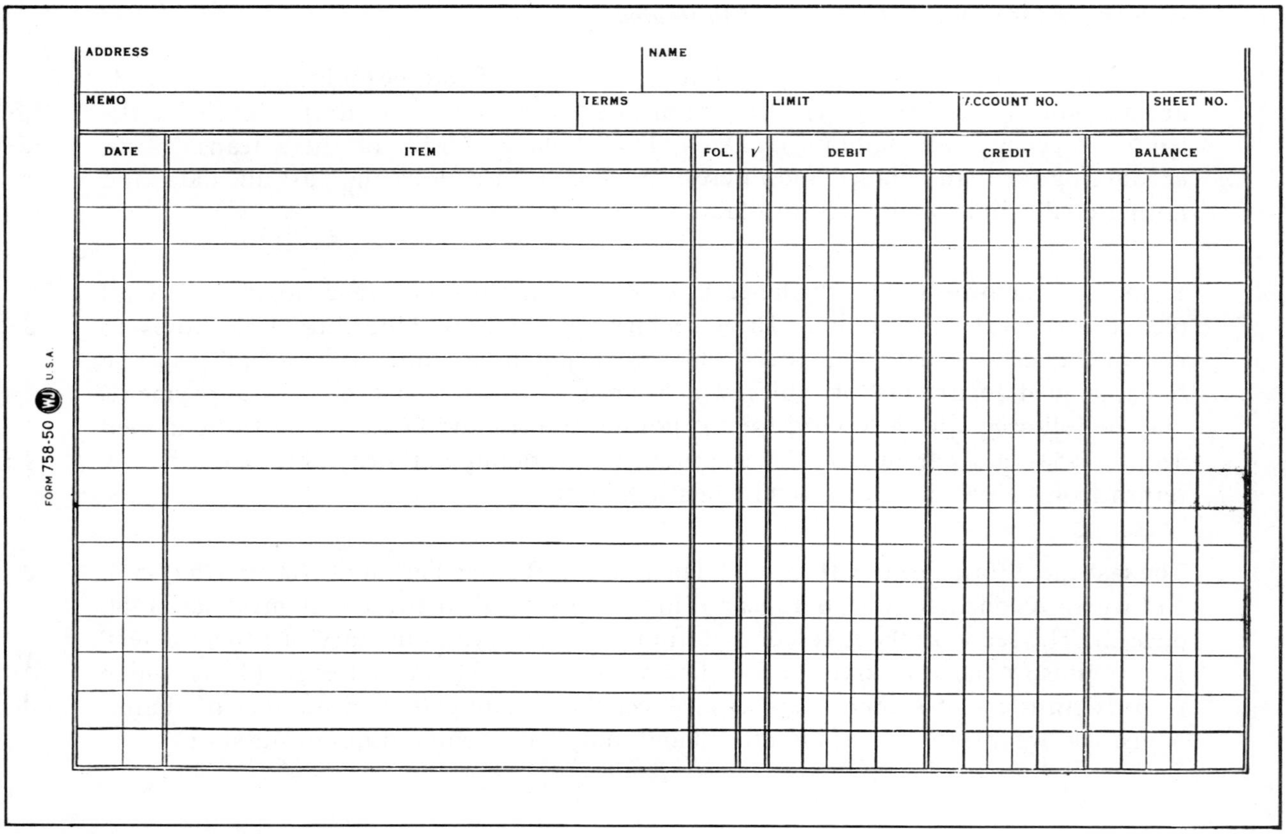

Figure J-1: CUSTOMER RECORD CARD

(Copyright by Wilson Jones Company. All rights reserved. Forms may be obtained, subject to supply, from Wilson Jones Company, 6150 Touhy Avenue, Chicago, Illinois 60648.)

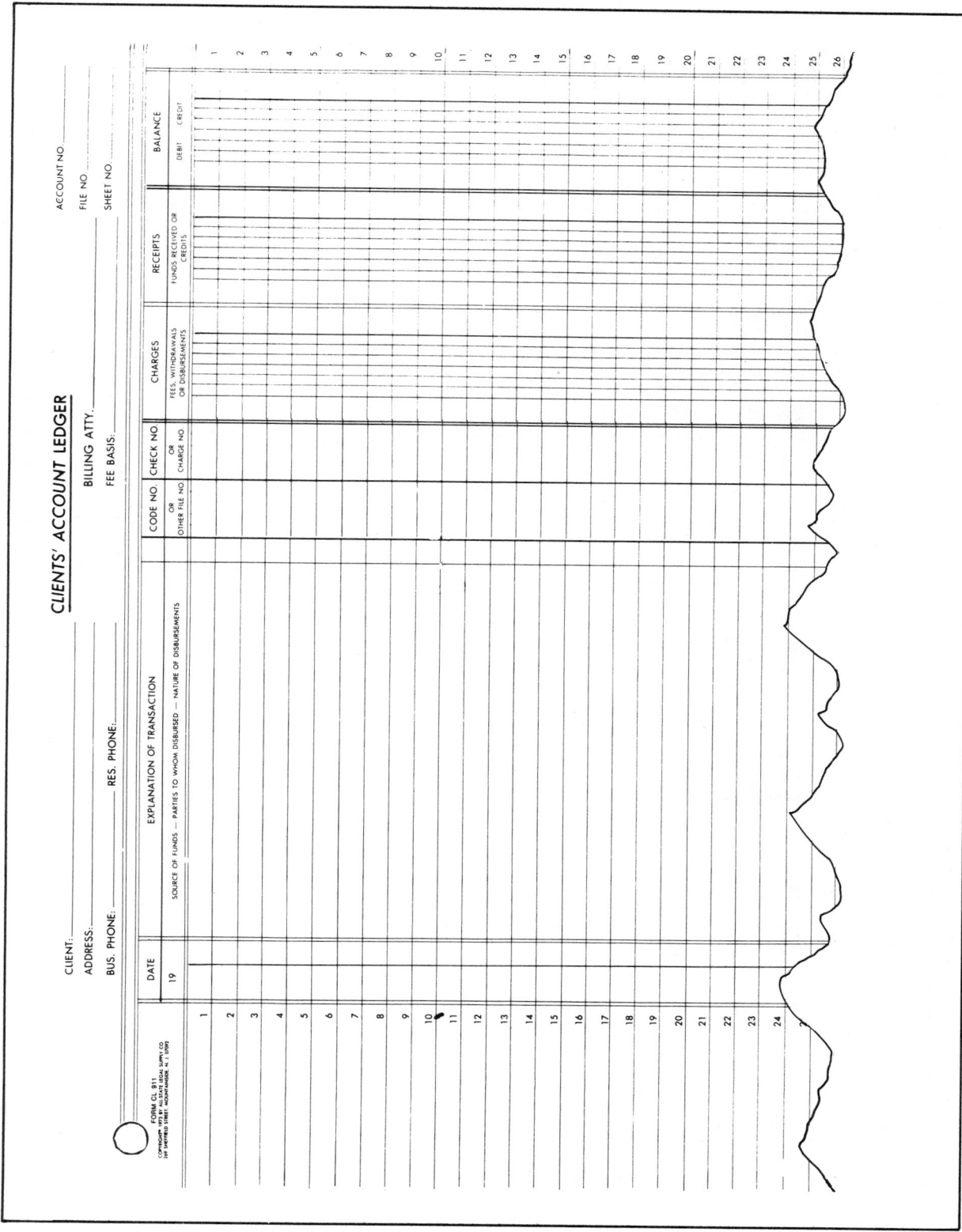

Figure J-2: CLIENTS' ACCOUNT LEDGER
(Copyright 1973 by All State Legal Supply Co., Mountainside, New Jersey 07092.)

819

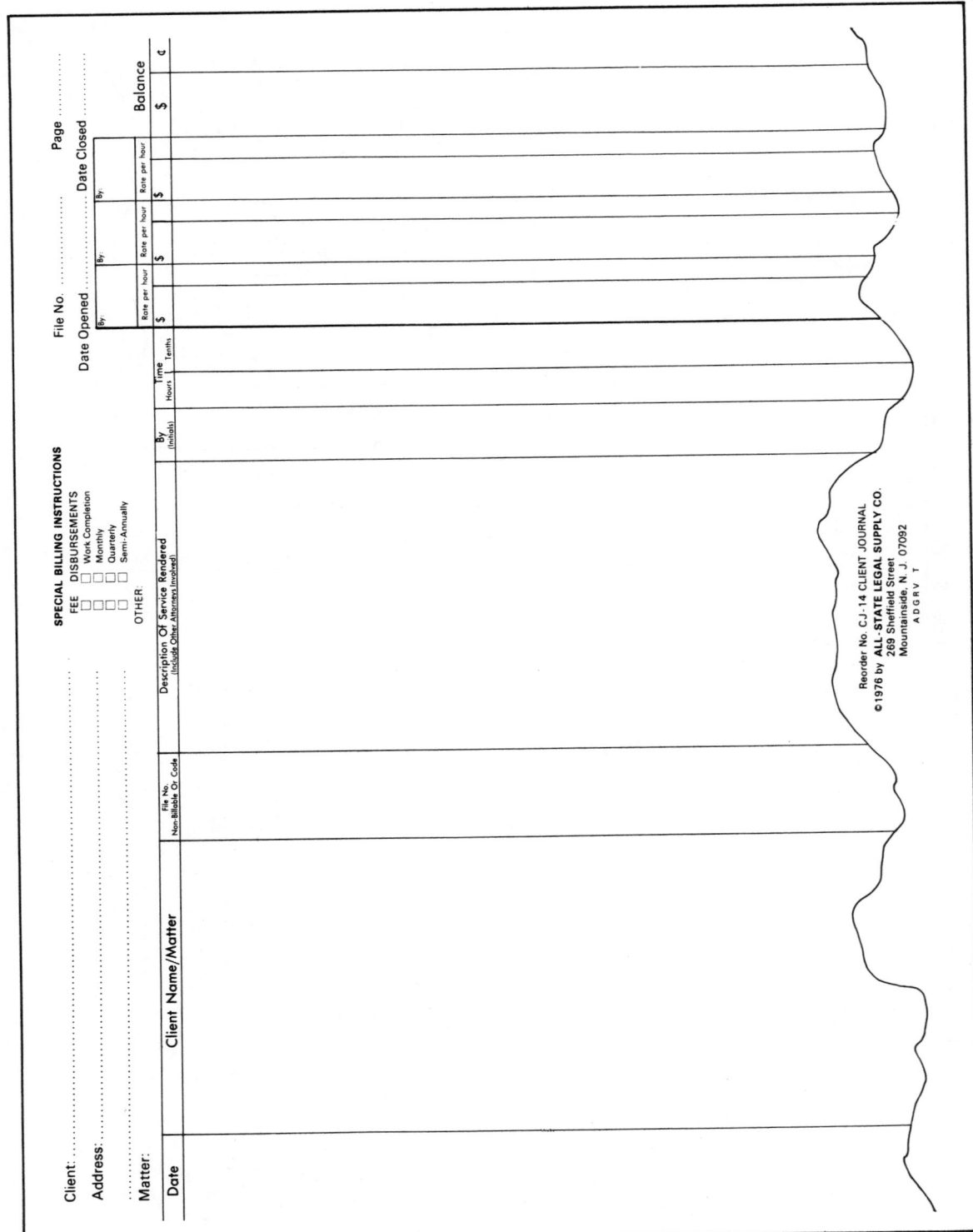

Figure J-3: CLIENT JOURNAL AND MICRO-RECORD OF SERVICES PERFORMED
(Copyright 1976 by All State Legal Supply Co., Mountainside, New Jersey 07092.)

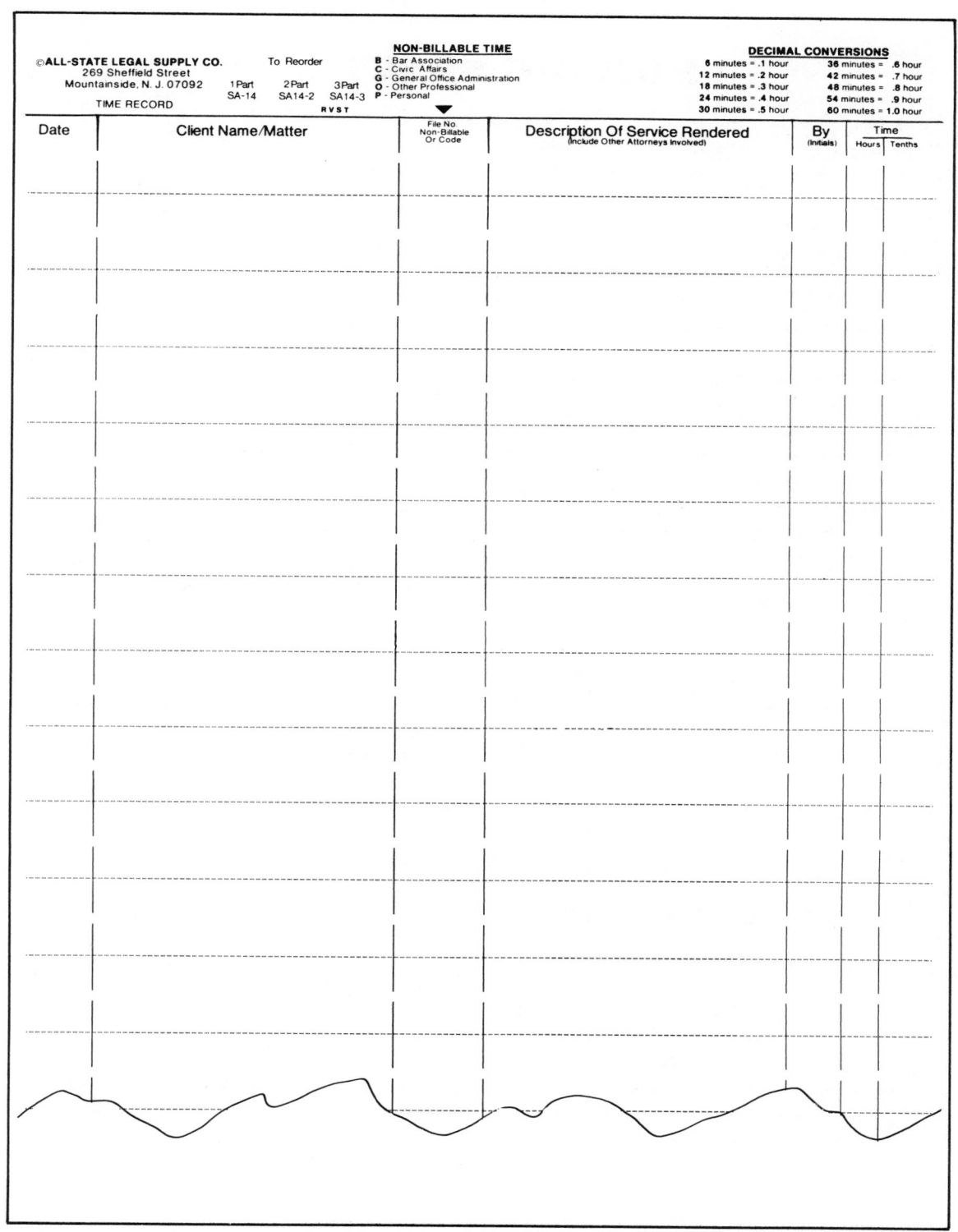

Figure J-4: INDIVIDUAL DESCRIPTION OF SERVICES PERFORMED AND NON-BILLABLE TIME
(Copyright by All State Legal Supply Co., Mountainside, New Jersey 07092.)

PRICING SHEET

PAGE NO._____ OF_____ PAGES

NAME		ARCH. OR CONTRACTOR		ESTIMATE NO.
LOCATION		TYPE OF WORK		
ESTIMATED BY	PRICED BY	EXTENDED BY	CHECKED BY	DATE

DESCRIPTION	QUAN.	@	MATERIAL	LABOR	SUB CONTRACT	EXTENSION
TOTALS						

FORM 365 REGENT STANDARD FORMS, INC. BELLMAWR, N.J. 08030

Figure J-5: PRICING SHEET
(Courtesy of Regent Standard Forms, Inc., Bellmawr, New Jersey 08031.)

Wedding Photography Contract

YOUR STUDIO NAME HERE
123 Main Street
YOUR TOWN, STATE and ZIP
Phone 123-4567

	DATE OF WEDDING	
BRIDE	GROOM	
STREET	STREET	
CITY	PHONE	CITY	PHONE
FUTURE ADDRESS			

	ADDRESS		TIME A.M. P.M.
PHOTOGRAPHER REPORT TO			
CEREMONY AT	ADDRESS		TIME A.M. P.M.
RECEPTION AT	ADDRESS		TIME A.M. P.M.
PRE-BRIDAL (DAY AND DATE)	TIME A.M. P.M.	LOCATION	
FORMALS (DAY AND DATE)	TIME A.M. P.M.	LOCATION	
NUMBER IN WEDDING PARTY	PARENTS ATTENDING		

STUDIO'S SERVICES TO INCLUDE

_____

_____

_____

_____

_____

_____

THE PAYMENTS NOTED BELOW ARE REQUIRED:

$ _____ ON ACCEPTANCE OF THIS CONTRACT

$ _____ DAYS BEFORE THE WEDDING

$ _____ ON RECEIPT OF PREVIEWS

$ _____ ON PLACEMENT OF FINAL ORDER

$ _____ BALANCE ON COMPLETION

$ _____ TOTAL CHARGES FOR SERVICES

IF THERE ARE ANY CHANGES IN THE SCHEDULE, NOTIFY US IMME-DIATELY. WE SUGGEST YOU CALL THE STUDIO ONE WEEK BEFORE THE WEDDING TO CONFIRM ALL ARRANGEMENTS.

- It is understood this studio is the exclusive official photographer, and others taking photographs will be permitted only at our discretion.
- No part of any order will be delivered until the balance is paid in full.
- The studio reserves the right to use negatives and/or reproductions for display, publication or other purposes. Negatives and previews remain the exclusive property of this studio.
- In the event of a postponement or cancellation of the wedding, the deposits paid are not refundable.
- The studio takes utmost care with respect to the exposure, development, and delivery of photographs. However, in the event the studio fails to comply with the terms of this contract, the studio's liability is limited to refund of deposits.

The terms of this contract are accepted by:

CLIENT _____ DATE _____

STUDIO _____ DATE _____

Thank You

Figure J-6: WEDDING PHOTOGRAPHY CONTRACT
(Available from New England Business Services, Inc., North Main Street, Groton, Massachusetts 01450; 1-800-225-6380.)

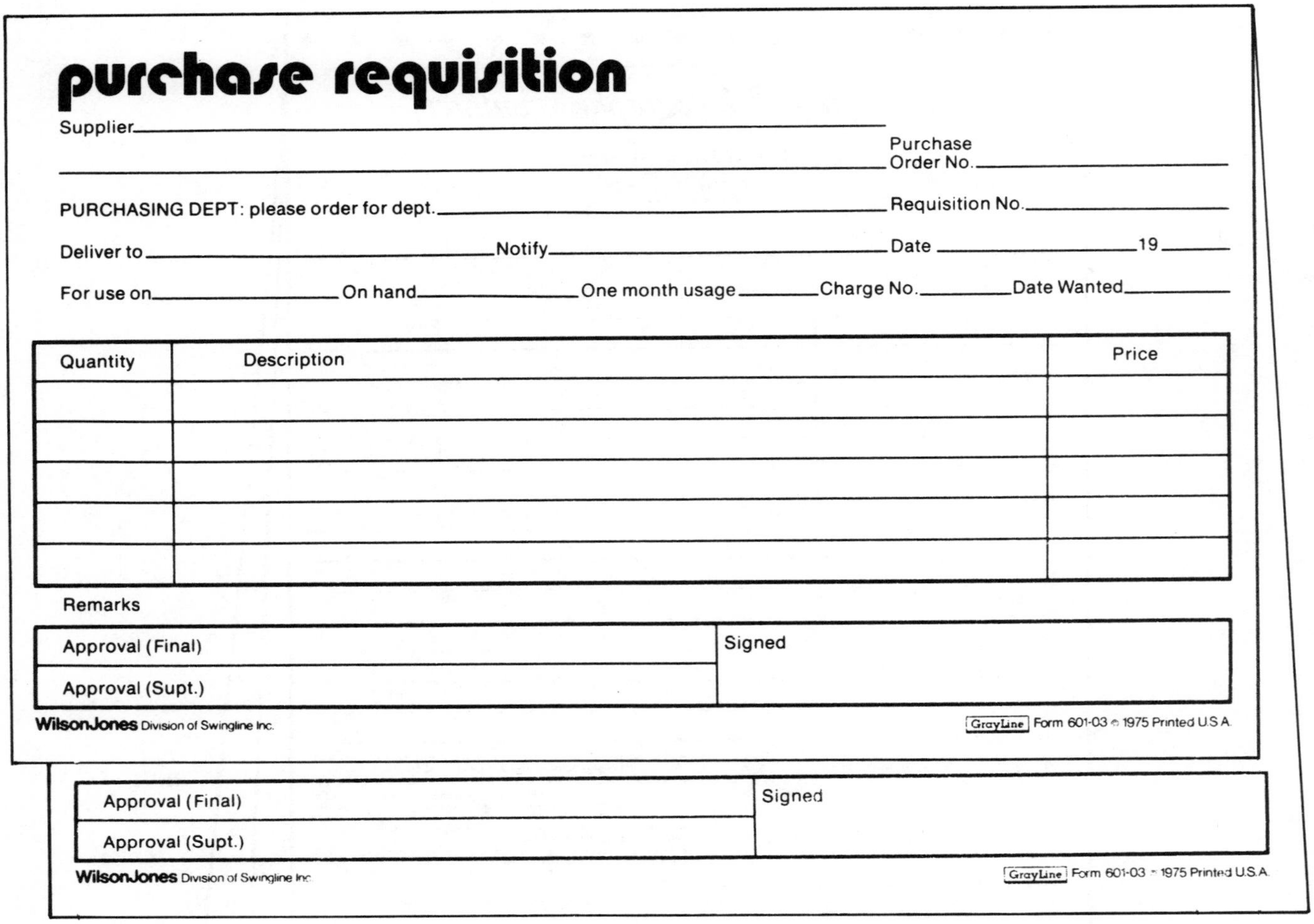

purchase requisition

Supplier_____

_____

PURCHASING DEPT: please order for dept._____

Deliver to_____Notify_____

For use on_____ On hand_____ One month usage_____ Charge No._____ Date Wanted_____

Purchase
Order No._____

Requisition No._____

Date _____ 19 _____

Quantity	Description	Price

Remarks

Approval (Final)	Signed
Approval (Supt.)	

WilsonJones Division of Swingline Inc.   GrayLine Form 601-03 © 1975 Printed U.S.A.

Approval (Final)	Signed
Approval (Supt.)	

WilsonJones Division of Swingline Inc.   GrayLine Form 601-03 © 1975 Printed U.S.A.

Figure J-7: PURCHASE REQUISITION
(Copyright 1975 by Wilson Jones Company. All rights reserved. Forms may be obtained, subject to supply, from Wilson Jones Company, 6150 Touhy Avenue, Chicago, Illinois 60648.)

ELECTRO-METHODS, INC.

P.O.BOX 54, 330 GOVERNORS HIGHWAY, SOUTH WINDSOR, CONN. 06074

TEL. (203) 289-8661
TWX (710) 425-6016

VENDOR •

PURCHASE ORDER

THIS NUMBER MUST APPEAR ON ALL INVOICES PACKING SLIPS PACKAGES AND CORRESPONDENCE RELATIVE TO THIS ORDER

CONN. STATE TAX EXEMPTION CERTIFICATE # 0658-559

THIS ORDER TAX EXEMPT: ☐ YES ☐ NO

DATE SHIPMENT REQUIRED AT ELECTRO-METHODS, INC.

NOTE •

PLEASE ENTER OUR ORDER FOR THE FOLLOWING, SUBJECT TO INSTRUCTIONS HEREIN AND ALL TERMS AND CONDITIONS PRINTED ON THE REVERSE SIDE:

DATE OF ORDER	REQUISITION NO	TERMS	F.O.B. SOUTH WINDSOR, CONN. OR	SHIP VIA	PREPAY ALL SHIPMENTS

ITEM	QUANTITY	PATTERN NO / PART NO	DESCRIPTION OF MATERIALS AND OR SERVICES TO BE SUPPLIED	PRICE

IMPORTANT INSTRUCTIONS:

1— PLEASE COMPLETE AND RETURN ACKNOWLEDGMENT PLY IMMEDIATELY CONFIRMING PRICE AND INDICATING EARLIEST SHIPPING DATE OF EACH ITEM.
2— RENDER INVOICES PROMPTLY AND IN TRIPLICATE.
3— THIS ORDER IS SUBJECT TO THE TERMS AND CONDITIONS PRINTED ON THE REVERSE SIDE HEREOF, AND NO EXCEPTIONS WILL BE ALLOWED WITHOUT WRITTEN PERMISSION OF THE PURCHASING DEPARTMENT.

ELECTRO-METHODS, INC.

COST ACCOUNTING

PURCHASING

Figure J-8: PURCHASE ORDER—COST ACCOUNTING
(Courtesy of Electro-Methods, Inc., South Windsor, Connecticut.)

STATE OF CONNECTICUT

Resale Certificate

I
WE HEREBY CERTIFY: That I we hold valid sellers permit No.................issued pursuant to the
Sales and Use Tax Act, that we are engaged in the business of selling

....

that the tangible personal property described herein we shall purchase from:

....

will be resold by me us in the form of tangible personal property; provided, however, that in the event any such
property is used for any purpose other than retention, demonstration, or display while holding it for sale in the
regular course of business, it is understood that I am we are required by the Sales and Use Tax Act to report and pay
tax, measured by the purchase price of such property.

   Description of property to be purchased:

....

....

....

Purchaser: ....

Address: ....

Dated:.................... 19........   By: ....

.... Connecticut

—PLIMPTON'S—

Figure J-9: RESALE CERTIFICATE
(Courtesy of Litton Office Product Centers.)

826

ELECTRO-METHODS, INC.

P.O. BOX 54, 330 GOVERNORS HIGHWAY, SOUTH WINDSOR, CONN. 06074

TEL. (203) 289-8661
TWX (710) 425-6016

ACKNOWLEDGED

SHIPMENT PROMISED

PURCHASE ORDER

THIS NUMBER MUST APPEAR ON ALL INVOICES, PACKING SLIPS, PACKAGES AND CORRESPONDENCE RELATIVE TO THIS ORDER.

CONN. STATE TAX EXEMPTION
CERTIFICATE # 0658-559

THIS ORDER TAX EXEMPT: ☐ YES ☐ NO

DATE SHIPMENT REQUIRED AT
ELECTRO-METHODS, INC.

PLEASE ENTER OUR ORDER FOR THE FOLLOWING, SUBJECT TO INSTRUCTIONS HEREIN AND ALL TERMS AND CONDITIONS PRINTED ON THE REVERSE SIDE:

DATE OF ORDER	REQUISITION NO.	TERMS	F.O.B. SOUTH WINDSOR, CONN. OR	SHIP VIA

ITEM	QUANTITY	PATTERN NO. / PART NO.	DESCRIPTION OF MATERIALS AND / OR SERVICES TO BE SUPPLIED	PRICE

DATE	FOLLOW-UP REMARKS	DATE	FOLLOW-UP REMARKS

PURCHASE ORDER FOLLOW-UP COPY

Figure J-10: PURCHASE ORDER FOLLOW-UP FORM
(Courtesy of Electro-Methods, Inc., South Windsor, Connecticut.)

827

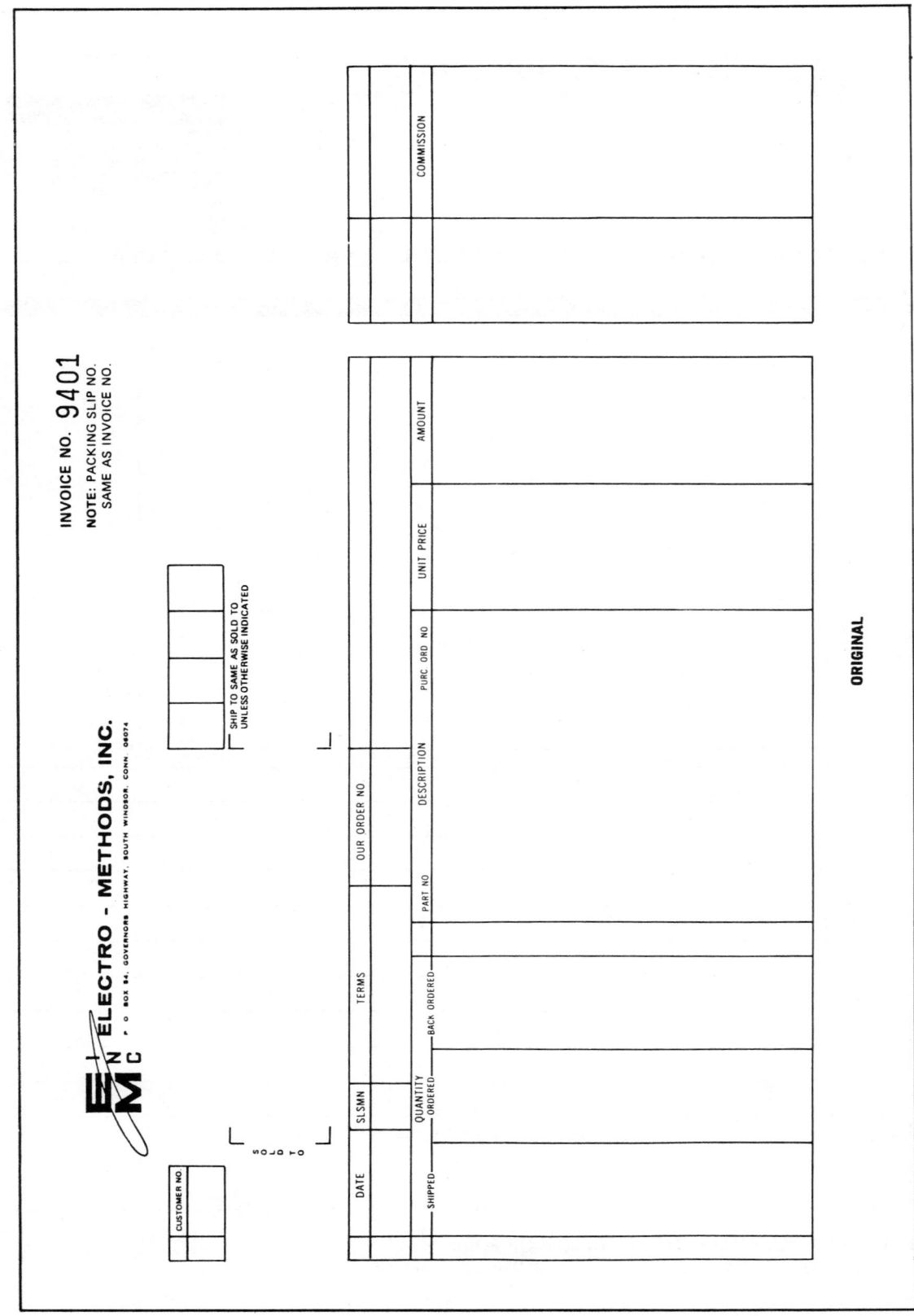

Figure J-11: INVOICE, BACK ORDER, AND COMMISSION FORM
(Courtesy of Electro-Methods, Inc., South Windsor, Connecticut.)

828

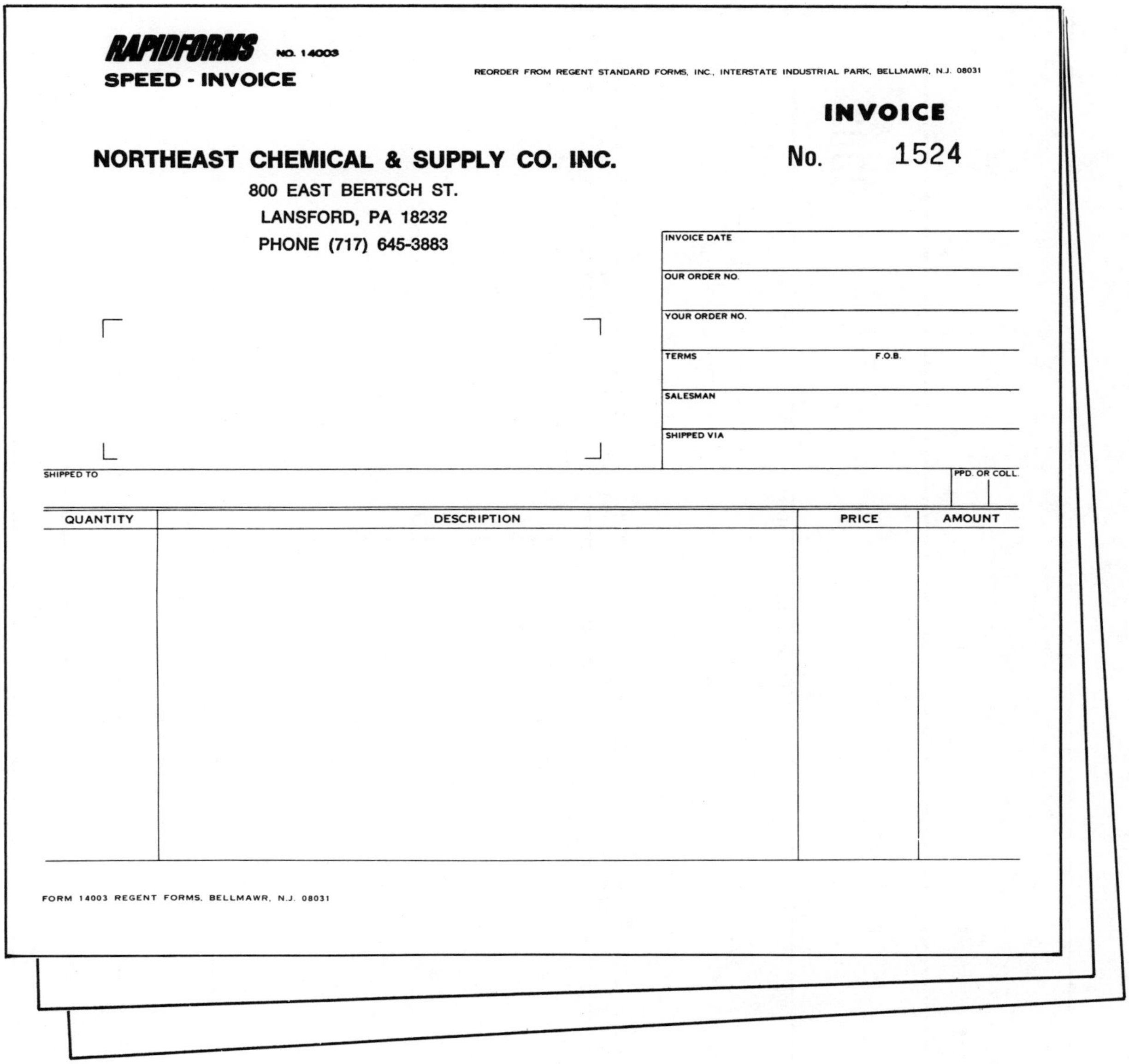

RAPIDFORMS NO. 14003

SPEED - INVOICE

REORDER FROM REGENT STANDARD FORMS, INC., INTERSTATE INDUSTRIAL PARK, BELLMAWR, N.J. 08031

INVOICE

NORTHEAST CHEMICAL & SUPPLY CO. INC.

No. 1524

800 EAST BERTSCH ST.

LANSFORD, PA 18232

PHONE (717) 645-3883

| INVOICE DATE |
| OUR ORDER NO. |
| YOUR ORDER NO. |
| TERMS | F.O.B. |
| SALESMAN |
| SHIPPED VIA |

SHIPPED TO | PPD. OR COLL.

QUANTITY	DESCRIPTION	PRICE	AMOUNT

FORM 14003 REGENT FORMS, BELLMAWR, N.J. 08031

Figure J-12: SPEED INVOICE
(Courtesy of Regent Standard Forms, Inc., Bellmawr, New Jersey 08031.)

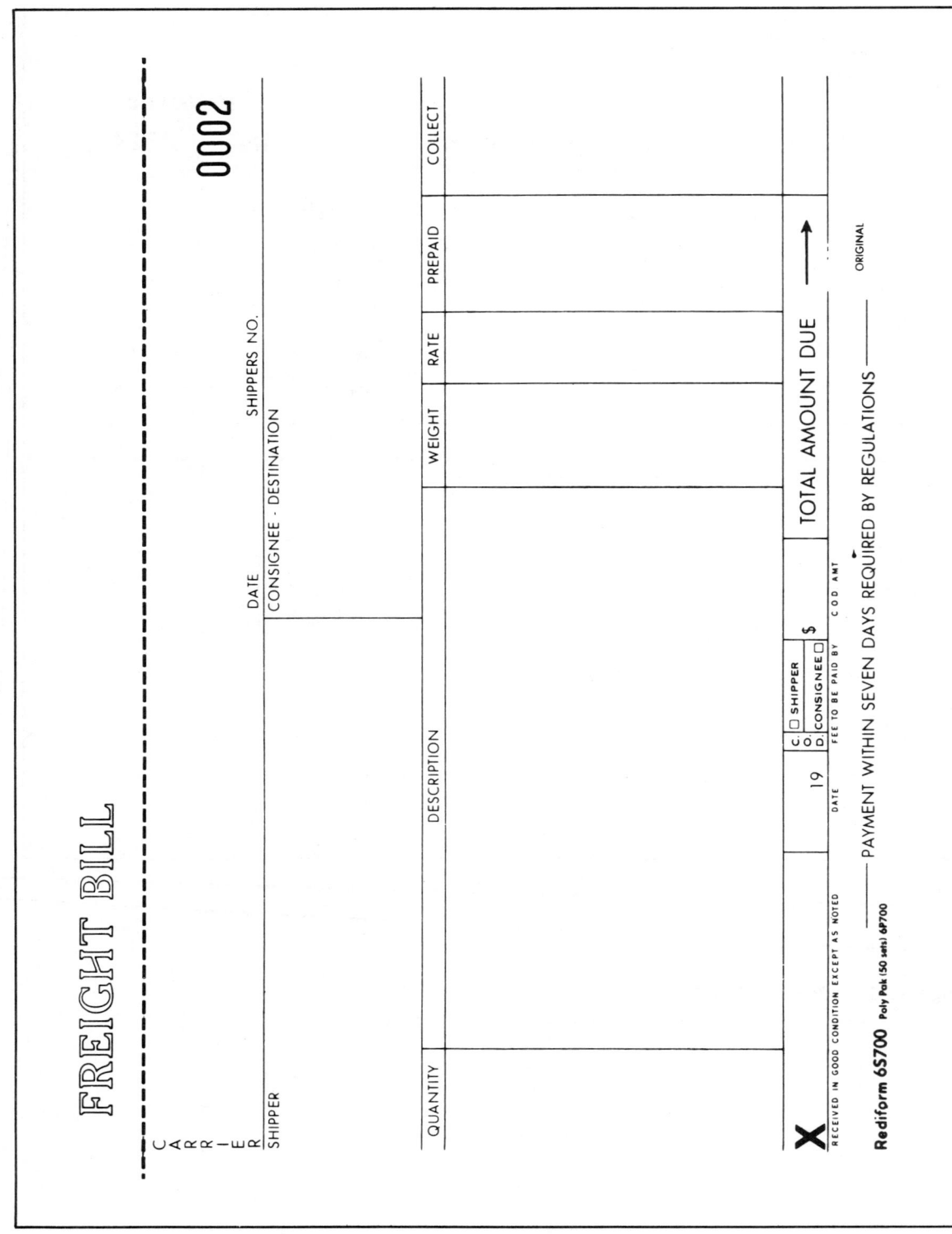

Figure J-13: FREIGHT BILL
(Courtesy of Rediform Office Products, Paramus, New Jersey 07652.)

830

ORIGINAL
Shipping Order and Freight Bill

No. **9885**

Carrier _____ Permit No. _____

Equip. No. _____ (Name must be same as shown on permit)
Carrying Capacity _____ Date _____ 19 ___

Point of Origin _____

Point of Destination _____

SHIPPER	CONSIGNEE
ADDRESS	ADDRESS
CITY	CITY

PKGS.	KIND	DESCRIPTION OF COMMODITIES	** WEIGHT	RATE	CHARGES

SHOW ALL NAMES IN FULL

SHIPPER

By

CARRIER:

Received in good condition except as noted
By Driver

CONSIGNEE:

Received in good condition except as noted
By

PAYMENT RECEIVED:
By

** Show each charge separately and what it represents. If other unit of charges, show per box, crate, bundle, bag, head, etc.

6H682 Rediform

ORIGIN
☐ TERMINAL STORE DOOR ☐
☐ AT RAILHEAD OFF RAILHEAD ☐

DESTINATION
☐ TERMINAL STORE DOOR ☐
☐ AT RAILHEAD OFF RAILHEAD ☐

ACCESSORIAL DOCUMENT NO.

AGREEMENT: ☐ Shipper's ☐ Receiver's
☐ TO LOAD ☐ TO UNLOAD ☐ Constructive Placement After 3:00 P.M.

Agreed By

C. O. D.	
C.O.D. Fee	
* Advances	
* Other Charges	
Prepaid	
Total To Collect	

Figure J-14: SHIPPING ORDER AND FREIGHT BILL
(Courtesy of Rediform Office Products, Paramus, New Jersey 07652.)

uniform b/l

0001

1st SHEET

(Uniform Domestic Straight Bill of Lading, adopted by Carriers in Official, Southern, Western and Illinois Classification Territories, March 15, 1922, as amended August 1, 1930, and June 15, 1941.)

UNIFORM STRAIGHT BILL OF LADING
ORIGINAL - NOT NEGOTIABLE

Shipper's No. _____

Agent's No. _____

RECEIVED, subject to the classifications and tariffs in effect on the date of the issue of this Bill of Lading,

at _____ 19 ____

from _____

the property described below, in apparent good order, except as noted (contents and condition of contents of packages unknown), marked, consigned, and destined as indicated below, which said company (the word company being understood throughout this contract as meaning any person or corporation in possession of the property under the contract) agrees to carry to its usual place of delivery at said destination, if on its own road or its own water line, otherwise to deliver to another carrier on the route to said destination. It is mutually agreed, as to each carrier of all or any of said property over all or any portion of said route to destination, and as to each party at any time interested in all or any of said property, that every service to be performed hereunder shall be subject to all the conditions not prohibited by law, whether printed or written, herein contained, including the conditions on back hereof, which are hereby agreed to by the shipper and accepted for himself and his assigns.

(Mail or street address of consignee - For purposes of notification only.)

Consigned to _____

Destination _____ State of _____ County of _____

Route _____

Delivering Carrier _____ Car Initial _____ Car No. _____

No. Packages	DESCRIPTION OF ARTICLES, SPECIAL MARKS, AND EXCEPTIONS	*WEIGHT (Subject to Correction)	CLASS OR RATE	CHECK COLUMN	
					Subject to Section 7 of conditions, if this shipment is to be delivered to the consignee without recourse on the consignor, the consignor shall sign the following statement:
					The carrier shall not make delivery of this shipment without payment of freight and all other lawful charges.
					_____ (Signature of Consignor.)
					If charges are to be prepaid, write or stamp here, "To be Prepaid."
					Received $_____ to apply in prepayment of the charges on the property described hereon.
					_____ Agent or Cashier.
					Per _____ (The signature here acknowledges only the amount prepaid.)

The requirements of General Order O.D.T. 18 have been complied with in the loading of this shipment, except as authorized by:

Charges advanced:

$ _____

*If the shipment moves between two ports by a carrier by water, the law requires that the bill of lading shall state whether it is "carrier's or shipper's weight."

NOTE - Where the rate is dependent on value, shippers are required to state specifically in writing the agreed or declared value of the property.

The agreed or declared value of the property is hereby specifically stated by the shipper to be not exceeding

per

_____ Shipper.

1

_____ Agent

Per _____

Per _____

Permanent postoffice address of shipper _____

(This Bill of Lading is to be signed by the shipper and agent of the carrier issuing same.)

Rediform 6S689

Poly Pak (50 sets) 6P689

Figure J-15: UNIFORM STRAIGHT BILL OF LADING
(Courtesy of Rediform Office Products, Paramus, New Jersey 07652.)

STRAIGHT BILL OF LADING—SHORT FORM—Original—Not Negotiable.

Shipper's No.

Carrier

Carrier's No.

RECEIVED, subject to the classifications and tariffs in effect on the date of the issue of this Bill of Lading,

at_____19____ from_____

the property described below, in apparent good order, except as noted (contents and condition of contents of packages unknown), marked, consigned, and destined as indicated below, which said carrier (the word carrier being understood throughout this contract as meaning any person or corporation in possession of the property under the contract) agrees to carry to its usual place of delivery at said destination, if on its route, otherwise to deliver to another carrier on the route to said destination. It is mutually agreed, as to each carrier of all or any of said property over all or any portion of said route to destination, and as to each party at any time interested in all or any of said property, that every service to be performed hereunder shall be subject to all the terms and conditions of the Uniform Domestic Straight Bill of Lading set forth (1) in Uniform Freight Classification in effect on the date hereof, if this is a rail or a rail-water shipment, or (2) in the applicable motor carrier classification or tariff if this is a motor carrier shipment.

Shipper hereby certifies that he is familiar with all the terms and conditions of the said bill of lading, including those on the back thereof, set forth in the classification or tariff which governs the transportation of this shipment, and the said terms and conditions are hereby agreed to by the shipper and accepted for himself and his assigns.

Consigned to_____

(Mail or street address of consignee—For purposes of notification only.)

Destination_____State_____County_____

Delivery Address ★_____
(★ To be filled in only when shipper desires and governing tariffs provide for delivery thereof.)

Route_____

Delivering Carrier   Car or Vehicle Initials   No.

No. Packages	Kind of Package, Description of Articles, Special Marks, and Exceptions	*Weight (Sub. to Cor.)	Class or Rate	Check Column	Subject to Section 7 of Conditions of applicable bill of lading, if this shipment is to be delivered to the consignee without recourse on the consignor, the consignor shall sign the following statement:
					The carrier shall not make delivery of this shipment without payment of freight and all other lawful charges.
					(Signature of Consignor.)
					If charges are to be prepaid, write or stamp here, "To Be Prepaid."
					Received $_____to apply in prepayment of the charges on the property described hereon.

*If the shipment moves between two ports by a carrier by water, the law requires that the bill of lading shall state whether it is "carrier's or shipper's weight."

NOTE—Where the rate is dependent on value, shippers are required to state specifically in writing the agreed or declared value of the property.

The agreed or declared value of the property is hereby specifically stated by the shipper to be not exceeding

_____ per _____

† "The fibre boxes used for this shipment conform to the specifications set forth in the box maker's certificate thereon, and all other requirements of Uniform Freight Classification."

† Shipper's imprint in lieu of stamp; not a part of bill of lading approved by the Interstate Commerce Commission.

Agent or Cashier

Per_____
(The signature here acknowledges only the amount prepaid.)

Charges Advanced:

$

Shipper, Per_____   _____Agent, Per_____

Permanent post-office address of shipper.

6S695 Rediform®

POLY PAK (50 SETS) 6P695

1

2

3

Figure J-16: STRAIGHT BILL OF LADING—SHORT FORM
(Courtesy of Rediform Office Products, Paramus, New Jersey 07652.)

THIS MEMORANDUM

THIS SHIPPING ORDER

(Uniform Domestic Order Bill of Lading adopted by Carriers in Official, Southern, Western and Illinois Classification territories, March 15, 1922, as amended August 1, 1930, and June 15, 1941.)

UNIFORM ORDER BILL OF LADING
(ORIGINAL)

Shipper's No._____

Agent's No._____

RECEIVED, subject to the classifications and tariffs in effect on the date of the issue of this Bill of Lading,

at_____ 19_____

from_____

the property described below, in apparent good order, except as noted (contents and condition of contents of packages unknown), marked, consigned, and destined as indicated below, which said company (the word company being understood throughout this contract as meaning any person or corporation in possession of the property under the contract) agrees to carry to its usual place of delivery at said destination, if on its own road or its own water line, otherwise to deliver to another carrier on the route to said destination. It is mutually agreed, as to each carrier of all or any of said property over all or any portion of said route to destination, and as to each party at any time interested in all or any of said property, that every service to be performed hereunder shall be subject to all the conditions not prohibited by law, whether printed or written, herein contained, including the conditions on back hereof, which are hereby agreed to by the shipper and accepted for himself and his assigns.

The surrender of this Original ORDER Bill of Lading properly indorsed shall be required before the delivery of the property. Inspection of property covered by this bill of lading will not be permitted unless provided by law or unless permission is indorsed on this original bill of lading or given in writing by the shipper.

(Mail or street address of consignee—For purposes of notification only.)

Consigned to ORDER of_____

Destination_____ State of_____ County of_____

Notify_____

At_____ State of_____ County of_____

Route_____

Delivering Carrier_____ Car Initial_____ Car No._____

NO. PACKAGES	DESCRIPTION OF ARTICLES, SPECIAL MARKS AND EXCEPTIONS	★ WEIGHT. (Subject to Correction)	CLASS OR RATE	CHECK COLUMN	
					Subject to Section 7 of conditions, if this shipment is to be delivered to the consignee without recourse on the consignor, the consignor shall sign the following statement:
					The carrier shall not make delivery of this shipment without payment of freight and all other lawful charges.
					(Signature of Consignor.)
					If charges are to be prepaid, write or stamp here, "To be Prepaid."
					Received $_____ to apply in prepayment of the charges on the property described hereon.
					Agent or Cashier
					Per_____ (The signature here acknowledges only the amount prepaid).

★ If the shipment moves between two ports by a carrier by water, the law requires that the bill of lading shall state whether it is "carrier's or shipper's weight."

NOTE—Where the rate is dependent on value, shippers are required to state specifically in writing the agreed or declared value of the property. **The agreed or declared value of the property is hereby specifically stated by the shipper to be not exceeding**

_____ per _____

Charges Advanced.

$_____

This is to certify that the above articles are properly described by name and are packed and marked and are in proper condition for transportation according to the regulations prescribed by the Interstate Commerce Commission.

The fibre boxes used for this shipment conform to the specifications set forth in the box maker's certificate thereon, and all other requirements of the Uniform Freight Classification.

1

_____ Shipper _____ Agent

Per_____ Per_____

Permanent post-office address of shipper:_____

6K 698 REDIFORM®

(This Bill of Lading is to be signed by the shipper and agent of the carrier issuing same.)

Figure J-17: UNIFORM ORDER BILL OF LADING
(Courtesy of Rediform Office Products, Paramus, New Jersey 07652.)

railroad b/l

1194 TRIP

(Uniform Domestic Straight Bill of Lading, Adopted by Carriers in Official, Southern, Western and Illinois Classification Territories, March 15, 1922, as amended August 1, 1930 and June 15, 1941.)

UNIFORM STRAIGHT BILL OF LADING   **Original—Not Negotiable**

Shipper's No. _____

Company   **Agent's No.** _____

RECEIVED, subject to the classifications and tariffs in effect on the date of the issue of this Bill of Lading, _____

at _____ 19____ from _____

the property described below, in apparent good order, except as noted (contents and condition of contents of packages unknown), marked, consigned, and destined as indicated below, which said company (the word company being understood throughout this contract as meaning any person or corporation in possession of the property under the contract) agrees to carry to its usual place of delivery at said destination, if on its own road or its own water line, otherwise to deliver to another carrier on the route to said destination. It is mutually agreed, as to each carrier of all or any of said property over all or any portion of said route to destination, and as to each party at any time interested in all or any of said property, that every service to be performed hereunder shall be subject to all the conditions not prohibited by law, whether printed or written, herein contained, including the conditions on back hereof, which are hereby agreed to by the shipper and accepted for himself and his assigns.

(Mail or street address of consignee—For purposes of notification only.)

Consigned to _____

Destination _____ State of _____ County of _____

Route _____

Delivering Carrier _____ Car Initial _____ Car No. _____

No. Packages	Description of Articles, Special Marks, and Exceptions	*Weight (Sub. to Cor.)	Class or Rate	Check Column	
					Subject to Section 7 of conditions, if this shipment is to be delivered to the consignee without recourse on the consignor, the consignor shall sign the following statement:
					The carrier shall not make delivery of this shipment without payment of freight and all other lawful charges.
					(Signature of Consignor)
					If charges are to be prepaid, write or stamp here, "To be Prepaid."
					Received $_____ to apply in prepayment of the charges on the property described hereon.
					Agent or Cashier

*If the shipment moves between two ports by a carrier by water, the law requires that the bill of lading shall state whether it is "carrier's or shipper's weight."

NOTE—Where the rate is dependent on value, shippers are required to state specifically in writing the agreed or declared value of the property. **The agreed or declared value of the property is hereby specifically stated by the shipper to be not exceeding**

_____ per _____

†"The fibre boxes used for this shipment conform to the specifications set forth in the box maker's certificate thereon, and all other requirements of Uniform Freight Classification."
†Shipper's imprint in lieu of stamp; not a part of bill of lading approved by the Interstate Commerce Commission.

Per _____
(The signature here acknowledges only the amount prepaid.)

Charges Advanced:

$_____

Shipper, Per _____ Agent, Per _____

Permanent post-office address of shipper. _____

Rediform®

6S 685

POLY PAK (50 SETS) 3P685

(This Bill of Lading is to be signed by the shipper and agent of the carrier issuing same.)

1

2

3

Figure J-18: RAILROAD BILL OF LADING
(Courtesy of Rediform Office Products, Paramus, New Jersey 07652.)

UNIFORM STRAIGHT BILL OF LADING **Original—Not Negotiable—Domestic**

Shipper's No.

Carrier _____ Agent's No. _____

RECEIVED, subject to the classifications and tariffs in effect on the date of the issue of this Bill of Lading.

at_____ 19_____ from_____

the property described below, in apparent good order, except as noted (contents and condition of contents of packages unknown) marked, consigned and destined as shown below, which said company (the word company being understood throughout this contract as meaning any person or corporation in possession of the property under the contract) agrees to carry to its usual place of delivery at said destination, if on its own railroad, water line, highway route or routes, or within the territory of its highway operations, otherwise to deliver to another carrier on the route to said destination. It is mutually agreed, as to each carrier of all or any of said property over all or any portion of said route to destination, and as to each party at any time interested in all or any of said property, that every service to be performed hereunder shall be subject to all the conditions not prohibited by law, whether printed or written, herein contained, including the conditions on back hereof, which are hereby agreed to by the shipper and accepted for himself and his assigns.

(Mail or street address of consignee—For purposes of notification only.)

Consigned to_____

Destination_____ Street_____ City_____ County_____ State

Routing_____

Delivering Carrier_____ Vehicle or Car Initial_____ No._____

Collect On Delivery

$_____ and remit to:_____

Street_____ City_____ State

No. Packages	Description of Articles, Special Marks, and Exceptions	*Weight (Sub. to Cor.)	Class or Rate	Check Column

C. O. D. charge to be paid by { Shipper ☐ Consignee ☐

Subject to Section 7 of conditions, if this shipment is to be delivered to the consignee without recourse on the consignor, the consignor shall sign the following statements:

The carrier shall not make delivery of this shipment without payment of freight and all other lawful charges.

_____ (Signature of Consignor.)

If charges are to be prepaid, write or stamp here, "To be Prepaid."

Received $_____ to apply to prepayment of the charges on the property described hereon.

_____ Agent or Cashier

Per_____ (The signature here acknowledges only the amount Prepaid.)

Charges Advanced:

*If the shipment moves between two ports by a carrier by water, the law requires that the bill of lading shall state whether it is "carrier's or shipper's weight." NOTE—Where the rate is dependent on value, shippers are required to state specifically in writing the agreed or declared value of the property.

The agreed or declared value of the property is hereby specifically stated by the shipper to be not exceeding _____ per _____

$_____

_____ Shipper, Per_____ _____ Agent, Per_____

Permanent post-office address of shipper.

Rediform®

6S 683

POLYPAK (50 SETS) 6P683

(This Bill of Lading is to be signed by the shipper and agent of the carrier issuing same.)

Figure J-19: DOMESTIC MOTOR CARRIER'S BILL OF LADING
(Courtesy of Rediform Office Products, Paramus, New Jersey 07652.)

STATE OF CALIFORNIA

DEPARTMENT OF FOOD AND AGRICULTURE

DIVISION OF MEASUREMENT STANDARDS

Weighmaster's Certificate of Weight and Measure

THIS IS TO CERTIFY, That the following described merchandise was weighed, measured or counted by a Public Weighmaster, and his signature is a recognized authority of accuracy, as prescribed by the California Business and Professions code, Division 5, Chapter 7.

DUPLICATE

5101

TRUCK LICENSE NO.

TRAILER LICENSE NO.

TRAILER LICENSE NO.

WEIGHING LOCATION

REMARKS

UNITS	COMMODITY	Weights		PRINT NAME OF PUBLIC WEIGHMASTER ABOVE ↑
		INITIAL GROSS		DATE
		GROSS	BY	DEPUTY
		TARE	BY	DEPUTY
MARK		NET	BY	DEPUTY
MERCHANDISE DELIVERED TO				
BUYER		ADDRESS		CARRIER
WEIGHED FOR				DRIVER'S NAME
SHIPPER OR SELLER		ADDRESS		

CHECK IF APPLICABLE: EARTH, STONE, SAND OR GRAVEL DRIVER ON ☐   OFF ☐   GROSS & TARE
FOR INTERSTATE HOUSEHOLD GOODS ONLY   DRIVER ON ☐   GROSS & TARE

6H-625 Rediform

STATE APPROVED 3-74

Figure J-20: CALIFORNIA WEIGHMASTER'S CERTIFICATE OF WEIGHT AND MEASURE
(Courtesy of Rediform Office Products, Paramus, New Jersey 07652.)

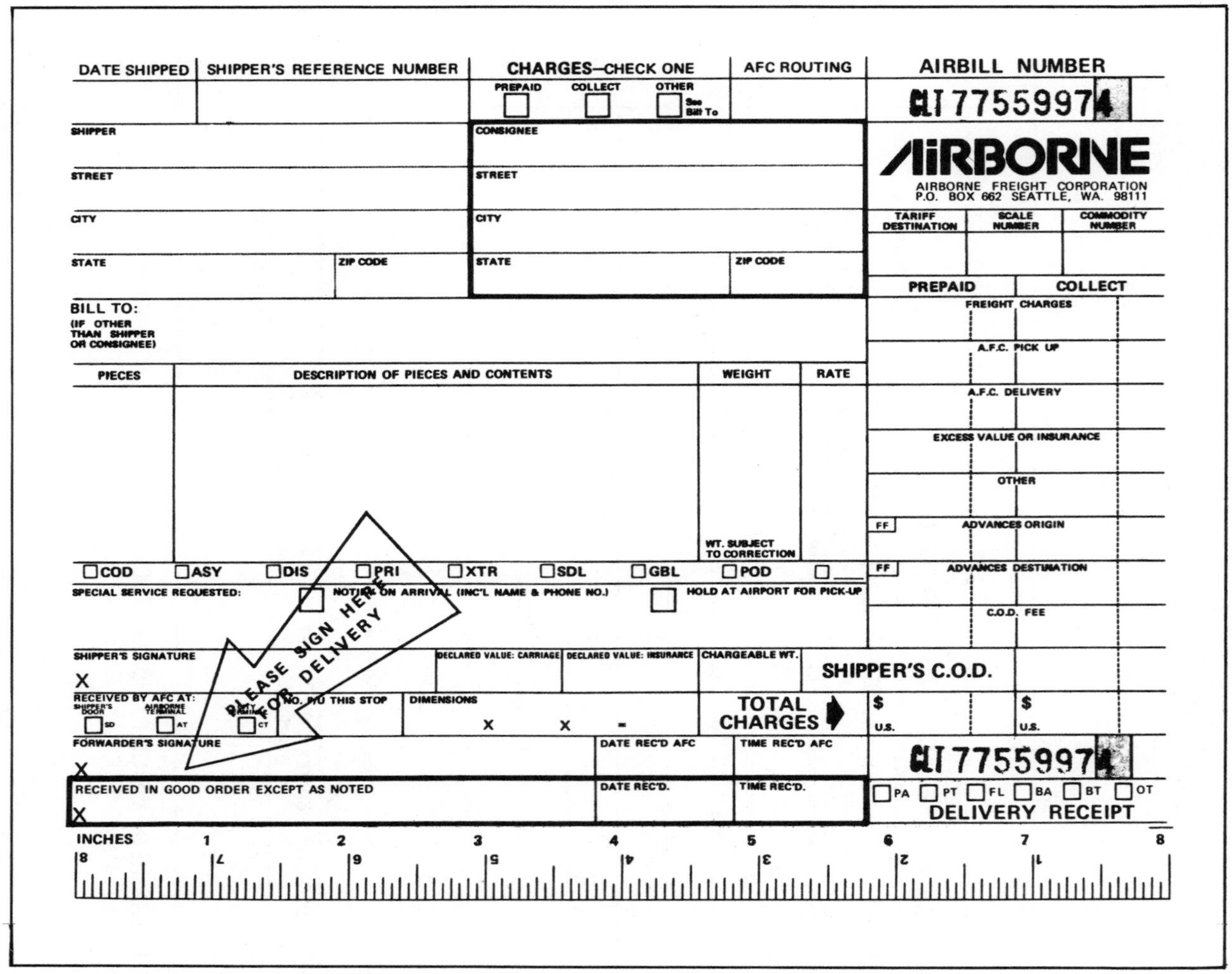

DATE SHIPPED | SHIPPER'S REFERENCE NUMBER | CHARGES—CHECK ONE | AFC ROUTING | AIRBILL NUMBER

PREPAID ☐ COLLECT ☐ OTHER ☐ See Bill To

CLI 77559974

SHIPPER | CONSIGNEE

STREET | STREET

CITY | CITY

STATE | ZIP CODE | STATE | ZIP CODE

AIRBORNE

AIRBORNE FREIGHT CORPORATION
P.O. BOX 662 SEATTLE, WA. 98111

TARIFF DESTINATION | SCALE NUMBER | COMMODITY NUMBER

BILL TO:
(IF OTHER THAN SHIPPER OR CONSIGNEE)

PREPAID | COLLECT

FREIGHT CHARGES

A.F.C. PICK UP

A.F.C. DELIVERY

EXCESS VALUE OR INSURANCE

OTHER

FF ADVANCES ORIGIN

FF ADVANCES DESTINATION

C.O.D. FEE

PIECES | DESCRIPTION OF PIECES AND CONTENTS | WEIGHT | RATE

WT. SUBJECT TO CORRECTION

☐COD ☐ASY ☐DIS ☐PRI ☐XTR ☐SDL ☐GBL ☐POD ☐___

SPECIAL SERVICE REQUESTED: ☐ NOTIFY ON ARRIVAL (INC'L NAME & PHONE NO.) ☐ HOLD AT AIRPORT FOR PICK-UP

PLEASE SIGN HERE FOR DELIVERY

SHIPPER'S SIGNATURE
X

DECLARED VALUE: CARRIAGE | DECLARED VALUE: INSURANCE | CHARGEABLE WT. | SHIPPER'S C.O.D.

RECEIVED BY AFC AT: SHIPPER'S DOOR ☐SD AIRBORNE TERMINAL ☐AT CITY TERMINAL ☐CT | NO. P/U THIS STOP | DIMENSIONS X X = | TOTAL CHARGES | $ U.S. | $ U.S.

FORWARDER'S SIGNATURE
X

DATE REC'D AFC | TIME REC'D AFC

CLI 77559974

RECEIVED IN GOOD ORDER EXCEPT AS NOTED
X

DATE REC'D. | TIME REC'D.

☐PA ☐PT ☐FL ☐BA ☐BT ☐OT

DELIVERY RECEIPT

INCHES 1 2 3 4 5 6 7 8

Figure J-21: DELIVERY RECEIPT FOR AIR FREIGHT
(Courtesy of Airborne Freight Corporation, Seattle, Washington.)

MERCHANDISE CLAIM

4759
PLEASE REFER TO ABOVE NUMBER WHEN CORRESPONDING

TO		DEPT.	DATE
STREET & NO.		INVOICE NO.	INVOICE DATE
CITY	STATE ZIP	AMOUNT OF INVOICE	

GENTLEMEN: WE MAKE CLAIM UPON YOU FOR THE FOLLOWING:

STOCK NO.	QUAN.	ITEM	PRICE	AMOUNT

DATE SHIPPED	PACKED BY	SHIPPED BY	TOTAL AMOUNT OF CLAIM ▶
REMARKS			

Rediform
3H 389

DATE APPROVED 19	BY	SIGNED

Figure J-22: MERCHANDISE CLAIM
(Courtesy of Rediform Office Products, Paramus, New Jersey 07652.)

DELIVERY RECORD

07008

FOR PICK-UP DELIVERY - MARK "PICK-UP" IN SALES MEMO COLUMN

REC'D FROM OR SHIPPER   ADDRESS   DATE

SALES MEMO	NAME	STREET NO.	STREET NAME	CITY (SPELL OUT IN FULL)	WGHT.	C.O.D.	NO. PKGS.		RECEIVED BY (FULL SIGNATURE)
								1	
								2	
								3	
								4	
								5	
								6	
								7	
								8	
								9	
								10	
								11	
								12	
								13	
								14	
								15	
								16	
								17	
								18	
								19	
								20	
								21	
								22	

ROUTE

TIME OUT / TIME IN   CARRIER   RECEIVED BY

EQUIP. NO.

DRIVER

| TOTAL WEIGHT | TOTAL TO COLLECT | TOTAL PACKAGES | FOR CARRIER |

6H 629 Rediform

Figure J-23: DELIVERY RECORD
(Courtesy of Rediform Office Products, Paramus, New Jersey 07652.)

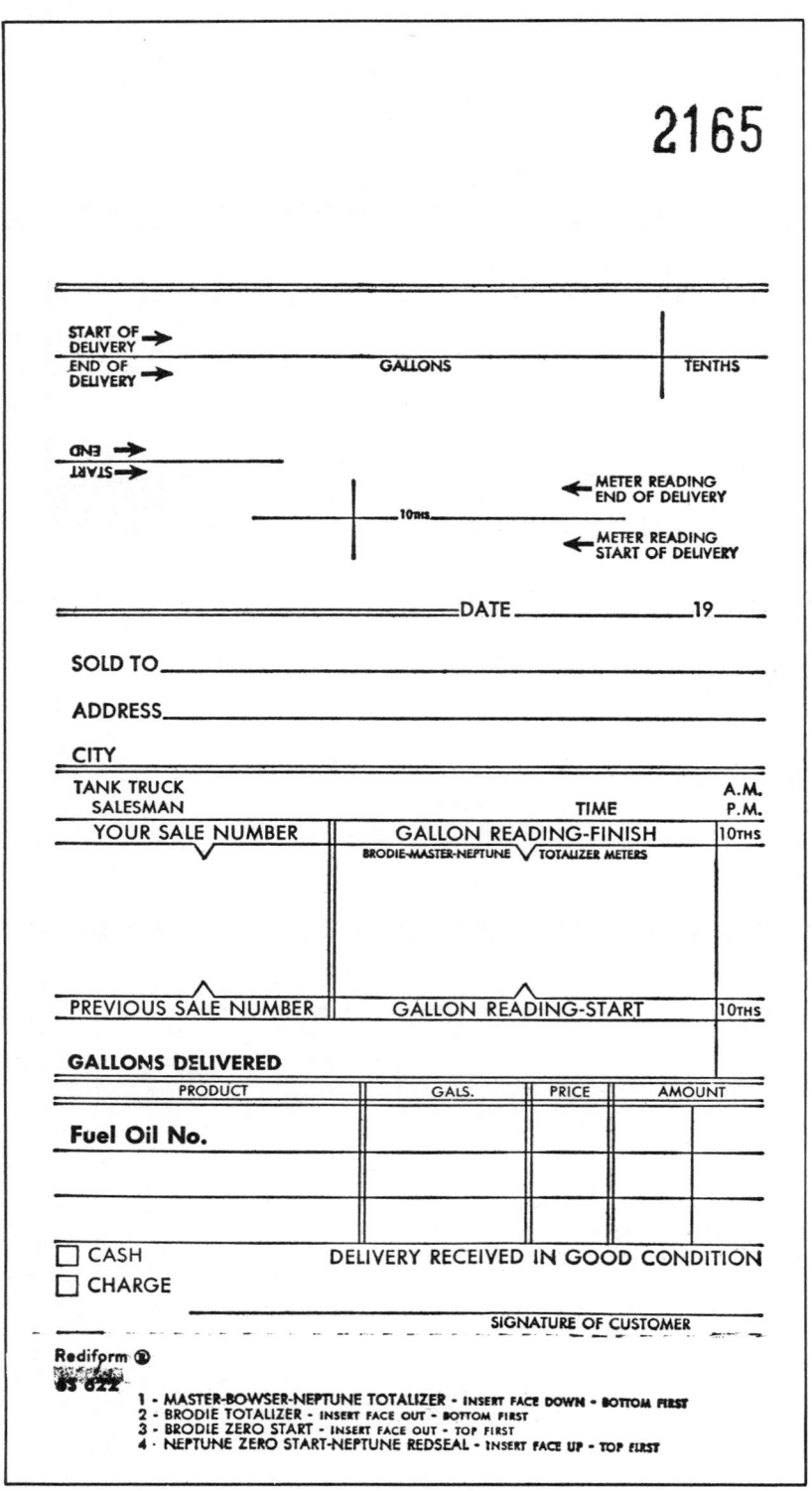

Figure J-24: FUEL OIL METERCHECK AND DELIVERY METHOD
(Courtesy of Rediform Office Products, Paramus, New Jersey 07652.)

CASH CONTROL REVIEW

Reviewed By _____ On _____

ATTACH RECOMMENDATIONS AND ANY SUPPORTING INFORMATION FOR LATER REVIEW.

Date of Last Review _____ By _____

1. Does person who opens mail list all checks and currency received before they are referred to Accounts Receivable? _____

2. Is this list used for or compared with cash receipts record? _____

3. Are receipts deposited in bank daily? _____

4. Are branch office collections deposited daily in local bank, subject only to withdrawal by corporate center? _____

5. Are transfers from one bank to another posted to general ledger accounts for cash or bank transfers? _____

6. Do the records provide a daily cash balance? _____

7. Are petty cash funds restricted to amounts reasonable and consistent with local operations? _____

8. Do disbursements in excess of a stated maximum require prior approval by officer or responsible person other than custodian of funds? _____

9. Are appropriate receipts, vouchers, or approvals obtained for all petty cash disbursements? _____

10. Are all checks prenumbered? _____

11. Are control procedures adequate for offices using a mechanical check signer? _____

12. Do supporting data accompany checks when checks are transmitted for signature? _____

13. Are supporting data canceled at time of payment to prevent subsequent misuse? _____

14. Is there a standard procedure for determining, before payment, that cash discounts allowable are taken? _____

15. Is accounting for cash and walk-in sales adequate? _____

Figure J-25: INTERNAL CHECKLIST FOR CASH CONTROL

C-P CASH REPORT

C-P

OFFICE CODE _____ (Office)
DATE

STATEMENT OF CONDITION		RECEIPTS (1)	DISBURSEMENTS (2)
14	Bank Balance		
15	Cash in Office		
16	ADV To Sub. Off		
19	Agents' Balances		
20	M.L. in Process		
21	ADV A/C Postage		
23			
24			
26	Notes (Inst. Bal.)		
27	ADV A/C Postage		
28	Total Debits		
29	Less Pending Items		
30	Net Due H.O.		
31	Previous Balance		
32	Transfer of Funds from H.O.		
32A			
33	Deposit to H.O. Account		
34	Adjusters' Drafts—Casualty		
	Adjusters' Drafts—Health		
	Adjusters' Drafts—Group-		
34A	Group Claim Credit Memos		
35			
36	CHECKS AND DRAFTS FOR DEPOSIT IN HOME OFFICE		
37	Premiums Life Other		
38	" Life		
39	" Health		
40	" U.S. COMMERCIAL — CANADA CASUALTY		
41	" PERSONAL — PROPERTY		
42	" Surety		
43	Comms.—Life		
44	" Health		
45	" U.S. COMMERCIAL — CANADA CASUALTY		
46	" PERSONAL — PROPERTY		
47	" Surety		
48	Comm. Pd. through Accrual		
49	Ben. Plan.—Agts. Remitt.		
50	Field Issued Checks—H.O. Acct.		
51	Tax and Other Withholdings		
52			

Figure J-26: C-P CASH REPORT
(Courtesy of The Travelers Insurance Company.)

J-26 (continued)

53	Installment Charges
54	Life Remittances
55	Cash Drawer Diff.
56	Agents' Diff.
57	Int. on Pol. Loans (Ded.)
58	Int. on Pol. Loans
59	Suspense Prem. Remitt.
60	
61	Direct Billing Diff.
62	Policy Loans
63	Policy Loan Repayments
64	Salaries
65	Expenses
66	
67	Scrip—Budget Plan
68	EMAP Agree.
69	Scrip—E.S.S.
70	
71	Advance Acct. Travel
72	Budget Plan—Cash Remit. Voucher
73	Div. to Policyholders
74	Real Estate Suspense
75	Budget Diff.—SDG
76	Mort. Loan Suspense
77	Data Center—Cash Remitt. Vo.
78	Adjusters' Drafts—Group—Illinois
79	Group Claim Credit Memos—Illinois
80	Undeliverable Checks
81	Deposit VO. R. R. Group Conv.
82	Cash Exchange Voucher
83	Cash Exchange Voucher—Canada
84	Modified ADP Comm.—Canada
85	Asgd. Risk Instlmt. Charges
86	Personal Lines Vouchers
87	Medicare Voucher
88	Direct Billing Diff. C-P
89	Multi Line ADP Comm.—U.S.
90	Presto Transfer Voucher
91	Premium Adjustment—LHFS
92	Commission Adjustment—LHFS
93	Casualty—Property Voucher
94	Life Voucher
95	Data Center Voucher
96	ADV. To AGTS-Career Life
97	ADV. To AGTS-Pers. Lines-Indy Co.
98	P.L. CPS Claim Credits
99	TOTALS

M-3151-1 REV. 6-78 PRINTED IN U.S.A.

ELECTRO-METHODS, INC.

SHEET No. 1952

Date

C.R.

DUPLICATE DEPOSIT

THE CONNECTICUT BANK
AND TRUST COMPANY
ROCKVILLE, CONNECTICUT

DR.

	DOLLARS	CENTS
BILLS		
COINS		
TOTALS		

NAME

CASH

SUB TOTALS

CHECKS

CR.
ACCOUNTS
RECEIVABLE

DOLLARS	CENTS

DR.
SALES DISCOUNTS

DOLLARS	CENTS

CR.
OTHER EXPLAIN

EXPLAIN	DOLLARS	CENTS

Figure J-27: DUPLICATE DEPOSIT
(Courtesy of Electro-Methods, Inc., South Windsor, Connecticut.)

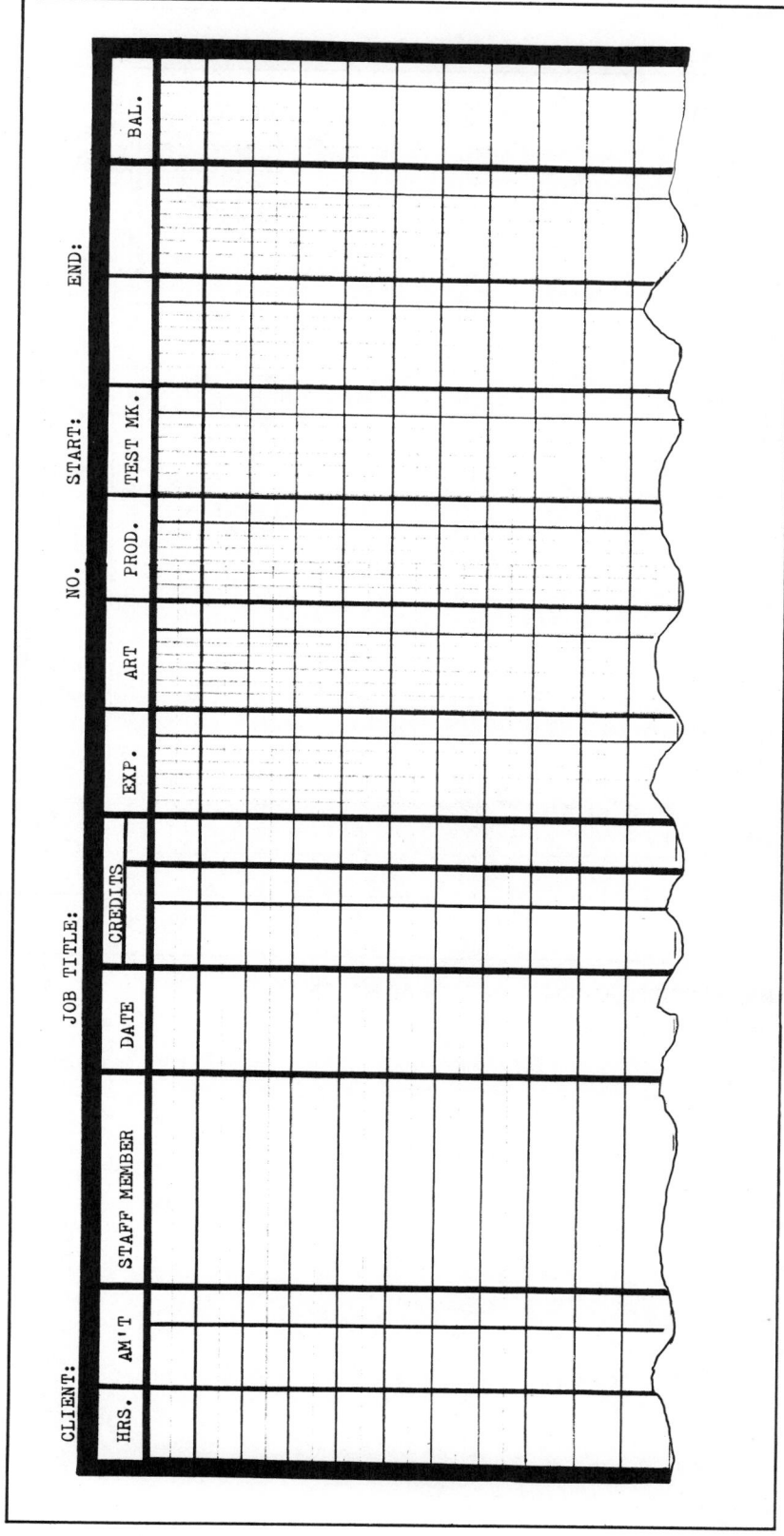

Figure J-28: COMBINATION COST AND ACCOUNTS RECEIVABLE SHEET

845

ACCT. TYPE _____

DAILY TRANSACTION JOURNAL AND TRIAL BALANCE

DATE _____

ACCOUNT IDENTIFICATION			REMARKS		DEBITS								CREDITS			SERV. CHG.	
ACCOUNT NUMBER	ABBREVIATED NAME	CURRENT BALANCE	STATUS FLAGS & HOLD FUNDS	Code	DEBIT	Code	DEBIT	Code	DEBIT	Code	DEBIT		Code	AMOUNT LAST DEPOSIT	DATE OF LAST DEP. MO DAY YR	GROSS AMT.	DATE LAST ACTIVE

DEBIT
30 (DM) DEBIT MEMO
31 (PC) ERROR CORRECT PRIOR STMT
32 (NSF) NON-SUFF FUND FEE
33 (SC) SERV CHG
34 (MS) MISC CHG
35 (LS) LIST TOTAL
36 (CT) CERT CHECK
37 (DC) DEF CORRECT
38 (RT) DEF D ITEM RET
39 (EC) ERROR CORRECT

CREDIT
50 CASH DEP
41 (PC) ERROR CORRECT PRIOR STMT
47 (DC) DEF CORRECT
48 (RV) REV ITEM NSF
49 (EC) ERROR CORRECT

BRANCH

STATUS FLAGS
D DORMANT
S STOP PAY
N NO POST

ACCT. TYPE
1 BUSINESS
2 PERSONAL
3 BUDGET

NO. OF ACCTS. CONTROL	OLD LEDGER BALANCE	NO. OF DEBITS	AMOUNT OF DEBITS	NO. OF CREDITS	AMOUNT OF CREDITS	NO. OF NSF CHECKS	AMOUNT OF NSF CHECKS	NO. OF UNP DEBITS	AMOUNT OF UNPOSTABLE DEBITS	NO. OF UNP CREDITS	AMOUNT OF UNPOSTABLE CREDITS	TOTAL SERVICE CHARGE	TOTAL NSF CHECK CHG.	TOTAL AMOUNT OVERDRAFT	NEW LEDGER BALANCE

Figure J-29: DAILY TRANSACTION JOURNAL AND TRIAL BALANCE
(Courtesy of Burroughs Corporation Office Products Group/Business Forms Division.)

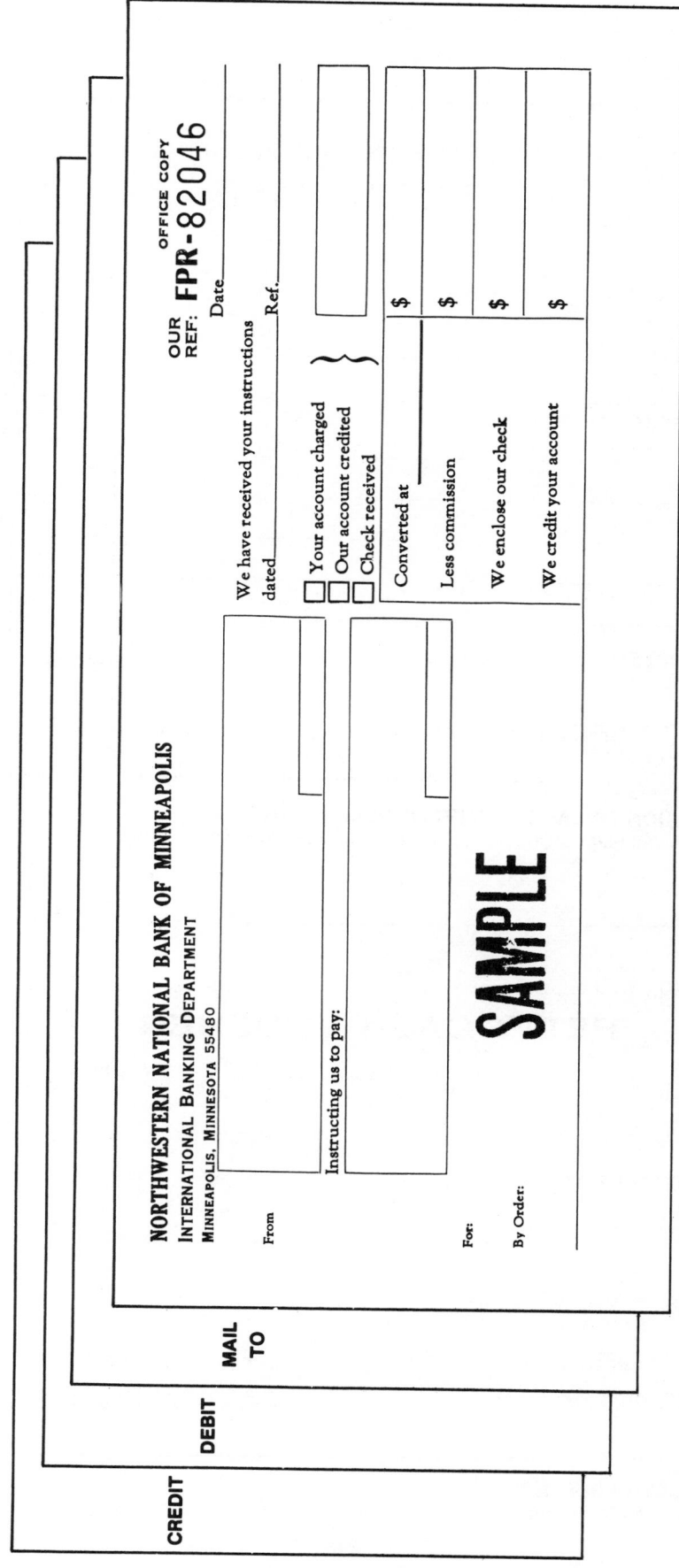

Figure J-30: BANK INSTRUCTION ON INTERNATIONAL TRANSACTION
(Courtesy of Northwestern National Bank of Minneapolis.)

847

PC 1—PETTY CASH VOUCHER

REQUISITION FOR AND RECEIPT OF

PETTY CASH

______________ 19 ____

NAME ______________________________

CHARGE TO ______________________ ________ FILE NO.

MATTER ______________________________

PURPOSE	EXPENSE	

DATE POSTED ______________ TOTAL $ ______

______________ APPROVED BY

______________ RECEIVED BY

Figure J-31: REQUISITION FOR AND RECEIPT OF PETTY CASH
(Copyright 1976 by All State Legal Supply Co., Mountainside, New Jersey 07092.)

FILE NO. .... AMOUNT $ ....

PETTY CASH VOUCHER

.... 19 ....

CLIENT ....

CHARGEABLE TO ....

FOR ....

....

.... *APPROVED BY*

.... *RECEIVED PAYMENT*

PC 2 - PETTY CASH VOUCHER

Figure J-32: PETTY CASH VOUCHER
(Copyright 1976 by All State Legal Supply Co., Mountainside, New Jersey 07092.)

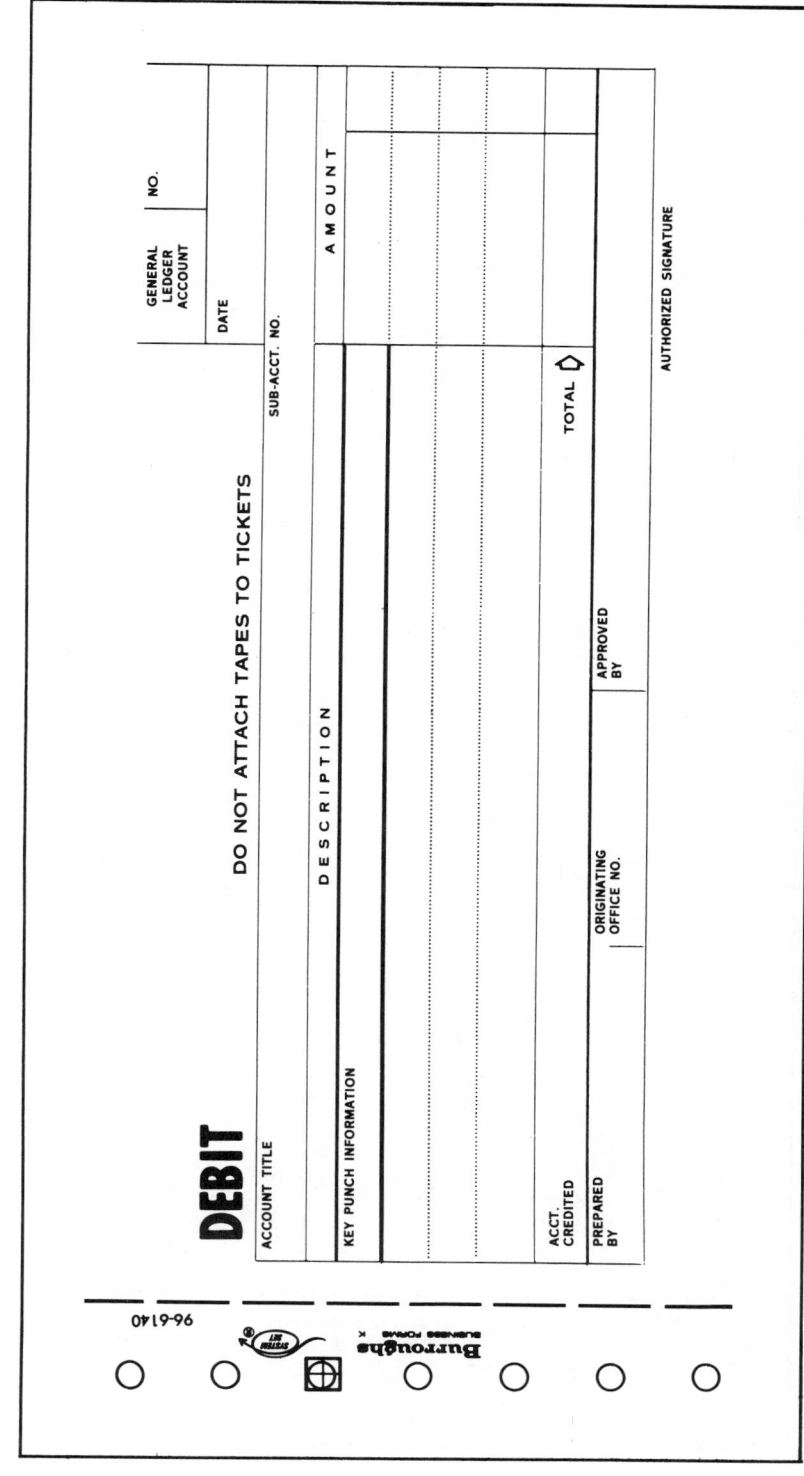

Figure J-33: DEBIT TICKET—GENERAL LEDGER
(Courtesy of Burroughs Corporation Office Products Group/Business Forms Division.)

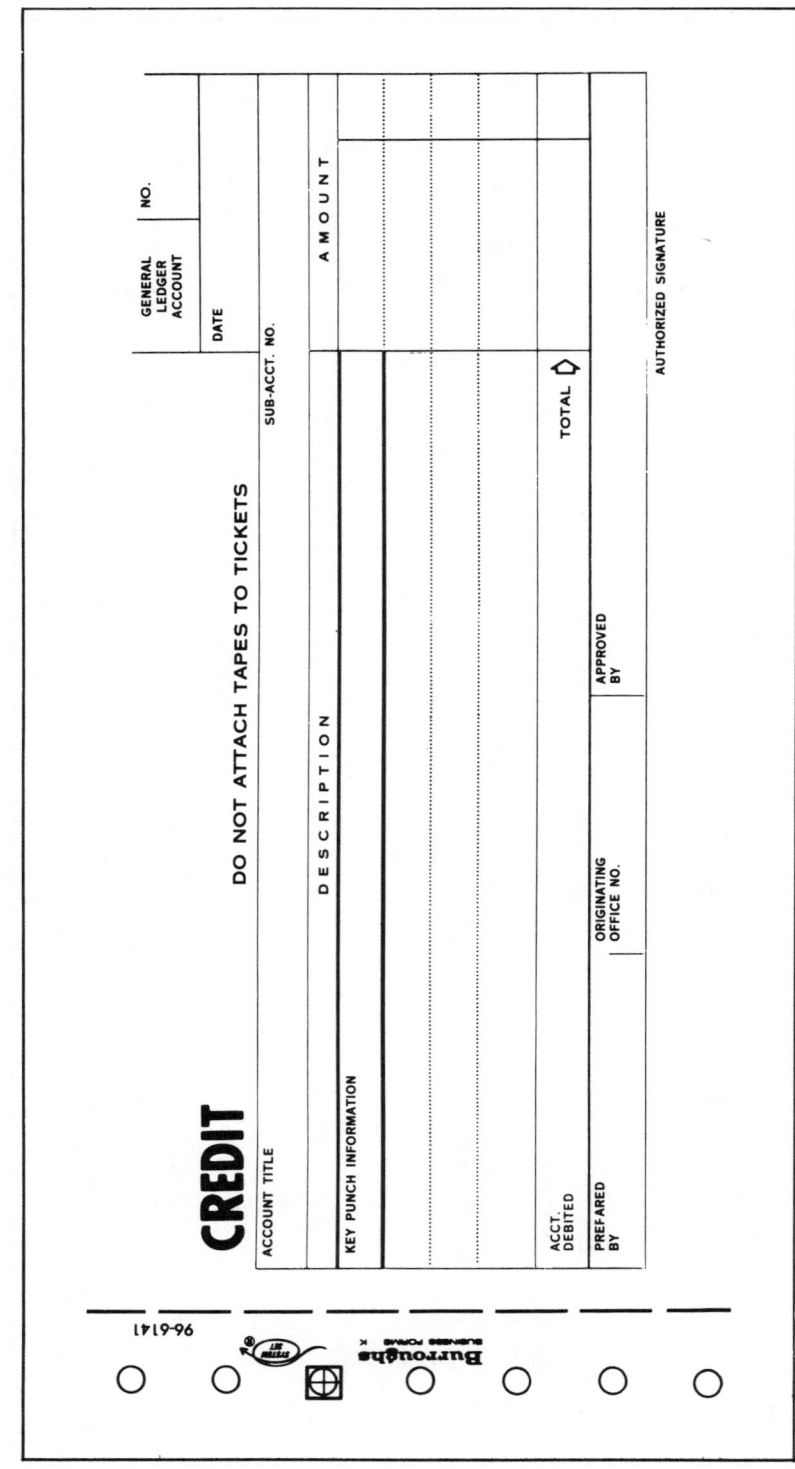

Figure J-34: CREDIT TICKET—GENERAL LEDGER
(Courtesy of Burroughs Corporation Office Products Group/Business Forms Division.)

TELEPHONE TOLL CALL RECORD

FILE NO. ....   DATE .... 19 ....

CHARGE TO: ....

PARTY CALLED: ....

PHONE NO. (   ) .... PLACE ....

SUBJECT MATTER OF CALL: ....

....

TIME: FROM .... .M.   TO .... .M.   ☐OUTSIDE PHONE

TO BE BILLED: YES☐   NO☐   TOLL CHARGE $ ....

BILLED☐   DATE ....   FEDERAL TAX $ _____

CALL MADE BY: ....   *TOTAL* $ ....

TCR - 15 — TOLL CALL RECORD   © 1976 ALL-STATE LEGAL SUPPLY CO., 269 SHEFFIELD ST., MOUNTAINSIDE, N. J. 07092

Figure J-35: TELEPHONE TOLL CALL RECORD
(Copyright 1976 by All State Legal Supply Co., Mountainside, New Jersey 07092.)

POSTAGE RECORD

.... 19 ....

CLIENT ....

Matter .... File No. ....

MAILED TO ....

ADDRESS ....

....

☐ Registered ☐ Certified Mail .. $ ....

☐ Regular Mail .... $ ....

☐ Other .... $ ....

TOTAL $ ____________________

ITEM MAILED ....

INSTRUCTIONS: ....

....

....

INITIALS ....

PR 10-POSTAGE RECORD

Figure J-36: POSTAGE RECORD
(Copyright 1976 by All State Legal Supply Co., Mountainside, New Jersey 07092.)

RAPIDFORMS NO. 82002

TRAVEL EXPENSE REPORT

TRAVEL EXPENSE REPORT

ATTACH RECEIPTS FOR LODGING AND FOR EACH ITEM OVER $25

NAME

LOCATION

FOR WEEK ENDING

DATE	SUNDAY	MONDAY	TUESDAY	WEDNESDAY	THURSDAY	FRIDAY	SATURDAY	EXPENSES TO BE PAID BY COMPANY	EXPENSES TO BE REIMBURSED TO EMPLOYEE
FROM									
.TO									
TO									
AUTO-MILEAGE									
AT ¢ PER MILE									
LODGING									
BREAKFAST									
LUNCH									
DINNER									
AIR/RAIL/BUS									
LOCAL CAB/BUS									
AUTO RENTAL									
GAS/OIL/LUB									
PHONE/TEL.*									
ENTERTAINMENT									
MISC GRATUITIES*									
TOLLS									
DAILY TOTAL									
SEND CHECK TO								SIGNED	

DATE	DETAILS OF (*) EXPENDITURES	AMOUNT

ACCTG. DISTRIBUTION

CASH ADVANCED		PERMANENT	
		TEMPORARY	
TOTAL EXPENSES	TO BE REIMBURSED		
BALANCE DUE		EMPLOYEE	
		COMPANY	

BALANCE PAID

WEEKLY TOTAL	APPROVED	VOUCHER NO.
	DATE PAID	CHECK NO.

ITEMIZED ENTERTAINMENT RECORD

DATE	ITEM	NAME OF PLACE/CITY & STATE	BUSINESS PURPOSE	PERSONS ENTERTAINED/BUSINESS RELATIONSHIP	AMOUNT

FORM 82002 REGENT FORMS, BELLMAWR, N.J. 08031

853

Figure J-37: TRAVEL EXPENSE REPORT
(Courtesy of Regent Standard Forms, Inc., Bellmawr, New Jersey 08031.)

Figure J-38: INDIVIDUAL TIME AND EARNINGS RECORD
(Copyright by Wilson Jones Company. All rights reserved. Forms may be obtained, subject to supply, from Wilson Jones Company, 6150 Touhy Avenue, Chicago, Illinois 60648.)

854

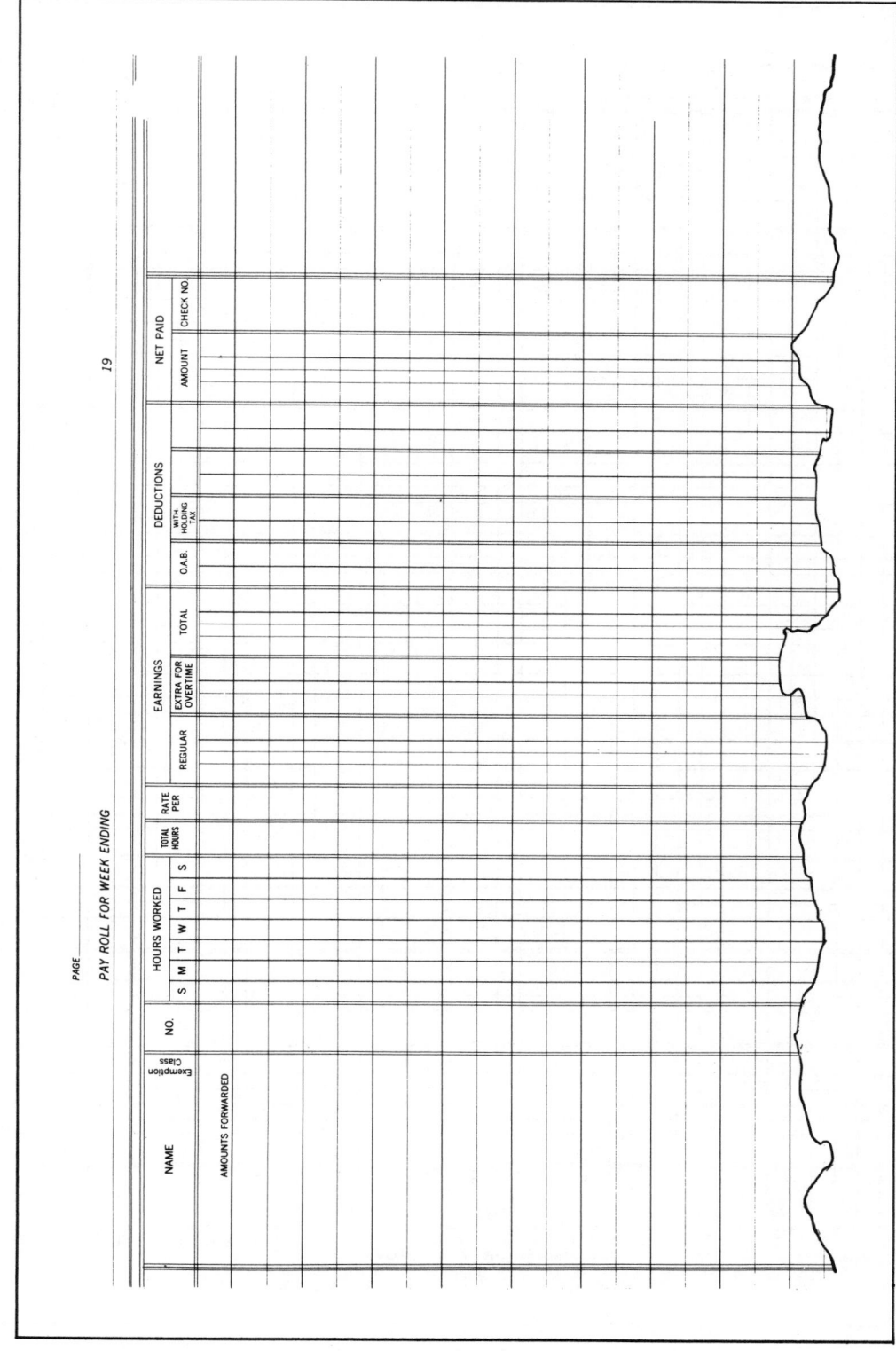

Figure J-39: QUARTERLY PAYROLL SUMMARY RECORD

855

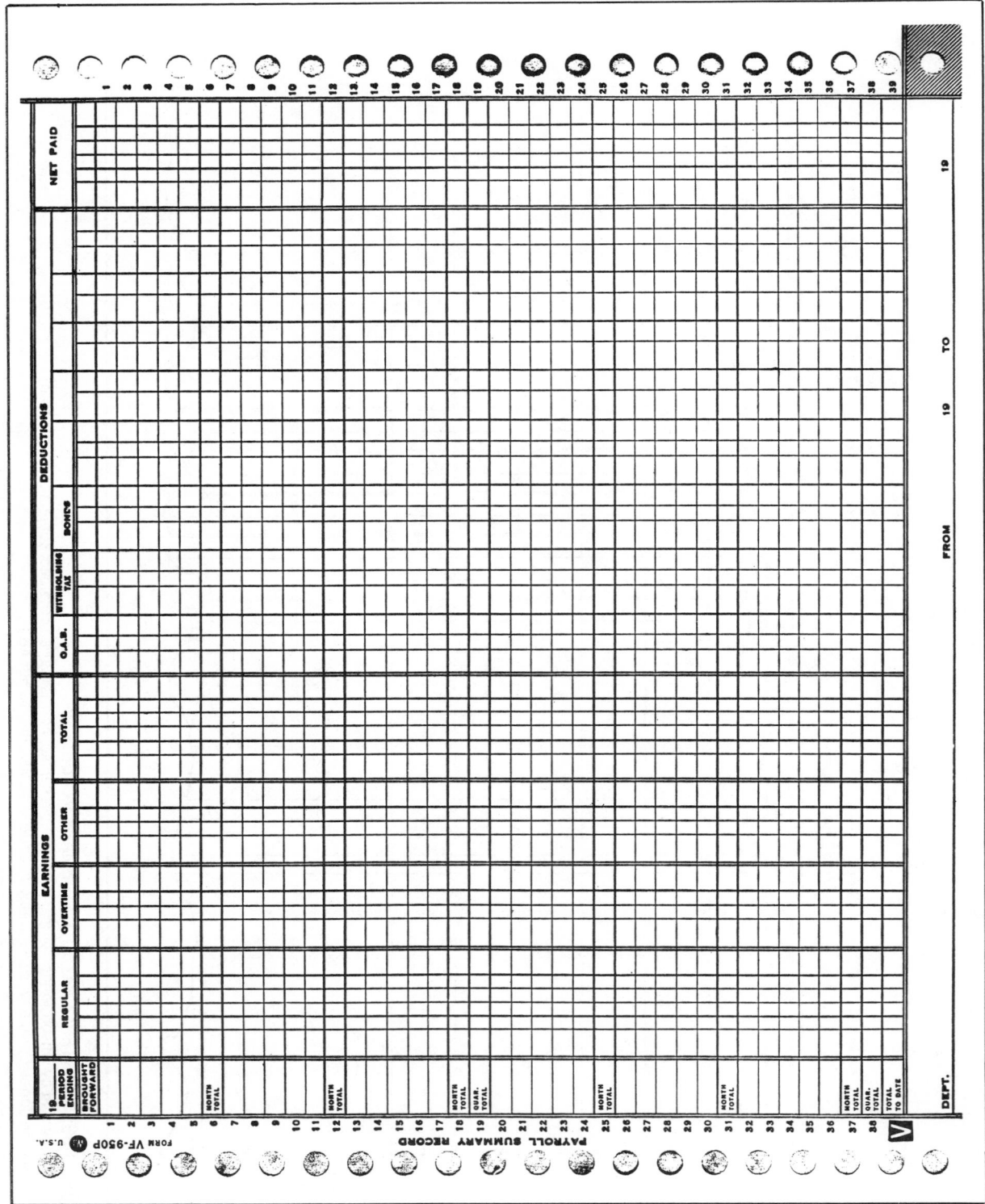

Figure J-40: WEEKLY PAYROLL LEDGER

856

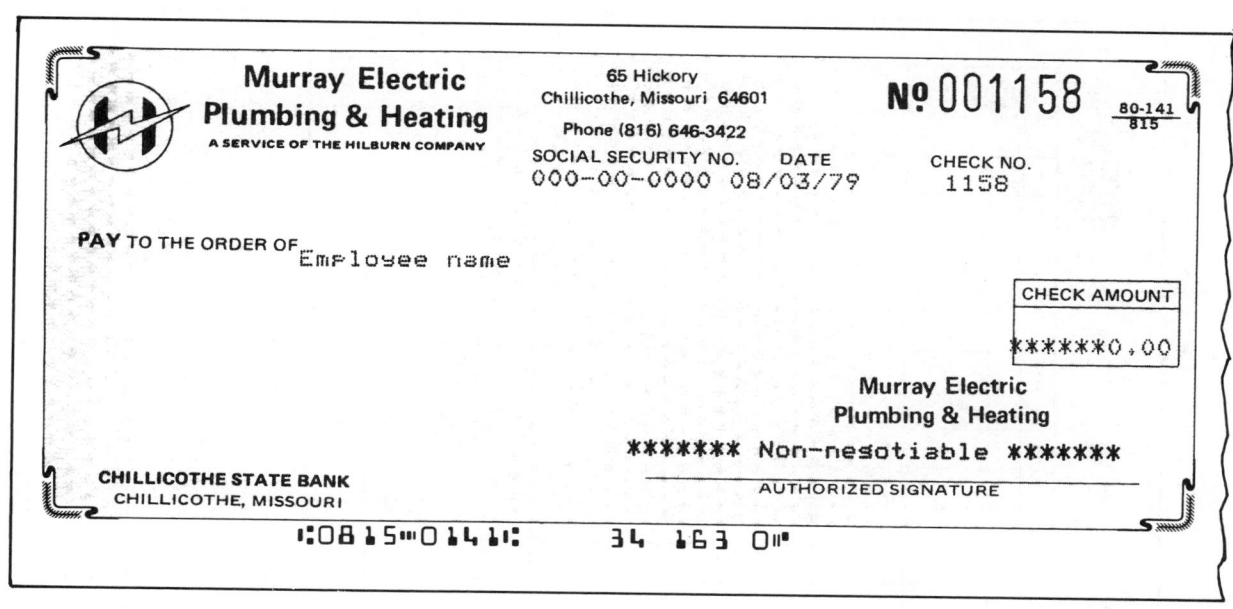

Figure J-41: CHECK AND DEDUCTIONS RECORD
  (Courtesy of Moore Business Forms, Inc.)

	TIME WORKED	DATE PAY PERIOD ENDING	CHECK ISSUED TO	GROSS AMOUNT	INC. TAX	SOC. SEC.				NET AMOUNT	CHECK NUMBER
			BALANCE FORWARD ⟶								
1											
2											
3											
4											
5											
6											
7											
8											
9											
10											
11											
12											
13											
14											
15											
16											
17											
18											
19											
20											
21											
22											
23											
24											
25											
26											
27											
28											
29											
30											
			TOTALS								

PAYROLL AND DISBURSEMENTS JOURNAL   RJPD-15

FORM NO. RJPD-15   PRINTED IN U.S.A.

PAYROLL AND DISBURSEMENTS JOURNAL

Figure J-42: PAYROLL AND DISBURSEMENTS JOURNAL
(Courtesy of Regent Standard Forms, Inc., Bellmawr, New Jersey 08031.)

	BANK BALANCE	DEPOSITS		1				
		AMOUNT	DATE					
1								
2								
3								
4								
5								
6								
7								
8								
9								
10								
11								
12								
13								
14								
15								
16								
17								
18								
19								
20								
21								
22								
23								
24								
25								
26								
27								
28								
29								
30								

MONTH OF_____ 19 _____ PAGE NO _____

9	10	11	12	13	14	
						1
						2
						3
						4
						5
						6
						7
						8
						9
						10
						11
						12
						13
						14
						15
						16
						17
						18
						19
						20
						21
						22
						23
						24
						25
						26
						27
						28
						29
						30

J-42 (front continued)

859

Figure J-42—Reverse Side

ANALYSIS OF MISC. COLUMN	✓				✓				✓				✓				✓			
ACCOUNT NO. OR DESCRIPTION																				
TOTALS																				

J-42 (reverse continued)

DISTRIBUTION OF OFFICE STAFF HOURS

WEEKLY

Function	Office Manager	Bookkeeper	Billing Clerk	Receptionist
Customer billing	–	–	30	–
Match and voucher vendor invoices	2	8	–	8
Examine and reconcile various output from ADP	2	4½	–	–
Answer telephone	–	–	2	8
File	–	4	6	–
Post to sales journal	–	3½	–	–
Write up cash receipts journal	–	3½	–	–
Write up cash disbursements journal	–	3½	–	–
Make bank deposit	2½	–	–	–
Bank reconciliations	–	1½	–	–
Open mail	–	–	–	4
Prepare sales and payroll tax returns	–	½	–	–
Post material and subcontract costs to job cards	–	1½	–	5
Post labor hours to job cards	–	1	–	5
Cost out jobs	7½	3½	–	–
Post general ledger	–	1½	–	–
Prepare ADP payroll transmittals	–	2½	–	10
Follow up on job inquiries, amendments and supplements	7½	–	2	–
Prepare monthly customer accounts receivable statements	2	–	–	–
Prepare daily reports	–	½	–	–
Prepare monthly inventory summary	2	½	–	–
Review and supervise office work	14½	–	–	–
TOTAL	40	40	40	40

Figure J-43: DISTRIBUTION OF OFFICE STAFF HOURS
(Courtesy of Gregory R. Stelmak.)

```
GENERAL MOTORS              ▐    01 00 321-1776  NMW   ▌    BASE REPORT        PAGE 1
SIC 3711                    ▐                          ▌    CONSOLIDATED
OFFICER: WRH                                                IN MILLIONS
LAST AUDITOR: DELOITTE, HASKINS & SELLS
```

DATE 0 TYPE OF AUDIT 00*AUDITOR NUMBER	12/31/74 CERTIFIED 3880	12/31/75 CERTIFIED 3880	12/31/76 CERTIFIED 3880	12/31/77 CERTIFIED 3880	12/31/78 CERTIFIED 2133
---CURRENT ASSETS---					
1*CASH	703.9	1,145.5	1,947.3	1,008.7	968.6
3 SHORT TERM INVESTMENT	634.3	2,237.4	2,677.6	2,231.3	3,086.2
10 NET RECEIVABLES-TRADE	1,641.0	1,703.3	1,785.3	2,184.5	2,745.2
19 NOTES REC- GMAC	1,359.8	1,639.4	2,173.8	2,496.6	2,893.5
28*TOTAL INVENTORY	6,404.7	5,690.9	6,327.8	7,175.7	7,576.7
33 TOTAL CURRENT ASSETS	10,743.7	12,416.5	14,911.8	15,096.8	17,270.2
---FIXED ASSETS---					
43 GROSS FIXED ASSETS	17,626.3	18,177.0	18,844.1	20,882.3	23,044.4
44 ACCUM. DEPRECIATION	10,593.0	11,091.1	11,883.0	12,679.4	13,438.8
46 NET FIXED ASSETS	7,033.3	7,085.9	6,961.1	8,202.9	9,605.6
51 INV/ADV IN AFFIL. & SUBS	1,551.6	1,624.2	1,872.2	1,945.0	2,275.8
54*PREPAID & DFD. EXPENSES	425.6	449.7	573.5	860.4	729.3
57 OTHER ASSETS	0.0	0.0	0.0	406.7	536.3
60 GOODWILL	32.5	26.1	24.2	0.0	0.0
61 TOTAL ASSETS	19,786.7	21,602.4	24,342.8	26,511.8	30,417.2
---CURRENT LIABILITIES---					
65 CURRENT MATURITY OF LTD	55.5	251.9	124.3	112.3	137.8
67 ACCOUNTS PAYABLE - TRADE	2,950.4	2,935.1	2,943.1	3,606.8	4,474.6
70 ACCRUALS	2,144.5	2,416.4	3,197.1	3,720.3	4,493.4
72 INCOME TAXES - PAYABLE	357.8	842.1	1,651.5	887.5	944.8
78 TOTAL CURRENT LIABS.	5,508.2	6,445.5	7,916.0	8,326.9	10,050.6
---NON-CURRENT LIABILITIES-					
79 LONG TERM DEBT	876.6	1,223.1	1,069.8	1,068.2	978.9
83 RESERVES AND CREDITS	527.6	517.3	479.4	472.8	614.5
85 OTHER LIABILITIES	430.3	396.6	592.0	1,023.5	1,384.4
94 TOTAL LIABILITIES	7,342.7	8,582.5	10,057.2	10,891.4	13,028.4
---NET WORTH---					
98*TREASURY STOCK	(86.7)	(62.6)	(99.6)	(146.5)	(181.1)
100 CAPITAL-PREFERRED STOCK	283.6	283.6	283.6	283.6	283.6
101 CAPITAL-COMMON STOCK	479.4	479.4	479.4	479.5	480.1
102 PAID-IN CAPITAL	767.0	767.0	770.3	772.1	792.0
103 RETAINED EARNINGS	11,000.7	11,552.5	12,851.9	14,231.7	16,014.2
108 NET WORTH	12,444.0	13,019.9	14,285.6	15,620.4	17,388.8
109 TOTAL LIABS. AND EQUITY	19,786.7	21,602.4	24,342.8	26,511.8	30,417.2
TANGIBLE NET WORTH	12,411.5	12,993.8	14,261.4	15,620.4	17,388.8
WORKING CAPITAL	5,235.5	5,971.0	6,995.8	6,769.9	7,219.6

**Figure J-44: BASE REPORT PRODUCED FROM AUTOMATED
FINANCIAL ANALYSIS SPREAD SHEETS**
(Courtesy of The First National Bank of Boston.)

DATE	12/31/74	12/31/75	12/31/76	12/31/77	12/31/78
---OPERATING STATEMENT---					
117 NET SALES - GROSS INCOME	31,549.5	35,724.9	47,181.0	54,961.3	63,221.1
123 DEPRECIATION	846.6	906.1	939.3	974.0	1,180.6
131 C.G.S.-NET OF DEPR.	26,918.7	29,889.7	38,031.4	44,441.1	51,275.7
132 TOTAL C.G.S.	27,765.3	30,795.8	38,970.7	45,415.1	52,456.3
133 GROSS PROFIT	3,784.2	4,929.1	8,210.3	9,546.2	10,764.8
137 TOTAL S, G, & A EXPENSE	1,363.9	1,333.7	1,759.7	1,997.3	2,255.8
142 AMORTIZATION	858.4	1,180.0	1,296.9	1,406.4	1,855.7
145 TOTAL OPERATING EXPENSE	2,222.3	2,513.7	3,056.6	3,403.7	4,111.5
146 OPERATING PROFIT	1,561.9	2,415.4	5,153.7	6,142.5	6,653.3
147 INTEREST EXPENSE	162.7	294.0	284.0	281.7	355.9
148 LOSS-TRANSL FGN CURR	45.6	27.1	0.0	0.0	0.0
149*OTHER EXPENSES	5.9	39.5	143.2	188.9	378.6
151 OTHER INCOME	215.0	180.0	559.4	377.7	424.7
153 PROFIT BEFORE TAXES	1,562.7	2,234.8	5,285.9	6,049.6	6,343.5
155 INCOME TAX	727.1	1,118.2	2,567.8	2,934.2	3,088.5
156 CURRENT TAXES	457.2	1,140.8	2,571.2	3,191.5	3,070.8
157* DEFERRED TAXES	269.9	(22.6)	(3.4)	(257.3)	17.7
161 EQUITY IN EARNS OF SUBS	114.4	136.6	184.7	222.1	253.0
162 NET PROFIT	950.0	1,253.2	2,902.8	3,337.5	3,508.0

---RECONCILIATION OF NET WORTH---					
NET WORTH BEGINNING		12,444.0	13,019.9	14,285.6	15,620.4
DECREASE(INCREASE) IN:					
TREASURY STOCK		24.1	(37.0)	(46.9)	(34.6)
INCREASE(DECREASE) IN:					
CAPITAL-PREFERRED STOCK		0.0	0.0	0.0	0.0
CAPITAL-COMMON STOCK		0.0	0.0	0.1	0.6
PAID-IN CAPITAL		0.0	3.3	1.8	19.9
PLUS: NET PROFIT		1,253.2	2,902.8	3,337.5	3,508.0
LESS:					
PREFERRED DIVIDENDS		(12.9)	(12.9)	(12.9)	(12.9)
COMMON DIVIDENDS		(688.4)	(1,590.5)	(1,944.8)	(1,712.6)
NET WORTH ENDING		13,020.0	14,285.6	15,620.4	17,388.8

Figure J-44 (continued)

GENERAL MOTORS   01 00 321-1776 NMW   BASE REPORT   PAGE 3
SIC 3711   CONSOLIDATED
OFFICER: WRH   IN MILLIONS

DATE	12/31/75	12/31/76	12/31/77	12/31/78
---CHANGES IN FINANCIAL POSITION---				
SOURCES OF WORKING CAPITAL				
NET PROFIT	1,253.2	2,902.8	3,337.5	3,508.0
DEPRECIATION	906.1	939.3	974.0	1,180.6
AMORTIZATION	1,180.0	1,296.9	1,406.4	1,855.7
CASH THROW	3,339.3	5,139.0	5,717.9	6,544.3
INCR(DECR) NON-CUR LIABS				
LONG TERM DEBT	346.5	(153.3)	(1.6)	(89.3)
RESERVES AND CREDITS	(10.3)	(37.9)	(6.6)	141.7
OTHER LIABILITIES	(33.7)	195.4	431.5	360.9
CAPITAL-PREFERRED STOCK	0.0	0.0	0.0	0.0
CAPITAL-COMMON STOCK	0.0	0.0	0.1	0.6
PAID-IN CAPITAL	0.0	3.3	1.8	19.9
TOTAL EXTERNAL SOURCES	302.5	7.5	425.2	433.8
TOTAL SOURCES	3,641.8	5,146.5	6,143.1	6,978.1
APPLICATIONS OF WORKING CAPITAL				
DIVIDENDS	701.3	1,603.4	1,957.7	1,725.5
CAPITAL EXPENDITURES	958.7	814.5	2,215.8	2,583.3
ADDS TO INTANG & MISC	1,173.7	1,295.0	1,382.2	1,855.7
INCR(DECR) IN NON-CUR-ASST				
INV/ADV IN AFFIL. & SUBS	72.6	248.0	72.8	330.8
PREPAID & DFD. EXPENSES	24.1	123.8	286.9	(131.1)
OTHER ASSETS	0.0	0.0	406.7	129.6
TREASURY STOCK	(24.1)	37.0	46.9	34.6
TOTAL APPLICATIONS	2,906.3	4,121.7	6,369.0	6,528.4
INCR(DECR) WORKING CAPITAL	735.5	1,024.8	(225.9)	449.7
REPORTED CAPITAL EXPEND	2,236.4	999.0	3,646.7	2,737.8
---CHANGES IN WORKING CAPITAL---				
INCR(DECR) CURRENT ASSETS				
CASH	441.6	801.8	(938.6)	(40.1)
SHORT TERM INVESTMENT	1,603.1	440.2	(446.3)	854.9
NET RECEIVABLES-TRADE	62.3	82.0	399.2	560.7
NOTES REC- GMAC	279.6	534.4	322.8	396.9
TOTAL INVENTORY	(713.8)	636.9	847.9	401.0
TOTAL INCR IN CUR ASSETS	1,672.8	2,495.3	185.0	2,173.4
INCR(DECR) CURRENT LIABS				
CURRENT MATURITY OF LTD	196.4	(127.6)	(12.0)	25.5
ACCOUNTS PAYABLE - TRADE	(15.3)	8.0	663.7	867.8
ACCRUALS	271.9	780.7	523.2	773.1
INCOME TAXES - PAYABLE	484.3	809.4	(764.0)	57.3
TOTAL INCR CURRENT LIABS	937.3	1,470.5	410.9	1,723.7
INCR(DECR) WORKING CAPITAL	735.5	1,024.8	(225.9)	449.7

Figure J-44 (continued)

```
GENERAL MOTORS            01 00 321-1776  NMW        BASE REPORT      PAGE 4
SIC 3711                                             CONSOLIDATED
OFFICER: WRH                                         IN MILLIONS

   DATE                 12/31/74   12/31/75   12/31/76   12/31/77   12/31/78

---SUMMARY FINANCIAL INFORMATION-------------------------------------------------
   QUICK RATIO            0.787      1.043      1.084      0.951      0.964
   CURRENT RATIO          1.950      1.926      1.883      1.813      1.718
   SALES/AVG WORKING CAP             6.375      7.277      7.985      9.038
   DAYS RECEIVABLES      18.984     17.402     13.811     14.507     15.849
   DAYS INVENTORY        84.195     67.450     59.266     57.670     52.719
   DAYS PAYABLES         38.785     34.787     27.565     28.987     31.135
   EBIT/INTEREST EXPENSE 10.604      8.601     19.612     22.475     18.823
   DEBT REPAYMENT +
     FIXED CHGS COVERAGE  6.474      3.168     10.594     12.668     10.728
   NET PROFIT/AVG T.N.W.             0.098      0.213      0.223      0.212
   TOTAL LIABILITIES/T.N.W. 0.591    0.660      0.705      0.697      0.749
   TOTAL LIAB - SUBTD DEBT/
     T.N.W. + SUBTD DEBT  0.591      0.660      0.705      0.697      0.749
   TANGIBLE NET WORTH   12,411.5   12,993.8   14,261.4   15,620.4   17,388.8
   CAPITAL FUNDS        12,411.5   12,993.8   14,261.4   15,620.4   17,388.8
   NET WORKING CAPITAL   5,235.5    5,971.0    6,995.8    6,769.9    7,219.6

---NOTES AND REMARKS------------------------------------------------------------
 00   CHANGE OF AUDITOR FROM
          1977  HASKINS & SELLS
          1978  DELOITTE, HASKINS & SELLS

  1   CASH
          1974  INCLUDES $303MM HELD FOR PMT OF INC. TAXES
          1975  INCLUDES $788MM HELD FOR PMT OF INC. TAXES
          1977  INCLUDES $715.3MM FOR PAYMENT OF INCOME TAXES

 28   TOTAL INVENTORY
          1977  SUBSTANTIALLY ALL DOMESTIC INVTYS AT LIFO
          1978  SUBSTANTIALLY ALL DOMESTIC INVTYS AT LIFO; LIFO RESERVE
                $1097.7MM

 54   PREPAID & DFD. EXPENSES
          1974  INCLUDES DFRD INC. TAXES $119M
          1975  INCLUDES DFRD INC. TAXES $27MM

 98   TREASURY STOCK
          1974  HELD FOR THE INCENTIVE PROGRAM
          1975  HELD FOR THE INCENTIVE PROGRAM
          1977  HELD FOR INCENTIVE PROGRAM

149   OTHER EXPENSES
          1977  INCLUDES $161MM PROV. FOR BONUS PLAN
          1978  INCLUDES $168.4MM PROVISION FOR BONUS PLAN

157   DEFERRED TAXES
          1974  INCLUDES INV. TAX CREDIT $10MM
          1975  NET OF DFRD TAX CREDITS
```

Figure J-44 (continued)

```
GENERAL MOTORS            01 00 321-1776  NMW          COMMON REPORT      P. 1
SIC 3711                                               CONSOLIDATED
OFFICER: WRH                                           IN MILLIONS
LAST AUDITOR DELOITTE, HASKINS & SELLS
```

DATE 0 TYPE OF AUDIT 00 AUDITOR NUMBER	12/31/74 CERTIFIED 3880	12/31/75 CERTIFIED 3880	12/31/76 CERTIFIED 3880	12/31/77 CERTIFIED 3880	12/31/78 CERTIFIED 2133
---CURRENT ASSETS---------					
1 CASH	0.036	0.053	0.080	0.038	0.032
3 SHORT TERM INVESTMENT	0.032	0.104	0.110	0.084	0.101
10 NET RECEIVABLES-TRADE	0.083	0.079	0.073	0.082	0.090
19 NOTES REC- GMAC	0.069	0.076	0.089	0.094	0.095
28 TOTAL INVENTORY	0.324	0.263	0.260	0.271	0.249
33 TOTAL CURRENT ASSETS	0.543	0.575	0.613	0.569	0.568
---FIXED ASSETS ----------					
43 GROSS FIXED ASSETS	0.891	0.841	0.774	0.788	0.758
44 ACCUM. DEPRECIATION	0.535	0.513	0.488	0.478	0.442
46 NET FIXED ASSETS	0.355	0.328	0.286	0.309	0.316
51 INV/ADV IN AFFIL. & SUBS	0.078	0.075	0.077	0.073	0.075
54 PREPAID & DFD. EXPENSES	0.022	0.021	0.024	0.032	0.024
57 OTHER ASSETS	0.000	0.000	0.000	0.015	0.018
60 GOODWILL	0.002	0.001	0.001	0.000	0.000
61 TOTAL ASSETS	1.000	1.000	1.000	1.000	1.000
---CURRENT LIABILITIES------					
65 CURRENT MATURITY OF LTD	0.003	0.012	0.005	0.004	0.005
67 ACCOUNTS PAYABLE - TRADE	0.149	0.136	0.121	0.136	0.147
70 ACCRUALS	0.108	0.112	0.131	0.140	0.148
72 INCOME TAXES - PAYABLE	0.018	0.039	0.068	0.033	0.031
78 TOTAL CURRENT LIABS.	0.278	0.298	0.325	0.314	0.330
---NON-CURRENT LIABILITIES-					
79 LONG TERM DEBT	0.044	0.057	0.044	0.040	0.032
83 RESERVES AND CREDITS	0.027	0.024	0.020	0.018	0.020
85 OTHER LIABILITIES	0.022	0.018	0.024	0.039	0.046
94 TOTAL LIABILITIES	0.371	0.397	0.413	0.411	0.428
---NET WORTH--------------					
98 TREASURY STOCK	(0.004)	(0.003)	(0.004)	(0.006)	(0.006)
100 CAPITAL-PREFERRED STOCK	0.014	0.013	0.012	0.011	0.009
101 CAPITAL-COMMON STOCK	0.024	0.022	0.020	0.018	0.016
102 PAID-IN CAPITAL	0.039	0.036	0.032	0.029	0.026
103 RETAINED EARNINGS	0.556	0.535	0.528	0.537	0.526
108 NET WORTH	0.629	0.603	0.587	0.589	0.572
109 TOTAL LIABS. AND EQUITY	1.000	1.000	1.000	1.000	1.000

Figure J-45: COMMON REPORT PRODUCED FROM AUTOMATED
FINANCIAL ANALYSIS SPREAD SHEETS
(Courtesy of The First National Bank of Boston.)

```
GENERAL MOTORS              01 00 321-1776  NMW       COMMON REPORT      P. 2
SIC 3711                                              CONSOLIDATED
OFFICER: WRH                                          IN MILLIONS

    DATE                    12/31/74    12/31/75    12/31/76    12/31/77    12/31/78

  ---OPERATING STATEMENT--------------------------------------------------------------
117 NET SALES - GROSS INCOME    1.000       1.000       1.000       1.000       1.000
123   DEPRECIATION              0.027       0.025       0.020       0.018       0.019
131   C.G.S.-NET OF DEPR.       0.853       0.837       0.806       0.809       0.811
132 TOTAL C.G.S.                0.880       0.862       0.826       0.826       0.830
133 GROSS PROFIT                0.120       0.138       0.174       0.174       0.170

137 TOTAL S, G, & A EXPENSE     0.043       0.037       0.037       0.036       0.036
142   AMORTIZATION              0.027       0.033       0.027       0.026       0.029
145 TOTAL OPERATING EXPENSE     0.070       0.070       0.065       0.062       0.065
146 OPERATING PROFIT            0.050       0.068       0.109       0.112       0.105

147 INTEREST EXPENSE            0.005       0.008       0.006       0.005       0.006
148 LOSS-TRANSL FGN CURR        0.001       0.001       0.000       0.000       0.000
149 OTHER EXPENSES              0.000       0.001       0.003       0.003       0.006
151 OTHER INCOME                0.007       0.005       0.012       0.007       0.007
153 PROFIT BEFORE TAXES         0.050       0.063       0.112       0.110       0.100

155 INCOME TAX                  0.023       0.031       0.054       0.053       0.049
156   CURRENT TAXES             0.014       0.032       0.054       0.058       0.049
157   DEFERRED TAXES            0.009      (0.001)      0.000      (0.005)      0.000
161 EQUITY IN EARNS OF SUBS     0.004       0.004       0.004       0.004       0.004
162 NET PROFIT                  0.030       0.035       0.062       0.061       0.055
```

Figure J-45 (continued)

```
GENERAL MOTORS                    █                    █         FUNDS FLOW ANALYSIS PG 1
CONSOLIDATED                                                          IN MILLIONS
OFFICER: WRH
```

DATE	12/31/75	12/31/76	12/31/77	12/31/78
OPERATING INFLOWS				
NET SALES	35,724.9	47,181.0	54,961.3	63,221.1
OTHER INCOME	180.0	559.4	377.7	424.7
GROSS OPERATING INFLOWS	35,904.9	47,740.4	55,339.0	63,645.8
OPERATING OUTFLOWS				
C.G.S. NET OF DEPR.	29,889.7	38,031.4	44,441.1	51,275.7
S., G. & A. EXPENSES	1,333.7	1,759.7	1,997.3	2,255.8
LOSS-TRANSL FGN CURR	27.1	0.0	0.0	0.0
OTHER EXPENSES	39.5	143.2	188.9	378.6
INCOME TAX	1,118.2	2,567.8	2,934.2	3,088.5
GROSS OPERATING OUTFLOWS	32,408.2	42,502.1	49,561.5	56,998.6
NET FUNDS FLOW FROM OPS	3,496.7	5,238.3	5,777.5	6,647.2
TRADE AND OPERATIONS FINANCING - INFLOWS				
INCR. T & O LIAB. ACCOUNTS				
ACCOUNTS PAYABLE - TRADE		8.0	663.7	867.8
ACCRUALS	271.9	780.7	523.2	773.1
INCOME TAXES - PAYABLE	484.3	809.4		57.3
RESERVES AND CREDITS				141.7
OTHER LIABILITIES		195.4	431.5	360.9
DECR. T & O ASSET ACCOUNTS				
TOTAL INVENTORY	713.8			
PREPAID & DFD. EXPENSES				131.1
GROSS T&O FNCNG INFLOWS	1,470.0	1,793.5	1,618.4	2,331.9
TRADE AND OPERATIONS FINANCING - OUTFLOWS				
DECR T & O LIAB ACCOUNTS				
ACCOUNTS PAYABLE - TRADE	15.3			
INCOME TAXES - PAYABLE			764.0	
RESERVES AND CREDITS	10.3	37.9	6.6	
OTHER LIABILITIES	33.7			
INCR T & O ASSET ACCOUNTS				
NET RECEIVABLES-TRADE	62.3	82.0	399.2	560.7
NOTES REC- GMAC	279.6	534.4	322.8	396.9
TOTAL INVENTORY		636.9	847.9	401.0
PREPAID & DFD. EXPENSES	24.1	123.8	286.9	
OTHER ASSETS			406.7	129.6
GROSS T&O FNCNG OUTFLOWS	425.3	1,415.0	3,034.1	1,488.2
NET FUNDS FLOW FROM T&O FIN	1,044.7	378.5	(1,415.7)	843.7

Figure J-46: FLOW OF FUNDS ANALYSIS
(Courtesy of the First National Bank of Boston.)

```
GENERAL MOTORS                    ■                ■      FUNDS FLOW ANALYSIS PG 2
CONSOLIDATED                                                    IN MILLIONS
OFFICER: WRH
```

DATE	12/31/75	12/31/76	12/31/77	12/31/78
EXTERNAL FINANCING INFLOWS				
DIVIDENDS FROM UNCSL SUB	67.6	0.0	110.3	0.0
CURRENT MATURITY OF LTD	251.9	124.3	112.3	137.8
INCR FINANCIAL LIAB ACCTS				
LONG TERM DEBT	346.5			
CAPITAL-COMMON STOCK			0.1	0.6
PAID-IN CAPITAL		3.3	1.8	19.9
DECR FINANCIAL ASSET ACCTS				
INV/ADV IN AFFIL. & SUBS			39.0	
TREASURY STOCK	24.1			
GROSS EXTERNAL FIN INFLO	690.1	127.6	263.5	158.3
EXTERNAL FINANCING OUTFLOWS				
INTEREST EXPENSE	294.0	284.0	281.7	355.9
CUR MAT LTD - LAST YEAR	55.5	251.9	124.3	112.3
DECR FINANCIAL LIAB ACCTS				
LONG TERM DEBT		153.3	1.6	89.3
INCR FINANCIAL ASSET ACCTS				
INV/ADV IN AFFIL. & SUBS	3.6	63.3		77.8
TREASURY STOCK		37.0	46.9	34.6
GROSS EXT FIN OUTFLOW	353.1	789.5	454.5	669.9
NET FUNDS FLOW FROM EXT FIN	337.0	(661.9)	(191.0)	(511.6)
NET FLOW BEFORE DISCRET EXP	4,878.4	4,954.9	4,170.8	6,979.3
DISCRETIONARY FUNDS OUTFLOW				
PREFERRED DIVIDENDS	12.9	12.9	12.9	12.9
COMMON DIVIDENDS	688.4	1,590.5	1,944.8	1,712.6
CAPITAL EXPENDITURES	958.7	814.5	2,215.8	2,583.3
ADDITIONS TO INTANGIBLES				
AND OTHER MISC FLOWS	1,173.7	1,295.0	1,382.2	1,855.7
NET DISCRET FUNDS FLOW	2,833.7	3,712.9	5,555.7	6,164.5
CHANGE IN CASH + EQUIV.	2,044.7	1,242.0	(1,384.9)	814.8
SUMMARY				
DAYS CASH + EQUIVALENT	38.100	39.718	23.861	25.966
T&O LIABS/TOTAL LIABS	0.828	0.881	0.892	0.914
NEW T&O LIAB/ALL NEW LIA	0.562	1.190	1.016	1.030
CASH FROM OPS/DISCR FLOW	1.234	1.411	1.040	1.078
CASH NEEDS FUNDED				
INTERNALLY	1.955	1.571	0.829	1.249

Figure J-46 (continued)

```
GENERAL MOTORS
CONSOLIDATED          ▮                    ▮        RATIO ANALYSIS
OFFICER: WRH

    DATE            12/31/74    12/31/75   12/31/76    12/31/77    12/31/78

LIQUIDITY
QUICK RATIO           0.788       1.043      1.084       0.951       0.964
CURRENT RATIO         1.950       1.926      1.884       1.813       1.718
SALES/AVG WORKING CAP             6.376      7.277       7.985       9.038
NET FIXED ASSETS/TNW  0.567       0.545      0.488       0.525       0.552
DAYS RECEIVABLES     18.985      17.403     13.811      14.507      15.849
DAYS INVENTORY       84.196      67.450     59.266      57.671      52.720
DAYS PAYABLES        38.786      34.788     27.565      28.988      31.135

LEVERAGE
LTD/CAPITALIZATION    0.066       0.086      0.070       0.064       0.053
LTD/TANG NET WORTH    0.071       0.094      0.075       0.068       0.056
CURR LIABS/T.N.W      0.444       0.496      0.555       0.533       0.578
TOT LIABS/T.N.W       0.592       0.661      0.705       0.697       0.749
TOT LIABS-SUB DEBT/
   T.N.W. + SUB DEBT  0.592       0.661      0.705       0.697       0.749

COVERAGE
EBIT/INTEREST        10.605       8.601     19.612      22.475      18.824
DEBT+FIXED CHGS COVER 6.474       3.168     10.595      12.668      10.728
CASH THROW/REPAYMENT+
      CAPITAL EXPNS               2.758      5.474       2.456       2.405

OPERATING PERFORMANCE
GROSS PROFIT/SALES    0.120       0.138      0.174       0.174       0.170
OPERATING PROF./SALES 0.050       0.068      0.109       0.112       0.105
PRETAX PROFIT/SALES   0.050       0.063      0.112       0.110       0.100
NET PROFIT/SALES      0.030       0.035      0.062       0.061       0.055

NET PROFIT/AVG T.N.W.             0.099      0.213       0.223       0.213
NET PROFIT/AVG CAP.               0.091      0.196       0.208       0.200
NET PROFIT/AVG NET
    TOTAL ASSETS                  0.061      0.126       0.131       0.123
NET PROFIT/AVG GROSS
    TOTAL ASSETS                  0.040      0.084       0.089       0.084
EARNINGS PER SHARE    3.318       4.370     10.090      11.601      12.181
OPERATING EPS         2.919       3.893      9.448      10.829      11.302

SALES/GROSS PLANT     1.790       1.965      2.504       2.632       2.743
SALES/NET PLANT       4.486       5.042      6.778       6.700       6.582
```

Figure J-47: RATIO ANALYSIS PRINTOUT
(Courtesy of The First National Bank of Boston.)

```
GENERAL MOTORS
CONSOLIDATED      ▮                       ▮        TREND ANALYSIS
OFFICER: WRH

PERIOD ENDING       12/74    12/75    12/76    12/77    12/78 STR AVG WGT AVG

SALES GROWTH RATE            0.132    0.320    0.164    0.150   0.191   0.180
COST GOODS/SALES    0.880    0.862    0.826    0.826    0.830   0.844   0.832
SELL,GEN+ADM/SALES  0.043    0.037    0.037    0.036    0.036   0.037   0.036
OTHER INC/SALES     0.007    0.005    0.012    0.007    0.007   0.007   0.007
OTHER EXP/SALES     0.000    0.001    0.003    0.003    0.006   0.002   0.004

CASH/SALES          0.022    0.032    0.041    0.018    0.015   0.025   0.021
RECEIVABLES/SALES   0.052    0.048    0.038    0.040    0.043   0.044   0.042
INVENTORY/SALES     0.203    0.159    0.134    0.131    0.120   0.149   0.131
PREPAID & DFD EXPS/SALES 0.013 0.013  0.012    0.016    0.012   0.013   0.013
OTHER ASSETS/SALES  0.000    0.000    0.000    0.007    0.008   0.003   0.005
NOTES REC- GMAC/SALES 0.043  0.046    0.046    0.045    0.046   0.045   0.045
ACCTS PAY/SALES     0.094    0.082    0.062    0.066    0.071   0.075   0.070
ACCRUALS/SALES      0.068    0.068    0.068    0.068    0.071   0.068   0.069
INC TAX PAY/SALES   0.011    0.024    0.035    0.016    0.015   0.020   0.019
OTHER LIABS/SALES   0.014    0.011    0.013    0.019    0.022   0.015   0.018

DEPR/PREV GROSS  PLANT        0.051    0.052    0.052    0.057   0.053   0.054
COM DIV/EARN AFTER PFD 1.039  0.555    0.550    0.585    0.490   0.643   0.553
INCOME TAX RATE     0.465    0.500    0.486    0.485    0.487   0.484   0.486
```

Figure J-48: TREND ANALYSIS FOR LOAN REVIEW AND ANALYTICAL PURPOSES
(Courtesy of The First National Bank of Boston.)

INSURANCE BUDGET REPORT

Budget Year 198____

Primary general liability .... _____

Primary liability on vehicles .... _____

Umbrella liability .... _____

Travel group accident .... _____

Furnaces & machinery .... _____

Other .... _____

Fire—buildings .... _____

Fire—plant & equipment .... _____

Fire—office fixtures & storage .... _____

Crime .... _____

Miscellaneous buildings & temp. structures .... _____

Aircraft hull coverage .... _____

Aircraft legal liability .... _____

Aircraft admitted liability .... _____

Other .... _____

Workmen's compensation—purchased coverage .... _____

Self-Insurance bonds .... _____

Figure J-49: INSURANCE BUDGET REPORT

SOURCES & USES OF FUNDS

	BEGINNING OF PERIOD	198
	END OF PERIOD	198

	START	END	SOURCES	USES
CASH				
CERTIFICATES OF DEPOSIT				
EUROCURRENCY DEPOSITS				
SOFT CURRENCY DEPOSITS				
OTHER TIME DEPOSITS				
TREASURY BILLS				
OTHER MARKETABLE SECURITIES				
ACCOUNTS RECEIVABLE (NET)				
NOTES RECEIVABLE (NET)				
INVENTORIES				
OTHER CURRENT ASSETS				
TOTAL CURRENT ASSETS				
GROSS FIXED ASSETS				
LESS: RESERVES FOR DEPRECIATION				
NET FIXED ASSETS				
PREPAIDS				
LAND				
OTHER				
✲ TOTAL ASSETS				
ACCOUNTS PAYABLE				
NOTES PAYABLE				
OTHER CURRENT LIABILITIES				
ACCRUED EXPENSES				
TAX LIABILITIES				
BONDS (%)				
BONDS (%)				
DEBENTURES				
OTHER LONG TERM DEBT				
COMMON STOCK				
RETAINED EARNINGS				
✲ TOTAL CLAIM ON ASSETS				

Figure J-50: SOURCES AND USES OF FUNDS

Burroughs
BUSINESS FORMS K

SYSTEM SET

96-6107

	DATE

TO:

AS PART OF OUR REGULAR AUDIT PROCEDURE WE ARE VERIFYING THE RECORDS OF OUR LOAN DEPARTMENT AND WOULD APPRECIATE YOUR ASSISTANCE.

ACCORDING TO OUR RECORDS AT THE CLOSE OF BUSINESS ON THE ABOVE DATE YOU WERE LIABLE, EITHER AS MAKER OR ENDORSER ON THE FOLLOWING NOTES:

PLEASE SIGN BELOW IF CORRECT AND MAIL IN THE ENCLOSED ENVELOPE.

ANY DIFFERENCES SHOULD BE REPORTED ON THE BACK OF THIS FORM.

Thank You

AMOUNT		COLLATERAL
		THIS IS **NOT** A BILL AND **NOT** A REQUEST FOR PAYMENT
THE ABOVE STATEMENT IS CORRECT	DATE	SIGNATURE AS FILED WITH THE BANK

Figure J-51: LOAN VERIFICATION REQUEST
(Courtesy of Burroughs Corporation Office Products Group/Business Forms Division.)

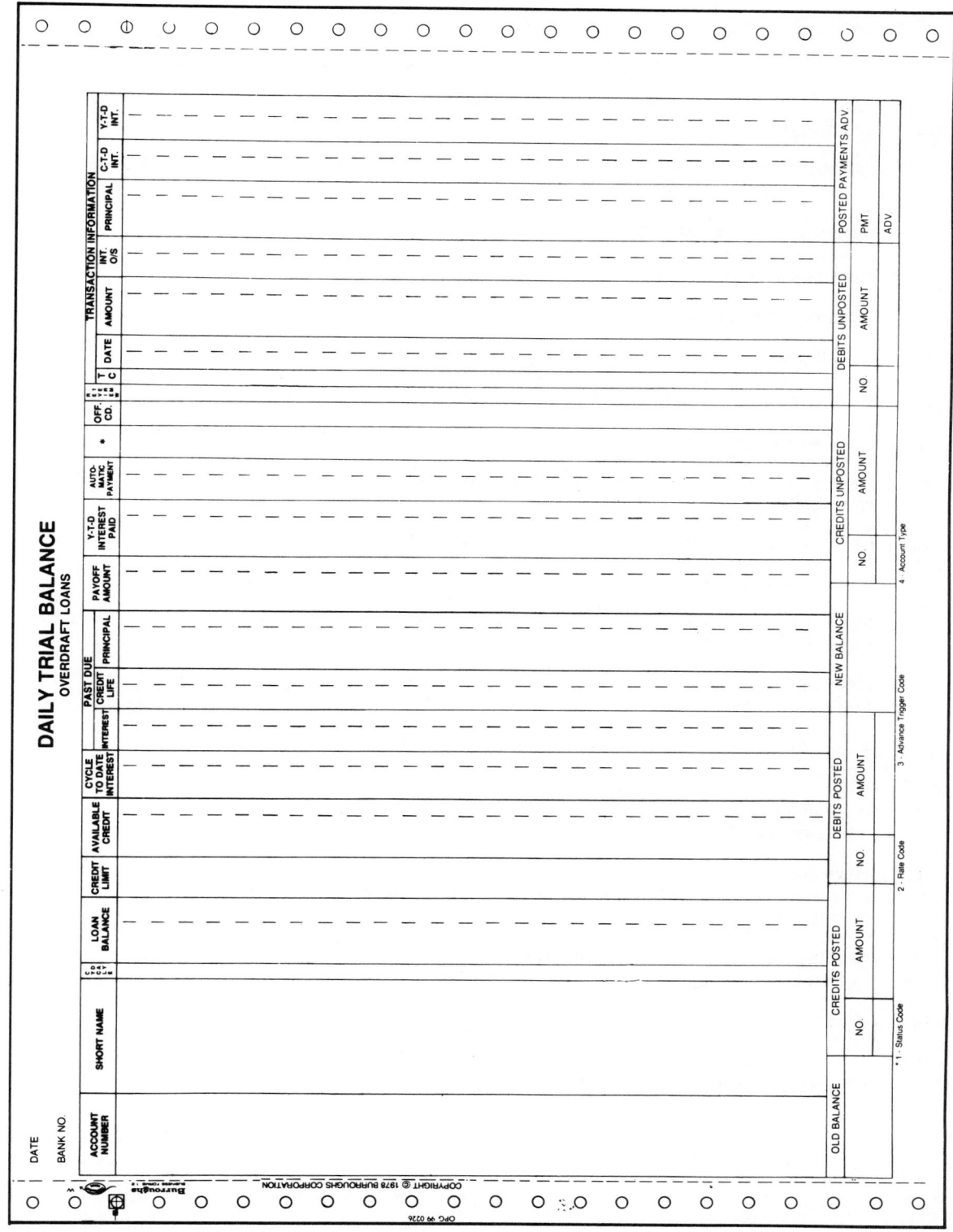

Figure J-52: DAILY TRIAL BALANCE FOR OVERDRAFT LOANS
(Courtesy of Burroughs Corporation Office Products Group/Business Forms Division.)

875

CHECKLIST FOR INTERNAL REPORTING

DATE OF REVIEW _____ BY _____

INSTRUCTIONS: APPEND SUPPORTING DATA, LISTS, OR MATERIAL AS REQUIRED.

1. Have trust indentures, loan agreements, major contracts, debenture and preferred stock provisions, and similar items been reviewed for compliance with all requirements? _____

2. Are any assets pledged, subject to lien or restriction? _____

3. Are all material contingencies, litigations, dividends in arrears, defaults, stock options, retained earnings restrictions, and similar items properly accounted for? _____

4. Have all data been obtained for SEC reports? _____

5. Have all inter-firm profits in transactions affiliated with related concerns been eliminated? _____

6. Have the bases of asset valuations been reviewed? _____

7. Is insurance coverage adequate for actual values of assets? _____

8. Have any changes in accounting policies occurred during the period since the last review? _____

9. Has our tax staff been consulted on current tax matters that require immediate attention? _____

10. Are we in compliance with the Foreign Corrupt Practices Act? _____

11. If statements do not agree with tax returns, have reconciling schedules been prepared? _____

12. Have suggestions for improvements in the internal control system or in financial reporting procedures been implemented or reviewed? _____

13. Are there any material deviations from company policies or procedure manuals found during this review? _____

14. When is the date of the next review? _____

15. Are there any other items of open business which will require attention? _____

Figure J-53: CHECKLIST FOR INTERNAL REPORTING

TYPE OF RETURN: DATE:

TO BE FILLED WITH: AT:

RETURN TO BE MAILED TO:

TO BE BILLED TO:

FISCAL YEAR ENDING:

ASSIGNED TO:

PREPARED BY/DATE:

APPROVED BY/DATE:

DATE MAILED:

EXTENSIONS GRANTED TO:

AMENDED BY/DATE

AMENDMENT APPROVED BY/DATE

AMENDED RETURN MAILED (DATE) ON:

IRS EXAMINATION (DATE) ON:

Figure J-54: RECORD FOR CORPORATE TAX RETURNS AND DECLARATIONS OF ESTIMATED TAXES

RECONCILIATION

FOR _____ MONTHS ENDING _____ 19 _____

NET WORTH AT BEGINNING OF PERIOD . . . . $ _____

PROFITS (LOSSES) BEFORE INCOME TAXES . . . . $ _____

LESS: RESERVES FOR INCOME TAXES . . . . _____

NET PROFITS (LOSSES) FOR PERIOD . . . . _____

    TOTAL . . . . $ _____

DEDUCTIONS:

    Dividends Paid (Preferred) . . . . _____

    Dividends Paid (Common) . . . . _____

ADJUSTMENTS: (Specify) _____

    _____ . . . . _____

    Additions:

    _____ . . . . _____

    _____ . . . . _____

    DEDUCTIONS:

    _____ . . . . _____

    _____ . . . . _____

    _____ . . . . _____

    _____ . . . . _____

    NET . . . . $ _____

NET WORTH AT END OF PERIOD . . . . $ _____

NET SALES FOR PERIOD . . . . $ _____

TOTAL DEPRECIATION FOR PERIOD . . . . $ _____

Figure J-55: RECONCILIATION OF NET WORTH

STOCKHOLDERS' EQUITY & RESERVES
AT

	198	198	198	198
__% PREFERRED, AUTHORIZED__ SHARES				
OUTSTANDING _____ SHARES				
PREMIUM OR DISCOUNT TO PAR VALUE				
A. TOTAL VALUE PREFERRED STOCK				
COMMON, AUTHORIZED _____ SHARES				
ISSUED _____ SHARES				
PAID-IN SURPLUS				
PAID-IN SURPLUS ON TREASURY STOCK				
B. TOTAL VALUE COMMON STOCK				
C. TOTAL VALUE (A) + (B)				
DONATED CAPITAL				
D. TOTAL (C) + DONATED CAPITAL				
RETAINED EARNINGS:				
RESERVE FOR PREFERRED RETIREMENT				
RESERVE FOR TREASURY STOCK				
RESERVE FOR SINKING FUND				
RES. DECLINE INVENTORY VALUE				
RESERVE ASSET REPLACEMENT				
RES. WORKING CAPITAL INVESTMENT				
RESERVE FOR EXPANSION				
RESERVE FOR CONTINGENCIES				
RESERVE FOR TRANSLATION LOSSES				
RES. EXTRAORDINARY LOSSES				
UNCOMMITTED FUNDS				
E. TOTAL RETAINED EARNINGS				
F. TOTAL (D) + (E)				
ADD: APPRAISAL SURPLUS				
SUBTRACT: TREASURY STOCK				
G. STOCKHOLDERS' EQUITY				

Figure J-56: STOCKHOLDERS' EQUITY

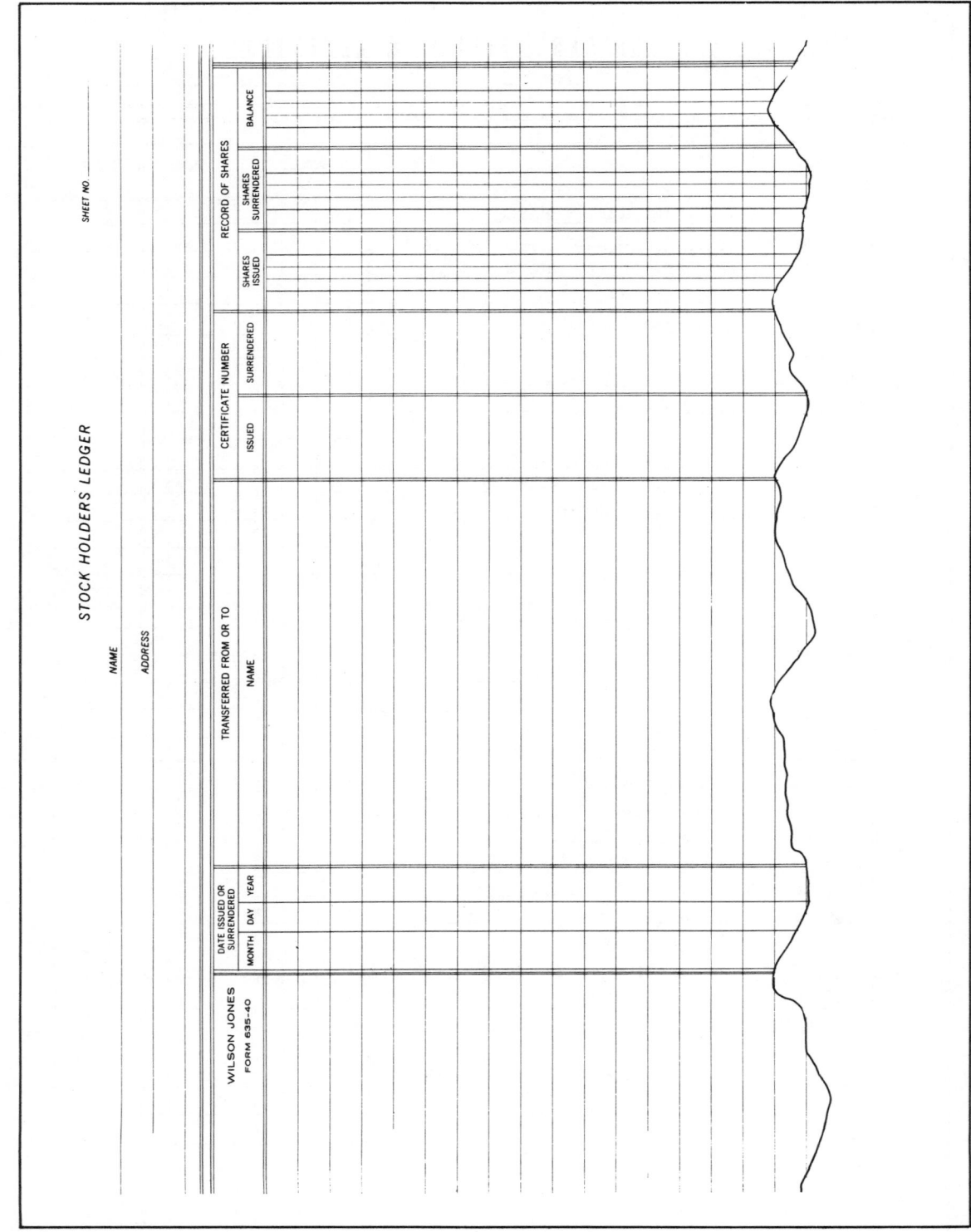

Figure J-57: STOCKHOLDERS' LEDGER

NONPROFIT ORGANIZATIONS— CONTROL, ADMINISTRATION, PLANNING

SECTION K FORMS

Nonprofit Organizations—Control, Administration, Planning

Figure   Page

Nonprofit Organizations—Control, Administration, Planning

Nonstock corporations are not necessarily nonprofit ones, although nonprofit corporations usually do not issue stock. Neither are nonprofit organizations exclusively religious, charitable, or educational institutions. They may include war veterans' organizations, social and recreational clubs, hospitals, cemeteries, civic associations, fraternal societies, labor organizations, agricultural organizations, research centers, homeowners' associations, business leagues, chambers of commerce, management companies, political candidate supporters.

The word "nonprofit," in practice a misnomer, designates tax exemption for it includes political bodies and their autonomous agencies as well. Therefore, this section brings together forms from various tax exempt entities, and organization proceeds along the general plan of this handbook. The most notable observation about this digest of forms is that nonprofit or tax exempt organizations encounter cognate control, planning, and management problems that firms not in this exclusive category also confront—and resolve.

By definition, these organizations would not engage in profit analysis as covered in Section B, but in practice this distinction, too, pales as profit-oriented companies involve themselves in traditionally nonprofit activities, and not-for-profit organizations become linked with profitable endeavors. Nevertheless, these entities apply controls—control of costs, control against funds misappropriation, administration controls, planning controls. Consequently, many forms appearing in this section can just as conveniently be subsumed into other sections but, presented separately, highlight participation of nonprofit enterprise management in control, planning, and administration solutions analogous to other firms. By the same token, management of a nonprofit endeavor will profit from other sections of this manual as well as from this section.

K-1   Produced in four copies, the Purchase Requisition (K-1) imposes various conditions on the initiator:

- (a)   three recommended vendors, when possible;
- (b)   chemicals listed alphabetically, laboratory equipment numerically;
- (c)   dates requisitioned and required;
- (d)   quote numbers (agency's and vendor's);
- (e)   terms of sale;
- (f)   description of material by quantity, unit price, and total amount;
- (g)   purpose for material ordered;
- (h)   signatures of initiator, department head, purchasing officer, and Director of Purchasing.

At the bottom of the form, space is allowed for accounting entries: fiscal year, fund to be charged, agency, identification or function, activity, amount to be charged, fund source, and project code.

K-2   For smaller orders of $200 or less, a Limited Value Purchase Order (K-2) suffices. This nine-copy model stipulates that all shipments be prepaid and that acceptance of the order by the supplier implies conformance with Executive Orders Numbers Three and Seventeen, which deal with labor discrimination and demands that the supplier list all employment openings with the State Employment Service, and further, that the contractor agrees and warrants that he (not he or she) will not discriminate on grounds of race, religion, sex, physical disability, etc. Routing of the nine pages:

- (a)   First copy to the vendor.
- (b)   Second to the purchasing unit.
- (c)   Third to data processing.
- (d)   Fourth to the originating department.
- (e)   Fifth to receiving.
- (f)   The last four are invoices—all routed to the purchasing department.

These last four copies (of K-2) are not pre-carboned except for a two-inch wide strip at the bottom which contains replicated information on charges and funding coding. Too, some patent differences with other commercial invoices arise. One question on the invoice asks whether the supplier is incorporated; if not, it must supply either a federal employer number or a social security number for federal reporting information. Another requests the vendor to supply separate invoices for each purchase order and advises that billing information will also appear on the check issued, which identifies the particular shipment. For control purposes, there is space for agency verification of charges (appearing in bold type), requiring signatures for goods received or services rendered, and expenditure authorized and properly chargeable. Shipping information also appears on the invoice. The invoice described above (in K-2) approximates the Vendor's Invoice (K-3).

K-3   Completed in quadruplicate, it must be signed in order to obtain payment.

K-4   On a less complicated level, the Textbook Requisition form (K-4), in sextuple, is a two-color **MONEY SAVER**. The left-hand side of the heading and columns one through five are in red; red areas are completed by the initiator. On carboned pages, various columns in red also highlight pertinent elements. The remainder of the form is printed in black letters, including columns six through ten on the first page, for ordering, inventory control, and reason for sales projections.

There are other TIME-SAVING FEATURES. Each copy is a different color. The bottom, pink copy, is retained by the initiator of the request. After the order has been processed, the third, blue copy, is returned to the initiator for his or her permanent records or for reference use in further correspondence. The blue copy, in its heading, also contains a coding key that relates to column seven—reasons for modifying the initiator's request. Because ordering and reordering take place at least twice each year, near reorder time the green copy is transmitted to the initiator, with column ten—showing number of items sold—highlighted to aid the initiator in reordering and to help in inventory maintenance.

When the order has been processed internally, a seven-page Bookstore Purchasing Form (K-5) is completed with copies distributed as follows:

K-5

    (a)   The original to the state controller.
    (b)   Next page to department charged (to accounts payable).
    (c)   Third to accounts payable.
    (d)   Fourth and fifth to the ordering bookstore.
    (e)   Sixth to the department (sent with order).
    (f)   Seventh retained for departmental records.

A national fraternity elicits six copies of its Official Order Form (K-6), all identical. Information required is straightforward, and standard merchandise is preprinted on the order as a TIME SAVER. Simpler still, the Purchase Request (K-7) used by the postal service actually is a small envelope which doubles as a purchase order, container for the money, and receptacle for requested stamps. For other postal services, a Carrier's Statement (K-8) summarizes both goods or services and monetary transactions. This dual-purpose form also is an envelope.

K-6

K-7

K-8

For interdepartmental transfers of materials, equipment, and supplies, a Transfer Voucher (K-9) is filed, in original, with the state comptroller, a duplicate goes to accounting, and one copy each goes to the department debited and credited. Credit and debit data appear at the bottom of the original and on each copy. With this procedure management can monitor all costs and equipment uses of each department, FORESTALL MISUSE of these items, and impede the siphoning off, by departments with large pipelines to funds, of surplus inventory and equipment for redistribution, which would circumvent planning and resource allocations.

K-9

Expenses, too, are closely controlled and allocated for proper purposes. Examples include:

    ◆   Request for Funds for Special Speakers (K-10), in duplicate, plus the file copy.
    ◆   Form for projected Local Expenses of Guest Speakers (K-11).
    ◆   Reservation Request for Guest Housing (K-12).

K-10
K-11
K-12

K-13
K-14 Travel expenses embrace a multistep process which begins with a Travel Request (K-13) and ends with a Request for Reimbursement of Expenses (K-14). Deceptively simple, these forms impose approval at various levels and from different directions, coupled with supporting documents and proof that travel ties in with purposes and time stated. As a further control method, absolute reimbursement limits for mileage, lodging, meals and tips (appropriately prorated on a per diem schedule by meal) establish expense boundaries. Besides travel expense approvals, repairs must be solicited, sanctioned and
K-15 scheduled (K-15).

K-16 For budgeting and planning purposes, actual revenue to date compared with budgeted revenue (K-16) for the period, and percent of budget computations appear in the last column of this next configuration. Such periodic analogical exercises encourage adjustments in expenditures and financial planning if revenues are behind or ahead. Also helpful would be a fourth column (even a fifth and sixth) that allows comparison of this year's revenue with last year's (or that of two or three preceding years) coupled with a variance analysis.

K-17
K-18 Cash flow transactions by quarter and project authorized provide an estimate of quarterly cash needs (K-17). The Capital Improvement Program Cash Flow (K-18), executed monthly, pairs actual and estimated cash receipts (including borrowing) and disbursements.

K-19 Key to nonprofit operation is tax exempt status. The sample California Exemption Application (K-19), along with sample articles of incorporation (signed by Doe, Roe, and Moe), must be filed by all organizations except certain political ones. Points emphasized (or sometimes overlooked by applicants) in this application are these:

(a) An authorized individual (officers, director, representative, or trustee) must sign the application.
(b) Financial statements of existing organizations, including *itemized* income and expenses, or a proposed budget of new organizations, must be attached.
(c) A detailed description of activities must be included.
(d) All organizing documents must accompany the application:
   (i) Articles of Incorporation;
   (ii) By-laws or Constitution;
   (iii) Trust Instrument.

A certificate of State Tax Exemption usually is filed with suppliers. Three examples include:

K-20
K-21
K-22
◆ Blanket Certificate of Exemption for Purchase of Materials, Tools, and Fuel (K-20).
◆ Multipurpose Certificate of Exemption (K-21).
◆ A Charitable and Religious Organizations Exemption Certificate (K-22).

A nonstock corporation incorporating in the State of Delaware will file a Certificate of Incorporation (and other documents) along the lines shown in the model (K-23). Like nonresident profit organizations, nonprofit ones, too, must qualify for doing business in or operating in a state in which the entity has not incorporated. The Application for Certificate of Authority (and accompanying instruction) (K-24) imposes the following conditions: **K-23** **K-24**

    (a)   Properly signed and notarized applications must be made in duplicate.

    (b)   The corporation must maintain a resident agent.

    (c)   A Certificate of Compliance, or Certificate of Good Standing, is required from the corporation's domicile state.

    (d)   Every nonresident must appoint the Commissioner of Commerce and Economic Development as Agent for Service of Process.

Do not confuse Item (d) above with Item (b). A separate form (K-25), and filing fee, is necessary to Appoint the Commissioner of Commerce and Economic Development as Resident Agent for Service of Process in Alaska. **K-25**

Of course, annual reports must be filed whether in Alaska (K-26) or in Delaware (K-27). Nonprofit organizations typically pay substantially lower franchise taxes (if any), and sometimes only a nominal filing fee, than do corporations organized for profit activities. (For instance, note fee differentials in Figures F-53 and F-56.) Despite a nonstock status, nonprofit organizations still must raise funds; one method, of course, is via a bond issue (K-28). (Another bond specimen appears in F-33.) **K-26** **K-27** **K-28**

Cash is cash, whether it belongs to a profit or a not-for-profit concern, and must be managed. On the Daily Cash Report (K-29), cash receipts, investment and loan proceeds are to be added to the beginning cash balance, and disbursements and investments purchased are to be subtracted from it, to arrive at a closing cash balance. This is done by category or fund. The seven-page form also excerpts the closing investment balance and notes payable for each transaction date. Control also crops up with Appropriation Disbursements (K-30). This form requires a voucher payment register number and date, check number and posting date, funds available and disbursed, and approval, among other information. **K-29** **K-30**

Some entities also insist on approval if employees engage in outside activity, whether remunerative or not. The Request for Approval (K-31), filed in quadruplicate, implicitly proscribes certain political activities. **K-31**

In the payroll and recruitment department, an early step begins with a Request for Recruitment Funds (K-32) followed at some point by an Equal Opportunity Information Request (K-33). The Employment Authorization (K-34) describes the type of vacancy, salary rate, personal data, method of payment, budgeting and payroll notations, plus five approvals. **K-32** **K-33** **K-34**

K-35

K-36
K-37

K-38

Temporary or part-time student labor also requires a Student Payroll Authorization (K-35) coupled with a Student Agreement (at the bottom of the same form). (This agreement may represent a good pledge for business concerns likewise to consider.) A Payroll Time Sheet (K-36) records in-and-out times for each pay period. Notice that both the employee and the supervisor must sign. The Labor Payroll Report (K-37) calls for the name of student and account to be charged and recapitulates time, rate, and amount for each payroll period. For an occupational accident or disease, a report (K-38) is filled out in detail by the operating unit head and forwarded to the state's Attorney General's office.

K-39
K-40

K-41

The other forms, which relate to payroll department functions only if additional payroll deductions result, are a state employee's Homeowner's Insurance Quotation form (K-39), and a state employee's Automobile Insurance Quotation form (K-40). In some instances the personnel or payroll department may supply additional forms on request, which would mean further involvement and higher operating costs for these departments. The last accounting design shown is a Motor Pool Vehicle request (K-41). This type of scheduling encourages MAXIMUM USE OF ASSETS, minimum investment in rolling stock, control against personal use of organization vehicles, COST-SAVING centralization of this function, and PROPER ALLOCATION OF COSTS among departments.

Form No. PUR 4 (Rev. 1/70)

The University of Connecticut

STATE OF CONNECTICUT

Purchase Requisition

PLEASE NOTE! INSTRUCTIONS
1. Restrict each requisition to one type of material.
2. Submit original and 2 copies. Keep 4th copy.
3. List chemicals alphabetically. Laboratory equipment and supplies numerically.
4. Double space between items. DO NOT REMOVE CARBONS!
5. Furnish at least 3 recommended vendors, when possible.

P.O. NO.

REQUISITION NO.

88931

VENDOR'S NAME AND ADDRESS

DELIVER TO DEPARTMENT

TEL. EXT.

DATE OF REQUISITION	DATE REQUIRED	OUR QUOTE NO.	F.O.B.	VENDOR'S QUOTE NO.	TERMS:

ITEM DESCRIPTION (GIVE COMPLETE & SPECIFIC DETAILS TO AVOID MISTAKES AND DELAYS)	QUANTITY	UNIT	UNIT PRICE	AMOUNT

RECOMMENDED VENDORS AND ADDRESSES

1.
2.
3.

ACCOUNTS CHARGEABLE - VENDOR PLEASE DISREGARD

ABOVE MAT'L TO BE USED FOR

FISCAL YEAR	FUND	AGENCY	SPEC. IDENT.	FUNC. TION	ACTIVITY	OBJECT MAJ	OBJECT MIN.	AMOUNT	FUND SOURCE	PROJ.
		7301								

REQUISITIONED BY

DEPT. HEAD APPROVAL

PUR. OFFICER APPROVAL

DIR. OF PUR. APPROVAL
DPA_____ PC_____

Figure K-1: PURCHASE REQUISITION
(Courtesy of the University of Connecticut.)

INVOICE for Goods Sold or Services Rendered to **THE UNIVERSITY OF CONNECTICUT**
BO-21A (PUR-5A)
REV. 9/77
(Comptroller's CO-17)
An Agency of the State of Connecticut

● U. CONN. PURCHASING DEPT., BOX U-76, STORRS, CONN. 06268

▼ FOR STATE AGENCY USE ▼

LIMITED-VALUE PURCHASE ORDER — 5. RECEIVING — *Not Valid for Orders Over $200* — Please mark all packages clearly with vendor's name

LIMITED-VALUE PURCHASE ORDER — 4. ORIGINATING DEPT. — *Not Valid for Orders Over $200* — Please mark all packages clearly with vendor's name

LIMITED-VALUE PURCHASE ORDER — 3. DATA PROCESSING — *Not Valid for Orders Over $200* — Please mark all packages clearly with vendor's name

LIMITED-VALUE PURCHASE ORDER — 2. UNIVERSITY PURCHASING — *Not Valid for Orders Over $200* — Please mark all packages clearly with vendor's name

LIMITED-VALUE PURCHASE ORDER
PUR-5A Rev. 9/77
(Comptroller's CO-94DP)

1. VENDOR
Not Valid for Orders Over $200
State of Connecticut
THE UNIVERSITY OF CONNECTICUT
Storrs, Connecticut 06268

Please mark all packages clearly with vendor's **name** and our Purchase Order No.

69636

1. All shipments on this order must be prepaid.   2. Acceptance of this order implies conformance with conditions on reverse side.

SHIP TO THE UNIVERSITY OF CONNECTICUT, *(Name of Department, Branch, etc.)*	*(Address)*	*(Attention of)*	REQUISITION DATE	DATE MAT'L REQUIRED

TO:

BILLING INSTRUCTIONS TO VENDOR
1. Claims against the University of Conn. must be presented on the 4-part invoice supplied by the University.
2. This order is exempt from Conn. Sales and Federal Excise taxes.
3. Send attached invoices to The University of Connecticut.
4. Submit invoices on day of shipment to insure prompt payment.

DIRECTOR OF PURCHASE AUTH. *(DPA, PC, CA, Exempt, etc.)*	DATE OF ORDER	YOUR QUOTE NO.	CASH DISC. TERMS	F.O.B. *(Delivered, unless noted here)*	DATE PROMISED

ITEM NO.	DESCRIPTION	QUANTITY	UNIT	UNIT PRICE	AMOUNT

Approved by the State Comptroller subject to availability of funds in existing appropriations.

BUYER'S INITIALS

APPROVED BY AGENCY AND FUNDS COMMITTED *(Signature of University Director of Purchases)*

RECOMMENDED VENDORS AND ADDRESSES
1.
2.
3.

NAME OF REQUISITIONER	APPROVED *(Signature of Department Head)*	APPROVED *(Signature of Dean or Director)*

FISCAL YR.	FUND	AGENCY	SP. ID.	FU.	ACTIVITY	MAJ.	MIN.	RES. FUNDS NO.	AMOUNT	ADJUSTMENT		ENCUMBRANCE	P.O. NO.	FU. S.	PROJ.
		7301								Debit	Credit				

Figure K-2: LIMITED VALUE PURCHASE ORDER
(Courtesy of the University of Connecticut.)

NOTICE TO VENDOR: A few days after this copy of the invoice is returned to you, you will receive payment for it from the State Comptroller. Keep this copy so that you will be able to identify the check issued in payment of this invoice and apply it properly to our account. The check will bear the same PAYMENT LIST NO. as shown here at the upper right.

State Agency: Please fill in below.		
FORM 1099 REPORT	PAYMENT LIST DATE	PAYMENT LIST NO.
☐ Yes ☐ No.		

Payment cannot be processed until this invoice is completed, signed, and submitted in quadruplicate.

VENDOR'S INVOICE

BO-21 Rev. 1/74

(Comptroller's CO-17)

Sold to State of Conn. through Purchasing Authority of

THE UNIVERSITY OF CONNECTICUT

Storrs, Connecticut 06268

VENDOR'S NAME AND ADDRESS →

(Enter address to which check is to be sent.)

State Agency: Please fill in below.		
FORM 1099 REPORT	PAYMENT LIST DATE	PAYMENT LIST NO.
☐ Yes ☐ No.		
REQ. FOR RES. OF FUNDS NO.		TRAVEL AUTHORIZATION NO.

Vendor: Please fill in below.

DATE OF INVOICE	PURCHASE ORDER NO.

Vendor: To insure proper identification of payment, insert your billing number below:

VENDOR'S NO.

VENDOR: If NOT incorporated, please fill in.→	YOUR FEDERAL EMPLOYER NO. (if your have one) Either →	YOUR SOC. SECURITY NO. (if no Employer No.) Or

SHIPPING INFORMATION

DATE SHIPPED	FROM (City and State)
VIA (Carrier)	F.O.B.
PREPAID OR COLLECT	TERMS

State Agency Signatures Below

COMMODITIES RECEIVED OR SERVICES RENDERED (Signature)

EXPENDITURE AUTHORIZED AND PROPERLY CHARGEABLE TO APPROPRIATIONS AS INDICATED BELOW (Authorized Signature)

PURCHASE ORDER		DESCRIPTION	QUANTITY	UNIT PRICE	AMOUNT
Date	Number				

This invoice is subject to _____ % Cash Discount if paid in _____ days.

VENDOR'S STATEMENT

(Conn. G. S. Sec. 3-117)

Please sign all copies in ink.

The above claim is just and correct and has not been paid; the whole labor has been performed or the articles furnished, and no commission, discount, bonus, reward or present of any kind has been promised, received or expected on account thereof by any officer of the State.

SIGNED (Vendor or Authorized Officer) X	TITLE	DATE SIGNED

TO BE FILLED IN BY EXPENDING AGENCY

Fiscal Year	Fund	Agency	Spec. Ident.	Func-tion	Activity	OBJECT		Document No.	Amount	ADJUSTMENT		Encumbrance	Ref. No.	Fund Source	Proj.
						Maj.	Min.			Dr.	Cr.				
		7301							/						

Figure K-3: VENDOR'S INVOICE

(Courtesy of the University of Connecticut.)

PLEASE FILL IN ALL RED AREAS BELOW:

DATE
SUBMITTED

DATE
LOGGED

TERM _____ YEAR _____

DEPARTMENT _____

COURSE AND
SECTION NUMBER _____

COURSE NAME _____

INSTRUCTOR _____

PHONE _____ U-BOX _____

Please put your estimate of total course enrollment here. This may vary from the quantity listed in column #5.

UConn Co-op
BOX U-19

TEXTBOOK REQUISITION

Please submit a requisition even if no textbook is to be used.

Please use a separate form for each course number. The same form may be used for multiple sections of the same course.

Instructor's estimate of the quantity of each title needed should show in column #5. This number may vary from total (estimated) course enrollment and/or vary title by title.

Your checkmark in column #4 is vital.

HOW THIS FORM WORKS

A. After processing this order, the Co-op will return the BLUE copy to the instructor indicating in column #6 the quantity of each title we plan to have available for the course. These quantities are based on our evaluation of past sales and enrollment figures.

B. Toward the end of the semester, the GREEN copy will be returned to the instructor showing in column #10 the number of copies sold.

IF POSSIBLE, PLEASE LIST
TITLES IN ORDER OF USE.

1 AUTHOR (LAST NAME FIRST, PLEASE)	2 TITLE AND EDITION (OR SUPPLY ITEM AND NUMBER)	3 PUBLISHER (OR VENDOR)	4 IS THIS BOOK REQUIRED YES / NO	5 EST. QUAN. NEEDED	6 STORE ORDER	7 REASON(S) FOR INCREASE OR DECREASE IN YOUR BOOK ESTIMATE	8 REORDER	9 COPIES LEFT	10 SOLD

FOR STORE USE ONLY

PRE-REGISTRATION

FALL _____ SPRING _____

FALL _____ SPRING _____

FALL _____ SPRING _____

CAPACITY _____

ENROLLMENT _____

PLEASE REFER TEXTBOOK QUESTIONS TO OUR BOOK DEPT. X 3537 OR 3727

№ 010720

COMMENTS:

CO-OP DUPLICATE COPY

SAVE FOR YOUR RECORDS OR RETURN TO CO-OP WITH YOUR COMMENTS

WHEN COMPLETED BY CO-OP SAVE FOR YOUR RECORDS

SAVE THIS COPY FOR YOUR RECORDS

PLEASE REMOVE LAST PLY (PINK) AND RETURN REMAINING COPIES INTACT

Figure K-4: TEXTBOOK REQUISITION
(Courtesy of the UConn Co-op.)

Bookstore Purchasing Form

FORM BO - 46

NAME AND
ADDRESS OF
CREDITOR

UCONN CO-OP
U-19

No. 35884

VOUCHER No.

DATE PAID

PRICE APPROVED

COMMODITIES RECEIVED

DEPARTMENT _____
U BOX _____
BUILDING _____
PHONE _____

THE STATE OF CONNECTICUT
Through the Purchasing Authority of
THE UNIVERSITY OF CONNECTICUT
STORRS, CONN.

DATE OF
INVOICE

INVOICE

RECIPIENT'S SIGNATURE_____ DATE FILLED_____ FILLED BY_____

TERMS

CONTROLLER

QUANTITY	DESCRIPTION	UNIT PRICE	AMOUNT
		TOTAL	
		DISCOUNT	
		POSTAGE	
		NET	
		VALIDATION	

Fiscal Year	Fund	Agency	Spec. Ident.	Func.	Activity	OBJECT Maj.	OBJECT Min.	List No.	Amount	ADJUSTMENT Dr.	ADJUSTMENT Cr.	Encumbrance	Ref. No.	Fund Source	Proj.
		7301													

STATE COMPTROLLER

DEPARTMENT CHARGED
(TO ACCOUNTS PAYABLE)

ACCOUNTS PAYABLE

CO-OP BOOKSTORE #1

CO-OP BOOKSTORE #2

DEPARTMENT (SEND
WITH ORDER)

DEPARTMENT (RETAIN)

Figure K-5: BOOKSTORE PURCHASING FORM
(Courtesy of the UConn Co-op.)

PLEASE TYPE ALL ORDERS

ORDER NO.   0747

MAIL COPIES 1, 2, 3, 4, 5, and 6 (DO NOT REMOVE CARBONS) TO MAN-
AGING DIRECTOR, 11500 OLIVE ST. ROAD, SUITE 142, ST. LOUIS, MO
63141. KEEP COPY 7 FOR CHAPTER FILES.

Add $2.50 order processing charge on all orders (for jewelry) under $30.00.

S
H NAME
I
P ST. & NO.
T
O CITY & STATE

ZIP CODE

CHECK TYPE OF DELIVERY DESIRED FOR JEWELRY:

Regular ☐

Special Delivery $2.00 additional ☐

Make checks payable to Beta Gamma Sigma.

Quan.	Serial No.	DESCRIPTION	Price	Extension	DO NOT WRITE IN THESE SPACES		
	#500	Miniature Key	$6.60				
	#501	Miniature Keypin	7.05				
	#502	Official Key	6.85				
	#503	Official Keypin	7.20				
	#504	Honorary Key	7.50				
	#600	Miniature Key Replica Lapel Pin	3.90				
	#601	Miniature Key Replica Lapel Button	3.90				
	#8	Tie Tack Assembly	3.65				
	#9	Adjustable Tie Chain	5.30				
	#10	Woman's Bracelet, Link Chain	4.60				
		For display of Keys 500 & 502					
			ENGRAVING $1.00 PER ITEM				
			TOTAL				

INSTRUCTIONS: Designate jewelry as "engraved" or "non-engraved". List serial No. of items as "502", "503", "8", etc.; directly below the
notation list persons to receive those items.

Full Name as it is to appear on Certificate Engrave first initials and full last name on keys. (Initials only engraved on #501 & #503)	Member inducted as: Jr., Sr., Masters, Doct., Fac., or Honorary	Month, Day, and Year Member Inducted. Engrave Year Date Only (as '74)	
			This order requested by:
			Chapter Secretary Date
			FULL name of University
			Engrave abbreviated name of University
			CERTIFICATE OF ELIGIBILITY
			I hereby certify that the above named juniors rank in the highest five percent of their class, the above named seniors rank in the highest ten percent of their class, and the above named graduate students receiving masters degrees rank in the highest twenty percent of their class and the above named doctoral candidates have completed all requirements for the degree. We have_____in the present junior class,_____in the present senior class, and_____in the present class receiving masters degrees.
			_____ Dean

Figure K-6: ORDER FORM
(Courtesy of Beta Gamma Sigma.)

U.S. POSTAL SERVICE
STAMP STOCK PURCHASE REQUEST

Dear Customer:

Customers of rural and star routes are expected to affix stamps to their greeting cards and letter mail deposited in rural boxes for collection by the carrier.

Your carrier has a supply of stamps, envelopes and postal cards and will fill your order. Use this envelope to assist you in your purchase.

Indicate the items desired.

Sign your name—print your address.

Enclose the necessary money and leave the envelope in the box.

The U.S. Postal Service and your carrier are pleased to render this service for your convenience.

POSTMASTER

NUMBER	DENOMINATION	AMOUNT
	10¢	
	15¢	
	Book 24-15¢ Stamps @ $3.60	
	Stamped Envelopes @ 18¢	
	Postal Cards @ 10¢	
SIGNATURE (Be sure to sign your name)		
YOUR ADDRESS (Please print)		
MANSFIELD CENTER, CT 06250		

Before destroying this envelope, please examine it carefully to be sure there are no stamps enclosed.

PS Form 4234 June 1978

Figure K-7: STAMP STOCK PURCHASE REQUEST

CARRIER'S STATEMENT

M

The following is a statement of the amount required for each of the items indicated and if there is any part that you do not understand, please call it to my attention.

Money Order		
Money Order Fee		
Postage on Letter		
Postage on Package		
Insurance Fee on Package		
Stamps		
Stamped Envelopes		
Postal Cards		
Register Fee		
C.O.D. Fee		
Certified Fee		
Postage Due Mail		
Total Amount Required		
Amount Received		
Balance Due You		
Balance Due the Carrier		

If there is a balance due you, the amount will be found in this envelope. If there is a balance due the carrier, please enclose it in this evelope and leave it in the box. Thank you.

CARRIER.

POST OFFICE	ZIP CODE
MANSFIELD CENTER, CT 06250	

PS Form 4245, Nov. 1977

Figure K-8: POSTAL CARRIER'S STATEMENT

UNIVERSITY OF CONNECTICUT
STORRS, CONN.
TRANSFER VOUCHER

TV No. 76572

DEPARTMENT CHARGED	University Box Number

THESE VOUCHERS TO BE USED BY DEPARTMENTS OF THE UNIVERSITY ONLY FOR ENTERING CHARGES AGAINST OTHER DEPARTMENTS OF THE UNIVERSITY.

VOUCHER NO.   DATE PAID

APPROVED FOR PAYMENT

Prepared By

DEPARTMENT CREDITED

Date Prepared

CONTROLLER

QUANTITY	DESCRIPTION	UNIT PRICE	AMOUNT

ACCOUNT(S) CHARGED

Fiscal Year	Fund	Agency	Spec. Ident.	Func-tion	Activity	Maj.	Min.	List No.	Amount	Ref. No.	Fund Source	Proj.
		7301										

(OBJECT spans Maj. / Min.)

ACCOUNT(S) CREDITED

Fiscal Year	Fund	Agency	Spec. Ident.	Func-tion	Activity	Maj.	Min.	List No.	Amount	Ref. No.	Fund Source	Proj.
		7301										

(OBJECT spans Maj. / Min.)

STATE COMPTROLLER'S COPY

ACCOUNTS COPY

DEPARTMENT CHARGED COPY

DEPARTMENT CREDITED COPY

Figure K-9: TRANSFER VOUCHER FOR SUPPLIES
(Courtesy of the University of Connecticut.)

THE GRADUATE SCHOOL
UNIVERSITY OF CONNECTICUT RESEARCH FOUNDATION
REQUEST FUNDS FOR SPECIAL COLLOQUIUM SPEAKERS

Department _____ U-Box # _____

Visitor's Name _____

Address _____

Professional Affiliation
(College or University) _____

Appearance Plan (e.g., special graduate colloquium, workshop, interdepartmental seminar)

_____

Topic: _____

Date of Appearance _____

Estimated fee and expenses $ _____

Other information regarding the special colloquium: _____

_____

_____

_____   _____
Department Head (Type Name)   Department Head Signature

Send 2 copies to: Hugh Clark, Associate Dean
                        Graduate School
                        U-133
                        Ext. 1861

Figure K-10: REQUEST FUNDS FOR SPECIAL COLLOQUIUM SPEAKERS
(Courtesy of the University of Connecticut.)

(Form No. RF-C-3)

LOCAL EXPENSES FOR GUEST SPEAKERS

THIS LETTER SHOULD BE SENT TO MR. HANNA ONE WEEK BEFORE THE EVENT

Mr. Edward Hanna
Asst. Vice President
　　for Financial Affairs, U-72

Dear Mr. Hanna:

　It is expected that _____ will entertain
　　　　　　　　　　　　　　　　　Name of Host & Position

(If FAC meal tickets are requested, host must be FAC member)

Name of Guest		Date(s)	Est. Cost	Location
_____	Breakfast*	_____	_____	_____
	Lunch*	_____	_____	_____
	Dinner*	_____	_____	_____

*Please specify where meals are to be eaten.

Position

_____
(cannot be State Employee)

LODGING AT _____ will be needed

on _____ estimated at $ _____ /night _____ (a total of $_____.)
　　Date(s)

　　　　(Lakeside reservations must be made by departmental secretary)

LOCAL TRANSPORTATION (_____)
　　　　　　　　　　　　Describe destination and mode of travel (Maximum $20.00)

is expected to be $ _____ .

Account to be charged is: 5.171-000-21-5001-35-016 for transportation and meals.

　　　　　　　　　　　　　　Sincerely yours,

　　　　　　　　　_____ , Head
　　　　　　　　　　　　　　Department of

Allowance for Meals:	Breakfast -	$1.00
	Lunch -	$2.00
	Dinner -	$5.00

cc: Hugh Clark, Associate Dean

Figure K-11: LOCAL EXPENSES FOR GUEST SPEAKERS
(Courtesy of the University of Connecticut.)

THE UNIVERSITY OF CONNECTICUT

Reservation Request for Guest Housing

Date of Request _____

Date of Arrival _____ Date of Departure _____ Total Number of Nights _____

Accommodations Requested: Lakeside Apt. _____ Lakeside Single _____ Whitney Hall _____

Name of Guest(s) _____

Purpose of Visit _____ _____

Charge to be paid by: _____ _____ _____ _____
                         Transfer Voucher   B012   Cash   Research Foundation Fund
                                                             (Whitney Only)

Name of Contact Agent if other than Dean/Director _____

Phone Extension of Contact Agent _____ Department _____

Signature of Dean/Director _____ U-Box Number _____

****

DETACH THIS PART FOR REFERENCE

Guest housing is available for occupancy after 2:00 p.m. Guests must vacate by 11 a.m. on the day of departure.

The key for *Lakeside* may be picked up in Room 109, on the ground floor of Hall Dorm on the same day of the arrival of the guest or the last work day preceding the arrival of the guest and may be left on the dresser by the guest on leaving. There is no Resident Manager in this facility.

The key for Whitney Hall may be obtained from the Resident Manager in her office at the time of registration and is returned to her upon vacating.

Figure K-12: RESERVATION REQUEST FOR GUEST HOUSING
(Courtesy of the University of Connecticut.)

(Form No. RF-TF-2)
Revised 10/77

UNIVERSITY OF CONNECTICUT RESEARCH FOUNDATION
FACULTY TRAVEL REQUEST

For AAUP Professional Development Award, check here (see memorandum of October 27, 1977, regarding such funds). Must be accompanied by letter of support from department head.

Person to be reimbursed   Title   Department

_____   _____   U-_____

Travel Period _____ Destination _____

Purpose of travel:

Presentation of invited paper	_____	PLEASE ATTACH COPIES OF
Serving as chairperson of a section	_____	CORRESPONDENCE, LETTER
Serving on a symposium panel	_____	OF INVITATION, OR OTHER
Presentation of contributed paper	_____	INFORMATION ABOUT
Attendance only	_____	MEETING. Include
Business meeting of professional society	_____	abstract of paper, if
Other (please explain) _____		available.

Title of paper _____

Professional society _____

COMPLETE SECTION A OR SECTION B

Section A	Section B
(No Grant or Contract Funds Are Available)	(Supplement to Grant or Contract Funds)

Domestic travel: air (   ) $\times \frac{2}{3}$ = _____

Foreign travel: air (   ) $\times \frac{2}{3}$ = _____

Rail _____

Auto (in lieu of bus) _____
           (Do not include limousine)

Registration _____
         (Do not include room and board)

Subsistence _____ (Not allowed)

Total _____

In accordance with the memorandum of September 2, 1975, I certify that no grant or contract funds are available to me to support the travel requested above.

In accordance with the memorandum of September 2, 1975, I certify that grant or contract funds are inadequate and the request below is supplementary.

Total cost of travel _____

Available from grant or contract _____

Supplement requested _____

For _____
      (Category of expenditure; follow
      "guidelines" under Section A)

_____
Applicant's Signature

_____
Applicant's Signature

_____
Department Head Signature

_____
Date

REQUESTS SHOULD BE SUBMITTED AT LEAST 4 WEEKS PRIOR TO THE DATE OF DEPARTURE. PLEASE SEND 1 COPY TO: Hugh Clark, Acting Vice President, U-133.

Figure K-13: FACULTY TRAVEL REQUEST
(Courtesy of the University of Connecticut.)

REQUEST FOR REIMBURSEMENT OF EXPENSES (Travel and Other)
INCURRED IN THE SERVICE OF THE STATE OF CONNECTICUT
BO-27 (CO-17XP-UC) REV. 7/72

For specific regulations governing reimbursable expenses, refer to the "STANDARD TRAVEL REGULATIONS" issued by the Department of Finance and Control.

Prepare in quadruplicate.

AGENCY NAME		AGENCY NO.	DATE PAID	PAYMENT LIST NO.
THE UNIVERSITY OF CONNECTICUT		7301		

Period Covered	FROM (Mo., day, yr.)	TO (Mo., day, yr.)		REQ. FOR RES. OF FUNDS NO.	TRAVEL AUTHORIZATION NO.

PAYEE'S CERTIFICATION	PAYEE'S NAME (First) ... (M. I.) ... (Last)	SOC. SEC. NO.	AMT. OF REIMB. REQUESTED (give details on reverse) $

HOME ADDRESS (No. and Street)   (Town)   (State)   (Zip Code)

I affirm that the reimbursements claimed herewith are just and that the travel indicated was officially necessary.

DATE	PAYEE'S TITLE	SIGNED (Payee)

Sec. 3-117 of the General Statutes requires receipts or vouchers for all expenditures exceeding five dollars. Please enter at right the total number of receipts and/or vouchers attached. ➤   NO. OF VOUCHER/RECEIPTS ATTACHED

ADVANCE FROM PETTY CASH (if applicable)

I acknowledge that the amount stated below was given to me as an advance against the amount of travel and other expenses shown herein as due to me.

AMOUNT $	SIGNED (Payee)

AGENCY'S CERTIFICATION

I certify that the services have been performed and the expenses incurred as stated in this account, except as noted; that they were necessary and proper; and that the amounts claimed are just and reasonable, except as noted.

DATE	APPROVED FOR $	SIGNED (Department Head)
SIGNED (Dean or Director)		SIGNED (Controller)

REMARKS, EXPLANATION OF UNUSUAL ITEMS, ETC.

PURPOSE OF TRIP

Fiscal Year	Fund	Agency	Spec. Ident.	Func.	Activity	Object Maj.	Object Min.	List No.	Amount	Adjustment Debit	Adjustment Credit	Encumbrance	Ref. No.	Fund Source	Proj.
		7301													
		7301													
		7301													
		7301													
		7301													
		7301													
		7301													
		7301													
		7301													
		7301													
		7301													

Figure K-14: REQUEST FOR REIMBURSEMENT OF EXPENSES
(Courtesy of the University of Connecticut.)

DATE (Mo., day)	TRAVEL		TRAVEL BY AUTOMOBILE					OTHER TRAVEL B-Bus R-Rail C-Cab O-Other	LODGING	MEALS B-Breakfast L-Lunch D-Dinner	MISC. (telephone, telegram, tips, etc.)	
	From	To	State-Owned		Personally Owned							
			MISC. EXPENSES (parking, tolls, gas, oil, repairs, etc.) AMOUNT		ODOMETER READING		NO. OF MILES	AMOUNT AT /MILE	AMOUNT	AMOUNT	AMOUNT	EXPLANATION	AMOUNT
					Start	Finish							
SUB-TOTALS →			$				TOTAL NO. OF MILES	$	$	$	$	$

GRAND TOTAL → $

Figure K-14 (continued)

905

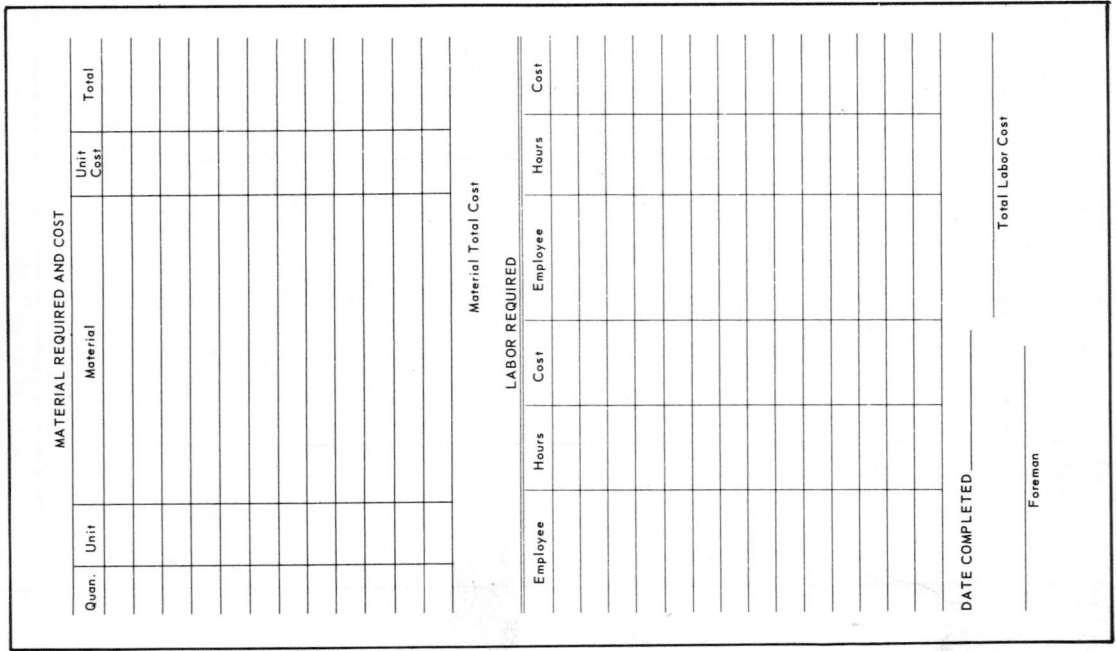

Figure K-15: **REQUEST FOR REPAIRS**
(Courtesy of the University of Connecticut.)

Figure K-15—Reverse Side

THE METROPOLITAN DISTRICT   File #13

WATER UTILITY FUND

REVENUE BUDGET

_____September_____ 19

	19 ACTUAL REVENUE	19 BUDGET REVENUE	% RECEIVED AS OF 9-30-
Sale of Water:			
Domestic	$ 5,620,894.59	$ 7,486,000	75.09
Commercial	1,726,359.05	2,270,000	76.05
Industrial	1,210,110.07	1,570,000	77.08
Public Authorities	600,012.94	766,500	78.28
Other Water Comp.	60,917.78	73,000	83.45
TOTAL WATER SALES	$ 9,218,294.43	$12,165,500	75.77
Other Revenue:			
Air Conditioning	$ -0-	3,000	0.0
Hydrant Maint.	190,815.00	255,000	74.83
Fire Services	157,676.81	204,000	77.29
Penalty-Water Bills	53,465.62	68,000	78.63
Rents-Water Property	14,961.20	13,600	110.00
Sales of Material	1,703.23	2,000	85.16
TOTAL OTHER REVENUE	$ 418,621.86	$ 545,600	76.73
Non-Oper. Revenue:			
Merchandising-Jobbing	$ 48,214.01	35,000	137.75
Interest-W.U. Investments	47,288.37	70,000	67.55
Interest-W.B. Investments	3,343.77	32,000	10.45
Interest-M.P. Assess.	5,217.04	4,000	130.43
Insurance Refunds	245,373.30	120,000	204.48
Miscellaneous	119,591.19	113,800	105.09
LESS:			
Loss-Recreation Areas	(66,450.53)	(81,500)	(81.53)
TOTAL NON-OPER. REV.	$ 402,577.15	$ 293,300	137.26
SUB TOTAL REVENUE	$10,039,493.44	13,004.400	77.20
Contributions	658,025.83	948,200	69.40
Depreciation Allowance	1,500,392.10	1,989,100	75.43
Retained Earnings	-0-	1,097,800	-0-
TOTAL ALL REVENUES	$12,197,911.37	$17,039,500	71.59

cc: EIC
     JRL   *Robert N French*
     RRB   Robert N. French,
                                  District Treasurer

Figure K-16: REVENUE BUDGET
  (Courtesy of Robert N. French, Treasurer, The Metropolitan District, Hartford, Connecticut.)

ASSESSABLE SEWER CONSTRUCTION FUND
STATEMENT OF CASH FLOW TRANSACTIONS

vs

C.I.P. BUDGET ALLOCATIONS AND PROJECTS AUTHORIZED IN PREVIOUS YEAR

ESTIMATED

	C.I.P. and PROJECTS	FIRST QUARTER	SECOND QUARTER	THIRD QUARTER	FOURTH QUARTER	REVISED
CASH BEGINNING	320,000	320,000	320,530	230,666	632,248	320,000
RECEIPTS:						
Sewer Assessment Collections	1,600,000	300,900	356,600	493,250	494,250	1,645,000
Sewer Assessment Interest	525,000	124,800	117,100	135,100	153,000	530,000
Outlet Charges	250,000	50,000	75,000	75,000	50,000	250,000
Sewer Connection Charges	75,000	15,000	22,500	22,500	15,000	75,000
Interest on Investments	25,000	5,000	5,000	7,500	7,500	25,000
Additional Borrowing During Year	500,000				250,000	250,000
Other Receipts	40,000	10,000	10,000	10,000	10,000	40,000
TOTAL RECEIPTS	3,015,000	505,700	586,200	743,350	979,750	2,815,000
TOTAL CASH AVAILABLE	3,335,000	825,700	906,730	974,016	1,611,998	3,135,000
DISBURSEMENTS:						
Construction of Sewers - 79 C.I.P.	259,800	29,300	33,600	221,800	154,000	438,700
Construction of Sewers - 78 PROJECTS	581,200	92,700	104,800	69,500	116,000	383,000
Construction - RETAINAGES	125,000	37,670	16,654	11,718	54,803	120,845
Interest on Notes	207,000		111,135			111,135
Bond Maturities	1,700,000	300,000	300,000	-0-	1,100,000	1,700,000
Bond Interest	277,000	40,500	104,875	33,750	97,375	276,500
Other Disbursements	20,000	5,000	5,000	5,000	5,000	20,000
TOTAL DISBURSEMENTS	3,170,000	505,170	676,064	341,768	1,527,178	3,050,180
CASH ENDING	165,000	320,530	230,666	632,248	84,820	84,820

Figure K-17: STATEMENT OF CASH FLOW TRANSACTIONS
(Courtesy of Robert N. French, Treasurer, The Metropolitan District, Hartford, Connecticut.)

CAPITAL IMPROVEMENT PROGRAM

PROGRAM CASH FLOW

PROGRAM _____

YEAR _____

		JAN	FEB	MAR	APR	MAY	JUN	JUL	AUG	SEP	OCT	NOV	DEC	TOTAL
CASH BEGINNING	ACT.													
	EST.													
RECEIPTS:														
TEMPORARY BORROWINGS	ACT.													
	EST.													
GRANTS	ACT.													
	EST.													
OTHER RECEIPTS	ACT.													
	EST.													
TOTAL AVAILABLE	ACT.													
	EST.													
DISBURSEMENTS:														
CONSTRUCTION & LABOR	ACT.													
	EST.													
NOTES REPAID	ACT.													
	EST.													
INTEREST PAID	ACT.													
	EST.													
TOTAL DISBURSEMENTS	ACT.													
	EST.													
CASH, ENDING	ACT.													
	EST.													
ACCRUED INTEREST	ACT.													
	EST.													
NOTES OUTSTANDING	ACT.													
	EST.													

Figure K-18: CAPITAL IMPROVEMENT PROGRAM—PROGRAM CASH FLOW
(Courtesy of Robert N. French, Treasurer, The Metropolitan District, Hartford, Connecticut.)

STATE OF CALIFORNIA
FRANCHISE TAX BOARD
SACRAMENTO, CALIFORNIA 95857
(916) 355-0392

EXEMPTION APPLICATION

For use by a principal officer or representative of the organization claiming exemption under Section 23701 of the Revenue and Taxation Code.

Every organization that claims to be exempt must furnish the information and data specified and pay the REQUIRED $10.00 APPLICATION FEE. If any organization fails to submit the information and data required, or pay the required fee, this application will not be considered on its merits and the organization will be notified accordingly. This application shall be open to public inspection in accordance with Section 26451.3 of the Revenue and Taxation Code.

See Instructions for FTB 3500 for guidance on completion and submission.

	DO NOT USE THESE SPACES
1a. Full Name of Organization	SERIAL NO.
b. Federal Employer Identification Number (See Specific Instruction 3, Item 1b.)	AMOUNT REMITTED
2. Complete Address (Number, street, city or town, State and Postal ZIP code)	TELEPHONE NUMBER

3a. Is the organization incorporated? ☐ Yes ☐ No	b. If "Yes," in which State?	c. Corporate Number:

4a. If not incorporated, what is form of organization? ☐ Now being incorporated ☐ Unincorporated association ☐ Trust	b. Date incorporated or organized	c. End of month in which the annual accounting period ends

5. If this organization or its predecessor previously applied for an exemption, enter "Granted" or "Denied" and date of determination (furnish copy of determination).
☐ California .... Date .... ☐ Federal .... Date .... ☐ Other State .... Date ....

6. Has organization filed Federal income tax returns? ☐ Yes ☐ No (If "Yes", state type of returns and years filed)

7a. Enter Revenue and Taxation Code Section under which exemption claimed (see instructions) Section 23701..................................

b. Primary activity of organization:

	Yes	No
8a. Are you a new organization? If "No," attach a statement indicating the name of your predecessor(s), the period during which it was in existence, and the reasons for its termination.		
b. Have you made or do you plan to make any distribution of your property or surplus to officers or members? If "Yes," attach a statement containing full details.		
c. Will any promoter, incorporator, founder, or member be employed by the organization? If "Yes," furnish complete details, including duties, responsibilities, qualifications, and compensation.		
d. Are you a membership organization? If "Yes," attach a statement which explains fully the qualifications for members, the different classes of membership, the number of members in each class, and the voting rights and privileges accorded each class		
e. Will any of the incorporators share any facilities with the organization? If "yes", attach a statement explaining in detail		
f. Will any property be rented, purchased, or transferred in any way from any of the incorporators? If "yes", attach a statement explaining in detail .		

NOTE: UNINCORPORATED ASSOCIATIONS OR TRUSTS SHOULD SECURE A FEDERAL EXEMPTION AND FURNISH A COPY OF THE FEDERAL EXEMPT DETERMINATION LETTER.

YOU **MUST** SUBMIT THE INFORMATION REQUESTED IN QUESTION 9, PAGE 2 OF THIS APPLICATION

Under penalties of perjury, I declare that I have examined this application, including accompanying schedules and statements, and to the best of my knowledge and belief, it is true, correct and complete.

_____ DATE	_____ SIGNATURE OF OFFICER OR REPRESENTATIVE	_____ TITLE
_____ PLACE SIGNED	[Versions of this form prior to (2-76) are obsolete and should be destroyed.]	

Section 23701 requires that each organization applying for exemption after December 31, 1969 MUST PAY A $10 APPLICATION FEE. Processing of the application cannot be completed until the application fee is received. DO NOT SEND CASH. ALLOW 45 DAYS FOR PROCESSING.

FTB 3500 (11-77)   Page 1

Figure K-19: EXEMPTION APPLICATION FOR CALIFORNIA NONPROFIT, NONSTOCK CORPORATION

9. YOU MUST ATTACH THE APPLICABLE INFORMATION REQUESTED:

a. If incorporated a **copy** of your endorsed articles of incorporation; if now being incorporated proposed articles must be furnished or if not incorporated, a copy of your constitution, articles of association, declaration of trust or other document setting forth your aims and purposes which is signed by the principal officers or trustees.

b. A **copy** of your bylaws or other similar code of regulations.

c. Complete statements of receipts and expenditures, and assets and liabilities for each of the last three annual accounting periods of operation (including those of your predecessor) or if a new organization, for that period for which you were in existence. Organizations that have not commenced operations or have been operating less than one year, see item "d" below.

d. A proposed budget showing expected income by source and areas of expenditures for the first year of operation if a newly formed organization or just commencing operations. **THE BUDGET IS REQUIRED BEFORE THE APPLICATION WILL BE PROCESSED** and should be based upon your most reasonable expectations.

e. A statement (in your own words) that states the specific purposes for which the organization was formed. (Do not quote the Articles of Incorporation or bylaws for this purpose.)

f. A statement which describes in detail the programs and activities which are presently carried on or will be carried on by the organization and how they will accomplish the specific purposes of the organization.

g. A statement explaining in detail each fund-raising activity and each business enterprise you have engaged in or plan to engage in, accompanied by copies of all agreements, if any, with other parties for the conduct of each fund-raising activity or business enterprise.

h. A statement which explains fully any specific activities that the organization has engaged in or sponsored and which have been discontinued. (Give dates of commencement and termination and the reasons for discontinuance.)

i. A copy of each lease, if any, in which you are the lessee or lessor of property (real, personal, gas, oil, or mineral) or in which you own an interest under such lease, together with copies of all agreements with other parties for development of the property.

j. Samples of any literature which the organization sells or distributes, and samples of any organizational advertising.

k. In addition to the above, one item (of 11 through 21) must be completed by most organizations according to the section under which exemption is being claimed. If you are claiming an exemption under a section indicated below, check item and furnish information or answer questions for that type of organization.

Labor, Agricultural or Horticultural organization under Section 23701a	(Answer Question 11)	____
Fraternal Beneficiary Society, etc., as described in Section 23701b, or Fraternal Society described in Section 23701l	(Answer Question 12)	____
Cemetery company or corporation chartered solely for burial purposes, as described in Section 23701c	(Answer Question 13)	____
Religious, Charitable, Scientific, Literary or Educational organization under Section 23701d	(Answer Question 14)	____
Business League, Chamber of Commerce, etc., under Section 23701e	(Answer Question 15)	____
Civic League, Social Welfare (including a veteran post or council), or Local Employee organization under Section 23701f	(Answer Question 16)	____
Social and Recreational organization under Section 23701g	(Answer Question 17)	____
Title Holding Corporation under Section 23701h	(Answer Question 18)	____
Voluntary Employees' Beneficiary organization under Section 23701i	(Answer Question 19)	____
Diversified Management Company under Section 23701m	(Answer Question 20)	____
Supplemental Unemployment Compensation Trust under Section 23701n	(Answer Question 21)	____

10. Attorney or representative to whom correspondence, concerning revision/amendment of articles or request for additional information should be mailed.

Name

Complete Address (Number, street, city or town, State and Postal ZIP Code) | Telephone:

11. If you are claiming exemption as a **Labor, Agricultural or Horticultural organization under Section 23701a,** submit an explanation of any services to be performed for your members. Cooperative organizations are not entitled to exemption, but may be allowed a special deduction under Sections 24404 and/or 24405.

12a. If you are claiming exemption as a **Fraternal Beneficiary Society, etc., as described in Section 23701b,** or a **Fraternal Society described in Section 23701l,** state whether the organization operates or plans to operate under the lodge system or for the exclusive benefit of the members of an organization so operating. Operating under the lodge system means carrying on activities under a form of organization that comprises local branches, chartered by a parent organization and largely self-governing, called lodges, chapters, or the like.

b. In the case of a **Subordinate or Local Lodge, etc.,** attach a certificate signed by the secretary of the parent organization, under the seal of that organization, certifying that the Subordinate Lodge is a duly constituted body operating under the jurisdiction of the parent body.

c. In the case of a **Parent or Grand Lodge,** attach a statement showing (1) the number of subordinate lodges in active operations, and (2) whether periodical meetings are actually held.

d. For **23701b organizations only,** attach a statement describing the types of benefits (life, sick, accident, or other benefits) paid or to be paid members.

Figure K-19 (continued)

13. If you are claiming exemption as a **cemetery company or corporation chartered solely for burial purposes**, as described in Section 23701c:

   a. Attach the following statements and/or documents:

      (1) Complete copy of sales contract or other document involved in acquisition of cemetery property by the organization.

      (2) Complete copy of any contract you may have which designates an agent to sell your cemetery lots.

      (3) Names of officers and directors of your organization from the date of incorporation to the present date indicating the period for which each held office.

      (4) Appraised value of cemetery property as of the date acquired. The appraisal should be obtained from sources other than the parties in interest.

   b. Do you have or do you plan to have a perpetual care fund? ☐ Yes ☐ No

      If "Yes," submit copy of federal exemption letter, and attach copy of the fund agreement and a statement giving nature of such fund (cash, securities, unsold land, etc.), manner in which and by whom the fund is or will be administered, and specific purposes for which it is used.

   c. Do you operate a crematorium? ☐ Yes ☐ No

---

14. If you are claiming exemption as a **Religious, Charitable, Scientific, Literary or Educational organization under Section 23701d**, answer the following questions. Attach statement explaining all "Yes" answers in "a" through "d."

	Yes	No
a. Did you receive or do you expect to receive 10 percent or more of your assets from any organization, group of affiliated organizations (affiliated through stockholding, common ownership, or otherwise), any individual, or members of a family group (brother or sister whether whole or half blood, spouse, ancestor, or lineal descendant)?		
b. Are you now, have you ever been, or do you plan to be engaged in carrying on propaganda, or otherwise advocating or opposing pending or proposed legislation?		
c. Do you participate or plan to participate in or intervene in (including the publishing or distributing of statements) any political campaign on behalf of or in opposition to any candidate for public office?		
d. Do you hold or plan to hold 10 percent or more of any class of stock or 10 percent or more of the total combined voting power of stock in any corporation?		

---

15. If you are claiming exemption as a **Business League, Chamber of Commerce, etc., under Section 23701e**, do you perform, or plan to perform, particular services for members, shareholders or others, such as furnishing credit reports, collecting accounts, inspecting products, conducting advertising, purchasing merchandise, or other similar undertakings? ☐ Yes ☐ No If "Yes," attach a detailed statement, including income realized and expenses incurred, regarding such activities. If engaged in advertising, attach specimen copies of material.

---

16. If a **Local Association of Employees**, attach a statement giving names and addresses of employers whose employees are eligible for membership in the association. If employees of more than one plant or office of the same employer are eligible for membership, give the address of each such plant or office.

---

17. If you are claiming exemption as a **Social and Recreational organization under Section 23701g**, answer the following questions and furnish the information requested.

	Yes	No
a. Have you entered or do you plan to enter into any contract or agreement for the management or operation of your property and/or activities? If "Yes," attach a copy of the contract or agreement		
b. Do you solicit or do you plan to solicit public patronage of your facilities by advertisement or otherwise? If "Yes," attach sample copies of such advertisements or other solicitations		
c. Are nonmembers other than bona fide guests of members permitted or will they be permitted to use the club facilities or participate in or attend any functions or activities conducted by the organization? If "Yes," attach a statement describing the functions or activities in which such nonmembers have participated or will participate, or to which they have been admitted or will be admitted. If such nonmembers have participated in or have been admitted to any functions or activities, state the amount received from such nonmembers, the expenses attributable to such functions, and the disposition made of net profits, if any, derived therefrom		
d. Do you rent or lease or do you plan to rent or lease any part of the club's property to others? If "Yes," attach a statement indicating the reason for such action or proposed action and the amount received or to be received. Also attach copies of the rental agreements or leases		
e. Have you ever sold or do you plan to sell any real property? If "Yes," attach a statement containing full details, including reasons for the sale(s) or planned sale(s), amounts received or to be received, and disposition or planned disposition of the proceeds		
f. Do you rent or lease, or plan to rent or lease any property from directors or members? If "Yes," attach a statement indicating reason for such action and amount paid or to be paid. Also furnish a copy of the lease or agreement		
g. Have you or will you derive any income from nonmembers, not explained above? If "Yes," furnish a statement separating the member and nonmember income for the past three years and a proposed budget separating member and nonmember income for the next period of operation		

   h. State total number of club members. If different classes of membership, explain dues, and privileges of each.

   i. If the organization is a **Homeowners Association**, furnish a copy of the Declaration of Covenants, Conditions and Restrictions, if applicable.

Figure K-19 (continued)

18a. If you are claiming exemption as a **Title Holding Corporation under Section 23701h**, attach a statement giving the complete names and addresses of the organizations for which title to property is held; the number of shares of capital stock held; and whether shares of stock have ever been held by persons other than such organizations. If stock was so held, include the years held and the total number of shares of each class of stock. Also, state whether the annual income (less expenses) is or will be turned over to the organization for which title to property is held and if not, the purpose for which such income is or will be held.

   b. Enclose a copy of an exemption letter (Federal or California) for each organization for which property will be held. If property will be held for organization(s) located in California, a California exemption letter must be furnished.

---

19. If you are claiming exemption as a **Voluntary Employees' Beneficiary organization under Section 23701i** attach a schedule of benefits available to members.

   a. Is each employee by or for whom contributions are made entitled to receive welfare benefits proportionate to the contributions by and/or for him?
   ☐ Yes   ☐ No If "No," attach a statement explaining in detail.

   b. Total number of persons entitled to receive benefits.

   c. Number of individual proprietors, partners, or self-employed persons entitled to receive benefits.

   d. Amount of income or receipts from members and employers of members for each year for which exemption is claimed.

   e. Amount of income or receipts from sources other than members and employers of members for each year for which exemption is claimed.

   f. Have you attached copies of the policies or certificates of membership issued by you? ☐ Yes   ☐ No

   g. Furnish a copy of the Federal determination letter.

---

20. If exemption is claimed as a **Diversified Management Company under Section 23701m**, state the date that the corporation was registered as a Diversified Management Company under Section 5 of the Federal Investment Act of 1940 (15 U.S.C.A.—§ 80a-8). Date_____.

---

21. If you are claiming exemption as a **Supplemental Unemployment Compensation Trust under Section 23701n**; attach a copy of the supplemental unemployment benefit plan and appurtenant agreements.

	Yes	No
a. Are benefits provided for individual proprietors, partners, or self-employed persons under the plan? If "Yes," attach a statement explaining in detail.		
b. Does the plan provide other benefits subordinate to the supplemental unemployment compensation benefits? If "Yes," attach a statement explaining in detail		
c. Do the benefits provided by the trust discriminate in favor of employees who are officers, shareholders, or persons whose principal duties consist of supervising the work of other employees, or highly compensated employees? If "Yes," attach a statement explaining in detail		

   d. Amount of income or receipts from members and employers of members for each year for which exemption is claimed.

   e. Amount of income or receipts from sources other than members and employers of members for each year for which exemption is claimed.

   f. Also furnish a copy of the Federal determination letter.

LOCATION OF FRANCHISE TAX BOARD OFFICES
EXEMPTS—INFORMATION: TELEPHONE (916) 355-0392

	Address	Zip Code
Bakersfield	1300 Seventeenth Street	93301
El Monte	9660 Flair Drive	91731
Fresno	2550 Mariposa Street	93721
Long Beach	3530 Atlantic Avenue	90807
Los Angeles	3200 Wilshire Boulevard	90010
Oakland	1916 Broadway	94612
Sacramento	1912 I Street	95814
San Bernardino	330 North D Street	92401
San Diego	1350 Front Street	92101
San Francisco	345 Larkin Street	94102
San Jose	1570 The Alameda	95126
Santa Ana	28 Civic Center Plaza	92701
Santa Barbara	41 Hitchcock Way	93105
Santa Rosa	447 College Avenue	95402
Stockton	31 E. Channel Street	95202
Van Nuys	8155 Van Nuys Boulevard	91402

TELEPHONE CALLS FROM WITHIN CALIFORNIA ARE TOLL FREE
Use Only the Corresponding Number Listed Below:

Sacramento Metropolitan Area *	Information	(916) 355-0370
	Forms	(916) 322-8932
Area Codes 209, 408, 415, 707, and 916	Information	(800) 852-7050
(except Sacramento)	Forms	(800) 852-7700
Area Codes 213, 714, and 805	Information	(800) 852-5711
	Forms	(800) 852-7700

* Also from outside California, but calls are not toll free.

OUT OF STATE OFFICES:

Chicago, IL	150 N. Wacker Drive	60606	(312) 332-4025
New York, NY	1271 Avenue of the Americas	10020	(212) 581-0100

Figure K-19 (continued)

5. Sample Articles—The following sample articles of incorporation are based on articles that have been filed with the Secretary of State and which have met the requirements for exemption.

(Sample Articles of Incorporation—See notes (a) thru (d))

ARTICLES OF INCORPORATION
OF
XYZ Church Corporation

I

The name of this corporation shall be *XYZ Church Corporation*.

II (See note (b))

The purposes for which this corporation is formed are:

(a) The specific and primary purposes are to operate a church for religious purposes.

(b) The general purposes and powers are to have and exercise all rights and powers conferred on nonprofit corporations under the laws of California, including the power to contract, rent, buy or sell personal or real property, *provided, however, that this corporation shall not, except to an insubstantial degree, engage in any activities or exercise any powers that are not in furtherance of the primary purposes of this corporation.*

(c) No substantial part of the activities of this corporation shall consist of carrying on propaganda, or otherwise attempting to influence legislation, and the corporation shall not participate or intervene in any political campaign (including the publishing or distribution of statements) on behalf of any candidate for public office.

III

This corporation is organized pursuant to the General Nonprofit Corporation Law of the State of California. This corporation does not contemplate pecuniary gain or profit to the members thereof and it is organized for nonprofit purposes.

IV

The principal office for the transaction of the business of this corporation is located in the County of _____, State of California.

V

The general management of the affairs of this corporation shall be under the control, supervision and direction of the board of directors. The names and addresses of persons who are to act in the capacity of directors until the selection of their successors are:

Name	Address
John Doe (typed)	(street, city and state)
Richard Roe	(street, city and state)
Nancy Moe	(street, city and state)

VI

The authorized number and qualifications of members of the corporation, the different classes of membership, if any, the property, voting and other rights and privileges of members, and their liability to dues and assessments and the method of collection thereof, shall be as set forth in the bylaws.

VII

The property of this corporation is irrevocably dedicated to _____ purposes and no part of the net income or assets of this organization shall ever inure to the benefit of any director, officer or member thereof or to the benefit of any private individual *. Upon the dissolution or winding up of the corporation, its assets remaining after payment of, or provision for payment of, all debts and liabilities of this corporation, shall be distributed to a nonprofit fund, foundation or corporation which is organized and operated exclusively for _____ purposes and which has established its tax exempt status under Section 501(c)(3) of the Internal Revenue Code. If this corporation holds any assets in trust, or a corporation is formed for charitable purposes, such assets shall be disposed of in such manner as may be directed by decree of the superior court of the county in which the corporation has its principal office, upon petition therefore by the Attorney General or by a person concerned in the liquidation, in a proceeding to which the Attorney General is a party **.

* (See note (c))   ** (See note (d))

IN WITNESS WHEREOF, the undersigned have executed these Articles of Incorporation, this_____day of_____, 19____.

_____
JOHN DOE

_____
RICHARD ROE

_____
NANCY MOE

STATE OF CALIFORNIA }
COUNTY OF_____ } ss.

On this_____day of_____19___, before me, _____, a Notary Public for the State of California, with principal office in_____County, personally appeared JOHN DOE, RICHARD ROE, and NANCY MOE, known to me to be the persons whose names are subscribed to the within Articles of Incorporation, and acknowledged to me that they executed the same.

IN WITNESS WHEREOF, I have hereunto set my hand and affixed my official seal on the day and year first above written.

_____
NOTARY PUBLIC
(NOTARIAL SEAL)

NOTES:

(a) General. These sample articles of incorporation are satisfactory for most new organizations desiring to form a corporation which should be entitled to an exemption from tax. They are also satisfactory with small changes for a constitution of an unincorporated association. If an unincorporated association is being incorporated, an Article VIII must be added before the IN WITNESS WHEREOF clause as follows: "The name of the unincorporated association which is being incorporated is *XYZ church association*." Also, an affidavit of subscribing persons must be included as part of the articles. See Corporation Code Section 9304(b). Article VII other than the IN WITNESS WHEREOF sentence is normally only desirable for organizations desiring an exemption under Section 23701d or 23701f of the Revenue and Taxation Code. See note (c) below. The details of the internal operations of the Organization should be covered in the bylaws.

Page 3

Figure K-19 (continued)

STATE OF CONNECTICUT
¹STATE TAX DEPARTMENT-SALES AND USE TAX DIVISION
HARTFORD, CONNECTICUT 06115

BLANKET CERTIFICATE OF EXEMPTION
FOR PURCHASE OF MATERIALS, TOOLS AND FUEL

Under Sec. 12-412 (R) General Statutes,

Revision of 1973, as amended

I hereby certify that all items checked in the squares below,

☐ **materials**

☐ **tools**

☐ **fuel**   **as defined by Regulation No. 12-426-11, as amended, purchased from**

. . . .
Name of Seller

Shall be purchased:

☐   To be used directly in agricultural production.

☐   To be used in an industrial plant directly in the actual fabrication of tangible personal property to be sold in the regular course of business.

☐   To be used directly in the furnishing of power to an industrial manufacturing plant.

☐   To be used directly in the furnishing of gas, water, steam or electricity when delivered to consumer through mains, lines or pipes.

☐   To be used directly in the fishing industry.

I further certify that I assume full liability for the payment to the State of any taxes, together with penalties and interest, that may be determined to be due on any purchases covered by this certificate. This certificate shall be considered a part of each order for materials, tools or fuel unless the purchaser shall advise seller to the contrary at the time the order is placed. The invoices, purchase orders or records covering all purchases made under this certificate shall be appropriately marked or stamped to indicate they are exempt purchases. The words **"Exempt under materials, tools and fuel certificate"** will satisfy this latter requirement.

This certificate shall remain in effect until revoked in writing by the purchaser. Blanket certificates should be renewed at three year intervals. It may also be used for individual exempt purchases rather than blanket use by filling out as far as applicable and marking thereon **"Individual purchase"** and listing on the reverse side the amount and date of the sale and the articles purchased.

Signed . . . .
           Name of Company or Individual

Permit No. (if any)

By . . . .

Title . . . .

Date . . . .

NOTE: The seller must support all sales made under this certificate by a separate invoice or record describing the articles purchased and the date and prices of the same. This certificate may be reproduced in print or type for use in making such exempt purchases. All applicable squares above must be checked or this certificate is void.

Summary

To be exempt from tax materials, tools and fuel must be in accordance with definitions of this regulation:

1.   Used directly in actual fabrication, or in agricultural production, or in the fishing industry, and:

2.   Such exemptions apply only to actual materials, tools or fuel and not machinery or replacement parts thereof, or equipment, furniture or fixtures which are taxable items.

¹Changed to Commissioner of Revenue Services and Department of Revenue Services by Public Act 77-614, effective January 1, 1979.

Figure K-20: BLANKET CERTIFICATE OF EXEMPTION
(Courtesy of Litton Office Product Centers.)

CERTIFICATE OF EXEMPTION

Date _____

The undersigned hereby claims exemption on otherwise taxable tangible personal property and services purchased, leased or rented from _____ and certifies that this claim is based upon the proposed non-taxable use of the items checked below:

_____ Sales of taxable property to organizations organized and operated for charitable, educational or religious purposes.

_____ Sales or use of taxable property the ultimate destination of which is outside and which will not be returned to any point within the State except in interstate commerce. The vendor himself must deliver such property outside the State or hire a common or contract carrier to do so.

_____ Other than above. Describe _____

Name _____ Address _____ City _____

Authorized Signature and Title _____

Figure K-21: CERTIFICATE OF EXEMPTION

916

CHARITABLE AND RELIGIOUS ORGANIZATIONS
EXEMPTION CERTIFICATE

"I HEREBY CERTIFY: that this organization is the holder of valid exemption permit No. . . . . . . issued pursuant to the Sales and Use Tax Act, that the tangible personal property described herein which I shall purchase or lease or the service(s) which I shall purchase from:

_____

_____ will be used exclusively by this organization

for the purposes for which it is organized and will not be resold:

Description of property or service(s):

_____

_____

_____

Purchaser _____

                     Name of Organization

By _____ Title _____

Address _____

Dated _____ 19 _____

at _____ "

Under "Description of property or service(s)" there may appear:

(1) Either an itemized list of the particular property to be purchased or leased, or

(2) An itemized list of particular service(s) to be purchased (a certificate thus describing the property and or service(s) is good until revoked in writing).

This certificate may be used for the purpose of a single purchase or lease, or it may be used as a blanket certificate for the purpose of a continuing line of purchases or leases, and the certificate should be plainly marked "Blanket Certificate."

The federal government, its agencies, the state of Connecticut and its subdivisions and their respective agencies may use this certificate by deleting "the holder of valid exemption permit number . . . . issued pursuant to" and insert "exempt under section 12-412A."

Figure K-22: CHARITABLE AND RELIGIOUS ORGANIZATIONS TAX EXEMPTION CERTIFICATE

(NON-STOCK)   NON-STOCK

C E R T I F I C A T E

O F

I N C O R P O R A T I O N

O F

_____

FIRST: The name of this Corporation is _____

_____

SECOND: Its Registered Office in the State of Delaware is to be located at _____

_____ , in the _____

County of _____. The Registered Agent in charge thereof

is _____

_____

THIRD: The nature of the business and, the objects and purposes proposed to be transacted,

promoted and carried on, are to do any or all the things herein mentioned, as fully and

to the same extent as natural persons might or could do, and in any part of the world,

viz:

Here should be stated, in general terms, the character of the particular business

to be carried on. Under Section 102 (a) (3) of the new law the following may be

stated in lieu of the old purpose clauses;

"The purpose of the corporation is to engage in any lawful act or activity

for which corporations may be organized under the general Corporation

Law of Delaware. "

Figure K-23: NONSTOCK CERTIFICATE OF INCORPORATION

FOURTH: The corporation shall not have any capital stock, and the conditions

of membership shall be as follows; VIZ: --

(In lieu of setting out the conditions of membership in the Certificate of Incorporation,

a statement may be inserted that the conditions of membership shall be stated in the

By-Laws.)

FIFTH: The names and places of residence of the incorporators are as follows:

NAMES   RESIDENCES

SIXTH: The activities and affairs of the corporation shall be managed by a Board

of Directors. The number of directors which shall constitute the whole board shall be

such as from time to time shall be fixed by, or in the manner provided in, the By-Laws,

but in no case shall the number be less than three. The directors need not be members

of the corporation unless so required by the By-Laws. The board of directors shall be

elected by the members at the annual meeting of the corporation to be held on such date

as the By-Laws may provide, and shall hold office until their successors are respectively

elected and qualified. The By-Laws shall specify the number of directors necessary to

constitute a quorum. The board of directors may, by resolution or resolutions, passed

by a majority of the whole board, designate one or more committees, which to the

extent provided in said resolution or resolutions or in the By-Laws of the corporation

shall have and may exercise all the powers of the board of directors in the management

of the activities and affairs of the corporation and may have power to authorize the seal

of the corporation to be affixed to all papers which may require it; and such committee

or committees shall have such name or names as may be stated in the By-Laws of the

Figure K-23 (continued)

corporation or as may be determined from time to time by resolution adopted by the board of directors. The directors of the corporation may, if the By-Laws so provide, be classified as to term of office. The corporation may elect such officers as the By-Laws may specify, who shall, subject to the provision of the Statute, have such titles and exercise such duties as the By-Laws may provide. The board of directors is expressly authorized to make, alter or repeal the By-Laws of this corporation.

The corporation may in its By-Laws, confer powers upon its board of directors in addition to the foregoing, and in addition to the powers and authorities expressly conferred upon them by the Statute, provided that the board of directors shall not exercise any power of authority conferred herein or by Statute upon the members.

SEVENTH: Meetings of members may be held without the State of Delaware, if the By-Laws so provided. The books of the corporation may be kept (subject to any provision contained in the Statutes) outside the State of Delaware at such place or places as may be from time to time designated by the board of directors.

EIGHTH: The corporation reserves the right to amend, alter, change or repeal any provision contained in this Certificate of Incorporation, in the manner now or hereafter prescribed by the Statute, and all rights conferred upon members herein are granted subject to this reservation.

WE, THE UNDERSIGNED, being each of the incorporators hereinbefore named, for the purpose of forming a corporation pursuant to Chapter 1 of Title 8 of The Delaware Code, do make this Certificate, hereby declaring and certifying that the facts herein stated are true, and accordingly have hereunto set our hands and seals this _____

day of _____, A. D. 19_____. _____

_____ (SEAL)

_____ (SEAL)

_____ (SEAL)

Figure K-23 (continued)

```
                        STATE OF ALASKA
                      APPLICATION FOR
                    CERTIFICATE OF AUTHORITY



Commissioner of Commerce
And Economic Development
State of Alaska



        Pursuant to the provisions of Section 10.20.480 of the Alaska Nonprofit
Corporation Act, the undersigned corporation hereby applies for a Certificate
of Authority to transact business in Alaska, and for that purpose submits the
following statement:

1.  The name of the corporation is_____
2.  The name which it elects to use in Alaska_____
    _____

3.  It is incorporated under the laws of_____
4.  The date of its incorporation is_____,
    and the period of its duration is_____
5.  The address of its principal office in the state or country under the laws
    of which it is incorporated is_____
    _____
6.  The address of its proposed registered office in Alaska is_____
    _____, and the name of its proposed
    registered agent 'in Alaska at that address is_____

7.  The purpose or purposes which it proposes to pursue in the transaction of
    business in Alaska Are:_____
    _____
    _____
    _____

8.  The names and respective addresses of its directors and officers are:


                    AT LEAST THREE DIRECTORS REQUIRED
    _____
                        Name                        Address
    _____
                    1 _____
    DIRECTORS       2 _____
                    3 _____
    _____
                    1 _____
    OFFICERS        2 _____
                    3 _____
    _____
                        IF MORE THAN 3 ATTACH LIST




    NOTE:  Please complete both sides of the application.

           Submit duplicate originals
```

Figure K-24: APPLICATION FOR CERTIFICATE OF AUTHORITY FOR NONPROFIT CORPORATION

9. The name and address of a person owning at least 5% of the shares or five per cent of any class of shares, and the percentage of the shares or class of shares owned by that person._____

_____

Dated_____, 19_____   _____
                                                        Exact Corporate Name

                                          By_____
                                                   President or Vice President

                                          Attest_____ _____
                                                   Secretary or Assistant Secretary

STATE OF   ss.
COUNTY OF

I,_____, a notary public, do hereby
certify that on this_____day of_____, 19____, personally
appeared before me_____, who being by me first duly
sworn, declared that he is the_____of_____
_____that he signed the foregoing document
as_____of the corporation, and that the statements therein
contained are true.

My Commission expires_____   _____
                                                   NOTARY PUBLIC

SEAL

Rev. 7/76

08-160

Figure K-24—Reverse Side.

APPOINTMENT OF THE COMMISSIONER OF COMMERCE AND ECONOMIC DEVELOPMENT OR HIS SUCCESSORS AS RESIDENT AGENT FOR SERVICE OF PROCESS IN ALASKA*

.... , a ....

(Name of Taxpayer)   (corporation, individual, etc.)

doing business under and by virtue of the laws of the (State) (Territory) (County) of ....

.... does hereby give consent to be sued in the Courts of the State of Alaska, and in compliance with the laws of Alaska, does hereby appoint, as (its) (his) agent for the service of process in all causes of action resulting from the taxpayer's failure or neglect to pay any Alaska taxes or license fees, the COMMISSIONER OF COMMERCE AND ECONOMIC DEVELOPMENT OR HIS SUCCESSORS, whose address is POUCH "D", Juneau, Alaska; and it is hereby agreed that service upon said Commissioner of Commerce and Economic Development or his Successors, shall be valid service upon the above named taxpayer as though such service were personally made upon said taxpayer within Alaska.

     IN WITNESS WHEREOF, the taxpayer hereto has signed this appointment at ....
(its) (his) principal place of business this .... day of ...., 19 ....

ATTEST:

                                          Name of Taxpayer ....

                                          By ....

                                          Title ....
                                          (A person authorized by appropriate by-laws, resolution, or otherwise to execute this document on behalf of the taxpayer herein.)

Subscribed and sworn to before me this .... day of ...., 19 ....

                                          ....

                                          Notary Public in and for ....

(SEAL)   My commission expires ....

*This appointment of a statutory agent for service of process in matters of taxes or license fees is in addition to and not in lieu of other statutes requiring the appointment of an agent.

(Filing Fee — Commissioner of Commerce and Economic Development $5.00)

REV. 9-75
08 — 182

Figure K-25: APPOINTMENT OF COMMISSIONER OF COMMERCE AS RESIDENT AGENT FOR SERVICE OF PROCESS IN ALASKA

NONPROFIT ANNUAL REPORT

YEAR	DATE	NUMBER	AMOUNT RECEIVED
	Sample X 05581		

For Use By The Commissioner Only

RETURN WITH REMITTANCE TO:
State of Alaska
Department of Commerce & Economic Development
CORPORATION SECTION
Pouch D
Juneau, Alaska 99811

**MAKE CHECKS PAYABLE TO DEPARTMENT
OF COMMERCE & ECONOMIC DEVELOPMENT**
TO ASSURE PROPER CREDIT, THIS NOTICE MUST BE RETURNED WITH
YOUR REMITTANCE. YOUR CANCELLED CHECK IS YOUR RECEIPT

- -

Do Not Detach For Office Use Only

STATE OF ALASKA
DEPARTMENT OF COMMERCE AND ECONOMIC DEVELOPMENT
CORPORATIONS SECTION
POUCH D — JUNEAU, ALASKA 99811
AUTHORITY: A.S. 10.20.620

(Type or print legibly)

NO. **X** 05581

NONPROFIT ANNUAL REPORT
For Year Ending December 31, 19 _____

NAME
OF CORPORATION _____ File No. _____

1. CORPORATION IF ORGANIZED UNDER THE LAWS OF THE STATE OR COUNTRY OF _____

2. ADDRESS OF PRINCIPAL CORPORATION OFFICE _____

3. REGISTERED AGENT _____
(FILE CHANGE ON FORM 08-184)

4. REGISTERED OFFICE IN ALASKA _____
(FILE CHANGE ON FORM 08-184)

5. CHARACTER OF BUSINESS IN WHICH CORPORATION IS ACTUALLY ENGAGED IN ALASKA _____

6. YOU MUST FURNISH THE NAMES AND ADDRESSES OF AT LEAST THREE DIRECTORS AND OFFICERS. IF DIRECTORS AND OFFICERS ARE THE SAME PEOPLE WRITE IN "SAME" IN THE DIRECTORS AREA.

		NAME	COMPLETE ADDRESS
DIRECTORS	1.		
	2.		
	3.		
OFFICERS	1. PRES.		
	2. V. PRES.		
	3. SEC.		
	4. TREAS.		

(If more space needed, attach list)

7. LIST THE REAL AND PERSONAL PROPERTY ASSETS OF THE CORPORATION, IF NONE SO INDICATE _____

LEGAL PROPERTY - BY LEGAL DESCRIPTION

PERSONAL PROPERTY - BY ESTIMATED VALUE

(IF MORE SPACE IS NEEDED, ATTACH EXHIBIT A)

8. LIST THE NAMES AND ADDRESSES OF EACH PERSON OWNING AT LEAST 5 PERCENT OF THE SHARES OR 5 PERCENT OF ANY CLASS OF SHARES, AND THE PERCENTAGE OF SHARES OR CLASS OF SHARES OWNED BY THAT PERSON. IF NONE, SO INDICATE _____

DATED _____ 19 ____ BY _____
PRESIDENT OR VICE PRESIDENT

ATTESTED BY _____ TITLE _____
SECRETARY

Figure K-26: NONPROFIT CORPORATION ANNUAL REPORT

DUPLICATE
STATE OF DELAWARE - 1978 ANNUAL FRANCHISE TAX REPORT - DELAWARE CORPORATION

THIS FORM PROPERLY COMPLETED AND EXECUTED TOGETHER WITH THE APPROPRIATE REMITTANCE. MUST BE FILED WITH THE SECRETARY OF STATE. FRANCHISE TAX SECTION. P.O. BOX 898. DOVER. DELAWARE 19901. ON OR BEFORE MARCH 1, 1979. RETAIN THE DUPLICATE FOR YOUR RECORDS. **PLEASE TYPE OR USE BLACK INK WHEN COMPLETING THIS FORM.**
UNLESS THIS FORM PROPERLY COMPLETED. WITH THE APPROPRIATE REMITTANCE IS RECEIVED IN THE OFFICE OF THE SECRETARY OF STATE ON OR BEFORE MARCH 1, 1979. A PENALTY OF $25.00 WILL BE IMPOSED. INTEREST AT THE RATE OF ONE PERCENT PER MONTH. AFTER MARCH 1, 1979, OF THE FRANCHISE TAX DUE IS ASSESSED DELINQUENT CORPORATIONS UNTIL TAX IS PAID

NAME

REGISTERED AGENT

ADDRESS

DATE OF INC.

Do Not Use

CAPITAL STATUS | Figures should be the same as reported in "Work Section" on reverse side.

(1) AUTHORIZED SHARES   (2)

DATE	DESIGNATION	NUMBER OF SHARES	PAR VALUE PER SHARE	ISSUED (IF NONE, SO STATE)	TOTAL GROSS ASSETS (IF NONE, SO STATE)

(3)

REMITTANCE DUE WITH THIS FORM (Payments made after _____, are not included)

		OFFICE USE ONLY	
A	Franchise Tax Due. (Enter amount from computation on back of report, not less than $20.00)	72 - 74 - 75	$ _____
B	Penalty of $25.00 If Applicable)	73 - 81	$ _____
C	Interest of 1% per month Total of Franchise Tax and Penalty. If Applicable	87	$ _____
D	**Add Filing Fee** (Check for at least $10.00 must accompany report)	71 - 80	$ _____ 10.00
E	Previous Credit		$ _____
F			$ _____
G			$ _____
	Total Payment Due _____ (Checks must be drawn on U.S. Bank - Money Order in U.S. Dollars		$ _____

Remit payment to "Secretary of State, Dover, Delaware." Exclusive of $10.00 filing fee. all payments shall BE NOT LESS THAN $20.00 NOR MORE THAN $110,000.00 for stock corporation. Non-Stock Corporations - Remit only $10.00 filing fee.

(4) Federal Employer Identification Number _____

(5) State Nature of Corporation's Business _____

(6) State Principal Place of Business Outside of Delaware _____

(7) State Appointed Date of Next Annual Meeting of Stockholders to Elect Directors _____

(8) DIRECTORS (IF NONE, SO STATE)   ADDRESS   TERM EXPIRES

(9) OFFICERS (IF NONE, SO STATE)   ADDRESS   TERM EXPIRES
PRESIDENT
VICE-PRESIDENT
VICE-PRESIDENT
SECRETARY
TREASURER
OTHER OFFICERS

(A separate sheet may be attached if space is insufficient to list all directors and officers. If directors and officers have not been elected please state.)

(PROFESSIONAL SERVICE CORPORATIONS - SUBMIT LIST OF SHAREHOLDERS)

Under penalties of perjury. I declare that I have examined this Annual Franchise Tax Report, including accompanying schedules and statements, and to the best of my knowledge and belief it is true, correct, and complete. If prepared by a person other than the taxpayer, his declaration is based on all information of which he has any knowledge.

_____ DATE   SIGN HERE ▶ SIGNATURE OF OFFICER, DIRECTOR (LISTED UNDER 8 OR 9 ABOVE), OR INCORPORATOR. IF NO OFFICERS OR DIRECTORS. MUST BE ORIGINAL SIGNATURE.   TITLE

_____ DATE   INDIVIDUAL OR FIRM SIGNATURE OF PREPARER   ADDRESS

FORM 1100

ALL ITEMS MUST BE COMPLETED IN ORDER TO PLACE REPORT ON FILE.

Figure K-27: DELAWARE ANNUAL FRANCHISE TAX REPORT

COMPUTATION OF FRANCHISE TAX

NOTE - ONE TAX YEAR EQUALS 365 DAYS

(Professional Service Corporations; corporations which have altered their authorized shares during the taxable year; corporations inactive during all or part of the taxable year; Regulated Investment Companies; See appropriate headings below.)

Two methods are provided for computing the tax, and the lesser tax is paid. One method is based on the authorized number of shares; the other is based on "assumed par value capital"

TAX ON AUTHORIZED NUMBER OF SHARES:

(10) Corporations having only authorized shares of no par value must use this method. Corporations having only authorized shares of a par value of more than $100.00 need not compute their tax on the basis of "assumed par value capital" since that method will result in a larger tax.

Total Authorized Shares	Tax
1,000 shares or less	$20.00
Over 1,000 but not over 3,000 shares	24.20
Over 3,000 but not over 5,000 shares	30.25
Over 5,000 but not over 10,000 shares	60.50
For each additional 10,000 shares or part thereof	30.25

FRANCHISE TAX COMPUTED ON
AUTHORIZED SHARES ·································· $ _____

TAX ON ASSUMED PAR VALUE CAPITAL   (WORK SECTION)

Corporations using this method must report issued shares as of the same date as total gross assets. For this purpose, treasury stock is considered issued.

MINIMUM TAX - Corporations with over 1,000 par value authorized shares, with 10 or less issued shares and no assets - pay $20.00.

Total gross assets must be reported as of the nearest date on which such amount is obtainable, but not earlier than Jan. 1, 1978, nor later than Dec. 31, 1978. Total gross assets shall be those 'Total Assets' reported to the United States on U.S. Form 1120, Schedule L, relative to the company's fiscal year ending in the calendar year prior to filing with the Secretary of State. Section 503, Title 8. If Schedule L has not been filed, please report assets which would have been reported.

The following method of computing the tax on assumed par value capital is to be used by corporations having only authorized shares with par value:

11. Total Gross Assets as of _____, 19___ .... * $ _____
12. Total number of issued shares .... * _____
13. Line 11 divided by line 12 (average gross asset value per share) .... $ _____
14. Number of authorized shares with par value less than or same as line 13 ...... _____
15. Line 13 multiplied by line 14 .... $ _____
16. Multiply all authorized shares with greater par value than the figure shown on line 13 by their respective par value . $ _____
17. Line 15 plus line 16 (assumed par value capital) .... $ _____
18. Total franchise tax due. $121.00 for each $1,000,000.00 or fraction thereof in excess of the figure shown on line 17 (e.g. tax on $1,500,000.00 is $242.00: 2 X $121 = $242.00). If the figure shown on line 17 is less than $1,000,000.00, the tax is prorated (e.g. tax on $500,000.00 is $60.50). ($500,000.00 ÷ $1,000,000.00 = $.50000 X $121.00 = $60.50) .... _____

The following method of computing the tax on assumed par value capital is to be used by corporations having both par value and no par value shares:

19. Tax on authorized no par shares as computed by the Authorized Number of Shares Method (see 10 above) .... $ _____
20. Total Gross Assets as of _____, 19___ .... * $ _____
21. Total number of issued shares (include issued shares with par and no par value) .... * _____
22. Line 20 divided by line 21 (average gross value per share) .... $ _____
23. Total number of authorized par value shares with par value less than or same as line 22 ...... _____
24. Line 22 multiplied by line 23 .... $ _____
25. Multiply all authorized shares with par value greater than the figure shown on line 22 by their respective par value . $ _____
26. Line 24 plus line 25 (assumed par value capital) .... $ _____
27. $121.00 for each $1,000,000.00 or fraction thereof in excess of $1,000,000.00 of the figure shown on line 26 (e.g. tax on $1,500,000.00 is $242.00: 2 X $121 = $242.00). If the figure shown on line 26 is less than $1,000,000.00, the tax is prorated (e.g. tax on $500,000.00 is $60.50). ($500,000 ÷ $1,000,000 = $.50000 X $121.00 = $60.50) .... $ _____
28. Total franchise tax due (Line 19 plus line 27) .... $ _____

29 Inactive Corporations (Tax shall not be reduced below $20.00)
A corporation which has not engaged in any of the business activities for which it was granted a certificate of incorporation for all or any part of the tax year is entitled to reduce its franchise tax for that portion of the year by one-half. To obtain this reduction, the corporation must set forth below the period of inactivity.
This corporation was not engaged, either within or without the State of Delaware, in any of the business activities for which it was granted a certificate of incorporation during the following portion of the tax year January 1, December 31, 1978:

PARTIAL YEAR ☐ _____, 19___ through _____, 19___
ENTIRE YEAR ☐

IF THE corporation was inactive for only a portion of the tax year, the tax is to be computed as follows: (1) compute the tax for the entire year in accordance with whichever method results in the lesser tax; (2) multiply the result obtained in step (1) by a fraction, the numerator of which is the number of days in the tax year during which the corporation was active and the denominator of which is 365: the result is the tax due for the active portion of the year; (3) multiply the result obtained in step (1) by a fraction the numerator of which is the number of days in the tax year during which the corporation was inactive and denominator is 365: multiply this figure by one-half, the result is the tax due for the inactive portion of the year. The sum of the amounts obtained in (2) and (3) is the franchise tax due and must be set forth in No. 3 (A) under REMITTANCE DUE WITH THIS FORM.

30. Regulated Investment Companies
Corporations which are Regulated Investment Companies, as defined by Section 851 of the Federal Internal Revenue Code, are eligible to base their tax, in addition to the methods outlined above, on average gross assets. "Average gross assets" is taken to be the mean of the gross assets on January 1 and December 31. The rate for such companies is $181.50 per annum for each $1,000,000.00 or fraction thereof in excess of $1,000,000.00 of the average gross assets during the taxable year.

The maximum tax imposed on Regulated Investment Companies is $55,000.00. (Proration and inactivity not applicable)

Average Gross Assets
January 1 $ _____
December 31 $ _____
Mean $ _____

31. New Corporations (Renewals Use Same Method)
Corporations incorporated on or after December 21, 1978 and before January 1, 1979 are required to file this annual franchise tax report and remit the $10.00 filing fee, but are not required to pay the franchise tax for the year 1978. Corporations incorporated during 1978, but before December 21, 1978, must compute their tax in accordance

with the instructions contained therein, and the result of that compilation is then to be multiplied by a fraction, the numerator of which is to be the number of days during which the corporation was incorporated during 1978, and the denominator of which is to be 365: the total number of days in the tax year. (e.g. Inc. July 30, 154 days ÷ 365 days = .421918). Tax shall not be reduced below $20.00, if incorporated before December 21, 1978.

32. Corporations Which Have Changed The Number of Authorized Shares During The Year
A corporation which has changed the number of its authorized shares during the tax year may also compute its tax in accordance with whichever of the alternative methods set forth above results in the lesser tax. However, whichever method is used, the tax must be computed separately for each period of the tax year during which a different number of shares, or different par value, was authorized. The tax resulting from each computation is to be multiplied by a fraction, the numerator of which is to be the number of days of the tax year during which that number of shares was authorized

and the denominator of which is to be 365, the total number of days in the tax year. The sum of the products of each multiplication is the Franchise Tax Due, and this amount must be set forth above on the line provided.
If a corporation which has changed the number of its authorized shares during the tax year elects to compute its tax by the assumed par value capital method set forth above, it must set forth on page 1 of this return under "Capital Status," and use in its computations, the number of its issued shares and its total gross assets as of a date within 30 days of each such change.

33. Professional Service Corporations
Professional Service Corporations subject to Section 1, Title 8, Chapter 6, compute their

tax according to the alternative methods set forth above. However, they are required to submit a list of all shareholders of the corporation together with this form and remittance.

34. Revision of Assessment
The Secretary of State is authorized to hear all complaints and appeals and all petitions for review of the assessment of franchise taxes. Form of petition for revision may be obtained from Secretary of State. Dover, Delaware.

* Use same figures reported in item No. 2 on front.

Figure K-27—Reverse Side

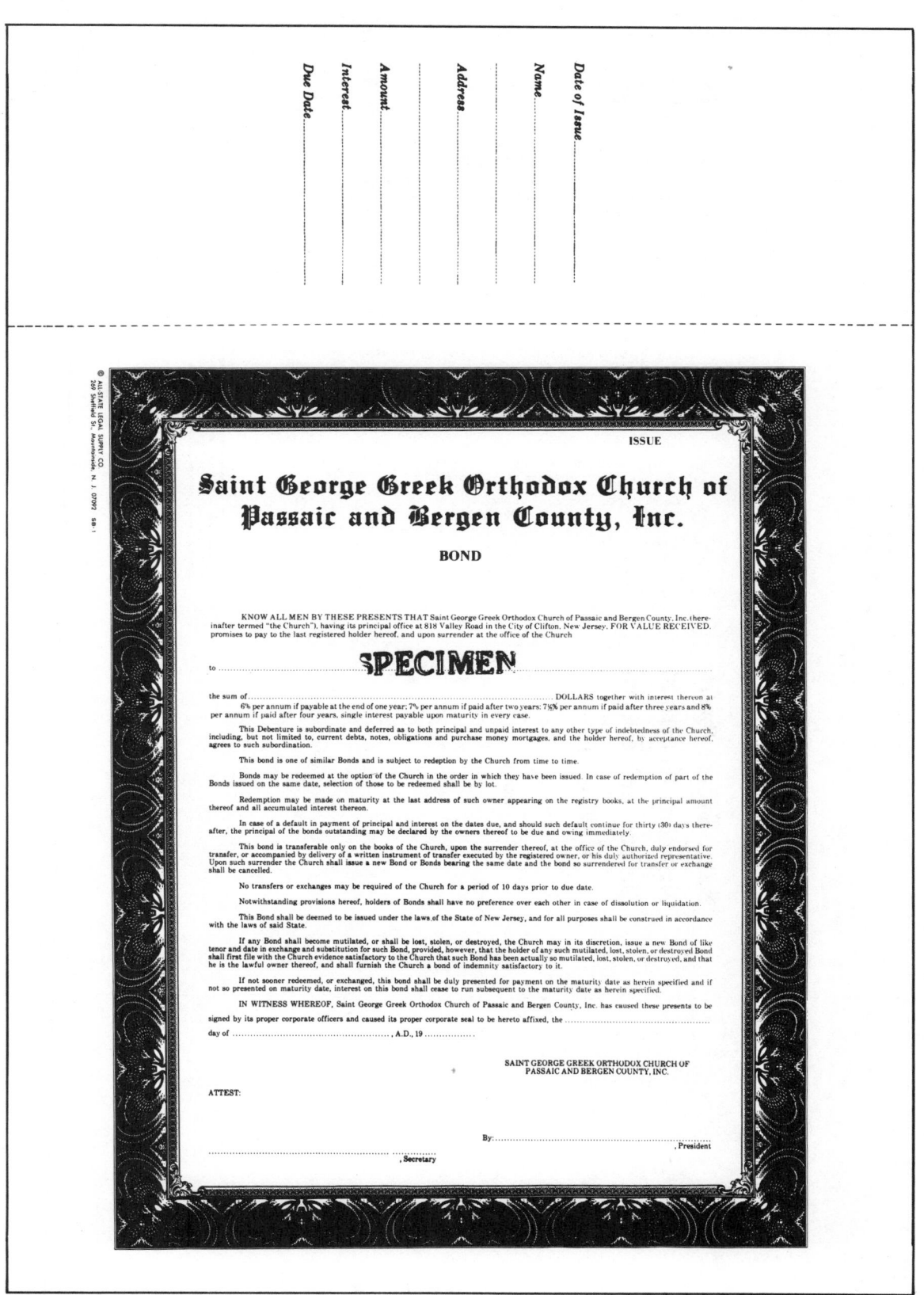

Figure K-28: CHURCH BOND

(Copyright by All State Legal Supply Co., Mountainside, New Jersey 07092.)

STATE OF NEW JERSEY, COUNTY OF ....) SS:

BE IT REMEMBERED, that on .... 19 ...., before me, the subscriber,

personally appeared

who, being by me duly sworn on h .... oath, deposes and makes proof to my satisfaction that .... he is the Secretary of

Saint George Greek Orthodox Church of Passaic and Bergen County, Inc., the Corporation named in the within Instrument; that ....

.... is the President of said Corporation; that the

execution, as well as the making of this Instrument, has been duly authorized by a proper resolution of the Board of Directors of the said

Corporation; that deponent well knows the corporate seal of said Corporation; and that the seal affixed to said Instrument is the proper corporate

seal and was thereto affixed and said Instrument signed and delivered by said President as and for the voluntary act and deed of said Corporation,

in presence of deponent, who thereupon subscribed h .... name thereto as attesting witness.

Sworn to and subscribed before me,   )
the date aforesaid   )

.... , Secretary

....

FOR VALUE RECEIVED .... *hereby sell, assign and transfer*

unto ....

all .... *right, title and interest represented by the within*

Bond, and do hereby irrevocably constitute and appoint ....

    Attorney to transfer said Bond on the books of the Church,
with full power of substitution in the premises.

    Dated the .... *day of* .... *, 19* ......

                 .... *(L. S.)*

In the presence of:

....

The signature to this assignment must correspond with the name as registered upon the books for the registry of the within instrument in every particular, without alteration or enlargement or any change whatsoever.

Saint George Greek Orthodox Church of Passaic and Bergen County, Inc.

BOND

INTEREST PAYABLE
Upon Maturity

PRINCIPAL AND INTEREST
Payable at the office
of the Church

Figure K-28: Reverse Side.

THE METROPOLITAN DISTRICT

DAILY CASH REPORT

Transaction
Date _____

FUND NO.	10	10	10	10	10				10
	C.B.T. 003-204-2 GENERAL FUND	H.N.B. T/A 011-1877 GENERAL FUND	C.B.T. T/A 005-849-1 GENERAL FUND	U.B.T. T/A 1-632-5041 GENERAL FUND	COL. BK T/A 640-189-4 GENERAL FUND				GENERAL FUND TOTAL
Beg. Cash Bal.									
Cash Receipts									
Invest. Rec.									
Note Proceeds									
SUB. TOTAL									
Disbursements									
Invest. Purchased									
Closing cash bal.									
Closing investment Balance									
Note Payable									

Figure K-29: DAILY CASH REPORT
(Courtesy of Robert N. French, Treasurer, The Metropolitan District, Hartford, Connecticut.)

THE METROPOLITAN DISTRICT

DAILY CASH REPORT

Transaction Date _____

FUND NO.	20 H.N.B. 010-9116 WATER BOND FUND	20 H.N.B. T/A 011-1877 WATER BOND FUND	20 C.B.T. T/A 005-849-1 WATER BOND FUND	20 U.B.T. T/A 1-632-5041 WATER BOND FUND	20 COL BK. T/A 640-189-4 WATER BOND FUND	20	20	20 WATER BOND FUND TOTAL
Beg. Cash Bal.								
Cash Receipts								
Invest. Rec.								
Note Proceeds								
SUB. TOTAL								
Disbursements								
Invest. Purchased								
Closing cash bal.								
Closing investment Balance								
Note Payable								

Figure K-29 (continued)

THE METROPOLITAN DISTRICT

DAILY CASH REPORT

Transaction Date _____

FUND NO.	30	30	30	30	30	30		30
	U.B.T. 1-632-5688 Assessable Fund	C.B.T. 003-310-3 Assessable Fund	H.N.B. T/A 011-1877 Assessable Fund	C.B.T. T/A 005-849-1 Assessable Fund	U.B.T. T/A 1-632-5041 Assessable Fund	COL. BK T/A 640-189-4 Assessable Fund		Assess. Fund TOTAL
Beg. Cash Bal.								
Cash Receipts								
Invest. Rec.								
Note Proceeds								
SUB. TOTAL								
Disbursements								
Invest. Purchased								
Closing cash bal.								
Closing investment Balance								
Note Payable								

Figure K-29 (continued)

THE METROPOLITAN DISTRICT

DAILY CASH REPORT

Transaction Date _____

FUND NO.	31 C.B.T. 003-401-0 DEBT EXPENSE FUND	31 HTFD. NAT. T/A 011-1877 DEBT EXPENSE FUND	31 C.B.T. T/A 005-849-1 DEBT EXPENSE FUND	31 COL. B&T 640-189-4 DEBT EXPENSE FUND	31 UBT - TA 632-504-1 DEBT EXPENSE FUND				31 TOTAL DEBT EXPENSE FUND
Beg. Cash Bal.									
Cash Receipts									
Invest. Rec.									
Note Proceeds									
SUB. TOTAL									
Disbursements									
Invest. Purchased									
Closing cash bal.									
Closing investment Balance									
Note Payable									

Figure K-29 (continued)

932

THE METROPOLITAN DISTRICT

DAILY CASH REPORT

Transaction Date _____

FUND NO.	50 C.B.T. 003-158-5 SEWER BOND FUND	50 H.N.B. T/A 011-1877 SEWER BOND FUND	50 C.B.T. T/A 005-849-1 SEWER BOND FUND	50 U.B.T. T/A 1-632-5041 SEWER BOND FUND	50 COL. BK T/A 640-189-4 SEWER BOND FUND	50	50	50	50 SEWER BOND FUND TOTAL
Beg. Cash Bal.									
Cash Receipts									
Invest. Rec.									
Note Proceeds									
SUB. TOTAL									
Disbursements									
Invest. Purchased									
Closing cash bal.									
Closing investment Balance									
Note Payable									

Figure K-29 (continued)

933

THE METROPOLITAN DISTRICT

DAILY CASH REPORT

Transaction
Date _____

FUND NO.	55	55	55	55	55			55
	C.B.T. 003-075-9 Hqts. Building Fund	H.N.B. T/A 011-1877 Hqts. Building Fund	C.B.T. T/A 005-849-1 Hqts. Building Fund	COLONIAL B&T 640-189-4 Hqts. Building Fund	U.B.T. 632-504-1 Hqts. Building Fund			TOTAL Hqts. BUILDING FUND
Beg. Cash Bal.								
Cash Receipts								
Invest. Rec.								
Note Proceeds								
SUB. TOTAL								
Disbursements								
Invest. Purchased								
Closing cash bal.								
Closing investment Balance								
Note Payable								

Figure K-29 (continued)

934

THE METROPOLITAN DISTRICT

DAILY CASH REPORT

Transaction
Date _____

FUND NO.	56	56	56	56	56				56
	H.N.B. 011-2240 GULLY BROOK	U.B.T. 01-632-504-1 GULLY BROOK	COLONIAL BANK & T 640-189-4 GULLY BROOK	CBT-TA 005-849-1 GULLY BROOK	HNB-TA 011-1877 GULLY BROOK				TOTAL GULLY BROOK
Beg. Cash Bal.									
Cash Receipts									
Invest. Rec.									
Note Proceeds									
SUB. TOTAL									
Disbursements									
Invest. Purchased									
Closing cash bal.									
Closing investment Balance									
Note Payable									

Figure K-29 (continued)

935

```
                  THE METROPOLITAN DISTRICT
                APPROPRIATION DISBURSEMENTS
                      WATER UTILITY FUND
          HARTFORD NATIONAL BANK & TRUST COMPANY
                        FUND # 20


                                  Voucher Payment Register #_____
                                  Voucher Payment Register Date_____


Amount Sewer $_____
Amount Water $_____
Total Disbursed 20-232-01_____


Voucher #_____ TO_____


Check #_____ TO_____ Void Check #_____
Posting Date_____


Funds Available_____
Checks Disbursed_____


Operator_____


Recorded_____


Posted_____


APPROVED_____



Prepared by_____
```

Figure K-30: APPROPRIATION DISBURSEMENTS
(Courtesy of Robert N. French, Treasurer, The Metropolitan District, Hartford, Connecticut.)

```
Form 1-SBA(c)                  THE UNIVERSITY OF CONNECTICUT
Rev. 1/77
                            SCHOOL OF BUSINESS ADMINISTRATION


           REQUEST FOR APPROVAL OF CONSULTING WORK OR OUTSIDE ACTIVITY

           (To be filled out in quadruplicate:  Two for the Dean's Office,
           one for the Department Head, and one for the staff member.)


   1.   Name of staff member_____Dept._____

   2.   Name and address of firm (or individual)_____

        _____


   3.   Description of work or project_____

        _____


   4.   Estimates of number of days and duration of engagement_____

        Starting_____ Terminating_____

   5.   Will University facilities be used? _____  _____
                                                    (Yes)            (No)
        If yes, please use Form 2, in addition to Form 1.  (These forms may be
        obtained from the Office of the Dean.)

   6.   Does the work or project interfere with your normal University duties?

        Yes_____   No_____

              I certify that my work as a
        consultant to the above concern        _____
        will not compromise the University       (Signature of Staff Member)
        in any of its relationships with
        the Federal government, nor will
        it interfere with any University        _____
        responsibilities.                          (Date)


- - - - - - - - - - - - - - - - - - - - - - - - - - - - - - - - - - - - -

        Comments by Department Head           Comments by Dean, School of
                                                 Business Administration


        _____      _____

        _____      _____

        _____      _____

        _____      _____

        _____      _____

        (Signature)        (Date)             (Signature)        (Date)
```

Figure K-31: REQUEST FOR APPROVAL OF CONSULTING WORK
(Courtesy of the University of Connecticut.)

UNIVERSITY OF CONNECTICUT RESEARCH FOUNDATION
REQUEST FUNDS FOR FACULTY RECRUITMENT

Department _____ U-Box _____

Candidate's Name _____

Address _____

Professional Affiliation
(College or University) _____

Candidate for what position? _____

Estimated Travel and Minor Incidental Expenses* _____

Appearance Plan (e.g., special graduate colloquium, workshop, interdepartmental seminar)

_____

_____

Topic _____

Date of Appearance _____

_____

Type Department Head Name

_____

Department Head Signature

_____

Date

SEND ONE COPY TO: Hugh Clark, Acting Vice President
                     U-133

*Do not include food, lodging or local (under $20) transportation. These may be requested on the Research Foundation's "Local Expenses for Guest Speakers" form, RF-C-3.

Figure K-32: REQUEST FUNDS FOR FACULTY RECRUITMENT
(Courtesy of the University of Connecticut.)

To be completed by Hiring Dept.

Search # ______________________

Job Title ______________________

Department ______________________

UNIVERSITY OF CONNECTICUT

EQUAL OPPORTUNITY INFORMATION REQUEST

A memorandum originating in the Office of the Secretary, U.S. Department of Health, Education and Welfare, states that Affirmative Action employers "are required to collect and maintain data on the race, sex and ethnic identity of all applicants for employment." We, therefore, ask you to complete the following questionnaire. PLEASE RETURN THIS FORM IN THE SEPARATE ENVELOPE PROVIDED. DO NOT RETURN IT TO THE RECRUITING DEPARTMENT. This information will be used only for the purpose of monitoring the success of our Affirmative Action Plan and will not be used to discriminate against any applicant. Thank you for your assistance.

NAME: ______________________________ DATE: ______________

Information on this position was made available to me from the following source:

______________________________ ______________________________

ETHNIC DATA:

These categories should not be interpreted as scientific or anthropological in nature. They were developed by the Federal government in response by both the Executive Branch and the Congress to provide for the collection and use of compatible, nonduplicated, exchangeable racial and ethnic data by Federal agencies.

_____ American Indian or Alaskan Native (A person having origins in any of the original peoples of North America).

_____ Asian or Pacific Islander (A person having origins in any of the original peoples of the Far East, Southeast Asia, or the Pacific Islands. This area includes China, Japan, Korea, the Phillippine Islands Samoa, or the Indian subcontinent).

_____ Black (A person having origins in any of the black racial groups).

_____ White (A person having origins in any of the original peoples of Europe, North Africa, or the Middle East).

_____ Puerto Rican (A person of Puerto Rican ancestry, regardless of race).

(over)

Figure K-33: EQUAL OPPORTUNITY INFORMATION REQUEST
(Courtesy of the University of Connecticut.)

-2-

_____ Chicano (A person of Mexican-American ancestry, regardless of race).
_____ Other Hispanic (A person of Cuban, Central or South American, or other Spanish culture or origin, regardless of race).

SEX: _____ Female   _____ Male

AGE: _____

MARITAL STATUS: _____ Married   _____ Single

If interviewed, please give us your opinion of your interview(s) by answering the following questions:

	YES	NO
Were you treated politely?	___	___
Were all questions job-related?	___	___
Did you feel that you were being treated in an unbiased manner?	___	___

COMMENTS: _____

_____

_____

THE UNIVERSITY OF CONNECTICUT DOES NOT DISCRIMINATE AGAINST ANY PERSON IN ITS EDUCATIONAL AND EMPLOYMENT ACTIVITIES ON THE GROUNDS OF RACE, COLOR, RELIGION, NATIONAL ORIGIN, SEX, MARITAL STATUS, ANCESTRY, AGE, OR PHYSICAL DISABILITY, INCLUDING, BUT NOT LIMITED TO BLINDNESS.

Figure K-33—Reverse Side

THE UNIVERSITY OF CONNECTICUT

EMPLOYMENT

AUTHORIZATION

Form # Pay 1 (Revised 2/77)

Name ☐ Mr. ☐ Miss
☐ Mrs. ☐ Ms. _____

Street _____

City & State _____ Zip _____

Social Security Number _____ Univ. Box No. _____

| DEPARTMENT: _____ | POSITION IDENTIFICATION
P.C. #: _____ | Related AAP Search
_____
(if any) |

The purpose of this authorization is to:

☐ REPLACE a previously submitted authorization, which will become voided.
☐ CHANGE some feature(s) of an existing authorization. Explain below under "Remarks."
☐ RENEW an appointment beyond its current ending date. Check one of next 2 boxes also.
☐ Fill a NEW POSITION.
☐ Fill the VACANCY of:_____ . If a renewal in the same PC#, write "Self."
☐ Employ by SPECIAL PAYROLL, not requiring a position.

Title of Position	Start-ing date	End-ing date*	Full time annual sal-ary RATE #	% of time emp.	Net annual salary rate	Main-ten-ance	Gross annual salary rate

Funding Ending Date if earlier than Appointment Date Shown Above: _____

*Last day on payroll; if permanent, write "P"   #For special payroll give total amount to be earned

TENURE STATUS   Years of prior academic service: _____
Length of probationary period: _____   MONTHS OF SERVICE PER YEAR: _____

Fund	Sp.l	Func	Activity	Maj	Min	FS	Proj	Bi-Weekly	Annual*	For Contracts, Grants, etc. Program name & Prin. Investigator	Terminal Date

*The sum of the amounts in this column should equal the "Net Annual Salary Rate"

PERSONAL DATA

If foreign national, exempt Social Security
☐ yes ☐ no (If yes, attach exemption form.)
(Only if unchanged and reported on a recent authorization, check ☐ and omit this section.)
Birthplace: _____
Birthdate: _____
Maiden or former name: _____
Veteran: ☐ WW II ☐ Korea ☐ Vietnam
Educational background:
Degree   Institution   Field of Study   Date

_____

(If degree is expected soon, give date in parentheses.)

☐ Married
☐ Single
☐ Widowed
☐ Divorced
☐ Separated

☐ Position type (Budget only)
METHOD OF PAYMENT
☐ Regular payroll   ☐ Special payroll   ☐ Hourly payroll

PRESENT (OR LAST PREVIOUS) EMPLOYMENT
Employer: (If Univ. of Conn., give department.) _____
Position de-scription or title: _____

FORMER STATE EMPLOYMENT
☐ Formerly (but not presently) employed by The University of Connecticut. Specify Payroll category:
☐ Unclassified ☐ Classified ☐ Special ☐ Student
☐ Formerly employed by another agency of the State of Conn.
Agency: _____
☐ Never employed by the State of Connecticut.

PERSONNEL:
P.C. # _____
Class code _____
Name or item # _____
_____
Emp. No. _____
Completed by _____

BUDGET:
Position and funds certified by
_____
Date _____

PAYROLL:
Date _____
Checked by _____

REMARKS:

APPROVED: Date
Department _____ Signed _____
Project _____ Dean or Director _____
Graduate School _____ Vice President _____
(required for graduate assistants)

Note to Dean: For Unclassified – 6 copies to Vice-President.
For Classified – 2 copies to Personnel.

Figure K-34: EMPLOYMENT AUTHORIZATION
(Courtesy of the University of Connecticut.)

Form Pay-2 (Rev. 7/74)
The Univ. of Conn.

STUDENT PAYROLL AUTHORIZATION

Name	Last	First	Middle	Maiden	Social Security Number
Home Address	Street	City	State	Zip Code	

Title of Position	Job Code #	Department	Date Effective

Birthdate	Birthplace		Connecticut Resident Since	Citizen	Alien	Marital Status (Single, Married, Widowed, Separated, Divorced)

Check and Complete Applicable Statements	☐ Never Employed by the State of Conn. (Including U. Conn.)	☐ Previously on Student Payroll at U. Conn.
	☐ Previously Employed by State of Conn., Other Than U. Conn. (Enter Agency Name.)	☐ Currently Employed by U. Conn. As: (Enter Present Title.)

Boxes in Heavy Outline for Payroll Use Only	Ending Date	Empl. No.	Fund	S. I.	F	Act.	Object Maj.	Min.	F. S.	Proj.	Rate	Dist. Code	Sec.	Univ. Box No.	Tax Code

Sex	Grammar School	High School (1, 2, 3, 4)	College (1, 2, 3, 4, Grad.)	Year Grad.	College Name	Major	Degree

Procedures have been followed to equalize student employment opportunities. This position was posted in the Student Aid Office on

_____

and this student was chosen as the best qualified of the resulting applicants.

_____   _____
(Date Signed)   (Department Head)

Student Aid Office Only	Budget Only	Payroll Only
Approved By	Certified By	Checked By
Date	Date	Date
College Dean/or Director		

- -

STUDENT AGREEMENT
Student Aid Office, Box U-116

All students engaged in work on campus are expected to fill out this section properly and completely.

Name (Last, first, middle, maiden)		
University or Commuting Address		
Title of Position	Job Code #	Rate Per Hour	Dates of Employment
Supervisor's Signature		Department	

I agree to report promptly for each scheduled working assignment and to notify my supervisor in advance when my absence is unavoidable. I understand that my supervisor has been urged to report on my work achievements for my permanent record. I agree to abide by the student labor regulations, copy of which is in the possession of my work supervisor.

Student's Signature	Date

Figure K-35: STUDENT PAYROLL AUTHORIZATION
(Courtesy of the University of Connecticut.)

THE UNIVERSITY OF CONNECTICUT
STUDENT PAYROLL – TIME SHEET
(Includes Workstudy)

Period Ending _____

_____
Print Student Name

_____
Student Signature

Remarks: _____

_____

_____

_____

_____

_____

Dept. Head Or
Supervisor
Signature: _____
Need Not Sign If Same Signature Will Appear On
Time Report—Student Payroll Prepunched Card

Form No. PAY-15 8/5/76

	A.M.				P.M.				Daily Total Hours
	IN	OUT	IN	OUT	IN	OUT	IN	OUT	
FRI									
SAT									
SUN									
MON									
TUE									
WED									
THU									
FRI									
SAT									
SUN									
MON									
TUE									
WED									
THU									

Total Hours For Period ↑

Figure K-36: STUDENT PAYROLL TIME SHEET
(Courtesy of the University of Connecticut.)

DEPARTMENT OF BUSINESS ADMINISTRATION

Record of Student Labor Payroll Report

Name of Student _____

Account charged _____

Payroll Period	Hours of work per week $\times$ rate	Total amount due

Figure K-37: RECORD OF STUDENT LABOR PAYROLL

Form AG-207

Case No. ....
(for office use only)

STATE OF CONNECTICUT
OFFICE OF ATTORNEY GENERAL
STATE CAPITOL
HARTFORD 15, CONN.

Approved
19

By ....
Philip L. Massicotte
Assistant to Attorney General
Workmen's Compensation

REPORT OF ACCIDENT OR OCCUPATIONAL DISEASE TO AN EMPLOYEE

Date of Report .... Date of Accident ....

DEPARTMENT REPORTING ....

SECTION OR DIVISION .... LOCATION ....

DIVISION HEAD FILING REPORT ....
(not injured person)   Title ....

Injured person's name ....

Address in full ....

Date of Birth: .... Sex ....
month   day   year

Occupation .... Title ....

Date of Employment ....

Was injury caused by the wilful and serious misconduct of injured or by his intoxication? .... If so, explain: ....

....

....

....

....

Did injury arise out of and in the course of injured person's employment? (Yes or No) ....

Is this an old injury aggravated by present employment? (Yes or No) .... If so, explain: When, Where and if injury was

compensible ....

....

....

....

....

Give name of attending physician, for old injury ....

Has injured returned to work? .... If so, when? ....

Give name of nearest relative and where (He or She) can be contacted   Phone No. ....

Name .... Address ....

Has this person been notified? (Yes or No) .... When? ....

TO BE FILLED OUT IN DETAIL BY DIVISION HEAD
FORWARD IMMEDIATELY TO:
ATTORNEY GENERAL'S OFFICE
STATE CAPITOL
HARTFORD 15, CONN.

Figure K-38: REPORT OF ACCIDENT OR OCCUPATIONAL DISEASE TO AN EMPLOYEE

2

ACCIDENT OR CAUSE OF INJURY

Date of accident .... Hour .... M   Date Stopped Work .... 19........

Place where accident occurred ....

City or Town ....

Did accident occur on State Property? (Yes or No) .... Private Property? (Yes or No) ....

If so, state what part of premises, establishment or buildings ....

....

Cause of injury ....

....

If caused by machinery or instrument, state name and type of same ....

If falling accident, state what caused fall ....

....

How did accident happen? Report in detail ....

....

....

....

....

....

....

....

....

Witnesses of accident:
Names   Where employed.

....

....

Name and address of attending Physician:

....

If taken to hospital, give name ....

Also state type of transportation and name of person or firm supplying same ....

....

[Signed] Name ....

Title ....

Figure K-38 (continued)

REPORT OF OCCUPATIONAL DISEASE 3

Name of Disease ....

Date of the first manifestation of a symptom of occupational disease ....

Nature of Disease ....

....

....

....

Previous condition of health ....

Was employee examined at the time of employment? (Yes or No) ....

If so; give date of examination .... By whom ....

Give date of examination just prior to first manifestation ....

Has employee ever received compensation previously for this disease? (Yes or No) ....

If so; give date of its first manifestation of a symptom ....

Give name of attending physician ....

Give name of employer at that time ....

Remarks by person filing Report ....

....

....

....

....

....

COMPENSATION STATUS

Able to work after Accident or Occupational Disease? (Yes or No) ....

Date removed from payroll .... Date Returned ....

Weekly wages for preceding 26 weeks ....

Weekly wages for preceding 26 weeks if employed in an institution:

    (a) Amount of cash received weekly: ....

    (b) Amount of cash weekly maintenance ....

        Total wages: ....

                    [Signed] Name ....

                                  Title ....

Figure K-38 (continued)

STATEMENT OF CLAIMANT
(Third Party)

What is your name .... Occupation ....

Address ....

Married or Single .... If married, name of husband or wife ....

In what company do you carry your insurance? ....

Kind of insurance carried ....

Place of accident .... Date and Time ....

Make of Auto .... Type .... Year .... License No. .... State ....

Name of Owner .... Age .... Address ....

Name of Driver .... Age .... Address ....

Names, Ages and Addresses of Occupants ....

....

Were you or anyone riding in your car injured ....

Names and Addresses of injured ....

Nature and Extent of injuries ....

....

....

Name and Address of Attending Doctor ....

Were there any witnesses to accident (Give names and addresses) ....

....

How did accident happen? Give full account stating speed and direction of each car ....

....

....

....

....

....

Nature of damage to your car ....

Amount for which you are making claim ....

Witness to: Signature of
Signature ....   Claimant ....

Dated .... 19........

Figure K-38 (continued)

CONNECTICUT STATE EMPLOYEES

HOMEOWNERS INSURANCE PROGRAM

To obtain a quotation, complete this form and return it today.　　　　CASE NUMBER _____

GENERAL INFORMATION

NAME (Exactly as it appears on house deed)　　　　　　　　　　　　TELEPHONE (HOME)　　AND　　(BUSINESS)

ADDRESS (No., Street, City or Town, County, State, Zip Code)

LOCATION OF PREMISES TO BE QUOTED (If different from above)

PRESENT AMOUNT OF INSURANCE　　|　DATE PRESENT POLICY EXPIRES (Mo., Day, Yr.)　　|　PRESENT COMPANY

SELECTION OF COVERAGES AND DWELLING INFORMATION

HOMEOWNERS

I OWN A HOME AND AM INTERESTED IN COVERAGE FOR $ _____

When choosing an amount of coverage for your home, it should be the replacement cost of the house (excluding the value of the land).

PLEASE COMPLETE THE FOLLOWING QUESTIONS:

Type of House: _____ (Ranch, Colonial, Split, etc.) ☐ ONE FAMILY ☐ TWO FAMILY

Number of Rooms: _____ (including _____ bedrooms) No. of Stories _____ No. of Baths _____

Year Built _____ If over 25 years old, have the following undergone major modernization in the last 10 years?

Heating ☐ YES ☐ NO　　Electrical ☐ YES ☐ NO　　Plumbing ☐ YES ☐ NO

Square Footage, excluding garage _____ (if known)

CHECK WHICH OF THE FOLLOWING APPLY:

☐ ATTACHED GARAGE　　　　　　　☐ STANDARD FIREPLACE　　　　　☐ CENTRAL AIR CONDITIONING
　☐ ONE CAR　☐ TWO CAR　　　　☐ ALUMINUM/VINYL SIDING　　　☐ CENTRAL HEATING SYSTEM
　　　　　　　　　　　　　　　　☐ UNFINISHED BASEMENT　　　　☐ FULLY ENCLOSED FOUNDATION
☐ ENCLOSED PORCH　　　　　　　☐ FINISHED BASEMENT　　　　　☐ WAVE WASH OR FLOOD EXPOSURE
☐ LARGE OPEN PORCH　　　　　　☐ UNFINISHED ATTIC (Full head room)　☐ POOL: Fenced? ☐ YES ☐ NO
☐ FULL WALL FIREPLACE

RENTERS

I RENT ☐ AN APARTMENT OR ☐ A HOUSE AND AM INTERESTED IN COVERAGE FOR $ _____

When choosing an amount of coverage for your personal property, it should be the actual cash value (allowing for depreciation).

Number of rental units in your building _____ (If 8 or more, estimate number)

ADDITIONAL INFORMATION

1. Construction of Building: ☐ FRAME　☐ MASONRY　☐ MASONRY VENEER (Brick over frame)　☐ OTHER _____

　Roof: ☐ TILE OR SLATE　☐ ASPHALT SHINGLES　☐ WOOD SHINGLES　☐ OTHER _____

2. Do you own any additional dwellings or apartment buildings? ☐ YES ☐ NO. If "YES", indicate (1) whether 1 or 2 family dwelling or apartment building, (2) if you occupy or rent it to others and (3) give address.

3. Do you operate a clerical office, professional office, studio or nursery, or do you give professional instruction? ☐ YES ☐ NO (If "YES", describe the nature and location of operation).

4. Have you had any losses to your house or property in the past 3 years? ☐ YES ☐ NO (If "YES", give dates/details).

5. Has any company declined, cancelled or refused to renew similar coverage for you in the past 3 years? ☐ YES ☐ NO (If "YES", give dates/details).

6. Distance to the nearest Fire Department _____ miles. Distance to the nearest Fire Hydrant _____ feet.

DETAILS TO QUESTIONS 1-5

STATE EXCEPTIONS

NEW YORK ONLY: Fire District _____

Co-insurance Applies: ☐ YES ☐ NO. Off Premises Theft applies: ☐ YES ☐ NO

CALIFORNIA BRUSH AREA ONLY: The minimum linear distance of any portion of the insured building(s) to Native Brush (Chaparral) or other natural vegetative growth is 400 feet, unless otherwise stated herein.

UNDER: ☐ 40 ft. ☐ 75 ft. ☐ 100 ft. ☐ 200 ft. ☐ 400 ft.

ALABAMA, FLORIDA, GEORGIA, SOUTH CAROLINA ONLY:

Premises are located: ☐ inside city limits ☐ inside fire district

☐ inside protected suburban area

SOUTH CAROLINA and MINNESOTA ONLY:

Insurable value of dwelling $ _____

I have read this request and declare the statements are true.
I understand that this is a request for a quotation only and that I am under no obligation.

SIGNATURE OF REQUESTER　　　　　　　　　　　　　　　　　　|　DATE

ES-223A REV. 1-79 PRINTED IN U.S.A.

Figure K-39: STATE EMPLOYEES HOMEOWNERS INSURANCE QUOTATION FORM

CONNECTICUT STATE EMPLOYEES

AUTOMOBILE INSURANCE PROGRAM

To obtain a quotation, complete this form and return it today.

CASE NUMBER _____

GENERAL INFORMATION

NAME (EXACTLY AS IT APPEARS ON DRIVER'S LICENSE)	TELEPHONE (Residence) (Business)	IN WHAT MONTH DOES YOUR PRESENT INSURANCE EXPIRE?
ADDRESS (No., Street, City. Town, State)	ZIP CODE	PRESENT INSURANCE COMPANY & ANNUAL PREMIUM

VEHICLE INFORMATION (Complete for all cars, pick-ups, trailers, motorhomes and campers registered in your or your spouse's name.)

VEH. NO.	YEAR	MAKE AND MODEL	COST WHEN NEW	VEHICLE IDENTIFICATION NUMBER	BODY STYLE 2 DOOR, 4 DOOR OR WAGON	NO. OF CYLIN-DERS	IF DRIVEN TO WORK, SCHOOL OR COMMUTING POINT– Miles One Way	Days Per Week	AVERAGE ANNUAL MILEAGE	IS YOUR CAR USED IN YOUR JOB
1.										
2.										
3.										
4.										

NOTE: Identify by vehicle number which vehicles are garaged away from above address. Give City and State: _____

COVERAGES (Please check Coverages you have now so that we can quote similar Coverages.)

SPLIT LIMITS

☐ $25,000/$50,000/$10,000

☐ $50,000/$100,000/$25,000

☐ $100,000/$300,000/$25,000

☐ Other _____

LIABILITY –OR– SINGLE LIMITS

☐ $50,000 per occurrence

☐ $100,000 per occurrence

☐ $300,000 per occurrence

☐ Other _____

Indicate if you have any Physical Damage Coverages and the Deductible amount.

VEH. NO.	COMPREHENSIVE		COLLISION	
	Yes	No	Yes	No
1.	$ DED.		$ DED.	
2.	$ DED.		$ DED.	
3.	$ DED.		$ DED.	
4.	$ DED.		$ DED.	

DRIVER INFORMATION (List yourself and all other licensed drivers residing in household.)

DRIVER'S NAME	OCCUPATION	DATE OF BIRTH	AGE	MARITAL STATUS	SEX	DATE FIRST LICENSED (If Less Than 3 Yrs.) Month-Year	PERCENTAGE OF MILEAGE BY DRIVER			
							VEH. 1	VEH. 2	VEH. 3	VEH. 4
							100%	100%	100%	100%

DRIVING RECORD (NOTE: Driving records are confirmed with the Department of Motor Vehicles.)

1. Has ANY driver in your household had a TRAFFIC VIOLATION, ACCIDENT or had license SUSPENDED or REVOKED in last 3 years? ☐ YES ☐ NO (If "Yes", give details/dates)

2. Has any company DECLINED, CANCELLED or REFUSED TO RENEW insurance for any driver during the last 3 years? (Note: Missouri residents are not required to answer this question.) ☐ YES ☐ NO (If "Yes", give details/dates)

3. Have ALL drivers under 21 years completed a DRIVER'S EDUCATION COURSE? ☐ YES ☐ NO (If "No", give Name)

DETAILS TO QUESTIONS 1, 2 AND 3 (you may also use this space to furnish information on additional drivers or cars.)

ADDITIONAL INFORMATION

1. Does any operator have any physical, medical or mental impairments? ☐ YES ☐ NO

2. Are you or any member of your household in the ASSIGNED RISK PLAN or the AUTOMOBILE INSURANCE PLAN? ☐ YES ☐ NO

3. Do you or any member of your household regularly use an auto NOT OWNED BY YOU? ☐ YES ☐ NO

4. Any FIRE, THEFT or VANDALISM losses in the past three years? ☐ YES ☐ NO

5. Does any vehicle have CRACKED or BROKEN GLASS? ☐ YES ☐ NO

6. Is any auto equipped with a factory-installed PASSIVE RESTRAINT system? If "YES", check one.

☐ Airbags–all front seat occupants protected.

☐ Passive belts–all front seat occupants protected.

☐ Other type–all front seat occupants protected.

☐ Any type–driver only protected.

7. Is your car parked on the street or in an open lot overnight? ☐ YES ☐ NO

8. Have you lived at present address less than 3 years? ☐ YES ☐ NO

9. Has any vehicle been specially painted, customized or altered, or equipped with racing type items? ☐ YES ☐ NO

10. Does any full-time student have a B average or better? (give name below) ☐ YES ☐ NO

Explain any "Yes" answers to Questions 1-10 here.

I HEREBY DECLARE THAT I PERSONALLY HAVE READ THIS REQUEST AND I DECLARE THAT THE STATEMENTS MADE ARE TRUE. I UNDERSTAND THAT THIS IS A REQUEST FOR A QUOTATION ONLY AND THAT I AM UNDER NO OBLIGATION.

SIGNATURE OF REQUESTER _____   DATE _____

ES-222A Rev. 6-79 Printed in U.S.A.

Figure K-40: STATE EMPLOYEES AUTO INSURANCE QUOTATION FORM

FORM MUST BE TYPED

MUST BE COMPLETELY CODED

Form MP-13 (Rev. 6/72)

SCHEDULING MOTOR POOL VEHICLES

COMPLETE AND PRESENT AT TIME OF VEHICLE PICK UP

REQUIREMENTS: Valid license; driver on University Payroll; trip must pertain to official State business.

DATE _____ DRIVER _____ DEPARTURE _____ A.M.
P.M. RETURN _____ A.M.
P.M.

DESTINATION _____ _____ _____
              Street   Town/City   State

REASON FOR TRIP _____

MATERIAL TO BE TRANSPORTED _____

NUMBER OF PASSENGERS _____

DEPARTMENT TO BE CHARGED _____ CODING _____

DEPARTMENT HEAD OR AUTHORIZED PERSON _____

Vehicle Will Not Be Held More Than ½ Hour After Scheduled Time Unless Notified

Figure K-41: SCHEDULING MOTOR POOL VEHICLES

Index